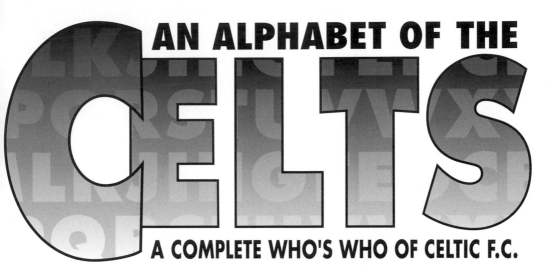

AN ALPHABET OF THE CELTS

A COMPLETE WHO'S WHO OF CELTIC F.C.

By Eugene MacBride, Martin O'Connor
& George Sheridan

Published by
ACL & POLAR PUBLISHING (UK) LTD

DEDICATION ONE:
In memory of my father, the Donegalman, Donncha Eoghain Ruaidh, who loved Celtic from his
soul and watched them 1916-1984; and in honour of my son Damian who loves them today.
E.A. MacB.

DEDICATION TWO:
To my wife Margaret, for her patient understanding of my lifelong obsession with football,
and to Phil and Liz, the next generation of torchbearers.
M. O'C.

DEDICATION THREE:
To the strikers/backbone/midfield of Marie, Claire and Julie and Denis the Sweeper.
G.S.

DEDICATION FOUR:
To the memory of Angus Potter whose love for Celtic transcends even death.

First published in Great Britain in 1994 by
ACL Colour Print & Polar Publishing (UK) Ltd
2, Uxbridge Road, Leicester LE4 7ST
England

Text © Copyright Eugene MacBride, Martin O'Connor and George Sheridan

Design © Copyright ACL & Polar 1994

ISBN 0 9514862 7 6

Edited by
Julian Baskcomb

Designed and Printed by
ACL Colour Print & Polar Publishing (UK) Ltd
2, Uxbridge Road, Leicester LE4 7ST
Telephone: (0116) 2610800

Photographs are courtesy of:
Celtic FC, Celtic View, George Herringshaw & Associated Sports Photography, Colorsport,
Empics Ltd, The Hulton Deutsch Collection, Sportapic Sports Agency, Daily Express, Daily
Record, David Munden Photography & Sportsline Photographic.

Many of the photographs reproduced are from original material in the files at Celtic FC, who
also retain the rights to official photocall pictures from the modern era taken by the appointed
Club Photographer. Most remaining photographs are from the private collection of the authors
or from albums owned by various Celtic supporters or players and their families who have
assisted in the compilation of this book. We have been unable to trace the sources of these
pictures, but any photographer involved is cordially invited to contact the publishers in writing
providing proof of copyright.

Cover photographs:
Front: (Clockwise): Jimmy McGrory, Sean Fallon, Billy McNeill, Dan Doyle, Kenny Dalglish, Charlie
Nicholas.
Back: Danny McGrain, Celtic FC 1954, Bert Peacock, Patsy Gallagher, Charlie Tully, Paul McStay,
Jimmy Johnstone, 'Packy' Bonner, Dan McArthur.

FOREWORD

by Sean Fallon, Freeman of Sligo.

Celtic was not just a football club to me, it was my home.
I spent more time there than I did at my own house. Even in my
playing days, if we were not asked to return in the afternoon,
then Bertie Peacock, Willie Fernie and myself often went back
and had some fun trying to take the ball off Willie who had
superb skill and control. Of course, when one talks of skill and
control, Charlie Tully immediately comes to mind. I think it is
fair to say that Charlie did more for Celtic FC and the great
support than any other player of my era. When Charlie joined
the club they were never more in need of a lift. The supporters
were hoping for just one outstanding personality and they got
their wish in Charles Patrick Tully. Charlie immediately caught
the imagination and everything he did was headlines in the
Scottish papers. The long-suffering Celtic support were again
walking tall when they weren't going wild with delight.
Charlie loved taking the mickey out of opponents. We were
playing Aberdeen one day at Celtic Park. Don Emery was marking Charlie who was having a
good game and giving Don the runaround. At last Charlie takes a complimentary ticket out of
his shorts pocket and waves it at the full-back: "Don, here's a comp. Would you not be better
watching me from the stand?"

When I finished playing, I started on the coaching side and bringing in new faces like Ian Young,
Tommy Gemmell, Jim Craig and some older ones like Ronnie Simpson and Bertie Auld. I signed
Danny McGrain the same day I saw him play against the English Schoolboys at Ibrox Park.
I went to Danny's home from Ibrox and waited until he arrived. He signed without any fuss.
I farmed him out to Maryhill Juniors for a year, then called him up. He went on to become one of
the greatest Celts ever, giving 20 years service to club and country. He was a great professional
and always projected an outstanding image, showing a great example to young players.

I signed Kenny Dalglish from under the noses of Rangers. Kenny lived opposite Ibrox Park.
In fact the day I signed Kenny almost cost me a divorce as I left my wife and three daughters
sitting for two hours in the car while I was in Kenny's home. I don't need to enlarge on Kenny's
career. The only thing I would add, he was farmed out to Cumbernauld Juniors for a year and
then called-up. A year at junior level did young players a lot of good - a pity this practice is
discontinued.

I am sure this book will be of high interest to the greatest supporters in football who, over the
years, have seen some great players wear the green and white colours with pride and distinction.
Now they can read of players that their dads and grandads and great-grandads used to talk
about which will no doubt bring nostalgic memories back and pride as well. It was their
forebears with their support many years ago that made it all possible. It is said that without
players there is no football club. I always believed that this should read: without supporters
there is no football club. Congratulations to the authors on their research which has called for
much dedication and I am sure will be appreciated by many readers.

Yours in Sport,
Sean Fallon

CONTENTS

A rainbow arched across the sky,
With many a colour bright,
Imports to the artistic eye
A thrill of pure delight.
The gifted artist with his brush
Can make his picture speak,
Depicting rosy tints that flush
On some fair sitter's cheek.
Italian skies oft, we are told,
Can boast a vivid blue;
A sunset in a blaze of gold
Has its admirers too.
Rich colours that Dame Nature blends
Give pleasures that won't cloy,
The plumage of our feathered friends
Can bring an inward joy.
But to my partial Celtic eyes
There's no more lovely sight:
A sunny day at the Paradise,
Ten jerseys green and white.

INTRODUCTION

Hugh Fletcher signed for Celtic 16 September 1952; Charlie Saunders 2 March 1953; Tom Hippsley 1 May 1953; Hugh Bryceland 19 January 1954; none of them is profiled in this book. We have tried to prepare a volume which may be useful to the researcher in 100 years time but, as with the doings of Jesus, if all the players who signed forms for Celtic had their careers summarised here, "I do not think the world itself would contain the books which would have to be written" (John Ch 21 v 25). As with golf, we have had to make the cut and decided to include only players who turned out for Celtic in the League (peacetime and wartime), the Scottish Cup, the League Cup and Europe. This means that Mick Gilhooley who was capped for Scotland at centre-half is not here; Mick O'Brien who played for both Irelands does not qualify; Ambrose Mulraney who was in the running for Scotland just after World War Two is not in; Ian White neither; nor, to our sorrow, Kinnaird Ouchterlonie, Johnnie Wilson, Tom Harvey, Jim Jackson, John Shearer or many many others all the way back to Charlie Gorevin and Pat Dowling of the early Celtic and Raymond McStay of 1994. Yet Dan Shea is here with George Washington Elliott, David Taylor, Dick Roose, men who only played for the club on loan and made their fame elsewhere. On the other hand, if a player makes his bow in the Glasgow Cup or the Charity Cup that debut is given to honour a time when these competitions attracted vast crowds and the ties were played with an appetite that often had the roaring crowd on its toes from start to finish. Once these Cups lose their importance in the '70s they no longer count as a player's debut (eg Charlie Nicholas) but this first appearance rates a mention in the text. The Drybrough Cup does however count as a debut (eg Steve Murray).

The following abbreviations have been used: SL = Scottish League; SC = Scottish Cup; SLC = Scottish League Cup; Eur = Europe; GC = Glasgow Cup; CC = Charity Cup; GL = Glasgow League; ICL = Inter-City League; RL = Regional (War) League; RLC = Regional (War) League Cup; SWC = Scottish War Cup; BB = Boys' Brigade; BC = Boys' Club; BG = Boys' Guild; CSC = Celtic Supporters' Club; SS = Senior Secondary. Three dots (...) signify a lost trail; [Luton Town] signifies the player is reputed to have signed for Luton in other sources but the authors have been unable to verify; d. June 1951 (?) means the date (in this case, of death) was obtained from another place but is not corroborated. The term 'on loan' has been used to cover temporary change of jersey colour at a time when players were at greater liberty to flit between clubs or between Scotland and England; for guest appearances during the First and Second World Wars; and for one-off transfers involving benefit matches. All quotes are from newspapers unless specifically ascribed. The text is dedicated firstly with respect to the Celtic players of the 106 years of the club's existence. We have not attempted to depict our Bhoys all as out and out heroes and master footballers. Pat McAuley was a master footballer; Peter McGonagle a Celtic hero. Dan Doyle was footballer and hero but there was at least one time he let the club down and badly. It gets said. The second dedication is to the Celtic fans, descendants of the immigrant Irish who founded the club. We have tried to produce a record which is informative and tells as much about each single player as we have been able to discover and space will allow. We wanted a work of quality which enhances Celtic's standing and does not insult the supporters' intelligence. A lot of hard labour and time has gone into the career paths and we have been reluctant to take from other sources without verifying wherever possible; the players' profiles are illustrated by reference to the actual games played between 28th May 1888 and 14th May 1994. Career path updates have been added after this date in the interests of topicality and one statistical exception is Pat McGinlay whose appearance figures are complete following his autumn 1994 move back to Hibernian. Celtic's record signing Phil O'Donnell is included, as is John O'Neill and Tosh McKinlay, but without appearance figures. Wherever feasible we have used quotes from the time eg to illustrate what splendid goalkeepers John Thomson and Willie Miller were. The work has been a labour of love and the authors look forward to the day when a new team will carry it forward to include Tommy Donegan, John McKnight, Highbury headmaster John McCourt, Tom Mooney, Joe Buchanan and a thousand others who wore the green and white. Bless 'em all!

ACKNOWLEDGEMENTS

First of all and especially, we want to thank the workers, ie the toiling porters of the Newspaper Library, Colindale, London NW for unrelenting good service with the 'Danger Barrows' over the time it has taken to prepare this volume. We were always helped with cheerful good humour and very often with endeavour way beyond the call of duty. Without them and that magnificent institution, the Newspaper Library, this book could not have happened.

Then : Rachel Steven for opening the door to the British Museum Reading Room; Colin Rowbotham, Steve Steventon and Lorraine Tillett who unveiled the mysteries of the word processor; Carla Stevens, Siobhan Crawley, Devon Weir, Anne Tutton, Omega B, for a steady supply of envelopes re-usable for sending print-outs to Glasgow and Leicester; boy wonder Danny Gallagher who supplied photos of Celtic players from his collection; Philippa Davidson who so kindly offered to read; Hana Roarty and Anne MacBride who asked how the tome was coming every time they wrote or 'phoned; Janet Beattie and Ross Morris for buying and sending everything marked "Celtic" they came across; wonderful Judy Schneider who found the disks the night they were lost; Jim MacBride who forwarded the most exotic programmes and brochures from Donegal and Glasgow; and No 1 Glenavon fan Ken Tyndall who lent his Old Firm sports library.

Next : Andrew Ward who took time out of a very busy schedule to transcribe a Willie Cook radio interview for us and provide valuable information on Joe McCulloch's war service alongside his father the great Tim Ward of Derby County and England; Neil Cowland for enhancing a Scottish Referee line-drawing of George Allan; Paul Taylor who kept chipping in with information the moment he came across anything new; Geoff Wilde who told us what we needed to know about Billy Semple and brought us up to date on Frank Walsh and Bobby Wraith; Mrs Phyllis Semple who supplied details of Billy's War Service; Denis Sheridan who interviewed George Carruth; George himself for invaluable detail on his dad, the magnificent Joe; David Potter whose voluminous writings on the Celts we trawled and especially the interview he did with Davie McLean shortly before the great Forfarman's death; David again for invaluable work done on Celtic births and deaths in the National Registry in Edinburgh; Miss

The Lisbon Lions - Celtic line up prior to European Cup final success.

Alison Potter for helping her dad speed the work and thus carry on the green and white tradition in a great Celtic family; Mrs Potter for her kindness in releasing David from his domestic duties; Brian Philp of the same National Registry for help with Jimmy Hay and Jimmy McIntosh; Tony Griffin for 'A Year in the Sun'; John Butterfield who is not only an expert on Woodrow Wilson's Theory of Cabinet Government but is just as much at home on the Celtic teams of the '70s and '80s; John worked for us in the New York Public Library and took some of our queries to the Celtic SC in Kearny, New Jersey for resolution; Ann Hynes who told us about John Mark Colquhoun's early schooling in Lancashire; Tony Byatt for his inquiries on Mick Davitt; Paddy O'Sullivan of Kirkcaldy CSC for his memories of Celtic matches; Mr Barney Duffy of Gweedore for putting us in touch with his nephew the effervescent Charlie Gallagher; the wonderful Hugh M. Brown who has a priceless and peerless collection of Celtic autographs and was able to put us in contact with countless players; Ms Alice Healy of Craigneuk for information on her brother Jimmy; Mrs Catherine Millar for help on the career of her husband the mighty Alex; Gerry Gallen (of the Era Bar, Craigneuk) and Joe Murphy (Bellshill) for assistance with players from the Lanarkshire coalfield; Brian Hunt for putting us in touch with Bobby Fisher; Colin Jose for help on Joe Kennaway; Tony Rae for details about his dad the darting Joe; Frank Glencross of Dalbeattie who volunteered his splendid collection of Celtic photographs and memorabilia as soon as he heard about the book; John Litster of Raith Rovers for help with George Johnstone; Patrick Sugrue for his memories of Frank O'Donnell at Spurs; Martin Boylan for Jimmy McStay's birth date; Gordon Dickson and Denis McCleary for the Celtic, Berwick Rangers connection; Jonathan Carolan for help with Mick McCarthy; U.U. Horningtoft, *eminence grise* of the Data Research Unit at *The Celt* fanzine; and above them all: Celtic historian par excellence, the nonpareil Pat Woods. It was Pat (however indirectly) who set the whole enterprise in motion at a Spurs versus Blackburn Rovers League Cup tie (1st November 1988). When he found a book was under way he then contributed with almost every scrap of printed information on the early Celtic he possessed and has been a treasure trove of detail for players' biographies.

Thirdly : wonderful John and Betty Butterly MBE who put us up in Glasgow in February 1993; the low-key but thoroughly efficient staff of the National Library of Scotland in Edinburgh; the ebulliently friendly staffs of the Scottish League offices in Glasgow and the National Registry in Edinburgh; Gregor Fisher (creator of the ineffable Rab C. Nesbit) who honoured us all unknown to himself by picking up some fiches we dropped in the Registry; Herbert Herrity, John Mennie and Terry Madden of the White Fathers in Edinburgh for accommodation in February 1994; David Capper, secretary of Sheffield United (help on Willie Falconer); Mark Chapman, Brentford FC historian whose generosity in research matters was overwhelming; the Enquiries Section of the Commonwealth War Graves Commission, polite and helpful people over and over.

Lastly, the glory men, the players: ex-Celtic reserve Johnnie Wilson who provided profiles on Celtic's intake of Fifers in the late 1930s; Jim Sharkey for an illuminating interview in Cambridge; Seton Airlie and Matt Lynch (who honoured us beyond belief with the original of his June 1946 letter from Jimmy Duncanson); Charlie Gallagher who could never have been more affable and collaborative and himself interviewed Bobby Carroll; Denis Connaghan; Frank Connor; John Gorman; Ian Lochhead; John and Nan Kurila; Atholl Henderson; Andy Young; Jackie Watters; Jimmy Sirrel; Johnny Paton; Johnny Bonnar; Eamon McMahon; Gil Heron who sent us his latest volume of poetry; Bobby Fisher; Bill Boland; Roddie MacDonald; Chris Shevlane; Frank McCarron; John Curran; George McCluskey; all those others too numerous to mention who gave time to speak to us on the 'phone; and the magnificent Frank Walsh who did a prodigious amount of legwork to trace players and procure photographs in the Wishaw area and himself gave us a totally informative interview in the most sequestered part of Bedfordshire in January 1994; Celtic great Sean Fallon who welcomed us to his home and provided the Foreword to this book; in terms of movement of players and fund of anecdote Sean was a true goldmine of information, always available and ready with his co-operation. To anyone and everyone who contributed in any way at all large or small and never forgetting our hard-working editors, Julian Baskcomb and Julia Byrne, snowed under by weekly updates: Thank you, thank you, thank you! Go raibh mile maith agaibh go leir! Celtic will be back!

ADAMS, David Robertson

Role: Goalkeeper 1902-12
6' 0" 14st.0lbs.
b. Oathlaw, 14th May 1883
d. Edinburgh, 29th November 1948

CAREER: Avonbridge FC/Vale of Carron FC/
Dunipace Juniors/CELTIC Dec 1902/retired
Mar 1912.

Debut v Hibernian (h) 1-0 (SL) 26.9.03

Davy Adams first turned out for Celtic at
Easter Road in the Inter-City League on April
11th 1903 as reserve goalkeeper to Andrew
McPherson. McPherson started as first choice
for 1903-04 but Davy was superlative against
Middlesbrough on tour (September 1st 1903)
and before the month was out, became Celtic's
No. 1 for the next eight years. Falkirk had
wanted him as a junior but Willie Maley
invited him to Ireland with Celtic for the
friendly with Bohemians on Boxing Day 1902
and he was fixed-up in Dublin. Jimmy
Brownlie (16 caps for Scotland) made 13 non-
competitive appearances for Celtic as a young
goalkeeper but was warned-off by James
Kelly: "You won't displace Davy Adams." Big
Davy was Celtic's most accomplished 'keeper
after Dan McArthur and before Charlie Shaw.
He kept goal for the six-in-a-row League side
1905-10 and was Celtic's last ditcher in the
Scottish Cup triumphs of 1904, 1907, 1908 and
1911. He was also
the last Celtic
'keeper to appear
in the hoops and
the first to wear a
distinguishing
yellow jersey (at Dundee on November 26th
1910?). According to Jimmy Quinn he did not
really "come out of his shell" until a great
game 2-1 against Rangers in the Glasgow Cup
final at Hampden (8th October 1904). Again in
the Glasgow Cup, in the second replay of the
final of 26th October 1907, he played Rangers
virtually on his own throughout the second
half for another 2-1 win. Occasionally after a
defeat, he had to run the gauntlet in Queen
Street station; "You're goalie nane!" "Maybe
so, but the Celtic executive don't know it yet".
Davy was allegedly "a martyr to rheumatism"
as well as subject to frequent bouts of
pneumonia but it was eye trouble that forced
his retirement. His final game coincided with
Patsy Gallagher's debut against St Mirren on
December 2nd 1911. The love in which the
faithful held him is evidenced by the roar that
went up when he appeared from the pavilion
unannounced to run the line for Celtic versus
Barnsley (3rd September 1912).

Appearances:
SL: 248 apps. 100 shut-outs.
SC: 43 apps. 24 shut-outs.
Total: *291 apps. 124 shut-outs (43%).*

Davy Adams (centre of the middle row) with his 1908 Celtic team-mates and the Charity, Scottish and Glasgow Cups.
The full line-up -
Back row (l to r):
T.White, J.Kelly, T.Colgan, J.McKillop, J.Grant, M.Dunbar.
Middle row:
W.Maley (Secretary), Young, Somers, McMenemy, Adams, Mitchell, Weir, R.Davis (trainer).
Front row:
Hamilton, McLeod, Loney, Hay, Quinn, McNair.

AIRLIE, Seton Montgomery

Role: Centre Forward 1942-47
6' 0" 12st.7lbs.
b. Carmyle, 22nd March 1920

CAREER: St Joseph's Tollcross/St Mungo Juveniles/Greyfriars/CELTIC (provisional) 17 May 1939/St Anthony's (farmed out) 1940/ Motherwell on trial (in error) 1941/CELTIC 28 Jan 1942 (Chelsea, Millwall & Aberaman loan 1942-43) (Derby County & Nottingham Forest loan 1943-44) (Notts County loan 1944-45-46)/ FC Cannes 20 July 1947/Worcester City cs 1950/Halesowen Town 1952/Malvern Town manager/Worcester City chief scout.

Debut v Hibernian (h) 2-1 (RL) 17.1.42
(scored once)

"The big fellow has everything we were lacking in the front line" (Jimmy McStay). "Dashing Celtic forward" Seton Airlie set Parkhead alight on his debut with a left foot drive from 25 yards fifteen minutes from time to secure Celtic's first points of 1942. He played in a forward line with a 1938 feel to it: Delaney and Crum; Airlie; Divers and Murphy. Seton might well have been the answer to the goals problem had not the Honourable Artillery Company (C.O. Ted Heath; MP 1950, PM 1970) conscripted him to shoot for them in the second week of March. At Stamford Bridge under Billy Birrel ("I loved playing for Chelsea"), he led the attack with another Glasgow great, Peter ("Ma Ba'") McKennan from Partick Thistle scheming the goals. Seton scored in a 2-1 win for the Pensioners on September 12th 1942 but was sent off near the end with George Summerbee of Portsmouth (father of Mike of Manchester City and England). As he was a registered Celt, the misdemeanor was dealt with not by the English authorities but by the SFA eighteen days later. Home on leave he played in the Rangers 8 Celtic 1 debacle of Ne'erday 1943 but was back to Ibrox the following 11th September for Rangers 0 Celtic 1. He played four times against Rangers in all, each time at Ibrox, but was also in the BAOR team which beat the Light Blues 6-1 in Hanover (17th October 1945). Seton was based in Hanover and played football for the Combined Services with the likes of Leslie Compton, Bryn Jones and Reg Lewis (Arsenal), Billy Hughes (Liverpool)

and the great Billy Steel (Morton) whose fame was just about to dawn. He turned out for Osnabruck in the Bundesliga ("They kept going same as we did"). Services football entailed vast amounts of travel throughout Germany (he even played in the 1936 Olympic Stadium, Berlin) and as deep into Eastern Europe as Poland and the Ukraine. Seton was demobbed in the winter of 1946 and came welcome home to the first team on 14th December when he scored two against Clyde at Parkhead. "I felt completely done-in, mentally and physically, my legs just didn't want to know. My one desire was for six months off." Although Jimmy McGrory was disinclined to hear of a rest, the player's condition took its toll, he was never again the old Seton Airlie. He played in the 1-1 draw at Ibrox on Ne'erday before 85,000 but had his last match for Celtic against Aberdeen at Parkhead the following day. He found a new appetite for the game in his two and a half seasons with Cannes and then took up employment in his profession as an engineer in Worcester where he now lives. By joining non-league Worcester City he was able to elude the transfer fee Cannes wanted for his services. There seems little doubt Seton Airlie might have done a fine job for Celtic. Once again, the war has a lot to answer for.

Appearances:
SL: 6 apps. 3 gls.
Total: *6 apps. 3 gls.*
RL: 10 apps. 2 gls.
RLC: 7 apps. 3 gls.
Total: *17 apps. 5 gls.*

Seton Airlie challenges Rangers' Bobby Brown.

AITKEN, Robert Sime

Role: Defence, Midfield 1974-90
6' 0" 13st.0lbs.
b. Irvine, 24th November 1958

CAREER: St Andrew's Academy Saltcoats/
Ayr United BC/Celtic BC/CELTIC S Form
1972/ CELTIC 5 June 1975/Newcastle United
10 Jan 1990/St Mirren player-coach 23 Aug
1991/ Aberdeen 24 June 1992.

*Debut v Stenhousemuir (a) 2-0 (SLC) 10.9.75
(sub)*

Aged 17, big Roy was "the new Duncan
Edwards, enormously strong, talented,
onfident." He was brought into the Celtic
team at Pittodrie on February 21st 1976 in
place of the off-form Roddie MacDonald. So
well did he succeed in plugging the leaks that
had developed in defence that Aberdeen
pulled Drew Jarvie off at half-time. Big Roy
arrived as of that game and never needed any
further nursing. Celtic had to adopt him on a
licence so as to play against Sachsenring in
East Germany (March 17th 1976) and Sean
Fallon was required in theory to report to the
dreaded Vopo on how Celtic were caring for
their 'child'. Roy played full-back, sweeper,
centre-back and supplied the midfield drive
lost after the passage of Davie Hay to Chelsea.
His commitment to the club was always so
utter he was unable ever to give less than his
best on the park. He played a vital role in
bringing the Double home in 1977 and was
indispensable to the Championship sides of
1979, 1981, 1982 and 1986. He won a second
Scottish Cup medal against Rangers on May
10th 1980 and in the final of 18th May 1985
versus Dundee United, it was his surge and
cross that enabled Frank McGarvey to head
the winner when for so long Celtic had looked
doomed. In 1988, he made his name for ever
as the man who captained Celtic to the
Centenary Year Double. In 1989, in the
Scottish Cup final of May 20th, still captain,
he played a specialist role to subdue the
threat of Mark Walters. According to
Rangers, he also nicked the throw-in that led
to Joe Miller's goal. He was Andy
Roxburgh's Scotland skipper (50 caps as a
Celt) and at club level he and McNeill
looked as potent a combination as McNeill
and Stein. Roy was made scapegoat for the

3-0 defeat by France in Paris (11th October 1989) and as Celtic's fortunes declined, the big man whose stated ambition was to end his football days at Parkhead, sought a transfer: "I will be free of the Parkhead terracing critics... of the media guys who wanted me out, of the referees who picked on me..." He took his verve and energy down to Newcastle as captain for £250,000 but fell out of favour on the arrival of Ossie Ardiles as manager. Davie Hay paid a further £225,000 for Roy to make a team out of St Mirren and Willie Miller no less to secure his unstinting enthusiasm for Aberdeen. He got a huge roar of acclaim when he came on for Steve Staunton and the Republic of Ireland in Packy Bonner's testimonial (12th May 1991). Roy Aitken is an all-time Celtic great. Celtic lost a lot more than just a player when he left Parkhead.

Appearances:
SL: 483 apps. 40 gls.
SLC: 82 apps. 6 gls.
SC: 55 apps. 4 gls.
Eur: 47 apps. 5 gls.
Total: *667 apps. 55 gls.*

ALLAN, George Horsburgh

Role: Centre-forward 1897-98
5' 10" 12st.4lbs.
b. *Linlithgow Bridge, 23rd April 1875*
d. *Earlsferry, Fife, 17th October 1899*

CAREER: Vale of Avon/Linlithgow
Athletic/Broxburn Shamrock 1893/
Bo'ness 1894/Leith Athletic 28 Mar
1895/Liverpool 29 Oct 1895/
CELTIC 1 May 1897/Liverpool
20 Apr 1898.

Debut v Hibernian (h) 4-1 (SL)
4.9.1897

Dod Allan

"Of splendid physique and a man to be
feared" Dod Allan, the first Liverpool player
to be capped for Scotland (3rd April 1897), got
goals for Celtic but the need to forage and
conform to their patient build-up and pattern-
weaving did not suit his style. He might have
looked lumbersome but was Powderhall class
as a sprinter and "a dribbler of versatility."
Like Quinn later, long-striding Dod wanted
the ball to chase. He helped Celtic to their
fourth Championship in 1898 but Liverpool
(who held his registration) gladly paid £50 to
have him back before the English season
ended. He got another year's football in but
was stricken by the "great white plague"
(tuberculosis) and stayed in Scotland to await
death after his condition was diagnosed. He is
buried in the Allan family grave in Linlithgow
cemetery.

Appearances:
SL: 17 apps. 15 gls.
SC: 2 apps. 1 gl.
Total: *19 apps. 16 gls.*

ALLAN, Thomas

Role: Centre-forward 1910-13
b. *Carluke, 9th October 1891*

CAREER: Law Volunteers/
Carluke Milton Rovers/
CELTIC 4 Jan 1910(Ayr
United loan 9 Apr 1910)
(Airdrie loan 28 May 1910)
(Vale of Leven loan 21 Oct
1911)/CELTIC 23 Nov 1912.

Debut v Hibernian (h) 0-0 (SL)
25.4.10

"Sturdy young player" Tom
Allan played friendlies and
benefit matches for Celtic
throughout the spring of
1910. On Willie Maley's
birthday, 25th April, in the
33rd Scottish League match
of the 1909-10 campaign he
took the field at Parkhead as
Jimmy Quinn's deputy in
a match which brought
home Celtic's tenth
Championship and
sixth in a row. He had
one more League game
as a Celt on 30th April 1910 but by the time
the new season opened he was at centre for
Airdrie in a 3-0 defeat at Parkhead. He was
open to transfer at £50 at Parkhead in the
summer of 1913.

Appearances:
SL: 2 apps. 0 gls.
Total: *2 apps. 0 gls.*

ANDERSON, Oliver

Role: Outside-right 1937-46
5' 7" 9st.6lbs.
b. *Glasgow, 13th May 1919*

CAREER: Calder St School/Glasgow 216 Coy
BB/Arthurlie July 1936/CELTIC 27 Apr 1937
(Hamilton Academicals loan 22 Feb 1941)
(Clyde loan 20 Dec 1941)(Morton loan)(Third
Lanark loan) - all during WW2/Alloa
13 September 1946/free 20 May 1947/
Third Lanark (trial) 2 Aug 1947/
Airdrie 5 Aug 1947/free 1948/Falkirk
Dec 1948/free 1949/Cowdenbeath
1950/Ards (trial) Dec 1950/Arbroath
1951/Kilmarnock (trial) Oct 1951.

Debut v Queen's Park (h) 0-1 (SL) 3.1.39

Oliver Anderson "the Tommy Walker
of the junior game" featured in the
Arthurlie Team of All Talents that won
the Scottish Junior Cup 5-1 against
Rob Roy at Celtic Park on 22nd May
1937 and was the most sought-after
junior of his time. He scored
Arthurlie's fourth and fifth goals, both
from penalties. He was a Scottish

Tom Allan (on the right) with John
Mitchell.

13

junior international during 1937-38 taking Johnnie Wilson's place after Johnnie signed provisionally for Celtic in September 1937. So persistent were the scouts, "like wasps around a honey jar", his mother was rumoured on the verge of a nervous breakdown. He could have gone anywhere but chose Celtic. Apart from football, he worked as a technician in the colour laboratory at Templeton's famous carpet factory on Glasgow Green, "By all the laws, Anderson should come up to the top by leaps and bounds." Then Hitler took a hand. The first draft of men under the Militia

Oliver Anderson

Training Act scooped him up in March 1939 and he was in the Royal Artillery by August 1st, a month before the outbreak of War. Celtic "paid him off" (i.e. made him a free agent for the Duration) in December 1939. He played for the SFA XI versus the Army at Galashiels on 16th March 1940 and was reported as having "filled-out... his play is a lot more purposeful than it used to be." Apart from his golden promise being interrupted by hostilities, he would complain he was never given the chance to settle in one position, that he was every manager's handyman. He played for Celtic reserves on January 15th 1944 before action with his anti-tank unit on D-Day 6th June 1944. He was strafed in France in September ("I got a bullet through the calf of my leg but that isn't going to stop me playing"). Oliver went into the Army as a private and emerged as a second lieutenant.

Appearances:
SL: 13 apps. 3 gls.
Total: *13 apps. 3 gls.*
RL: 3 apps. 1 gl.
Total: *3 apps. 1 gl.*

Ian Andrews

ANDREWS, Ian Edmund

Role: Goalkeeper 1988-90
6' 2" 13st.0lbs.
b. Nottingham, 1st December 1964

CAREER: Nottingham Forest schoolboy/ Mansfield Town app.1980/Leicester City Sept 1981(Middlesbrough loan Jan 1984)(Swindon Town loan Jan 1984)/CELTIC 23 July 1988 (Leeds United loan 13 Dec 1988)(Southampton loan Dec 1989)/Southampton 7 Feb 1990/ Bournemouth 5 Sept 1994.

Debut v Hearts (h) 1-0 (SL) 13.8.88

Alex Miller tried to sign Ian Andrews for Hibs in October 1987 after he had lost his place at Filbert Street to the veteran Paul Cooper. Liverpool and Spurs had also shown an interest. Aberdeen made inquiries when Jim Leighton moved to Manchester United in May 1988 but big Ian became Celtic's for £300,000 after Packy Bonner's back operation of July 12th 1988. He played against Ajax in the Viareggio Tournament (31st July 1988) and against Cruzeiro in the Centenary Match the following Sunday. He looked the part and had a magnificent Premier League debut but then came the 5-1 defeat at Ibrox on August 27th 1988. McNeill faulted his 'keeper for just one counter on a day of scant protection from centre-backs McCarthy and Aitken. Big Billy wanted to keep faith but as the defence leaked goals, media and fans were unrelenting and Ian was dropped as of 24th September 1988. And Hibs? They had bought Andy Goram instead.

Appearances:
SL: 5 apps. 1 shut-out.
SLC: 2 apps. 0 shut-outs.
Eur: 1 app. 0 shut-outs.
Total: *8 apps. 1 shut-out. (13%)*

ARCHDEACON, Owen

Role: Outside-left 1982-89
5' 9" 10st.8lbs.
b. Greenock, 4th March 1966

CAREER: St Columba's High School (Port Glasgow)/Celtic BC/Gourock United/ CELTIC 20 Aug 1982/Barnsley 16 June 1989.
Debut v Motherwell (h) 4-2 (SL) 10.4.84 (sub) (scored once)

"Owen is a gem of a player. His attitude and skill are a tribute to his club" (Andy Roxburgh March 1984). Owen Archdeacon was Scotland Youth Player of the Year in June 1984 and reckoned by Alex Ferguson and Jim McLean the young star most likely to succeed. His

Owen Archdeacon

chief claim on the Celtic memory came on April 4th 1987 when he used his great speed off the mark to rob Rangers goalkeeper Woods of a Jimmy Nicholl pass-back and score the final goal in a much-appreciated 3-1 win. He was also in the team at Love Street on May 3rd 1986 when Celtic knocked the Premier League Championship out of Hearts' hands at the very death. At Barnsley, 'Dancer' is a highly valued player: "He can play quite happily on the left side of midfield and at left-back. No matter where he plays, his performances are almost always top quality - and the bonus is, he scores goals!" (Mel Machin 1992). Owen's speciality was the banana-bend cross or corner with Murdo MacLeod thundering in on the end to hit a net-bursting volley.

Appearances:
SL: 76 apps. 8 gls.
SLC: 4 apps. 1 gl.
SC: 4 apps. 0 gls.
Eur: 3 apps. 0 gls.
Total: *87 apps. 9 gls.*

ARNOTT, Walter

Role: Full-Back 1895
5' 9" 12st.6lbs.
b. Pollokshields, 12th May 1863
d. 18th May 1931

CAREER: Pollokshields Athletic/Ashfield/ Queen's Park May 1882/ Pollokshields Athletic 1 Jan 1884/Queen's Park 17 Jan 1884/ Kilmarnock Athletic Oct 1884/Corinthians 1889/Ballina FC 1889/Linfield 1891/Third Lanark & Queen's Park 1892/St Bernard's 1893(CELTIC loan 1895)/Notts County Feb 1895.
Debut v Third Lanark (h) 4-4 (SL) 23.2.1895

Wattie was a freelance footballer who played where the whim took him but who is normally identified with the heyday of Queen's Park (twice English Cup finalists) and Scotland. He was essentially a Queen's Park player but a knight errant helping out other clubs on request and frequently travelling to Ireland 'on business'. He did so with or without the approval of the SFA who banned him from the Scottish Cup in 1889 for a foray into Erin that saw him play without permission. He guested for Celtic in place of Jerry Reynolds when the team was going through a bad patch and even with the great Wattie in defence, had to battle back from 1-4 down. He brought an Irish Cup medal away from his stint with Linfield and played for Notts County in the English Cup. He was extremely fast and renowned for his ability to win the ball in a chase then pivot and clear almost in the one movement. An all-round sportsman, he even yachted in the Clyde regatta. He won 10 full caps against England between 1884 and 1893.

Appearances:
SL: 1 app. 0 gls.
Total: *1 app. 0 gls.*

Wattie Arnott

ATKINSON, John

Role: Outside-left 1909
b. Cambuslang, 5th December 1884

CAREER: Scottish Amateurs 1903/Hamilton Academicals 11 Mar 1903/Queen's Park Feb 1905/Hamilton Academicals Aug 1905/ (CELTIC loan Apr 1909)/(Partick Thistle loan 19 Mar 1910)/Hamilton Academicals again 30 Apr 1910.

Debut v Morton (h) 5-1 (SL) 22.4.09
(scored twice)

Celtic emerged from the Scottish Cup final replay (the Hampden Riot) on April 17th 1909 with eight League games to complete in 11 days before the season closed. When Davie Hamilton was injured versus Accies on April 21st Celtic secured the services of this Douglas Park amateur to play against Morton the following day. The young medical student scored the first and the fourth goals. He qualified as a doctor in October 1910, obtained a practice in Co.Durham and was still playing football in the north-east of England in 1912.

Appearances:
SL: 1 app. 2 gls.
Total: *1 app. 2 gls.*

AULD, Robert

Role: Outside-left 1955-61/Midfield 1965-71
5' 8" 10st.10lbs.
b. Maryhill, 23rd March 1938

CAREER: Springbank School/ Partick Thistle Boys Supporters' Club/Panmure Thistle/Maryhill Harp/CELTIC 2 Apr 1955 (Dumbarton loan 17 Oct 1956)/ CELTIC again 3 June 1957/ Birmingham City 1 May 1961/ CELTIC 14 Jan 1965/free 29 Apr 1971/Hibernian 6 May 1971/coach 1973/Partick Thistle manager 12 June 1974/ Hibernian manager 18 Nov 1980/dismissed 2 Sept 1982/ Hamilton Academicals co-manager 3 Feb 1983/manager 14 May 1983/ dismissed 10 Jan 1984/Partick Thistle manager 2 Apr 1986/resigned 17 July 1986/Dumbarton manager 21 Jan 1988/ dismissed 12 Sept 1988.

Debut v Rangers (a) 0-1 (CC) 1.5.57

The upturn in Celtic's fortunes in the mid-60s is represented almost as much by Bertie Auld as by the great Jock Stein himself. Bertie was "speed, ball control, distribution," in short, midfield genius. Sean Fallon cajoled chairman Kelly into bringing him back from Birmingham. "We were playing mile-a-minute stuff at the time and he complemented Bobby Murdoch by slowing things down. He could take two or three people out of the game with a pass." Kelly recognised Bertie's undoubted talent but deplored his temper. Bertie had tangled with the biggest (Maurice Cook and Ron Yeats) and laid out the best (Johnny Haynes). Against Holland with Scotland on May 27th 1959 he was ordered off in the last minute "for pushing a Dutch player with a foot in the face." On another notorious occasion, August 15th 1960, Korean veteran and Ibrox hatchet man Harold Davis pulled the fallen Auld up by his hair. Celtic players rushed in, not so much to help Bertie, as to prevent his sending-off. Bertie did not often dither over his retaliation! Kelly relented under Sean

Fallon's pressure and Bertie rewarded him not only with a personality change but with both equalisers in the Scottish Cup final of April 24th 1965 versus Dunfermline. With Bobby Murdoch he ran the midfield for Stein and was a huge favourite with the Celtic support. So changed a character was he that when he was ordered-off in Montevideo on November 4th 1967, he knew he'd done nothing wrong and didn't bother leaving the field. He won five Championship medals 1966-70, three Scottish Cup 1965, 1967, 1969 and four League Cup 1966, 1967, 1968, 1969. Bertie had known the depths with Celtic. Under Stein he scaled the crests. At Lisbon, after the European Final, cavorting in the dressing-room, he demanded of Sean Fallon: "I was your best man out there, wasn't I? Admit I was your best man!" His release in April 1971 came as a shock. The team carried him shoulder high on May 1st, the 14th anniversary of his debut, while the crowd went crazy and Bertie wiped away the tears. 'Ten-thirty' was an all-time Celtic great.

Appearances:
SL: 176 apps. 53 gls.
SLC: 47 apps. 20 gls.
SC: 31 apps. 11 gls.
Eur: 25 apps. 1 gl.
Total: *279 apps. 85 gls.*

The Celtic party for the trip to America in the summer of 1951.

Back row (left to right): Charlie Tully, John McGrory, John McPhail, Joe Baillie, Jimmy Mallan, Jock Weir, Bobby Evans, Roy Milne, Alec Rollo and Bertie Peacock.

Front: Bobby Collins, Sean Fallon, John Millsopp and Willie Fernie.

BAILLIE, Joseph

Role: Left-Half 1945-54
5′ 9″ 11st.3lbs.
b. Dumfries, 26th February 1929
d. Maryhill, 23rd March 1966

CAREER: St Roch's school/St Roch's Juniors/
CELTIC 15 Dec 1945/Wolverhampton
Wanderers 1 Nov 1954/Bristol City June 1955/
Leicester City 10 June 1957/Bradford PA June
1960.

Debut v Queen of the South (a) 1-3 (SL) 14.9.46

Joe Baillie

"Baillie for craft, Evans for graft, Stein for dependability." A Jimmy Gribben discovery and one of new manager McGrory's first signings, Joe Baillie was a slater by trade but a footballer born. "More a half-forward than a half-back," he joined Celtic when the club's fortunes were seldom worse. A junior international, he was much sought after and was one of the few 'captures of the season' to live up to his early reputation. He understudied the great Pat McAuley and when Pat was suspended for 14 days on March 8th 1948, Joe came into the team and was part of "the best Celtic side seen at Motherwell in years" in the 0-3 win of March 20th. McAuley returned for the Scottish Cup semi-final of March 27th versus Morton at Ibrox although Joe felt he might have done enough to deserve the chance. He became Celtic's first choice at left-half as of November 19th 1949 when McAuley put himself in bad odour by asking for more money when on top wages. "After the silky touch of McAuley, Joe at times looked awkward and immature... he improved game after game." Joe played in the Danny Kaye Charity Cup final of May 6th 1950 at Hampden when Celtic beat Rangers 3-2. He was in the team that ended the years of dearth by winning the Scottish Cup 1-0 versus Motherwell on 21st April 1951 before 133,343 at Hampden, the youngest Celtic side ever to lift the trophy. Joe went to McCarthyite America with Celtic in the summer of 1951 and knew what it was like to be loved when Celtic fans mobbed the team off the Liverpool train at the Central Station on June 30th 1951. He was back at Hampden on August 1st when Celtic beat Aberdeen in the final of the St Mungo Cup after being 2-0 down. Joe was rejected for National Service on account of cartilage trouble but did his bit as a Bevin Boy. By January 1952 he was up at five each morning and down the mine at Twechar an hour later. His career as a Celt was effectively ended on November 22nd 1952 when he was carried off in 15 minutes at Broomfield with torn ligaments. He went to the World Cup in Switzerland with Celtic and went to Malenkov's Moscow with Wolves both in 1954 (Stan Cullis bought him on repute without having seen him in action). He died tragically by drowning in the River Kelvin. His son Brian aged 15 was interesting Celtic in 1975.

Appearances:
SL: 107 apps. 0 gls.
SLC: 31 apps. 1 gl.
SC: 13 apps. 0 gls.
Total: *151 apps. 1 gl.*

BAILLIE, William Alexander

Role: Centre-half 1982-91
6′ 2″ 12st.0lbs.
b. Hamilton, 6th July 1966

CAREER: Burnbank BC/CELTIC 20 Aug
1982/(Toronto Blizzard loan cs 1990)/CELTIC
again 30 Aug 1990/St Mirren 6 June 1991/free
Apr 1993/Dunfermline Athletic 10 Aug 1993/
retired July 1994/Strathclyde Police.

Debut v Falkirk (a) 2-0 (SL) 22.12.87 (sub)

Big Lex was the son of ex-Rangers pivot Doug Baillie and first played for Celtic in the Glasgow Cup against Queen's Park on May 14th 1985. He came on as a second-half substitute in Davie Provan's Testimonial against Nottingham Forest (30th November 1987) and made a strong impression. Of outsiders, only his father was meant to know in advance he was in the team to play Souness' Rangers in the vital Premier League match of 2nd January 1988 at Parkhead (when he broke a couple of Chris Woods' ribs as they went up together for a corner). He made an excellent deputy for

McCarthy and ran big Mick neck and neck for a first team place until he was short with the pass-back that gave Dundee an equaliser when every point was precious (13th February 1988). He came in for McCarthy during the traumatic autumn of 1988 and although Keith Wright outpaced him to set up a Tommy Coyne goal for Dundee on September 24th the fans booed angrily when he was replaced by Billy Stark late on. He carried the blame for the 3-1 defeat at Easter Road the following week. Lex served the Celtic reserves well in his long patient stint at Parkhead (for a good while as captain and never afraid to make himself heard). Ligament trouble in August 1989 saw him off to Canada for rehabilitation but on return (26th August 1990) his chances against Paul Elliott were few. When he started alongside Elliott against Hibs on September 8th it was his first game for Celtic in 18 months. Versus St Mirren on November 17th 1990, Billy McNeill hailed him as "the best". He played his last game for Celtic in Packy Bonner's testimonial on May 12th 1991. Davie Hay took him to Love Street for £90,000.

Lex Baillie

Appearances:
SL: 32 apps. 1 gl.
Eur: 1 app. 0 gls.
Total: *33 apps. 1 gl.*

BAINES, Roy

Role: Goalkeeper 1976-79
6' 0" 11st.7lbs.
b. Derby, 7th February 1950

CAREER: Woodpecker Bar FC Derby/Roe Farm FC Derby/Derby County/ Hibernian 9 Sept 1968/free 1972/ Morton 9 Aug 1972/ CELTIC 28 Oct 1976/Morton 8 Mar 1979/ free by oversight May 1983/ St Johnstone 3 Aug 1983/free 27 Apr 1985/Tranent Juniors manager 1985.

Debut v Dundee United (h) 2-0 (SL) 26.3.77

Brian Clough freed Roy Baines on his arrival at Derby as manager but Celtic invited the big Bobby Moore look-alike for a trial at the end of June 1968. Stein had a full quota of goalies and commended the Englishman to Bob Shankly at Easter Road where he signed after a month's trial. Roy came to Celtic Park eventually in exchange for Andy Ritchie and £10,000 but was never able wholly to displace Peter Latchford. He made his debut when Peter twisted his ankle against Rangers on 19th March 1977 (one English goalie replacing another) and saved a Hamish McAlpine penalty at 0-0. He did his bit to bring home big Jock's 10th League title with Celtic. Benny Rooney offered him a much mitigated ('continental') training schedule to come back to Cappielow (as opposed to a 200 mile round trip daily) and Roy went back down the Clyde for the best years of his career. He is at present Mine Host of the Keeper's Arms, Tranent (Davy Adams' old stamping-ground) and an enthusiastic supporter of Edinburgh Monarchs speedway team.

Appearances:
SL: 12 apps.
6 shut-outs.
SLC: 3 apps.
0 shut-outs.
SC: 1 app.
1 shut-out.
Total: *16 apps.*
7 shut-outs
(44%).

Roy Baines

BARBER, Thomas

Role: Half-back 1918
5' 8" 11st.3lbs.
b. Derby, 20th February 1888
d. Nuneaton, 18th September 1925

CAREER: Todd's Nook Board School/
Hamotley FC/West Stanley FC 1904/Bolton
Wanderers May 1908/Aston Villa 24 Dec
1912/(CELTIC loan 23 Aug 1918)/(Partick
Thistle loan 27 Dec 1918)/(Linfield & Belfast
Celtic loan Jan 1919)/Stalybridge Celtic 1919/
Crystal Palace 1920/Merthyr Town 1920/
Walsall 1921/Darlaston 1922/Hinckley United
1922/retired 1923.

Debut v Clyde (a) 3-0 (SL) 31.8.18

There were 122,000 spectators at the English
Cup Final at Crystal Palace on 19th April 1913
when Tom Barber scored the only goal (a
looping header from 30 yards following a
Charlie Wallace corner, the way Clem
Stephenson had dreamed Villa would score)
versus Sunderland with ten minutes to go.
When War broke out in 1914 he joined the
Footballers' Battalion but after leg wounds on
the Western Front was laid-up in Aberdeen
Infirmary in Aug 1916: "I'll never be able to
play football again." He recovered sufficiently
to play for England versus Scotland in the
Haig Hospital Fund International at Celtic
Park on June 8th 1918. Sent to work in

*Tom Barber, then of Aston Villa, with 'The
Footballers' Battalion' during the First World War.*

*Back row (left to right): Bairnsfather (Croydon
Common), Jones (Birmingham & Brighton), Booth
(Brighton), Beech (Brighton), Lonsdale (Southend
& Grimsby), J.Smith (Chesterfield), unknown,
Martin (Grimsby), Sheldon (Man Utd &
Liverpool).*
*Front: Gallagher (Spurs), Capt. Bell
(Southampton), Capt. Woodward (Chelsea), Major
Buckley (Derby), Wheelhouse (Grimsby), Barber
(Aston Villa), Bullock (Huddersfield).*

munitions at Glasgow, Tom ("a first-class man
without a doubt") helped the Celts to two
wins out of two but went down with pleurisy
in September 1918. He came back to take
McMenemy's place on November 23rd.
Partick Thistle were so confidently expected to
beat Celtic for the first time ever for points
that the queues stretched outside Firhill until
half-time. Celtic won 0-1. His last game for
Celtic was a 3-1 defeat at Motherwell. Tom
was stricken with tuberculosis and went too
early to his grave.

Appearances:
SL: 5 apps. 0 gls.
Total: *5 apps. 0 gls.*

BARCLAY, Graham

Role: Goalkeeper 1973-77
6' 0" 11st.7lbs.
b. Bothwell, 11th April 1957

CAREER: Hamilton
Amateurs/Blantyre Victoria
1973/CELTIC 19 Aug 1973/
(Dunfermline Athletic loan 25
July 1975)/free 30 Apr 1977.

Debut v Clydebank (h) 4-1 (SC)
15.2.75

Graham Barclay

In 1974 Jock Stein was
already planning his Celtic
side of 1977 and its
goalkeeper was professional guitarist
Graham Barclay. Rangers were interested but
at 16 he was a Celtic player and "a great
prospect" who had obviously been told to
work with '77 in mind. He first played for
Celtic against Preston North End on August
2nd 1974 the day Bobby Charlton made his
come-back to first-class football. His
performances for Scotland Pro Youth were
seldom short of brilliant but when Celtic (two
teams, four goalkeepers) released him in the
spring of his prospective golden year he had
played a mere ten reserve games in all. Ally
Hunter was dropped for the Clydebank Cup-
tie and Denis Connaghan's cartilage was
playing up so Graham went into the team. He
was mostly employed keeping his hands
warm, and two days later Peter Latchford
arrived at Parkhead, recommended by Don
Revie. He received no offers until Eric Smith
asked him to assist Hamilton Academicals just
before Christmas. Graham had by then opened
a successful Gentlemen's Outfitters with his
brother, his Saturdays were fully taken-up,
and at the age of 20, he said no.

> **Appearances:**
> *SC: 1 app. 0 shut-outs.*
> **Total:** *1 app. 0 shut-outs.*

BARRIE, James

Role: Full-back 1930
5' 10" 11st.10lbs.
b. Old Kilpatrick, 20th October 1902

CAREER: Duntocher Hibernian 1921/
Kirkintilloch Rob Roy 1922/Duntocher
Hibernian 1923/Dumbarton (trial) 15 Feb

1923/Queen's Park 27 Feb
1923/Clydebank Jan 1924/
Bethlehem Steel USA 1926/
New Bedford USA 1928/Fall
River USA 1929/CELTIC (trial)
4 Feb 1930/free 14 July 1930/
Halifax Town 28 July 1930/
Worcester City Aug 1933/
Cowdenbeath 11 Jan 1934.

Debut v Airdrie (h) 1-2 (SL)
5.2.30

Jimmy Barrie, "a Baillieston
product and a good one", came
to Celtic recommended by the
great Bill Harper, ex-Hibs and
Scotland 'keeper and went
straight into the team for a mid-week fixture
with the Waysiders. This was the notorious
clash in which John Thomson took such a
brutal kicking from Skinner of Airdrie and
Peter McGonagle of Celtic also broke teeth,
jaw and collarbone. Celtic were desperate for
full-backs but Jimmy was tried just the once.

> **Appearances:**
> *SL: 1 app. 0 gls.*
> **Total:** *1 app. 0 gls.*

BATTLES, Bernard

Role: Full-back, half-back 1895-97; 1898-1904
5' 11" 13st.10lbs.
b. Springburn, 13th January 1875
d. Glasgow, 9th February 1905

CAREER: Linlithgow Juniors/Bathgate
Rovers/Broxburn Shamrock/Bathgate FC
1893/Hearts 1 Sept 1894/CELTIC 8 June 1895/
(Liverpool loan 28 Mar 1896)/Dundee 1 May
1897/Liverpool 28 Mar 1898/CELTIC 3 Oct
1898/Kilmarnock 11 June 1904.

Debut v Dundee (a) 2-1 (SL) 10.8.1895

> *"Brave Battles! Brilliant on the football field*
> *Best of defenders before the threatened goal*
> *Strong in attack and steadfast in control*
> *When greatest pressed, the least inclined to yield."*

(Lines by another Celtic player, perhaps Sandy
McMahon, on the occasion of Barney's death).
Celtic played Rangers in the Glasgow Cup
final at first Cathkin on November 21st 1896:
"...fouls were numerous... Celtic were always
the aggressors." One week later Celtic had
Hibs at Parkhead in a vital League match. The
entire Celtic team wanted the press box

cleared of their critics but only Battles, Divers and Meehan saw it through and refused to strip. Celtic took a high moral line: the trio were suspended until season's end and their wages cut drastically. Barney had offers to go to England but had given his word to Dundee. He broke his wrist on 28th January 1898 and played the following two matches with his arm in splints and held in a sling. Dundee put Hearts (their tormentors of earlier in the season) out of the Cup 3-0 on February 5th and then a week later gifted the League to Celtic by beating Rangers in a match Ibrox had to win. "St Bernard Battles, Patron of Parkhead" proclaimed the newspapers. "... surely after today, the Celts will forgive and forget the dressing-room revolt?" That autumn, Celtic were in such doldrums James Kelly and Willie Maley were each thinking of a come-back. Instead, the club ate humble pie and brought the mighty Barney home from exile.

"Back to the Celtic again
Let us join in the happy refrain
Out with your rattles
For Big Barney Battles
Is back with the Celtic again!"

Celtic revived. Barney was total inspiration every game he played. In the Scottish Cup final of April 22nd 1899 against Rangers it was he who admonished the maimed Jack Bell to stay on the field and Jack set up Celtic's second goal. Scotland rewarded him with a full set of caps (three) in 1900-01 (the sensation of the day in that he replaced Rangers crack full-back Nicol Smith). 'Gentle Barney' was a robust performer, especially when out-paced, and a marked man with referees and opposing supporters. He died suddenly at home in Glasgow's Gallowgate after a bout of influenza. His coffin was carried out of Sacred

Heart Bridgeton by Doyle, McMahon, Campbell and Orr, then followed by an enormous cortege of 2,000 while another 40,000 lined the route to Dalbeth on Sunday February 12th in mute testimony to the love they bore a great, great Celt. He is buried in lair 412, section 3A, nowadays overgrown and virtually inaccessible.

"Now by the graveside,
under Spring's soft
skies
In grief we stand, with
hearts broken
And heads bowed".

Appearances:
SL: 110 apps. 6 gls.
SC: 26 apps. 0 gls.
Total: *136 apps. 6 gls.*

♣ **Celtic note:** *Barney Battles junior was born posthumously and himself fathered a son on February 28th 1940. Barney's own father once demanded free entrance at Tynecastle: "I am the man that put the bone in him!"*

BAUCHOP, James Rae

Role: Wing-forward 1906-09
5' 10" 11st.8lbs.
b. Sauchie, 24th May 1886
d. Bradford, 13th June 1948

CAREER: Sauchie FC May 1902/Alloa 30 May 1904/CELTIC 2 Jan 1906/(Norwich City loan 15 May 1907)/(Crystal Palace loan Mar 1908)/Derby County 21 May 1909/Tottenham Hotspur May 1913/Bradford PA Dec 1913/(CELTIC loan Ne'erday 1918)/(Rangers loan Jan 1918 (did not play))/(Bradford City loan 14 Sept 1918)/Doncaster Rovers 1922/Lincoln City Sept 1923/retired 1924/Bradford PA trainer 1924.

Debut v Falkirk (h) 7-0 (SL) 6.1.06 (scored once)

Jimmy Bauchop joined the six-in-a-row side as a deputy winger and impressed at once as a "cool and effective" exponent on right or left. He went on the 1906 club tour of Europe, took a bad knocking-about in Berlin on May 27th and was down with a severe bout of food poisoning in Budapest on June 3rd. Jimmy was unable to command a regular first-team place and according to Jimmy Quinn, "We were sorry to see him go." He was destined to peak in England where he flourished as an inside-left with a dynamite shot, hat-tricks a speciality. Wherever he went he was a huge pull with the fans and his transfer always regarded as "the catch of the season." He was

Jimmy Bauchop

famed for "splendid crosses, grand outfield work and deadly shooting." Jimmy Quinn and Steve Bloomer were both ardent admirers of his work. In the search for a replacement for Quinn, Maley watched him at centre for Spurs at Anfield on November 23rd 1913. He played centre for Celtic on Ne'erday 1918 but was tightly marked on a day when Celtic had all the pressure but could not score.

Appearances:
SL: 14 apps. 5 gls.
Total: *14 apps. 5 gls.*

BEATTIE, Richard

Role: Goalkeeper 1954-59
5' 11" 11st.2lbs.
b. Glasgow, 24th October 1936
d. Old Kilpatrick, 15th August 1990

CAREER: Lusset Juveniles/Duntocher Hibernian cs 1954/CELTIC 26 Sept 1954/ (Rangers loan 11 Mar 1959)/Portsmouth 10 Aug 1959/Peterborough United 29 May 1962/ St Mirren 4 Jan 1963/not retained 30 Apr 1964/Brechin City as free agent 15 Aug 1964 (one game only).

Debut v Falkirk (a) 1-1 (SLC) 3.9.55

Dick Beattie played his first game for Celtic in the Floodlight Friendly for the Championship of the East End versus Clyde at Shawfield on October 20th 1954. He arrived at Parkhead unable to cope with high balls but was prepared to work at his game and as a result his name is associated forever in the Celtic memory with October 19th 1957 when Celtic not only retained the League Cup but hammered Rangers 7-1 into the bargain. As Bonnar's successor, he was brave, athletic and

skilful. He had three impossible saves versus Hibs at Easter Road right near the start of the match on 29th December 1956 and then the game of his life at the same venue versus Reilly, Baker and Ormond on November 23rd 1957 a match during which he even got behind an Eddie Turnbull penalty. There was the occasional bad day. He was having a magnificent game for a 10-man Celtic versus Clyde in the Glasgow Cup on August 20th 1958 when he hit a short goal kick to Dunky MacKay with five to go. Dunky played it back, Dick fumbled and in came Johnny

Dick Beattie

Coyle: 1-1. He had been cutting Tommy Ring's crosses out all night. A minute later he missed his first: 1-2 for Clyde. Against Motherwell on January 2nd 1959 he lost another two goals in the last two minutes for a 3-3 draw that signalled the end for Beattie as Celtic's 'keeper. Dick and his distinctive orange jockey cap took off to England and trouble in the shape of Jimmy Gauld. He pleaded guilty to two charges of taking a bribe (both in England) and was sent down for nine months at Mansfield on January 26th 1965. He did his time and went back to earning his livelihood as a welder including a stint in Algiers. He skippered St Mirren at Parkhead on March 9th 1963 and came out to a huge ovation.

Appearances:
SL: 114 apps. 29 shut-outs
SLC: 28 apps. 10 shut-outs
SC: 14 apps. 4 shut-outs.
Total: *156 apps. 43 shut-outs (28%).*

BELL, Andrew

Andy Bell

Role: Goalkeeper 1951-55
5' 11" 12st.0lbs.
b. 14th July 1932

CAREER: 69 Coy Ruchill BB/Victoria Thistle Juveniles 1949/Hearts (trial) Aug & Sept 1949/ Arthurlie Sept 1949/ CELTIC 27 Aug 1951/ Army Dec 1953/free Apr 1955/Airdrie 8 Aug 1955/ St Johnstone 8 Sept 1956/ free 1957/Albion Rovers 14 Sept 1957.

Debut v Dundee (a) 1-2 (SL) 20.10.51

After losing three goals to Rangers in the League Cup semi-final of October 13th 1951, Johnny Bonnar was dropped, his deputy Alex Devanney passed-over, and the job of Celtic goalkeeper before 30,000 fans at Dundee given to 20-year old apprentice engineering draughtsman and opening bat for Barr & Stroud, Andy Bell, who had made his debut for Celtic reserves also at Dens Park only a fortnight before. He was taken aboard the team bus by skipper John McPhail. "Boys, meet your new goalie." Of the entire first team squad he knew only Jock and Donald Weir but neither was present (Tully was dropped for the first time). The week following his Dundee

ordeal the young 'keeper faced at Parkhead the most redoubtable forward line ever to represent the Hibs: Smith and Johnstone; Reilly; Turnbull and Ormond. He held out until 12 minutes from time. Rangers were his undoing on Ne'erday 1952 and when Sonny Hunter returned from Switzerland, Andy reverted to Celtic's No. 3 goalkeeper. He enjoyed his finest hour with Bonnar injured and Hunter dropped, against Rangers in the Scottish League on September 19th 1953 when he lost a goal in 20 minutes, saw Celtic equalise at once, then took everything Ibrox could throw at him for the rest of the game: "... swallow-diving to grasp a Paton header... hurling himself across goal to tip over a Waddell piledriver... saving point-blank again from Waddell." Andy lost his place when he damaged his shoulder against Drumcondra on October 5th 1953 and although he took over as Celtic goalie again playing League and Cup when Bonnar cracked a bone in his hand (February 17th to March 13th in the Double Year of 1954) the demands of Military Service and the signings of Beattie and McCreadie meant his effective career as a Celt was over.

Appearances:
SL: 25 apps. 3 shut-outs.
SC: 3 apps. 0 shut-outs.
Total: *28 apps. 3 shut-outs (11%).*

BELL, James

Role: Goalkeeper 1890-91
b. Mauchline, 30th March 1866

CAREER: Hurlford/Mauchline FC 1884/Ayr FC/Mauchline FC Aug 1887/Dumbarton 1888/CELTIC Aug 1890/Hurlford 1891/ Kilmarnock Apr 1894.

Debut v Hearts (a) 5-0 (SL) 23.8.1890

Jamie Bell was Celtic's very first League goalkeeper. Stop-gap James McLaren, a magnificent left-half, had given an "inglorious display" in the 1-4 defeat by Renton the previous week but that very

Jamie Bell

first points game was expunged from the record. Jamie Bell was played in too much of a hurry: he was not a complete fortnight clear of his last club engagement and for that Celtic were deducted four points on September 4th 1890. He played the whole of the first League season but the club moved to secure Tom Duff for 1891-92. When Celtic were at Seamill Hydro in October 1966, Sean Fallon was shown a medal by a man working nearby, won by his grandfather playing for Celtic. It was for the Glasgow Cup at 2nd Hampden (Cathkin Park) on February 14th 1891 when the cry went up: "Celtic have won a Cup at last!" It belonged to the goalie on that auspicious day: Jamie Bell.

Appearances:
SL: 15 apps. 4 shut-outs.
SC: 7 apps. 2 shut-outs.
Total: *22 apps. 6 shut-outs (27%).*

BELL, John

Role: Winger 1897-1900
5' 11" 12st.7lbs.
b. Dumbarton, 6th October 1869

CAREER: Dumbarton Union/Dumbarton 1887/Everton 1893/CELTIC 13 Aug 1898/ New Brighton Tower Nov 1900/Everton 1901/ Preston NE 1903/retired 14 Sept 1908/Preston NE manager-coach 1909/to Canada Mar 1911.

Debut v Third Lanark (h) 2-1 (SL) 20.8.1898

"A thrusting winger, a precision passer, a defence buster as the mood took him," Jack Bell had made Celtic suffer plenty from his destructive speed as a Dumbarton player (eg; in the 0-8 defeat of Ne'erday 1892 when he scored two) and Glasgow was stupefied that Willie Maley should have bought him for the phenomenal outlay of £300 to replace Jimmy Blessington. So much so, the *Evening Times* rushed out a special edition. Everton fans wanted rid of their Scots and Jack had promised himself to Celtic on May 4th 1898 if manager Dick Molineux succumbed to the pressure. Ibrox came in for him but he kept his word to Celtic. In the Scottish Cup final versus Rangers on April 22nd 1899 he was a passenger from the 55th minute and made frequently as if to come off. The Celtic fans howled at the very idea and Battles gestured at him he must stay. Jack persevered and set up the move that culminated in the second

Jack Bell

goal: Celtic 2 Rangers 0. He played (and scored) in the Rosebery international of 7th April 1900 against England at Celtic Park in a forward line (he was inside-left and Johnny Campbell inside-right) regarded as "the finest attack that ever represented Scotland." A week later he played versus Queen's Park throughout the 'Hurricane Final' of 14th April 1900 and got a vital point for Celtic just before the interval to send them in 3-1 up with the gale to face in the second half. Celtic won 4-3. Jack was alive and well in Wallasey 1951.

Appearances:
SL: 35 apps. 16 gls.
FSC: 11 apps. 7 gls.
Total: *46 apps. 23 gls.*

BENNETT, Alexander

Role: Forward 1903-08
5' 8" 11st.6lbs.
b. 20th October 1881
d. 9th January 1940

CAREER: Stonelaw High Grade School Rutherglen/Rutherglen Woodburn/ Rutherglen Glencairn/Hearts (trial) 20 Apr 1903/CELTIC 21 Apr 1903/Rangers 9 May 1908/Scottish Rifles 12 Jan 1917/(Ayr United

Alec Bennett

loan as "Thomson" 6 Nov 1917)/Dumbarton 11 Mar 1918/Albion Rovers 13 July 1920/3rd Lanark manager Aug 1921/resigned 23 May 1924/Clydebank manager May 1924/resigned July 1926.

Debut v Partick Thistle (h) 2-1 (SL) 15.8.03 (scored once)

Celtic went through to Gorgie Road on April 20th 1903 and took a 3-0 skinning from Hearts in the Inter-City League. Hearts had a trialist centre out hiding his identity under the pseudonym Johnston. He pulled Celtic apart on the pitch but travelled back to Glasgow with them on the train. The following day under his real name Alec Bennett he was a Celtic player signed and sealed but with a proviso which allowed his release for £50 at any time. He played his first game for Celtic in the Inter-City League versus Dundee at Parkhead on May 2nd 1903. He missed the Scottish Cup of April 16th 1904, officially because he had 'flu, unofficially because Celtic's opponents Rangers were already tapping him. He played in the great forward line of Bennett, McMenemy, Quinn, Somers and Hamilton for the first time in the Inter-City league versus Rangers at Parkhead a fortnight later (a match which counted for four points). This was the Celtic forward line which won the League

rubber against Rangers at Hampden on May 6th 1905, the first of Celtic's six Flags in a row and the first of Alec's four Championship medals won with Celtic. He won two Scottish Cup medals with Celtic: 3-0 against Hearts on April 20th 1907 and 5-1 (he opened the scoring) against St Mirren on April 18th 1908 when, in rampant form, he ran the Buddies ragged. He also scored the goal at Ibrox that won the Championship for Celtic one week later. He joined Rangers as a free agent under his agreement but Jimmy Quinn believes he was perfectly happy where he was, just unable to withstand siren voices from Govan. His departure broke the hearts of the faithful, not so much because it was to Rangers, but because it meant the loss of a genuine footballer, a total trier, whose "every movement had a meaning and a purpose". Celtic played Partick Thistle in the Charity Cup on May 2nd 1908 at Parkhead and after the game (in which Alec did not play) a fan penetrated the pavilion, inquired which were Bennett's boots and began to extract the laces. He winked to the Icicle McNair: "I'll keep these. Just a wee souvenir."

Appearances:
SL: 126 apps. 47 gls.
SC: 26 apps. 6 gls.
Total: *152 apps. 53 gls.*

♣ **Celtic note:** *Alec played 18 times for Scotland when caps were a rarity. His grandson, prop-forward Sandy Carmichael MBE, played rugby 50 times for Scotland and toured twice with the British Lions.*

BIGGINS, Wayne

Role: Striker 1993-94
5' 11" 11st.7lbs.
b. Sheffield, 20th November 1961

CAREER: Lincoln City app. 1979/pro. 1980/ free 1981/Matlock Town 1981/King's Lynn 1982/Matlock Town 1983/Burnley Feb 1984/ Norwich City Oct 1985/Manchester City July 1988/Stoke City 10 Aug 1989/Barnsley 1 Oct 1992/CELTIC 24 Nov 1993/Stoke City 24 Mar 1994.

Debut v Motherwell (h) 2-0 (SL) 24.11.93 (sub)

Veteran striker 'Bertie' Biggins was Lou Macari's first signing as manager of Celtic and came to Parkhead in part-exchange for Andy

Wayne Biggins

BIRRELL, James

Role: Outside-left 1938-39
5' 7" 10st.10lbs.
b. Dunfermline, 19th September 1916

CAREER: Blairhall Colliery/Third Lanark (trial) 1937/CELTIC 3 Jan 1938/(East Fife loan 3 Nov 1939)/registration cancelled 31 Aug 1940/... Dunfermline Athletic Aug-Oct 1941.

Debut v Clyde (n) 3-0 (GC) 15.10.38

Jimmy Birrell was part of the Celtic intake of 1938 that included Tom Harvey, James McMillan, Johnnie Wilson (all Blairhall Colliery) and Harry Keenan of Cambuslang Rangers and Clyde. His career was a short one but at least he got a medal - and Glasgow Cup medals were hard-won and cherished in 1938. He took Frank Murphy's place before a crowd of 43,976 at Hampden as the first newcomer into the great side of 1938 and was acclaimed "Celtic's latest left-wing sensation." Chairman Tom White watched Celtic beat a very good Clyde team and declared it the best Parkhead side of his experience. Jimmy took on the Bully Wee defence and sent over the "picture cross" from which Delaney headed the first goal three minutes after half-time. On the outbreak of War in 1939 he returned to Fife to do his bit as a miner. He scored five goals for East Fife against Stenhousemuir (and Willie Buchan) on December 16th 1939.

Appearances:
SL: 6 apps.
2 gls.
Total: *6 apps.*
2 gls.

Jimmy Birrell

Payton. He was signed at 3.30pm and took the field at 8.55pm the same day as a Celtic substitute. It was the start of his second period of service under manager Macari (whom he helped win the Autoglass Trophy with Stoke at Wembley on 16th May 1992). Doug Baillie watched him versus Raith Rovers at Parkhead on November 27th 1993: "He is a big, strong, hard-working lad who, like his near-namesake Biggles, is better in the air than on the ground." Bertie scored two for Celtic against St Patrick's Athletic at the Richmond Ground, Inchicore on January 12th 1994 but failed to disturb any riggings in the Scottish Premier. Ex-Celtic coach Joe Jordan took him back to Stoke for £125,000 on the transfer deadline day of 1993-94.

Appearances:
SL: 9 apps. 0 gls.
SC: 1 app. 0 gls.
Total: *10 apps. 0 gls.*

BLACK, John

Role: Centre-forward 1911-12
5' 10" 12st.0lbs.
b. Glasgow

CAREER: Govanhill Avondale/Benburb/
CELTIC 28 Sept 1912/(Thornliebank loan
24 Apr 1912)/(Abercorn loan 8 Sept 1912)/
(Belfast Celtic loan May 1913)/Clyde 2 May
1914/(Wishaw Thistle loan 21 Apr 1916)/
(Abercorn loan 6 May 1916)/Clydebank 8 Aug
1916/Abercorn 31 July 1917/(St Mirren loan
27 Oct 1917)/Dumbarton Harp 5 Aug 1918/
Dumbarton 12 June 1919/Albion Rovers Jan
1920/Abertillery Town Aug 1920/Bathgate
8 Feb 1922/Dumbarton Harp 17 Sept 1923.

Debut v Hibernian (h) 3-1 (SL) 28.10.11

"A host in himself," John Black was a
blacksmith by trade and tried out for Celtic at
Dumfries the same day as Patsy Gallagher and
Willie Angus, the future VC. He and Angus
were signed but Patsy was rejected
(temporarily) as too wee. At centre-forward,
Gunner Willie Nichol was standing in for
Jimmy Quinn but when neither was fit,
Johnny Black played. "He shapes well but is
apt to wander a little." His one counter for
Celtic was a "smart goal" from a Travers
back-heel on 28th October 1911. With
Abercorn he knocked in the hat-trick that gave
the Paisley club the Qualifying Cup 4-1 versus
Arbroath at Cathkin on January 25th 1913
after a saga of games played and postponed.
Jimmy Blessington took him to Belfast at a
time when Celtic were desperate for a centre
to understudy Quinn. Clyde paid Parkhead
£10 for Johnny's services.

Appearances:
SL: 4 apps. 1 gl.
Total: *4 apps. 1 gl.*

BLACK, William

Role: Half-back 1904-05
5' 9" 12st.0lbs.
b. Flemington, 16th May 1878

CAREER: Dalziel Rovers 1900/Queen's Park
1903/CELTIC 21 Apr 1904/Everton 29 May
1905/(Broxburn loan 4 Aug 1906)/Everton
again Dec 1906/Dumbarton 26 Aug 1907/
Kilmarnock 8 June 1908/Hamilton
Academicals 26 Aug 1909/Ayr Parkhouse

4 May 1910/Ayr United 12 Aug 1910/
Annbank 1 May 1913/Thornhill Sept 1914.

*Debut v Port Glasgow Athletic (a) 4-1 (SL)
27.8.04*

It was Celtic's boast they never poached from
Queen's Park; then they signed Bob Campbell
and University student Willie Black but to the
mind of Maley neither Spider turned out to be
much of a catch. Willie Black was brought to
Parkhead as cover for Sunny Jim Young and
Jimmy Hay in the first Championship season
of the 6-in-a-row. Young, Loney and Hay, the
most famous half-back line in the club's
history was frequently Black, Loney and Hay
or Young, Loney and Black. And they were
loyal to him. When he was carried off crippled
versus Partick Thistle in a wild tough match
just days before Christmas 1904, Sunny Jim
went looking for James Sommen, the guilty
Jag, and joined Willie (but ordered-off, not
carried-off) in the pavilion shortly after.
Another leg injury seriously threatened his
career at Everton.

Appearances:
SL: 10 apps. 0 gls.
SC: 1 app. 0 gls.
Total: *11 apps. 0 gls.*

BLACKWOOD, John

Role: Centre-forward 1899-1900
b. Maine, USA, c 1877

CAREER: Petershill/CELTIC 21 Sept 1899/
(Partick Thistle loan 28 October 1899)/
CELTIC again 2 May 1900/Woolwich Arsenal
9 May 1900/Reading May 1901/QPR 1902/
West Ham United 1904/Royal Albert 2 Sept
1905.

Debut v Hearts (h) 0-2 (SL) 30.9.1899

John Blackwood and Willie McOustra both
played a trial for Celtic versus the Kaffirs,
tourists from the Orange Free State at
Parkhead on 21st September 1899 and were
signed after the game. John was described as a
"very old-looking junior". He took over the
centre-forward position from Johnny
Campbell against a no-nonsense Hearts team
on September 30th 1899 but was so far out of
his depth that Barney Battles moved up front
in the second half. John played to a backdrop
of the spanking new Grant Stand "looking
splendid in cream." He was not meant for

Celtic but scored goals for Thistle and seems to have been much sought after in the English Southern League.

Appearances:
SL: 1 app. 0 gls.
Total: 1 app. 0 gls.

BLAIR, Daniel

Role: Inside-forward 1924-27
5' 7" 11st.0lbs.
b. Glasgow, 2nd February 1905

CAREER: St Anthony's/CELTIC 6 Sept 1924/ (Ayr United loan 29 Oct 1926)/free 22 Aug 1927/Glasgow Perthshire 1927.

Debut v Morton (a) 0-1 (SL) 1.11.24

Dan was "a wee one but tricky." "I have seldom seen a young fellow with better judgement in his passes." In the club tradition long-cherished that a Celtic player could fit in anywhere, Dan Blair made his debut at outside-left at Cappielow where he could observe the fighting on the terraces close at hand and mingle with fans seeking refuge down his flank. He was watched from the stand by a Third Lanark forward with a crocked shoulder: Tommy McInally veering towards a second term at Parkhead if young Blair didn't look like filling Patsy Gallagher's boots. In Dan's next game on December 20th 1924, that is exactly what he was required to do but with no Patsy "Celtic were like sheep without a shepherd." When Maley decided to retire the Atom, it was McInally got the nod, not Dan Blair, the wee boy hailed not so long before as "the new McMenemy."

Appearances:
SL: 3 apps. 0 gls.
Total: 3 apps. 0 gls.

BLAIR, John

Role: Outside-right 1910

CAREER: Cliftonville Olympic/Cliftonville Apr 1904/Belfast Celtic Jan 1908/CELTIC Oct 1910/Motherwell Dec 1910/Belfast Celtic 1911/Linfield 1912/Shelbourne Dec 1912/ Cliftonville 1914/retired 1915.

Debut v Third Lanark (h) 0-0 (SL) 19.11.10

John Blair was an amateur who had played for Ireland against Wales in 1907 and Scotland

and England in 1908. When he came over to work in the yards at Clydebank, Celtic snapped him up and his debut was eagerly awaited. He played only one game in a forward line reading Blair, McMenemy, Quinn, Johnstone and Kivlichan. "Had he been a left-winger, or a half-back or a back, he would, perhaps, have been of more value to Celtic." He failed to make enough of a mark but went on to play six times for Motherwell.

Appearances:
SL: 1 app. 0 gls.
Total: 1 app. 0 gls.

BLESSINGTON, James

Role: Inside-right 1892-98
5' 8" 11st.6lbs.
b. Linlithgow, 28th February 1874
d. Newton Abbott, Devon, 18th April 1939

CAREER: Hibernian 1889/Leith Hibernian 1891/Leith Athletic 1891/(St Bernard's loan Aug 1892)/CELTIC 27 Aug 1892/(Preston NE loan 18 Feb 1898)/Preston NE cs 1898/Derby County June 1899/Bristol City Nov 1899/ Luton Town 1900/Leicester Fosse May 1903/ manager Jan 1907 until Apr 1909/...Belfast Celtic coach 1913-14/Works Football (Luton) by Mar 1918/Abertillery Town manager June 1921.

Debut v Pollokshaws Athletic (a) 7-2 (GC) 17.9.1892

Son of a quarryman, Jimmy Blessington dropped his apprenticeship as a blacksmith to join Celtic during the traumatic summer of 1892 when it looked as if they were going to lose four top men: McCallum, McMahon, Madden and Brady. Leith alleged the Glasgow Irishmen had poached him: "On his own admission Celtic badgered him to join them." While Nottingham Forest were going to all lengths to conceal McCallum and McMahon, Celtic had Blessington in hiding in Glasgow to stop Leith making contact until they managed to play him at Johnstone on August 24th: "He applied to join us when the Hibs broke up...We offered him Alec Brady's place and sent a rep to ask why he didn't want it. The rep brought Blessington back with him." The SFA exonerated Celtic but suspended the new Celt until 15th September 1892 for a version of events that would not tally. He was inside-right week after week without fail in Celtic's

Jimmy Blessington

first two Championship seasons of 1892-93-94 and honoured with four caps by Scotland for whom he scored some vital goals. This ideal professional was rarely in trouble on or off the park but did clash with the Parkhead executive in August 1897 over his other job: employment by a bookie. Celtic were more inclined to put him out of the game than let him stay with Preston but the player had too many offers from non-League clubs for Parkhead to prevail. Jimmy Kelly told him: "If you were dead, we'd need to replace you." Jimmy was unable to take up a coaching appointment in Germany on the outbreak of War in 1914 and served in the Merchant Navy on the Atlantic route for a time and got out to Celtic Park whenever he docked in Glasgow. He resumed his trade as an electrician in Luton before taking over the running of the Victoria Hotel, St Peter's Port, Guernsey in the 1920s. Some of his medals (and beautiful!) were on show at the People's Palace during the Celtic Centenary Exhibition in 1988.

Appearances:
SL: 82 apps. 31 gls.
SC: 17 apps. 7 gls.
Total: *99 apps. 38 gls.*

BODEN, Alexander

Role: Centre-half 1943-56
5' 11" 12st.0lbs.
b. Hardgate, 13th August 1925

CAREER: Duntocher St Mary's BG/ CELTIC 12 Aug 1943/Army Nov 1943 (Dumbarton loan 1945)(Forres Mechanics loan 13 Oct 1946)/demobbed Oct 1946/ (Cowdenbeath loan 5 Dec 1946)/Ayr United 8 Sept 1956/ Clydebank coach 29 June 1958/CELTIC coach 15 July 1958/asst. trainer 1961/scout & coach 18 June 1967.
Debut v Third Lanark (h) 3-1 (SLC) 23.8.47

An unmistakable presence with his straight back, red hair and gap-toothed grin, Alec Boden was the first of Celtic's genuine stopper centre-halves as of 1948. He had been a Sergeant PTI in the Forces and was regularly entrusted with the pre-season training. Alec was seldom a classic centre-half but was always a battler and an out-and-out jersey player. He and outside-right Johnny Gribbon joined Celtic at the same time from Duntocher St Mary's but Alec (having almost signed for Wolves who were creaming off the best of Scottish juvenile talent during the war years) was

Alec Boden in 1949 versus Rangers at Ibrox.

called up almost at once to fight Hitler. In the Army he lost two cartilages, both from the same knee. He went on loan to Cowdenbeath because of a plethora of centre-halves at Parkhead: Corbett, McMillan and Mallan. At Ibrox on 16th October 1948, under the eye of Rangers' special guest, Mr de Valera, Alec cannoned a clearance off Billy Williamson's back that looped into the air 20 yards out and over the head of a stranded Willie Miller for a freak goal to put Celtic 1-0 down in a vital League Cup-tie. For 1949-50 he took over as skipper from Pat McAuley. He tore his kneecap versus Raith Rovers at Parkhead two days after Christmas 1952 and did the same again at Tynecastle on Valentine's Day 1953. Alec was popular with the executive and was chosen inside-left instead of Bertie Peacock against East Fife at home on March 23rd 1952; between September 11th and October 2nd 1954 he was entrusted with Fernie's position at inside-right "to bring repose to the forward line" (a stint which included the 3-3 home draw versus Wolves in the Champions' match of September 20th). Worse, on Christmas Day, he was played at outside-right versus Clyde at Parkhead, a position "I have never played before in my life" (although he scored just before half-time). He is immortalised in the half-back line, Evans Boden and Baillie of the team that won the Scottish Cup on April 21st 1951.

Appearances:
SL: 122 apps. 2 gls.
SLC: 20 apps. 0 gls.
SC: 16 apps. 0 gls.
Total: *158 apps. 2 gls.*

♣ **Celtic note:** *As a Celtic scout Alec was directed to have a look at a boy called Vic Davidson with Glasgow United. Alec reported favourably but recommended Celtic keep an eye also on Vic's team mate - Kenny Dalglish.*

BOGAN, Thomas

Role: Outside-right 1946-48
5' 8" 11st.0lbs.
b. Glasgow, 18th May 1920
d. 23rd September 1993

CAREER: Strathclyde 1937/Blantyre Celtic 1939/Renfrew 1943/Hibernian 11 Sept 1943/CELTIC 1 Feb 1946/Preston NE 30 Sept 1948/Manchester United 26 Aug 1949/Aberdeen 8 Mar 1951/Southampton 12 Dec 1951/Blackburn Rovers 22 Aug 1953/Macclesfield Town June 1954.

Debut v Hibernian (h) 0-1 (RL) 2.2.46

"The player with the greatest burst of speed I ever encountered was Tommy Bogan... he could gather a ball and sweep past you almost in one movement." (Davie Shaw, June 11th 1955). Willie McCartney set out to build for Hibs a team to rival Celtic's of 1938 and in Tommy Bogan recruited a junior who burst upon the senior scene as the fastest thing in boots. He was capped for Scotland against England at Hampden on April 14th 1945 but twisted his knee when he somersaulted over Frank Swift in a lightning first minute attack and was carried off (Leslie Johnston substituted). He scored a magnificent but unavailing last minute goal against Rangers in the 2-3 League defeat (the boycott match) of September 7th 1946; Jack Cantwell crossed deep from the right; George Hazlett touched on to Tommy who hit a net-buster on the volley past Bobby Brown without the ball having touched the ground. After

Tommy Bogan

a broken right leg (October 26th 1946), Tommy's best season for Celtic was 1947-48 when some days "he played like three wingers" and had the crowd on tiptoe every time he got the ball: "Celtic supporters have taken Bogan to their hearts. He looked a match-winner on his own and every time, almost, he got possession, there was a great expectant roar." Tommy refused a transfer to Deepdale on July 21st 1948 just at the time Celtic were instructed by the SFA that Pat Buckley was St Johnstone's own and Bobby Collins must join Everton. Bob Kelly: "Perhaps we should have him declared a Preston player". New coach, the famed Jimmy Hogan met the Celtic players for the first time on August 3rd 1948: "The good ship Celtic will set sail on August 14th." Tommy: "There'll be some passengers aboard this ship." He was not a wholly contented man at Parkhead and said later he could never understand why he had left Hibs. He was Johnny Carey's first signing at Blackburn Rovers.

Appearances:
SL: 34 apps. 5 gls.
SLC: 9 apps. 3 gls.
SC: 4 apps. 0 gls.
Total: *47 apps. 8 gls.*
RL: 3 apps. 1 gl.
RLC: 5 apps. 0 gls.
Total: *8 apps. 1 gl.*

♣ **Celtic note:** *Tommy won the John Wylie Silver Medal and Prize for Best Student in the Year Stow College of Printing (18th October 1943).*

BOLAND, William

Role: Inside-right 1944-45
5' 8" 11st.0lbs.
b. 30th November 1919

CAREER: Muirkirk Higher Grade/Auchinleck Talbot 1935/Muirkirk Juniors 1937/Muirkirk Hibs 1942/CELTIC 6 Sept 1944/free 13 Dec 1945/Muirkirk Hibs Jan 1946.

Debut v Clyde (a) 0-0 (RLC) 24.2.45

Bill Boland

Bill Boland was a "sturdy junior" drafted into the Celtic big team in place of John Divers to partner the great Delaney in the League Cup of 1944-45. Bill, a miner all his working life, had to do a double shift on a Monday to be free to play football on a Saturday. He played three trials as a centre for Scottish Schools Under-15's and was playing junior for Auchinleck before his sixteenth birthday. Junior football in Ayrshire closed down between 1939 and 1942 and Muirkirk Hibs were a juvenile side but playing in the junior grade. Bill had two trials for Celtic (in both of which new Bhoy Bobby Evans participated) and was signed after the second. He played the first four games out of six in the League Cup qualifying sections and scored his first goal for Celtic with a "terrific shot" against Falkirk on March 3rd as Celtic played their 15th game in a row without defeat. Against Thistle at Firhill on March 10th 1945, he "revealed the coolness of a veteran" when after nine minutes he "beat the defence before scoring" with a beauty of a shot from outside the box to win the match for Celtic. He surrendered his place to Pat McAuley on 24th March and travelled as reserve with the team to Brockville. With that his moment as a Celtic first-teamer passed. However vague Jimmy McGrory's plans for the team on succeeding Jimmy McStay, they did not include the Bhoy from Muirkirk. Bill celebrated the Golden Jubilee of his marriage with a surprise party thrown by friends in the Walfrid Restaurant in September 1993.

Appearances:
RLC: 4 apps. 2 gls.
Total: *4 apps. 2 gls.*

BONE, James

Role: Striker 1974-75
5' 10" 11st.8lbs.
b. Bridge of Allan, 22nd September 1949

CAREER: Stirling High School/Fallin BB/Bannockburn/Airth Castle Rovers 1967/Partick Thistle 28 May 1968/Norwich City 29 Feb 1972/Sheffield United 21 Mar 1973/CELTIC 18 Feb 1974/Arbroath 10 Jan 1975/St Mirren 2 Feb 1978/Toronto Blizzard 1979, 1980/free May 1982/Hong Kong Rangers 8 June 1982/Hearts 3 Aug 1983/Arbroath player-manager 21 Feb 1985/St Mirren asst. manager 16 Dec 1986/dismissed 22 Feb 1988/Dundee United coach 24 Feb 1988/Airdrie manager 19 May 1989/resigned 14 May 1991/Power Dynamo (Kitwe Zambia) coach as of 16 May 1991/Lenasia Dynamos (Johannesburg) coach Mar 1992/St Mirren manager 25 May 1992.

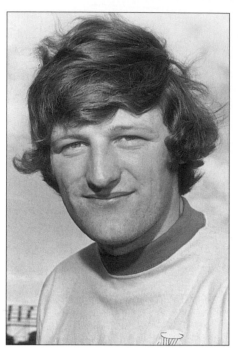

Jimmy Bone

Debut v Hearts (h) 1-0 (SL) 2.3.74 (sub)

Jock Stein sent shock waves of anticipation through Scottish football when he signed Jimmy Bone to freshen up a Celtic forward line gone stale. Jimmy scored 21 goals in his time at Parkhead of which 20 were for the reserves. By the end of March 1974 he was out of the squad and in September open to offer as not having "fitted into the scheme of things...not sharp enough...too much work on the weights in England." Jimmy admitted he received nothing but kindness at Parkhead yet "Somehow I never thought of myself as a Celt." He recovered all his deadliness before goal as skipper at Arbroath and as a man-manager (the fight with Frank McGarvey of 18th September 1987 apart) from Bannockburn Amateurs to the African continent has enjoyed outstanding success.

Appearances:
SL: 7 apps. 1 gl.
SLC: 3 apps. 0 gls.
SC: 1 app. 0 gls.
Total: *11 apps. 1 gl.*

BONNAR, John

Role: Goalkeeper 1948-58
5' 9" 12st.0lbs.
b. 11th January 1924

CAREER: Holy Cross Academy Edinburgh/ Polkemmet Juniors 1945/ Arbroath 18 Oct 1946/CELTIC 13 Aug 1948/Dumbarton 18 Aug 1958/ St Johnstone 8 Sept 1959/retired 1960.
Debut v Clyde (a) 4-0 (SL) 6.11.48

Johnny Bonnar was a shale-miner and much sought-after as a junior. His parents were from the same part of Donegal from which his namesake and fellow-goalkeeper Packy was to emerge in the late 1970s. He "seemed inspired" on his debut for Arbroath versus Cowdenbeath on October 19th 1946. Celtic bought him as cover for Willie Miller after Rolando Ugolini's departure for Middlesbrough. At the start of 1949-50 Johnny held out for better terms and Manchester City considered him a possible replacement for the great Frank Swift until he re-signed on September 5th. Alex Devanney had become Celtic's second choice 'keeper in the meantime and Johnny spent most of his Saturdays sitting in the stand. Willie Miller injured his hand before 44,238 at Tynecastle on Hogmanay 1949 but it was "Tiger" (as Tully called him) not Alex who was nominated to replace him. Sports reporters with a short memory and little judgement were soon calling him "Celtic's best since John Thomson." "He's not a big lad but he makes up for it by his catlike ability and magnificent anticipation." Johnny was a competent goalie but inconsistent and never wholly assured of his place against George Hunter and Andy Bell. He dropped a corner in the first round of the Scottish Cup at Methil on January 27th 1951 and the strong-going East Fife went 1-0 up. Johnny had 'flu for the replay and Sonny Hunter took over in goal. "I know I've been off form lately. A spell in the reserves will do me good. I wish George Hunter the best of luck." He turned into gold in May 1953 after talk of Celtic's interest in Jimmy Cowan. He had a great game against Queen's Park in the

John Bonnar, Jock Stein and Jimmy Walsh with the Coronation Cup in 1953.

final of the Charity Cup on May 9th 1953 and thus secured his place in the no-hope Parkhead side included in the Coronation competition only because the Celts were such crowd-pullers. This "jewel of a 'keeper" broke the hearts of Arsenal, Manchester United and a great Hibs team in that order. His game so inspired Celtic that had Puskas' Hungarians been in Glasgow the Tims might well have beaten them too. In the race with Hearts for the League in 1954, against Partick Thistle at Firhill on March 20th, in a match Celtic had to win to stay in contention, he made four world-class saves, the first when Celtic were 1-0 down. At Easter Road on April 17th, the day the League was won, Celtic scored at the start of each half and for the rest of the game Johnny played Hibs on his own. On April 23rd 1955, he went up too early to intercept Archie Robertson's fluke corner in the last two minutes of the Cup final versus Clyde for a 1-1 draw. Celtic now turned to Dick Beattie as a last line of defence. Johnny became first organiser of the Celtic Development Fund (31st March 1963). To fans of his era he will always be "Coronation" Bonnar.

Appearances:
SL: 120 apps. 33 shut-outs.
SLC: 38 apps. 10 shut-outs.
SC: 22 apps. 6 shut-outs.
Total: *180 apps. 49 shut-outs (27%).*

Goalkeeper John Bonnar watches as an effort from Falkirk's Davidson goes wide in February 1955 at Brockville Park.

Pat Bonner

BONNER, Patrick Joseph

Role: Goalkeeper 1978-to date
6' 2" 13st.1lb.
b. Clochglas, nr Kincasslagh, Co.Donegal, 24th May 1960

CAREER: Rosses Rovers GAA/Keadue Rovers Mar 1975/Leicester City (trial) 1975-76/Celtic (trial) 1977/CELTIC 14 May 1978/ free 16 May 1994/agrees to join Kilmarnock 13 June 1994/ CELTIC again 19 July 1994.

Debut v Motherwell (h) 2-1 (SL) 17.3.79

'Packy' Bonner was Jock Stein's last signing for Celtic. Jock was fallible in his appreciation of goalkeepers but lived long enough to realise he'd endowed the club with one of its all-time best. Such was young Bonner's form Celtic let Roy Baines return to Morton to make way for him. Packy played in Danny McGrain's Testimonial versus Manchester United on August 4th 1980 and had a magnificent game including a save from Steve Coppell in the penalty shoot-out. "Speaking as a former centre-half, he's like having a brick wall behind you" (Billy McNeill). Packy was Celtic 'keeper in the Championship sides of 1981, 1982, 1986 and 1988 and won Scottish Cup medals in 1985 and 1989 as well as a League Cup medal in 1982. The big Rosses man was rock solid (bad back and all) in the European Nations' Cup of 1988 and his performance in the defeat of England at Stuttgart on June 12th 1988 (which united all men of good will both sides of the Border) was hailed as part of Ireland's best reason to celebrate since Eoghan Ruadh's victory at Benburb 1646. He entered hospital for an operation on his back and missed the traumatic start to 1988-89. *Not the View* published a photograph of Packy on the cover with the caption "Get Well Soon". He returned to the first team at Tynecastle on October 22nd 1988. Again in the World Cup 1990, he re-asserted his status as National Hero when he saved Timofte's penalty at 4-4 in the shoot-out against Romania on June 25th 1990 and helped send Ireland through to Rome and the quarter-finals. Agent Liam Brady negotiated his new contract with Celtic in 1991 then joined him at Parkhead as manager. After 155 successive games in three years he was dropped for the Airdrie match of 23rd November 1991. So good was Gordon Marshall's form, Packy did not get another

chance until 19th September 1992 when he let in four at Falkirk in a nine-goal match which was also his 400th Scottish League game for Celtic. He surpassed Charlie Shaw's record of 420 League games in the draw 0-0 versus Thistle at home 20th February 1993 and played his 600th competitive game for the club versus Aberdeen at Pittodrie on November 9th 1993. Even so there was a feeling abroad that 'Bonner has lost decisiveness and confidence for some time now'. Packy conceded two bad goals against Aberdeen on 19th January 1994 and a 'camouflaged axeing' let in new signing Carl Muggleton. For Eire, the big Donegalman won his 70th cap versus Russia at Lansdowne Road on March 23rd and moved to within one of Liam Brady's cap record in the 0-1 defeat of Holland at Limburg on 20th April. Three days later, he again won his place back in the Celtic side after a 13 match lay-off. The rumour is he learned of his free transfer in the Parkhead car park just back from the 1-1 draw at Aberdeen on May 14th. An official version said his release was to cut the wage bill. The news, a month before Packy played for Eire in the USA World Cup, stunned supporters of the green and white all over the world. They had anticipated him playing hundreds more games for his beloved Celtic. On his 34th birthday under the new lights at Lansdowne Road he equalled Brady's record as most-capped FAI international and broke it at the same venue 1-3 versus the Czech Republic on June 5th 1994. He won his 77th cap in Orlando on July 4th 1994 when his mistake just before half-time gave Holland a 2-0 lead which proved unassailable and put Ireland out of the World Cup. Having secured an agreement to become a Kilmarnock player, one of new manager Tommy Burns' widely welcomed first acts was to bring Packy back to Celtic for 1994-95. He captained his country versus Liechtenstein on October 12th 1994 - his 78th cap. He ranks quite simply as one of Celtic's best-ever goalkeepers.

Appearances:
SL: 463 apps. 172 shut-outs.
SLC: 60 apps. 26 shut-outs.
SC: 49 apps. 31 shut-outs.
Eur: 35 apps. 14 shut-outs.
Total: *607 apps. 243 shut-outs (40%).*

BOYD, Thomas

Role: Full-back 1992 to date
5' 11" 12st.8lbs.
b. Glasgow, 24th November 1965

CAREER: Celtic BC/Motherwell 'S' form/
Motherwell YTS 9 Sept 1983/Chelsea 21 May
1991/CELTIC 6 Feb 1992.

Debut v Airdrie (h) 2-0 (SL) 8.2.92

Had Tommy Boyd joined Celtic as a cash
transfer, he might have represented the best
value pound for pound since Murdo MacLeod
or Davie Provan. He came as a straight swap
for Tony Cascarino and Celtic fans were
convinced that Celtic had achieved by far the
better bargain. The ex-Motherwell skipper
who had lifted the Scottish Cup for the
Steelmen on May 18th 1991 made an
immediate impression and did much to
assuage the pain of Anton Rogan's departure
to Sunderland. Although right-footed, he

Tommy Boyd

preferred left-back but was asked to play on
the starboard side at the start of 1992-93 so as
to accommodate Dariusz Wdowczyk. His
understanding with John Collins seemed for a
time to rival that of McGrain and Dalglish.
After the McCann/Dempsey takeover of
March 5th 1994 various members of the Celtic
staff, playing and non-playing, disclosed how
desperately close they had been to making
their disaproval bluntly plain to the Seven
Gnomes on the Old Board. Tom's was the first
voice to go public against the new defensive
playing style inaugurated by manager Lou
Macari: "Myself and two other senior players
had a frank talk with Chic Bates, the assistant
manager, about the need for a better balance
and an awareness that there's more to this
game than just avoiding losing" (19th March
1994). 1993-94 had not been the best of seasons
for Tom perhaps because Macari had to stifle
his attacking flair. He is not at his best in a
more cautious role. Tom was once proclaimed
the first Scots 'Yopper' to go from the dole to
the top of his profession.

Appearances:
SL: 93 apps. 1 gl.
SLC: 8 apps. 0 gls.
SC: 6 apps. 0 gls.
Eur: 8 apps. 0 gls.
Total: *115 apps. 1 gl.*

BOYLE, James

Role: Inside-right 1890-93
b. Springburn, 11th July 1866

CAREER: Towerhill Apr 1888/CELTIC
1890/Clyde Mar 1893/Woolwich Arsenal
29 Nov 1893/Dartford 1897.

Debut v Vale of Leven (a) 1-3 (SL) 24.1.1891

Dapper Jimmy Boyle should have made his
League debut at home on 27th December 1890
but because of frost the match for points
against St Mirren was played as a friendly (he
scored). Likewise on January 3rd 1891 the state
of the pitch deprived the Cowlairs game of
League status (Jimmy scored again). He made
his official debut in a 10-man side and defeat
at Alexandria (Mick McKeown missed his
train!). He won a Glasgow Cup medal when
Celtic beat 3rd Lanark 4-0 at 2nd Hampden on
St Valentine's Day 1891, the first major trophy
ever brought home to Parkhead. He was
inside-left to Johnny Campbell at Cambuslang

Jimmy Boyle

on March 7th 1891 but made way for Duke McMahon with 15 minutes to go. Celtic lost 3-1 but the McMahon-Campbell left-wing combination had been discovered and Jimmy Boyle's shift of position its occasion. An engineer by profession, he took a job in Woolwich and skippered the Gunners against Celtic at the Manor Field Plumstead on February 15th 1897 when the green and white stripes staged a fighting come-back and won a famous victory 4-5.

Appearances:
SL: 9 apps. 0 gls.
Total: *9 apps. 0 gls.*

BOYLE, John

Role: Full-back 1933-38
5' 9" 11st.4lbs.
b. 24th December 1913

CAREER: Armadale Thistle/Bathgate/ CELTIC 21 Feb 1933/free 1938/Hibernian 6 June 1938/Hamilton Academicals 10 July 1939/free 7 Aug 1942.

Debut v Queen of the South (h) 5-0 (SL) 22.8.36

An injury to Jock Morrison in the Celtic Public Trial of August 1st 1936 gave John Boyle his opportunity in the first team as partner to Bobby Hogg after George Paterson and Willie Hughes had both had a try. John was "a big-kicking back ... set for big things." Morrison

John Boyle

recovered in time for the Champions' Match versus Sunderland on 16th September. John Boyle had the extraordinary distinction of displacing Bobby Hogg on March 27th 1937, the rare example, perhaps unique, of Larkhall Bobby's taking the field at left-back. The Scottish selectors were seeking a left-back for the team against England and this was Celtic's attempt to let Bobby impress on the other side of the defence. In the event, he got little to do

on the day and Andy Beattie played in the 3-1 win at Hampden on April 17th 1937. Major Frank Buckley was reported very keen on taking John Boyle to Wolves in the close season of 1938 but it was the great Willie McCartney who persuaded him his future lay with the immense Hibs side being built at Easter Road.

Appearances:
SL: 10 apps. 0 gls.
Total: *10 apps. 0 gls.*

BOYLE, Robert

Role: Goalkeeper 1912-13
5' 9" 11st.0lbs.
b. Cowie

CAREER: Cowie Wanderers 1911/CELTIC 30 Sept 1912/Alloa 9 Dec 1913/to USA July 1914/ ...McKeesport FC (Pittsburg) by 1991-20.

Robert Boyle

Debut v Partick Thistle (a) 3-2 (SL) 30.9.12

Celtic were in a kicking match at Dundee in the League on September 21st 1912 and had big panther goalie John Mulrooney incapacitated for a month. They experimented with Motherwell reserve Frank Mitchell in the Glasgow Cup the following week before Plean boy and Scottish junior international Bob Boyle was spotted at the Stenhousemuir Tryst Fair and pitched straight into the League team. According to Patsy Gallagher, Robert had "a bad attack of nerves" (after a good first half) versus Rangers in the Glasgow Cup final at Hampden before 80,000 fans on October 12th 1912 and lost two soft goals in a 3-1 defeat. He played professional soccer in the USA (had the game of his life in the US Cup in St Louis on 1st February 1920) and served with the Canadian Field Artillery in France during the Kaiser War.

Appearances:
SL: 10 apps. 1 shut-out.
Total: *10 apps. 1 shut-out (10%).*

BRADY, Alexander

Role: Inside-right 1891-92
5' 7" 12st.0lbs.
b. Cathcart, 2nd April 1865
d. Renton, 19th October 1913

CAREER: Dundee Harp/Renton/Partick Thistle 1888/Sunderland Sept 1888/Burnley Oct 1888/Sunderland May 1889/Everton Nov 1889/(Broxburn Shamrock loan 1890)/CELTIC 10 Aug 1891/Sheffield Wednesday 3 Sept 1892/Clydebank 10 Aug 1899/Renton 14 Aug 1901.

Debut v Hearts (a) 1-3 (SL) 15.8.1891

Alec Brady was a man in much demand in England and was suspended in September 1889 for two months as having signed two forms; one for Burnley and one for Everton, a ploy that Dan Doyle so successfully exploited. English football has always drained the Scottish game of its talent so Celtic caused a sensation as early as 1891 by bucking the trend and poaching Everton skipper

Alec Brady

Dan Doyle and his team-mate "a wee barrel of a man," Alec Brady. They came up to Glasgow to interview John Glass after a mystery paragraph in one of the Liverpool papers. Celtic's enterprise was Everton's "coolness to freeze mercury" but Brady, "a glutton for work," joined Neil McCallum on the Parkhead right and within days the papers were asking: "Is there any team in Britain can draw crowds so well as Celtic?" His name is perpetuated in the Celtic memory as inside-right of the first Parkhead side to lift the Scottish Cup (April 9th 1892) and set the East End to dancing in the streets. Alec got married during 1891-92 and both he and Johnny Madden tried to join Sheffield Wednesday during the close season for the extra money. Glass and Willie Maley stumbled across riveter Madden but Wednesday smuggled Alec into hiding in Boston Lincs until he took the field in their first ever English League game (3rd September 1892). This early-day Puskas won an English Cup medal with the Owls at Crystal Palace on April 18th 1896.

Appearances:
SL: 19 apps. 4 gls.
SC: 5 apps. 6 gls.
Total: *24 apps. 10 gls.*

BRESLIN, Patrick

Role: Centre-half 1899
b. Maryhill, 2nd October 1881

CAREER: Johnstone Hibernian/Johnstone FC 1898/CELTIC (trial) Jan 1899.

Debut v Dundee (h) 4-1 (SL) 7.1.1899

Pat Breslin tried-out for Celtic on the last day of the 18-game League campaign in the year Rangers won the Championship without dropping a point. Tom Hynds and Barney Battles had been sharing the centre-half spot but the hunt was on for somebody permanent and Pat was offered his chance in the rain before "a poor turn-out" in a line reading Hynds, Breslin and Orr. 'Scanty' Hynds was back at centre-half for the Scottish Cup at Dalbeattie the following week and before the end of January Celtic had secured Harry 'Beef' Marshall on loan from Hearts.

Appearances:
SL: 1 app. 0 gls.
Total: *1 app. 0 gls.*

BRITTON, Gerard Joseph

Role: Striker 1988-92
6' 1" 11st.0lbs.
b. Glasgow, 20th October 1970

CAREER: Celtic BC/CELTIC 15 May 1987/ (Reading loan 28 Nov 1991)/(Partick Thistle loan 4 Aug 1992)/Partick Thistle 10 Aug 1992/ Dundee 11 Jan 1994.

Debut v Dundee United (a) 1-3 (SL) 8.12.90 (sub)

"I need a big striker. Where am I to find him?" (John Lambie 30th November 1991). In the opinion of some, Gerry Britton never received the chance he deserved in all his time at Celtic Park. He scored 122 goals in 143 starts and 53 substitutions with the reserves but got small chance to show what he could do in the first team. He made his unofficial debut with Stuart Balmer in the Penzance FC Centenary match of 5th March 1989. He won two Glasgow Cup medals with Celtic (2-0 versus Rangers Hogmanay 1989 and 3-2 versus Partick Thistle on January 23rd 1991 when he scored the hat-trick). John Lambie bought him for £100,000 at the start of a season where want of a goalscorer was again to be a major

Gerry Britton

problem at Parkhead and the 33-year old McAvennie would be brought back as a stop-gap. "The tireless Britton" scored the final goal in the 3-0 defeat of Rangers that kept Thistle in the Premier Division (4th May 1993). "He gathered the ball, went round Maxwell and rolled it into an empty net." Gerry married a grand-daughter of Mick Davitt in June 1993. Ex-Celt Jim Duffy took him to Dundee.

Appearances:
SL: 2 apps. 0 gls.
SC: 2 apps. 0 gls.
Total: *4 apps. 0 gls.*

BRODIE, John

Role: Outside-left 1916-19
5' 6" 11st.0lbs.
b. Dumbarton, 5th January 1896

CAREER: Maryhill Juniors/Dumbarton Harp 14 Sept 1915/CELTIC 9 June 1916/(Ayr United loan Sept 1917)/(Dumbarton loan Jan 1918)/(Dumbarton Harp loan 26 Oct & Feb 1918 & 26 Oct 1918)/Chelsea June 1919/free Apr 1920/Dumbarton Harp 11 May 1920.

Debut v Clyde (h) 3-1 (GC) 21.9.18

Intended by nature for inside-forward, John Brodie had two games for the Celtic big team

each time out of position on the left wing, yet was hailed as "the other Browning". He made his Scottish League debut at Falkirk on September 28th 1918 and scored the goal that put Celtic 0-2 up midway through the second half. Thus he did his bit to bring home the Championship of 1919. He and Johnny Browning went to Chelsea together. "He did not get a chance to show his paces at Celtic Park. The amount of talent already there when he arrived obscured him."

Appearances:
SL: 2 apps. 1 gl.
Total: *2 apps. 1 gl.*

BROGAN, Francis

Role: Outside-left 1960-64
5' 10" 9st.10lbs.
b. Stepps, 3rd June 1942

CAREER: St Joseph's Dumfries/St Mungo's Academy Mar 1959/Celtic Teenagers 4 Aug 1959/CELTIC 1 Nov 1960/St Roch's (farmed-out) 1960/Ipswich Town 11 June 1964/Morton (trial) 30 July 1971/Halifax Town Nov 1971/retired June 1973/Blantyre Celtic coach.

Debut v Clyde (n) 1-1 (CC) 9.5.61

Frank Brogan was a Chartered Accountant who could run the 100 yards in 10.1 seconds. Celtic had long finished scouring the earth for an outside-left when he enlisted as one of Jock Stein's colts. Frank joined a queue behind Alex Byrne that included Auld, Hughes, Carroll, Mackle and Jeffrey. An attacking winger who scored goals he was the best of the bunch in the opinion of many. He made his debut at Hampden in the Charity Cup final and helped

Frank Brogan (second left) scored Celtic's 5000th league goal. He is pictured here with J. Delaney (scorer of the 4000th), J.McGrory (3000th) and A.McLean (2000th).

secure a six-month tenure of the famous old trophy (1887) for Celtic. On his League debut against Hearts (February 21st 1962) "he showed up the other forwards with delightful play". Frank's corner kicks were Charlie Gallagher class. Nevertheless, his participation at times was not entirely to management's satisfaction and he was as often out of the Celtic team as in it. Jackie Milburn took him to Ipswich where his speed, dig and urgency were hugely appreciated. He missed most of 1970-71 with a broken ankle, tried a come-back with Morton (where he walked out before a match) then Halifax. When the bone snapped again, he knew nature was warning him it was time to call quits.

Appearances:
SL: 37 apps. 13 gls.
SLC: 1 app. 1 gl.
SC: 9 apps. 3 gls.
Eur: 1 app. 0 gls.
Total: *48 apps. 17 gls.*

Below: Jim Brogan measures a pass during the 1973 Scottish Cup Final with Rangers.

BROGAN, James

Role: Left-half, left-back 1963-75
5' 10" 11st.3lbs.
b. 5th June 1944

CAREER: Dumfries St Joseph's/St Roch's 17 Aug 1962/CELTIC 11 Sept 1962/free 4 June 1975/Coventry City 20 Aug 1975/ Ayr United 9 Mar 1977/retired 1 Nov 1977.
Debut v Falkirk (a) 0-1 (SL) 21.9.63

"Jim Brogan is possibly one of the most dynamic young men in the car sales business and his vitality and enthusiasm are shared by all his highly efficient staff..."
(Advertisement 1971).

Jim Brogan CA is the ex-schoolboy fly-half and Celtic footballer who became a millionaire businessman and never for a moment ceased to be a jersey player. He succeeded John Clark in the Celtic team as a runner and grafter, a player who relished combat. When Celtic put Leeds out in the semi-final of the European Cup at Hampden on April 15th 1970, Jock Stein

complimented his left-half: "Jim Brogan used to chase the game, now he reads it." Jim made his Celtic debut just after the 1-5 defeat of part-timers Basle in the Cup-winners' Cup but so "clueless, craftless" were the Bhoys at Brockville that the disgruntled support left for home convinced the Swiss were second-rate juniors. Stein made the difference and Jim collected seven Championship medals for the seasons 1968-74, Scottish Cup medals for 1969, 1971 (both versus Rangers), 1972 and 1974. On a lower note, he also played in the European Cup final versus Feyenoord in Milan on 6th May 1970. His best year was 1971 when he was runner-up to Martin Buchan as Scottish Player of the Year, had an outstanding match against the English League (March 17th), and won four full Scotland caps culminating in a Wembley appearance on May 22nd, a game he finished nursing a hairline fracture of the leg. As a full-back, he popped up in the penalty box to head a last-gasp winner for Celtic against Rangers (2-1) on January 3rd 1972. Jim was an assiduous trainer and the type of professional who never took the field unless exuding fitness and total physical readiness (and it showed). Pat McCluskey and Andy Lynch were both laying claim to his place in 1975 and although Jim professed surprise, it was no shock that Stein allowed him to go on a free. He skippered Celtic versus Rangers in his final match to celebrate Glasgow's 800th birthday on May 10th 1975 (and got a broken rib). With customary thoroughness he moved home and family down to England to take a proper crack at succeeding with Coventry. Given his track record as Jim Brogan Enterprises he might well have made Celtic an excellent Chief Executive in 1990.

Appearances:
SL: 213 apps. 6 gls.
SLC: 57 apps. 2 gls.
SC: 38 apps. 0 gls.
Eur: 31 apps. 1 gl.
Total: *339 apps. 9 gls.*

BROWN, Hugh

Role: Left-half 1916-21
5' 6" 10st.4lbs.
b. Glasgow, c 1896
d. 4th August 1952

CAREER: Anderston Thornbank/ St Anthony's/CELTIC 8 Nov 1916/ (Clackmannan loan 1920)/free 1921/ Dunfermline Athletic 7 July 1921/Partick Thistle 7 Oct 1921/Merthyr Town 5 Nov 1921/[Dunkeld & Birnam 11 Jan 1924].
Debut v Raith Rovers (a) 4-1 (SL) 2.12.16

Hugh Brown

"Small but a terrier in work," "clever young half-back," Hugh Brown may well have got the ball over the line within two minutes of his debut but the goal was credited to Jimmy McColl who made sure. Hugh came into the team for Private John McMaster at the end of the year of the Somme and quickly appealed to the faithful as a 100 per center. He had *"pluck to spare," "with dainty touches," "The skill a half requires/Yet proves a rock/A stumbling block/ To many fancied fliers./May years bring caps/And no mishaps/May fortune never frown/May fate be kind/To one inclined/To play the game like Brown".* Hugh was a constant in the Celtic team during the neck-and-neck struggle with Rangers for the Championship of 1919 when the League Flag came to Parkhead at the last gasp on May 10th. "Celtic's Jimmy Wilde" surrendered his place to McMaster on Johnny's return from the Army but why a star like Hugh was so abruptly dispensed with is a mystery. He was "on top of his form" with Merthyr in 1921-22.

Appearances:
SL: 98 apps. 1 gl.
Total: *98 apps. 1 gl.*

BROWN, John

Role: Outside-left 1911-13
5' 11" 12st.3lbs.
b. Dysart
d. 7th December 1943

CAREER: Clackmannan Juniors/Hearts o'
Beath 1906/Alloa 24 May 1907/Falkirk 6 Apr
1909/CELTIC 7 June 1911/(Chelsea loan
26 Dec 1912)/Chelsea 8 Mar 1913/(Falkirk
loan 15 Sept 1915 until Apr 1916)/Royal Navy
1916/Raith Rovers Mar 1919/Dunfermline
Athletic 1919/(Falkirk loan 1919)/
Clackmannan Mar 1920/Falkirk 2 Apr 1921/
Clackmannan 9 Apr 1921/Lochgelly United
17 May 1921/trainer July 1922/player again
6 Sept 1922/manager May 1923/Dundee
masseur-trainer July 1926 until 1935 and
during World War Two.

Debut v Airdrie (h) 3-0 (SL) 15.8.11 (scored once)

Ex-pit laddie John Brown, "fast and clever on
the ball, a fine shot and most accurate in his
crossing" was "the most in and out player I
ever saw" (Patsy Gallagher). Like Billy
Meredith, Johnny played with a toothpick in
his mouth and was bought as cover for Davie
Hamilton in the period of transition between
the six-in-a-row side 1905-10 and the four-in-a-
row 1914-17. Almost at once Hammie was
understudying John. Jimmy Quinn scored the
hat-trick in the 3-0 defeat of Rangers on
Ne'erday 1912: "Travers fed Brown and Brown
fed Quinn all three goals besides keeping
Rangers at full stretch throughout." He was
capped by the Scottish League at

Middlesbrough on 17th February 1912 (master
of tact Willie Maley described the Andy
Cunningham-Johnny Brown left wing as the
Scots' weakest link) and won a Scottish Cup
medal on April 6th when his header made the
second goal for Patsy Gallagher. For the most
part he was an unsatisfactory winger, too
much of the touch player, and reminded many
of Willie Groves. He was a different man
entirely at centre: "In the middle, Brown was
like a lion with dash and pluck he never
shows on the wing" (versus Partick Thistle,
September 30th, 1912). He saw action in World
War I and was invalided home in September
1917. After football he ran a confectionery
business in Glencraig. "A splendid masseur,"
he was Dundee trainer under manager Alec
McNair.

Appearances:
SL: 40 apps. 7 gls.
SC: 7 apps. 3 gls.
Total: *47 apps. 10 gls.*

BROWN, William

Role: Inside-left 1916-1919
5' 7" 10st.6lbs.
b. Glasgow, c 1895

CAREER: Cambuslang
Rangers/Parkhead
Juniors 5 July 1916/
CELTIC 6 Sept 1916/(Vale
of Leven loan Nov 1917 &
1918-19)/free June 1919/
Dundee 12 July 1919/King's Park 12 Mar
1920/Cowdenbeath 2 Sept 1920/ Lochgelly
United 8 July 1922.

Willie Brown

*Debut v Kilmarnock (a) 1-1 (SL)
12.10.18 (scored once)*

"Crack inside-forward" and junior
internationalist Willie Brown was
inclined to play "too close a game."
He saved an invaluable point in a
Championship season with an
equaliser five minutes from time on
his debut. He played inside-left to
George Elliott on his second and
final game for Celtic a week later, a
3-0 defeat at Ibrox. At Dundee,
Willie was inside man to Alex
Troup who made so many goals for
Dixie Dean at Everton and his signing "gave cause for satisfaction".

*John Brown about to score in the 1912 Scottish Cup semi-final
victory over Hearts at Ibrox.*

He joined Lochgelly in 1922 after they had appealed in the press for players. He played - and scored - against Celtic in the Scottish Cup in Fife (13th January 1923) one of the first-ever matches filmed. Willie was alive and well and writing to the *Celtic View* in 1967.

Appearances:
SL: 2 apps. 1 gl.
Total: *2 apps. 1 gl.*

BROWNING, John

Role: Outside-left 1911-19
5' 6" 11st.7lbs.
b. Dumbarton,
29th November 1888

CAREER: Glasgow Perthshire/Bonhill Hibernian Aug 1908/ Dumbarton Harp 20 Aug 1908/Vale of Leven 1 Oct 1909/CELTIC 24 Apr 1911/ (Dumbarton Harp loan 4 Aug 1911)/(Vale of Leven loan 20 May 1912)/CELTIC again 28 Oct 1912/Chelsea 12 June 1919/free 1920/ Vale of Leven 7 June 1920/Dumbarton 3 Sept 1920/Vale of Leven 22 Aug 1922/retired 1924.

Debut v Third Lanark (a) 1-0 (SL) 2.11.12

Johnny Browning, a baker to trade, was a dour Son nicknamed 'Smiler' for irony but still did a good Harry Lauder impression that enlivened many a dull jaunt for Celtic. He was the "Catch of the Season" 1912-13 and Davie Hamilton's true successor at outside-left. He played his first game for Celtic in the Inter-City League at Dens Park on October 30th 1912 (scored) and was the left-winger of the four-in-a-row team although signed originally as an inside-left. He won a Scottish Cup medal versus Hibs on April 16th 1914 when he registered two of Celtic's four goals. He was out with leg problems most of 1918-19, played his last game for Celtic on March 1st 1919, then did severe damage to his knee cartilage with Chelsea on 6th September 1919. He managed only five games for the Pensioners, the last on 14th February 1920 before being freed. He was involved with ex-Ranger Archie 'Punch' Kyle in an attempt to fix the result of Lochgelly United versus Bo'ness on March 22nd 1924. Time with hard labour followed but Johnny came out of jug smiling on August

15th 1924 and was applying to coach in Bavaria in April 1925. His son John was on Celtic's books during August 1932 and gave Liverpool good service pre-World War Two.

Appearances:
SL: 210 apps. 63 gls.
SC: 7 apps. 2 gls.
Total: *217 apps. 65 gls.*

BUCHAN, William Ralston Murray

Role: Inside-forward
1933-37
5' 11" 11st.3lbs.
b. Grangemouth,
17th October 1914

CAREER: Grange Rovers/ CELTIC 12 Jan 1933/ Blackpool 15 Nov 1937/ (CELTIC loan 14 Oct 1939)/ (Stenhousemuir loan Nov 1939) /RAF May 1940/(Manchester United loan 1940-41)/(Leicester City loan 1941-42-43)/(Manchester United loan 1942-43)/(Hamilton Academicals loan Jan 1943)/(Fulham loan 1943-44)/(Hamilton Academicals loan Jan 1945)/(Stenhousemuir loan Aug 1945)/Blackpool again 12 Jan 1946/ Hull City 16 Jan 1948/Gateshead 24 Nov 1949 /coach Oct 1952/free June 1953/Coleraine player-manager 22 July 1953/resigned 9 Jan 1954/East Stirling (player) 10 Sept 1955.

Debut v Queen of the South (a) 2-3 (SL) 12.8.33

Willie Maley made a dash by car to Grangemouth in January 1933 to sign Willie Buchan before Rangers could beat him to it. Young Buchan was "the most promising newcomer to senior football since Tommy McInally...all the ability...a deadly shot...more active than McInally ever was...capture of the year...can go into the first team any time." Willie's "control and distribution were things to wonder at"; he could run, dribble, pass, score, be a striker or a midfield general and the Celtic fans loved him. On January 28th 1933 his presence in a Celtic Alliance side pulled 10,000 fans to Firhill for an ordinary reserve game versus Partick Thistle and 39,000 for a 2nd XI Cup replay versus Rangers on April 24th. He was a penalty king and (albeit often using a tearing run-up!) master of the "silky, side-foot push" right or left but always well out of the 'keeper's reach as against Clyde on 29th February 1936. Never a blaze away type of player, Willie liked to score goals without actually disturbing the rigging of the net. The ball over the line was enough. The 1937 Scottish Cup final before a British record crowd of 146,433 will always be Willie Buchan's: "It was the only time in my life when I felt I was in danger of passing out on the

Willie Buchan

park...when we ran out of the tunnel we were hit by a wall of noise. It was deafening and frightening...we could not communicate with one another...yet it all died down once the whistle sounded". He orchestrated a continual change of tactics that kept a very good Aberdeen side guessing and unsettled. It was his drive parried by George Johnstone that set Johnny Crum up for the first goal. Willie got the winner himself from a Delaney-McGrory move. His transfer to Blackpool in a deal knocked out in a matter of hours on a Saturday night was like a betrayal of faith by the Celtic executive. "It may take Celtic a long time to locate his like again." Blackpool beat Stockport County 9-2 in the English League War Cup on February 8th 1941. Ephraim (Jock) Dodds scored eight, Willie Buchan set them up, every one. He played for Scotland in the 0-4 defeat by England at Hampden on April 17th 1943. Willie was not a long time at Celtic Park but his impact was startling as much as his loss was grievous. He must qualify easily as an all-time Celtic great.

Appearances:
SL: 120 apps. 51 gls.
SC: 14 apps. 8 gls.
Total: *134 apps. 59 gls.*
RL: 1 app. 0 gls.
Total: *1 app. 0 gls.*

BUCKLEY, John

Role: Outside-right 1978-83
5' 9" 10st.7lbs.
b. East Kilbride, 18th May 1962

CAREER: Queen's Park/ CELTIC 1 May 1978/(Partick Thistle loan 30 Mar 1983)/ Partick Thistle 19 Aug 1983/ Doncaster Rovers 9 July 1984 /Leeds United July 1985/ (Leicester City loan Mar 1987)/ (Doncaster Rovers loan 17 Oct 1987)/Rotherham United Nov 1987/Partick Thistle 19 Oct 1990 /Scunthorpe United 17 July 1991 /Rotherham United Feb 1993/ retired 18 July 1993.

Debut v Arbroath (h) 4-1 (SLC) 1.9.82

John Buckley "a cracking player...one of the fastest in Scottish football" won a Glasgow Cup medal versus Rangers on May 13th 1982. He was reserve to Davie Provan throughout his time with Celtic. A dribbling winger, he went to Firhill as a makeweight in the Brian Whittaker transfer and was "outstanding in most of his games for Thistle." Billy Bremner paid £30,000 to take him to Doncaster where he was known as 'Roadrunner' for his pace. With Rotherham he gained a Division Four Championship medal in 1989. John Lambie paid £65,000 for his renewed services to Firhill in 1990. Poor John nearly died after fracturing his skull in his second spell playing for Rotherham versus Plymouth on March 11th 1993 and was

John Buckley

in a coma for several days. Surgery was needed to remove a blood clot from the brain. John recovered to lead a normal life but occasional numbness in his arm signalled he was no longer up to the demands of the first class game and at 31 John hung up his boots.

Appearances:
SLC: 1 app. 0 gls.
Total: *1 app. 0 gls.*

BURNS, John

Role: Outside-right 1918-20
5' 7" 11st.10lbs.
b. c 1895

CAREER: St Anthony's/CELTIC (provisional) 1 Apr 1918/full 22 July 1918/(Dumbarton loan 1918)/(Dumbarton Harp loan 1918)/ (Hamilton Academicals loan 1918)/(Vale of Leven loan Mar 1919)/(Dumbarton Harp loan 27 Sept 1919)/free May 1920/Queen of the South 10 Dec 1920/reinstated amateur 15 Aug 1922/East Stirling Aug 1922/Canada 1922.

Debut v Hibernian (a) 3-0 (SL) 17.8.18

"A likeable lad with a cunning foot enough," John Burns played for the Scottish Juniors who beat their English counterparts 2-1 at Firhill on March 30th 1918. This "crack young forward" was a stop-gap for Andy McAtee detained with the artillery assisting the Italians in the Alps north of Venice. "He crosses a fine ball but lack of physique may count against him." Despite a "sparkling display" against Hamilton Academicals on December 21st 1918, John lacked the "force, fire, fearlessness..." of his performances as a junior and "has not been a real success on the right-wing." McAtee was home by mid-January 1919 and bar an appearance in round one of the Victory Cup (1st March 1919) John Burns was a Celtic reserve thereafter. He was described as a "dandy inside-left" at East Stirling in September 1922.

Appearances:.
SL: 13 apps. 4 gls.
Total: *13 apps. 4 gls.*

BURNS, Thomas

Role: Midfield 1973-89
5' 11" 11st.3lbs.
b. Glasgow, 16th December 1956

CAREER: St Mungo's Academy/St Mary's BG/Eastercraigs Amateurs 1970/CELTIC S form 1970/Celtic BC 1970/CELTIC 23 Aug 1973/Maryhill Juniors (farmed out)/Salisbury (Rhodesia) (Harare, Zimbabwe) CSC loan cs 1975/(Blackpool loan 1 Feb 1983)/Kilmarnock 7 Dec 1989/player-assistant-manager 18 Sept 1991/caretaker-manager 6 Apr 1992/player-manager 27 Apr 1992/resigned 11 July 1994/CELTIC manager 12 July 1994.

Debut v Dundee (h) 1-2 (SL) 19.4.75 (sub)

"Burns does the simple things effectively... has a tremendous vision to open the game up." Jock Stein signed Tommy as a full professional in 1974 and envisioned him as a first team man of 1977: "Doesn't he have class! The way he passes the ball he could develop into another Baxter or Auld!...His left foot makes the ball talk!" Sure enough Tommy won his first Championship medal in 1977, won another in 1979 and his first Scottish Cup badge against Rangers in 1980. He was the schemer of the Flag sides in 1981 and 1982. In the Feyenoord tournament at Rotterdam 1982, Ruud Gullit, Wim van Hanegem, Wim Kieft all played but the Man of the Series was "Twists and Turns" Tommy Burns. He won his first cap against Northern Ireland at Hampden on May 19th 1981. His control was "impeccable" and "he showed a willingness to take defenders on" but Tommy himself felt he drifted out of the game in the second half which cost him his place at Wembley on May 23rd although he travelled in the squad with McGrain and Provan. Tommy had to wait until 1988 for a crack at the English. Scotland were short of real class for the 1982 World Cup and Tommy, the man who could thread a needle with his left foot, was having his best season yet. On May 14th Stein announced his name in the initial 40 from which the squad for Spain would be picked but, despite a fair game versus Wales at Hampden on May 24th, Tommy seemed unable to do enough to impress big Jock

and was ultimately not selected for the final party of 22. Against Sporting Lisbon in the European Cup on November 2nd 1983, Celtic took the field 2-0 down from the first leg. Tommy ran amok. Celtic won 5-0. Dinamo Kiev took precautions against that sort of performance on October 22nd 1986; they whacked Tommy both hard and early. By then he had another Scottish Cup medal (1985) and another Championship (1986) badge for his collection. This out-and-out Celt celebrated the Centenary Year by scheming the Double home. The way Tom played football had to be seen to be believed. Celtic could be running about about like headless chickens then on would come the substitute Burns. Rationality restored. At Parkhead on November 12th 1988, "he guided a free kick into the heart of the Rangers defence, a slanting and deceptive ball and one which so baffled Butcher that the big England defender glanced it into his own net for the equaliser." Tommy played his last game for Celtic during the first half-hour of the friendly versus Ajax of 6th December 1989 before being summoned off to admit the heir apparent, Steve Fulton. He removed his boots and threw them to the Jungle in farewell. At Rugby Park, the fans chanted his name from beginning to end of the match against Hamilton Academicals on 25th April 1992 demanding he be made manager. He duly took Killie into the Premier Division on May 15th 1993. Tommy Burns is an all-time Celtic great who in July 1994 to widespread approval was appointed manager at Parkhead in succession to Lou Macari.

Appearances:
SL: 353 apps. 52 gls.
SLC: 70 apps. 15 gls.
SC: 43 apps. 11 gls.
Eur: 34 apps. 3 gls.
Total: *500 apps. 81 gls.*

Left: Tommy as player and manager

BYRNE, Alexander

Role: Outside-left 1954-63
5' 9" 11st.4lbs.
b. Greenock, 4th June 1933

CAREER: Gourock Juniors/Royal Engineers (Malvern)(Cheltenham Town loan)/CELTIC 25 Sept 1954/Morton 22 June 1963/Queen of the South 12 Feb 1964/Hellas FC (Australia)/Juventus FC (Australia) player-coach/Hellas FC player-coach.

Debut v East Fife (a) 0-2 (SL) 9.3.57

Alec Byrne, a dazzling winger of speed and control, symbolises the Seven Lean Years between 1958 and 24th April 1965 when Celtic's successes were restricted to the occasional Glasgow Cup or a share of the Charity Trophy (9th May 1961). "Byrne is assured of a great future at the Paradise," wrote John McPhail on March 16th 1957. Alec played centre in the Army and first came into the Celtic side as replacement for Billy McPhail, badly injured versus Dundee on March 5th 1957. On his day as a left-winger, he might rip a defence to rags. Against 3rd Lanark in a fourth round replay of the Scottish Cup before 50,000 at

Alec Byrne

Hampden on a Wednesday afternoon, March 14th 1962, with two minutes to play and Celtic 3-0 up, he gathered the ball in midfield, beat man after man at pace, cut in, and unleashed a thunder of a shot past Jocky Robertson in the Hi-Hi goal. He was Celtic's answer to the loss of Fernie but was never encouraged completely to believe in his own innate ability to dribble the heart out of the opposition and to exploit it. What might not Stein have made of Alec Byrne? This gentleman of a player who worked full shifts daily in the shipyards at Greenock and trained the nights at Port Glasgow and Cappielow was destroyed by barracking even when directed at colleagues and not at him. He is remembered with respect by the long-suffering support of the time.

Appearances:
SL: 70 apps. 22 gls.
SLC: 9 apps. 0 gls.
SC: 19 apps. 8 gls.
Eur: 2 apps. 1 gl.
Total: *100 apps. 31 gls.*

BYRNE, Paul

Role: Striker 1993 to date
5' 10" 11st.0lbs.
b. Dublin, 3rd June 1972

CAREER: Bluebell United (Dublin)/Oxford United YTS 1986/pro. 1988/free 1990/Arsenal Oct 1990/free Apr 1991/Bangor Nov 1991/ CELTIC 26 May 1993.

Debut v St Johnstone (a) 1-2 (SL) 6.10.93

Paul Byrne made his Celtic debut in the defeat at Perth that at last persuaded manager Liam Brady it was time to offer his resignation. Paul came from Bangor for £70,000 trailing clouds of glory as both Northern Ireland Player of the Year and Northern Ireland Young Player of the Year. "I signed him for Celtic when no-one else would touch him. He has terrific ability; he operates well on the right of midfield and is a great crosser of the ball" commented Brady in March 1994 whilst simultaneously questioning Paul's temperament. Paul's first full match for Celtic was against Dundee with Frank Connor in charge on October 10th 1993. He proved willing to run with the ball at defenders and showed a deftness in the parting pass hardly excelled by Nicholas or Paul McStay. It was his cross, skimmed perfectly across the Sporting defence on October 20th 1993, that enabled Creaney to score and sent Celtic to Lisbon 1-0 up in the UEFA Cup. Against Rangers in the League at Ibrox on October 30th 1993, "The perfect weight of Byrne's passes suggested that the player carries a finely calibrated set of scales inside his head." Paul scored his first goal for Celtic only on January 19th 1994 and got the first goal under the new McCann regime against St Johnstone on March 5th 1994. He was in the Eire squad against Russia at Lansdowne Road on March 23rd but did not get a game and failed to make the Irish squad for the World Cup. He made a welcome return to the first team as a goal purveyor in the League Cup semi-final success versus Aberdeen on 26th October 1994.

Appearances:
SL: 22 apps. 2 gls.
SC: 1 app. 0 gls.
Eur: 2 apps. 0 gls.
Total: *25 apps. 2 gls.*

Paul Byrne

CAIRNEY, Charles

Role: Right-half 1949-50
5' 8" 10st.6lbs
b. Blantyre, 21st September 1926

CAREER: HM Forces/Cambuslang Rangers 1947/CELTIC 14 Mar 1949/free 6 May 1950/ Leyton Orient 27 July 1950/Barry Town 1951/ Bristol Rovers July 1953/Headington United cs 1955/Worcester City 1955-56/East Stirling 24 Oct 1957/Celtic Old Crocks 11 June 1969.

Debut v Raith Rovers (h) 2-2 (SL) 1.10.49

Chic Cairney was understudy to the great Bobby Evans. He had a magnificent game against Brentford (Paterson, MacDonald, Paton) in the friendly of September 26th 1949 and when Bobby was in Belfast with Scotland on the first Saturday of October 1949, Chic got his chance against a fine Raith Rovers side and did well. His next big day was at Upton Park on October 17th. Celtic lost 5-2 but received an extraordinary compliment: "They showed how football used to be played in this country before it was sacrificed on the altar of bash and speed and inspired West Ham to play likewise only West Ham played it faster." Chic gave a hundred per cent wherever he went and made a redoubtable skipper at Worcester City.

Chic Cairney

Appearances:
SL: 1 app. 0 gls.
Total: *1 app. 0 gls.*

CAIRNEY, James Mougan

Role: Inside-forward 1922-23
b. Calton, 29th November 1902

CAREER: Duntocher Hibernian/St Anthony's cs 1922/ CELTIC 27 Sept 1922/ (Arbroath loan 15 Mar 1923)/free 11 May 1923/Arthurlie 29 Aug 1923/

Jim Cairney

Whittall's Carpet Factory Worcester (Mass. USA) FC 1924/Boston (Mass. USA) FC Aug 1924.

Debut v Partick Thistle (h) 4-3 (SL) 7.10.22

"A brilliant inside man," Jim Cairney is said to "have pleased" by coming on at some point in the away friendly versus Newcastle on September 27th 1922. Celtic signed him after the game. Although inside-left in a sensationally revamped Celtic forward line "he did nothing out of the ordinary on his League debut" but was in the Scottish Cup side that won 2-3 at Lochgelly in the first round (January 13th 1923). The following week, Celtic tried out a personal friend of Jim's at inside-right, a Garngad boy who had been on loan to Clydebank, name of McGrory. Jim Cairney sought his fame in the States and Tommy Muirhead watched him playing a great game of football there in early July 1924 and signed him for Boston.

Appearances:
SL: 3 apps. 0 gls.
SC: 1 app. 0 gls.
Total: *4 apps. 0 gls.*

CALLACHAN, Henry

Role: Full-back 1925-27
b. Madras, India, 9th April 1903
d. Leicester, 11th February 1990

CAREER: Kirkintilloch Rob Roy/Parkhead Juniors/CELTIC 11 Aug 1925/(Alloa loan 25 Aug 1925)/(Beith loan 18 Aug 1926)/Leicester City 24 Sept 1927/Tunbridge Wells Rangers Aug 1930/Burton Town Aug 1931/[Market Harborough].

Debut v Dundee (h) 0-0 (SL) 31.10.25

"A very stylish full-back...plays as McNair played - the ball comes to him more often than he goes to it...he knows the art of taking up position...McNair's successor." Harry Callachan was the son of a soldier and one of the first juniors for whom Celtic paid a fee: £50. He was signed as cover for Willie McStay and Hugh Hilley and was in the Celtic team immediately prior to the Cup final of 1926

Harry Callachan

CALLAGHAN, Thomas

Role: Midfield 1968-76
6' 1" 11st.10lbs.
b. Cowdenbeath, 6th December 1945

CAREER: St Columba's School Cowdenbeath/ Lochore Welfare/Dunfermline Athletic 22 Sept 1962/CELTIC 22 Nov 1968/(San Antonio Thunder loan cs 1976)/Clydebank 4 Nov 1976 /free 29 Apr 1977/Galway United manager 1977-78/Partick Thistle coach.

Debut v Partick Thistle (a) 4-0 (SL) 23.11.68

Jock Stein never picked a team but he tried to include Willie Fernie: a powerful runner with ball control prepared to come through from the back, go at a defence and destroy it. At Dunfermline under Stein, Tid Callaghan was a crunching tackler with a mean streak until he broke his leg (November 5th 1966). At Parkhead Jock used him as his workhorse, carrying the ball deep down the left. He was a long time in awe of the Lisbon Lions and it was not until January 9th 1970 that the Jungle was first chanting his name. One week later Stein had to warn him he was still dithering in admiration for Bertie Auld. Jim Craig and Jim Brogan did not go on the American tour of 1970 so Bobby Murdoch played sweeper and Tid got a proper chance to show what he could do as link-man with Willie Wallace. By 1972 his game was at its zenith and at the San Siro Milan he showed running power and control that tore at the Inter defence (5th April 1972). Against Rangers at Ibrox on August 30th 1973, "he ran his legs off...One day Tommy Docherty must take a look at this man Callaghan." Like George McCluskey, he is underestimated as a Celt but his talent was enormous. He was versatile in defence and midfield and above all was no problem, a total professional, dedicated to his game and the club he loved, Celtic. He has Championship medals for 1969 to 1974 and Scottish Cup badges for 1971, 1972 and 1974 (as well as for 1968 with Dunfermline). Some player, Tommy Callaghan.

when they were advised "to shake off their apathy or whatever it is," in a 0-0 draw versus Partick Thistle. He returned to the Celtic side that lifted the Championship (the last for 10 years) on April 14th 1926. The crowd showed small enthusiasm after the harsh disappointment of the Cup final defeat by St Mirren. Hugh Hilley's health was in decline at the start of 1927-28 but when Peter McGonagle took his place it looked as if Callachan would be spending a third season idle. Then Willie Orr appeared in Scotland looking for talent. He returned to Leicester with Harry. "I got a great right-back" (April 1928), but only three appearances followed for the Foxes.

Appearances:
SL: 11 apps. 0 gls.
Total: *11 apps. 0 gls.*

Appearances: .
SL: 172 apps. 14 gls.
SLC: 52 apps. 7 gls.
SC: 32 apps. 6 gls.
Eur: 28 apps. 6 gls.
Total: *284 apps. 33 gls.*

*Right:
Tommy
Callaghan*

CAMERON, James Scott

Role: Outside-right 1932-33
5' 8" 11st.0lbs.
b. Lochee, 27th May 1906
d. Dundee, 16th December 1935

CAREER: Lochee Central/Dundee Harp/
Montrose Oct 1928/Dundee Harp Nov 1928/
Dundee United 28 Dec 1928/Chester cs 1931/
Shelbourne 1931/CELTIC 2 May 1932/free
1933/Arbroath 6 Aug 1933/Forfar Athletic
5 Oct 1934.

Debut v Aberdeen (h) 3-0 (SL) 13.8.32
(scored once)

Jimmy Cameron

Dundee United played
Jimmy Cameron at
outside-right on
December 29th 1929 and
"he so delighted the 2,000
hardy spectators that they
completely forgot about
the snowstorm."
Throughout 1932 the
clamour of the Celtic fans
was for 'made players' ie
seasoned professionals so
Willie Maley signed Jimmy Cameron. He was
a right-footer, but given the job of solving
Celtic's perennial problem at outside-left.
Against Aberdeen on his debut "he found it
well-nigh impossible to get his crosses in.
Time and again he smacked the ball against a
defender." Jimmy was "a player above the
ordinary" but "...he turns back oftener than I
would like and by the time the ball comes
across, the defenders are in position." Jimmy
dropped into the reserves then broke his ankle
in January 1933. A fruiterer in Dundee, he was
not destined for a long life. Within weeks of
his projected marriage, he played one bitter
December 7th for Forfar versus Edinburgh
City at East Pilton. The glacial weather
produced an ice-field of a pitch. Jimmy scored
his last goal in football from a penalty to make
it 2-2 at half-time. All the way home to
Dundee he had to stand freezing in the
corridor of an unheated train. Within days he
was stricken with pneumonia and in a short
time was dead.

Appearances:
SL: 4 apps. 2 gls.
Total: *4 apps. 2 gls.*

CAMPBELL, John

Role: Forward 1890-95 & 1897-1903
5' 9" 11st.10lbs.
b. June-Dec 1872
d. 2nd December 1947

CAREER: Possil Hawthorn/Benburb 1888/
CELTIC Easter 1890/Aston Villa 1895/CELTIC
1 May 1897/Third Lanark 22 Aug 1903/retired
1906.

Debut v Battlefield (h) 7-1 (GC) 20.9.1890

Saracen Street man Johnny Campbell ("a
better passer than a dribbler; his dribbling is
straight, go-ahead") could (and did) play

anywhere in the forward line but lives in the Celtic memory as left-wing partner to Duke McMahon. Some commentators were convinced Johnny was wasted when not played at centre: "Why Celtic will not employ him in the middle is one of these points that passeth understanding." He was not naturally left-footed and used to pull the ball onto his right before the cross. Johnny played his first game for Celtic on a tour match versus Bolton Wanderers at Pike's Lane on 4th April 1890. He was in the first Celtic side to lift the Scottish Cup in 1892 and was an essential to the Championship sides of 1893 and 1894. He left Parkhead in 1895 "through the stupid action of a very prominent committee man," according to Willie Maley. The Italian sports magazine *Guerin Sportivo* of January 1989 lists him as the joint top League scorer in Europe for 1895-96 on 20 goals. He was a cherished member of Villa's Double side of 1897 but when Tom Maley asked him to come home he seems to have responded with little hesitation. He was inside-right in the Celtic side which beat Rangers 0-4 at Ibrox in a superlative League show on September 27th 1897: "I am as proud to-day as when I helped Aston Villa to win the Cup." With Johnny back, Celtic took the League again in 1898 and the Cup in 1899 and 1900. He was inside-right in the team that beat England 4-1 wearing Lord Rosebery's primrose and white at Celtic Park on April 7th 1900, when Scotland fielded one of her finest ever forward lines (Jack Bell was inside-left). Apart from the above, Johnny is a man of some other interesting firsts: first (and only?) Celtic reserve to score 12 goals in a game; first man to hansel St James' Park Newcastle with a goal (September 3rd 1892); first man to score a League goal at the present Villa Park (15th April 1897); first Celtic player to be sued for 'palimony' (and lose) (24th March 1898); the one and only ex-Celt to win a Scottish Cup medal with Third Lanark (1904). Johnny Campbell was an all-time Celtic great.

Appearances: .
SL: 169 apps. 87 gls.
SC: 46 apps. 22 gls.
Total: *215 apps. 109 gls.*

CAMPBELL, Robert Gordon

Role: Full-back 1905-06
6' 0" 12st.0lbs
b. Ellon, 27th January 1883
d. Glasgow, 31st May 1943

CAREER: Kintore Village FC/Crosshill Winton/Rutherglen Glencairn 1902/Queen's Park Victoria XI 1904/Queen's Park 23 Aug 1904/CELTIC 26 June 1905/Rangers 13 Jan 1906/Kilmarnock 30 July 1914/Ayr United 29 Dec 1915/retired 1917/Rangers director Oct 1926.

Debut v Motherwell (h) 3-1 (SL) 19.8.05

"In R.G. Campbell, Celtic may have gained a back with greater promise than any youngster since the late Nicol Smith." Like Billy Foulke, RG Campbell's nickname was "Baby" (for "Baby Elephant"). He almost gave the game up with knee trouble when with Glencairn. He played for Queen's Park against Celtic the day Hampden was opened (October 31st 1903); "Campbell, of the crimson stockings, who has the reputation of being a pure intellectual and a scrupulously fair type of amateur did a few things not equalled by Nic Smith or Isaac Begbie at their worst." He made his next impact on Celtic with his first goal for Queen's Park, a last-minute screamer from 40 yards out at Parkhead in the League on October 29th 1904 to salvage the Spiders a 1-1 draw. For such a big man his debut for Celtic saw him "as nervous as a bride at the altar." Celtic played Rangers at Ibrox on October 21st 1905 and lost 3-2; "Catch of the Season" Campbell was their Achilles heel. Rangers knew where his heart lay and paid £350 for his services which included casting him at centre as the

John Campbell

Ibrox counterpart of Jimmy Quinn (he scored six in the 1-7 defeat of Morton in a friendly). He also played his cricket (for Clydesdale) handy to Hampden and Ibrox until he moved to live in Hyndland in April 1910. Bob was an assiduous worker for the Glasgow Wesleyan Brotherhood and had ideas in advance of his time as to how football could be improved: allow the goal from a corner kick; a goal and not a penalty when the ball has been fisted out; two defenders instead of three for offside (November 1911). Celtic played Rangers for his benefit at Ibrox on August 19th 1912. Big Bob collapsed and died in Bath Street.

Appearances:
SL: 11 apps. 0 gls.
Total: *11 apps. 0 gls.*

CANNON, Bernard

Role: Outside-left 1947-48
5' 7" 11st.7lbs
b. 4th May 1922

CAREER: Buncrana Amateurs/Mile End Athletic/Blantyre Celtic/ CELTIC 5 Mar 1947/ free 4 May 1948/Derry City cs 1948/Alloa Aug 1950.

Debut v Hibernian (a) 0-2 (SL) 12.4.47

Buncrana boy Barney Cannon played a trial for Celtic versus Aston Villa in Birmingham on 1st March 1947 and was booked for the club the day after the death of chairman Tom White. Barney was the sixth winger signed by Celtic

Barney Cannon

during 1946-47 after Hugh Doherty and Tommy Hughes (both Dundalk), Ronnie Mitchell (Renfrew Waverley), Jackie Jordan (Queen's Park) and Frank Quinn (Saltcoats Victoria). Outside-lefts were suddenly in plentiful supply at Parkhead and he found himself competing for a big team game with Johnny Paton, Konrad Kapler and George Hazlett. Barney's moment of glory lies with Derry City on April 16th 1949 when he played in the Irish Cup final against Glentoran (Bertie Peacock, Danny Blanchflower) and scored a superb goal, Derry's third, in a 3-1 win. His 40-yard run and raging shot were remembered by

soccer connoisseurs in the bars of the Walled City with awe and gratitude long years after. Barney played for Derry City at Parkhead on 24th April 1950.

Appearances:
SL: 3 apps. 0 gls.
Total: *3 apps. 0 gls.*

CANTWELL, John

Role: Centre-forward 1946-47
b. 21st November 1923
d. 24th March 1989

CAREER: Glenboig St Joseph's/CELTIC 26 July 1946/free Apr 1947/Dumbarton 9 June 1947/free 1950/Morton Aug 1950/free 1951/ Stenhousemuir 30 Aug 1951/free 1952.

Debut v Clyde (a) 2-2 (SL) 14.8.46 (scored twice)

Jack Cantwell was a juvenile of 23 just out of the Navy when he tried out for Celtic in a Central War Relief Fund match against Morton at Cappielow on June 8th 1946. He had already played trials for Third Lanark with Clyde, Hibernian and Bury all interested. He was "a grafter of the McGrory type" and

Jack Cantwell

opened the scoring in 17 minutes. Things looked good indeed when he scored two in two minutes against Clyde in the League on August 14th. He also scored in the 1-4 defeat by Third Lanark (September 4th 1946) when the bulk of the support staggered out of the ground in a daze, shocked into silence at the dismal shambles just witnessed. The militant minority made for the main entrance to demand words of chairman White. Jimmy McMenemy put his finger on the problem: too many apprentices, not enough journeymen. Jack was freed after only a season when he disputed new terms.

Appearances:
SL: 8 apps. 5 gls.
SLC: 1 app. 0 gls.
Total: *9 apps. 5 gls.*

CARLIN, James

Role: Outside-left 1897
b. Kinning Park, 8th December 1877

CAREER: Stevenston Thistle/Paisley Celtic/
CELTIC 13 Oct 1896/Victoria United 3 May
1897/Reading 18 Nov 1897/Clyde 17 Mar
1898/Stevenston Thistle 29 Sept 1898/Glossop
1899/Arthurlie 9 Mar 1900/reinstated amateur
14 Aug 1900/Barnsley Dec 1900.

Debut v Dundee (h) 0-1 (SL) 20.2.1897

For the vital penultimate match of the
Championship 1897, Celtic had included John
Neilson from Abercorn only to discover at the
last moment he was ineligible. James Carlin
was drafted in from the reserves but found the
standard beyond him. Celtic lost to a last-
minute goal. It was not the first time James
had been made strip in a hurry. On the day of
the Players' Strike of 28th November 1896,
Davie Meikleham was sent to Cathkin by
express hansom to bring Tom Dunbar to
Parkhead. So who took Dunbar's place
courtesy of Queen's Park Strollers? Answer:
James Carlin.

> **Appearances:**
> *SL: 1 app. 0 gls.*
> **Total:** *1 app. 0 gls.*

CARROLL, Robert

Role: Outside-right 1959-63
5' 7" 10st.10lbs.
b. 13th May 1938

CAREER: Partick Thistle Boys Supporters'
Club 1953/Campsie Black Watch 1955/Irvine
Meadow Mar 1956/CELTIC 22 Sept 1957/St
Mirren 1 Feb 1963/Dundee United 29 July
1965/Coleraine 8 July 1967/Queen of the
South 17 Nov 1967/Irvine Meadow 19 June
1968.

Debut v Partick Thistle (h) 1-2 (SLC) 12.8.59

"He may not be a Puskas on the ball but give
him just one glimpse of goal and he hits 'em
just as hard and true as the Hungarian
master." Railwayman Bobby Carroll was a
prolific goalscorer as a junior. With him on the
right wing Irvine Meadow won the Scottish
Junior Cup in 1959 just before he was called
up to be a Kelly Kid. Bobby was never less
than a whole-hearted trier but played "for one

bad lot being licked by another bad lot." At
Broomfield on October 1st 1962, he was
placing the ball for a corner when a black
puddin' came flying through the air and
flopped on the pitch beside him. Voice from
the crowd: "Aye, an' that makes two o' ye!"
(Paddy Crerand couldn't play on for
laughing!). One of Bobby's problems at
Parkhead was conscientiousness, like trying to
have a decent sleep before a game. The wee
man just couldn't drop off and found he was
far better off making a late night of it and
going to bed exhausted. The goal of his career
was scored against Everton on January 27th
1960 at Parkhead, a tight, sharp angle and a
raging shot high into the roof of the net. He
also scored Celtic's first goal in European
competition against Valencia in Spain (Fairs
Cities' Cup 26th Sept 1962).

> **Appearances:**
> *SL: 61 apps. 20 gls.*
> *SLC: 12 apps. 4 gls.*
> *SC: 4 apps. 1 gl.*
> *Eur: 1 app. 2 gls.*
> **Total:** *78 apps. 27 gls.*

Bobby Carroll

CARRUTH, Joseph

Role: Centre-forward 1936-45
5' 9" 11st.7lbs.
b. 12th March 1914
d. 26th November 1988

CAREER: Springburn United/Petershill cs 1936/CELTIC 14 Aug 1936/(Hearts loan 25 Mar 1940)/(Albion Rovers loan 9 Aug 1940)/ St Mirren (trial) 6 Sept 1941/(Vale of Clyde loan 12 Dec 1941)/free 22 Jan 1945/Stirling Albion (trial) 11 Aug 1945/free 7 Sept 1945/ Jordanvale Hearts coach by 1948.

Debut v Falkirk (a) 3-0 (SL) 5.12.36 (scored once)

"Joe Carruth is the nearest deputy to Quinn and McGrory Celtic have discovered. He has their same heart for leadership...how the Parkhead crowd just love a trier." Joe trained at Parkhead and worked-out in Johnny McMillan's gym in Sauchiehall Street against all comers, not excluding the professionals. He was the reason Celtic felt they could let McGrory go after Joe's brilliant game and hat-trick against Hamilton Acas on September 4th 1937. On April 9th 1938 he weaved his way Buchan-style through the Motherwell defence and walked the ball into the net for "Parkhead's goal of the season." His shoulder charges on Joe Kennaway gave a robust new dimension to the Public Trial of 9th August 1938. For what happened at Ibrox on Ne'erday

1939 before a record crowd of 118,567 there is one version says Delaney and Watters were involved but another sees Carruth only: "He got the ball in his own penalty area, beat the first man by lifting it over his head; the second, he pushed the ball one way and ran the other; he dummied three players with one move, tricked another two, walked round Dawson and shot. Even Bill Struth congratulated him." Joe was operated-on for cartilage in December 1940 and in his first game back scored four goals for Albion Rovers in a 5-2 defeat of Morton (8th March 1941). He was one of only five Celts to be a guest of the club at both Jubilee dinners at the Grosvenor 15th June 1938 and Glasgow City Chambers 11th April 1988. He has also the distinction of having played for Stirling Albion in their inaugural match in August 1945. The new Quinn, the new McGrory, but why Joe, this one hundred per cent centre-forward either faded or Celtic lost faith is a mystery. He was working long shifts in Hydepark Loco Works that left little time for proper training. This may be a part of the answer.

Appearances:
SL: 39 apps. 28 gls.
SC: 3 apps. 2 gls.
Total: *42 apps. 30 gls.*
RL: 14 apps. 5 gls.
Total: *14 apps. 5 gls.*

Joe Carruth's wedding. Best man is Jackie Watters (seated).

CASCARINO, Antony Guy

Role: Striker 1991-92
6' 2" 13st.0lbs.
b. St Paul Cray, 1st September 1962

CAREER: Crockenhill (Kent League) Mar 1981
/Gillingham Jan 1982/Millwall 23 June 1987/
Aston Villa 16 Mar 1990/CELTIC 19 July 1991
/Chelsea 6 Feb 1992/free 17 May 1994/
Olympique Marseille 19 July 1994.

Debut v Dundee United (a) 4-3 (SL) 10.8.91

Liam Brady inherited a team in June 1991
containing a proven goalscorer Tommy Coyne
and a boy of promise, Gerry Creaney, but
within a month was spending £1.1million on
Tony Cascarino who had scored a mere 12
goals in 50 games for Aston Villa. Although
Tony seemed to think there was more to his
game than goalscoring, his luck did not turn
in the Scottish Premier. He got his first goal on
October 5th 1991 against Hearts at Celtic Park
when "many had thought they might go to
their graves without seeing Cascarino put a
ball in the net." He came on as substitute,
scored and was sent off, all within six minutes!
His second counter was the famous equaliser
(he had been on the park just three minutes)

Tony Cascarino

versus Rangers at Ibrox on November 2nd
1991. The big striker played his last match for
Celtic against the New Zealand XI on
February 4th 1992: "Celtic played too much
football to suit my game." Despite reports of a
free transfer (March 22nd 1994) it was his two
flick headers down that produced both
Chelsea goals against Luton on April 9th 1994
and took the Blues into the FA Cup final. Tony
came on for Mark Stein with 12 minutes to go
at Wembley (May 14th) but Chelsea were 3-0
down and chasing a lost cause in the incessant
rain. His only appearance in the World Cup
finals in the USA was for the last 15 minutes
of Ireland's 2-0 exit from the competition
versus Holland at Orlando (July 4th 1994).
Television commentator Liam Brady meant no
disrespect but included Tony in his list of Irish
strikers who lacked pace.

> **Appearances:**
> *SL: 24 apps. 4 gls.*
> *SLC: 1 app. 0 gls.*
> *SC: 1 app. 0 gls.*
> *Eur: 4 apps. 0 gls.*
> **Total:** *30 apps. 4 gls.*

CASEY, James

Role: Sweeper/Midfield 1974-80
6' 0" 11st.5lbs.
b. Ruchazie, 2nd August 1957

CAREER: St Gregory's/Celtic Amateurs/
CELTIC S form 20 Jan 1972/Maryhill Juniors
(farmed-out)/CELTIC May 1974/Phoenix
Inferno 29 Nov 1980/Arbroath 29 Jan 1981/
retired summer 1983.

*Debut v Stenhousemuir (h) 1-0 (SLC) 24.9.75
(sub)*

Ben Casey signed full-time for Celtic as part
of the projected nucleus of 1977 but suffered
sore initially from torn ligaments and muscle
problems. He was drafted into the party for
Singapore and Australia when Dalglish
refused to travel as of 8th July 1977. He got his
chance after Pat Stanton's injury when he
played first as sweeper against Chelsea on
August 15th 1977 but in Stein's words "came
under great strain." Chosen as central
defender versus Rangers for the Scottish Cup
final of 10th May 1980 when MacDonald and
McAdam were suspended, he damaged his
ankle the Tuesday before Hampden and had
to drop out in favour of Mike Conroy. Jim

Jim Casey

Celtic added several thousands to the gate for a humdrum League fixture by introducing James Cassidy as guest star. James was a most popular talent wherever he played and his departure for Glasgow Hibs was much resented in Kilmarnock. He trained under the great distance runner Paddy Cannon in his time at Oatlands and "led the Bolton line with dash and brilliance." At Molineux the December previous to his playing for Celtic he cracked a goalpost with a shot. From then on he never played but the crowd was urging him: "Shoot, Cassidy!" When Joe Cassidy joined the Trotters in 1924 he was geed on by the fans: "Go, Cass! Go!" the same cry Jimmy had heard in the 'nineties. At 5'7" Jimmy was the tallest of the Bolton forwards. His son James junior tried out at Burnden Park in the 1920s, the decade of the Three Cups, but without his father's success.

Appearances: .
SL: 1 app. 0 gls.
Total: *1 app. 0 gls.*

CASSIDY, Joseph

Role: Centre, Inside-left
1893-95
5' 8" 11st.7lbs.
b. Dalziel,
30th July 1872

CAREER: Motherwell Athletic/ Blyth FC 1890/Newton Heath 6 Mar 1893/(CELTIC loan 27 May 1893)/CELTIC 3 June 1893/Newton Heath Mar 1895/ Manchester City 20 Apr 1900/ Middlesbrough 8 May 1901/Workington player-coach 1906/ retired Nov 1906.

Joe Cassidy

Debut v Rangers (n) 5-0 (CC) 27.5.1893

"Strong and burly," Joe Cassidy from Motherwell gave Celtic a couple of seasons of his time and did not leave empty-handed. He won a Charity Cup medal immediately and on February 24th 1894 was in the team that won Celtic's second Flag. There was also a Glasgow Cup medal at 1st Cathkin Park in a 2-0 win over Rangers on November 17th 1894. He played his last game on February 16th 1895 at Tynecastle for a Celtic side penetrated by dressing-room

played indoor football in the States but was unable to settle and at Arbroath walked out on the Red Lichties for over a year. His finest hour was with Scottish schoolboys, the 2-4 win at Wembley on June 9th 1973.

Appearances:
SL: 11 apps. 0 gls.
SLC: 7 apps. 0 gls.
SC: 3 apps. 1 gl.
Eur: 5 apps. 0 gls.
Total: *26 apps. 1 gl.*

CASSIDY, James

James Cassidy

Role: Centre forward 1892
5' 7" 11st.7lbs.
b. Dalry, 2nd December 1869

CAREER: Kilmarnock Athletic 1888/ Kilmarnock Feb 1889/Glasgow Hibernian 7 Sept 1889/Bolton Wanderers Nov 1889/ (Carfin Shamrock loan 1890)/(CELTIC loan 14 May 1892)/retired summer 1898.

Debut v Leith Athletic (h) 2-0 (SL) 14.5.1892

discord. Hearts won 4-0. Willie Maley says he prospered in Motherwell after retirement.

Appearances:
SL: 28 apps. 13 gls.
SC: 8 apps. 4 gls.
Total: *36 apps. 17 gls.*

CASSIDY, Joseph

Role: Inside-left, Centre 1912-23
5' 7" 11st.0lbs.
b. Cadder, 10th October 1896
d. 23rd July 1949

CAREER: Westthorn School Dalbeth/Vale of Clyde/CELTIC 16 Oct 1912/(Vale of Atholl loan 25 Oct 1913)/(Kilmarnock loan 30 Oct 1913)/(Abercorn loan 12 Dec 1913)/(Ayr United loan 26 Dec 1913)/(Ayr United loan 9 May 1914)/2 Black Watch (HLI) 1915/ (Reading loan 12 Feb 1915)/Scottish Horse (Lovat's Scouts) 1916/(Clydebank loan 18 Sept 1915 & Jan 1919)/Bolton Wanderers 9 Aug 1924/Cardiff City 19 Oct 1925/Dundee 19 Aug 1926/Clyde 22 June 1928/free 12 Jan 1929/ Ballymena United 29 Jan 1929/Dundalk 2 Apr 1931/ Morton 6 Aug 1931/free 1 Sept 1931/ Dundalk 26 Sept 1931/Morton 22 Jan 1932.

Debut v Motherwell (a) 0-1 (SL) 15.3.13

The Inter-City League was the place for blooding youngsters and Celtic gave a trial to "Smith" at inside-left versus Hibernian on October 16th 1912. "Smith" was a 16 year old, real name Cassidy, "surely the smallest and cleverest thing ever to appear in a Celtic jersey." Joe lost some good years to fighting the Kaiser but made a startling reappearance from France on Hogmanay 1918 and walked straight into the team at Ibrox the next day. He was Celtic spirit incarnate and the fans worshipped him especially at Ibrox on Ne'erday 1921 when he got both goals in the 0-2 win. "His second goal was so beautifully taken, Rangers supporters could scarcely forebear to cheer." He broke his jaw against Rangers in a clash with Billy McCandless on October 28th 1922. On Armistice Day, Celtic

JOE CASSIDY
(Celtic)

crashed 1-4 to Ayr United. Joe was back the following week at Broomfield, handsome face held together in sticking plaster and bandages. Hibs reached the final of the Scottish Cup in 1923 without conceding a goal. Then they met Cassidy. Joe had scored three at Lochgelly (2-3), four against Hurlford (4-0), two against East Fife (2-1) and it was not until the 4th round that any other Celt (Adam McLean) produced a Cup goal. Against the powerful Motherwell side in the semi-final, Joe gave Celtic a dream start with a strike in 30 seconds. In the 64th minute of the final of 31st March Hibs yielded to a Cassidy header at the Mount Florida end of Hampden. Should not Bill Harper have come off his line quicker? "It was a goal all the same. I had my eyes glued on the ball. I could have brought it down and placed it where I liked." Truly, Celtic's 1923 triumph was Cassidy's Cup. Jimmy McGrory acknowledges Joe Cassidy as his mentor in the art of heading a ball and picks him at inside-left in his all-time team. Joe was an artistic inside man made to function at centre on Tommy McInally's first departure 1922. He left home when he left Celtic and was never the same player elsewhere. Nevertheless, at Dundee, "He set a style of football among the players associated with him in the team at that time that was noticeable even after he left." His transfer following on John Gilchrist's transformed Celtic into a club prepared to sell itself into mediocrity. During Celtic's great year of 1938, Joe was employed as an attendant at 'Victoria Falls' in the Glasgow Empire Exhibition at Bellahouston Park. News of his comparatively early death in 1949 was met with shock and anguish by the fans of his era.

Appearances: .
SL: 189 apps. 91 gls.
SC: 15 apps. 13 gls.
Total: *204 apps. 104 gls.*

♣ **Celtic note:** *Trooper Cassidy won the Military Medal in November 1918 and an Irish Cup medal with Ballymena 2-1 versus Belfast Celtic on 31st March 1929.*

CATTANACH, David

Role: Half-back 1963-72
5' 9" 11st.0lbs.
b. Falkirk, 27th June 1946

CAREER: St Modan's High School 1961/
Stirling Albion ground staff 25 July 1961/
Woodburn Athletic (farmed-out) 1961/Stirling
Albion 29 June 1962/CELTIC 19 Aug 1963/
Falkirk 20 Jan 1972/free own request 15 July
1974/Stirling Albion coach.

Debut v St Mirren (h) 5-0 (SL) 9.4.66

Davie Cattanach is another successful
businessman who might well have made
Celtic a fine Chief Executive on December 19th
1990. He was pursued by Manchester United,
Liverpool and Aston Villa as a schoolboy and
capped as an amateur for Scotland versus
England (23rd February 1962). He spent all his
time at Annfield playing just for love of the
game. He made his Celtic debut with no
"pre-match publicity" in place of Bobby
Murdoch and his "cool, workmanlike display"
drew the applause of the fans and "illustrated
the depth of Celtic's reserve strength." Celtic

Davie Cattanach

needed four goals for the ton and Davie
brought the best out of Jim Thorburn with a
drive at 0-0. His business career took off while
at Parkhead and he was probably the first
Celtic player to park a 3.5 litre Jaguar outside
the main entrance! He came close to glory as a
member of Big Jock's squad on a May
afternoon in Lisbon besides having a
grandfather James Friel who was a cousin of
Patsy Gallagher. His best run in the team was
at right-back instead of Jim Craig during the
first month of 1968 but it was his fluffed
pass-back that let Pat Gardner in to score
Dunfermline's second goal and knock Celtic
out of the Cup on January 27th. When Auld
and Gemmell were sent home from the US
tour in 1970, Davie was summoned out to join
the squad on May 21st and played in the 3-1
defeat by Eintracht at Randalls Island the next
day and the following two matches in
Bermuda. In 1989 "local publican" Davie
Cattanach put up £350,000 in an attempt to
buy out the board of Falkirk FC and although
the offer was refused on 22nd December 1989,
his bid had a lot of popular support among
the fans.

Appearances:
SL: 13 apps. 1 gl.
SLC: 2 apps. 0 gls.
SC: 3 apps. 0 gls.
Eur: 1 app. 0 gls.
Total: *19 apps. 1 gl.*

CHALMERS, Paul

Role: Striker 1980-86
5' 10" 10st.3lbs.
b. 31st October 1963

CAREER: St Helen's Primary Bishopbriggs/
Eastercraigs Amateurs/Celtic S form 1979/
CELTIC 9 Oct 1980/(Bradford City loan 27 Jan
1986)/Nottingham Forest (trial) Aug 1986/
St Mirren 4 Sept 1986/Swansea City Dec 1990
/Dunfermline Athletic 28 Aug 1992/Hamilton
Academicals 7 July 1993.

*Debut v Morton (h) 4-0 (SL) 19.2.85 (sub)
(scored once)*

Paul Chalmers, son of the great Steve, "and
built for speed like his father," hit the back of
the net so prolifically for Celtic reserves he
was given his place on the bench versus Ghent
in the Cup-Winners' Cup tie of October 3rd
1984. When he scored all four goals in the 4-0

Paul Chalmers in action against Dundee United.

CHALMERS, Stephen

Role: Forward 1959-71
5' 9" 10st.12lbs.
b. Glasgow, 26th December 1936

CAREER: St Mungo's Primary/St Roch
Senior Secondary/Brunswick BC/
Kirkintilloch Rob Roy 1953/Newmarket
Town on National Service/Ashfield 1956/
CELTIC 6 Feb 1959/(Glentoran loan (v
Dukla Prague) 6 Dec 1965)/Morton player-
coach 9 Sept 1971/Partick Thistle player
5 Oct 1972/free 29 Apr 1975/Celtic coach
26 July 1975/(St Roch loan 2 Aug 1975)/
Celtic Pools organiser 1979.

Debut v Airdrie (h) 1-2 (SL) 10.3.59

In 1963 Jimmy Delaney (rightly) criticised
Steve Chalmers as a head-down player
with no idea of how to pace his game. Jock
Stein took Steve's speed and as with all
else, harnessed it to a plan. The transformed Chalmers responded initially with
three of the second-half goals in the 5-1 win
over Rangers on January 3rd 1966. He is
nowadays immortalised as a Lisbon Lion
and scorer of the single most important
goal in the club's history five minutes from
time on May 25th 1967.
His pace in the middle of
the attack at the Estadio
da Luz that Thursday
afternoon gave Inter no
rest. Steve was constantly
in the thick of it pushing
up against the Milan
defenders in a way that
must have made the great
Delaney proud. He scored
another memorable goal:
the last against Rangers in
the Scottish Cup final of
April 26th 1969, a solo run
down the left and a shot
at the near post which
made it 4-0 for Celtic and
and revenge at last for the
drubbing of April 14th
1928. It was his third
Scottish Cup medal to set
alongside 1965 and 1967.
He won League medals

defeat of Hearts reserves at Tynecastle on
February 12th 1985, it brought his total to 29 in
24 matches. His next counter was in his debut
for the first team. "This is a proud and happy
day for me" said Steve. The goal's ascription
was disputed but Celtic awarded it to Paul.
Davie Hay complimented him after the
game at Fir Park on 19th October 1985:
"He came on as sub and looked better
than a couple of international strikers"
(ie Johnston and McClair). It cost St
Mirren £20,000 to take him to Paisley.
He received a ball from Mick
McCarthy full in the face at Love
Street on November 26th 1988 and
sustained a broken nose with horrific
injuries necessitating stitches inside
and outside nose and mouth. Paul
was out of hospital in the course of
the week looking a mess but ready
to resume training and demanding
a place in the team the following
Saturday. Swansea bought his
transfer for £110,000. He won a
Welsh Cup medal 2-0 versus
Wrexham on May 18th 1991.

Appearances: .
SL: 4 apps. 1 gl.
Total: *4 apps. 1 gl.*

Celtic Chalmers!
Dad Steve and son Paul.

Steve Chalmers scores the goal which brought the European Cup to Britain for the first time and, wearing an Inter Milan shirt (below), celebrates with the other Celtic scorer on that memorable night in Lisbon, Tommy Gemmell.

for each season of 1965-69 and League Cup medals for each year 1965 to 1969 inclusive. And what other Celt can claim to have scored against Brazil (25th June 1966 at Hampden) in the first minute with a "blazing shot"? Steve is usually associated with speed and readiness to shoot but he was also a menace in the air and could head a ball with the power of McGrory as witness the opening goal in the first semi-final of the Scottish Cup versus Rangers at Ibrox on April 2nd 1960. Steve's header from a Colrain corner beat George Niven as comprehensively as any Mochan thunderbolt. His Celtic career virtually ended with the broken leg sustained in the League Cup final against St Johnstone on October 25th 1969. Steve was the utter professional, totally dedicated to his game, a courteous gentleman (he gave his League Cup medal of October 29th 1966 to

John Hughes whom he had come on for) and a credit to his father David (a Celtic prospect but who went to Clydebank and played alongside the great McGrory on loan there). His 241 goals for Celtic (all-told) was a post-war club record until surpassed by Bobby Lennox on November 24th 1973. He was also a good enough golfer to be champion of his club (Cawdor) and play in the Scottish Amateur. This unassuming chap and out-and-out trier is a Celtic all-time hero.

Appearances:
SL: 261 apps. 155 gls.
SLC: 58 apps. 31 gls.
SC: 47 apps. 29 gls.
Eur: 39 apps. 13 gls.
Total: *405 apps. 228 gls.*

CLARK, John

Role: Centre-forward 1903
b. Edinburgh, 24th July 1880
d. Belvidere Hospital, 16th June 1906

CAREER: Holytown Thistle/Clyde 19 May 1902/(CELTIC loan 14 Mar 1903)/Clyde 4 May 1903.

Debut v Morton (a) 2-0 (SL) 14.3.03 (scored once)

Celtic's 1902-03 season was empty and bare by the time John Clark was borrowed from Clyde for the injured Johnny Campbell. His full name was John Clark Watson, son of Horatio Watson but as a footballer he was simple John Clark. He played his last game for Celtic on April 4th in the Inter-City League and then returned to the Bully Wee. He was still a Clyde first-teamer when he died just two seasons later of enteric fever. Celtic played a benefit for his family against Clyde at Shawfield on August 29th 1906.

> **Appearances:**
> SL: *2 apps. 1 gl.*
> **Total:** *2 apps. 1 gl.*

CLARK, John

Role: Left-half 1958-71
5′ 8″ 11st.5lbs.
b. Bellshill, 13th March 1941

CAREER: Chapelhall BG/Larkhall Thistle 31 Oct 1957/Birmingham City July 1958/free 12 Aug 1958/Larkhall Thistle 12 Aug 1958/ CELTIC 8 Oct 1958/Morton 12 June 1971/ CELTIC coach 1973/Aberdeen asst. manager 17 Jan 1978/CELTIC asst. manager 29 May 1978/dismissed 5 July 1983/Cowdenbeath manager 26 Mar 1984/resigned 17 Dec 1985/ Stranraer manager 7 Jan 1986/Clyde manager 30 July 1986/resigned 2 May 1992/Shotts Bon Accord manager 25 May 1993.

Debut v Arbroath (a) 5-0 (SL) 3.10.59

John Clark played a trial for Jock Stein on September 20th 1958 after Larkhall Thistle had refused the deal offered by Birmingham and joined a Celtic reserve half-back line reading Crerand, McNeill and Clark. He put Hibernian out in the 4th round of the Scottish Cup with the only goal of the replay in extra time at Easter Road on March 15th 1961 and was rewarded by being preferred to Bertie Peacock

for the two finals versus Stein's Dunfermline (22nd and 26th April 1961). As a Kelly Kid he was too often played at right-half when it was patently obvious to the terracing he was far more comfortable and instinctive on the left. He came into his own when the Big Man returned to Celtic Park and scrapped 2-3-5. He needed a sweeper and chose John Clark. On April 24th 1965 when Celtic's glorious Steintime began with the Cup final win over Dunfermline, John took a bang on the face in the 50th minute but carried on to the day's glorious finale like a latter-day Hugh Hilley, his nostrils plugged with cotton-wool and the blood spattering his jersey. John probably 'arrived' as the player Jock Stein wanted him to be in the semi-final of the Cup Winners'

John Clark

Cup against Liverpool at Parkhead on April 14th 1966 when the wee man bestrode the Celtic defence like a colossus. On tour with Celtic in St Louis at the end of May 1966, he was nominated for the Scotland pool against Portugal and Brazil. Against the World Champions at Hampden on June 25th, he "played... as expected to play - far from overawed by the big names on the field. He was calm and cool when others were losing their head..." At Lisbon on May 25th 1967 he was in his element. At one point, Ronnie Simpson dashed out of goal and back-heeled the ball to Luggy. The wee sweeper just brushed the crisis away. Once McNeill went into management, the man he wanted at his elbow was the one who had seldom been far from it in his playing days: John Clark. Lisbon Lion Clark was an essential component of the greatest team in the history of the Celtic. He won League medals 1966, 1967 and 1968 but had lost his place to Jim Brogan as of March 2nd 1968, the first of the Lions to yield to a cub. He won a second Scottish Cup medal in 1967 and was on the bench in 1969. His display against Brazil in 1966 proved so effective the great Pele recognised the Brush at once when their paths crossed years later in the lobby of a New York hotel.

Appearances:
SL: 185 apps. 1 gl.
SLC: 62 apps. 1 gl.
SC: 31 apps. 1 gl.
Eur: 40 apps. 0 gls.
Total: *318 apps. 3 gls.*

CLARK, Joseph McGhee

Role: Outside-left 1912-13
b. Maryhill, 4th May 1892

CAREER: St Anthony's/Motherwell (trial) 20 Jan 1912/CELTIC 27 Jan 1912/(Cowdenbeath loan 28 Aug 1912)/Abercorn 18 Sept 1913/ Renton 17 Sept 1914.

Debut v Third Lanark (h) 3-1 (SL) 3.2.12 (scored once)

"St Anthony's crack outside-left" Joe Clark ("of whom much is expected") was a Holy Cross, Crosshill boy, perhaps more intent on securing his future in the business field than on the football pitch. He came into the team just as Andy Donaldson moved to Airdrie and Willie Angus, the future VC left-half, to Vale of Leven. He deputised for Johnny Brown on each of his two first-team appearances with Paddy Travers as his inside man. He may have spent some time with Preston in 1912-13 but this has not been verified. He was part of a young intake that included Peter Johnstone, John Young and Willie Glover. By 1917 Joe was fighting the Kaiser.

Appearances:
SL: 2 apps. 1 gl.
Total: *2 apps. 1 gl.*

CLIFFORD, Hugh

Role: Half-back 1892-93
b. Carfin, 8th April 1873

CAREER: Hibernian 1888/Derby County/ Carfin Shamrock 20 Apr 1889/Stoke 1890/ CELTIC May 1892/Stoke Sept 1893/Carfin Shamrock 25 Aug 1894/Motherwell 27 Nov 1894/Liverpool 24 Apr 1895/Manchester City 4 July 1895/retired 1896/Carfin Rovers 7 Sept 1897/re-instated amateur 8 Aug 1899.

Debut v Leith Athletic (h) 2-0 (SL) 14.5.1892

Celtic confidently expected Hugh Clifford to join them from Carfin Shamrock but he opted for Stoke. He is credited with having advised Celtic to think about young McMahon at Hibernian as a colt ungainly to the eye but a dream to play with. Hugh Clifford was brought in to fill the gap left by the departure of peerless Peter Dowds to Aston Villa in May 1892. He was in the Celtic side that played at Stoke on November 7th 1892 billed as "The Greatest Team on Earth" (lost 5-0). He was displaced in the Championship side of 1892-93 by Tom Dunbar. Hugh's grandson, John Clifford, an outside-left with Our Lady's High and Carfin Harp joined Celtic in November 1949.

Appearances:
SL: 5 apps. 0 gls.
Total: *5 apps. 0 gls.*

COEN, Joseph Leo

Role: Goalkeeper 1931-32
5' 11" 13st.6lbs.
b. Glasgow, 4th December 1911
d. 15th October 1941

CAREER: Bellahouston Academy/Mosspark

Joe Coen

Amateurs/Parkview United 1929/Clydeholm Juniors 1930/Clydebank (seniors) 16 Oct 1930 /CELTIC 7 Mar 1931/(Clydebank loan 22 Apr 1931)/(Nithsdale Wanderers loan 9 May 1931) /(Stenhousemuir loan 16 Mar 1932)/free May 1932/Guildford City 1 Aug 1932/ Bournemouth 1932/free 14 May 1934/Luton Town cs 1934.

Debut v Clyde (h) 1-1 (SL) 10.10.31

Joe Coen had "the same flair for the spectacular" as the man he understudied John Thomson, "the same confident manner in cutting out a cross or lifting the ball from the head of an opposing forward." Joe played for Glasgow Schools against London in 1928-29 and worked as a timekeeper's clerk in the yards at Clydebank. He played trials for Morton and Partick Thistle before joining Celtic and was reserve to Thomson until the arrival of Johnny Falconer. When Thomson died, it was Falconer took over in goal. Joe got his chance after Johnny broke a finger against Rangers in the Glasgow Cup at Ibrox (7th October 1931) and was Celtic's 'keeper for the next two weeks while Joe Kennaway got married and sailed from the States. Kennaway was in goal on Hallowe'en 1931 as Thomson's

lineal successor. Joe Coen's career burgeoned at Kenilworth Road where he was a highly-regarded last line. He joined the RAF as Luton's first-team goalkeeper and was killed while training to be a pilot. Joseph Leo Coen is on the Footballers' Roll of Honour for World War Two. He is buried in Holy Trinity Churchyard, Biscot, Luton, Bedfordshire.

> **Appearances:** .
> *SL: 3 apps. 0 shut-outs.*
> **Total:** *3 apps. 0 shut-outs.*

COLEMAN, James

Role: Full-back 1888

CAREER: Dumbarton Athletic 12 June 1886/ CELTIC Aug 1888/Dumbarton Athletic Sept 1888/Morton/Glasgow Hibernian Sept 1889/ Nottingham Forest Nov 1889.

Debut v Shettleston (h) 5-1 (SC) 1.9.1888

James Coleman "the elder", of William Street, Dumbarton, was billed to play for Celtic in the first round of the World Exhibition Cup at Gilmorehill on August 1st 1888 but Dumbarton club-men were so active in the X-arena, nothing happened. James did not play. He did play for Dumbarton Athletic against Celtic in the second round of the Cup (which did not actually exist) on August 21st 1888 then deputised for Paddy Gallagher in the first-ever Celtic side to participate in the Scottish Cup (the day after Jack the Ripper claimed his first victim). He was back with his home town team when they played Celtic in a friendly on September 8th 1888 but was one of the recruits to the alternative Celtic, Glasgow Hibs, when they started up on Rutherglen Road. He is described as "a back of the first water...one who will be selected yet for honours." James was a rivetter in the yards who became a barman in Green Street, Calton, in September 1889.

> **Appearances:** .
> *SC: 1 app. 0 gls.*
> **Total:** *1 app. 0 gls.*

COLEMAN, John

Role: Outside-left 1888-93
5' 6" 11st.0lbs.
b. Cardross, 3rd January 1870
d. 4th May 1927(?)

CAREER: Cathcart/Netherlee 1887/Vale of Leven Hibs 1887/Hibernian Sept 1887/ CELTIC June 1888/reserves trainer 2 Nov 1895.

Debut v Shettleston (h) 5-1 (SC) 1.9.1888

A friend of the Maleys, little Johnny Coleman played outside-left in the Hibs team that hanselled first Celtic Park against Cowlairs on May 8th 1888. He played in Celtic's second only game against Dundee Harp on June 9th 1888 (and scored the solitary goal) having missed the opener on 28th May. Against Dundee Harp on October 8th 1888, "he wrought so hard" he used up two pairs of shorts. Frequently the butt of colleague Willie Groves' mordant in-match commentary, he

Johnny Coleman

played for the infant Celts in the Snow Final versus Third Lanark on February 2nd 1889 at what we now call Cathkin Park and again in the replay on the 9th, each time as inside-forward to Tom Maley. He was virtually retired when the Cup was won in 1892 and managed but one game in the first Championship season of 1893. He succeeded Jimmy Curtis in charge of the reserves and was warned: "Only Cullen, Tom Dunbar and James Orr are any use. The rest are downright rubbish." By 1901 he was into the Craze of the Age, building bikes, not far from Parkhead, at Bellgrove Cycles, 129 Sword St, Dennistoun. When War broke out in 1914, he was over age but wangled his way to the King's Shilling. "What age are you?" "How old do you think I am?" The recruiting sergeant's clerk hazarded a guess. "Aye, that'll do. Put me down for that."

Appearances:
SL: 7 apps. 2 gls.
SC: 11 apps. 1 gl.
Total: *18 apps. 3 gls.*

COLLIER, Austin

Role: Left-half 1941
5' 7" 10st.10lbs.
*b. Dewsbury,
24th July 1914*

CAREER: Upton Colliery 1935/ Frickley Colliery cs 1937/Mansfield Town May 1938/free Apr 1939/ York City May 1939/ (Partick Thistle loan

Austin Collier

20 Aug 1940)/(CELTIC loan May 1941)/(Third Lanark loan 9 Oct 1941)/(East Fife loan July 1942-43)/(Partick Thistle loan 1942-43)/ Aberdeen (trial) 7 Aug 1943/(Partick Thistle loan 1943-44)/(Hibernian loan 15 Jan 1944)/ Queen of the South 14 Nov 1946/free Apr 1947/Rochdale 24 May 1947/Halifax Town Nov 1947.

Debut v Queen's Park (a) 5-2 (CC) 21.5.41

PT Instructor Private (later Sergeant) Austin Collier, an Englishman in the HLI, made his debut for Partick Thistle on August 24th 1940 and played for the British Army against the Polish at Firhill on September 2nd 1940. "What he lacks in height, he atones for in stocki-ness...a rare grafter, assiduous in attention to his forwards." Austin had a great season 1940-41 but went to Celtic for the sake of "joining a better firm." Indeed, Celtic were reproached for poaching him. He looked the perfect replacement for George Paterson RAF (his style and his cultured left peg reminded many of George) but lost his place as early as the end of September to Joe McLaughlin. Alan Breck of the *Evening Times* once called him "one of the most enthusiastic little fellows I know." Austin was stationed in Italy in 1944 and played for the British Army versus France in Naples in the autumn; he was also in the United Services that held Matt Busby's unbeaten Army XI touring round the Mediterranean to a 2-2 draw in 1945.

Appearances:
RL: 3 apps. 0 gls.
Total: *3 apps. 0 gls.*

COLLINS, Alexander

Role: Right-back 1888
b. Port Glasgow, 26th February 1866

CAREER: CELTIC 1888/Clydesdale Harriers XI loan 23 Feb 1889.

Debut v Clyde (h) 9-2 (SC) 8.12.1888

"I worked at Hyde Park locomotive shop from six in the morning until 5.30 at night, trained two nights a week. Absence from a practice meant no game on a Saturday" (10th January 1937). Alec, also known as Abe, Collins of 580½ Springburn Road, filled the problem position of right-back for the early Celtic and was "a decided improvement in the team" (September 4th 1888). He was picked for the replay of the protested 5th Round Scottish Cup tie after Clyde had beaten Celtic 0-1 on 24th November 1888. The following week Celtic had another squeak in the sixth round at Merchiston Park against East Stirling who led 1-0 until three minutes from time with Jimmy Kelly echoing "Isn't this terrible! Isn't this terrible!" Once again Alec played right-back. His first appearance for Celtic was in a merit friendly at Mavisbank against Airdrie on August 11th 1888, a good day not to be playing for Celtic reserves who lost 1-9 to Rangers. He also played in the Glasgow Exhibition Cup final of September 6th 1888 when Celtic lost 2-0 to Cowlairs. He was right-back for the Strollers XI that won the Reserve Cup 13-1 versus St Mirren on 21st February 1891, a Cup Celtic were not to lift again until 1935 when Alec aka Abe was picking-up his pension.

Appearances:
SC: 2 apps. 0 gls.
Total: *2 apps. 0 gls.*

COLLINS, Francis J.

Role: Goalkeeper 1921-22
b. c 1897

CAREER: Wanderers FC Dublin/Jacob's FC Dublin 1918/CELTIC 2 May 1921/Jacob's FC 1922.

Debut v Dumbarton (h) 4-0 (SL) 6.9.21

Frank Collins, "clean, clever, sturdy," was signed as cover for Charlie Shaw after putting up the shutters for junior Ireland versus

Frank Collins

Scotland at Parkhead on March 12th 1921. Frank met the Celtic party in London on its way to the Battlefields on May 21st 1921 and played his first game for the club versus R et C Athletique in Paris on May 28th. As a Celtic reserve he was capped for Ireland versus Scotland at Parkhead (4th March 1922) but was open to transfer at the end of the season: "Charlie Shaw's too good to give that Dublin lad a look-in." Back in Erin he played for the League of Ireland and won a full Free State cap against Italy on April 23rd 1927. He was still turning out for Jacob's in 1932.

Appearances:
SL: 2 apps. 1 shut-out.
Total: *2 apps. 1 shut-out. (50%).*

COLLINS, John

Role: Left Midfield 1990 to date
5' 7" 10st.10lbs.
b. Galashiels, 31st January 1968

CAREER: Gala Academy/St Margaret's BC/Celtic BC/Hutchison Vale BC/Hibernian Jan 1984/CELTIC July 12 1990.

Debut v Ayr United (h) 4-0 (SLC) 22.8.90

"Collins is one of the rare players around who can play and is also willing to run until he has no puff left" (Ian Paul 25th April 1994).

"Collins appears to revel in the extra responsibility when Paul McStay is missing" (Alex Gordon 25th April 1994). Hibernian played Billy McNeill's Manchester City in a pre-season friendly on August 3rd 1984 and fielded a 16-year old boy from the ground staff: John Collins, ex-Celtic Boys Club. Rumour said Celtic could have had him were the club but willing to meet his travel expenses from the Borders. Parkhead was poised to sign him in 1988 when to everyone's surprise, John contracted himself to Hibernian for another two years on March 2nd with a promise not to seek a transfer during that time. His transfer cost Celtic £1,000,000, a lot more than his weekly train fare a few years previously! John Collins has won no medals at Celtic but no one is more regularly nominated Man of the Match for his "inexhaustible contribution." He is a skilful, diligent player and above all, amenable; always prepared to do the unglamorous ball-winning chores as required even at left-back, like a model professional. He has also had his moments. Celtic started 0-2 down against Cologne in the home leg of the UEFA Cup first round on September 30th 1992. Collins ran amok like Tommy Burns against Sporting Lisbon and Celtic took the tie 3-2 on aggregate. To the immense relief of the Celtic faithful, John followed skipper McStay's example of the previous summer and on August 7th 1993 committed himself to a further three years with the club. He damaged knee ligaments versus Young Boys in Berne in the UEFA Cup on September 14th 1993, an injury which did nothing to alleviate Celtic's problems culminating in the resignation of manager Liam Brady on October 6th. Against Rangers on March 20th 1993 he opened the scoring with "a gem of a goal" from his wrong foot, his right, in the 2-1 win. He took over the Celtic captaincy from McStay on April 23rd 1994 and seemed to revel in the role as well as providing the side with its new fulcrum. He led Celtic out at Ibrox in the Murray lock-out match of April 30th 1994 as "the roofs of the stands were almost lifted by rousing renditions of Hello, Hello, The Sash and Derry's Walls" (Graeme Stewart). "It may be foolish to read too much into the body language but Collins also possesses the skill to command" (Kevin McCarra). He also scored another goal "a free-kick, the like of which you would be lucky to see in Rio's Maracana Stadium ...with one flick of his left foot the ball was launched like a net-seeking missile into the top corner of the Rangers goal (Tom English). He bent "this delicious free-kick" round a nine man wall from 20 yards, a goal that stunned 45,000 Ibrox fans into such silence "as would not have been out of place in a monastery" (Graeme Stewart). Again at Ibrox, he scored with another that curled round the wall and left Goram totally stranded on August 27th 1994. How a team can carry two outstanding talents like Paul McStay and John Collins yet win nothing season after season is one of football's modern mysteries.

Appearances:
SL: 154 apps. 28 gls.
SLC: 14 apps. 0 gls.
SC: 13 apps. 1 gl.
Eur: 7 apps. 1 gl.
Total: *188 apps. 30 gls.*

John Collins

COLLINS, Robert

Role: Forward 1949-58
5' 4" 9st.6lbs.
b. Govanhill, 16th February 1931

CAREER: Polmadie Primary/Calder St SS/
BB/Polmadie Hawthorn Juveniles/Pollok
Juniors 8 Aug 1947/CELTIC 25 Apr 1949
(declared void)/Pollok 26 Aug 1948/CELTIC
27 Aug 1948/Everton 12 Sept 1958/Leeds
United 8 Mar 1962/Bury 22 Feb 1967/Morton
(trial) 29 July 1969/Morton 7 Aug 1969/
Ringwood City (Melbourne) 9 Aug 1971/
Hakoah (Sydney) Oct 1971/Wilhelmina
(Melbourne) (all player-coach)/Oldham
Athletic player-coach Oct 1972/Shamrock
Rovers loan/retired 20 Apr 1973/Oldham asst.
manager 20 Apr 1973/Huddersfield Town
manager 2 July 1974/resigned 23 Dec 1975/
Leeds United coach July 1976/Hull City coach
July 1977/Hull City caretaker-manager 1 Oct
1977/manager 17 Oct 1977/dismissed 10 Feb
1978/ Blackpool coach Mar 1978/resigned
May 1978/Barnsley coach Oct 1980, caretaker-
manager 8 Feb 1984, manager June 1984,
dismissed July 1985/Guiseley Celtic manager
Sept 1987/resigned Sept 1988

Debut v Rangers (h) 3-2 (SLC) 13.8.49

The Celtic sensation of 1949 was Bobby
Collins, "the Wee Barra" cast as an outside-
right but who "itched to do a great deal more
than is expected of a winger... He must be at
inside-right or inside-left to give top value."
This view was virtually unanimous on the
terracing but Manager McGrory seemed
mesmerised by wee Bobby's one-step corner
kicks and on the wing he stayed despite a
"rave match" as inside man versus Hearts on
17th September and a Celtic side transformed
when John McPhail was injured and Bobby
came in from the right wing against Queen of
the South on Christmas Eve 1949. At last
against Morton at Cappielow on October 28th
1950 he was allowed to play his natural game
(for the third time only and scoring every
time) as partner to outside-right Jock Weir.
Jock and Bobby were Celtic's right wing
against Motherwell in the Scottish Cup win of
April 21st 1951. Bobby's shooting was always
a feature of his game "and would do credit to
a man twice his size." He became Celtic's
penalty taker and scored with two spot-kicks
against Aberdeen at Pittodrie on December
29th 1951, the month he began work as a
Bevin Boy down the Valleyfield pit in Fife,
doing his ball-work at Cowdenbeath after a
day on the seam. He hit top form in the
Coronation Cup of 1953, sank three penalties
against Aberdeen at Parkhead on September
26th 1953, and helped Celtic to the Double of
1954 although not in the side that won the
Cup. He played in the first Scottish final
against Clyde in 1955 but was dropped
without explanation for the replay (rumour
said he had too aggressively shoulder-charged
Ken Hewkins, the Clyde 'keeper in the first
game). Celtic lost the Cup 0-1. He was unfit
for Hearts at Hampden in April 1956 and the
7-1 defeat of Rangers in the League Cup final
on October 19th 1957 was virtually his Celtic
swan song. Strange to relate, he was the
solitary Celt below form throughout that
glorious autumn afternoon. The word was he
had to be sold to help pay for the new
Parkhead floodlights. His stay with Everton
(who lost him because of a lack of liaison in
1949) was a mere hiatus before his career
really resumed at Elland Road. Don Revie
made him skipper of the great team he was
building and Bobby revelled in his new role of
midfield general. "The Wee Barra" became
"The Lord Mayor of Leeds" and players like
Jackie Charlton and the Leeds fans of the time
swear by Bobby Collins as one of the United

Right-wing pair Bobby Collins (left) and Willie Fearnie doing a bit of heading practice.

all-time greats. He returned to play for Scotland at Wembley after a six year absence on 10th April 1965 and skippered Leeds there on May 1st versus Liverpool in the FA Cup final. His best years were suddenly behind him when he had his thigh broken versus Juventus in Turin on October 6th of that same year. He appeared at the Celtic Supporters' Association rally on December 5th 1965 to a huge ovation. He was beloved of the faithful in his time and many a heart was broken when he left Celtic Park.

Appearances:
SL: 220 apps. 80 gls.
SLC: 62 apps. 26 gls.
SC: 38 apps. 10 gls.
Total: *320 apps. 116 gls.*

COLQUHOUN, John Mark

Role: Outside-right 1983-85
5' 7" 10st.0lbs.
b. Stirling, 14th July 1963

CAREER: SS Aidan & Oswald Primary Royton Lancs/St Modan's High School/ Grangemouth International BC/Stirling Albion 9 July 1980/CELTIC 21 Nov 1983/ Hearts 24 May 1985/Millwall 5 Aug 1991/ Sunderland 9 July 1992/Hearts 27 July 1993.

Debut v Hearts (a) 3-1 (SL) 17.12.83

John Mark is the son of John Colquhoun who was on Celtic's books between 1957-59 but made his name with Oldham. John Mark was

John Colquhoun

COLRAIN, John

Role: Centre-forward 1953-60
6′ 0″ 13st.0lbs.
b. Glasgow, 4th February 1937
d. 14th July 1984

CAREER: Sacred Heart Bridgeton BG/
St Mungo's Academy 1951/Ashfield 1952/
CELTIC (provisional) 20 Nov 1953/St
Anthony's (farmed-out) 1954/Duntocher
Hibernian (farmed-out) 1955/Army 1955/
CELTIC (full) 22 July 1957/Clyde 18 Nov
1960/Ipswich Town 23 May 1963/Glentoran
player-coach 30 July 1966/free 6 July 1968/
St Patrick's Athletic 1968-70/Manchester City
scout 1972/Partick Thistle scout.

Debut v Rangers (h) 0-1 (SL) 1.1.58

an early Davie Hay signing as cover for the
injured Davie Provan and at Parkhead was
employed wide on the right, not as the striker
in the No. 7 shirt who had scored 51 goals in
102 appearances for Stirling Albion. The day
he signed for Celtic he had been scratching
about for a UEFA Cup ticket to Nottingham
Forest versus Celtic and was hoping to go
down to the game on a Stirling CSC bus.
Instead he travelled with the team. He scored
a goal to savour all his life in a pre-season
friendly against Arsenal on August 4th 1984, a
raking glory of a shot high into the net that
left Pat Jennings helpless. Hearts came looking
for Davie Provan in May 1985 and were told
John was available. At Tynecastle he was
encouraged to resume his Annfield role and
once again began to "slip through the middle
like a ghost in a snowstorm." John Mark
Colquhoun was the player with a conscience
who went to the touch-line to try to silence the
mindless racial chants of Hearts fans against
Paul Elliott at Parkhead (22nd September
1990).

Appearances:
SL: 29 apps. 3 gls.
SLC: 3 apps. 0 gls.
SC: 1 app. 1 gl.
Eur: 2 apps. 0 gls.
Total: *35 apps. 4 gls.*

With his height and weight, John Colrain was
hailed as the new Hooky McPhail "and the
best young prospect in the game," before he
had even played a game for Celtic. After
Bobby Collins he had the hardest wallop at
Celtic Park but could not head the ball and
was not explosively fast either. Nevertheless
he combined gloriously with the budding
talents of Jackson, Conway, Divers and Auld
as the "crafty leader" in Jock Stein's all-
conquering reserve side of 1957-58. When

John Colrain

Collins left, big John stepped into the first team but within days was carrying the can for a 3-1 defeat at Aberdeen (27th September 1958). John was not cut out to be a thrusting centre. He might have done Fernie's job as midfield general but was categorised too early and could not conceive of himself as other than an out-and-out forward either until Clyde moved him to left-half. He created one of the best teams Glentoran have ever had. With Glens he played midfield at Ibrox in the European Cup (11th October 1966) and "blanketed the pitch as solidly as a wall." When he was sacked (over terms) an E.G.M. demanded his reinstatement. This dapper man once so charmed a great crooner with his conversation that he received a standing invitation to drop in on Mr Sinatra any time.

Appearances:
SL: 44 apps. 20 gls.
SLC: 4 apps. 2 gls.
SC: 10 apps. 1 gl.
Total: *58 apps. 23 gls.*

CONN, Alfred

Role: Forward 1977-79
5' 10" 11st.2lbs.
b. Edinburgh, 5th April 1952

CAREER: Prestonpans Primary/Tynecastle Athletic/Leeds United app (registration cancelled own request) 1967/Rangers ground staff 18 July 1967/Musselburgh Windsor (farmed-out)/Tottenham Hotspur 15 July 1974/CELTIC 1 Mar 1977/free 30 Apr 1979/Derby County 8 May 1979/free 11 May 1979/Hercules Alicante (trial) July 1979/Pittsburgh Spirit by Christmas 1979/San Jose Earthquakes 31 Mar 1980/Hartford Hellions 1980/Hearts 7 July 1980/Blackpool 10 Mar 1981/Motherwell 10 Aug 1981/retired June 1984.

Debut v Aberdeen (a) 0-2 (SL) 5.3.77 (sub)

Alfie Conn, son of a famous father, was one of Jock Stein's sensation signings; "We needed strengthening with Europe in mind...he's four players in one, he can play on either wing, in midfield or as a striker." Alfie (his name was

thundered out by the Scottish support at Wembley on May 24th 1975) signed for Celtic first on a month's approval. Rangers were experiencing a goal famine and the Ibrox fans had been chanting Conn's name as a hint to the management he was available at Spurs during the two home games prior to his signing for Celtic. Regardless of his antecedents (he had been ordered off against Celtic at Ibrox on September 11th 1971) he received a rapturous welcome from the Parkhead fans on his home debut against Partick Thistle (March 9th 1977) but took a verbal battering on his return to Ibrox ten days later. On his best days Conn thrilled fans with his rich skills and dribbling, but such memorable days were too few. He was a huge success on the tour of Australasia in the summer and looked the ready-made replacement if the rumours about Dalglish and Liverpool proved well-founded. But Alfie had been dogged by problems with his knees since his Rangers days and the trouble persisted at Celtic. He was stretchered off against Dundee United at Parkhead on the opening day of the season (13th August 1977) and operated on for cartilage two days later. He was too seldom the explosive player his father was and the absence of a

Alfie Conn

high workrate due to knees or temperament made no appeal to Terry Neill at Spurs or to Billy McNeill when he succeeded Stein. Alfie Conn holds two Scottish Cup medals: for Rangers versus Celtic 1973 and Celtic versus Rangers 1977.

Appearances:
SL: 32 apps. 7 gls.
SLC: 10 apps. 1 gl.
SC: 6 apps. 0 gls.
Eur: 1 app. 0 gls.
Total: *49 apps. 8 gls.*

CONNACHAN, James

Role: Centre-forward 1896-98
5' 8" 11st.12lbs.
b. Glasgow, 29th August 1874

CAREER: Glasgow Perthshire/Duntocher Hibernian/CELTIC 27 Feb 1897/free 15 Oct 1898/Airdrie 24 Oct 1898/Newton Heath 28 Oct 1898/Glossop Feb 1899/Leicester Fosse May 1900/Nottingham Forest 1901/Morton 3 Oct 1901/Renton 14 Aug 1902/Britannia FC (Canada) 1906/Dumbarton Harp 11 Dec 1907/ retired summer 1908.

Debut v St Mirren (a) 0-2 (SL) 13.3.1897

Jamie Connachan began to play for Celtic in the Glasgow League on February 27th 1897 as the cycle track was being planned for the World Championships, the Celtic Charity was being transformed into a Limited Company and moves were afoot to bring a galaxy of stars from England to get the new business venture off to a booming start. Once the Anglos arrived there was no room for Jamie in the big team and the wage bill had to be cut. On October 15th 1898 he was part of a whole-sale clear-out of reserves. Extremely fast, he was "a demon in spikes" with a "go-ahead style" much like Dod Allen who deprived him of his place in the first team.

> **Appearances:**
> SL: 1 app. 0 gls.
> **Total:** 1 app. 0 gls.

CONNAGHAN, Denis

Role: Goalkeeper 1963-64; 1971-77
6' 2" 11st.6lbs.
b. Glasgow, 9th January 1945

CAREER: Holyrood Senior Secondary 1960/ CELTIC (provisional) 3 May 1963/Yoker Athletic (farmed out) cs 1963/free Apr 1964/ Yoker Athletic 1964/Queen of the South (trial) 22 Aug 1964/Renfrew Juniors 1965/St Mirren 10 June 1966/Baltimore Bays 13 Apr 1967/ St Mirren 15 Mar 1968/CELTIC 25 Oct 1971/ Morton guest 14 Aug 1976/Clydebank Mar 1977/free Apr 1977/Ayr United 3 Aug 1977/ Morton 5 Sept 1977/Clyde 29 July 1979/ Arthurlie 1980/retired 1981.

Debut v Dunfermline Athletic (a) 2-1 (SL) 27.10.71

"Connaghan...safe...agile...brave...fields the ball with the deliberation of a tennis player about to serve." Denis was released at the end of his first period at Parkhead on account of a surfeit of goalkeepers and made his fame at Love Street where his rapport with the St Mirren fans meant his departure for Baltimore was not wholly appreciated. For Jock Stein goalkeepers were always a headache and Denis was bought to pressure Evan Williams after the 4-1 League Cup debacle against Partick Thistle on October 24th 1971. He made his debut despite the handicap of a nose bro-ken in training. Stein insisted on goalies who made themselves heard. Against Aberdeen at Pittodrie on November 6th, Denis came out to field a Joe Harper cross; McNeill thought he was still on his line and headed the ball gently goalwards to gift the Dons a 1-1 draw. He made his Old Firm debut in the 2-1 League win of January 3rd 1972 when Jim Brogan

Denis Connaghan

scored in the last minute and Denis went crazy in the Celtic goal. His concentration had a tendency to lapse and in March 1973 he was first to admit: "I haven't shown any form at all since Celtic bought me." Evan Williams took over again in goal as of January 22nd 1972 until he lost five at Hampden against Hibs in the Drybrough Cup final of August 5th. Denis went into the team for the friendly versus Spurs on August 7th and was the 'keeper at Stirling on the 12th when Stein invaded the terracing to get the party songs to stop. Again Williams came back (September 9th) but in January 1973 Celtic bought Ally Hunter which meant Denis saw no more first team action until the Scottish Cup tie versus Motherwell at Parkhead on March 10th 1974 when Hunter declared unfit with a leg injury. Denis had still to play on a losing side with Celtic and made some superlative saves in the replay on March 13th including a stupendous dive and twist to turn a Goldthorp header over the bar. Ally Hunter came back but had a nightmare against Dumbarton in the 3-3 League match of March 30th. Denis now took over as first team goalie, played against Basle on March 20th and in both European Cup semi-finals against Atletico 'Atrocioso' with an utter glory night in Spain when he defied the Madrid attack until 12 minutes from time. He was between the sticks for the Celtic side that won the 9th Championship in a row at Falkirk on April 27th 1974. Denis played in three Hampden finals: won a Scottish Cup medal versus Dundee United (4th May 1974); a Drybrough Cup medal against Rangers (3rd August 1974) when he saved penalties from Parlane and McLean in the shoot-out; a loser's medal in the Junior final with Arthurlie versus Pollok (16th May 1981). He was selected to play for Junior Scotland versus Eire on October 4th 1980 but was unfit on the day. Denis Connaghan was always a popular character and the best of clubmen.

Appearances:
SL: 32 apps. 11 shut-outs.
SLC: 15 apps. 8 shut-outs.
SC: 4 apps. 3 shut-outs.
Eur: 5 apps. 0 shut-outs.
Total: *56 apps. 22 shut-outs (39%).*

CONNELLY, George

Role: Utility 1964-76
6' 1" 12st.0lbs.
b. 1st March 1949

CAREER: St Serf's School/St Margaret's Secondary School (Dunfermline)/Tulliallan Thistle 1963/CELTIC (provisional) 9 July 1964/(full) 19 June 1965/(Falkirk loan 14 July 1976)/free 18 Oct 1976/Tulliallan Thistle 11 Aug 1978/Sauchie FC 4 Mar 1982.
Debut v Dunfermline Athletic (a) 2-1 (SL) 30.4.68 (sub)

"Somebody will have to invent a position this kid can't play...Connelly is perhaps the greatest discovery made by Celtic since the War." George Connelly was the kid Jock Stein sent out before the Cup-Winners' Cup tie with Dinamo Kiev on January 12th 1966 before 64,000 to entertain with a nerveless display of keepie-uppie round the track. He turned out for Celtic in the home friendly with Newcastle on March 8th 1968 but had an unhappy first appearance and was replaced by Chalmers. Stein had utter faith in him and when Hughes was unfit and

George Connelly

George Connelly scores the goal which gave the Celts victory at Leeds in the European Cup semi-final.

Johnstone suspended, gave him his place against Rangers in the Scottish Cup final of April 26th 1969 (when he robbed Greig for the third goal right on half-time). Against Fiorentina in the European Cup in Florence (March 18th 1970) he went into the Celtic side without a previous first team outing to his credit all season and played like a veteran. He was Celtic's Beckenbauer, a ball-playing centre-half, destined for greatness while maturing in the shadow of McNeill. He shocked Leeds with the winning goal within 58 seconds of the start of the European Cup semi-final (1st April 1970) at Elland Road. Against Inter Milan at the San Siro also in the European Cup (5th April 1972) he allowed the great Boninsegna barely a kick. He was "a colossus" against Rangers in the League Cup at Hampden on September 16th 1972 and a year later when Celtic lost 1-0 at Ibrox, "every worthwhile move started from Connelly." He had a magnificent "dominating" first game for Scotland against Czechoslovakia on September 26th 1973 "with searching passes to both wings." The Scottish Football Writers nominated him their Player of the Year for 1973 and George had nowhere else to go but up as Big Billy's successor at centre-half, Celtic captain and Scottish international. The fatal day was June 20th 1973 when he walked out on the Scotland party boarding the plane for Berne at Glasgow airport allegedly worried over his wife who was expecting their first

baby. He went missing from club training for the first time on November 16th 1973. "A very complex character," said Stein. "Maybe he has some problem of his own." A broken ankle, a clean fracture, against Basle on March 20th 1974 put paid to his playing in the World Cup at Munich. With that and the departure of his . best pal Davie Hay to Chelsea, his professional behaviour deteriorated rapidly: "I just want to be unknown...I can't put up with the pressures and publicity of football...my wife's fed-up with me...I don't care what happens." "I'm more often in Connelly's house than I am in my own mother's" (Jock Stein). The genius came off the Celtic pay-roll as of 27th September 1975 but was given a chance to make a new start with Falkirk the following summer "contrite, teetotal, eager to show his skills again away from Premier League pressure." George managed to cope through August and September but was so unfit on October 12th he had to be replaced at half-time. He took labouring jobs but made a return to football where it had all begun at Tulliallan. SJFA team manager John Hughes weighed him up as a Scottish junior cap prospect with Sauchie in 1979.

Appearances:
SL: 136 apps. 5 gls.
SLC: 63 apps. 4 gls.
SC: 25 apps. 2 gls.
Eur: 30 apps. 2 gls.
Total: *254 apps. 13 gls.*

CONNOLLY, Bernard

Role: Centre-forward 1913-19
5′ 7″ 11st.0lbs.
b. Glasgow, 27th June 1894

CAREER: Vale of Clyde/CELTIC 11 Feb 1913
/(Dumbarton Harp loan 1913)/(Vale of Atholl
loan 27 Dec 1913)/(Vale of Leven loan 20
March 1914)/(Ayr United loan 13 May 1914)/
(Wishaw Thistle loan 13 Nov 1915)/
(Clydebank loan 19 Feb 1916)/(Stevenston
United loan 30 Sept 1916 & 8 Nov 1916 & 16
Dec 1916 & 19 Jan 1917)/(Dumbarton Harp
loan 5 May 1917)/Army 1917/Cambuslang
Rangers 1919.

Debut v Clyde (h) 1-0 (CC) 3.5.13

Barney signed for Celtic after a trial versus the
Cameronians from Maryhill Barracks the day
after the bodies of Scott, Wilson and Bowers
were found at the South Pole. His ordeal by
fire was on May 10th 1913 in the Charity Cup
final versus
Rangers at
Celtic Park.
Rangers were
two up in six
minutes but by
half-time
Peerless Patsy
had got one
back for Celtic.
The second half
was Barney's.
He scored
immediately
and his winner
was a Jimmy
Quinn special, a
burst at speed
through the
Rangers defence
then a crashing

Barney Connolly

shot. Quinn's
knees were
wrecked and the hunt was on for his
successor. Barney was highly admired by the
great Celt and got his chance but by October
1913 Celtic's forwards were "stingless... A
scoring centre must be found." Barney's
moment had passed.

> **Appearances:**
> *SL: 13 apps. 4 gls.*
> **Total:** *13 apps. 4 gls.*

CONNOLLY, Patrick

Role: Outside-right 1921-32
5′ 8″ 11st.0lbs.
b. Hamilton, 14th April 1901
d. Hairmyes Hospital, 18th February 1969

CAREER: Kirkintilloch Rob Roy/CELTIC
2 Dec 1921/(Third Lanark loan 30 Jan 1924)/
(Shelbourne loan 4 Nov 1930)/(Morton loan
5 Nov 1931)/(Armadale loan 21 Jan 1933)/
Hibernian 6 Feb 1933/free 30 Apr 1933/
Airdrie Oct 1933/Bo'ness 8 Nov 1934.

Debut v Clyde (a) 1-1 (SL) 3.1.22

Paddy Connolly 'The Greyhound', Andy
McAtee's successor, was one of the fastest
right wingers in the Celtic story. Against Hibs
in the Scottish Cup final of March 31st 1923
Celtic defended at the start and once the storm
had been weathered Connolly was given his
head down the wing, "cantering like a Lincoln
winner." It was his cross (but from the left) set
Joe Cassidy up for the only goal (at the Mount
Florida end). Willie McStay prescribed the
same formula of hold-them-then-hit-them for
the semi-final against Rangers two years later
(March 21st 1925). When Wilson and Alec
Thomson began to set Paddy loose, he started
going past the likes of Tully Craig and Billy
McCandless like an icy draught and getting
crosses in that were tailor-made to McGrory
and McLean. Paddy was a Celtic hero, beloved
of the fans but in 1928 his long embroilment
with Celtic over reduced terms began. Paddy
would hold out each season then re-sign but
by 1932 he was training at Albion Rovers in
despair. As his dash diminished he became
much more of a combination player (eg at
Morton) but at the top of his game as a
tearaway winger with a devastating cross
(which he worked hard to develop after a poor
start), he was vastly appreciated by the
roaring fans of the mid-twenties. Jimmy
McGrory puts him on
the right wing in his
all-time Celtic team.
Paddy died in
Hairmyres hospital after
a long illness.

> **Appearances:**
> *SL: 259 apps. 39 gls.*
> *SC: 37 apps. 7 gls.*
> **Total:**
> *296 apps. 46 gls.*

Paddy Connolly

CONNOR, Francis

Role: Goalkeeper 1960-62
5' 8" 11st.0lbs.
b. Blantyre, 13th February 1936

CAREER: Polkemmet Juniors 1952/
Kilmarnock (trial) summer 1953/Armadale
Thistle July 1954/Blantyre Celtic autumn
1954/HM Forces Mar 1956/(Third Lanark loan
4 Jan 1958)/Dundee United (trial) 22 Aug 1959
/CELTIC (trial) 4 Jan 1960/CELTIC 19 Mar
1960/free 2 May 1961/re-signed 24 July 1961/
free again 1 May 1962/Portadown May 1962/
St Mirren 13 Nov 1963/free 30 Apr 1964/
Third Lanark (trial) Aug 1964/free 21 Sept
1964/Derry City 1964/Portadown 1967/
Albion Rovers 9 Aug 1968/trainer-coach 13
Jan 1969/Cowdenbeath trainer 26 Oct 1974/
Alloa coach Nov 1974/Cowdenbeath manager
17 Feb 1976/CELTIC coach 17 Sept 1977/
Berwick Rangers manager 6 Nov 1980/
Motherwell asst. manager 16 July 1982/
CELTIC coach-asst. manager 4 July 1983/
dismissed 2 Feb 1986/Raith Rovers manager
c14 Feb 1986/Hearts asst. manager 2 Nov
1990/left 15 May 1993/CELTIC coach 10 June
1993/acting-asst. manager 6 Oct 1993/acting-
manager 8-26 Oct 1993/first team coach Dec
1993.

Debut v Partick Thistle (a) 3-2 (SLC) 12.8.61

Frank Connor

"Quiet man from Airdrie" with "ranting and
raving image" who loved playing in goal (but
was just on the small side), Frank Connor did
his National Service, played a trial for Celtic
reserves versus Rangers on January 4th 1960
and pulled Max Murray down for a penalty
within ten seconds of kick-off. With Derry City
he won the Irish League and the Gold Cup in
1965. As a coach/manager he was prized by
most of the footballers he worked with as "one
of the best motivators of young players there
is" (Mark Reid). He was acting-manager at
Cowdenbeath till player power demanded he
get the whole job; at Berwick they swore by a
man who was prepared to do a seven-hour
round journey by bus and train to supervise
training five nights a week. In his first stint at
Celtic (September 1977) he was responsible for
the development of the likes of Bonner,
Nicholas, Crainie, Halpin, and Peter Mackie.
He was taken on by Desmond White hours
before David Hay was appointed manager.
There were rumours of a relationship not

exactly close and in the end it was Frank who
had to go. Jock Wallace believed in him
enough to employ him at Motherwell and Joe
Jordan at Hearts, then Liam Brady at Celtic to
bring on the reserves. He was the players'
choice to succeed Brady: "We would say 'Give
him the job now.' We all regard him as the
boss, and treat him as such. He would make
you play during the night for him. Frank has
kicked a few backsides around here and we
will give our blood, sweat and tears for him"
(Peter Grant 19th October 1993).

Appearances:
SL: 2 apps. 1 shut-out.
SLC: 6 apps. 0 shut-outs.
Total: *8 apps. 1 shut-out (13%).*

♣ **Celtic note:** *According to Mark McGhee,
Frank is no stranger to what Kevin McCarra calls
gnomic utterance; "We allow laughing and joking
but we'll have no joviality."*

CONNOR, John

Role: Centre-forward 1932-34
5′ 7″ 10st.9lbs.
b. Garngad, 7th September 1911
d. 28th May 1994

CAREER: St Roch's School/St Roch's BG/St Roch's Juniors 1930/CELTIC (trial) 18 Aug 1931/CELTIC 6 June 1932/(Airdrie loan 23 Nov 1932)/free 30 Apr 1934/Airdrie 6 June 1934/(Albion Rovers loan 15 Mar 1935)/Plymouth Argyle 31 May 1936/Swansea Town 1938/Queen of the South 27 June 1939/(Airdrie loan 29 July 1940)/(Third Lanark loan Oct 1940-41-42-43)/(Dundee United loan Aug 1944)/(Raith Rovers loan Sept 1944)/Queen of the South again 1945/free 1946/Alloa June 1946/free own request 19 Nov 1946/St Johnstone 28 Nov 1946/free Apr 1947/British Railways Works Teams 1948/St Roch's match secretary 6 Apr 1948/manager Apr 1948/resigned c10 Dec 1948/...Metro-Vickers coach by 1955/Celtic Old Crocks 1949-59.

Debut v Queen's Park (a) 1-4 (SL) 17.9.32

Garngad boy John Connor used to do an early morning roll delivery to have sixpence to pay himself in at Celtic on a Saturday. At St Roch's he took over from Hugh Mills: "a very useful head near goal...shapes well in the outfield." A two-footed player, John was the third junior centre-forward recruited by Celtic in the first six months of 1932 after Crum and Paterson but was mooted as the solution to Parkhead's quest for a successor to Adam McLean. For Airdrie he scored 22 goals at centre to save the Waysiders from relegation. Back with Celtic he was played at inside-left and received a free at the end of 1933-34 after a severe cartilage operation. Airdrie lent him to Albion Rovers for the last six games of 1934-35 to help keep them in Division One. John scored eight goals and Rovers survived. Jimmy McGrory scored 50 League goals in 1935-36, top in Europe.

John Connor

Second to him in Scotland was John Connor of Airdrie (he got five in the 6-2 defeat of Dunfermline on February 22nd 1936 with Tom Lyon at inside-right). He remained a steady goalscorer, "a darting opportunist," and a totally reliable team man, dedicated to keeping himself fit and putting in the whole 90 minutes for his wages. He served with the Black Watch in Perth in 1946 and gave up the St Roch's job in order to get himself a regular game of football on a Saturday.

Appearances:
SL: 4 apps. 1 gl.
Total: *4 apps. 1 gl.*

CONROY, Michael

Role: Left-half 1953-60
5′ 8″ 10st.5lbs.
b. Port Glasgow, 5th August 1932

CAREER: St Columba's Juveniles Port Glasgow/St Anthony's 1949/CELTIC (trial) 10 Jan 1953/CELTIC 13 Jan 1953/free 30 Apr 1960/retired 1960.

Debut v St Mirren (h) 3-2 (SL) 11.4.53

Jet-haired Mike Conroy lasted six years as a part-timer at Celtic without ever achieving the regular first-team spot his talent deserved. By

Mike Conroy Snr

1959 only Evans and Peacock had been on the books longer. He lost two years to National Service and for the rest was plagued by injuries. He damaged a "hinge" in his ankle which Alec Dowdells called "an unheard-of injury" and after a smack in the face with the ball in the reserves in 1956 even his eyesight was threatened for a time. He went full-time for 1959-60 and immediately strained an ankle tendon in pre-season training. He was freed at last in 1960 and advised on medical grounds to pursue the game no further. He was Celtic's scout in the Greenock area until July 1975 and honoured by the Kearny New Jersey CSC as their special guest in 1982.

Appearances:
SL: 7 apps. 0 gls.
SLC: 1 app. 0 gls.
Total: *8 apps. 0 gls.*

CONROY, Michael

Role: Midfield 1978-82
5' 9" 11st.7lbs.
b. Johnstone, 31st July 1957

CAREER: Port Glasgow Juniors 1978/ CELTIC 10 Apr 1978/Hibernian 11 Oct 1982/ free 9 May 1984/Blackpool 1 Sept 1984/ Wrexham July 1986/Leyton Orient July 1987/ Cork City player-asst. manager 1988/ dismissed summer 1993.

Debut v Hibernian (a) 1-4 (SL) 15.4.78
(scored once)

Like his Celtic father, Mike Conroy junior was a hard grafter who could also play a bit. He had three reserve games for Celtic before displacing Ronnie Glavin in the big team on a day when Hibs carried the fight to Celtic and attacked in waves. His finest hour was in the Scottish Cup final of May 10th 1980 when Celtic (already gone off the boil in the League) were required to play without a recognised centre-half, both MacDonald and McAdam being under suspension and Ben Casey injured. Manager McNeill told Mike he was going in as central defender and until kick-off made him practise every day jumping against giants (MacDonald and McAdam). On the day at Hampden he was a five-star man and beat Derek Johnstone eight times out of nine in the air. He left for Easter Road with two League Championship badges for 1979 and 1981 and his 1980 Cup medal. "It was a tremendous

Mike Conroy Jnr

wrench leaving Celtic...Celtic were in my blood." Mike was player-manager of the Cork City side that shocked Celtic 2-0 on August 23rd 1991 during the pre-season tour of Ireland under new boss, Liam Brady and even put himself on for the final five minutes.

Appearances:
SL: 66 apps. 9 gls.
SLC: 14 apps. 3 gls.
SC: 6 apps. 1 gl.
Eur: 3 apps. 1 gl.
Total: *89 apps. 14 gls.*

CONWAY, James

Role: Centre-forward 1956-61
5' 10" 11st.0lbs.
b. Motherwell, 27th August 1940

CAREER: Scottish Schoolboys u-14s 1954/ Coltness United 1956/CELTIC (provisional) 23 Aug 1956/(full) 27 Aug 1957/(Rangers loan 11 Mar 1959)/Norwich City 30 Apr 1961/ Southend United 29 Oct 1963/Partick Thistle 30 June 1965/free 1966/Portadown player-manager 1967/Bolton Wanderers trainer-coach 12 Oct 1968/scout 1977.

Debut v Falkirk (a) 1-0 (SL) 7.9.57

"Fast, elusive, with a great wallop in both feet," Jim Conway was an apprentice engine fitter, up at six o'clock daily, putting in a full day's work then making the dash from Wishaw to Parkhead to train. He was Joe Baker's successor at Coltness and West Ham wanted him after three games for the Dahlias. However much "a five-star proposition" he seemed, Jimmy McGrory remembered John McGrory's broken leg on top of a broken apprenticeship and resisted all the boy's pleas to go full-time. He insisted he get a trade. Jim had "a wonderful gift of instant control of an

Jim Conway

awkward ball...is adept at luring opposing centre-halves out of position...causes quite a fair-sized gap down the middle." He had a flat-footed running style and although "deficient in heading" had some beautiful touches. He served in Celtic reserves under Jock Stein and scored four to bring the Big Man his first ever trophy as a Boss, the 2nd XI Cup of March 21st 1958 when wee Rangers were annihilated 8-2 on aggregate. He took over from Billy McPhail as of August 9th 1958 but could not make the goals come in the same abundance in the first team. Jim was too easily caught on the ball and when he did eventually complete his apprenticeship and could go full-time, Norwich City stepped in with £10,000 and bought his transfer to Carrow Road. His enormous promise was not fulfilled at Celtic but never once did he offer an ounce less than his best endeavour. His presence in the team always raised the hopes of the long-suffering fans of the time. Jock Stein tried to sign him for Dunfermline on August 20th 1963. Charlie Tully brought him over to Portadown.

Appearances:
SL: 32 apps. 9 gls.
SLC: 10 apps. 4 gls.
SC: 1 app. 0 gls.
Total: *43 apps. 13 gls.*

♣ **Celtic note:** *Jim Conway took size 8 in a shoe, 6½ in a football boot.*

CONWAY, John

Role: Inside-right 1938-46
5′ 8″ 11st.0lbs.
b. Kinglassie, 30th September 1921

CAREER: Glencraig Celtic/CELTIC 27 Oct 1938/(Alloa loan 1940)/(Raith Rovers loan 1941)/RAF Aug 1942/(St Mirren loan 29 Aug 1942)/(Fulham & Derby County loan 1942-43)/(Raith Rovers loan 4 Mar 1944)/(St Johnstone loan 1945)/Stirling Albion (trial) 8 July1946/free 13 Dec 1946.

Debut v Hamilton Academicals (h) 2-2 (RL) 10.8.40

"Strong and tireless," John Conway from Lochgelly was an Edinburgh University student training to be a teacher. He was on Celtic's Fife "waiting list" at the age of 17 until an unfounded rumour reached Parkhead that he was signed for Bradford. Celtic rushed into action to secure him on a provisional form. He was virtually forgotten about until he scored two goals for Alloa at the end of 1939-40. Jimmy McStay played him from the start of 1940-41. "Celtic have struck oil... Conway is undoubtedly one of the most thrustful inside men thrown up since the start of the War." John won a Glasgow Cup medal versus Rangers at Ibrox on 28th September 1940. His last hurrah for Celtic was at Hampden on a sun-drenched Saturday (June 1st 1946) versus Rangers again in the Victory Cup semi-final. John was a surprise choice at outside-left in a Celtic side bereft of Delaney and Jackie Gallacher. The score was 0-0 but Johnny Paton took the left-wing spot in the notorious replay of June 5th.

John Conway

Appearances:
RL: 24 apps. 5 gls.
SWC: 1 app. 0 gls.
Total: *25 apps. 5 gls.*

CORCORAN, Patrick

Role: Outside-right 1918
5' 9" 11st.4lbs.
b. Glasgow, 16th June 1893

CAREER: Mossend Hibernian 1911/
Clyde 27 Aug 1912/Shelbourne 8 Mar
1913/Clyde 3 May 1913/(Shelbourne loan
28 Dec 1914)/(Royal Albert loan 23 Sept 1915)
/(Hamilton Academicals loan 2 Aug 1916)/
(Renton loan 10 Feb 1917)/(Albion Rovers
loan 23 Oct 1917)/(CELTIC loan 26 Oct 1918)/
(Royal Albert loan 16 July 1919)/Hamilton
Academicals 3 Sept 1919/Bathgate 5 July 1920
/Plymouth Argyle Oct 1920/Luton Town
5 Oct 1926/registration cancelled 14 Oct 1926/
Bathgate 3 Nov 1926/East Stirlingshire 16 Mar
1927.

Debut v Dumbarton (a) 5-0 (SL) 26.10.18

The Spanish 'flu
epidemic raged through
Europe in the closing
stages of World War
One taking as pitiless
a toll of life as the
battlefields themselves.
The least of its effects
was to make tatters of
team selections for the
Scottish League. At
Boghead on the last
Saturday of October
1918, the kick-off was delayed for half-an-hour
while Sons and Bhoys tried to patch two sides
together. Celtic lent Dumbarton Tom
McGregor and borrowed a winger from
Albion Rovers. Celtic skipper Charlie Shaw
knew the man well: he bore the scar where
Paddy Corcoran had opened his head with a
kick in the Scottish Cup (10th February 1914).
This rolling stone stopped long enough at
Plymouth to be "spoken of as the best outside
forward ever seen at Home Park," and earned
selection for the Anglo-Scots versus the Home
Scots in the International Trial (20th March
1924). Paddy missed a season at Plymouth
with a groin injury but his transfer to Luton
was refused by the English League on grounds
of compensation already received for "total
disablement."

Appearances:
SL: 3 apps. 0 gls.
Total: *3 apps. 0 gls.*

CORRIGAN, Edward

Role: Inside-left 1924-26
5' 7" 11st.0lbs.
b. New Monkland, 18th May 1900

CAREER: St Anthony's/Petershill/CELTIC
22 Oct 1924/(Ayr United loan 28 Nov 1925)/
(St Bernard's loan 20 Jan 1926)/Dundee 21
Sept 1926/St Bernard's 25 Jan 1927/free
summer 1927.

Debut v Rangers (h) 0-1 (SL) 25.10.24

Ned Corrigan

"Have Celtic found Patsy
Gallagher's successor?
How many clubs were
after this boy?" (January
1923). For his first
game as a Celt and a
senior, Ned Corrigan
was not only thrown
in against Rangers, he
was played out of
position at outside-left.
For the first 45 minutes
he was nowhere but
came on to have quite a
game in the second half.
Unfortunately it did not
presage a bright future with the
club.

Appearances:
SL: 4 apps. 0 gls.
Total: *4 apps. 0 gls.*

COWAN, Joseph

Role: Centre-forward 1929-32
5' 7" 11st.0lbs.
b. Prestonpans, 25th February 1910
d. Windygates, 18th April 1991

CAREER: Aberhill Public School (Methil)/
Markinch Rangers/Wellesley Juniors/CELTIC
23 Sept 1929/Raith Rovers 29 July 1931/freed
by Scottish League June 1934/East Fife 28 June
1934/free Apr 1938.

Debut v Aberdeen (a) 1-1 (SL) 24.1.31
(scored once)

"Nippy leader" Joe Cowan was signed from
Wellesley after twelve goals in his first five
appearances as a junior. No sooner had he left
for Glasgow than up in Fife Pat Duffy put
Frank O'Donnell in his place and Celtic signed

him as well. Joe's services were quickly superfluous and he took off again for the Kingdom to score goals at a prolific rate for Raith Rovers and East Fife. Joe was prone to injury but had such a season for Rovers in 1932-33 that Everton were watching him as a prospective understudy to the great 'Dixie' Dean. As Rovers' team form slumped in 1933-34, Joe's service dried-up and he came in for his share of barracking. East Fife knew the potential was still there and took him to Bayview. The Methil club were playing Dumbarton at home on September 29th 1934 and led 1-0 at half-time thanks to Joe. A word of encouragement in the dressing room at the interval and he scored six more in the second half. He scored six against King's Park on March 14th 1936. Joe played against Celtic in the Scottish Cup at Methil on February 27th 1937 but '37 was Celtic's year and they won 0-3 (the same day as future Celtic chairman and figure of probity Desmond White was ordered-off for a punch on Andy McCall at Hampden). East Fife won the Cup in 1938 but Joe was injured as of March 5th. He was a foundry grinder and played works football after Bayview.

Appearances:
SL: 1 app. 0 gls.
Total: *1 app. 0 gls.*

COYLE, Ronald

Role: Centre-half 1979-87
5' 10" 11st.0lbs.
b. 4th August 1964

CAREER: Celtic BC/ CELTIC Jan 1979/ (Clyde loan 26 Aug 1986)/(Middlesbrough loan 9 Dec 1986)/ Middlesbrough 3 Mar 1987/ Rochdale 14 Aug 1987/ Raith Rovers 7 Jan 1988.

Debut v Dundee (h) 0-1 (SL) 4.5.85 (sub)

"Huffy" Coyle was in the Scottish Schoolboys Under-15 side with Paul McStay, Paul Nicholas and John Sludden in the 4-5 win over England at Wembley on June 7th 1980. A big stopper-type centre-half, he looked more a six-footer than a mere five-ten. He was thrown in at Tannadice in the 4-2 Premier League defeat of January 4th 1986 when "the defence looked

"Huffy" Coyle

like a sieve." He might have succeeded very well at Parkhead if Celtic had been able to blood him without the pressure but David Hay opted for a Nescafé Instant policy and bought experience in the shape of Mick McCarthy. Middlesbrough paid £5,000 for Ronnie's signature. Frank Connor took him to Stark's Park and he was part of Jimmy Nicholl's team that won promotion to the Premier League in 1993.

Appearances:
SL: 2 apps. 0 gls.
Total: *2 apps. 0 gls.*

COYNE, Brian

Role: Central defence 1977-79
6' 0" 12st.0lbs.
b. Gorbals, 13th December 1959

CAREER: Celtic BC 1971/St Roch (farmed-out) 1976/CELTIC 1977/Shrewsbury Town July 1979/ Motherwell 1980/ Worcester City 1983/ Newtown (Wales) player-manager.

Debut v Clydebank (h) 5-2 (SL) 17.4.78 (sub)

Brian Coyne worked his way through the ranks of Celtic Boys' Club from U-12 level to U-16 when he travelled with the first group to visit the USA. At St Roch's this tall, dark-haired defender came under the astute guidance of ex-Tim Willie O'Neill. His one and only appearance for his beloved Celtic was as a replacement for Tommy Burns (a substitution wrongly ascribed to Alfie Conn in the record books). His good friend Johnny Doyle commended him to Ally McLeod at Fir Park and under Davie Hay as manager, Brian gained a First Division League Champions' medal with Motherwell in 1981-82. Jock Wallace dropped him from his plans for the Steelmen and Brian went to Worcester to link up with ex-Celt Seton Airlie. He is currently a club manager in the

Brian Coyne

Coyne and Charlie Nicholas and scored 23 goals. ("When I play with Charlie Nicholas it means a lot more running...Tommy and I halve the workload"). His prodigious heading ability produced a great goal in 13 minutes to level the scores against Borussia Dortmund in the home tie of the UEFA Cup (November 3rd 1992). He missed most of 1992-93 with injury but made his come-back against Dundee on the last day of the season (15th May). He was unable to make managers Brady or Macari offer him a contract commensurate with his worth and Gerry played out his last days at Celtic wide on the right. Jim Smith took his fine, but sometimes dormant, ability to Fratton Park for employment as an out-and-out striker at £600,000. The hoops had to be peeled from his back. "Lou Macari basically pushed me out. He has his own ideas and unfortunately his ideas and my talent didn't mix ... My allegiance to the club will never die, I am

Celtic born and bred." Gerry was a product of the Celtic conveyor belt same as Fulton, McCarrison, Britton, Whyte, Archdeacon, Davie Elliot and Mathie. When he left Parkhead, there was a feeling it was time to take a look at the belt.

Appearances:
SL: 112 apps. 36 gls.
SLC: 10 apps. 8 gls.
SC: 10 apps. 8 gls.
Eur: 10 apps. 3 gls.
Total: *142 apps. 55 gls.*

CRERAND, Patrick

Role: Right-half 1957-63
5' 8" 11st.7lbs.
b. Glasgow, 19th February 1939

CAREER: St Luke's Ballater St/Holyrood Senior Secondary/Duntocher Hibernian/ CELTIC 7 Aug 1957/Manchester United 6 Feb 1963/retired 1971/coach 27 Aug 1971/asst. manager 2 Jan 1973/resigned 8 Dec 1975/ Northampton Town manager 22 July 1976/ resigned 4 Jan 1977/Manchester United scout.

Debut v Queen of the South (h) 3-1 (SL) 4.10.58

"I wouldn't leave Celtic for England, Italy or anywhere in the world even if they gave me £10,000" (May 1961). Paddy Crerand was an utter gentleman off the park but in the heat of battle had some formidable temper. His troubles began when he was ordered-off playing for Scotland in Bratislava (May 14th 1961) for an alleged head-butt. The SFA imposed a week's suspension as of August 12th 1961. Bratislava was followed by a fist-fight at Brockville and a second early bath at the Falkirk Fives of July 29th 1961. Bob Kelly now added four weeks suspension without pay onto the SFA sentence (August 1st 1961). Paddy served his time but was next involved in the fracas versus Uruguay of May 2nd 1962 at Hampden when an unidentified Scotland player punched referee Holland in a melee. Celtic ordered him to write an apology to the SFA for remarks to newspapers but the SFA refused his account as inadequate and ordered him to write again. Having reached the depths, Paddy now experienced the zenith of his Celtic career with the match of his life against the great Real Madrid and Puskas at

Gerry Creaney

Paddy Crerand

Celtic Park (September 10th 1962), a performance which produced the screaming headline: Is Crerand The Greatest Right-Half In The World? Old-timers rated him the best passer of a ball at Parkhead since Jock Gilchrist. His form slumped after a five-star performance versus Wales at Cardiff (October 20th 1962) probably because he was being tapped by English clubs and an awful first-half versus Rangers on Ne'erday 1963 was followed by a petulant half-time 'barney' with Sean Fallon. On January 29th he asked for a transfer: "I want to be a Busby Babe." What happened next no one knows for sure: Paddy happy to go; Paddy in tears to be going; Paddy mesmerised by the aura of Busby; Paddy pleading with McGrory to stay; Paddy being advised by "a Glasgow businessman" to join United. Still to-day the ambiguity persists: that he loves Celtic is the received wisdom; yet in July 1992 his freesheet newspaper column in Manchester was apparently willing the undecided Paul McStay to come to Old Trafford.

Appearances:
SL: 91 apps. 5 gls.
SLC: 13 apps. 0 gls.
SC: 14 apps. 0 gls.
Eur: 2 apps. 0 gls.
Total: *120 apps. 5 gls.*

CRILLY, William

Role: Centre-forward 1922
5' 3" 9st.0lbs.
b. Cowcaddens, 1903

CAREER: R.& J. Dick 1918/Cambuslang Rangers 1919/Alloa 5 Nov 1920/CELTIC 6 May 1922/Alloa 19 Sept 1922/to USA 23 Apr 1923/New York Giants 6 May 1923/ Indiana Flooring Club 1924/New York Giants 1925/New York Hispano 1927/Alloa Aug 1929/USA Nov 1930/Brooklyn Wanderers 1931/New York Americans 1931/Bohemians' Queen's Club 1932/Nassau (Long Island) 1933 /Brooklyn Hispanos 1934/St Mary's Celtic (USA) 1935.

Debut v Hamilton Academicals (h) 2-1 (SL) 26.8.22

"Crilly is slippery as an eel, elusive as the will o' the wisp, fleet as a rumour ...is to Scottish football what Jimmy Wilde is to boxing" (1921). The Cowcaddens "Electric Spark" gave Rangers a bad shock in the Scottish Cup before 54,000 at Ibrox (February 19th 1921) and helped Alloa to promotion in 1922 (he scored six against King's Park at Stirling on November 19th 1921). Celtic were about to be rid of Tommy McInally for the first time so although Willie was a far cry from the normal run of Celtic centres in stature and style the club dispensed with John Connor (signed July 1921) and Tully Craig to obtain his services and took him on tour to Prague and Berlin. He had a powerful shot and was remarkably quick on his feet but when the League started "the ease with which Crilly was knocked off the ball upset the balance of the attack." Back he went to Alloa. "Celtic were not dissatisfied - the little fellow wanted to be back with his pals" (Crilly did not know this). Willie became a naturalised US citizen in the 1920s and went to prison in the

Willie Crilly

UK in 1930 for infringing the Aliens Act. He was deported back to the States and played for Brooklyn Wanderers against Celtic on tour (June 7th 1931). This mite of a man who longed to be home in Scotland, became a friend of the great ex-World Heavyweight Champion Jack Johnson. By 1935, Willie had scored over 1000 goals in his career.

Appearances:
SL: 3 apps. 0 gls.
Total: *3 apps. 0 gls.*

♣ **Celtic note:** *Willie played on Sundays for a Glasgow Meat Market side called the Pale Ale. Teams staked themselves to win and outside betting was heavy. Games were played on Glasgow Green or Soda Waste (near Shawfield) and huge crowds were common. You can talk about the Rangers/And how they never fail/But if you want to see good football/Just watch the real Pale Ale.*

CRINGAN, William

Role: Centre-half 1917-23
5' 8" 11st.12lbs.
b. Ponfeigh,
15th May 1890
d. 12th May 1958

Willie Cringan

CAREER: Douglas Water Thistle/ Sunderland 10 June 1910/(Wishaw Thistle loan 20 Aug 1915)/(Ayr United loan 7 Jan 1916)/ (CELTIC loan 5 May 1917)/CELTIC 18 Sept 1917/RFA May 1918/Third Lanark 5 Oct 1923 /Motherwell 10 May 1924/free 17 Feb 1925/ Inverness Thistle 6 Mar 1925/free May 1925/ Belgium coach summer 1925/Bathgate 12 Nov 1925.

Debut v Rangers (a) 2-0 (CC) 12.5.17

"*It's a pity how Celts/Must keep tightening their belts...*" (Sept 1923). Willie Cringan was in Sunderland's Cup final team with Charlie Buchan on April 26th 1913 at the Crystal Palace when Tom Barber scored the only goal for Villa. He returned home to work in the mines for the War effort but was caught up in red tape and was arrested at least twice by the constabulary for so-called 'desertion' after games for Celtic. He went into the Services in May and was back down the pit in August. He had a blinder at Ibrox in just his second game

for Celtic in a triangle with Gallagher and McMenemy on May 12th 1917 (his first match was the previous Saturday at Fir Park for Motherwell Charities). "The finest pivot in Scotland" played in Charlie Shaw's Championship side of 1919 and then led Celtic to the Flag of 1922. He was the kind of club servant who would wrestle off his bed with 'flu in order to turn out for Celtic. After serious injury he was got ready by Eddie McGarvie in the space of days to go out and shackle Hugh Ferguson in the semi-final of the Scottish Cup at Ibrox on March 10th 1923 ("too high praise cannot be given the Celtic centre-half"). Willie lifted the Scottish Cup at Hampden versus Hibernian just three weeks later on March 31st 1923. Like Charlie Shaw two years before, he represented a conference of the players to Willie Maley about the possibility of bonuses after an all-round wage cut in August 1923. Maley took the request to Chairman White. The humble petition transformed dramatically into a pistol held to the head of the executive and Cringan into the bearer of an ultimatum. Willie was soon dropped and quickly transferred. He took it on the chin: "Celtic are strengthening the side. They don't need me any more." He got on with playing his favourite other sport of quoits and became Scottish champion on September 1st 1926. Willie Cringan was a great Celt in every sense who merited a lot better of the club he loved and had served so well. He became landlord of the Star Inn, Bathgate.

Appearances:
SL: 202 apps. 8 gls.
SC: 12 apps. 1 gl.
Total: *214 apps. 9 gls.*

♣ **Celtic note:** *Jimmy Cringan, Willie's wee brother, who played for Birmingham in the English Cup final of 1931, was on Celtic's books as of August 6th 1921 but was freed.*
♣ *Willie was the uncle of Jimmy Davidson, centre-half of Partick Thistle and Scotland (1954 and 1955).*

CRONE, William

Role: Inside-forward 1913-16
5' 7" 11st.0lbs.
b. Dublin, c 1892

CAREER: Belfast Celtic 1912/CELTIC 18 Nov 1913/Distillery Oct 1916/Glentoran Oct 1917.

Debut v Hamilton Academicals (h) 1-0 (SL) 22.11.13

Handsome Billy Crone was drafted into the magnificent Celtic double side of 1913-14 as cover for Gallagher and McMenemy. He was "the smartest forward on view" when the Irish League lost 1-2 against the Scottish (with McNair, Dodds, McAtee and Gallagher) in Belfast on November 5th 1913. He made his debut on the day Charlie Shaw equalled Tom Sinclair's record of eight consecutive shut-outs. He was in the Celtic party that toured Austria-Hungary and Germany on the eve of War in 1914. Having "crossed the Irish Sea with a fame he has never been able to live up to," he developed into quite an adequate performer for the four-in-a-row team as partner to McAtee or Browning and was no stranger to the goals column. Distillery and Glentoran both claimed Billy on his return home, each asserting Maley had promised he was theirs. He belonged to a famous Belfast footballing family. His uncle, another Billy Crone, played for Distillery versus Celtic (22nd April 1889).

Appearances:
SL: 17 apps. 9 gls.
Total: *17 apps. 9 gls.*

CROSSAN, Bernard

Role: Inside-left, Outside-left 1890; 1895-97
b. c 1869
d. 24th December 1917

CAREER: Benburb 1889/CELTIC by 16 Aug 1890/Preston NE 1 Jan 1891/Third Lanark cs 1891/St Bernard's 1892/CELTIC 5 June 1895/ reinstated amateur 2 Aug 1898.

Debut v Hearts (a) 5-0 (SL) 23.8.1890

Cardinal Newman was just five days cold when Barney took the field at outside-left in Celtic's very first League match on August 16th 1890 and very first points defeat, later expunged from the record. He was "a bow-legged little man, hen-toed, strongly built with a pleasant face and a stutter," and an even better card sharp than Dan Doyle. Barney succumbed to the temptation of English gold at the end of 1890 but came home from Preston under the SFA amnesty of summer 1891 that brought Doyle and Brady to Celtic. He won a Scottish Cup medal with

St Bernard's on April 20th 1895. In his second period with Celtic "he did not come up to expectation" but twice he was called into the team in crisis: on the day of the Three Players' Strike (28th November 1896) and against Arthurlie at Barrhead in the infamous Scottish Cup defeat of January 9th 1897 when Celtic started with seven men and were two down before Barney was thrust onto the field still in his everyday trousers; he joined John King in central defence and together they "were as open as a barn door." He is the Celtic player who used a chair as his opponent ("Just tell us in your own words, Crossan") to demonstrate his innocence of foul play to a Referees Committee. After retirement, he ran a grocer's in Glasgow High Street.

Appearances:
SL: 8 apps. 3 gls.
SC: 7 apps. 4 gls.
Total: *15 apps. 7 gls.*

♣ **Celtic note:** *Renton protested the result of the 1895 Scottish Cup final on the grounds that Crossan had participated in an unauthorised match, Edinburgh Fish Merchants versus Butchers in summer 1894 for which admission money had been charged. Renton produced witnesses who had seen Barney playing. St Bernard's pleaded mistaken identity and produced the lookalike who was being confused with Barney. Appeal dismissed. (Fact: Barney played for the Fishmen).*

CROZIER, James Paterson Lyle

Role: Outside-left 1928-29
5' 7" 11st.0lbs.
b. Milton, Glasgow, 29th October 1906

CAREER: Ashfield/Hull City June 1927/ CELTIC 18 Aug 1928/(Forfar Athletic loan 29 Aug 1928)/(Ayr United loan 17 Jan 1929)/ Derry City 4 July 1929/left Feb 1930/Ashfield (Intermediate) 8 Aug 1930/Brechin City 3 Oct 1931/Morton (trial) 9 Apr 1934.

Debut v Dundee (h) 2-1 (SL) 29.12.28

"Crozier can turn on a three-penny bit. When the young fellow gathers strength to get the ball well across he will be about the best winger I ever

Jimmy Crozier

played with" (Jimmy Howieson of Hull City August 1927). Jimmy Crozier "the Bargain Buy of the Year at £50," got his first game for Celtic at Dunoon in a 3-0 defeat by Rangers (September 12th 1928) and made his League debut in snow and rain at Parkhead before playing at a frozen Ibrox on Ne'erday 1929. Rangers opened their Archie Leitch stand which is now a listed building and all the mismanagement of the 1920s caught up with Celtic: they were overtaken for the first time ever 26-25 in Scottish League matches won. McCallum came in again at outside-left, Willie Gray got a chance, Bob McWilliam and Willie Hughes were tried, Peter Kavanagh was signed but Jimmy Crozier had crossed his last ball for Celtic.

Appearances:
SL: 2 apps. 0 gls.
Total: *2 apps. 0 gls.*

CRUM, John

Role: Forward 1932-42
5' 7" 10st.4lbs.
b. 1st January 1912
d. Hyndland, 6th July 1969

Johnny Crum

CAREER: Argyle Thistle/Ashfield/CELTIC 25 Feb 1932/Morton 9 Aug 1942/free 4 May 1946.

Debut v Motherwell (h) 4-1 (SL) 22.10.32 (scored twice)

Railwayman Johnny Crum was a quintessential striker with two good feet besides being a jersey player giving his all for Celtic. On his debut he was "cool, confident, afraid of nothing ...He beat Alan Craig repeatedly in the air ...and he can shoot." Johnny's game was dig, brains and artistry. He is immortalised as a member of two great Celtic forward lines: Delaney and Buchan; McGrory; Crum and Murphy (1937) and Delaney, MacDonald, Crum, Divers and Murphy (1938). MacDonald, Crum and Divers were described as "as tricky as a colony of monkeys." He opened the scoring versus Aberdeen in the 1937 Scottish final (April 24th): Buchan shot, George Johnstone parried but Crum, ever dangerous, pounced, and Hampden erupted. At Ibrox a year later, in the final of the Exhibition Trophy versus Everton (June 10th 1938) he beat Ted Sagar's dive in the 6th minute of extra time then ran behind the goal to do a jig of joy for the Celtic end. Johnny won Championship medals in Willie Lyon's teams of 1936 and 1938 and played for Scotland at outside right at Wembley on April 4th 1936 before 93,267 fans. Eddie Hapgood committed virtually the only foul in the game when he took the wee Celt out in the 76th minute "as he was flashing through to tap home a Dave McCulloch pass." Johnny was still receiving treatment behind the goal when Tommy Walker scored the equaliser from the penalty spot. His game shaded in 1938-39 against opponents who used heavily physical tactics on the lightweight Celtic forwards but his full transfer in 1942 came as a real surprise to his staunch support. When Celtic were in the doldrums during World War Two, Johnny performed some prodigious scoring feats for Morton, and seldom failed against Celtic ("They thought they didn't need me"). He scored six against St Mirren at Cappielow on Ne'erday 1943 as Celtic were going down 8-1 at Ibrox. He, John Kelly and Gerry McAloon were in the Morton side that beat Rangers 4-2 at Ibrox on November 11th 1944 after being 2-1 down at half-time. Jock Stein played against him then and remembered him as "still a very good and brainy centre-forward". In

retirement he worked as a salesman in Neil
Tuley's sports shop at 105, West Regent Street.
He was also the punters' friend and advised a
heavy bet on Celtic (virtually without a hope)
to lift the Coronation Cup in May 1953. He
never appeared at Supporters' Association
Rallies but the applause was deafening and
prolonged (and Johnny very touched). He was
club pianist in the tradition of Peter Somers
and Duggie Livingstone. His Celtic versus
Everton jersey was on show under glass at the
People's Palace Celtic Centenary Exhibition in
1988. Johnny Crum was a great, great Celt.

Appearances:
SL: 190 apps. 73 gls.
SC: 21 apps. 15 gls.
Total: *211 apps. 88 gls.*
RL: 54 apps. 19 gls.
SWC: 2 apps. 2 gls.
RLC: 13 apps. 2 gls.
Total: *69 apps. 23 gls.*

CULLEN, Joseph

Role: Goalkeeper 1892-97
d. 27th October 1905

CAREER: St Francis'
School Cumberland
St/Stanley Swifts/
Benburb/CELTIC 1 Jan 1892
/Tottenham Hotspur 11 May
1897/Lincoln City 16 Sept 1899
until 20 Jan 1900.

Debut v Cowlairs (h) 4-1 (SC) 23.1.1892

Joe Cullen

"Cullen's ringing laughter at Madden's sallies
brought the salt to our eyes. Christmas bells
take a back seat when Joe starts." Legend has
it that Joe Cullen was pulled out of the crowd
by Dan Doyle at 1st Cathkin Park on January
2nd 1892 and told to get stripped, and was
playing. In fact Tom Maley signed him for
Celtic at 70 South Shamrock Street
immediately after Celtic's 0-8 fiasco versus
Dumbarton on Ne'erday 1892 and Joe became
Celtic's main goalkeeper in succession to Tom
Duff. He was a capable performer in a
dangerous age for goalkeepers (he also
survived the big explosion at Higginbotham's
Works just months after joining Celtic) but
Willie Maley says his nerve was never the
same again after Johnny Campbell (ex-Renton)
kicked him unconscious at Sunderland
(September 5th 1892). He was the first Celtic

goalkeeper to win a Scottish Cup medal (April
9th 1892) and the first to keep at New Celtic
Park (August 20th 1892). He was superseded
by the great Dan McArthur and moved to
Spurs as one of nine Scottish imports in the
summer of 1897. His death from pneumonia
was as sudden and unexpected as Barney
Battles' later. He had been watching the Celtic
players training only days before. He died just
hours before his mother. He is buried at
Dalbeth but the grave is unregistered. Like a
later 'keeper, John Mulrooney, Joe as a
character was ebullient and effervescent,
always ready for a laugh or a song.

Appearances:
SL: 58 apps. 15 shut-outs.
SC: 15 apps. 5 shut-outs.
Total: *73 apps. 20 shut-outs (27%).*

♣ **Celtic note:** *His Scottish Cup final
runners-up medal of February 17th
1894 was picked up in the street in
Brisbane, Australia about 1925 and
sent to Willie Maley. Maley kept it on
his desk at Parkhead until one night
the office was burgled. A few months
later Joe's medal was returned in the
post and went this time into Maley's
collection of sporting memorabilia.*

CULLEY, James

Role: Goalkeeper 1941-42
5' 11" 12st.0lbs.
b. Croy, 1915

CAREER: Camelon Juniors/Hibernian 22 Apr
1934/free 30 Apr 1938/Lincoln City 1938/
Alloa 25 July 1939/CELTIC loan Nov 1941/
CELTIC 29 Jan 1942/ ... Torrance BC match
secretary by 1947-48.

Debut v Falkirk (a) 1-0 (RL) 15.10.41

Jimmy Culley was Hibs' goalie before the
great Jimmy Kerr and served at Alloa under
Jimmy McStay. He played at Brockville in
November 1941 in place of Willie Hunter,
detained on essential war work. Opposing him
at centre-forward for Falkirk was a man called
Bob Rooney destined for a far longer career at
Parkhead (1960 to 1977) than goalkeeper
Jimmy. Jimmy Culley represents an interim
stage in the Celtic goalkeepers' line of
succession. He was concussed in the Celtic
public trial of August 1st 1942 but his deputy

was also unwell so Jimmy soldiered on until he gave way to Joe Kennaway's true successor (recovered from tonsilitis) on August 22nd - the splendid Willie Miller.

Appearances:
RL: 15 apps. 4 shut-outs.
RLC: 7 apps. 1 shut-out.
Total: *22 apps. 5 shut-outs (23%).*

CUNNINGHAM, John

Role: Outside-left 1889-92
b. Glasgow, circa 1873
d. 1910

CAREER: Benburb/CELTIC (trial) May 1889/ Burnley Nov 1889/Glasgow Hibernian 18 Dec 1889/CELTIC 1890/Partick Thistle 1892/ Hearts Oct 1892/Rangers 1892/Glasgow Thistle Mar 1893/Preston North End Sept 1893/Sheffield United May 1897/Aston Villa June 1898/Newton Heath Oct 1898/Wigan County 1899/Barrow Aug 1901.

Debut v Cowlairs (a) 5-0 (SL) 29.4.1891

"Cunningham has a penchant for turning directly at goal, wriggling, twisting like an eel." Johnny from 16 Shamrock Street first turned out for Celtic in place of Neil McCallum versus Bolton Wanderers on May 23rd 1889. Two days later the Celtic colt proved himself "the right stamp" against Preston

John Cunningham

North End. He made his main fame at Deepdale. Celtic played a double-header versus Sheffield United for the unofficial British Championship in March and April 1898. The Blades won the first leg 1-0 and the second was a draw 1-1. United's inside-left for the latter game was Johnny Cunningham. The puzzle is that Willie Maley should speak of him as "destined to have a very short football career but which might have been a very fine one"; yet elsewhere: "He was the best-known of our Benburb captures."

Appearances:
SL: 7 apps. 0 gls.
SC: 1 app. 0 gls.
Total: *8 apps. 0 gls.*

CURLEY, Thomas

Role: Outside-right 1960-65
5' 7" 10st.10lbs
b. Glasgow, 11th June 1945

CAREER: St Aloysius School, Chapelhall/ Portsmouth June 1960/CELTIC groundstaff Sept 1960/CELTIC 27 Nov 1961/free 1965/ Brentford Sept 1965/Crewe Alexandra Aug 1967/Hamilton Academicals 7 Aug 1969/free 22 Nov 1969/retired.

Debut v Hearts (a) 2-4 (SL) 26.9.64

Speedy, dark-haired Tommy Curley joined Pompey just a fortnight after leaving school but returned homesick to Scotland after three months and joined the Celtic ground staff. He played his one League game with six future Lisbon Lions in the team at a point when Celtic's chances of winning the European Cup were about as remote as the fall of Communism. He saw more regular employment with Brentford and Crewe but when Tommy Ewing's new broom went into action at Hamilton, he was one of the first to be swept away. As a Celtic Colt he played against a Schools XI at Barrowfield on April 2nd 1962 when the Colts forward line read: Jimmy Johnstone and Ramsay Brown; George McBride; Gerry Sweeney and Tommy Curley. He was back at Barrowfield for a 6-0 win over Rangers on August 29th 1963 in the Combined Reserve League. Tommy scored the last two, one of them a penalty. His marker was Billy Mathieson. At present, he is a councillor with Monklands District.

Appearances:
SL: 1 app. 0 gls.
Total: *1 app. 0 gls.*

CURRAN, John

Role: Half-back 1892-94
b. Bellshill

CAREER: Benburb/CELTIC cs 1892/ Liverpool 6 Oct 1894/Hibernian 14 Nov 1895/ Motherwell 17 Jan 1896.

Debut v Renton (a) 2-0 (SL) 25.3.1893

John Curran "a sturdy miner from Bellshill," broke into Celtic's League team in place of secretary-player Maley and was right-half in the side that won the Charity Cup 5-0 versus

Rangers (May 27th 1893). He played against Clyde on Christmas Day 1893 under Celtic's first lights, against Rangers in the Scottish Cup final defeat of February 17th 1894 but was a happy man again when Celtic won their second Flag the following Saturday. Celtic played Hearts at Tynecastle in a friendly (May 19th 1894) when John was accused of "shady tactics" and being "part of the rough element" introduced into the Celtic team and by implication a "bad loser." He left for Liverpool after a disagreement with the Celtic top brass.

Appearances:
SL: 21 apps. 0 gls.
SC: 5 apps. 0 gls.
Total: *26 apps. 0 gls.*

CURRAN, John

Role: Right-back 1958-62
6' 4" 12st.7lbs.
b. 21st May 1940

CAREER: St Mungo's Academy/Drumchapel Amateurs 1957/Ruchazie Hearts 1958/ Duntocher Hibernian 1958/CELTIC 6 Nov 1958/free 1 May 1962/Derry City 1 Oct 1962/ free 1963/Maryhill Harp 31 July 1963-1966/ CELTIC BC team manager 1980-1986/CELTIC scout 1986.

Debut v Clyde (h) 1-1 (SL) 26.9.59

"He's built like George Young, he's known as John Charles to his school pals and right now (1957) he's being groomed to succeed Bobby Evans at Celtic Park." John Curran was an "enthusiastic never-say-die" Kelly Kid vying for a place at full-back with Dunky MacKay and John Donnelly not to mention a reserve centre-half called Billy McNeill. John trained under Jock Stein and on his debut (a part-time professional), he was "most competent" and looked "like following in the great tradition of Parkhead defensive stars". A "top-rater" with Duntocher Hibs he represented Glasgow RC schools as a 12-year old against Lanarkshire in September 1951 at outside-right with future Scotland great Frank McLintock as his inside man. Celtic took him on the trip to Sunderland (January 30th 1960) along with two other tyros, Bobby Murdoch and Tommy Henderson to get a taste of the "big time" (Celtic lost 7-1). John is second only to Ian McWilliam as the tallest Celt to play for the first team (and never on a losing side). He went to Derry City still a

John Curran

part-timer but career pressure and difficulties with travel to Ireland saw him revert to junior football in the green and white hoops of Maryhill Harp. "Afterwards I concentrated on my full-time professional career and combined this with following my former team-mates throughout the glorious Stein years." With Celtic Boys' Club, John assisted in bringing young players like John Collins, Gerry Creaney and Joe Miller through their forma-tion years. He is at present Assistant Director of Personnel with Strathclyde Regional Council which has over 100,000 employees and is the largest local authority in Europe.

Appearances:
SL: 4 apps. 0 gls.
Total: *4 apps. 0 gls.*

CUSHLEY, John

Role: Centre-half 1960-67
5' 11" 12st.0lbs.
b. Hamilton, 21st January 1943

CAREER: Our Lady's High/Blantyre Celtic (did not play)/CELTIC 7 July 1960/West Ham United 17 July 1967/Dunfermline Athletic

18 Sept 1969/free 30 Apr 1972/Dumbarton 29 June 1972/free 10 Jan 1976/CELTIC coach 25 July 1978/Dumbarton asst. manager 29 June 1979/Clyde asst. manager 11 Aug 1986/ resigned 2 May 1992.

Debut v Kilmarnock (a) 0-6 (SL) 27.3.63

Our Lady's High Under-15's in 1957-58 had a half-back line of Benny Rooney, John Cushley and Bobby Murdoch. "Fast-tackling" centre-half Cushley realised early there was more to life than football and took Highers in English, Spanish, Latin and History as a prelude to MA in Modern Languages at Glasgow University 1964. Thus he was on the plane to Spain with manager McGrory (August 11th 1964) as interpreter on Celtic's futile bid to bring the great Di Stefano to Parkhead. Big John spent his days at the Paradise as understudy to Big Billy and turned Raich Carter down when he tried to buy him for Middlesbrough in August 1965 after a "5-star performance" versus ex-Spurs great Bobby Smith on trial for FC Austria in Vienna (May 26th 1965). His most protracted run in the first team was after

McNeill's injury at Hamilton (November 20th 1965) when he slotted in so well mighty Caesar was hardly missed. He played in the 5-1 defeat of Rangers on January 3rd and in both games against Kiev although Big Billy was available for the second (26th January 1966) and did in fact play but wearing the No.4 shorts. John dropped out himself through injury on February 5th 1966 and was sidelined again until January 18th 1967 as a result of ligament damage done on Bermuda (May 14th 1966). He was in the squad for Lisbon and assigned a specialist role by Stein just before the match: to get the Inter-Milan party off the Celtic benches. He went to West Ham after the European Cup as successor to Ken Brown and was hugely popular with the Hammers fans who nicknamed him Wilbur in honour of his near namesake, the little Irish genius, Cush. John never neglected his off-the-field career and even branched out as a teacher of "Mechanised Book-keeping" and Accounting. All his frees were at his own request to facilitate teaching jobs. There was no club was not sorry to lose him and that included Celtic. His father was Ned Cushley for many years secretary-manager of Blantyre Celtic.

Appearances:
SL: 30 apps. 0 gls.
SLC: 5 apps. 0 gls.
SC: 1 app. 0 gls.
Eur: 5 apps. 0 gls.
Total: *41 apps. 0 gls.*

John Cushley at home with his collection of Frank Sinatra records.

DALGLISH, Kenneth Mathieson

Role: Utility 1967-77
5′ 8″ 10st.10lbs.
b. Dalmarnock, 4th March 1951

CAREER: Glasgow United/Possilpark YMCA
1962/Drumchapel Amateurs/CELTIC
(provisional) 4 May 1967/Cumbernauld
United (farmed-out) 20 July 1967/CELTIC (full
professional) 29 Apr 1968/Liverpool 10 Aug
1977/ player-manager 30 May 1985/resigned
22 Feb 1991/Blackburn Rovers manager 12 Oct
1991.

Debut v Hamilton Academicals (a) 4-2 (SLC)
25.9.68 (sub)

"Dalglish's best position? Och, just let him out
on the park" (Jock Stein). Kenny Dalglish was
told he was playing one hour before kick-off
in the Scottish Cup semi-final versus Airdrie
on April 7th 1971. It was his fifth game for
Celtic yet his third for the club at Hampden.
"He had a hand in both goals ... he has the
power and mobility to be the new Bobby
Murdoch." Kenny was signed by Sean Fallon
taking his wife and three daughters out down
the coast for a wedding anniversary meal.
Sean asked them to wait a minute and a solid

Kenny Dalglish
happy as
Blackburn
Rovers'
manager,
August 1994

two hours later (the
boy was huffing
with his father)
emerged with the
signature of one of
the most instinctive footballers ever to grace
the British game. Kenny ("seldom in the thick
of the action ...like a fly-half waiting for the
ball from a scrum") arrived in the three
matches against Rangers at Ibrox August 14th,
August 25th and September 11th 1971. Celtic
won them all and "Dalgleish" (sic) scored in
each. He had an outstanding first season (won
the first of his 102 caps versus Belgium on
November 10th 1971) but Stein worried for
him. He was taken off before the end against
Aberdeen on March 11th 1972 and Big Jock
consulted with Tommy Docherty to pull him
out of the Scottish team to play the English
League at Middlesbrough four days later:
"He's missed nothing all season and he needs
a rest." Kenny ("always moving on to the ball,
always facing the play, always with a clear
picture of where everybody is") won League
medals for 1972, 1973, 1974 and 1977. He won
his first Scottish Cup in 1972, another in 1974,
"master-minded" the defeat of Airdrie in 1975
and lifted the trophy for Celtic in 1977. After
the Scottish Cup semi-final against Dundee on
April 3rd 1974 Stein proclaimed him "on the
verge of greatness." All the same, he had a disappointing World Cup in Munich and it was
not until October 5th 1974 that he truly discovered real form again. He took over as skipper
from Billy McNeill in 1975. "Celtic are short on
class ...he has to work like a slave ...wins the
ball in his own penalty box ...in midfield ...gets
shots in on goal ...makes telling passes from all
three positions" (March 1976). Kenny had no
obvious weaknesses. He scored goals; he made
goals; he defended; he attacked; he was fearless; he was very seldom on the injured list. In
1977 he skippered Celtic to the Double and
most fans agreed with manager Stein that the
team was 1967 quality again with a personnel
able to compete with the best in Europe.
Kenny too seemed to have Europe in his sights
to judge from his addresses (fervently
applauded) to the Supporters' Associations
but the club with which he won the European
Cup in 1978 was Liverpool (Bill Shankly had
rejected him at 15!) and not Celtic. It was the
timing of his departure that left the bitter taste.
With him, anything might have been possible
in 1977-78. Without him, the season crumbled
to nothing. He played his last game at East

Kenny Dalglish

End Park on the evening before he became a Liverpool player. Stein stood glum-faced at the top of the Dunfermline dressing room steps staring down as the all-time Celtic great took the field. The end of Dalglish presaged the end of Stein.

Appearances:
SL: 204 apps. 112 gls.
SLC: 60 apps. 35 gls.
SC: 29 apps. 11 gls.
Eur: 27 apps. 8 gls.
Total: *320 apps. 166 gls.*

♣ **Celtic note:** *Kenny lost his medal at the end of the 1977 final. Police found it in the umbrella of a man in an invalid chair whom he had gone to greet. Next, both he and Stein attempted to board the Rangers bus by mistake, Kenny carrying the Scottish Cup!*

DAVIDSON, Andrew

Role: Left-half 1913-14
5' 9" 11st.7lbs.
b. c 1892

CAREER: Allan Glen's High School/ Rutherglen Glencairn/CELTIC 19 Apr 1913/ (Vale of Atholl loan Oct 1913)/(Wishaw Thistle loan Jan 1914)/St Mirren 9 May 1914/(South Shields loan 8 Jan 1916)/reinstated amateur 8 Aug 1916/South Shields Oct 1917/Glasgow University XI 1919/South Shields 1919-20.

Debut v Clyde (a) 1-0 (SL) 5.1.14

A medical student at Glasgow University, Andrew Davidson joined Celtic a fortnight before Johnny McMaster but it was the great McMaster who took John Mitchell's spot at left-half. Andrew got into the side in place of skipper Sunny Jim Young in a strong-going team January 1914 at Shawfield in snow and slush; played behind Patsy Gallagher when the Atom got a hat-trick against Dumbarton at Parkhead January 12; and participated one week later in Celtic's first win at Dundee in 12 years with a Browning goal ten minutes from time. Sunny Jim came back but McMaster was suspended and Andrew went in again for the game of his life versus Morton at Parkhead on February 14. His last game as a Celt was against Falkirk at Brockville on February 28 1914 when the Bhoys lost their first match since 15 September 1913 and their first goal since two weeks before Christmas. Thus he made a fair contribution to the Double side of 1914. Andrew qualified as a doctor in April 1916 and became Captain Davidson RAMC during the Great War. Although "still useful" with South Shields in 1919-20, he played for Glasgow University at right-half versus Aberdeen University on February 28th 1920 and seemed "lacking in training ...his play was shaky at times."

Appearances:
SL: 5 apps. 0 gls.
SC: 1 app. 0 gls.
Total: *6 apps. 0 gls.*

DAVIDSON, James Wilkie

Role: Outside-right 1892-95
5' 8" 11st.2lbs.
b. Edinburgh, 25th October 1873

CAREER: Leith Athletic/CELTIC 1892/ Burnley 7 July 1895/Lincoln City Mar 1897/ Tottenham Hotspur May 1897/Brighton United 1898/Burnley Apr 1900 until 1902.

Debut v Rangers (a) 2-2 (SL) 24.9.1892 (scored once)

James 'Tooty' Davidson

Celtic imported Tom Towie from St Bernard's about the same time as James ('Tooty') Davidson but Towie was ineligible for League games. Tooty played in the League, Towie in the Cup, and it was Towie who played in the two Scottish finals of 1893. Tooty was inside-left to Johnny Campbell in the Celtic side that won its first League flag at Leith on May 9th 1893. He lost his place to Johnny Madden the following (Championship) season after a fearful 5-0 thumping by Rangers in the League in September and got only the occasional game thereafter. His last was the benefit match for the Oul' Giniral, James McLaren, Celt of '88, on June 22nd 1895. Tooty was a much-appreciated player at Turf Moor.

Appearances:
SL: 21 apps. 8 gls.
Total: *21 apps. 8 gls.*

DAVIDSON, Robert

Role: Full-back 1898-1902
5′ 9″ 12st.0lbs.
b. West Calder

CAREER: West Benhar Juveniles/Albion Rovers/ Dykehead Aug 1894/CELTIC 28 June 1898/(Belfast Celtic loan Nov 1899)/ Manchester City 9 Aug 1902/Airdrie 10 Sept 1904/Bathgate 8 Aug 1910/to Australia 1911/ Balimba Rangers (Queensland) Sept 1912.

Debut v Hibernian (h) 1-2 (SL) 27.9.1898

"I don't suppose Celtic ever had a player whose heart was so much in the team or one more anxious to see his side win. No one bears a Celtic loss more hard." 'Big Bob' joined Celtic when the full backs were Welford and Storrier with Dan Doyle standing by. By December he was threatening the places of both full-backs but for

Bob Davidson

the Cup final versus Rangers on April 22nd 1899, the executive went for experience and Bobby missed match and medal. He would have played in the final of April 14th 1900 but a knee wrench two days before meant he had to call off. Celtic got him a medal and a week later, his brother Andy, also a full-back, won an English one with Bury 4-0 versus Southampton. He was a good back but like Battles, suffered against real pace as possessed by Marky Bell of Hearts (November 17th 1900). He was Tom Maley's second signing for Manchester City after Sandy Turnbull and was fined £25 (a lot!) and suspended (end of May 1906) until New Year 1907 by the English FA as one of several City players who had been paid over the £4 limit. Airdrie ignored the sentence and continued to play him. Celtic played his benefit at Broomfield on August 25th 1909.

Appearances:
SL: 43 apps. 0 gls.
SC: 13 apps. 0 gls.
Total: 56 apps. 0 gls.

DAVIDSON, Victor

Role: Forward 1968-75; Midfield 1979-81
5′ 9″ 10st.5lbs.
b. Glasgow, 8th November 1950

CAREER: Glasgow United/CELTIC ground staff 20 July 1967/CELTIC 12 Dec 1967/ Giffnock North (farmed-out)/Ashfield (farmed-out) Dec 1967/CELTIC 18 May 1968/ free 1 May 1975/Motherwell 3 June 1975/ Blackpool 18 July 1978/CELTIC 31 Mar 1979/ Phoenix Inferno 1981.

*Debut v St Mirren (a) 3-2 (SL) 18.4.70
(scored once)*

Once young Vic began to score goals for Celtic reserves, Sean Fallon transformed "one of the most promising youngsters of them all" from midfielder into striker in 1970. By 1971 Vic was "the new John White." "You don't know how he's going to beat you ...no hint ...he runs at you and past you in one" (Davie Sneddon). Stein wasn't so sure: "He's a stick-out in the reserves but he still has a lot to learn about first-team football" He knew Vic was too easily brushed-off the ball at top level. Vic

Vic Davidson

points to the 1-2 defeat by Rangers (14th September 1974) as the beginning of the end of his first period at Parkhead. He experienced "bad feeling" and was demoted to "sub and scapegoat." He ascribed his failure at Parkhead to too high an expectation of his talent: "If I didn't have an outstanding game I knew I was out again ... I was afraid to try anything." "Towards the end of my time ... I wasn't giving Celtic everything ... I wasn't putting in 100% ... I was demoralised by reserve team football and I'd lost respect from my team mates and for myself." Billy McNeill paid £30,000 to bring him back to Celtic in a Bertie Auld role but again the club-player bond failed to gel. Vic now lives in Denver, Colorado, and is a naturalised US citizen.

Appearances:
SL: 39 apps. 17 gls.
SLC: 10 apps. 2 gls.
SC: 5 apps. 2 gls.
Eur: 12 apps. 3 gls.
Total: *66 apps. 24 gls.*

DAVITT, Michael

Role: Full-back 1935-41
5' 8" 10st.7lbs.
b. 22nd October 1912
d. 24th February 1973

CAREER: League Hearts/ Baillieston Juniors June 1933/St Francis Juniors 1934/CELTIC 8 June 1935/free 1941/ Renfrew Juniors 11 Oct 1941.

Debut v Ayr United (h) 4-1 (SL) 26.3.38

Michael Davitt "of fine build" started off as a juvenile inside-forward but was at centre-half for St Francis versus Cambuslang Rangers in a Cup match (May 15th 1934) when Scott Duncan watched him for Manchester United. He was a surprise

Michael Davitt

replacement for John Morrison at left-back on a day when Celtic needed 9 points from 7 games for the 1938 Championship. "Davitt was not at all at home in the position. It would have been better if Willie Lyon had dropped behind and Davitt been given his rightful place." It was his solitary match for the Celtic big team bar the pre-season trial of August 6th 1937 when he played for the Green and White in a half-back line reading: Lynch, Lyon and Davitt. His granddaughter married Gerry Britton in the summer of 1993.

Appearances: .
SL: 1 app. 0 gls.
Total: *1 app. 0 gls.*

DAWSON, Daniel

Role: Half-back 1932-38
5' 8" 11st.0lbs.
b. Larkhall, 26th June 1912

CAREER: Larkhall Thistle/CELTIC 4 June 1932/Queen of the South cs 1938/(Hamilton Academicals loan 1940- 41)(Third Lanark loan 27 May 1941)/Queen of the South 1942.

Danny Dawson

Debut v Queen's Park (h) 3-1 (SL) 30.9.33

"He's a stuffy boy, wee Dawson, and a cute 'un." "A more whole-hearted player does not exist." Danny was hailed as "another Jimmy McMullan with all McMullan's craft" and was signed as cover for Peter Wilson and "ready for the first team at any time." When Wilson went to Hibs, it was Chic Geatons who took over at right-half and when Geatons was unavailable, John Morrison. Danny, "who sent Parkhead fans into ecstasies with his whole-hearted displays," suffered a serious left knee injury in the

Scottish Cup 2nd round replay against Thistle (February 13th 1935) and was not back in training for virtually an entire year. He played against Sunderland with "terrier-like enthusiasm" in the home leg of the Champions' match (30th September 1936). When Willie Hughes moved to Clyde, Danny was seen as his replacement utility man but knee trouble struck again in November 1937.

Appearances:
SL: 17 apps. 3 gls.
SC: 3 apps. 0 gls.
Total: *20 apps. 3 gls.*

DEANS, John Kelly

Role: Striker 1971-76
5' 8" 10st.8lbs.
b. Linwood, 30th July 1946

CAREER: Neilston Juniors 1965/Motherwell 19 Oct 1966/CELTIC 30 Oct 1971/Luton Town 17 June 1976/(Carlisle United loan 2 Feb 1977)/(Partick Thistle loan 16 Mar 1977)/ Juventus (Adelaide) cs 1977/Shelbourne Nov 1977/Juventus (Adelaide) cs 1978/Partick Thistle (trial) 15 July 1980.

Debut v Partick Thistle (a) 5-1 (SL) 27.11.71 (scored once)

'Dixie' Deans in action during the 1974 Scottish Cup Final with Dundee United.

Celtic were fined £50 for signing Rangers fan 'Dixie' Deans because he still had four weeks of a six week suspension to serve (and was entertaining thoughts of giving up the game). Stein wanted a gutsy front runner and Dixie was another of his "sensation" signings. He became a good boy with Celtic and was ordered-off but once, with the reserves on April 28th 1975. He is remembered as the Celt who ballooned the very first spot-kick over the bar in the shoot-out against Inter-Milan in the semi-final of the European Cup at Parkhead (April 19th 1972) when Inter went through 4-5. Celtic had prepared for penalties at Seamill and Dixie had scored every time. (Not to worry. He was applauded vociferously on to the field three days later and at the end of the match, the fans chanted his name; to hear "Dixie! Dixie!" roared out in glory by a big crowd at Parkhead was an unforgettable experience). This "chunky wee striker" was always "the punters' favourite", with as big a heart as Joe Carruth in his time. On May 6th 1972 he registered a straight hat-trick versus Hibs in the Scottish Cup final. James Kelly had done it for Renton in 1888; Jimmy Quinn for Celtic in 1904 and now Dixie. In the League against Partick Thistle on November 17th 1973 he scored six goals, the first four coming in a row. Both teams autographed the match ball and Dixie took it home. Dixie gave his all for Celtic all the time including two front teeth (versus St Johnstone on January 17th 1976 when he spat out and played on, blood spilling down his jersey). He was a restless, hungry player, a rogue elephant of a centre, who ran at defences and gave them no rest. For such a small man he was total menace in the air. "Deans has tremendous elasticity which makes him able to climb higher than some of the biggest opponents he meets" (Joe Aitchison). Dixie was capped against East Germany on October 30th 1974 and versus Spain on November 20th, each time at Hampden. When he wasn't playing for Scotland he followed them with enthusiasm.

Appearances:
SL: 126 apps. 89 gls.
SLC: 23 apps. 11 gls.
SC: 21 apps. 18 gls.
Eur: 14 apps. 6 gls.
Total: *184 apps. 124 gls.*

DELANEY, James

Role: Outside-right, centre-forward 1933-46
5' 9" 11st.3lbs.
b. Cleland, 3rd September 1914
d. Cleland, 26th September 1989

CAREER: Cleland St Mary's 1933/Wishaw Juniors trial 1933/Stoneyburn Juniors 1933/ CELTIC 9 Sept 1933/Manchester United 8 Feb 1946/Aberdeen 15 Nov 1950/Falkirk 4 Dec 1951/Derry City 12 Jan 1954/Cork Athletic player-manager 21 Dec 1955/Elgin City 28 Sept 1956/retired 19 Apr 1957.

Debut v Hearts (a) 0-0 (SL) 18.8.34

"Jimmy Delaney was the greatest inspirational footballer I ever played with or saw. No game was ever lost with Jimmy in the team" (Johnny Paton, December 1993). World War Two in the Celtic story is the era of Jimmy Delaney. Jimmy succeeded Bertie Thomson on the Celtic right and one year three days later scored the opener for Scotland versus England at Hampden in the George V Silver Jubilee international. He scored three goals when Celtic beat Rangers 4-2 in the Charity Cup final at Hampden on May 9th 1936 and was apprehended by manager Maley in the tunnel; "Don't let this go to your head!" On two successive Saturdays in April 1937 he played before an aggregate of 300,000 spectators at Hampden, first with Scotland and then with Celtic. He was outside-right in the Celtic side that beat Everton in the final of the Exhibition Trophy on June 10th 1938. Then Celtic played Arbroath at home on April 1st 1939. Jimmy's left arm was stamped on in a melée and both bones shattered so badly that surgeon Mr Beattie wanted to amputate. Celtic players mobbed Attilio Becci at the time but Jimmy absolved him later: "He was blameless..." Jimmy made his come-back on August 2nd 1941 and took on the entire burden of the Celtic attack: "Delaney was here, there and everywhere. He lifted Celtic to victory ...Celtic's problems are all forward, only Delaney in the least dangerous ...stop Delaney you stop Celts ...Delaney carried the Celtic attack on his shoulders ...if you take Delaney out of the match, Celtic were impossible winners." As Malky MacDonald said: "You didn't play with Jimmy Delaney, you played to him."A crowd of 500 people outside 6 Carlton Place chanted "We Want Delaney!" (April 12th 1944) while inside the selectors picked the team for England at Hampden. Jimmy (for long unable to obtain insurance) played in the 2-3 defeat of April 22nd 1944 in front of 133,000 fans, the day Montgomery, the conqueror of Rommel, appeared unannounced and received a tumultuous roar as he came on field to meet Delaney. Jimmy raced home after the match. His infant son, Michael, died that same evening. There was consternation among the faithful in May 1945 when Rex of the

" For peace sake, Fatzinfire, find out if Delaney's in the team ! "

Sunday Mail revealed Maestro was perfectly fit but not in the team simply because he had asked for a rise on his top scale of £2 a week. Mr White and the directorate had taken dudgeon. Tommy Bogan was bought and Jimmy's days as a Celt with the only club he really loved were numbered. Matt Busby met him at Motherwell station and took "the greatest match-winner in the game" to Old Trafford. Busby was team-building. For Celtic the parting with this all-time great was another incomprehensible lurch towards disaster.

Appearances:
SL: 143 apps. 68 gls.
SC: 17 apps. 5 gls.
Total: *160 apps. 73 gls.*
RL: 121 apps. 76 gls.
RLC: 24 apps. 11 gls.
Total: *145 apps. 87 gls.*

♣ **Celtic note:** *April 13th 1946; Scotland 0, England 0 with a minute to go at Hampden. Jackie Husband flights a free kick out on the left across the Mount Florida end goal. Willie Waddell touches it into the box and Jimmy Delaney crashes it into the net behind Frank Swift. Hampden is bedlam. Delaney does it again!*

DEVANNY, Alexander Stark

Role: Goalkeeper 1949-52
5' 11" 11st.0lbs.
b. 25th July 1930

CAREER: Dennistoun Juveniles/Glasgow Perthshire 8 July 1949/ CELTIC 15 Aug 1949/free May 1952/Berwick Rangers 28 June 1952/free 30 Apr 1955/Northampton Town 6 July 1955/ St Mirren June 1955/Alloa 18 Aug 1957/free 1961.

Alex Devanny

Debut v Forfar Athletic (h) 4-1 (SLC) 15.9.51

Maryhill boy Alex Devanny started as an out-side-left but toured London with Dennistoun Juveniles in the summer of 1949 and was encouraged in his calling as a goalie by none other than the great Ted Ditchburn of Spurs and England. He was called up from Perthshire when Johnny Bonnar would not accept terms for the start of 1949-50. "Celtic reckon he will be one of their best-ever

captures." Alex was reserve 'keeper when Willie Miller was injured against Hearts on December 31st 1949 but Bonnar got the nod to take over in the first team. Once George Hunter appeared on the scene, Alex was demoted to third choice goalie but moved up as Bonnar's reserve in 1951 when Hunter went off to Switzerland. Bonnar was injured in the 3-3 draw with Newcastle at Parkhead 12th September 1951 and Alex played against Rangers at Ibrox in the "Best Behaviour, Please" match of 22nd September (1-1) before a crowd of 85,000. He had his last game in the Glasgow Cup final at Hampden two days later. He stood transfixed to give Billy McPhail a free header for Clyde's opener in 3 minutes and carried the can for the 2-1 defeat while Willie Miller (head in bandages) performed miracles at the other end.

Appearances:
SL: 1 app. 0 shut-outs.
SLC: 2 apps. 0 shut-outs.
Total: *3 apps. 0 shut-outs.*

DEVLIN, James

Role: Outside-right 1890-91 & 1894-95

CAREER: Blackstoun Rangers/CELTIC Oct 1890/Abercorn/Paisley Celtic Sept 1893/ CELTIC Sept 1894/Royal Albert May 1895/ Chorley Sept 1895/Dundee 1 May 1896/ Sunderland 9 Nov 1897/Arsenal Dec 1897/ Airdrie 13 Aug 1898/Third Lanark 30 Aug 1898/Albion Rovers 14 Aug 1899/British Army Dec 1899/Albion Rovers 15 Aug 1901.

Debut v Dumbarton (a) 2-0 (SL) 9.3.1895

James Devlin was inside-right for Celtic reserves when they won the 2nd XI Cup 13-1 versus St Mirren (February 21st 1891) and took Neil McCallum's place versus Blackburn Rovers (October 1st 1891). Celtic were in the throes of their worst run since February 1889, without a win since January 2nd 1895 when he was reintroduced for the injured Johnny Campbell at Boghead in March. He played for Royal Albert in a friendly versus Celtic at Larkhall (May 21st 1895) and scored the first goal in a 3-5 defeat.

Appearances:
SL: 2 apps. 1 gl.
Total: *2 apps. 1 gl.*

DEVLIN, John

Role: Inside-right 1895

CAREER: Mossend Celtic/CELTIC Mar 1895/ Airdrie Aug 1895/Chorley Sept 1895/Airdrie 29 Nov 1895/Tottenham Hotspur Dec 1895/ Millwall Nov 1897/Third Lanark 2 May 1898/ Albion Rovers 14 Aug 1899/British Army Dec 1899/Albion Rovers 15 Aug 1901/Nithsdale Wanderers 23 May 1902/Lanemark 25 Mar 1905/retired 1907.

Debut v Leith Athletic (h) 4-0 (SL) 16.3.1895 (scored once)

John Devlin tried-out for Celtic in the League team just one week after his brother in place of Jimmy Blessington. His debut was marred by an horrendous leg break for John Marshall, the Leith right-winger, early in the first half. The snap was so distinct the entire south stand (the Jungle) winced. John Devlin played again for Celtic the following week in an Old Firm match at Ibrox. A depleted Celtic side drew 1-1 after taking the lead in the second half. The Devlins allegedly joined the Army for the Boer War and saw service in South Africa.

Appearances:
SL: 2 apps. 1 gl.
Total: *2 apps. 1 gl.*

DIVERS, John

Role: Forward 1893-96; 1898-1901
5' 8" 10st.2lbs.
b. 19th September 1873(?)
d. 1910(?)

CAREER: Vale of Clyde/ Benburb/Hibernian/ CELTIC 14 Sept 1893/ Everton 1 May 1897/ CELTIC 15 Oct 1898/ (Hibernian loan 26 Sept 1901)/Hibernian 16 Nov 1901/retired 1904/Bohemians trainer 1904.

Johnny Divers

Debut v Hurlford (h) 6-0 (SC) 25.11.1893

"He's an artist, I tell you. It's a treat to watch him play. His only fault is, he's too artistic at times. He does too much" (Willie Maley in the stand at Bramall Lane 14th October 1893). "Divers is like a battery, stimulating others till all are as lively as himself ...The amount of work he gets through in 90 minutes is

astounding." Apart from a superb work rate Johnny "hit his shots as from the cannon's mouth." He was one of the three strikers who refused to strip for trainer J.J. Mullen on November 28th 1896 unless the press box was cleared of reporters from the *Glasgow Evening News* and its ancillary, the *Scottish Referee*. He followed Barney Battles back to Parkhead to pull the team out of a trough in October 1898 and was at centre in the side that beat Rangers in the Cup final of 22nd April 1899. As a member of the Hibs team that defeated Celtic in the final of 26th April 1902, he had a specialist role: to stop Duke McMahon jumping at corners. Johnny (allegedly discovered during a bounce game on the old Celtic Park) was a whole-hearted Celt who never shirked. Willie Maley says it was only lack of physique that restricted him to gaining just one Scottish cap.

Appearances:
SL: 64 apps. 31 gls.
SC: 23 apps. 9 gls.
Total: *87 apps. 40 gls.*

DIVERS, John

Role: Inside-left 1932-45
5' 11" 11st.10lbs.
b. Clydebank, 6th August 1911
d. Western Infirmary, 8th June 1984

CAREER: Clydebank BG/Linwood St Conval's/Rothesay Royal Victoria 1930/ Renfrew Juniors 1931/CELTIC 2 Dec 1932/ (Morton loan 1942)/free 1 Sept 1945/Oldham Athletic trial Sept 1945/Morton 6 Oct 1945/ free May 1947/Oldham Athletic 19 Aug 1947/ Morton again 15 Oct 1947/Chairman Players' Union 1947/Morton player-coach 8 Mar 1949/ Portadown player-manager 30 Sept 1950/ suspended by club Nov 1950.

Debut v Clyde (h) 2-1 (SL) 2.4.34

John Divers

Bob Kelly nominates Tommy McInally as his all-time Celtic inside-left and as reserve: Patsy Gallagher's nephew, loose-limbed, long-striding Johnny Divers. This "big strong lump of a lad" had to go on the Celtic transfer list before making the grade. Manager Maley circulated English clubs: "He is not taking the game seriously enough. He would be a different player away from Glasgow." When McGrory retired in December 1937, Johnny Crum moved to centre and Johnny Divers came in permanently as a member of the Championship side of 1938. A scheming inside-forward with a booming shot, he put Celtic ahead against Rangers at Parkhead on Ne'erday with a glorious goal and shot a second into Jenkins' empty net for a 3-0 win with eleven minutes to go and the fog descending. Against an intensely physical Sunderland side in the Glasgow Empirex tournament first round replay (May 26th 1938), he "played the kind of football you can't buy with money." Scotland capped him versus Ireland in Belfast on October 8th 1938. His fitness fell away with War work (he would arrive at Parkhead on a Saturday in his overalls straight from the shipyards) and when he rejoined Celtic from Morton after "intensive training," it was as a left-half. "His employment made a big difference ...that untiring stride, the two-footed command of the gliding pass, alert anticipation of the opposition to go through on his own." Along with the genius was the grafter: "Divers ...working furiously to check attacks and turn them about." This inside-left of the great team of '38 was one of the first players to whom manager McGrory offered a free. Morton were not slow to take advantage of a great football brain. Joe McLaughlin called him "one of the greatest coaches I've ever met ... the brains of the Celtic team ... I never met a man who could lay a pass on like Johnny ... he played inside-forward but operated as a fourth half-back passing the ammo, and how he passed it!" Morton beat Celtic 4-0 at Cappielow on January 17th 1948. Johnny Divers scored the opening goal. "The ease with which he finds the open space makes defensive work a pleasure" (Morton centre-half, ex-Celt Alex Millar).

Appearances:
SL: 75 apps. 44 gls.
SC: 7 apps. 4 gls.
Total: *82 apps. 48 gls.*
RL: 93 apps. 37 gls.
SWC: 2 apps. 1 gl.
RLC: 20 apps. 6 gls.
Total: *115 apps. 44 gls.*

John Divers

DIVERS, John

Role: Inside-left 1957-66
5' 11" 12st.8lbs.
b. Clydebank, 8th March 1940

CAREER: St Patrick's High School Dumbarton /Glentyan Thistle 1955/CELTIC 7 July 1956/ Renfrew Juniors (farmed-out) 1956/free 30 Apr 1966/Partick Thistle 30 Sept 1966/ free 1969/Strathclyde University XI 1969-70.

Debut v St Mirren (h) 2-2 (SL) 16.11.57 (scored once)

John Divers, son of John Divers 1938, grand-nephew of Patsy Gallagher, supplanted Sammy Wilson of the October 1957 side and became one of John McPhail's "three wonder boys - Jackson, Colrain and Divers." He oozed class but also worked hard and was at his best when the going was heavy. His stamina was affected by a blood flow problem throughout 1959-60 yet by August 1960 had gained a yard after massage treatment. He had a magnificent season 1961-62; "Divers would not disgrace a Scottish jersey ... he could even make us forget about Denis Law. He has skill, enthusiasm and the discipline to benefit any team. Not only is he scoring goals, he is chiselling the openings so beautifully" (March 1962). So much so, John found himself in the squad for the 'revenge' match versus Uruguay at Hampden (2nd May 1962) and came on as second-half substitute

for the Scottish League against the Italian in Rome (14th November 1962). Besides his skill as a goalmaker he also had a thunderous shot which might turn a match. Bobby Murdoch got his first chance with Celtic when John turned up at Parkhead for the start of the season against Hearts on Saturday 11th August 1962 minus his boots (size 8½) used at Hampden with the Glasgow XI in midweek. He was dropped on the spot, Charlie Gallagher was ordered to strip, and the fabulous Bobby given his debut. When Jock Stein took over, John was largely a "forgotten man" but "proved still a handy reserve to have around" with a brilliant goal versus Motherwell on August 18th 1965 and showing "a speed of turn and shot that astounded the Celtic support" against Dundee three days later. He was now studying physiotherapy and his mind was no longer wholly on the game. He could still hit them, e.g., a glory of a free-kick high into the postage stamp corner of the net for Partick against Hibs (January 11th 1969) from fully 30 yards!

Appearances:
SL: 171 apps. 80 gls.
SLC: 26 apps. 8 gls.
SC: 28 apps. 11 gls.
Eur: 7 apps. 3 gls.
Total: *232 apps. 102 gls.*

DOBBIN, James

Role: Midfield 1979-84
5' 8" 10st.7lbs.
b. Dunfermline, 17th September 1963

CAREER: Whitburn BC/CELTIC 'S' form Jan 1979/CELTIC 9 Oct 1980/(Motherwell loan Feb 1984)/Doncaster Rovers 16 Mar 1984/ Barnsley 18 Sept 1986/Grimsby Town 15 July 1991.

Debut v Arbroath (h) 4-1 (SLC) 1.9.82
(scored once)

"He is a silky player with a great touch" said Billy Bremner who paid £25,000 to take Jim Dobbin to Doncaster. Besides this, Jim had "a great talent for scoring spectacular goals." He made his debut as replacement for another great ball-player: Paul McStay. McStay came back from injury and apart from the pre-season tour of Switzerland and Germany in 1983, it was another year and another League Cup before Jim got a second chance (August

27th 1983), the humiliating 0-0 home draw versus Brechin City. On his League debut he "passed the ball around like a champ" and scored with one of his raging shots in seven minutes versus St Johnstone at Muirton on December 3rd 1983. As captain of Grimsby he

Jim Dobbin

stopped Kevin Keegan's Newcastle achieving a record 14 wins in a row by scoring the only goal of the match at St James' Park on October 23rd 1992.

Appearances:
SL: 3 apps. 2 gls.
SLC: 4 apps. 1 gl.
Total: *7 apps. 3 gls.*

DOCHERTY, James

Role: Inside-forward 1947-50
5' 8" 11st.7 lbs.
b. Clydebank, 22nd April 1926

CAREER: Coatbridge St Pat's 1946/Renfrew Jnrs 1947/HM Forces 1947/CELTIC 15 Dec 1947/free 6 May 1950/Northampton Town 22 July 1950/Stirling Albion 10 Aug 1951/ Arbroath 8 Dec 1951/Alloa 4 Aug 1952/free 1953/Llanelly July 1953/Distillery 1954/ Stranraer 27 Oct 1955.

Debut v Clyde (h) 2-1 (SL) 18.4.49

"Docherty is a prospect for the future, astute, tall, well-built, deliberate, intent always on doing the right thing" (18 April 1949). Jimmy played half-back as a juvenile and was reckoned a better prospect in 1946 than Frank Brennan at the same stage. He played inside-left to Tully on the Highland Tour of 1949 then inside-right to Leslie Johnston and Tommy Docherty. He went to London with Celtic to play Millwall for groundsman Bill Moor's benefit 25 April 1949, a friendly that developed into a fracas. The 20,000 crowd at the Den sang "Dear Old Pals" while the referee lectured the teams. Two days later he came on for Leslie Johnston as substitute at Notts County and left the pitch at the end with an ovation for both sides ringing in his ears. Jimmy's free transfer in 1950 came as a surprise to the Celtic fans.

Appearances:
SL: 2 apps. 0 gls.
Total: *2 apps. 0 gls.*

DOCHERTY, James

Role: Centre-forward/outside-right 1954-56
5' 8" 11st.7lbs.
b. 13th April 1934

CAREER: Duntocher St Mary's BG/Duntocher Hibernian/CELTIC (provisional) 21 Oct 1954/demobbed 5 Jan 1955/(Alloa loan 21 Dec 1955)/free 1956/Alloa 1956.

Debut v Falkirk (a) 1-1 (SLC) 3.9.55

Ex farm-worker Jimmy Docherty, with "McGrory's shoulders and power", ("the nearest approach I have seen to Jimmy McGrory for a long time") made his Celtic debut as a centre flanked by Fernie and Tully in one of the more infamous Falkirk - Celtic encounters at Brockville (and all-ticket at that).

Bairns' left-back Ian Rae was ordered-off in the first half after a clash with Tully. Right on half-time Falkirk next lost future Rangers star Bobby Morrison with cartilage trouble after a Tully tackle. The Bairns played the second half with nine men. The press reported the pitch as showered with bottles but the Celtic Supporters' Association could count only four items of glassware, one of them contributed probably by Falkirk fans. "Terrified" Falkirk players were not so intimidated as to hitch a lift back to Glasgow on the Celtic bus. The Supporters' Association decided to hit the Brockville club where it hurt for not controlling their hooligans and decided to stay away from the League match on 10th September. Jimmy Docherty helped put Thistle out of the Glasgow Cup on the eve of the

Jimmy Docherty

boycott and made his Old Firm debut 24 September 1955 as outside-right at Ibrox in a 0-0 draw. Dick Beattie made his first save in the 87th minute and George Niven was not much busier. Quite a contrast to Falkirk. Jimmy was a highly valued man at Alloa.

Appearances:
SL: 1 app. 0 gls.
SLC: 1 app. 0 gls.
Total: *2 apps. 0 gls.*

DOCHERTY, John

Role: Goalkeeper 1896; 1897; 1898-1900

CAREER: Glasgow Wanderers/Vale of Leven 1 Sept 1894/Dumbarton 1895/(CELTIC loan 15 Feb 1896 & 6 Nov 1897)/CELTIC 7 May 1898/free May 1900/reinstated amateur 14 Aug 1900/Vale of Leven 1900/Renton 14 Aug 1909/retired 1910.

Debut v Dundee (a) 2-1 (SL) 6.11.1897

Dan McArthur had taken one of his customary kickings versus Rangers on October 30th 1897 in the Glasgow Cup semi-final and Celtic were without a 'keeper for Dundee so John Docherty was borrowed from Dumbarton. Celtic took the points but only thanks to a magnificent stop by goalie John in the last minute from Keillor. John might have ended his third phase at Parkhead in a blaze of glory with a Glasgow Cup medal (May 12th 1900) but Rangers were on top form at 2nd Hampden (Cathkin Park) and took the trophy 5-1. John was freed and Celtic signed Willie Donnelly of Clyde as McArthur's understudy. Vale of Leven played his benefit against Renton on August 20th 1908.

Appearances: .
SL: 11 apps. 0 gls.
Total: *11 apps. 0 gls.*

DOCHERTY, Thomas Henderson

Role: Right-half 1948-49
5' 7" 11st.8lbs.
b. Glasgow, 24th April 1928

CAREER: St Paul's Shettleston BG/Shettleston Juniors 1945/HLI July 1946/demobbed 12 July 1948/CELTIC 26 July 1948/Preston NE 4 Nov 1949/(Third Lanark loan 12 May 1956)/Arsenal 23 Aug 1958/Oxford University coach /Barnet FC coach (both part-time as Arsenal player)/Chelsea coach 10 Feb 1961/player 30 Aug 1961/manager 27 Sept 1961/(Prague FC Sydney loan 1 July 1965)/Rotherham United manager 22 Nov 1967/Queen's Park Rangers manager 6 Nov 1968/left 5 Dec 1968/Aston Villa manager 18 Dec 1968/dismissed 19 Jan 1970/Hull City asst. manager 2 July 1971/ Scotland manager 12 Sept 1971/Manchester United manager 22 Dec 1972/dismissed 4 July 1977/Derby County manager 17 Sept 1977/ Queen's Park Rangers manager 11 May 1979/ left 6 May 1980/reinstated 15 May 1980/ dismissed 7 Oct 1980/Sydney Olympic manager Dec 1980/left 20 June 1981/Preston NE manager 22 June 1981/dismissed 3 Dec 1981/Melbourne coach July 1982/Sydney Olympic manager Sept 1982/left 1 Sept 1983/ Wolverhampton Wanderers manager 8 June 1984/dismissed 4 July 1985/Altrincham manager 28 Sept 1987/resigned 4 Feb 1988/ Burnley scout 6 June 1989.

Debut v Rangers (h) 0-1 (SL) 21.8.48

"When I was a youngster, it was my one and only ambition to play in a green and white jersey. When I was transferred it was one of the great disappointments of my life. I'd go back gladly if the chance came along" (August

Tommy Docherty

2nd 1958). Ex-Sergeant Tommy Docherty came home from Palestine and signed for Celtic as a ball-playing centre-half. He was thrown in at outside-right against Rangers in an attempt to break a goal drought. Tommy over-elaborated in his attempts to run the legs off Tiger Shaw so went back to the reserves as understudy to Bobby Evans. He made the first team again on October 23rd 1948 when Evans was making his debut with Scotland at Cardiff. Tommy showed total promise along with his partner Joe Baillie on the left. He was at centre-half on November 27th 1948 for Alec Boden and sat in on one of chairman Kelly's pre-match pep talks. His presence in the side was always distinctive. No spectator was ever unaware that the sandy-haired kid was on the field, so much did he look the part and so driving was his energy. John Kerr who had recommended the O'Donnells to Preston in 1935 again tipped off Deepdale there was another Scottish gem at Parkhead.

Appearances:
SL: 9 apps. 2 gls.
Total: 9 apps. 2 gls.

DODDS, Joseph

Role: Left-back 1908-20; 1921-22
5' 8" 11st.10lbs.
b. Carluke, 14th July 1887
d. 14th October 1965

CAREER: Braidwood United/Carluke Milton Rovers/CELTIC 13 May 1908/(Kilmarnock loan Sept 1908 & 28 Apr 1909)/RFA 51HD 20 Mar 1918/(Fulham loan 23 Mar 1918)/(Ayr United loan 20 April 1918)/(Queen of the South loan April 1918)/Cowdenbeath 4 Aug 1920/CELTIC 2 May 1921/resigned 22 Aug 1922/(Queen of the South loan player-manager 25 Oct 1922)/reinstated amateur 1923/Queen of the South 15 Aug 1923/retired 16 Aug 1928/CELTIC asst. trainer 9 Nov 1936.

Debut v Dundee (h) 2-0 (SL) 10.10.08

"There's a full-back playing football whom everybody knows/He partners gentleman McNair, the essence of repose/He plays a clean and clever game and never fears a foe/So the best way to describe him is to call him Fearless Joe."

"I am of the opinion Joe Dodds did not get full justice from the selectors. He should have got more caps than he did. A feature of Joe's play was that when he went for the ball, he used to get it. If he shouted 'This is mine!' a goalie could be sure the ball wasn't coming his way. He was great with his head, force and direction being always just right. McNair and Dodds were the best club pair I ever had in front of me" (Jimmy Brownlie 15th February 1941). Originally a forward, rollicking Joe Dodds was "the mobile column of the Celtic defence, pushed out to meet the first shock of the enemy's attack." He signed for Celtic as left-half or centre-half and converted into the speediest left-back the club has ever had ("He can beat the fastest wingers with a yard or two to spare"). Joe began to establish himself in the Celtic side as of January 1909 and played as centre-half in both Scottish finals versus Rangers (April 10 and 17th). The Cup was withheld and Celtic's dash for the Championship began, eight games in 11 days, with Joe playing in seven. He first teamed up with Eck McNair at full-back in a friendly at Dundee on August 30th 1909 but only when Jimmy Hay departed for Newcastle in 1911 did the great McNair and Dodds combination properly come into play. The Charity Cup final (Rangers 2, Celtic 1) of May 10th 1911 established Joe as a great left-back. He won Scottish Cup medals in 1911, 1912 and 1914 and belonged to the 4-Championships-in-a-row team 1914-17 with other League medals won for 1909, 1910 and 1919. His three full caps for Scotland all came in 1914 and he was in the side that beat England 3-1 at Hampden on April 4th. Joe served in France in the Kaiser War and as Driver Dodds of the Royal Field Artillery led Celtic out to an almighty roar against Hibs in the League on December 28th 1918 when "the best Celtic team so far this season" collected two more points towards the Championship. Joe's free kicks were Gemmell/MacLeod/ Wdowczyk class, "the ball in the back of the net before the defenders had time to turn." He left Celtic for more money in the Central League at Cowdenbeath and left a second time when the club failed to honour the promise of

a benefit made to bring him home to Parkhead. He was an all-time Celtic great and must rank as one of the fastest backs the club has ever had. There is nowhere an account of his having a bad day. He went to school with Willie Angus, VC, DCM.

Appearances:
SL: 351 apps. 29 gls.
SC: 27 apps. 1 gl.
Total: *378 apps. 30 gls.*

DOHERTY, Hugh

Role: Outside-right 1946-47
5' 7" 10st.12lbs.
b. Buncrana, May 5th 1921

CAREER: Buncrana Celtic/Derry City Nov 1939- May 1940/temporary retirement/Buncrana Celtic Aug 1942/ Dundalk Oct 1945/CELTIC 23 Aug 1946/Blackpool 1947/(Raith Rovers loan 13 Jan 1949)/retired late 1949.

Debut v Queen of the South (h) 2-0 (SL) 4.1.47

Hugh ('Dickie') Doherty was spotted at Dundalk by Tommy Bogan and gave Celtic his signature as an amateur. He displaced Bobby Evans at outside-right, sustained a cut temple on his debut but played with the blood pouring down his face. The wound took five stitches and Hugh turned out against Queen's Park the following Saturday in a scrum cap. He played for Celtic (Division A) in the Scottish Cup at Dens Park versus Dundee (Division B) on January 25th 1947. Celtic were a goal down when Hugh received the ball in the penalty area on half-time but hit a trintler into the hands of the astonished Reuben Bennett. Throughout the interval "Doherty's miss was the talk of the town." Despite the club's attempts to make him accept money, Hugh remained obdurate for better terms and went home to Buncrana in May 1947. With Blackpool, he consented to turn professional but his prospects as a right-winger were small; prior to Hugh, in May 1947, the Seasiders had signed another outside-right - the immortal Stanley Matthews. Injuries forced his retirement while with Raith Rovers.

Appearances:
SL: 3 apps. 0 gls.
SC: 1 app. 0 gls.
Total: *4 apps. 0 gls.*

DOHERTY, John

Role: Goalkeeper 1937-39
6' 3"
b. 1917

CAREER: St Eugene's FC (Derry)/Derry City May 1934/CELTIC 1 Nov 1937/Coleraine July 1939.

Debut v Queen's Park (h) 0-1 (SL) 3.1.39

As an amateur at Derry City, John 'Pot' Doherty was understudy to ex-Celtic goalie Jock Wallace and took over from Tom Doyle in the Celtic reserves. He got his chance after Kennaway had taken a knocking-about in the Ne'erday match at Ibrox 1939. His debut match was Queen's Park's first win over Celtic in 12 years. His second and last appearance was on the occasion of a Joe Carruth hat-trick versus Partick Thistle in a 3-1 win at Parkhead.

Appearances:
SL: 2 apps. 0 shut outs.
Total: *2 apps. 0 shut-outs.*

DOLAN, Francis

Role: Centre-half 1890-94
b. Old Monkland, 24th April 1870
d. 12th February 1933

CAREER: CELTIC 1890/
Coatdyke Gaelic 5 Sept 1894.

Frank Dolan

Debut v Cowlairs (h) 2-0 (SL) 14.3.1891

Frank Dolan was understudy to Jimmy Kelly when he made his first appearance for the Celtic big team with Paddy Gallagher on his right and Willie Maley to his left. Kelly was still unfit the following week but the opposition was Rangers at Parkhead so the selectors went for experience and ex-Hib Jimmy McGhee. The papers made noises about Celtic's reluctance to trust young Frank for the big occasion. He got one more chance on April 4th in the League at Love Street, then back came Kelly and Frank reverted to permanent reserve. With his brother Mick in goal, Frank was in the Celtic Crusaders side that beat St Mirren Strollers 13-1 in the final of the Reserve XI Cup (21st February 1891).

Appearances:
SL: 2 apps. 0 gls.
Total: *2 apps. 0 gls.*

DOLAN, Michael

Role: Goalkeeper 1888-94
b. Uddingston, 30th September 1868
d. 27th July 1910

CAREER: Drumpellier 1886/CELTIC May 1888/Uddingston FC as of 3 Nov 1888 & 7 Sept 1889/Coatdyke Gaelic 1894.

Debut v Rangers Swifts (h) 5-2 (Inaugural Match) 28.5.1888

It was the boast of Lord Provost Thomas A. Kerr of Glasgow in the 1950s that he had lived up the same close as the Dolan brothers (401 Gt Eastern Road). Mick, a worker at Parkhead Forge, had greatness thrust upon him of a Monday evening in late May 1888. "Lanarkshire's best goalkeeper" while with Drumpellier, of the original Celtic team against Rangers, he was one regarded as not a match for the enterprise ahead and soon lost his place to Willie Dunning. He was still reserve on New Year's Day 1892 when Tom Duff let in 11 (three chalked-off) against Dumbarton and Joe Cullen was signed. He had played in the Glasgow Cup final versus Clyde at 1st Cathkin Park on December 12th 1891. Celtic won 7-1 and goal-nets were used for the first time ever in any Scottish final. Mick is therefore probably the first Celtic goalie to pick a ball from the back of the net after Bowie of Clyde scored in the 48th minute to make it 2-1 as the snow came down in pancakes.

Appearances: .
SL: 3 apps. 1 shut-out.
SC: 1 app. 0 shut-outs.
Total: *4 apps. 1 shut-out (25%).*

DONALDSON, Andrew

Role: Inside-left 1911-12
5' 6" 10st.7lbs.
b. Airdrie, 5th June 1884(?)

CAREER: Ashfield/Motherwell 8 Aug 1906/ Airdrie 1 May 1908/CELTIC 29 April 1911/ Airdrie 1 Feb 1912/Third Lanark 15 Aug 1918 /Airdrie 5 Jan 1920/St Johnstone 29 July 1920 /Dykehead 17 Jan 1922/Motherwell trainer.

Debut v Third Lanark (h) 5-2 (CC) 6.5.11
(scored once)

Andy McAtee had a reputation for silence but McAtee was a gabber compared with Andy Donaldson. Andy "the personification of pluck" did his talking on the field as witness four goals for Airdrie versus Rangers on January 4th 1915 at Ibrox. Within days of signing for Celtic he was

Andy Donaldson

playing his football as far afield as Dresden, Prague, Budapest and Vienna on the tour of 1911. Brother Walfrid met the players at Folkestone on the way home (30th May 1911) and travelled up with the Bhoys to London so it's possible that Celtic's founder and Sunny Jim Young's best pal, the taciturn Andy, exchanged compliments. Andy was a competent footballer but competition for a place was intense against Paddy Travers and Jimmy McMenemy. Patsy Gallagher made his debut on December 2nd 1911 and Andy's prospects dimmed further.

Appearances:
SL: 17 apps. 5 gls.
Total: *17 apps. 5 gls.*

DONLEVY, Patrick

Role: Centre-half 1898

CAREER: Kilsyth Emmet/Duntocher Hibernian/Glasgow Perthshire 1896/CELTIC 28 Mar 1898/free 15 Oct 1898/Airdrie 19 Oct 1898/Thornliebank 1 Sept 1899/Arthurlie 5 June 1900/Thornliebank 20 Aug 1902/ retired 1903.

Debut v Hibernian (h) 1-2 (SL) 26.9.1898

Pat Donlevy had two interesting games for Celtic: the first on January 11th 1898 versus Rangers at Barrowfield for the "Engineers' Strike Fund"; and his League debut which saw Hibs get a free kick that Robertson put over the bar. The referee ordered a retake and this time Burns got a touch for Hibs' equaliser (a goal direct from a free was illegitimate in 1898). Pat was part of the massacre of reserves on October 15th 1898.

Appearances:
SL: 1 app. 0 gls.
Total: *1 app. 0 gls.*

DONNELLY, John

Role: Full-back 1955-62
5' 9" 11st.0lbs.
b. West Lothian, 17th December 1936

CAREER: Bathgate St Mary's 1950/Broxburn Celtic Juveniles 1953/Armadale Thistle/ CELTIC 16 Jan 1956/Preston NE 11 April 1962 until 1966.

Debut v Rangers (a) 0-2 (GC) 19.8.57

Celtic carried several youngsters on the USA tour of 1957 including ex-inside-right John Donnelly. John got his chance in the States, twice against Spurs. Regular right-back Mike Haughney stayed on in America but Frank Meechan took big Mike's place until he gifted Hibs the opening goal in five minutes at Easter Road (August 17th 1957). John Donnelly became Celtic's new right-back two days later

John Donnelly

and exactly two months by date before the match at Hampden that would establish his name for ever in the Celtic memory of a team beginning: Beattie, Donnelly and Fallon. He had a great game against Johnny Hubbard on his debut and looked set to be Celtic's right-back for years ahead but was called-up to do National Service in mid-July 1958 and replaced by an extremely fine back indeed: his friend and fellow US tourist Dunky MacKay. It was with deep disappointment Celtic fans realised John was not going to be in the Preston NE team for the Cup final versus West Ham on May 2nd 1964. John had all the virtues of a good defender except perhaps pace and was sometimes exposed by very fast wingers like Billy Muir of Kilmarnock (23rd August 1961).

Appearances:
SL: 31 apps. 0 gls.
SLC: 9 apps. 0 gls.
SC: 3 apps. 0 gls.
Total: *43 apps. 0 gls.*

DONNELLY, Simon Thomas

Role: Striker 1992 to date
5' 9" 10st.12lbs.
b. Glasgow, 1st December 1974

CAREER: Stonelaw High School/Clyde BC 1988/Queen's Park BC/Celtic BC/CELTIC groundstaff July 1992/CELTIC 27 May 1993.

Debut v Hibernian (a) 0-0 (SL) 19.3.94 (sub)

Simon Donnelly

"Donnelly has a knack of lunging to beat a defender to the ball but producing a deft touch when he makes contact. Catcalls from the crowd broke out as he glided away from Richard Gough's clutches on several occasions" (Kevin McCarra May 1st 1994). Lou Macari's use of Simon Donnelly was his first sign of encouragement to the younger players at Parkhead. "He has shown plenty of get-up-and-go. If I see that in others they'll get their chance. Donnelly looks the frail type but he's fearless and he's scored regularly." Simon, son of Tom Donnelly who played for Rangers and Motherwell, has 'fast feet'; he gets the ball under control quickly and shoots on the instant, a style reminiscent of that quintessential striker, Joe McBride. He "ran the show" at Ibrox on April 30th 1994 when David Murray put an embargo on the presence of Celtic fans. "He was asked to perform by playing up front against Rangers on his own for much of the match. His task was to hold the ball against Richard Gough... Donnelly accepted the challenge. He ran across Rangers' defensive line constantly and was always available to take possession and then invite challenges which he often escaped... perfectly balanced to ride the tackle and move on... Rarely has a young player emerged with such impact and provided Donnelly can be tutored in the bizarre ways of football life, he should have the opportunity to reach the heights of excellence and could become one of the finest players our game has produced in many years" (James Traynor May 2nd 1994). In a testimonial against Manchester United at Old Trafford on May 16th "Donnelly first dispossessed Keane, then rounded Bruce before calmly sliding the ball past Walsh..." For his second goal "he spotted Walsh off his line and beat the 'keeper with an audacious chip. It was, by any standards, a stunning double contribution from one so young" (Hugh Keevins).

Appearances
SL: 12 apps. 5 gls.
Total: *12 apps. 5 gls.*

DONNELLY, William

Role: Goalkeeper 1900-01
b. Magherafelt, Co Derry, 1872
d. 1st August 1948

CAREER: St Mungo Juniors/Vale of Clyde/ Hibernian 25 Oct 1893/Clyde 27 June 1895/ Liverpool May 1896/Clyde 22 June 1898/ CELTIC 2 Aug 1900/Belfast Celtic Aug 1901.

Debut v Third Lanark (h) 5-1 (SL) 24.9.1900

Garngad boy Willie Donnelly faced 21 penalties for Clyde and saved 19. He was signed as cover for McArthur and first took over as Dan's deputy when the wee demon took a boot in the face from Kitey McPherson (Rangers) in the Glasgow Cup on September 22nd 1900. Dan was injured again at Dundee (22nd December 1900) and Willie went on Celtic's Christmas tour to Blackburn and Grimsby. McArthur played in the 1-0 defeat of Rangers in "the Cup-tie of the Century" (12th January 1901) but was rendered comatose with 15 minutes to go. Willie now took over and saw Celtic on their way to the Cup with clean sheets against Kilmarnock and Dundee. McArthur had a shut-out in the semi-final against St Mirren on March 23rd but a poor final versus Hearts when Celtic lost 4-3 (April 6th 1901). Celtic now turned to the histrionic Bob McFarlane of Grimsby Town as the wee man's successor. Willie crossed to his native Ireland but was one of four players suspended by Belfast Celtic after a 3-2 defeat by Derry (2nd November 1901). He was a steelworker in the Blochairn works in the 1920s.

Appearances:
SL: 3 apps. 0 shut-outs.
SC: 2 apps. 2 shut-outs.
Total: *5 apps. 2 shut-outs (40%).*

DONOGHUE, John

Role: Left-back 1926-30; 1932
5' 7" 10st.8lbs.
b. New York, 22nd January 1903
d. 11th July 1971

CAREER: St Francis Jnrs/Shawfield Jnrs/
CELTIC 11 June 1926/(Third Lanark loan
1927)(Cowdenbeath loan 21 Sept 1927)/
(Belfast Celtic loan 11 Oct 1929-30 April 1930)/
Wrexham 13 July 1930/free 1932/CELTIC
12 Aug 1932/ Excelsior de Roubaix 29 Sept
1932-30 June 1933.

Debut v Hibernian (a) 2-3 (SL) 25.9.26

John Donoghue

Peter McGonagle
was taken off with
cartilage trouble
against Motherwell in
the League 7 April
1928 and ruled out of
the Scottish Cup final
for the following
Saturday. John
Donoghue, born in the
States of Irish parents,
had made a brilliant
start for Celtic as
Jimmy McStay's
deputy at centre-half ("I liked in particular the
way he covered for colleagues in moments of
pressure ...he will go far") including a
Glasgow Cup medal versus Rangers in a
hurricane 9 October 1926. He was assigned
McGonagle's place at left-back for Hampden
but on the day had a torrid second half against
Sandy Archibald in top form. Like his wee
friend ex-Celt Johnny Paton with whom he got
a contract in France, John seems never to have
had his fill of Parkhead. At the pre-season trial
of 9th August 1932 (a try-out that finished like
a Cup-tie) Johnny Falconer came off with
sciatic nerve after five minutes and ex-Celt
Donoghue took the goalie's jersey for the
Greens. Four days later he was centre-half for
the reserves at Pittodrie. When Celtic played
at Roubaix 27th May 1934 and Peter
McGonagle was interviewed for the press it
was John Donoghue who acted as his
interpreter.

Appearances:
SL: 42 apps. 1 gl.
SC: 8 apps. 0 gls.
Total: *50 apps. 1 gl.*

DORNAN, Henry

Role: Left-back 1941-44
5' 8" 11st.0lbs.
b. 14th February 1916

CAREER: Ardeer Recreation July 1934/
Kilmarnock 10 Aug 1939/(Dumbarton loan
1939 & 31 Aug 1940)/ (CELTIC loan 17 May
1941)/(St Mirren loan May 1944 & Feb 1945)/
Kilmarnock Apr 1945/free Apr 1947/Arbroath
25 Sept 1947/free 1948/Queen of the South
9 Aug 1948.

Debut v Queen's Park (a) 5-2 (CC) 21.5.41

When Celtic left-back Roy Milne was called-
up to the RAF and the defence of the Empire
in India, Willie McStay caused a lot of grief to
Dumbarton by recruiting their on-loan full-
back Harry Dornan to take his place. Celtic's
right-back was Bobby Hogg who had been
collecting partners since 1931: Hogg and
McGonagle, Hogg and Donoghue, Hogg and
Morrison, Hogg and Milne, and now (until
Harry damaged his knee ligaments first match
of the season August 14th 1943): Hogg and
Dornan. The injury to his leg enforced Harry's
temporary retirement. By the time the
Kilmarnock player was fit again, Pat
McDonald was Hogg's partner and Harry
dropped into the reserves to play in front of
Rolando Ugolini. He gave Celtic their money's
worth as a consistent and reliable servant in a
time of duress.

Appearances:
RL: 56 apps. 1 gl.
RLC: 10 apps. 0 gls.
Total: *66 apps. 1 gl.*

DOWDS, Peter

Role: Utility 1889-92; 1894-95
b. c1871
d. Johnstone, 3rd September 1895

CAREER: Broxburn Shamrock/CELTIC Feb
1889/Aston Villa May 1892/Stoke July 1893/
CELTIC 5 May 1894.

Debut v Hearts (a) 5-0 (SL) 23.8.1890
(scored once)

"To the present generation [1931] Peter Dowds
is not even a name, but to old-timers he was
the greatest-ever, at home in any and every
position, the equal of a Doyle or Kelly in

defence, of Madden on the right, Campbell on the left, Cassidy at centre..." (Willie Maley, drawing on sentiments expressed at Peter Dowds' funeral in 1895). Peter Dowds played in Celtic's very first League match (later expunged), the 1-4 defeat by Renton on

Peter Dowds

August 16th 1890. He was a left-sided player but any gap that needed to be filled Peter took it. With Peter Dowds aboard, the good ship Celtic now began to haul in the silver and landed its very first trophy, the North-Eastern Cup, 6-1 against a hard, strong Cowlairs side at Barrowfield (May 11th 1889). Dowds was centre when the first major trophy, the Glasgow Cup, was won, 4-0 against Third Lanark on Valentine's Day 1891 and right-half when it was retained against Clyde ten months later. He scored goals with "cute back-heels", overhead kicks and sheer pace. He graced the first Celtic side to lift the Scottish Cup 5-1 versus Queen's Park at Ibrox (April 9th 1892) again at centre. Celtic were now in the running for the Double but Dowds missed his train and Celtic two vital points and the Flag at Leith on April 18th 1892. The SFA then voted down professionalism and Aston Villa offered Peter top wages. Celtic were in despair and countered with a pub and thirty bob a week. English comment was scathing: "See the height to which these amateur clubs go." Almost two years to the day of his departure he was back to New Celtic Park and in the team that hanselled brand new Love St on September 8th 1894. He virtually disappeared from the side thereafter and in November it was announced he had "chest trouble." Celtic had brought home a very sick man. He played his last game versus Manchester City at Hyde Road Ardwick (December 1st 1894) in a thick fog to which the experts attributed the rapid failure of his health as consumption took its grip. Bar Jimmy McGhee, Celtic had to wait on the arrival of the young Alec McNair about ten years on for a player who might remotely match the versatility of Peter Dowds. He and

McNair stand as probably the most available men the Parkhead club has ever had. Even then, Alec never scored goals like Peter.

Appearances:
SL: 36 apps. 18 gls.
SC: 13 apps. 3 gls.
Total: *49 apps. 21 gls.*

♣ **Celtic note:** *Col John Shaughnessy remembered Peter as a tobacco-chewer during a match. He would remove the wad as he went for a high ball!*

DOWIE, John

Role: Midfield 1977-79
6' 0" 11st.7lbs.
b. Hamilton, 12th December 1955

CAREER: Calder Blantyre/Rangers 'S' form 1969/ground staff 1971/free 1972/Fulham 4 Aug 1972/CELTIC 6 Sept 1977/(Houston Hurricane loan cs 1978)/free 30 Apr 1979/Doncaster Rovers July 1979/Clyde 5 Dec 1981 /Doveton (Australia) 1982/Brunswick Juventus (Australia) 1983.

Debut v Rangers (a) 2-3 (SL) 10.9.77

John Dowie

"I was shattered when Rangers released me ... I was Rangers daft," said John Dowie on signing for Celtic. John was another of Stein's sensation signings and cost £25,000 from Fulham. He was never a Fulham regular and the nearest he came to glory at Putney was consideration for the Lilywhites' bench at the Cup final of 1975 versus West Ham. John was signed to strengthen the squad for Europe already fatally weakened by the departure of Dalglish and injury to Stanton and probably because Big Jock now found there were "a lot more £100,000 players in Scotland than I realised."

Appearances:
SL: 14 apps. 0 gls.
SLC: 3 apps. 0 gls.
SC: 1 app. 0 gls.
Total: *18 apps. 0 gls.*

DOYLE, Daniel

Role: Left-back 1891-99
5 '11" 12st.0lbs.
b. Paisley, 16th September 1864
d. Glasgow, 8th April 1918

CAREER: Rawyard Juniors/Darngavil/Slamannan Barnsmuir/Broxburn Shamrock/Hibernian 1886/Broxburn Shamrock 1887/East Stirlingshire 1887/Sunderland cs 1888/Hibernian 1 Sept 1888/(Hearts loan-one game-1888)/Newcastle East End 1888/Grimsby Town Dec 1888/Bolton Wanderers April 1889/Everton Aug 1889/CELTIC 10 Aug 1891/reinstated amateur 8 Aug 1899/President Mossend Hibs.

Debut v Hearts (a) 1-3 (SL) 15.8.1891

Everton had already nominated Dan Doyle captain for season 1891-92 when Celtic poached him for a pre-season friendly at Springburn (August 10th 1891). According to the myth Dan made no demands nor discussed terms, he was simply glad to become a Celt. In fact so seductive was the scenario painted by President Glass, Doyle burst out laughing: "Hold on, John! Don't put my name above the door until I've got the licence!" It was not his first contact with Celtic. He had played right-back in the Hibs team which hanselled the first Celtic Park against Cowlairs on May 8th 1888 with Mick McKeown as his partner. During the summer of 1890, as a registered Everton player, he

Dan Doyle

agreed to sign for both Celtic and Bolton and accepted close season wages from Parkhead, Pike's Lane and Goodison without the least compunction. According to Dan, Celtic and Bolton were both breaking the rules anyway by paying him a single penny. The glee at Parkhead that they had actually landed a star like 'Ned' (his nickname with the Celtic players) was reflected in the crowds that now began to follow the green and white. Dan Doyle was left-back in the first Celtic side to ever win the Scottish Cup (April 9th 1892). He won League Championship medals with Celtic in 1893 and 1894 and captained Scotland against England at Parkhead on April 7th 1894, the second Celt after James Kelly to lead his country out. Nobody told Doyle what to do. When Arthurlie put Celtic out of the Scottish Cup on January 1897, despite an affected reconciliation, he was on strike for more money and did not bother to turn up. He played for Scotland versus England at the Crystal Palace (April 3rd 1897) in a 1-2 win: "Lambie captained the Scottish team but Doyle bossed it." He received his club wages a year in advance by secret arrangement; he would linger in England after friendlies when he should have been at Parkhead training; even the redoubtable JH McLaughlin covered up for him as Celtic chairman. Dan chided anyone and everyone. He once demanded of the great Jimmy Kelly: "How the hell did you get your reputation with the rubbish you're playing today?" His fortunes faded after football. His Bellshill whisky business folded and he had to resort to labouring. Willie Maley visited him in the Glasgow Cancer hospital just hours before he died. Dan showed him his legs emaciated and gaunt: "Ah, well, they made a little bit of Celtic history."

Appearances:
SL: 112 apps. 4 gls.
SC: 21 apps. 2 gls.
Total: *133 apps. 6 gls.*

♣ **Celtic note:** *Grimsby Town v Stevely 12th January 1889; Dan collided with Stevely forward and Derbyshire cricketer William Cropper who was carried off and died the next day.*

DOYLE, Francis

Role: Left-half 1926-28
5' 8" 11st.0lbs.
b. Glasgow, 20th November 1901
d. 19th May 1965

CAREER: Vale of Clyde 14 Mar 1920/Fulham 18 Aug 1923/free 1926/CELTIC 23 Mar 1926/...retired Aug 1933.

Debut v Queen's Park (a) 6-1 (SL) 28.8.26

Frank Doyle

A Willie Orr discovery and "a tip-top inside-forward with Airdrie," Frank Doyle was offered the chance of joining up at Parkhead after Celtic's "blood-less surgeon" Eddie McGarvie had helped cure the cartilage trouble Frank thought had ended his career at Fulham. He had been training at Dens Park and on the point of signing for Dundee when his father offered him a share in the family outfitters' business as an inducement to stay in Glasgow. His play was "serviceable, extremely serviceable" and his moment of glory came at Fir Park in the Scottish Cup fourth round on March 3rd 1928. A raging Doyle shot ("a beauty of a goal") broke the deadlock in the 55th minute and

was greeted by at least one old-timer with a shout of "Good old Dan!" Frank was in the team at inside-left in place of the suspended Tommy McInally ("I'm not suspended, I've resigned!"). 'Snally' had walked out of Seamill during the week unable to take a practical joke by the players. Frank was essentially a reserve throughout his time at Parkhead and left in 1928 after a dispute over terms. He was idle throughout 1928-29 and took over the family shop on retirement.

Appearances: .
SL: 17 apps. 2 gls.
SC: 4 apps. 1 gl.
Total: *21 apps. 3 gls.*

DOYLE, John

Role: Winger 1976-81
5' 8" 10st.0lbs.
b. Caldercruix, 11th May 1951
d. Kilmarnock, 19th October 1981

CAREER: Viewpark BG/Viewpark FC/Ayr United 1968/CELTIC 15 Mar 1976.

Debut v Dundee (a) 1-0 (SL) 20.3.76

Johnny Doyle was fast "goes past the back on sheer speed, gets his crosses in." He also had a temper and knew the inside of the SFA offices well. He was under suspension when Celtic signed him at Glasgow airport on the way to East Germany to play Sachsenring. He became an enormous favourite with the faithful, an old-style battling Celt, "a running, tackling, up and down one-man riot." Against Arbroath on August 28th 1976 "he received the ball with his back to goal, turned, beat three men, and hammered home from the tightest angle." He was man of the match against Rangers on November 11th 1978: "Doyle has never played better in a Celtic jersey. He never stopped running, he took some stick, but he kept coming back for more." For all his perpetual motion on the park, this was a man who hated training. Celtic won the Championship against Rangers at Parkhead on 21st May 1979. They won it with ten men because in a moment of madness, 11 minutes into the second half, Johnny Doyle kicked Alec MacDonald lying prone with Rangers leading 0-1. He was stunned with remorse and could barely be persuaded to join in the celebrations at the end. Against St Mirren in the Scottish Cup 4th round replay (February 20th 1980) he was

A change of sport for John Doyle (left) and Peter Latchford.

"absolutely non-stop" and scored the winner in the first minute of extra time. On November 1st 1980 he played Rangers on his own at Ibrox but lost 3-0. To some extent his star waned with the coming of Davie Provan. Aged only 30 he was electrocuted in a domestic accident. Celtic played in Ipswich on November 3rd following his death and the fans staged a spontaneous two minutes silence for Johnny Doyle in the centre of the East Anglian town. He is buried in Grassard Road cemetery Kilmarnock. John Doyle was True Grit. "He was a wee gem" (Mary Mills).

Appearances: .
SL: 118 apps. 14 gls.
SLC: 33 apps. 14 gls.
SC: 18 apps. 7 gls.
Eur: 11 apps. 1 gl.
Total: *180 apps. 36 gls.*

DOYLE, Thomas

Role: Goalkeeper 1935-38
b. Uddingston, 30th September 1915(?)

CAREER: New Stevenston Athletic/Blantyre Celtic 1935/CELTIC 19 Nov 1935/(Arbroath loan 9 Oct 1936)/free 1938/Rochdale

1938/Stockport County 1939/free 1946.
Debut v Third Lanark (a) 2-4 (SL) 6.4.37

Joe Kennaway was hurt in the semi-final of the Cup versus Clyde at Hampden on April 3rd 1937 and did not play again until the final itself three weeks later. Motherwell man Tom Doyle, according to Willie Maley, "the most attractive junior goalie in years," took his place for the three intervening League games. In the first one he wore a black armband for Willie Kivlichan dead the day before. Tom had the distinction on October 6th 1937 of going down to Roker Park for the Cup-winners' match and keeping a clean-sheet in a 0-2 win versus Sunderland. His last game for Celtic was a defeat at Arbroath on October 9th 1937, the day Attilio Becci gave Jimmy Delaney a hint of things to come; the Parkhead maestro spent the second half in Arbroath Infirmary while X-rays probed the extent of damage done. Tom served in the Forces 1940-46 and played for "Celtic 1938" in the 1950s. He broke two ribs in the cause of charity on June 9th 1956.

Appearances:
SL: 5 apps. 0 shut-outs.
Total: *5 apps. 0 shut-outs.*

DRUMMOND, James

Role: Inside-left 1901-02
b. Bellshill, 24th April 1891

CAREER: Bellshill Athletic/CELTIC 23 May 1901/Manchester City 1 Feb 1902/Partick Thistle Oct 1903/retired 1905.

Debut v Morton (a) 2-1 (SL) 24.8.01

Sandy McMahon had a high opinion of Jimmy Drummond, a fruit of Celtic's first youth policy and signed as his prospective successor. Jimmy played first for Celtic versus Hibs in the first round of the Glasgow Exhibition Cup on August 21st 1901 (and scored). He showed "passing ability above the average" and played in the final against Rangers on September 9th when Celtic lost a trophy nowadays on display behind glass at Parkhead. Jimmy had problems with injuries throughout the autumn, managed a League game against Hearts on November 2nd but looked "painfully unfit." However when Manchester City came in for Willie McOustra, they paid "enormous prices" (£600) to take him and Jimmy Drummond south together. At City he seemed "awkward and slow" and soon dropped into the Combination side.

Appearances: .
SL: 4 apps. 1 gl.
Total: *4 apps. 1 gl.*

DUFF, Thomas

Role: Goalkeeper 1891-92
b. Ayr, 18th May 1867

CAREER: Cartvale/ Morton 25 Sep 1886/ Cowlairs 1887/CELTIC Aug 1891/Cowlairs Jan 1892/retired Mar 1895/ Northern 1895-96.

Debut v Hearts (a) 1-3 (SL) 15.8.1891

Tom Duff

Tom Duff was a "quiet and gentlemanly" player (October 1887). Sandy McMahon describes him as "a great goalie had he only put his mind to it." According to Willie Maley he was the first goalie to bring Celtic peace of mind that the position was adequately filled. Tom was in the Cowlairs team that played the inaugural match on first Celtic Park against

Hibs on May 8th 1888. Celtic coveted him from the day they beat Cowlairs 8-0 in the Scottish Cup 22nd September 1888. In spite of the score he had a great game. His goalkeeping in the North-Eastern Cup for Cowlairs against Celtic at Dalmarnock Street 18th January 1890 was "magnificent." His Celtic appearances are not many because of a terrible soaking against Dumbarton in the League 6th September 1891 leading to rheumatics. He played only two games out of the 14 immediately prior to the 0-8 disaster of Ne'erday 1892. On that day Celtic used goal nets at Parkhead for the first time and poor Tom, having presumably celebrated the New Year late if not to excess, had to retrieve the ball eleven times in a 0-8 defeat (three goals were struck off). The Celtic reaction was apoplectic and he was summarily dismissed.

Appearances:
SL: 8 apps. 3 shut-outs.
SC: 1 app. 1 shut-out.
Total: *9 apps. 4 shut-outs (44%).*

DUFFY, John G.

Role: Inside-forward 1948-54
5' 10" 10st.12lbs.
b. Dundee, 24th August 1929

CAREER: Dunkeld Amateurs/CELTIC 4 Aug 1948/St Anthony's (farmed-out)/RAF 1949/ (Arbroath loan 7 Aug 1953)/free 30 Apr 1954/Southend United 23 May 1954/ retired 1961.

Debut v East Fife (a) 1-4 (SL) 21.3.53

John Duffy "the kind that can play anywhere" came into the Celtic side at a time when form was so unbelievably bad there was a strong feeling it was immoral that they should be contesting the Coronation Cup "and against Arsenal at that ...7-1 conquerors of Hibs!" John had played everywhere for Celtic reserves bar centre-forward and goalkeeper but made no startling difference to big team form. On his debut, he lost Tully, his wing partner in 65 minutes when Charlie was crashed into the surrounds by Don Emery and taken off with a black eye and concussion. His next game was at Dundee two weeks later at inside-right to Jimmy Walsh. Celtic now lost 4-0, destroyed by the genius of Billy Steel. Hugh Nelson of Arbroath watched him at Dens Park and was impressed enough to ask Celtic to let the Red Lichties (with Bill Rennet) have him on loan. Southend played two benefits for this "grand fellow on and off the park", versus Portsmouth on April 27th 1959 and against an All-Stars XI on May 1st. It is thought that after Southend John became a school-teacher in Dundee. He may well be the John Duffy who represent-ed Celtic at Davie McLean's funeral just before Christmas 1967.

John Duffy

Appearances: .
SL: 2 apps. 0 gls.
Total: 2 apps. 0 gls.

DUFFY,
Robert McFarlane Davidson

Role: Half-back 1935-47
5' 8" 11st.0lbs.
b. Dundee, 19th April 1913

CAREER: Dundee St Joseph's 1932/Lochee Harp 1933/CELTIC 5 Oct 1935/(Dundee loan Oct 1939)/RAF 1940/(Blackpool loan 6 Feb 1941)/(Fulham loan 1941-42)/(Hamilton Academicals loan 24 April 1942)/(Rochdale loan 1942-43)/(Dundee United loan 31 May 1944)/(Newcastle United loan 1944-45)/(Leeds United loan Sept 1945)/free April 1947.

Debut v Hamilton Academicals (h) 3-3 (SL) 16.1.37

Geatons, Lyon and Paterson is one of the most famous half-back lines in the Celtic story and it was Bertie Duffy's personal misfor-tune to arrive at the club when he had little chance

Bertie Duffy

of displacing either Chic at right-half or smiling George at left. Lynch, Millar and Duffy was as good a reserve half-back line in 1938 as Crerand, McNeill and Clark twenty years later. Bertie was a left-half (Dawson, Lyon and Duffy) in the side that retained the Charity Cup 3-4 against Queen's Park on May 15th 1937. Mac Dodds put the Spiders 3-2 ahead with ten minutes to go. Willie Lyon congratulated his old team-mate on the prospect of a medal at last. McGrory equalised in 84 and Lyon himself got the winner a minute later! In December 1944, Bertie was being tipped as "a potential Scottish international." It is a high compliment surely that in 1945 Celtic had to wrangle with Newcastle and Rochdale over who held his signature (Rochdale claimed a free transfer from Parkhead) while PTI Sgt Bertie Duffy RAF was also in demand at Leeds.

Appearances:
SL: 4 apps. 0 gls.
Total: 4 apps. 0 gls.

DUNBAR, Michael

Role: Inside-left 1888-93
b. Cathcart, 30th October 1863
d. Glasgow, 6th September 1921

CAREER: Busby Linwood/Busby Cartvale 1884/(Netherlee loan 1884)/Cowlairs 2 Oct 1886/Hibernian Sep 1887/CELTIC May 1888/retired 1893/CELTIC director 13 April 1897.

Debut v Rangers Swifts (h) 5-2 (Inaugural Match) 28.5.1888

Celtic's first ever schemer was Mick Dunbar of Durham Terrace, Busby. The eldest of three brothers (he was followed by James and Tom) and the son of Martin Dunbar who worked in the calico factory, he was inside-left in the Hibs team that played the inaugural match on first Celtic Park against Cowlairs (May 8th 1888). Tall and spindly, he was teak-hard nonetheless, a real grafter who scored goals but not enough to be the compleat footballer. His goals came on "high days and bonfire nights." Maley describes him as the most affable of companions: "I remember once on a journey to England in our first year, when Mike and I were enjoying the comforts of a good bed after a tiring journey, a knock came to the door and a voice announced letters for the secretary. I, lying at the front of the bed, was too comfortable to rise and shouted I would get them when I came down to breakfast. My bedfellow, however, insisted on my rising, and when I refused, planted his feet in the small of my back and I found myself dumped on the floor to the detriment of my bones." Mick was capped for Scotland as a Cartvale against Ireland in Belfast on March 20th 1886. He became a very successful publican with two licences in the Gallowgate (72 and 429) and another at 32 Main St. He lived at 89 Armadale St and is buried at Dalbeth section 12, lair 203.

Mick Dunbar

Appearances: :
SL: 15 apps. 4 gls.
SC: 17 apps. 6 gls.
Total: *32 apps. 10 gls.*

DUNBAR, Thomas

Role: Right-back 1890-91; 1892-97
b. Busby, 18th August 1868
d. 28th April 1908

CAREER: Rutherglen 1887/Hibernian 7 Jan 1888/Busby Cartvale/CELTIC 1890/(St Mirren loan Oct 1890)/Rangers 7 Nov 1891/ CELTIC by 16 July 1892/reinstated amateur 3 Aug 1897/Busby Cartvale Feb 1898.

Debut v Rangers (a) 2-1 (SL) 2.5.1891

Tom Dunbar was Mick's wee brother and played in the last major game on Old Celtic Park on June 1st 1892 (the Charity Cup final) but not for Celtic, rather as left-back for Rangers. He then played in the very last match on the old pitch (16th July 1892) this time as a Celtic player against Clyde in aid of the Gweedore Eviction Fund. The SFA made

noises about his return to Parkhead from Ibrox at the same time as Jimmy Blessington's transfer was under investigation. Tom rates as one of Celtic's faithful reserves, a big team man only if Reynolds or Doyle was injured or there was a players' strike and he had to be fetched in (from Cathkin) to play as on November 28th 1896. He married a niece of John Glass and ran the Ritz bar at Glasgow's Charing Cross, a pub which stayed in the family for 70 years. He was capped against the Irish League in 1895. At the time of Mo Johnston's signing for Rangers, Tom's 86-year old daughter was claiming him as Rangers' first Catholic signing but the Busby man is further down that particular queue.

Appearances: :
SL: 51 apps. 3 gls.
SC: 9 apps. 1 gl.
Total: *60 apps. 4 gls.*

DUNCAN, Adam Scott Mathieson

Role: Outside-right 1919
5' 8" 11st.10lbs.
b. Dumbarton, 2nd November 1888
d. 3rd October 1975

CAREER: Dumbarton Academy/Dumbarton Oakvale/Dumbarton Corinthians/Clydebank Juniors/Shettleston Juniors/Dumbarton Nov 1905/Newcastle United Mar 1908/Rangers 13 Sept 1913/RFA Jan 1917/(CELTIC loan Jan 1919)/(Partick Thistle loan Feb 1919)/ Dumbarton 15 July 1919/Cowdenbeath 1920/ retired 1922/Hamilton Academicals secretary-manager July 1923/Cowdenbeath secretary-manager July 1925/Manchester United manager June 1932/Ipswich Town manager 12 Nov 1937/secretary summer 1955/retired May 1958.

Debut v Third Lanark (a) 3-2 (SL) 4.1.19

Rangers were just a neck in front in the League race New Year 1919 yet told Scott Duncan to please himself as to whether he helped Celtic out for two fixtures

Scott Duncan

(January 4th and 11th) as partner to Jimmy McMenemy (who had extended the invitation). Celtic won both matches and by the final whistle of the second had cut Rangers' lead to a point with a game in hand. In November 1936, as manager of Manchester United, Scott Duncan went to Dublin to sign Bohemians' centre, Benny Gaughran. Celtic beat him to it but he came away with another Irishman for Old Trafford: Johnny Carey. Scott's career in football was of prodigious length but finally he retired to Helensburgh.

Appearances:
SL: 2 apps. 0 gls.
Total: *2 apps. 0 gls.*

DUNCAN, David Millar

Role: Outside-left 1942-44
5' 8" 11st.8lbs.
b. 21st November 1921
d. 11th January 1991

CAREER: Woodside Amateurs 1935/Milton o' Balgownie 1935/ Lochgelly Albert 1938/ Wolverhampton Wanderers trial 1939/ Raith Rovers May 1939/ (Hearts loan autumn 1942)/CELTIC 17 Dec 1942/(East Fife loan

Davie Duncan

16 Aug 1943)/East Fife c 13 Nov 1944/ Raith Rovers 6 Jan 1954/free Apr 1955/Crewe Alexandra Aug 1955 /Brechin City Feb 1956/retired May 1959.

Debut v Motherwell (h) 3-2 (RL)
19.12.42 (scored once)

"He used his chances with a minimum of fuss, maximum of intent ...a terrier of a left-foot ...Celtic have found that winger" (19th December 1942). Davie Duncan, expert at penalties, free kicks and long throws, first came to Jimmy McStay's attention in the War Cup with his pile-driver shooting when Raith put Celtic out over two legs (24th February and 2nd March 1940). He was Celtic's goalscorer (he got the equaliser for 1-1) in the 8-1 disaster at Ibrox on

Ne'erday 1943. By February 20th 1943 the outside-left sensation was playing inside-right in the reserves despite the fact that "Parkhead's greatest need is for a free-running left-winger." Hugh Long took over at outside-left. After the War, both Davie Duncan and Long, Celtic rejects, were capped for Scotland, Davie three times for his fast, uncompromising displays as a left-wing raider in the very fine East Fife side of the time. He played for the Scottish League in the 1-1 draw at Newcastle on St Patrick's Day 1948 and was the first Division B player to win a full Scottish cap (versus Belgium at Hampden on April 28th 1948). He seldom failed to turn it on for Celtic either at Bayview or on his visits to Parkhead. "It made true Celts squirm that Parkhead gave him a free transfer" (13th November 1948).

Appearances:
RL: 10 apps. 3 gls.
RLC: 4 apps. 0 gls.
Total: *14 apps. 3 gls.*

DUNCAN, James B.

Role: Outside-left 1951-55
5' 9" 10st.10lbs.
b. c 1932

CAREER: King's Park Secondary/Mearns Amateurs/Strathclyde Juniors 1948/free/ Baillieston Juniors/CELTIC 22 Jan 1951/Army 2 Feb 1955/free Apr 1955 /St Mirren 22 June 1955 /Dundee United 8 Aug 1957/Albion Rovers 5 Aug 1958/free May 1959 /Dundee United 1959/ Stranraer 2 Feb 1961.

Debut v St Mirren (a) 2-1
(SL) 1.11.52 (scored once)

League games apart, smiling Jimmy Duncan ("refreshing dash and approach") had two remarkable starts near the launch of his career. He played in the farewell match (for the Mater Hospital) against Elisha Scott's

Jimmy Duncan

magnificent Belfast Celtic (May 17th 1952) and also against Peter Doherty's Doncaster Rovers (November 22nd 1952) the night Celtic played for the first time under floodlights in the UK in the 20th century. In goal for Rovers was an 18-year old Magherafelt boy, Harry Gregg. Jimmy was kept out of the Celtic big team first by Charlie Tully and Bertie Peacock and then by Neil Mochan. He had his best run during September/October 1953. He played at Ibrox on September 19th 1953 when the crowd gave a display of bottle-throwing at half-time. He was in the Celtic party to see the Magyars destroy England at Wembley (25th November 1953) and also went as the club's guest to the World Cup in Switzerland in 1954.

Appearances:
SL: 8 apps. 2 gls.
SLC: 1 app. 0 gls.
Total: 9 apps. 2 gls.

DUNCAN, William

Role: Goalkeeper 1910
5' 10" 14st.0lbs.
b. Kilsyth, 14th March 1880

CAREER: Condorrat Hearts/Strathclyde/ Airdrie 16 June 1903/(Clyde loan 1910)/ (CELTIC loan 15 Mar 1910)/St Mirren 10 Dec 1910/USA Feb 1913/reinstated amateur 13 Aug 1915/Bethlehem Steel (USA) 1915/ Boston FC (USA) trainer Oct 1924.

Debut v Third Lanark (h) 2-0 (SL) 16.3.10

Davy Adams went down with pneumonia at the end of February 1910. Celtic experimented with Jimmy Quinn's brother Phil in a couple of friendlies, then played Dick Roose in the Scottish Cup versus Clyde. Willie Duncan, "a man of ample proportions," a quarter-miler and a splendid goalie ("Brownlie's equal") was brought in from Airdrie to do service on the run-in to the sixth championship in a row. At the end of the season he returned to Broomfield but in the meantime the Waysiders had discovered Jock Ewart. Willie was now redundant and returned unsigned to his work as a sett-maker at Alnwick in Northumberland. When Davy Adams again took ill on the eve of the Glasgow Cup final versus Rangers (October 8th 1910) he was summoned to make the dash to Hampden. For all his haste Celtic lost 3-1. Willie played some fine football for St Mirren, taking his chance

when crack 'keeper Grant was down with pleurisy and reserve McBirnie had a broken leg. Tommy Muirhead met him in the USA in 1924 and Willie was home for a holiday New Year 1927.

Appearances:
SL: 9 apps. 6 shut-outs.
Total: 9 apps. 6 shut-outs (67%).

DUNN, William

Role: Centre-forward 1933-35
5' 10" 10st.4lbs.
b. Glasgow, 9th October 1910
d. Glasgow, 7th September 1980

CAREER: Ashfield/CELTIC 6 Feb 1933/Brentford 7 June 1935/Southampton May 1937/(Bo'ness loan 24 Sept 1938)/Raith Rovers 29 Sept 1938/(Dumbarton loan 2 Dec 1939)/RAF 1941.

Debut v St Johnstone (a) 1-1 (SL) 23.9.33

One of nine footballing brothers, Lambhill boy Willie Dunn was a free-scoring junior with Ashfield. He opened his senior career on a day when Jimmy McGrory was injured and played against the sensational Chile/Peru touring team at Parkhead on October 4th 1933. Celtic won but the Latins were a total novelty: no stopper, no striker, the entire emphasis on ball play and fluid team work. Willie scored plenty

Willie Dunn

for the reserves but could not get the ball in the net for the first team no matter how well he led the line. Brentford took him down to play in the English First Division but again it was with the reserves he made his mark as understudy to Dave McCulloch. Southampton were keen for him to stay in 1938 but he refused terms. He cost Raith Rovers £750 which was quite a sum of money at the time. Willie played for Rovers at inside-left in the 4-0 defeat of Celtic in Kirkcaldy on January 7th 1939 but did not score. Waterford wanted him in 1946.

Appearances:
SL: 9 apps. 2 gls.
Total: *9 apps. 2 gls.*

DUNNING, William

Role: Goalkeeper 1888
6′ 0″ 13st.0lbs.
b. Arthurlie, 2nd January 1865
d. Southampton, 4th January 1902

CAREER: Johnstone Juniors/ CELTIC 1888/Glasgow Hibernian 1889 & 1890/Bootle 1890/Aston Villa July 1892/ retired 1895.

Debut v Shettleston (h) 5-1 (SC) 1.9.1888

According to Veteran in the *Evening Times'* History of Celtic (1931) only one member of the team against Abercorn at Gilmorehill on August 1st 1888 in the World Exhibition Cup was "without a suitor" ie not being pursued by another club. This was Howwood man Willie ("cool at goal") Dunning, brought into the side in place of Mick Dolan. No reflection on Willie. It was just that everyone seemed already suited to 'keepers. He played his last game for Celtic in a North-Eastern Cup-tie (December 29th 1888) on Southcroft Park Rutherglen before being replaced by John Kelly. His fame was made with Aston Villa as a "strong, tall, daring" goalkeeper in an age when it was a dangerous calling indeed. He won a League championship medal with Villa in 1894 but retired from ill-health. He sought a warmer, drier clime in South Africa but ended his days working as a docker at Southampton. He was dead of TB just after his 37th birthday.

Appearances:
SC: 6 apps. 1 shut-out.
Total: *6 apps. 1 shut-out (17%).*

DZIEKANOWSKI, Dariusz

Role: Striker 1989-92
6′ 1″ 12st.13lbs.
b. 30th September 1962

CAREER: FSO Cars/Widzew Lodz/Legia Warsaw/CELTIC 14 July 1989/Bristol City 14 Jan 1992/Legia Warsaw autumn 1993/ contract cancelled winter 1994/FC Yverdon Sports (Switzerland) trial spring 1994/ FC Cologne summer 1994.

Debut v Hearts (a) 3-1 (SL) 12.8.89

Willie Dunning

"He was unpredictable, sometimes greedy ... but for sheer natural talent, no player had made such an impact since Charlie Nicholas in his youth. I was awestruck by him" (Paul Elliott). Big Jacki, "the George Best of Poland," "the Playboy of the Eastern World," hit Parkhead with the impact of a Tully. "His ball control is phenomenal, he's strong, he's desperate to do well for the club ...He's a natural entertainer." (Roy Aitken August 3rd 1989). "He had a contempt for the mundane" (Graham Spiers). Against Moscow Dinamo on August 5th 1989, "he pirouetted, levitated and lashed a volley high into the net to the delighted apoplexy of the spectators." "Every time Dziekanowski got the ball there was a roar from the Jungle" (August 22nd 1989). He hit four goals against Partizan Belgrade in the Cup-Winners' Cup on September 27th 1989 but the rest was anti-climax. When he scored against Motherwell on January 30th 1991 it was his first goal since September 8th. His pattern was a good first half-year, then disillusionment, then loss of form. His disciplinary record as a Legia player and a Polish international was hardly golden but according to Billy McNeill "the player has been rebelling because of what he considers injustice." "To Dziekanowski, a quiet night in was a prospect of intolerable anguish. He homed in on the strobe lights. He hit the town. He hit the high spots." McNeill was prepared to make allowances but not Liam Brady. Brady played him just the once, as substitute for Joe Miller with 12 minutes to go at Fir Park on October 8th 1991. Ex-Celt Jimmy Lumsden

("It cheers me up just watching his natural ability") paid £250,000 to take him to Bristol City. Jacki started brightly, his "bewildering close control dragging Leicester all over the place until Desmond Lynam was beside himself in homage" (January 25th 1992). The six-months syndrome struck again and by August Jacki was talking transfers: City lacked ambition enough for Disco King. As a Celtic player he was capped eleven times for Poland.

Appearances:
SL: 48 apps. 10 gls.
SLC: 9 apps. 7 gls.
SC: 7 apps. 1 gl.
Eur: 2 apps. 4 gls.
Total: *66 apps. 22 gls.*

Dariusz 'Jacki' Dziekanowski

EDVALDSSON, Johannes

Role: Utility 1975-80
6' 3" 14st.4lbs.
b. Reykjavik, Iceland, 3rd September 1950

CAREER: Valur Reykjavic/Capetown City 1972/Valur Reykjavic 1972/Metz (France)/ Holbek (Denmark) 1974/CELTIC 8 Aug 1975/ Tulsa Roughnecks 2 Feb 1980/FC Hannover 96 1981/Motherwell 21 Aug 1982/free Mar 1984/ Throttur (Iceland) coach 1984.
Debut v Aberdeen (h) 1-0 (SLC) 9.8.75

In June 1975 Jock Stein began to hint about an international centre-half, a big continental, who might be on his way to freshen up the Celtic. Jock had his car crash on July 5th but Shuggie tried out for Sean Fallon on the Irish tour at the end of the month. He was still a trialist when he scored the only goal of the game that beat Derby County at Parkhead (August

Johannes Edvaldsson

2nd 1975). On October 6th during the League Cup semi-final against Partick Thistle, he received the ultimate accolade: the Celtic fans chanting his name at Hampden. He would play wherever he was asked without demur. He was almighty in the Double side of 1977 and a big reason why Celtic thought they could do well again in Europe. In August 1978 he and Roddie MacDonald were being hailed as "one of the best centre-back pairings in Britain" but at other times their lack of pace was painful as against Archibald and Harper of Aberdeen. 'Shuggie' always kept something special in reserve for an Old Firm match. He came on as substitute on October 27th 1979: "One look at Edvaldsson and Rangers' defence got edgy." If there is the remotest sense in which he did not fulfil his potential at Celtic Park, it must surely be down to his greatest asset - his versatility. Shuggie was so adaptable that ultimately there was no one position he ever retained for long and which he could call his own. Jock Wallace was patently glad to get him. He signed him on the pitch at Fir Park. As a Celtic player Shuggie was capped 16 times for Iceland.

Appearances:
SL: 127 apps. 24 gls.
SLC: 35 apps. 8 gls.
SC: 13 apps. 0 gls.
Eur: 13 apps. 4 gls.
Total: *188 apps. 36 gls.*

ELLIOT, David

Role: Left Midfield 1987-91
5' 9" 11st.0lbs.
b. Glasgow, 13th November 1969

CAREER: Celtic BC/CELTIC 13 May 1987/ Partick Thistle 30 July 1990/St Mirren 7 June 1991.

Debut v Hamilton Academicals (h) 2-0 (SL) 7.1.89 (sub)

"Wing wizard" Davie Elliot, "the fastest player in Scottish football" (1991) was in the Celtic side that won the BP Youth Cup in 1987. Partick Thistle paid £75,000 for him then transferred him and Chic Charnley together for George Shaw, Mark McWalter and

Davie Elliot

£250,000. With Thistle he was a roaring success in Division One but found his game harder to master in the Premier League. Falkirk wanted him but Jimmy Bone demanded £250,000. "He's a natural winger and a player I would have loved to bring to Brockville" (Jim Jeffries 25th October 1994).

Appearances:
SL: 6 apps. 0 gls.
Total: *6 apps. 0 gls.*

ELLIOTT, George Washington

George Elliott

Role: Centre-forward 1918
5' 9" 11st.8lbs.
b. Sunderland, 7th January 1889
d. Middlesbrough, 27th November 1948

CAREER: Redcar Crusaders/ South Bank/Middlesbrough 3 May 1909/ (Bradford City & Fulham loan during WW1)/ (Bradford Park Avenue loan 17 Mar 1917)/ (CELTIC loan 19 Oct 1918)/retired May 1925.

Debut v Rangers (h) 0-3 (SL) 19.10.18

Middlesbrough came to Parkhead on March 21st 1914 and beat a depleted Celtic 1-3, the day Jimmy McColl went home from the match to find his mother Bridget dead aged 38. George Elliott, England international centre, scored the third goal to clinch the match. His next appearance at Celtic Park four and a half years later was not so fortunate: Celtic were awarded a penalty when two down. George was assigned to take it. Johnny Hempsey saved. Until Wilf Mannion (whom Celtic tried to sign) and George Hardwick he was the greatest player Middlesbrough had ever had. By October 7th 1922, he was leading scorer in the English First Division on 10 goals and rumoured to be coming back to Celtic in exchange for Jock Gilchrist. George was a Cargo Superintendent at Middlesbrough Docks both during his playing career and after.

Appearances:
SL: 1 app. 0 gls.
Total: *1 app. 0 gls.*

ELLIOTT, Paul Marcellus

Role: Centre-half 1989-91
6' 2" 14st.1lb.
b. Lewisham, 18th March 1964

CAREER: Woodhill Primary/Blackheath
Bluecoat School/Charlton Athletic 1 July 1980
/Luton Town 9 Mar 1983/Aston Villa 2 Dec
1985/Pisa July 1987/CELTIC 3 July 1989/
Chelsea 8 July 1991/retired May 1994.
Debut v Motherwell (h) 1-1 (SL) 23.9.89

Paul Elliott first played at Celtic Park with
Aston Villa on August 2nd 1986. While he was
in Italy, Brian Glanville of the *Sunday Times*
commended him as the best centre-half
England had. Billy McNeill bought him as
replacement for Mick McCarthy and Paul

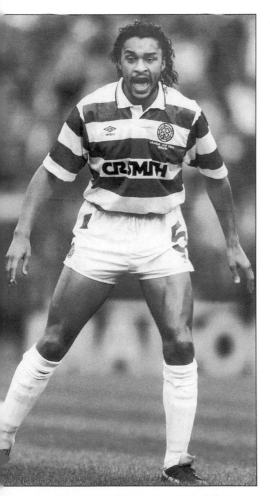

Paul Elliott

made it sound as he was coming to Celtic for
little or no pay: "I've made a reasonable
amount of money out here but my next move
has to be with medals in mind rather than
cash." With injuries and poor form he did not
start well but hit his game on Sunday 25th
February 1990 when Celtic put Rangers out of
the Scottish Cup in the fourth round at
Parkhead. From that moment on the Jungle
loved this "big, ruthless type of player...a
driver-on." On St Patrick's Day 1991 in the
Scottish Cup quarter-final, he took a ball full
in the face from Iain Ferguson, spat out blood,
changed his jersey and carried on. Celtic fans
deluged Bobby Robson with letters recom-
mending an England cap despite the fact that
Paul was embroiled with the club in a breach
of contract action for £158,000 that caused him
to ask for a transfer (December 19th 1990) and
was eventually settled out of court (April 29th
1991). He was nominated Scottish Players'
Player of the Year on May 18th 1991 and
captained England 'B' versus Switzerland two
days later. He left Celtic to return to London
and £4,000 a week. "Billy McNeill said the
club would break the bank to keep me but I
said it did not matter. I had been away from
my family too long." At the end of Packy
Bonner's benefit on May 12th 1991 and chants
of "Paul Elliott Must Stay!" the Jungle invaded
the pitch to hoist him aloft in a last effort to
make him think again. In vain. Paul was off to
Chelsea, where he played his last game of
football on 5th September 1992 as the result of
a cruciate ligament injury to his right knee
sustained in a clash with Dean Saunders at
Anfield. Paul took action against Saunders in
the High Court in London on 23rd May 1994.
His disciplinary record at Celtic was brought
into play against him: 14 bookings in 1989-90.
Paul countered with a mere five in 45 matches
in 1990-91. More however, rested on proving
intent and the case was lost on 10th June and
Paul faced costs of £500,000.

Appearances: .
SL: 52 apps. 2 gls.
SLC: 5 apps. 3 gls.
SC: 8 apps. 0 gls.
Eur: 1 app. 0 gls.
Total: *66 apps. 5 gls.*

EVANS, Robert

Role: Right-half, Centre-half 1944-60
5' 8" 12st.0lbs.
b. Glasgow, 16th July 1927

CAREER: Sir John Maxwell's Primary/BB/
Maxwell Thistle/Thornliebank Methodist/
St Anthony's 24 Jan 1944/CELTIC 23 July 1944
/Chelsea 20 May 1960/Newport County
player-manager 23 May 1961/
dismissed as manager 21 Mar 1962/player
contract cancelled 19 July 1962/Morton
23 July 1962/Third Lanark player-coach
12 June 1963/dismissed 28 May 1964/
recalled as player-manager 22 June 1964/
dismissed 1 June 1965/Raith Rovers
14 Aug 1965/retired 14 Dec 1967.

Debut v Albion Rovers (a) 1-0 (RL) 19.8.44

"Evans was willing to graft until he dropped...
Evans throws everything he has into a match...
where the ball was, there was the red head of
Evans... it was Evans made the match memo-
rable... Best half-back display seen in years."
Bobby Evans was "a team in himself" with
energy, spirit and stamina rivalled only by
Harry Mooney of Third Lanark. He did twice

Bobby Evans in action.

the work of any one else on the park yet until
1951, bar caps for Scotland, his efforts and
enthusiasm bore next to no reward in a poor
Celtic side. ("It must be shattering to put so
much into a game and get nothing out of it").
Bobby played in attack until the famous relegation battle versus Dundee at Dens Park on
April 17th 1948. When manager McGrory
asked him to
persevere at right-half for 1948-49, Bobby
flared-up: "You'll put me out of the game!"
Instead the switch put him into the Scottish
team against Wales on October 23rd 1948 and
also into the sides that won so gloriously at
Wembley on April 9th 1949 (1-3) and April
14th 1951 (2-3). He had a magnificent
Coronation Cup tourney in 1953 and the
match of his life against Lawrie Reilly of Hibs
in the final (20th May 1953). He was virtually
an ever-present in the Double season of
1953-54 and was the first Celtic captain to raise
the League Cup over his head for the fans to
see (Hallowe'en 1956). He became captain of
Scotland on June 15th 1958 during the World
Cup in Sweden against France and led his
men out at Wembley on April 11th 1959. Jock
Stein's ankle problem had seen Bobby move to
centre-half in imitation of Billy Wright at
Wolves. The great galloper now became a class
defender, so polished that some Celtic fans
wondered how the gangly McNeill, "tall, pale

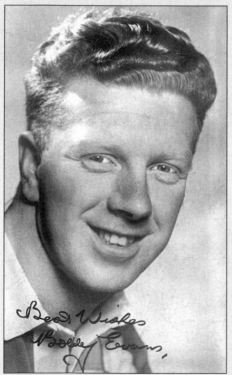

and all legs," good as he was, could ever possibly replace him. Scotland lost 0-4 versus England on April 19th 1958. But for Younger in goal and Evans at centre-half it might have been a disaster on a par with some of the Wartime massacres. Near the end of his international career (6th May 1959) his Scotland team beat West Germany 3-2. It was Ginger Evans versus the great Uwe Seeler that night at Hampden and Bobby gave one of his finest ever performances. Bobby Evans is an all-time Celtic great. He is the most-capped Celt (48 for Scotland,

25 for the Scottish League) after McGrain and McStay. Middle-aged men of 1994 deem it an inestimable privilege to have seen him play.

Appearances:
SL: 384 apps. 9 gls.
SLC: 87 apps. 1 gl.
SC: 64 apps. 0 gls.
Total:
535 apps. 10 gls.
RL: 13 apps. 0 gls.
SLC: 1 app. 1 gl.
Total: *14 apps. 1 gl.*

♣ **Celtic note:** *Bobby's distinctive mark (and Joe Baillie's) was the hoops worn outside his shorts. He adopted this Queen's Park style on tour in the US 1951 to be cooler in the heat.*

Bobby Evans (left) and Billy Wright lead out their teams for the Scotland-England clash in 1959.

FAGAN, William

Role: Inside-forward
1934-37
5' 11" 11st.7lbs.
*b. Musselburgh,
20th February 1917
d. Wellingborough,
29th February 1992*

CAREER: Balgonia
Scotia/Wellesley
Juniors Mar 1934/

Willie Fagan

CELTIC 8 June 1934/
Preston NE 14 Oct 1936/ Liverpool 23 Oct
1937/RAF 1939/(Aldershot loan 1939-40)/
(CELTIC loan Jan 1942)/(Chelsea loan 28 Aug
1943)/(Northampton Town loan 1942-43)/
(Reading loan 1944-45)/(Crystal Palace loan
1945-46)/Distillery player-manager 4 Jan
1952/Weymouth player-manager July 1952/
retired 1955.

Debut v Dunfermline Athletic (a) 3-1 (SL) 16.3.35

Auburn-haired Willie Fagan dripped
class like his uncle Jean McFarlane:
"He has a glorious habit of merely
flicking the ball, invariably finding
his man, when surrounded by two or
three opponents." Tommy Muirhead
took Willie to Preston to join the
O'Donnells for £3,500 the kind of
money which would have bought a
row of new houses going up in
Clarkston at the time. Liverpool
(George Kay) paid £8,000 for him a
year later after he had played (and
lost) at Wembley in the 1937 Cup final
(May 1st) under the gaze of his old
Celtic team-mates newly beaten 8-0
by Motherwell with Frank O'Donnell
at centre and Hugh O'Donnell his
wing partner on the left. Willie Fagan
was booked to guest for Celtic versus Rangers
on September 6th 1941. Liverpool had given
their consent but Scottish League
secretary McAndrew banned the loan. Willie
did manage to turn out over Ne'erday 1942.
He has the distinction of playing in a War-time
League South Cup final at Wembley (April
15th 1944) when Chelsea and Charlton were
introduced to Eisenhower who was just weeks
away from giving the go-ahead for D-Day.
Charlton won 3-1, same score as Sunderland
over Preston in 1937. Willie refused to leave
Anfield for Bradford Park Avenue as Len

Shackleton's replacement when Shack moved
to Newcastle in 1946. Instead, he was a key
man in the Liverpool side that won the League
in 1947. Willie returned to Wembley with
Liverpool on 29th April 1950 but again, no
luck. Arsenal won 2-0. After football he
worked for HM Prisons.

Appearances:
SL: 12 apps. 9 gls.
Total: *12 apps. 9 gls.*
RL: 2 apps. 1 gl.
Total: *2 apps. 1 gl.*

FALCONER, John Stevenson

Role: Goalkeeper 1931-33
5' 10" 11st.0lbs.
b. Govan, 14th November 1898

CAREER: Plantation Hearts/Ibrox Waverley/
Gower Thistle/St Anthony's 1919/
Cowdenbeath 13 June 1921/free 26 Dec 1930/
CELTIC 15 Aug 1931/free 1933/East Stirling
trial 5 Aug 1933/free 30 Apr 1934/Creetown
1934/Stranraer Nov
1935/retired Feb 1936
/Hull City scout.

*Debut v Queen's Park
(h) 2-2 (SL) 12.9.31*

Johnny Falconer

Celtic had coveted
Kinning Park boy and
Rangers fan Falconer
since the summer of
1922 when he had
done some great
goalkeeping for the
Parkhead five-a-side
teams. He saved a
Dixie Dean penalty
with the Scottish
League versus the
English at Ibrox on
March 10th 1928 but a
split kneecap against Hearts (October 13th
1928) at Tynecastle put him out of the game
until March 1930. Celtic signed him much as
heir apparent to pave the way for John
Thomson's big money transfer. His reviews
were mixed in the weeks that followed
Thomson's fatal accident of September 5th
1931, either "brilliant" or "did not give full
satisfaction" and there was a move to bring
Peter Shevlin home from Shelbourne. Johnny's
new silver kneecap was not up to the

demands of the first-class game but he made a capable deputy to Joe Kennaway. Malky MacDonald pays tribute to him as a trainer, willing to put in long hours to bring young players back to fitness after injury. He was always massively popular with the fans for his courage as witness the rolling applause when he was led off at East End Park with a torn shoulder muscle when with East Stirling on Hogmanay 1933.

Appearances:
SL: 7 apps. 2 shut-outs.
SC: 1 app. 0 shut-outs.
Total: *8 apps. 2 shut-outs (25%).*

Willie Falconer

FALCONER, William

Role: Utility 1994 to date
6' 1" 12st.10lbs.
b. Aberdeen, 5th April 1966

CAREER: Lewis United/Aberdeen 9 Apr 1982/Watford 17 June 1988/Middlesbrough 16 Aug 1991/Sheffield United 10 Aug 1993/ CELTIC 9 Feb 1994.

Debut v Hearts (a) 2-0 (SL) 12.2.94

Willie Falconer was Lou Macari's fourth Celtic signing after Biggins, Muggleton and Martin: "Obviously I don't expect Willie to set the world on fire but he represents a step in the right direction. We are so short of players." Willie made his debut at Tynecastle when Celtic won their first points of 1994. According to press reports, it was the discovery by Kevin Kelly that the Bank of Scotland was refusing to meet the first instalment of Falconer's £350,000 transfer fee from Bramall Lane that prompted the Celtic chairman to demand the resignations of co-directors David Smith and Chris White and invoke at last the aid to the club of Fergus McCann and Brian Dempsey. Played up front, Willie got his first goal in eight starts against Dundee United at Tannadice in the 1-3 Premier League win of March 2nd 1994. He made his Old Firm debut in the Ibrox lock-out match on April 30th 1994. Along with the other Celtic freshmen, Lee Martin and Barry Smith, big Willie was booked but played his part in a fine team performance for the 1-1 draw. Willie scored a fine third goal for Celtic against Manchester United in Mark Hughes' testimonial on May 16th 1994 with some dazzling footwork that totally baffled the Reds' defence 16 minutes from time.

Appearances:
SL: 14 apps. 1 gl.
Total: *14 apps. 1 gl.*

FALLON, John

Role: Goalkeeper 1958-72
5' 11" 12st.3lbs.
b. Blantyre, 16th August 1940

CAREER: CELTIC 11 Dec 1958/Fauldhouse United (farmed-out) 1958/Motherwell 29 Feb

1972/free Apr 1972/Morton 15 Aug 1972/
retired 12 Oct 1972/Blantyre Celtic coach 1975
/resigned 19 Aug 1976/Blantyre Celtic coach
again Jan 1977.

Debut v Clyde (h) 1-1 (SL) 26.9.59

"There have been few more likeable or human
characters at Celtic Park than John Fallon"
(David Potter). John was the first breakthrough to the big team of Jock Stein's
coaching school and was a signed Celt before
he even had a junior club. He was all Celtic,
agony and ecstasy, unable to act cool,
indifferent and "professional" and was even
admonished by the Greenock police for
gestures of delight to the Celtic support
(March 7th 1964). He first lost his place to
Ronnie Simpson versus Barcelona on
November 18th 1964 but was restored to the
first team on 16th January 1965. He produced
two wonder saves in the Scottish Cup final of
April 24th versus Dunfermline; one from Alex
Edwards at 2-2 in the 60th minute and the
other at full length from John McLaughlin
twelve minutes later. At the final whistle he
swung from the crossbar in ecstasy. Ronnie
Simpson became Stein's first-choice 'keeper on
September 25th 1965 but John
was first to tear onto the field to
embrace his Celtic pals as the
great European journey ended
in Lisbon on May 25th 1967. On
his best days he was a miracle
'keeper and had the papers
crying out for Scotland to cap
him: "Have you ever seen a
'keeper pick them out of the air
the way he did?" (versus
Manchester City August 4th
1970). Against Real for Di
Stefano's benefit in Madrid
(June 7th 1967) he displayed
class that was preternatural. He
had his nightmares, as against
Rangers on January 2nd 1968
when he seemed to gift both
goals. He redeemed all with
two shut-outs; a blinding
performance in a blizzard at the
San Siro versus AC Milan in the
European Cup (February 19th
1968); and in the Scottish Cup
final of April 26th 1969 as
Rangers launched "one massive
attack after another", Fallon
refused to yield. He saved

point-blank from Persson on the quarter-hour
and went full-length to Ferguson's feet in the
33rd minute immediately after saving from
Greig. At the end, the Celtic players presented
him to the fans and John made a formal bow.
Like many professionals of his generation,
John Fallon saw little harm in a cigarette. In
the preparation for the Fiorentina match on
March 17th 1970, Big Jock put him and Evan
Williams through a practice bout described by
one observer as "murderous." As John toiled
and strained and the shots rained in, the
abstemious Stein encouraged him from the
heart: "That'll teach ye no' to smoke before
trainin'!" In the League Cup final versus
St Johnstone on October 25th 1969, with Celtic
leading 1-0, he had two outstanding saves
right at the end, the second, from Benny
Rooney, quite enormous and it won Celtic the
Cup.

Appearances:
SL: 114 apps. 32 shut-outs.
SLC: 36 apps. 13 shut-outs.
SC: 14 apps. 6 shut-outs.
Eur: 20 apps. 10 shut-outs.
Total: *184 apps. 61 shut-outs (33%).*

John Fallon

FALLON, Sean

Role: Full-back, Centre-forward 1950-58
5' 8" 12st.6lbs.
b. Sligo, 31st July 1922

CAREER: Sligo St Mary's Juniors 1944/
Craobh Ruadh GAA/Coolers GAA/Longford
Town Aug 1946/McArthur's FC cs 1947/Sligo
Distillery cs 1947/Sligo Rovers (from
Longford) Aug 1948/Glenavon 11 Aug 1949/
CELTIC 21 Mar 1950/retired 2 Aug 1958/
coach 27 Nov 1959/first team coach 1961/
assistant-to-the-manager 20 Aug 1962/asst.
manager 31 Jan 1965/acting-manager July
1975/Chief Scout 3 June 1976/left CELTIC
28 May 1978/Dumbarton asst. manager
16 Sept 1978/director 6 Dec 1978/team
manager 11 Apr 1980/resigned 30 Apr 1981/
unpaid director 3 Feb 1982/Clyde director
1986.

Debut v Clyde (a) 2-2 (SL) 15.4.50

Willie Maley watched two-goal Sean Fallon at
centre lead the fight-back in the St Mungo Cup
final on August 1st 1951: "He was out of
position but has the same never-say-die spirit
as Jimmy Quinn." Sean: "I was just an
ordinary player with only a big heart and a
fighting spirit to recommend me." Sean Fallon
scored an own goal on his debut but played
right-back for Celtic in the Scottish Cup final
(April 21st 1951). "As I walked off Hampden
Park I felt I had got everything out of life I had
ever wanted. I had become a member of the
famous Celtic FC and holder of a Scottish Cup
badge all in one year." Not for nothing was he
known as the Iron Man. Sean's goal-line
clearances were often miraculous: "How
Fallon kept upright after heading out from
Stables at 1-0 was astonishing" (Celtic 5,
Dundee 0; 13th December 1952). Against
Aberdeen in the final of April 24th 1954,
"rugged as his native Sligo shore," he led the
attack and thundered through with 27 minutes
to go. For Sean nothing was hopeless. *The
Evening Times* reported Preston versus West
Bromwich Albion at Wembley on May 1st 1954
under the headline: "Oh for a Fallon to waken
up this Wembley final!". With Eire he won
eight caps, five at full-back and three as No 9.
As centre he went against the French "like a
battering-ram" at Dalymount (November 16th
1952) and scored in 20 minutes. Celtic
rewarded his whole-hearted endeavour with

the captaincy on December 13th 1952 but
Sean's left arm was chronically susceptible to
cracks and breaks and he had to surrender the
skipper's role most of the time to his chosen
deputy Jock Stein. A broken collarbone against
Hearts on October 24th 1953 kept him out
much of the 1953-54 Double Season. He went
off in the 65th minute then returned with his
arm in a sling to play out the match at outside-
left; "It wasn't as if it was a broken leg!" He
made his comeback as centre on St. Patrick's
Day to try to solve Celtic's goal crisis in a 0-6
win at Airdrie. A knee injury ended his career.
He was helped off during the pre-season trial
of 1958 just 10 months after a team starting
Beattie, Donnelly and Fallon had triumphed
7-1 over Rangers at Hampden. Thereafter he
rendered service of a value as incalculable as
Steve Callaghan's in the 20s and 30s in terms
of the men he signed like Gemmell, Macari,
Hay, Connelly, McGrain, Dalglish, Bonner
with an adventure, large or small, attached to
each. He was on holiday in 1976 when the
dramas unfolded at Parkhead and went
unconsulted on his demotion to (Accelerated)
Youth Development Officer. He enjoyed a new
lease of life with Dumbarton and in December
1980 was negotiating with Johann Cruyff to
come to Boghead for £2,000 a week. It was a
brave try but the Dutchman opted for New
York Cosmos instead. Sean's epitaph? "I can
never hope to find words to express my
feelings at becoming a member of the Celtic
Football Club." The support offered him a
Testimonial Dinner in gratitude at the Forte
Crest Hotel in Glasgow on October 31st 1993.
Bertie Peacock paid tribute to the Iron man
and George Young was among the guests.

Appearances:
SL: 177 apps. 8 gls.
SLC: 46 apps. 4 gls.
SC: 31 apps. 2 gls.
Total: *254 apps. 14 gls.*

♣ **Celtic note 1:** *Sean was the one Celt to speak
out like a Cassandra amid the euphoria of April
1970: "Feyenoord are a first-class team in every
way. We didn't spot a single weakness" (April 27th
1970).*
♣ **Celtic note 2:** *Sean won the Henry Cup for
long distance swimming in Sligo on August 24th
1947. He "overcame stiff opposition."*

Sean Fallon

FARRELL, Patrick

Role: Half-back 1896-97
5' 9" 11st.4lbs.

CAREER: Ligoneil FC/
Belfast Celtic 1894/
Distillery 1895/CELTIC 1
Aug 1896/Arsenal 4 May
1897/Brighton United cs
1898/Distillery Aug 1900
/Brighton & Hove Albion
31 July 1901 until 1904.

Pat Farrell

Debut v Arthurlie (a) 2-4 (SC) 9.1.1897

The "merely useful" Pat Farrell (with a 1896
Cup winners' medal from Distillery) was
pulled into the Celtic first team to make up
numbers on the fateful day at Barrhead when
they went crashing out of the Scottish Cup in
the first round, a result as shocking as Berwick
Rangers 1, Glasgow Rangers 0 sixty years on.
Celtic's stars were on strike and they started
with seven men. Arthurlie had narrowed the
pitch and sent their lads out to get "stuck-in".
The best period of Pat's career was during his
second spell at Distillery when he was capped
versus Scotland and Wales in 1901. He was
also much appreciated at Brighton where he
was famed not just as a footballer but as the
man to have your money on when it came to
challenge races at the sprints.

Appearances:
SC: 1 app. 0 gls.
Total: *1 app. 0 gls.*

Neil Ferguson

FERGUSON, Cornelius

Role: Left-half, left-back
1940
5' 7" 10st.7lbs.
*b. Carronshore,
3rd July 1920*

CAREER: Grange
Rovers/Alloa 14 July
1938/(CELTIC loan
8 Aug 1940)/RAF 1941/Alloa again 26 June
1946/free own request 6 Feb 1948.

*Debut v Hamilton Academicals (h) 2-2 (RL)
10.8.40*

"I have never seen a wing-half coming out so
often with the ball after a tackle than Neilly

Ferguson." New manager Willie McStay
borrowed Neil Ferguson from his old club
Alloa for the first two games of 1940-41. It was
a distracting time to be playing football.
August 13 was Adler Tag (Eagle Day), when
Goering unleashed the Luftwaffe to bomb
British airfields. Neil, who played football in
the Forces in the same unit as Tommy Walker,
resumed his career with Alloa but retired to
concentrate on his business as a grate-builder.
He was reported in the Southern General
troubled with the arteries in his leg February
1952 while Alloa supporters went all out to
raise funds in his benefit.

Appearances:
RL: 2 apps. 0 gls.
Total: *2 apps. 0 gls.*

FERGUSON, George

Role: Full-back 1945-48
5' 8" 11st.4lbs.

CAREER: St Anthony's
1944/CELTIC 9 Mar
1945/Dumbarton 31
Aug 1948.

George Ferguson

Debut v Partick Thistle (h) 3-0 (RL) 7.4.45

George Ferguson was left-back in the very first
team picked by Jimmy McGrory. He made his
Old Firm debut on September 8th 1945 at
Ibrox and with the score 2-2 fluffed a clearance
and let the deadly Venters in to beat Miller
from 20 yards. He kept his place the following
week in the side that gave McGrory his first
win as Celtic manager 2-0 against Hamilton.
Thereafter George was mainly a Celtic reserve.
He was one of the "revolutionary changes" in
the team of January 10th 1948 "but seldom
kicked true or with reasonable length even
from open position." He was on the retained
list for 1948-49 but before August was out was
on his way to Dumbarton to join Celtic old
Bhoys Lynch, Cantwell and Donegan. George
was left-back in the Sons' team that lifted the
Festival of Britain Quaich at Firhill 3-0 versus
Ayr United (6th August 1951), Dumbarton's
solitary prize won in the 'fifties.

Appearances:
SL: 5 apps. 0 gls.
Total: *5 apps. 0 gls.*
RL: 6 apps. 0 gls.
Total: *6 apps. 0 gls.*

FERGUSON, John

Role: Centre forward 1895

CAREER: Jordanhill Juniors 1894/CELTIC (trial) Mar 1895/Blackburn Rovers Apr 1895/Hibernian 14 Aug 1895 /Third Lanark 13 Mar 1896/Partick Thistle 17 Oct 1896 until 1899.

Debut v Leith Athletic 6-5 (SL) 30.3.1895 (scored once)

John Ferguson scored all four goals for Junior Scotland versus Ireland in Belfast on February 9th 1895 and played his one and only game for Celtic as a stand-in for the injured Johnny Madden. At half-time the score stood 4-4. Divers scored for Celtic in the second half and with three minutes to go John Ferguson made it 4-6 after Boyd of Leith had been sent off. Leith drew back to 5-6 in the last minute so it was hardly a game the young trialist could forget. He played in a friendly at St Mirren (April 20th 1895) and scored again. He then joined Hibs and was centre in the side that beat Celtic 4-2 at Easter Road on August 24th 1895 when the resurrected Hibernian unfurled their Division Two Championship flag at half-time.

Appearances:
SL: *1 app. 1 gl.*
Total: *1 app. 1 gl.*

FERNIE, William

Role: Inside-forward 1948-58; 1960-61
5' 9" 10st.10lbs.
b. Kinglassie, Fife, 22nd November 1928

CAREER: BB/Aberdeen & Raith Rovers (trial) 1945/Leslie Hearts/CELTIC 12 Oct 1948/ Kinglassie Colliery (farmed-out)/ Middlesbrough 1 Dec 1958/CELTIC 6 Oct 1960 /St Mirren 24 Nov 1961/free 1 May 1963/ Partick Thistle (trial) 19 Aug 1963/Alloa 16 Sept 1963/free 19 Oct 1963/Fraserburgh Dec 1963/Coleraine (Bertie Peacock) 30 Jan 1964/Bangor (Charlie Tully) by Nov 1964/ retired 1965/CELTIC coach 18 June 1967/ Kilmarnock manager 9 Oct 1973/dismissed 20 Oct 1977.

Debut v St Mirren (a) 1-0 (SL) 18.3.50

"Willie, you're inclined to hold the ball too long. Even so, I think you'll play for Scotland" (Celtic trainer Jimmy Gribben) "The fastest inside-forward I've seen all season is Willie Fernie... both on and off the ball he outstrips most defenders" (Bobby Evans January 1953). "The crowd howled for Fernie's magic and Tully let him take over on the wing" (November 10th 1956). Willie Fernie variously described as "the Wizard of the Weave" and "Scotland's Stanley Matthews" was a "nagging tooth" of an attacker always ready to run at the defence and made an impression as a destroyer that never left Jock Stein. He could

Willie Fernie

have gone anywhere but Celtic scout Pat Duffy was the one football figure to visit him in hospital after a broken jaw at Easter Road with Leslie Hearts in June 1948 and Willie signed for Celtic. He was an elegant long-striding inside-forward who lent the Celtic strip the dignity of evening dress. It was one of his deep devastating runs that set up Sean Fallon's winning goal in the Scottish final of April 24th 1954 versus Aberdeen. In an almighty game at Easter Road on December 29th 1956, Eric Smith made it 2-2 in the 72nd

FERGUSON, William

Role: Outside-left 1895-97

CAREER: Jordanhill Juniors 1893/Maryhill Juniors 1894 /CELTIC 16 Mar 1895/ Burnley 20 Feb 1897/ Manchester City Nov 1899.

Debut v Rangers (a) 1-1 (SL) 23.3.1895

Willie Ferguson, "The Bag o' Tricks," of 11, Temple Place, Maryhill was "a little black-headed man, of ludicrous appearance, ungainly gait, but could play..." He became Celtic's regular outside-left at the time of the 11-0 rout of Dundee (depleted) on October 26th 1895 and linked-up with Sandy McMahon as effectively as Johnny Campbell

before him. In a famous Glasgow Cup semi-final on an Ibrox quagmire (November 16th 1895), Celtic went in at half-time 3-1 down against Queen's Park until Ferguson took over in the second half as "the star of the front rank, the coolest man of the 25,000 present." The 4-2 defeat in the Scottish Cup at Arthurlie (January 9th 1897) sounded his knell at Parkhead. He told a fellow Maryhill man: "Leaving Celtic is like leaving home." He was suspended at Burnley October 1899 "for failing to observe training instructions." Willie was in another kind of training at Cromarty Camp May 1916 preparing to go to France with his battalion.

Appearances:
SL: 25 apps. 11 gls.
SC: 2 apps. 1 gl.
Total: *27 apps. 12 gls.*

---

minute. From the kick-off Fernie dribbled right into the Edinburgh penalty box like an all-elegance Patsy Gallagher and set Neilly Mochan up to score Celtic's third. Patsy was an eel, Willie went past players straight-backed with a wiggle of his hips. He came in for the injured Tully at outside-left in the Coronation Cup final at Hampden versus Hibs on May 20th 1953 and added a second medal to his Charity Cup badge won also at Hampden 11 days before. He was inside man to Bobby Collins then John Higgins in the Double side of 1954 and on April 18th 1953, had been travelling reserve with Scotland at Wembley. He played in the two World Cups of 1954 (Switzerland) and 1958 (Sweden) and brought the same elegance to the dark blue of Scotland as he did to the green and white of Celtic. If Willie had a fault it was over-elaboration but he was prepared to work at feeding quicker even to the extent of trying to shorten his stride on the Parkhead terraces at the end of 1954. He scored five goals against Queen of the South at Palmerston on January 22nd 1955. The first three were disallowed so Willie walked the next two into the net and challenged the referee each time with a stare. He started 1956-57 in almighty form and ripped Dunfermline apart 6-0 any way he felt like on September 12th. He was in the first Celtic team ever to win the League Cup on October 31st 1956 and had a fantastic match in the Scottish Cup at Ibrox when Rangers were put out 0-2 on February 19th 1957. He

dropped back alongside Bobby Evans as of the Public Trial of August 3rd 1957 and schemed the 7-1 destruction of Rangers from right-half at Hampden on October 19th 1957. In the last minute he slotted a penalty home by selecting as his target George Niven's bunnet placed just inside the right-hand post at the Mount Florida end. He was so at home on an ice-covered Stark's Park on January 25th 1958 that even Raith Rovers supporters applauded. He went to Middlesbrough to set the goals up for Brian Clough (and help finance the new Parkhead floodlights). Clough was not an easy partner but eventually admitted Willie was one of the finest providers he ever had. But Fernie missed the dressing-room patter at Celtic and was brought back as an old head to bring on the youngsters. He had slowed down too much to suit Parkhead yet helped St Mirren to the Scottish Cup final of 1962 (with an eighth minute goal versus Celtic in the semi-final at Ibrox March 31st 1962). He coached Kilmarnock to play the beautiful game like Malcolm MacDonald before him but when he was sacked during a bad patch, bought a taxi and was lost to football there-after. Willie Fernie is one of the most elegant ball-players to have graced the hoops and an all-time Celtic great.

Appearances:
SL: 219 apps. 54 gls.
SLC: 59 apps. 10 gls.
SC: 39 apps. 10 gls.
Total: *317 apps. 74 gls.*

FILIPPI, Joseph

Role: Right-back 1977-79
5' 10" 11st.5lbs.
b. Ayrshire, 3rd November 1953

CAREER: Prestwick Star 1968/Ayrshire Schools 1969/Coventry City 1969/Ayr United 1 Aug 1970/CELTIC 4 Nov 1977/Clyde 21 Dec 1979/free 2 May 1981/Glenafton Athletic 30 June 1981.

Debut v Motherwell (a) 3-2 (SL) 5.11.77

Danny McGrain's chronic foot trouble began with an injury against Hibs on October 1st 1977. Celtic brought Joe Filippi in as his replacement and gave Ayr United Brian McLaughlin and £15,000. Joe, one of twin boys and son of a native Italian who became a headmaster in Cumnock, signed for Celtic the day after his 24th birthday: "What a fantastic present to get!" An apprentice draughtsman,

Joe Filippi

he hated the cooped-up existence and gave up life in an office to train as a plater and welder. Celtic had a miserable season unable to compensate for the loss not only of McGrain but of Dalglish and Pat Stanton. Joe gifted Rangers the start of a goal at Parkhead on November 12th 1977 but set the equaliser up for Tom McAdam. No matter how well Joe played, McGrain's absence was always felt. Murmurings in the Jungle began to intensify and he lost his place to Alan Sneddon as of February 6th 1978. He was out of the team until August 16th with McGrain's come-back then in the offing. From January 1979 on Joe was essentially a Celtic reserve.

Appearances:
SL: 32 apps. 0 gls.
SLC: 8 apps. 0 gls.
SC: 2 apps. 0 gls.
Total: *42 apps. 0 gls.*

FINDLAY, Robert

Role: Outside-left 1900-01
5' 9" 11st.7lbs.
b. Galston, 29th March 1877
d. Bayonne, USA, 13th August 1926

CAREER: Kilmarnock Rugby XI/Kilmarnock 18 May 1897/CELTIC 8 Aug 1900/free 1 Nov 1901/Kilmarnock 1 Nov 1901/Dundee 2 Nov 1904/Motherwell 10 June 1905/Hamilton Academicals 30 Apr 1907/Port Glasgow Athletic 22 Apr 1908/St Bernard's 10 Aug 1909 /retired Apr 1911.

Debut v Morton (a) 3-2 (SL) 18.8.1900 (scored once)

Rab Findlay

"Findlay has pluck but is unfit" (September 28th 1901). Jack Bell's departure in the summer of 1900 left Celtic bereft of an outside-left. Divers, Battles and Gilhooly were all tried before Celtic splashed out £150 on Rab Findlay, "an acquisition of note." His first game for the green and white vertical stripes was also Morton's first in the Scottish League. A brave and fearless raider, Rab was dogged constantly by cartilage trouble and did not properly strike form until the first round of the Glasgow Cup on September 15th 1900. Celtic were two up with 15 minutes to go, Rangers hit back with three goals in 11 minutes and Celtic equalised on the whistle. The knee kept him out of the side for long periods and gave Jimmy Quinn his chance (eg in the Scottish Cup final of April 6th 1901). Rab on song was a great favourite with the crowd for his thrusting style: "Findlay has no equal with danger shots from any angle or any distance." Rab was interviewed for the Motherwell manager's job on April 22nd 1911 but Johnny Hunter won it. Rab's son played soccer for the USA in the Olympics at Paris 1924 and Amsterdam 1928.

Appearances:
SL: 14 apps. 5 gls.
SC: 3 apps. 2 gls.
Total: *17 apps. 7 gls.*

FISHER, James

Role: Outside-right 1898-1900
5' 5" 11st.0lbs.
b. Denny, 23rd December 1876

CAREER: Vale of Forth/King's Park Feb 1892
/East Stirling 19 June 1895/St Bernard's
12 May 1896/Aston Villa 11 May 1897/
CELTIC 27 Aug 1898/(Preston NE loan 28 Jan
1899)/(East Stirling loan 2 Dec 1899)/CELTIC
again Feb 1900/Newton Heath 12 Oct 1900/
King's Park 14 Mar 1902/Vale of Leithen 4 Dec
1902/Fulham 1903/retired 1904.

Debut v St Mirren (h) 4-1 (SL) 3.9.1898

Cud Fisher was a flying winger who joined
Celtic within two weeks of another galloper
Jack Bell. Would Celtic now abandon the
careful pattern-weave style copied from Proud
Preston and favoured since the 8-0 massacre of
Cowlairs (September 22nd 1888)? (Answer: Of
course not). Cud made his debut on the day of
the Battle of Omdurman. The club found they
had paid Villa good money for a winger
unable to get his crosses in and afterwards
unable to shoot. Against Clyde on a rain-
lashed Parkhead (November 5th 1898) Celtic
were leading 5-2 when Cud did score but was
so blatantly offside Clyde at first refused to
re-start. Celtic then took the score to 9-2 with
four minutes to go but this time the Bully Wee
left the field. Celtic stood around and waited
in the rain till the ref blew for time. Cud, "one
of the most disappointing catches ever landed
at Parkhead," served with the Royal Engineers
in the Kaiser War.

> **Appearances:**
> *SL: 10 apps. 3 gls.*
> **Total:** *10 apps. 3 gls.*

FISHER, Robert

Role: Centre-forward 1942
5' 7" 10st.10lbs.
b. New Herrington, 9th July 1919

CAREER: Herrington YMCA summer 1938/
Langley Park Villa/Shildon FC 2 Mar 1939-
Sept 1939/New Herrington FC/Royal
Engineers/CELTIC 6 Apr 1942/free 23 Oct
1942/Eppleton CW 1946/West Auckland/
retired.

*Debut v Partick Thistle (a) 3-1 (RL) 6.4.42
(scored once)*

Soldier Robert Fisher was an amateur footballer from the Durham County League, who
showed "strength, speed, promise" on top of a
goal within 30 seconds of his debut. This first
match of his was described by chairman Tom
White "as worth
every penny of
the patronage."
Celtic signed the
"strong-going little
Englishman" as a
professional
immediately after.
Bobby had been
with the BEF in
France and was
evacuated not from
Dunkirk, but
Saint-Nazaire in
1940. He was
recommended to
Celtic by a Sergeant McGuckin. Although
unwilling, he was part of the strike before the
League Cup semi-final versus Rangers on May
2nd 1942. The Celtic players had gathered at
St Enoch's Square only to be told (this is Alex
Dowdell's version) there would be no
complimentaries; their friends must pay at the
turnstiles. This resulted in a marked reluctance
to get changed at Hampden until Chairman
White appeared brandishing his Corona cigar:
no player was going to hold a gun to his head!
According to Bobby the Celts wanted bonus
money commensurate with being in the semi-
final but his own immediate ambition was to
make his mark against Rangers. Bobby played
four times for Celtic in the Summer Cup of
1942 and in the Charity Cup versus Third
Lanark on April 25th when he created "a
delicious opening" for Frank Murphy's goal in
50 minutes. His last game for Celtic was
versus QP at Hampden on August 15th 1942
just four days before the Dieppe Raid, the
bloody try-out for D-Day. He left for Gibraltar
where he spent one and a half years. His registration was cancelled just as the Second Battle
of Alamein started. He followed the invading
troops ashore in Europe in June 1944. Like Jim
Welford before him Bobby also played cricket
for County Durham, most notably against the
touring New Zealanders in 1949.

Robert Fisher

> **Appearances:**
> *RL: 2 apps. 1 gl.*
> *RLC: 1 app. 0 gls.*
> **Total:** *3 apps. 1 gl.*

Tynecastle (October 20th 1934) was the best Jimmy McMenemy had ever seen. He played five times for the Irish Free State and gave "a masterly display...always safe" against Germany at Dalymount on Sunday October 18th 1936. He got into deep trouble back at Tynecastle in a reserve game just over a month later (November 28th). Under intense provocation, Fox drop-kicked a ball point-blank towards the jeering mass behind his goal. There was a pitch invasion, Fox himself was head-butted, then arrested and charged with assault. At the trial in Edinburgh Burgh Court on February 1st 1937, left-back Jack Doyle and left-half Bertie Duffy both denied the ball had hit a spectator. Both testified it had hit the surrounding wall only. To no avail. Defendant fined £2 with the option of 20 days! Fox returned to Ireland and won two more FAI Cup medals in 1941 and 1947. His team, Cork United (Cork City reformed) were League champions in 1941, '42 and '43.

Appearances:
SL: 6 apps. 4 shut-outs.
Total: *6 apps. 4 shut-outs (67%).*

♣ **Celtic note:** *The fan who spat tobacco over Tully at Tynecastle on October 25th 1952, sixteen years on, was likewise fined £2 on a charge of Breach of the Peace.*

FORAN, Joseph W.

Role: Inside-forward 1891-93
b. Paisley

CAREER: Greenlaw Strollers/CELTIC 1890/ (St Mirren loan 28 Mar 1891)/Johnstone FC 17 Apr 1894 & 31 Aug 1894/Paisley Celtic 3 May 1895/reinstated amateur 13 Aug 1895/ Paisley Celtic 31 Aug 1895.

Debut v Leith Athletic (h) 2-0 (SL) 14.5.1892 (scored once)

Joey Foran was inside-left for the Celtic Crusaders who won the Reserve XI Cup 13-1 versus St Mirren Strollers on February 21st 1891 (St Mirren scored first). On his debut he played outside-left in place of Johnny Campbell as partner to guest star Jimmy Cassidy of Bolton Wanderers. He was also in the team that played the final match on First Celtic Park (July 16th 1892) this time at out-side-right to Brady in Alec's last show before the dash to Sheffield. When Celtic's League

programme opened on August 20th 1892 Sandy McMahon was still in Nottingham and Joey came in for him at inside-left in a team labelled the "nebulous hypothesis" before the match.

Appearances:
SL: 2 apps. 1 gl.
Total: *2 apps. 1 gl.*

FRASER, Robert

Role: Full-back 1948-49
5' 9" 11st.0lbs.
b. Dundee, 21st December 1925

CAREER: Dundee Anhorage/Lochee Harp/ CELTIC 10 Jan 1948/free 1949/Hearts 5 May 1949/free 1951/Northwich Victoria Aug 1951/ St. Johnstone 1 Aug 1953/Montrose 1954.

Debut v Hibernian (h) 2-4 (SL) 3.4.48

Bert Fraser ("half a dozen scouts are sitting on his doorstep") was signed for Celtic aged 23 by second team coach Chic Geatons. Against Queen of the South colts on 14th February 1948 his kicking was "well-timed and placed, every ball had a mission ... his tackling could still be tightened up." He had another fine game for the wee team against a Thistle wing of Jimmy Walker and Willie Sharp on March 6th 1948, Walker in particular being no slouch. There was "a potential first-team player here." On his one appearance for the Celtic big team (in direct opposition to Eddie Turnbull) his game was "promising but rather slow." Hearts snapped him up when Celtic let him go.

Appearances:
SL: 1 app. 0 gls.
Total: *1 app. 0 gls.*

FULLARTON, Alexander Sutherland

Role: Right-back 1916
5' 9" 11st.12lbs.
b. Stevenston, 6th June 1895

CAREER: Saltcoats Victoria/CELTIC 29 May 1916/(Stevenston United loan Oct 1916)/ CELTIC again 5 Apr 1917/Clydebank 24 July 1917/Stevenston United 13 Aug 1918/ Kilmarnock 12 June 1920/Stevenston United 29 July 1921/Kilwinning Rangers 1922/Ardeer Recreation 1930/retired 1932.

Debut v Clyde (a) 5-0 (SL) 28.4.17

"He has the makings of another Hughie Watson whom I never saw play but have heard a lot of" (Patsy Gallagher). April 21st 1917: Champions Celtic lose a home game 0-2 to Kilmarnock and end a sequence of 62 League matches without defeat stretching back to November 20th 1915. Killie's two goals severely dent Celtic's defensive record and mean they are leaking 0.5 of a goal per game on average throughout 1916-17. For the last match of the season the following week Alex Fullarton, "a right-back of rare physique and style," came in for Eck McNair to bolster the crumbling defence. He had played a trial for Celtic in a Red Cross Charities Match at Victoria Park Saltcoats on May 10th 1916. Alex's debut was in the last match of the last title triumph of the four-in-a-row team. With Kilwinning in August 1924 he was "a great defender... worth watching."

Appearances:
SL: 1 app. 0 gls.
Total: *1 app. 0 gls.*

FULTON, Stephen

Role: Midfield 1987-93
5' 11" 12st.8lbs.
b. Greenock,
10th August 1970

CAREER: Celtic BC/ CELTIC 15 May 1987/ Bolton Wanderers 13 July 1993/ (Peterborough United loan 27 Dec 1993)/ Falkirk 11 Aug 1994.

Debut v St Mirren (h) 7-1 (SL) 8.10.88 (sub)

Steve Fulton, "with that vision given only to the few," found himself in the Premier League squad as early as October 24th 1987 for the home match against Dundee United. According to Billy McNeill he had an "absolute blinder" against Liverpool in the Dubai Cup (April 4th 1989) and "never for a

Steve Fulton

moment seemed out of his depth. He's going to be a really great player, I'm convinced of it." Versus Hibs in the semi-final of the Scottish Cup on April 16th 1989 he gave McIntyre such a skinning to set-up goals for Walker and McGhee that right-back Tommy was taken-off after 35 minutes. Steve won the Mr Superfit award, his "sheer adventure, running and power" shading even Paul McStay on the day. The match heralded "the emergence of a fine new Celt." Tommy Burns started the game versus Ajax at Parkhead on December 6th 1989 but after half an hour was taken off and replaced by his heir apparent, Steve Fulton. Gary Gillespie was very impressed on his own debut (August 17th 1991): "Some of the passes being knocked about were great and young Fulton was hitting the ball everywhere and always available to receive it. He looked a hell of a good player." Against St Johnstone on April 11th 1992 he scored his first Premier League goal in 45 games with a thunderbolt from 25 yards and got an ovation all to himself as he was substituted in the 81st minute. "He makes great passes, sixty, seventy yard rakers. He's so capable of switching the play. We've encouraged his all-round game" (Tommy Craig). Steve clearly had a football brain, and with a left foot as educated as Tommy Burns', could pass with pin-point accuracy but after six seasons at Parkhead he had remained 'promising' for far too long. Bolton paid £300,000 for his potential, yet by November, Morton were angling to get him on loan from the Burnden Park reserves.

Appearances:
SL: 74 apps. 2 gls.
SLC: 9 apps. 1 gl.
SC: 6 apps. 3 gls.
Eur: 4 apps. 0 gls.
Total: *93 apps. 6 gls.*

McMenemy's... cool artfulness... judgement of a veteran... no superior as a passer of the ball but where does he get the strength to shoot?" 30 August 1913: "Gallagher twisted and turned at will, slipped passes and back-heeled in the most tantalising manner..." Scottish Cup semi-final 10 February 1914: "Gallagher was everywhere, untiring, unafraid..." 4 November 1916: "Gallagher's goal was struck with such force it hit the back of the net and came out." 25 November 1916: "Once in either half, Anderson and Gallagher rolled on the ground in each other's embraces in the intensity of desire - the one to score, the other to save." 6 January 1917: "The most talked-about player in the trenches is Patsy Gallagher" (Sgt. Downie VC on a visit to Parkhead). 23 February 1918: "hampered on every side" versus Morton at Parkhead on the half hour, the Mazy Meanderer dribbled his way through and fell into the net with the ball. 19 September 1921: Patsy receives the ball from a kick-off takes it all the way himself without a Hib touching and scores "with a gentle tap" past Bill Harper at Easter Road. 11 April 1925, Scottish Cup final vs Dundee, Celtic are a goal down with 20 minutes to go: "...he jinked, jouked, hurdled, swerved, dribbled, jumped, fell, got up, ran on, jinked again, stumbled, jouked once more, went over his wilkies with the ball still grasped between his feet and suddenly, he was over the line, him and the ball, past an astonished Jock

Britton, and Hampden to the last 75,000th man was rising in starry-eyed tribute to a genius in bootlaces. The momentum of the wee green devil meant he was caught in the net and had to be pulled out by his far-from-unhappy colleagues..." (Minutes later he almost went through again). Reporter: "You're as good as ever, old man." Patsy: "Tell me something I don't know. I'll play for years yet." In fact, Celtic, probably to save on wages, retired him without his knowledge on July 29th 1926, after he had missed much of the season with a dicky knee. Peerless Patsy was irate: "I'm as right as rain! The idea of being finished has never entered my head!" The club had made an awful mistake but Patsy refused to relent. The Bhoy became a Bairn. He had a cluster of nicknames: "The Mighty Atom"/(*Up an' at 'em/Pat from Donegal*), "The Mazy Meanderer", "The Tiny Bit o' Grit" plus the utmost admiration of his fellow professionals, the men who whacked him on the park and whom he whacked back - but whenever possible on the referee's blind side! Davie McLean acknowledged him as the best ever and at his funeral ex-Ranger 'Tireless' Tommy Cairns spoke his epitaph: "He was the greatest wee ****** that ever kicked a ba'."

Appearances:
SL: 432 apps. 187 gls.
SC: 32 apps. 9 gls.
Total: *464 apps. 196 gls.*

Patsy Gallagher up to his tricks in the 1912 Cup semi-final with Hearts at Hampden.

GALLAGHER, William Patrick

Role: Inside-right 1938-49
5' 9" 11st.7lbs.
b. Renfrew, 29th June 1919
d. 16th October 1982

CAREER: Whiteinch School/Renfrew
Beechwood/St Anthony's by 20 Mar 1937/
CELTIC (provisional)1937/(full) 5 May 1938/
Royal Engineers/free Apr 1949/Falkirk
17 May 1949/Ayr United Aug 1950/
St Johnstone 27 Aug 1952/free 30 Apr 1953/
Inverness Thistle 1953.

Debut v Hamilton Academicals (a) 2-6 (RL) 2.9.44

Willie Gallagher was the eldest of Patsy's five
boys and the father of Kevin of Dundee
United, Coventry City and Blackburn Rovers.
His playing style much resembled that of his
cousin, the great Johnny Divers. "I learned my
game as a ball boy at Celtic Park. Bright
prospects should be made ball boys, the
apprentice as close as possible to the journey-
man." His father was allegedly opposed to his
joining Celtic for fear of the inevitable
comparisons. Willie was big-built and
although he possessed a superb football brain,
was considered on the slow side (perhaps
more studied than slow; he could turn on the
gas when he wanted. His father Patsy was no
slouch, and son Kevin opened the scoring for
Dundee United in the 1988 Scottish Cup final
by out-sprinting Roy Aitken). The War tore the
heart out of Willie's career. He had a great
debut in a triangle of Malcolm MacDonald,
Delaney and Gallagher, playing beautiful
football until suddenly Accies took control. He
was probably better suited at half-back than
inside-forward. As right-half he was ordered-
off against Queen's Park at Hampden on
January 11th 1947. Inside-left Evans dropped
back into Willie's slot and had a blinder. Patsy
was at Dens Park on April 17th 1948 to see
Celtic son Willie play against Dundee son
Tommy in a match Celtic had to win to avoid
relegation. Willie started 1948-49 in fine style
in the League Cup. He was inside-right on
September 11th when Celtic beat Hibs 1-0, a
match watched by Manny Shinwell MP, the
first time he had seen Celtic in action since
Hibs beat them 0-1 at Parkhead in the Scottish
Cup final of April 26th 1902. Willie was in the
team that beat Rangers 3-1 a fortnight later
and put Celtic 2-1 up right on half-time, this
match watched by Dr Robert Davitt, son of the
great Michael Davitt who laid the shamrock
sod on Celtic Park on March 19th 1892. Willie
lost his place after the 3-6 destruction by
Clyde on October 9th. One week later, minus
Willie, Celtic played at Ibrox in front of yet
another special guest (invited by Rangers!) -
the Taoiseach, Eammon de Valera.

Appearances:
SL: 29 apps. 0 gls.
SLC: 6 apps. 3 gls.
SC: 4 apps. 2 gls.
Total: *39 apps. 5 gls.*
RL: 18 apps. 3 gls.
Total: *18 apps. 3 gls.*

Willie Gallagher (right) with his famous father, Patsy, and brother Tommy of Dundee.

1906. He played a trial against Clyde at Shawfield on January 4th 1905 and scored the winner five minutes from time. His start in League football was a damp one: players forced to leave the field for shelter in a torrential thunderstorm during the first half. He went on the missionary journey to the Highlands and then on the Continental tour both in May 1906. Celtic played Southampton in Budapest on June 4th 1906 and Ned played full-back with Donnie McLeod. He received a medal "the size of a plate" to commemorate the 1-0 win. Derby wanted both him and Jimmy Bauchop but the two pals were not reunited until Bradford City in 1913. Ned "stiffened up the half-back line" at Dumbarton during the Kaiser War. He coached in Spain after retirement then worked for British Celanese in Spondon near Derby.

'Ned' Garry

Appearances:
SL: 6 apps. 1 gl.
Total: *6 apps. 1 gl.*

GEATONS, Charles

Role: Right-half 1927-41
5' 11" 12st.0lbs.
b. Lochgelly, 16th July 1907
d. Lochgelly, 20th June 1970

CAREER: Lochgelly Celtic Juveniles 1926/Lochgelly Celtic 1927/CELTIC 29 Oct 1927/retired 1941/part-time coach July 1945/full-time coach 8 Oct 1946/reserve team coach 1 Aug 1948/resigned 8 Aug 1950/Blackburn Rovers scout.

Debut v Aberdeen (h) 2-2 (SL)
16.3.29

On his debut (at right-back) "Geatons acquitted himself well... got rid of the ball as Alec McNair used to do... with judgement."

Chic Geatons (born Gattens) was recommended to Celtic by Peter Gildea and signed by wonder scout Steve Callaghan. He started shakily (without the pace for a full-back) but worked hard on his game and endeared himself to the support by his whole-hearted attitude. He is immortalised in the half-back lines of 1931-34 (Wilson, McStay and Geatons) and 1935-38 (Geatons, Lyon and Paterson). It was Graham Robertson's failing health in 1930 that let Chic in at left-half. He won Scottish Cup medals in 1931 and 1933. When Peter Wilson went to Hibs in 1934, Chic took over on his natural side, the right. He was a magnificent striker of the dead ball but his glory goal was just after the Dundee equaliser at Parkhead on December 10th 1932. He beat man after man then hit a raging shot into the net from outside the penalty box. He won two Championship medals in 1936 and 1938 and another Cup medal in 1937. Johnnie Wilson tells how Chic was playing with Celtic reserves at Shawfield on March 5th 1938 when the news came through the big team was losing 0-2 to Kilmarnock in the third round of the Scottish Cup. Chic feigned injury to get over to Parkhead and gee the Celtic on. (Back at Clyde, the Geatonless reserves went down 4-2). As the team of 1938 began to lose its balance and snap on heavy pitches against defenders intent on destroying its rhythm, Chic doubled his work rate and "played like a youngster. His amazing running power put hair on his bald bits." When he went off injured versus Clyde in the Glasgow Cup on September 11th 1940, "it was like the loss of a cotter pin to the Celtic machine." He played his last game in a 0-4 Regional League defeat by Hibs on October 26th 1940 when not a single foul was registered against Celtic in the whole 90 minutes and just five against Hibs. Chic resigned Celtic on being assigned the reserves in the North-Eastern section of Division C after Jimmy Hogan's retirement in 1950.

Appearances:
SL: 286 apps. 13 gls.
SC: 33 apps. 0 gls.
Total: *319 apps. 13 gls.*
RL: 26 apps. 2 gls.
Total: *26 apps. 2 gls.*

GEDDES, John

Role: Right-back 1927-29
5' 10" 11st.0lbs.
b. Lochgelly, 11th April 1908

CAREER: Lochgelly Celtic/CELTIC Oct 1927/
Gillingham 1929/Rhyl 1930/Tunbridge Wells
Rangers 1932/Bolton Wanderers (trial) Aug
1933/Rotherham United (trial) Sept 1933/
...Newry Town Sept 1935.

Debut v Aberdeen (h) 2-2 (SL) 25.2.28

"A stalwart back...of high reputation," John
Geddes got his first chance in the Celtic big
team at the age of 18 because Willie McStay
was on international duty against Ireland at
Firhill (watched by 54,723!). He was partnered
by another debutant at left-back, Tom Sinclair.
The boys received another chance in the last
game of the season versus Raith Rovers at
Parkhead. Raith won 0-3 and that was the end
for John and Tom. John had better luck in
England and tried-out at Burnden Park as a
centre-half.

Appearances:
SL: 2 apps. 0 gls.
Total:
2 apps. 0 gls.

GEEHRIN, Patrick

Pat Geehrin

Role: Full-back 1910-11
5' 9" 11st.7lbs.
b. Musselburgh, c 1889

CAREER: Bonnyrigg Thistle/CELTIC 11 Apr
1910/(Alloa loan 19 Sept 1910-Mar 1911)/
Bristol City Sept 1911/Alloa 6 July 1912/
Armadale 5 May 1914.

Debut v St Mirren (a) 1-1 (SL) 18.3.11

"A really good man to fall back on," Pat
Geehrin played his one and only game for the
Celtic big team as deputy for Jimmy Hay and
partner for Alec McNair at full-back. Celtic
went on a Continental tour on May 13th 1911
but young Pat did not travel for the disaffect-
ed Dun Hay. Celtic pulled in Jock Davie of
Hamilton Academicals as Hay's replacement.

Appearances:
SL: 1 app. 0 gls.
Total: *1 app. 0 gls.*

GEMMELL, Thomas

Role: Full-back 1961-71
6' 2" 13st.10lbs.
b. Craigneuk, 16th October 1943

CAREER: Meadow Thistle Amateurs 1957/
Coltness United 24 Oct 1961/CELTIC
25 Oct 1961/ Coltness United (farmed-out)
1961/Nottingham Forest 17 Dec 1971/free
25 Apr 1973/Miami Toros 1973/Dundee
1 July 1973/manager 12 June 1977/
resigned 24 Apr 1980/Bannockburn FC
manager 10 Oct 1984/Albion Rovers
manager 3 Jan 1986/resigned Dec 1988/
Albion Rovers manager again 1 Apr 1993/
resigned 26 Jan 1994.

Debut v Aberdeen (a) 5-1 (SL) 5.1.63

T.G. was spotted at 16 by Eddie McCarroll
who tipped off Sean Fallon. Sean found
himself in a race with Malky MacDonald
representing Brentford. Tommy must rate
as surely the best full-back ever to pull on
the green and white. He could defend, he
could attack, and what other full-back has
scored a goal in each of two European Cup
finals? His shooting was thunderous. He
was timed at 71.55mph on January 12th
1981 which beat the 69.9mph established in
his prime. There was no possibility a
'keeper could fathom his spot kicks: "I took
penalties like a golf shot. I pictured the
target and made sure I hit it. If I didn't
know where the ball was going, neither did
the goalie." He struck one penalty so hard
against the World Champions Feyenoord at

Tommy Gemmell with the Scottish Cup in 1969.

Hampden on February 9th 1971 that he was collecting the ball himself before goalie Treytel had even made a move to turn. He made life a misery for a wonder boy Rangers winger: "Gemmell never has easier games than against Henderson... he handles him almost casually." There were moments of aberration like the pass that stranded John Clark in Novi Sad and let Stanic in to win for Vojvodina (March 1st 1967); the lob without looking from 22 yards that sailed over Simpson's head and put USSR into the lead against Scotland at Hampden (May 10th 1967). Nevertheless, France-Football voted Big Tam the Sixth Best Player in Europe on Christmas Day 1967 and had he been judged only on his performance against England at Wembley on April 15th, his place would have been well merited. A poll of sports journalists in Hungary and Brazil nominated him the best right-back in the world in the spring of 1970. As Tommy himself put it of the Leeds forwards at Elland Road in the European Cup semi-final first leg (April 1st 1970); "I got tired of dispossessing them." With the onset of fame Tommy's life-style grew far from frugal with a Corsair 200E, a Daimler, a white S-type Jag all in the same season 1967-68. By October 27th 1969 he held three Scottish Cup medals, four League Championship, four League Cup, one

European Cup, had been capped for Scotland and was on the transfer list at his own request. Playing against Germany in Hamburg on October 22nd, Tam took a flying kick at Haller in retaliation near the end of the game and was sent off. Celtic disciplined him by giving Davie Hay the left-back position for the League Cup final against St Johnstone three days later and relations between club and player were thereafter never the same. In May 1970 Jock Stein spoke of how "Players who want to play for Celtic must be protected against those who don't...success affects p eople in different ways, not always for the best." At Nottingham Forest, he was skipper during 1972-73 but a lawn-mower accident on March 24th seemed to have scuppered his further prospects on the Trent. He bounced back with Dundee and complained that the Celtic wall was not far enough back for a free kick on October 13th 1973. The referee agreed and then Tam stole an extra yard. He won the League Cup with the Dark Blues against Celtic on an Arctic day at Hampden (December 15th 1973). As he raised the trophy, Big Tam received an unworthy Ibrox-style razzing from the diehard Celtic support. Tommy Gemmell must walk into any Celtic team of any era. He is an all-time great and then a whole lot else. As a footballer he was far larger than life.

Tommy Gemmell scores Celtic's goal in the 1970 European Cup Final defeat by Feyenoord in Milan.

Jock Stein called him "The best left-back in the world" but Tam was ever more than that. With Gemmell in defence, Celtic never seemed a mere eleven men equally matched by eleven others. He brought new dimensions to every game he played and regularly chased the likes of Lennox, Wallace and Hood at the top of the goalscorers' list. He is certainly the most versatile, adaptable and athletic full-back Celtic have ever had.

Appearances:
SL: 247 apps. 37 gls.
SLC: 74 apps. 10 gls.
SC: 43 apps. 5 gls.
Eur: 54 apps. 12 gls.
Total: 418 apps. 64 gls.

♣ **Celtic note:** Tommy took 34 penalties for Celtic and missed just three.

GIBSON, Andrew

Role: Inside-forward 1912
b. Glasgow

CAREER: Kelvinhaugh/Strathclyde Juniors Jan 1911/Southampton 29 July 1911/CELTIC (trial) 10 Apr 1912/Leeds City Sept 1912.
Debut v Kilmarnock (h) 2-0 (SL) 13.4.12 (scored once)

Andrew Gibson "played a fine game and scored a good goal" on his debut (the Titanic was just two days away from its iceberg!). He was signed for Southampton by manager George Swift who reckoned him the best junior he had ever seen. Saints suspended him for breach of discipline just after March 9th 1912 and whatever he did, his services were no longer wanted. Celtic too had admired him as a junior and let him try out at inside-left for the absent McMenemy. On the day of his debut, the 1912 Scottish Cup, won at Ibrox versus Clyde the previous Saturday, was paraded with pride by small boys with bugles, some of them in bare feet.

Appearances:
SL: 2 apps. 1 gl.
Total: 2 apps. 1 gl.

GIBSON, John

Role: Outside-right 1976-78
5' 7" 9st.6lbs.
b. Hull, 23rd December 1950

CAREER: Clydebank BG/Clydebank Star/ Partick Thistle 21 Nov 1967/Ayr United 23 Nov 1974/St Mirren 31 Aug 1976/free 6 Dec 1976/CELTIC 7 Dec 1976/free 29 Apr 1978/East Fife 26 July 1978/free 16 Oct 1980/ Forfar Athletic 1980/Stirling Albion 30 July 1981/free Oct 1981/Sauchie Juniors 31 Oct 1981.
Debut v Ayr United (h) 3-0 (SL) 18.12.76 (sub)

Partick Thistle were playing Ferranti Thistle in the Scottish Cup on January 27th 1974 and took Gibson off to put Steve Chalmers on. "Controversial winger" Gibson refused to shake hands as they crossed and Thistle fined him £20. This was just one of Johnny's "five breaches of discipline" in 1973-74 and added to his "involvement over the years in several incidents." "Very fast, blessed with great

Johnny Gibson

skills," he was transferred to Ally MacLeod's Ayr United for two Dougs, Somner and Mitchell but carrying a cartilage problem which meant several operations. Jock Stein was watching a St Mirren reserve match when Johnny caught his eye just three weeks before he was freed. He became another of Big Jock's sensation signings, "a fair wee player" but who suffered from "over-ambition." His dad was Alec Gibson, full-back of Clyde and Stirling Albion. Young John was born in England when John senior was playing with Hull and just as the Scot Nats were getting ready to lift the Stone of Scone from Westminster Abbey.

Appearances:
SL: 4 apps. 1 gl.
Total: *4 apps. 1 gl.*

GILCHRIST, John Wotherspoon

Role: Right-half 1919-23
5' 9" 11st.4lbs.
b. Glasgow, 30th March 1899
d. February 1950 (?)

CAREER: Strathclyde 1917/St Anthony's 1918/CELTIC 20 May 1919/Preston North End 26 Jan 1923/(Carlisle United loan Jan 1924)/Third Lanark 30 July 1924/dismissed 18 Sept 1924/(Dunfermline Athletic loan 19 Sept 1924)/released 13 Oct 1924/(Bathgate loan 4 June 1925)/(Brooklyn Wanderers loan Aug 1925)/(Chicago Bricklayers loan Oct 1925).

Debut v Dumbarton (h) 3-1 (SL) 18.8.19

"A fine, strapping, upstanding lad... nderstands the half-back game...he has the proper tap, the proper glide and if he doesn't turn out the goods, he'll have himself to blame." "I had not seen before, and have not seen since, a man who so consistently made the ball nurse the ground. Whether a pass was to travel five or 25 yards, the ball did not rise more than inches above the turf..." Jimmy McMenemy rated Jock Gilchrist "a worthy successor to Sunny Jim Young." Jock brought a touch to the game that had "the grace and finish of an artist." He had a fine conceit of himself as a player (however much on the slow side) and an individual. Like Davie McLean before him, Jock refused to be dictated to by Willie Maley but made the familiar mistake of confusing civility with servility. Maley (in shirt sleeves, snappish): "I'd like to speak to you." Gilchrist: "I'll let you speak to me when you're better dressed." He was picked for Scotland at Villa Park in the 0-1 defeat of England on April 8th 1922 and as in the case of Mick McKeown, an international cap did nothing to mollify a prickly temperament. On Tuesday January 22nd 1923 (after three carpetings) the club suspended their international half-back sine die for "wilful inattention to training" (he had missed most recently the previous day but had allegedly been spotted at the boxing in the evening). Jock celebrated his transfer in champagne (not at the Bank; he and Maley were not talking) but from the moment he left Parkhead his career plunged downhill fast. He cost Preston £4,500, a top fee for its time. At Deepdale he was in trouble almost at once as "leaden feet" and the biting tongue again manifested themselves. He went up for transfer on September 14th 1923 and when he showed no sign of being chastened, received two weeks

notice on January 4th 1924. At Third Lanark he was dismissed as "palpably inefficient" although still on the retained list in 1928. Properly disposed, he might have given Celtic years and years of good service. As it was, his premature departure let in Peter Wilson.

Appearances:
SL: 127 apps. 6 gls.
SC: 7 apps. 0 gls.
Total: *134 apps. 6 gls.*

GILFEATHER, Edward

Role: Half-back 1923-26
6' 1" 11st.12lbs.
b. Auchterderan, 2nd June 1903

CAREER: Glencraig Celtic 1921/Cowdenbeath (trial) 18 Mar 1922/Cowdenbeath 18 May 1922/CELTIC 21 Sept 1922/(Cowdenbeath loan 5 Oct 1922)/(Ayr United loan 23 Mar 1923)/(Dundee Hibernian loan 6 Aug 1923)/ (Dundee United loan 26 June 1924)/(Alloa loan 25 Aug 1925)/Hibernian 25 June 1926/ Clydebank 1931/retired 6 Feb 1932/Leith Athletic 14 Aug 1933/retired 11 Jan 1934.

Debut v Queen's Park (h) 4-1 (SL) 13.10.25

"Bushy-haired" Eddie Gilfeather, "strength with genuine ability," "a capture for any team," was a virtual unknown throughout his time with Celtic. So much so, the papers reported his debut as 'Gilfillan'. Celtic had no reserve side and Eddie signed two one-year contracts at Tannadice before moving to Easter Road on a full transfer and establishing his name as a household word. He was a competent midfielder but with a tendency some days "simply to boot the ball up the middle every time he is in possession." For a tall man he took a boot no bigger than McGrory's: size 6. He was the players' billiards champion during his time at Parkhead. Knee trouble forced his retirement from football. He was rescued from drowning at Arbroath in the summer of 1925.

Appearances:
SL: 2 apps. 0 gls.
Total: *2 apps. 0 gls.*

GILGUN, Patrick

Role: Centre-forward 1924-25
5' 9" 11st.4lbs.
b. West Shotts, 30th December 1901

CAREER: Law Scotia/CELTIC 5 Jan 1924/ (Vale of Leven loan 28 Jan 1924)/(East Stirling loan 12 June 1924)/Brighton & Hove Albion 1925/Norwich City 18 Aug 1926/ Sittingbourne FC July 1927/ Lloyds FC (Sittingbourne) December 1932.

Debut v Clydebank (h) 1-2 (SL) 4.3.24

"Promising youngster" Paddy Gilgun made his debut on the day when Jimmy McGrory came to Parkhead and reminded Celtic of his existence with an equaliser just before half-time for doomed Clydebank. Paddy was a "thrustful type" who liked to run at defence and possessed a powerful drive. He became a Celtic goalscorer on April 26th, the last match of the League programme 1924 when the attendance was so dismal Hibs took the guarantee back to Edinburgh only. "He parted with the ball when he should have held it but under astute Parkhead tuition this fault will soon be remedied." At East Stirling in March 1925, "he clings rather long to the ball and what he accomplishes in sixty movements could easily be done in two or three." Nevertheless he was missed at Firs Park when he moved down to England.

Appearances:
SL: 3 apps. 1 gl.
Total: *3 apps. 1 gl.*

GILHOOLY, Patrick

Role: Forward 1896-1901
5' 7" 11st.7lbs.
b. Draffan, 6th July 1876
d. Cleland, 20th February 1907

CAREER: Vale of Avon Juveniles/Larkhall Thistle/Cambuslang Hibernian/CELTIC 10 Oct 1896/Sheffield United 10 Sept 1900/ Tottenham Hotspur Sept 1901/Brighton & Hove Albion 1904/retired 1905.

Debut v Hibernian (h) 1-1 (SL) 28.11.1896
(scored once)

Paddy Gilgun

Rosy-cheeked, jet-haired Pat Gilhooly was the darling of Parkhead, *"a Celtic idol in his day, proud to be clad in the loved green and white"* and made his first appearance on the occasion of the Three Players' Strike. In his obituary, Tom Maley speaks of "a singularly winning personality...he made friends wherever he went." John Conway, the Celtic poet of 37, Harvie Street, Bridgeton, wrote of him as *"...this prince among men, with kindly heart and his winning ways"*. There seems also to have been a touch of the Dan Doyles in this Larkhall boy's character. He was probably a deliberate absentee the day Celtic kicked off with seven men in the Scottish Cup disaster at Arthurlie (9th January 1897). Just over a year later he is charged with "swollen head" and selfish play: "Gilhooly forgets he has mates... he exhausts himself with dribbling."

Pat Gilhooly

He lacked pace yet 'arrived' as an outside-right at Ibrox on 27th September 1897 when Celtic won 0-4 in the League. He played with Dan Doyle, Harry Marshall and Bernard ('Pat') Breslin (Hibs) for "the spoiled Rangers team" (the other seven) that represented the Scottish League versus the English at Villa Park 9th April 1898 and won a joyous victory; *"With modest merit and skilful play/He won his cap 'gainst great England's might."* When he went on the transfer list on 1st September 1900, rumour said he had worked it by his refusal to try. Some were glad to see the back of him: "A great favourite but discipline must be enforced... Celtic Park has been the happy hunting ground of the deadhead at all times... That is changed... A free lift is now a thing of the past...'tis time." Celtic claimed receipt of just £150 for him and Tom Turnbull together but nearer £400 was bruited in the bars. He gave up football at Brighton with ill-health and entered the Western Infirmary on 16th January 1907 for "a serious operation." His case was hopeless and he was sent home to Cleland. *"He talked of the old days on his dying bed/How the green and white were his earliest love/Green is the earth that haps his head/White is the soul that has gone above."*

Appearances:
SL: 46 apps. 17 gls.
SC: 4 apps. 3 gls.
Total: *50 apps. 20 gls.*

GILLAN, George

Role: Inside-left 1940-41
5' 6" 9st.0lbs.
b. 21st June 1919

CAREER: Saltcoats Victoria 1937/Arthurlie 1938/Alloa 19 June 1939/(CELTIC loan 7 Aug 1940)/Motherwell 7 Aug 1941/Ayr United 4 Dec 1945/free Apr 24 1946/Hamilton Academicals 12 Sept 1946/free Apr 1951/Berwick Rangers 4 Aug 1951/free June 1952/Wigtown & Bladnoch 24 Jan 1953/Ardeer Thistle coach 1955/Ardeer Recreation coach by 1959.

Debut v Hamilton Academicals (h) 2-2 (RL) 10.8.40 (scored once)

"One of the shrewdest players in the game... Celtic find a star ready-made" were the verdicts on George Gillan's first performance as partner to Frank Murphy on the Celtic left. George scored the 60th minute goal that won him a Glasgow Cup medal on September 28th 1940 in an inspired Celtic performance 0-1 versus Rangers at Ibrox. He scored two against Motherwell in a 4-1 win on January 25th 1941, the day the papers proclaimed "Celtic's revival is complete" and "Gillan... the livewire of the Celtic attack." He was the occasion of a pitch invasion versus Airdrie on March 22nd 1941 when players on both sides "went berserk in the second half" and the crowd joined in when wee George was hacked to the ground with ten minutes to go. Celtic wanted to buy "the natty little inside man" outright but it was Motherwell (having rejected him as a junior for too wee) who stumped up the actual money. George gave them

George Gillan

fruitful service throughout the war and helped bring the Summer Cup to Fir Park 1-0 versus Clyde at Hampden on July 8th 1944. When not playing football he was involved in building Sherman tanks. Having been his boss at Alloa and Celtic Jimmy McStay brought him also to Hamilton Academicals where he played inside man to Doc Fitzsimons. George applied for the Motherwell manager's job in 1955. He coached Bobby Lennox at Ardeer.

Appearances:
RL: 23 apps. 8 gls.
RLC: 7 apps. 2 gls.
Total: *30 apps. 10 gls.*

GILLESPIE, Gary Thomson

Role: Centre-half 1991-94
6' 3" 13st.0lbs.
b. Bonnybridge, 5th July 1960

CAREER: Grangemouth International BC/Falkirk 30 May 1977/Coventry City (trial) 23 Jan 1978/ Coventry City 1 Mar 1978/ Liverpool July 1973/ CELTIC 15 Aug 1991/free 17 May 1994/Coventry City trial 17 Aug 1994.

Debut v Falkirk (h) 4-1 (SL) 17.8.91 (scored once)

Elegant and gracious, brilliant but brittle, Gary Gillespie was one for the connoisseur. At Falkirk (where he was allegedly Rangers-daft) he had "the same sort of cool as Alan Hansen." At Coventry he was "a hell of a prospect." He became Joe Fagan's first big money signing but it took him over seven years to play 200 games for Liverpool ("Gary Gillespie has pulled out because of injury"). Celtic were reported as taking an interest as early as October 1984. He took Mark Lawrenson's place in the first minute of the European Cup final the night of the Heysel Stadium disaster 30th May 1985 and was also in the team at Hillsborough on April 15th 1989. Gary, who cost Celtic £925,000 always had plenty time on the ball but was sometimes almost too languidly casual as when he surrendered Motherwell a last-minute equaliser on January 30th 1993. When Celtic had to win the UEFA Cup-tie versus Cologne (September 30th 1992) a poll of fans beforehand favoured a battling defender like Galloway rather than one with Gary's cultured approach: "Naw - this isnae the game for him. We need people are gonnae dae somethin'." 1993-94 saw Gary playing more regularly in Celtic's first team. The secret seemed to be a patented energy tablet

Gary Gillespie

recommended by physiotherapist Brian Scott. He might well have needed a pill to banish the night-mares from the Ne'erday 1994 match when he and Wdowczyk posed statuesque to gift Rangers two goals in the opening minutes. Rumours subsequently that he was on £3,000 a week were hotly denied but the exact figure remained a secret. He was freed, nevertheless, to ease the burden on the wage bill.

Appearances:
SL: 69 apps. 3 gls.
SLC: 3 apps. 0 gls.
SC: 6 apps. 0 gls.
Eur: 8 apps. 0 gls.
Total: 86 apps. 3 gls.

GILLIGAN, Samuel Anderson

Role: Centre-forward 1903-04
5' 10" 12st.0lbs.
b. Dundee, 18th January 1882

CAREER: Belmont Athletic/Dundee Violet 1902/Dundee 2 May 1903/CELTIC 10 Sept 1903/Bristol City 1904/Liverpool 1910/ Gillingham player-manager July 1913 until 1915/(Dundee Hibernian loan 28 Oct 1916)/ Dundee Hibernian 7 Nov 1917/Forfar Athletic 4 Sept 1919.

Debut v Hibernian (h) 1-0 (SL) 26.9.03

Queen's Park opened Hampden against Celtic on October 31st 1903 and the centre who took first kick-off on the virgin turf was Sam Gilligan, one of four footballing brothers. He was bought as cover for Alec Bennett but the Rutherglen genius moved to inside forward and Sam became Celtic's regular spearhead despite "a lack of confidence at close quarters." On Boxing Day 1903 "after many disappointing

Sam Gilligan

displays" he got a hat-trick against Port Glasgow Athletic. In 1904 Sam reverted to second-choice centre and when it was decided not to risk Bennett against Rangers in the Scottish Cup final of April 16th 1904, Quinn led the line. At Bristol City he was an enormous favourite and kicked-off in the English Cup final of April 24th 1909 versus Manchester United at the Crystal Palace (City lost 0-1). There was public outcry when he was transferred to Liverpool. It was his goal against Oldham at Boundary Park on April 27th 1912 that kept the Reds in the First Division. Sam was resident in Vancouver by 1969 at least.

Appearances:
SL: 13 apps. 13 gls.
SC: 1 app. 0 gls.
Total: *14 apps. 13 gls.*

GILMARTIN, Hugh

Role: Inside-right 1944-46
b. Port Glasgow, 12th March 1924

CAREER: Market Star/CELTIC 24 Oct 1944/ free 1946/Hamilton Academicals 20 Aug 1946 /free 1947.

Debut v Albion Rovers (h) 5-0 (RL) 2.12.44

Alan Breck of the *Evening Times* watched the second match Hugh Gilmartin played for Celtic on December 9th 1944: "I have never seen a Celtic team that depended so little on the arts of inside-forward play...these present-day Celts have no ball-play or combination...they beat a man by holding or pushing...I hope - with peace just around the corner - the Celtic people realise how much they have to do." Hugh had one more game for the club, a 1-2 defeat versus Partick Thistle in the League Cup 31 March 1945. Jimmy McStay must have had faith because he took him to Douglas Park after release from Celtic.

Appearances:
RL: 2 apps. 0 gls.
RLC: 1 app. 0 gls.
Total: *3 apps. 0 gls.*

GLANCEY, Lawrence

Role: Centre-forward 1922-23
b. Cowdenbeath, 29th July 1902

CAREER: Cowdenbeath St Bride's/Hearts o' Beath Nov 1921/Cowdenbeath (trial) 10 Dec 1921/Hibernian (trial) 7 Jan 1922/CELTIC 21 Jan 1922/(Clackmannan loan 19 Apr 1922)/ (Cowdenbeath loan 12 May 1922)/Bo'ness 28 July 1923.

Debut v Motherwell (h) 2-0 (SL) 15.3.22

"A much wanted junior," "strong, robust, tall, a shot in either foot," Lawrence Glancey scored "four beautiful goals" on only his second outing with Beath versus Dunfermline Juniors on December 3rd 1921. He was almost a Cowdenbeath player until Celtic stepped-in. He scored two in a reserve match versus Aberdeen and was signed the same day. He started his first and only League game before a crowd of 8,000. The gates were opened at half-time and 10,000 unemployed poured in. Cowdenbeath, having been dished by Tom White over admission to Division One in 1919, brought a charge against Celtic on December 14th 1923 that they had offered Glancey monetary inducements. Celtic: Cowdenbeath made an offer; we topped it. (Case dismissed).

Appearances:
SL: 1 app. 0 gls.
Total: *1 app. 0 gls.*

GLASGOW, Samuel Little

Role: Full-back 1920-22
5' 9" 11st.0lbs.
b. Leadhills, 15th April 1897

CAREER: Leadhills/Nithsdale Wanderers 28 Aug 1920/CELTIC 11 Nov 1920/(Nithsdale Wanderers loan 5 Feb 1921)/(Dykehead loan 6 Oct 1922/St Johnstone 1 Dec 1922/Dykehead Oct 1923.

Debut v Clydebank (a) 2-0 (SL) 8.1.21

"A big fellow with a kick like a horse. A trifle slow...get on your toes, my lad!" (Match notes 15th April 1923). Celtic were "fighting like tigers" for every point in the new year 1921 to prevent Rangers getting too far ahead in the race for the Flag. Sam Glasgow made his debut on a soaking wet day when Alec McNair and Willie McStay were both injured.

He got his second chance on February 12th 1921 when McStay was with Scotland versus Wales at Pittodrie. Celtic beat St Mirren 6-0 which gave Sam a 100% League record as a Celt and a 100% clean sheet as a defender. Sam was a quarter-miler and (despite the 1923 match notes) no slouch on the track.

Sam Glasgow

Appearances:
SL: 2 apps. 0 gls.
Total: *2 apps. 0 gls.*

GLAVIN, Ronald

Role: Midfield 1974-79
5' 9" 11st.6lbs.
b. Glasgow, 27th March 1951

CAREER: Lochend Rovers 1967/Partick Thistle 1 Feb 1968/CELTIC 15 Nov 1974/ Barnsley 5 June 1979/free 1984/Belenenses (Portugal) 3 Aug 1984/Barnsley coach 10 July 1985/dismissed Mar 1986/Stockport County player-coach 30 Aug 1986/caretaker-manager 3 Nov 1986/resigned 6 Nov 1986/ Cowdenbeath match-to-match contract 22 Nov 1986/St Louis Steamers USA 8 Mar 1987.

Debut v Airdrie (h) 6-0 (SL) 16.11.74 (scored once)

Celtic reserves were shocked 4-1 by Partick Thistle colts on March 24th 1970 and three of the goals were scored by Ronnie Glavin.

Ronnie was in the Jags' senior side that repeated the dose in the League Cup final of October 23rd 1971. Jock Wallace was alleged to be interested in taking him to

Ronnie Glavin

Rangers "but R.G. was R.C. so nothing was done." At Firhill, Ronnie was the free man in midfield but at Parkhead was required to do his share of marking until the arrival of Pat Stanton. He became his own man once more in a free-running role as successor to Tommy Callaghan. He fed off the chances created by Dalglish and Joe Craig and became a goalscorer again in 1976-77 which meant he made a big contribution to the landing of the Double. His other reward was a full cap for Scotland against Sweden on April 26th 1977 but an injury in the third minute cost him his Cup final place against Rangers on May 7th. He was hugely popular at Barnsley as an attack-minded midfielder: "I'm doing what I'm good at, getting forward, supporting the front men... I had a chance to go to Manchester United but my ambition was always to play for Celtic. In retrospect, I was daft." His transfer value was £400,000 in 1981 but he went to Portugal as a free transfer. He later played indoor football for his wee brother Tony's team in the USA.

Appearances:
SL: 101 apps. 35 gls.
SLC: 29 apps. 3 gls.
SC: 12 apps. 8 gls.
Eur: 7 apps. 2 gls.
Total: *149 apps. 48 gls.*

GOLDIE, Hugh

Role: Half-back 1897-99
5' 7" 11st.10lbs.
*b. Dalry,
10th February 1874*

CAREER: Hurlford Thistle 1890/St Mirren 3 Sept 1894/Everton 1895/free 1897/CELTIC 1 May 1897/free 7 Jan 1899/ Dundee 3 Feb 1899/Barry Town 1899/Millwall 1899/Dundee 2 June 1900/New Brompton 1902/retired 1904.

Hugh Goldie

Debut v Clyde (h) 2-1 (GC) 18.9.1897

As a centre-back Jim Welford always preferred Hugh Goldie over anyone else to cover the wing to his right. Hugh came to Celtic when the new Limited Company was importing 'dons' galore from England so as to make as sudden an impact as Mr Souness at Ibrox 89 years on. Hugh took no time to make his mark. He was in the Celtic team that won 0-4 versus Rangers with 31,000 fans packed tight into old Ibrox in the League on September 27th 1897 when "the finest football played in Scotland this season" was seen. He won a Championship medal for 1897-98 but became part of the budget cuts when "St Bernard Battles, Patron of Parkhead" was brought home on October 3rd 1898. His high-energy profile made a great impression at Millwall but he had some drink-related training problems with New Brompton.

Appearances:
SL: 25 apps. 0 gls.
SC: 2 apps. 1 gl.
Total: *27 apps. 1 gl.*

GOLDIE, Peter

Role: Full-back, half-back 1953-58
5' 9" 11st.8lbs.
b. Dumbarton, 7th June 1934

CAREER: Vale Emmet/ Duntocher Hibernian June 1952/CELTIC
9 May 1953/free 1958/Aldershot 13 June 1958.

Debut v Partick Thistle (h) 5-1 (SL) 17.12.55

Peter Goldie

"A new Peter Wilson in the making," Peter Goldie, provisional signing and still a junior, broke his leg on October 17th 1953 but Celtic kept faith and called him up when the fracture healed. He got his initial chance as Mike Haughney's partner at left-back followed by a run at right-half when Jock Stein was injured in March 1956 and Evans moved to pivot. He played against the Busby Babes at Parkhead in a very bad-tempered benefit for the Cheshire Homes on April 16th 1956 but, for the Scottish Cup final versus Hearts five days later, Eric Smith was preferred at right-half. Celtic lost 1-3 in the League to Queen of the South just one week later and the fans vented their pent-up wrath on the directors' box (Queen of the South had lost 9-1 to Partick Thistle just days before). The shake -up was drastic: Alec Boden for Peter Goldie at right-half. Peter went a year without a first-team game until the return of Queen of the South on April 29th 1957. At Aldershot he went part-time and worked in the aircraft establishment at Farnborough.

Appearances:
SL: 13 apps. 0 gls.
SC: 1 app. 0 gls.
Total: *14 apps. 0 gls.*

GOLDIE, William

Role: Goalkeeper 1960
5' 11" 11st.0lbs.
b. Newmains, 16th March 1937

CAREER: L.Pieters 1951/Ardeer Thistle June 1952/Motherwell (trial) 2 Jan 1954/Rutherglen Glencairn 1955/Clyde (trial) 23 Feb 1956/ Airdrie Mar 1956/Army (Kenya) 1958/ CELTIC (trial) 15 Jan 1960/CELTIC (month trial) 28 Jan 1960/free 2 Mar 1960/CELTIC again 26 Aug 1960/free 26 Oct 1960/Albion Rovers 24 Jan 1961.

Debut v Airdrie (a) 0-2 (SL) 1.10.60

Schoolboy internationalist Willie Goldie was a competent, sometimes brilliant goalkeeper, whose best days were with Airdrie. He joined Celtic in August 1960 as cover for John Fallon when Haffey and Connor were unfit. He figures in an extraordinary story that illustrates Bob Kelly's idiosyncratic approach to team selection. As the Celtic coach made its way to Broomfield, Willie was spotted in the street, Celtic scarf on, en route to the game. He was taken aboard the team bus and so impressed was the future Sir Bob by Willie's dedication that John Fallon was dropped forthwith and Willie given his big team chance. Result? "Goldie gave away the goals like free soap coupons." Willie lost a leg as a result of an accident at work on June 25th 1962 but plays a mean game of golf. The Old Course at St Andrew's knows the power of his truly massive drives.

Appearances:
SL: 1 app. 0 shut-outs.
Total: *1 app. 0 shut-outs.*

GORMAN, John

Role: Full-back 1964-70
5' 9" 11st 0lbs.
b. Winchburgh,
16th August 1949

CAREER: Uphall
Saints 1963-65/CELTIC
(provisional) 19 Oct
1964/CELTIC (full)
19 Dec 1967/Carlisle
United 8 Sept 1970/
Tottenham Hotspur
11 Nov 1976/free own
request Mar 1979/
Tampa Bay Rowdies
1979-80-81-82/Phoenix
Inferno 1982-83-84-85/
Gillingham asst.
manager 1985/Leyton
Orient coach 1988/
Swindon Town coach
1991/manager 4 June 1993.

John Gorman

Debut v Hamilton Academicals (a) 4-2 (SLC)
25.9.68

Originally a left-midfielder, John Gorman
played in Celtic reserves alongside Hay,
Dalglish, Macari and McGrain when, to quote
his own words, "Celtic were a great side."
Celtic took him to the European Cup final in
Milan (May 6th 1970) to get the feel of the big
time but John was denied the opportunities
offered Dalglish, Vic Davidson and McGrain
who were on the trip. He was competing for a
place in the first team against Craig and
Gemmell, Hay and Brogan, but got just one
chance in all the time he was at Celtic Park.
He made his Celtic debut on the same night as
Kenny Dalglish. John started the game but
Kenny only came on at half-time (for Charlie
Gallagher). Carlisle offered him the chance of
first team football. "I was Celtic daft, I still am
and I was sorry to leave." At Brunton Park he
was three times nominated fans' Player of the
Year and was in the side that won promotion
to Division One in 1973. Spurs paid £60,000 for
John and manager Keith Burkinshaw
described him as "a marvellous servant, a
perfect example of the true professional; lots of
natural ability and enthusiasm; never gave less
than one hundred per cent." Gorman was
however sidelined for long spells by serious
ligament trouble in his left knee and

Tottenham eventually released him to
play in the United States. Glenn Hoddle
was clearly impressed however. When he
took over at Swindon in 1991 his ex-team-
mate Gorman was brought in as coach to
help teach the Town the beautiful game.
When Hoddle moved on to Chelsea shortly
after winning Swindon promotion to the
Premiership via the 1993 play-off final
at Wembley, Gorman was offered the
manager's job at the County Ground.
Despite bravely remaining true to John's
pure footballing principles Swindon
struggled and were relegated a year later.

Appearances:
SLC: 1 app. 0 gls.
Total: *1 app. 0 gls.*

GORMLEY, Philip

Phil Gormley

Role: Centre-forward
1948-50
5' 6" 11st.0lbs.
b. Greenock,
13th October 1924

CAREER: Klondyke
Athletic Juniors 1946/
Kirkintilloch Rob Roy
1947/CELTIC 3 Jan 1948 /free Apr 1950/
Aldershot Aug 1950/Dundee United 31 July
1953.

Debut v Aberdeen (h) 1-0 (SL) 10.1.48

Celtic were so hard up for a centre at the start
of 1948 they even had thoughts of Billy
Williamson of Rangers before Jock Weir was
bought from Blackburn. Phil Gormley was a
left-half converted to centre at Rob Roy (for
whom he scored six against Clydebank on
December 6th 1947) and was drafted-in as
"surprise choice" for the injured Frank Walsh
and Joe Rae in Celtic's "relegation scrap"
versus Aberdeen. He was "dead game and
very direct. But, like most Celtic centres of
recent years, was acknowledged no planned
support." Centre-half Willie Corbett secured
both points from a penalty on the day. Phil
joined the reserves and broke his leg just over
a year later on February 5th 1949.

Appearances:
SL: 1 app. 0 gls.
Total: *1 app. 0 gls.*

GOULD, John Daniel

Role: Outside-right 1939-40
5' 8" 11st.0lbs.
b. 16th December 1919

CAREER: Neilston Victoria/Third Lanark
(trial) Nov 1937/Arbroath Apr 1938/(CELTIC
loan 11 Nov 1939)/(Albion Rovers loan
15 Aug 1940)/(Morton loan 1 Feb 1941)/
(Raith Rovers loan 9 Sept 1941)/(Dumbarton
loan 13 Dec 1941)/(Raith Rovers loan 1942-43)
/(Third Lanark loan 20 May 1943)/Arbroath
again 9 Mar 1944/free 26 Apr 1947/Ayr
United 26 Apr 1947/Stenhousemuir 27 Jan
1948.

Debut v Morton (a) 1-1 (RL) 11.11.39

Barrhead boy and apprentice engineer with
G&J Weir of Cathcart, John Gould was in the
Arbroath team (as wing partner to John
McInally) the day Delaney had his arm broken
(April 1st 1939). West Ham had watched him
the week before and Newcastle were openly
interested. Arbroath were offered £4,000 for
his full transfer but on the outbreak of war,
Celtic got his services on loan for free. He was
Willie Maley's last signing and brought to
Parkhead at a time when Celtic were losing
every Saturday game they played. At

Arbroath he
"would persist
in trying to beat
the man twice"
and had been
encouraged to
play the raiding
winger and go
for goals but
was "timid
when it came to
shooting." John
made a bright
start (in
drenching rain)
then faded,
unable to fit-in
and by mid-
December Celtic
had scratched a
mere four
points from
nine games.

John Gould

With the advent of Jimmy McStay as manager
in February 1940 he seems to have fallen
completely out of favour. Celtic now reverted
to the policy of a different winger a week as
long as his name was John but not Gould:
John Kelly, John Crum, John Watters.

Appearances:
RL: 15 apps. 4 gls.
SWC: 2 apps. 1 gl.
Total: *17 apps. 5 gls.*

GRAHAM, John Lang

Role: Inside-right 1903-04
b. Dalry, 7th August 1881

CAREER: Kilmarnock Rugby XI 1898/
Kilmarnock 5 June 1900/Bristol Rovers May
1902/CELTIC 1 May 1903/Millwall May 1904
/Accrington Stanley Apr 1905/Hamilton
Academicals Dec 1906.

Debut v Hibernian (a) 2-0 (SL) 5.9.03

Mick Dunbar made a trip to Bristol at the end
of April 1903 to secure some Ayrshire men
regarded by the press as "plain done" before
they left Scotland: Bobby Muir and Johnny
Graham. He signed these two and took Jim
Young as well because he was homesick. Muir
and Young made a certain fame at Parkhead
but Graham was destined to understudy the
genius McMenemy. He played his last game
for Celtic in a club benefit at Arthurlie on May
12th 1904 and scored in a 1-1 draw.

Appearances:
SL: 4 apps. 0 gls.
Total: *4 apps. 0 gls.*

GRANGER, John

Role: Full-back, half-back
1922-25
5' 7" 11st.0lbs.
*b. Dumbarton,
16th July 1899*

CAREER: Vale of Leven
Juniors/Dumbarton
9 May 1921/Vale of
Leven 1 Oct 1921/CELTIC 15 Feb 1922/
(Armadale loan 8 Feb 1924)/(Forfar Athletic
loan Sept 1924)/free 1925/Vale of Leven
15 June 1925/Dumbarton 12 July 1926/ free
25 Dec 1926/Melbourne Caledonian May
1927/Ards 19 July 1931.

John Granger

Debut v Falkirk (a) 0-0 (SL) 17.2.23

John was Celtic's first-choice deputy at full-back and half-back when season 1923-24 began and the DM was 20,000,000 to the Pound. Willie Cringan was down to travel as 12th man to Aberdeen on 29th September 1923 but was in bad odour over a request to management for bonuses and John Granger travelled instead. His last game for the Celtic big team was in the opening League match of the 1924-25 season on August 16th at Dens Park. He sailed for Australia on May 4th 1927 but was back in Scotland and looking for a club by February 21st 1930. On June 23rd 1938 he turned out at left-half for Patsy Gallagher's Charity XI at Holm Park, Yoker.

Appearances:
SL: 13 apps. 0 gls.
Total: *13 apps. 0 gls.*

GRANT, Peter

Role: Midfield 1982 to date
5' 10" 11st.4lbs.
b. Bellshill, 30th August 1965

CAREER: St Aloysius Chapelhall/Celtic BC 1976/CELTIC S form 1977/CELTIC 27 July 1982.

Debut v Rangers (a) 0-1 (SL) 21.4.84

"I've seen more meat on a butcher's pencil but this kid got stuck in and wasn't slow at lambasting more experienced colleagues" (Celtic v Hibernian 28th April 1984). "Grant is the scuffler in the Celtic team...his responsibility is to win the ball and allow more glamorous talents to exploit the rewards of his hardness and all-consuming commitment" (1988). Peter Grant "bristled with promise" in his early days at Parkhead as a "tigerish competitor... noted for his ball-winning ability and great appetite for the game... a midfield work-horse who gets things done and helps others play." His proudest moment was probably after the League was clinched at Parkhead versus Dundee on April 23rd 1988. He had broken his foot against St Mirren 18 days before but the packed house chanted and chanted his name until he came out on sticks and joined the team. During '87-88 he had been one of the most improved players in the side but after the triumphs of the Centenary season his progress slowed and talk of a transfer to Norwich or Dundee over a

new contract resulted. "Yet, when the ball starts rolling on a Saturday, Grant banishes all thoughts of money from his mind and gives his all. The most important thing for players like Grant is the greater good of the club..." (James Traynor 30th November 1992). It was his persistence led to Joe Miller's goal in the Scottish Cup final of May 20th 1989. He was capped first against England as a substitute on May 27th 1989 and started against Chile three days later. Peter's favourite position is centre-midfield and he possesses a long-range wallop in the tradition of Geatons, Lynch, Peacock which he uses too seldom. Peter Grant is an

Peter Grant

out-and-out jersey player who loves Celtic with every breath he takes. After 14 moons of contracts, Peter signed up to Celtic for three more years on 10th September 1993. He took some flak for the first two Rangers' goals in the Ne'erday 1994 disaster, was stretchered off with torn knee ligaments on 15th January (Celtic versus Aberdeen abandoned for fog) and was out of the game until the Rangers-fans-only Old Firm clash at Ibrox on April 30th. Despite the lay-off Peter "tackled and blocked with unlikely stamina" and punched the air at the end to celebrate a performance by his beloved Celtic that totally upset the odds.

Appearances:
SL: 283 apps. 10 gls.
SLC: 31 apps. 2 gls.
SC: 26 apps. 1 gl.
Eur: 25 apps. 0 gls.
Total: *365 apps. 13 gls.*

GRASSAM, William

Role: Inside-forward 1903
5' 10" 12st.0lbs.
b. Larbert,
20th November 1878

CAREER: Redcliffe Thistle 1896/Maryhill 1897/ Burslem Port Vale July 1899/ West Ham United 1900/CELTIC 1 May 1903/Manchester United 28 Sept 1903/Leyton FC 1905/West Ham United Dec 1905/ Brentford Aug 1909/free Mar 1911.

Debut v Hibernian (n) 5-0 (CC) 21.5.03

Maryhill boy Willie Grassam was West Ham skipper and a goal-scoring inside-forward when he joined Celtic at the same time as Bobby Muir, Johnny Graham and Sunny Jim Young. His first competitive match was at first Cathkin in the green and white stripes. Next time he appeared for Celtic on August 17th 1903 it was in the new hooped strip that gave the team "a very youthful appearance." Willie's best football was played in his two stints at West Ham (which was a brand new club when he joined first) and where he was ultimately replaced only by the great Dan Shea.

Appearances:
SL: 2 apps. 0 gls.
Total: *2 apps. 0 gls.*

GRAY, Alexander

Role: Outside-left 1912-18
5' 6" 10st.7lbs.
b. Bainsford, 11th September 1892

CAREER: East Plean United/Stenhousemuir 15 Aug 1910/CELTIC 11 May 1912/(Alloa loan 20 Mar 1913)/(Ayr United loan 17 May 1913)/CELTIC again 29 Apr 1914/(Ayr United loan 31 Aug 1914)/(Falkirk loan 8 Mar 1917)/ Kilmarnock 16 Oct 1918/Ayr United 24 Apr 1919/Stenhousemuir 20 Aug 1920/Johnstone Oct 1920/Vale of Leven 26 May 1922/ Arthurlie 15 Feb 1922/ Stenhousemuir 27 Sept 1922.

Debut v Kilmarnock (a) 2-0 (SL)
31.8.12 (scored once)

"He's extra," said fellow Stenhousemuir man Alec McNair when Celtic signed Alex Gray "a fast and tricky winger" "to solve the outside-left problem." Alex sailed for the tour of Scandinavia in June 1912 although never aboard a boat of any sort before in his life. He took the place of John Brown in the second match when Celtic employed what a Copenhagen paper called their "short-passing Spil" against the

Willie Grassam

Danish Olympic XI preparing for the Games in Stockholm. On January 25th 1913 Alex played against Airdrie in one of the most colourful forward lines ever to represent the Celtic: Gray and Gallagher; Quinn; Browning and Brown. The Broomfield goalie was also Brown. Alex was a moulder to trade; by 1915 he was making hand grenades.

Appearances:
SL: 13 apps. 4 gls.
SC: 1 app. 0 gls.
Total: *14 apps. 4 gls.*

GRAY, John Lyon

Role: Inside-right 1900-02
b. Stenhousemuir, 4th May 1881

CAREER: Elder Park/CELTIC 28 Aug 1900/ Cape Caledonians May 1902.

Debut v Third Lanark (a) 2-1 (SL) 1.9.1900
(scored once)

"Celtic expect much from the Stenhousemuir laddie..." "Gray has speed and judgement but is no advance on Gilhooly." John Gray was involved in one piece of excitement while playing for Celtic at Paisley on January 19th 1901 just three days before Queen Victoria died. Celtic crossed over 1-4 up against St Mirren but the Buddies fought back to 3-4 with two quick goals in the second half. Then McMahon kicked out at Brandon and the crowd invaded the pitch. In the melee, Celtic president John Glass was assaulted but Celtic held out for the points. John emigrated to South Africa in 1902 to work for the Imperial Railway company at Salt River.

Appearances:
SL: 2 apps. 0 gls.
Total: *2 apps. 0 gls.*

GRAY, Stuart

Role: Left Midfield 1989 to date
5' 10" 11st.0lbs.
b. Harrogate,
18th December 1973

CAREER: Celtic BC/ CELTIC 'S' form Nov 1989 /CELTIC ground staff July 1990/Giffnock North AFC /CELTIC 7 July 1992/ (Bournemouth loan 17 Feb 1994).
Debut v Aberdeen (h) 1-0 (SL) 1.5.93

Stuart Gray

Stuart Gray is the son of the famous Scottish international Eddie Gray, who was a key part of Don Revie's great era at Leeds United. Stuart was one of the tyros blooded at the end of the fruitless 1992-93 season. He played as an orthodox left-winger and was complimented by assistant manager Craig: "It was smashing to see young lads like Gray doing so well." What the punter saw was a boy able to beat his man on the outside but instead of going fast into space, checking, passing back and losing valuable momentum. He was also booked for time-wasting. Stuart is possessed of a powerful long-range shot and used it to effect to keep Alan Main on his toes for Dundee United in the Reserve League Cup final won by Celtic at Tannadice on 18th April 1994. He was virtually an ever-present in the second team during 1993-94 and was allegedly

well-regarded by manager Macari. He came on for the injured John O'Neill (16 minutes) at Old Trafford in the Mark Hughes Testimonial match (16th May 1994) when Celtic beat the Reds 1-3.

Appearances:
SL: 1 app. 0 gls.
Total: *1 app. 0 gls.*

GRAY, William

Role: Centre-forward 1927-29
5' 9" 12st.0lbs.
b. Maryhill, 30th May 1907

CAREER: Wyndford Star/Maryhill Hibernian 1927/CELTIC 9 Aug 1927/Hamilton Academicals 17 Aug 1929/Colwyn Bay 1930/ Hamilton 27 Feb 1932/Maryhill Juniors June 1935.
Debut v Dundee (a) 1-0 (SL) 11.8.28

'Wuggy' Gray, the Human Siege Gun, played his third game for Celtic in broiling heat. "The crowd was thunderstruck by the rocket force of Gray's shooting... John Thomson saved the game, Gray won it." Willie was brought to Parkhead to replace McGrory (expected to join Arsenal any time) but stepped into the team as immediate cover for the departed Tommy McInally. He had been a prolific scorer as a junior with four goals in the Scottish Junior Cup final on May 26th 1928 versus Jock Stein's beloved Burnbank. He scored with a famous penalty at Cathkin in the last minute for a 2-2 draw in the League on September 24th 1928. Referee Campbell Bilney had seen Jimmy McGrory kicked by a Thirds player although he did not know

'Wuggy' Gray

which one. Q. Who kicked McGrory? A. The Unknown Warrior. Why Celtic lost faith is not clear. Willie went to Hamilton for £250, met Celtic at Douglas Park on August 31st 1929 and scored twice.

Appearances:
SL: 26 apps. 12 gls.
SC: 5 apps. 0 gls.
Total: *31 apps. 12 gls.*

GROVES, William

Role: Centre-forward
1888-90 & 1896
5' 8" 11st.0lbs.
b. Leith, 9th November 1869
d. Edinburgh, 13th February 1908

CAREER: Thistle FC/Leith Harp/Hibernian 1886/CELTIC Aug 1888/West Bromwich Albion 25 Oct 1890/Aston Villa Sept 1893/Hibernian 26 Aug 1895/ CELTIC 29 Nov 1896/Rushden 1898.

Willie Groves

Debut v Shettleston (h) 5-1 (SC) 1.9.1888

> *"There's one that wants a-watchin'*
> *They call him Willie Groves*
> *He's wonderful to look at*
> *As about the field he roves*
> *Ah, he beats my comprehension*
> *Real admiration I have felt*
> *He's a dasher, he's a smasher*
> *He's a bould, bould Celt!"*

"Darlin' Willie," "as genteel a centre-forward as ever kicked a ball" was Celtic's initial superstar, the huge favourite of the first Celtic fans for his "famous, fast, cork-screw runs". He was inside-right in the Hibs side that lifted the Scottish Cup at 2nd Hampden (Cathkin Park) on February 12th 1887, a victory that inspired Brother Walfrid and John Glass with the idea of a Hibernian side in Glasgow. He was at centre when Hibs hanselled first Celtic Park against Cowlairs on May 8th 1888. Willie Maley describes him as "swarthy, well-fea-tured, well set-up." Willie had devastating speed and a thunderous shot to go. "Groves electrified the spectators by some of his runs" (versus Dumbarton Harp August 8th 1888). He was a touch player, described in the context of the time as "dainty, lady-like, rather timid." One irate Irishman bellowed at him: "What are you dancing about for? Can't you

hit it a welt like McKeown?" He had a sharp tongue on the pitch and kept a commentary going, a lot of it coded but much of it to let Johnny Coleman know the stinker he was having. Paddy Gallagher and Mick McKeown were "thick-witted Hibernians." When they bridled, he apologised: "It's my lisp. I said quick-witted, not thick-witted." He played for Celtic initially on August 1st 1888 against Abercorn in the World Exhibition Cup at Gilmorehill and played centre in both Scottish Cup finals of February 1888. It was a magnificent run and shot by Darlin' Willie that put Rangers out in the first round of the Scottish Cup at old Celtic Park in "the first titanic struggle between the clubs" on September 6th 1890. Although Celtic had set him up in a pub at 29 Taylor Street, the lure of English gold proved too strong and he missed the game with Abercorn in Paisley on October 25th 1890 to slip away to England. He won the English Cup with WBA on March 19th 1893 and the League with Aston Villa in 1894. His health broke with the onset of TB and he was in Bournemouth in August 1894 for the sea air but forbidden ever to play again on medical advice on November 10th. He had five games for Hibs during 1895-96 and turned out twice for Celtic in December 1896 but by now was a spent force. He was so ill by September 1899 that Willie Maley opened a subscription list on his behalf. He was working as a labourer for Edinburgh Corporation at the end of 1903 and died in utter penury.

Appearances:
SL: 4 apps. 3 gls.
SC: 14 apps. 13 gls.
Total: *18 apps. 16 gls.*

♣ **Celtic note:** *Willie Groves signed forms for Everton dated 18 July 1889 (witness D. Doyle; "Give me Dan's terms and I'll sign") but repented and got Tom Maley to break his honeymoon and plead for him at the SFA. He could not play for WBA until he served a month's suspension. WBA were to transfer him to Everton in 1893 but Villa made him the first £100 transfer and paid a £50 fine on top to get him.*

HAFFEY, Francis

Role: Goalkeeper 1958-64
6' 0" 11st.6lbs.
b. Glasgow, 28th November 1938

CAREER: Campsie Black Watch/CELTIC (trial) Ne'erday 1958/CELTIC 18 Feb 1958/ Maryhill Harp (farmed-out) 1958/Swindon Town 9 Oct 1964/free 1965/St George-Budapest FC (Sydney) 28 June 1965/Hakoah (Sydney)/Sutherland FC player-coach by 1976.
Debut v Third Lanark (h) 4-1 (SL) 30.4.58

"Is Haffey an improvement on Beattie?" was the question until Celtic knocked Rangers out of the Scottish Cup on February 28th 1959 and Bobby Evans approached the big 'keeper with his hand held out in congratulation at the end. It was Haffey versus Rangers again in the Charity Cup semi-final of May 2nd 1959. He was "Haffey the Barrier, Haffey the Cat, Haffey the Hero" on Ne'erday 1960 when he even saved a Billy Little spot-kick up in the postage stamp corner in the 59th minute. Against England at Hampden (9th April 1960) he saved another penalty this time from Bobby Charlton but the referee ordered a re-take. He did not accept the 9-3 humiliation at Wembley of April 15th 1961 as casually as Denis Law has made out. So affected was he that John Fallon expected to be in the Cup final side versus Dunfermline the following Saturday. Frank rescued his career from the catastrophe and carried on. As a Celtic goalie he is associated with moments of high comedy. 3rd February 1962: he tries to steer a free kick smartish to Dunky MacKay and puts it in his own net; 17th March 1962: furious rowing with Crerand and McNeill and the ref has to calm down all three; 2nd March 1963: he throws a pass-back between his legs to Jim Kennedy as he staggers out of the penalty box with the ball; 13th April 1963: Frank duffs a clearance right to McDonald's feet for Raith's equaliser in the Scottish Cup semi-final; 26th October 1963: penalty for Celtic 9-0 up against Airdrie; fans chant for Haffey; Frank ambles up, cannonball shot, Roddie McKenzie's save is stunning, Frank applauds. But otherwise the man was brilliant. Only he and McNeill stood between Celtic and a real thrashing in the Scottish Cup final replay of 15th May 1963. A broken ankle against Partick Thistle in the Glasgow Cup (13th November 1963) signalled the end of his career with Celtic. Frank (who always just happened to have his music with him) commenced a new career as a cabaret performer in Australia and took a vivid interest in Australian Rules football.

Appearances:
SL: 140 apps. 41 shut-outs.
SLC: 24 apps. 9 shut-outs.
SC: 34 apps. 10 shut-outs.
Eur: 3 apps. 1 shut-out.
Total: *201 apps. 61 shut-outs (30%).*

Frank Haffey

HALPIN, John William

Role: Outside-left 1978-84
5' 9" 11st.0lbs.
b. Broxburn, 15th November 1961

CAREER: Celtic BC/Armadale Thistle/ Hibernian (trial) 1978/CELTIC 5 Sept 1978/ (South China loan May 1983)/(Sunderland loan 16 Aug 1984)/Carlisle United 24 Oct 1984/free 16 May 1991/Rochdale July 1991/ Gretna 1993.

John Halpin

Debut v Queen of the South (h) 4-0 (SC) 23.1.82 (scored once)

John Halpin was a speedy, direct winger who first played for Celtic in the Glasgow Cup 3-2 defeat of Clyde on May 8th 1979. Despite a splendid tour of Germany and Holland in July 1980 when he (as likewise Charlie Nicholas) "sweated himself in as a genuine first team squad man," a series of injuries meant he was seldom closer to the first team than its fringes during his time at Parkhead. He scored 18 goals in 27 games for the reserves in 1983-84 but like John Gorman decided to try his luck at Carlisle where he was vastly more appreciated and played 82 games. He suffered two broken legs, the second in January 1987 so bad that he was off until November and almost decided to retire on specialist's advice.

Appearances:
SL: 7 apps. 0 gls.
SLC: 5 apps. 0 gls.
SC: 1 app. 1 gl.
Eur: 1 app. 0 gls.
Total: *14 apps. 1 gl.*

HAMILL, Michael

Role: Centre-half 1916; 1918
5' 8" 10st.7lbs.
b. 19th January 1889
d. c 19th July 1943

Mickey Hamill

CAREER: Hardinge St School/St Paul's Swifts/Belfast Rangers/Red Hand FC/Belfast Celtic 1908/(CELTIC loan (Dublin) 28 Dec 1910)/Manchester United 31 Dec 1910/(Belfast Celtic loan cs 1913)/Belfast Celtic (still a United player) 1914/(CELTIC loan 19 Oct 1916)/(Manchester United loan 2 Dec 1916)/ (CELTIC loan 9 Dec 1916)/Distillery 1916/ (CELTIC loan 18 May & 25 May 1918)/ Manchester City 1 Oct 1920/Belfast Celtic 1924/Fall River FC USA June 1924/Belfast Celtic 1926/retired 1930/Distillery manager Aug 1934.

Debut v Morton (h) 0-0 (SL) 21.10.16

Born in Leeson Street just off the Falls Road, Mickey Hamill, "cool finesse... a class defender," was one of the most instinctive footballers ever to grace the green and white: "He could do as he liked with the ball... clever trapping, accurate passing, back-heeling... wonderful headwork... fantastic display." Celtic wanted him in 1910 but he was already pledged to Manchester United. At Old Trafford, trainer Geordie Livingstone warned him he was yards too slow for the English game and set him doing 25-yard sprints and only 25-yard sprints in training until he was sick and tired of speeding-up. In his second season, Mickey played right-half behind Billy Meredith. He won his first cap versus England in 1912, the first of five and developed into the fast-moving pivot with long, accurate passes to his wingmen. Celtic fans were crazy about him in his short spells at Parkhead and unable to comprehend a certain coolness in the Scottish press: *Och! Michael avick/You have many a trick/As a half back you rank with the best/And we call you our own/Though you're only on loan/From the dear little isle of the West./You get praise now and then/From the knights of the pen/But often in mood circumspective/You may wonder with me/Why the scribes all agree/Your play is just 'quietly effective.'* Mickey led Belfast Celtic (with Willie McStay) to their first Irish Cup triumph in the third game against Linfield at Grosvenor Park on April 4th 1918. From Glasgow, Mickey took a Charity Cup medal away with him on 25th May 1918 to go with his 1916 Championship medal as mementos of his time with Celtic. He played for Ireland against Scotland in the Victory International at Ibrox on March 22nd 1919 (when he toyed with Jimmy Gordon) and amused the crowd with his cry of (Belfast) "Celtic's ball!" at throw-ins. He also played for the English League in another of the Victory Internationals. His last appearance at Parkhead was in Jimmy McMenemy's testimonial on January 6th 1920. The mystery of his death by apparent drowning in the Lagan Canal at Lisburn is still unsolved. Mickey lived at 116, Falls Road.

Appearances:
SL: 7 apps. 0 gls.
Total: *7 apps. 0 gls.*

HAMILTON, David

Role: Outside-left 1902-12
5' 6" 10st.2lbs.
b. Glasgow, 21st October 1882
d. Glasgow, 23rd January 1950

CAREER: League Hibernian Juveniles/ Cambuslang Hibernian/CELTIC 25 Apr 1902/ (Clyde loan 1 May 1902)/(Ayr FC loan 1902)/ Dundee 6 Dec 1912/Bathgate 3 Nov 1913/ retired 1914.

Debut v Hearts (h) 3-1 (CC) 19.5.02 (scored once)

"COPE'S" "CLIPS" CIGARETTES

No. 405.— HAMILTON, D. Celtic

Noted Footballers

Celtic played Hearts in the Inter-City League on February 1st 1902 with South Side boy "Wilson" a junior internationalist trying out at outside-left. It was an impressive trial. "Wilson" even opened the scoring. He was in the team again versus Blackburn Rovers on April 16th 1902 for the Ibrox Disaster Fund with "Smith" (alias J.McMenemy) at inside-right. He missed a badge against Hibs in the final of the Charity Cup (31st May 1902) but was left-winger in the team that relieved Rangers of the 1901 Exhibition Cup at 2nd Hampden on one of Celtic's glory nights, June 17th 1902. Celtic went down to play Liverpool on September 1st and Manchester City on September 2nd 1902. "Hamilton's speed and dash were a feature of Celtic's English games... Hamilton has no equal for speed." He lined up in Celtic's greatest ever front five: Bennett, McMenemy, Quinn, Somers and Hamilton for the first time in an Inter-

City League match on 30th April 1904 and set-off on the journey to six Championships in a row at Meadowside versus Partick Thistle on August 20th 1904. Davie won Scottish Cup medals in 1904, 1908 and 1911. He played in both Finals of the Riot Year 1909. He thrived on the service produced by Peter Somers and won the Ne'erday 1906 match versus Rangers with a run and shot reminiscent of the great Billy Groves. Tom Sinclair got his hands to it but couldn't stop it.

He was ordered-off for "obscene and threatening language" (ie "I wish I had a revolver") to referee JB Stark at Easter Road 5th October 1907. For this he received two months suspension. Davie was the team's singer with Peter Somers as accompanist on the piano. He had long patches of sheer excellence. At other times, he couldn't get a cross in. But he still rates as a great, great Celt.

Appearances:
SL: 221 apps. 53 gls.
SC: 39 apps. 7 gls.
Total: *260 apps. 60 gls.*

♣ **Celtic note:** *Alec Maley tells of a Celtic player, he thinks it was Davie Hamilton, being smacked in the face before a Scottish Cup final by Jimmy Quinn as an antidote for nerves. Which particular final he does not say.*

HANCOCK, Stephen

Role: Forward 1970-74
5' 8" 11st.3lbs.
b. Sheffield, 10th September 1953

CAREER: St Anthony's School Edinburgh/ CELTIC 'S' form 16 May 1968/Newtongrange Star (farmed-out) 1970/CELTIC 25 Sept 1970/ free 1974/ Hibernian (trial) 1974/Sheffield Wednesday 1974/free 1975/Hearts (trial) July

1975/Hearts Nov 1975/free 29 Apr 1976/ Meadowbank Thistle 1977/free 1979/ Stenhousemuir 29 June 1979/ Forfar Athletic 1 Aug 1981/resigned 13 Nov 1982.

Debut v Sliema Wanderers (a) 2-1 (EC) 3.11.71 (sub)

Steve Hancock was a fantastic prospect. He won three junior caps with Newtongrange Star and the Junior Player of the Year Cup on May 17th 1971. What happened? "I thought I

Steve Hancock

knew better than Jock Stein. He wanted me to move to digs in Glasgow from my home in Edinburgh. I didn't think this was necessary. Now I know I was wrong" (3rd November 1982). Stein dropped him from the reserves and Steve's odyssey away from Parkhead began. John Hagart persuaded Hearts to try him. Steve turned out against Celtic on August 13th 1975 and pounced on a Latchford mistake in 15 minutes. When Meadowbank freed him he was on the point of going back to his work as a taxi driver. Stenhousemuir took him to Ochilview where he scored 50 goals in two seasons. Forfar paid £12,000 for him (big money for the Loons) and he took them into the semi-final of the Scottish Cup in 1982 with the goal that knocked-out Hearts. He retired suddenly to sell insurance on Saturdays.

Appearances:
Eur: 1 app. 0 gls.
Total: *1 app. 0 gls.*

HANNAH, Robert

Role: Inside-forward 1974-77
5' 10" 11st.10lbs.
b. c 1958

CAREER: Celtic BC/CELTIC 22 July 1974/ Bellshill Athletic (farmed-out) 1974/free 30 Apr 1977/Ayr United 4 July 1977/ St Johnstone 22 May 1979/East Stirling 18 Jan 1980.

Debut v Ayr United (a) 5-3 (SL) 1.5.76 (sub)

Jock Stein wrote in the *Celtic View* of April 2nd 1975; "To be honest, we have slipped more than I thought possible. Changes will have to be made." He then went on to mention three hopes of the future - Burns, Casey and

Hannah. "Exciting young prospect" Robert Hannah was in the Celtic Under-17 team that won the European Youth Cup at Celtic Park on April 15th 1974 just before he joined the ground staff. He and Tommy Burns went to Salisbury, Southern Rhodesia (Harare, Zimbabwe) in the summer of 1975 to play there for six weeks at the request of the local Celtic SC. He played in the Scottish Professional Youth team that beat France 0-1 in the final of the Cannes International Tournament on April 19th 1976. Andy Roxburgh praised his non-stop running and Jack Harkness forecast that young Hannah "will certainly play in the Celtic first team before '75-76 is out" and sure enough he did, each time as a substitute, once for Burns on his debut and next for Edvaldsson two days later. Previously he had been in the squad for both legs of the Cup-Winners' Cup tie against Sachsenring (3rd and 17th March 1976). He travelled with Celtic to Krakow for the UEFA Cup match with Wisla (29th September 1976). What happened thereafter to all Bobby's fine promise is a mystery.

Appearances:
SL: 2 apps. 0 gls.
SLC: 1 app. 0 gls.
Total: *3 apps. 0 gls.*

HASTIE, John

Role: Inside-left 1910-12

CAREER: Glenbuck Cherrypickers 1907/Nithsdale Wanderers 1909 (did not play)/Glenbuck Cherrypickers Sept 1910/CELTIC 9 Nov 1910 (Raith Rovers loan13 July 1911)/CELTIC 30 Apr 1912/Nithsdale Wanderers 21 Nov 1912.

Debut v Dundee (a) 0-1 (SL) 26.11.10

John Hastie

Robert Hannah

Dundee went into the lead in the 89th minute of John Hastie's first game in a Celtic jersey. Willie Kivlichan equalised at once but the ref was adamant: time-up, no goal! His third game on 10th December 1910 was just four days before Amundsen reached the South Pole in the race with Scott. His first goal for the club was against Belfast Celtic in a 0-1 win (27th December 1910). He won a Scottish Cup medal with Celtic in the replay against Hamilton Academicals at Ibrox on April 15th 1911. Celtic took him on the Continental tour of 1911 and John played his last game at Montmartre, Paris against Etoile Rouge (28th May 1911).

Appearances:
SL: 16 apps. 3 gls.
SC: 3 apps. 1 gl.
Total: *19 apps. 4 gls.*

HAUGHNEY, Michael

Role: Right-back 1949-57
5' 11" 12st.0lbs.
b. Paisley, 10th December 1926

CAREER: Dalkeith St David's/Newtongrange Star/CELTIC 20 Jan 1949/retired 1957/free Apr 1958.

Debut v Rangers (h) 3-2 (SLC) 13.8.49
(scored once)

Mike Haughney's mother was a niece of the magnificent Peter Dowds and Mike had a trial for Celtic as a juvenile as early as 1944. He played outside-left on his debut. Rangers equalised 2-2 in the 62nd minute and Celtic switched the forward line by sending Haughney to centre. Within eight minutes he had reduced the Rangers end to silence and exalted the Celts to bedlam with a raging shot past Bobby Brown. To the great regret of coach Jimmy Hogan big Mike was a student and a part-timer: "He has the hardest and most accurate shot I've seen in years, if he could train regularly, he would soon achieve top grade." Mike became known as "the man who can only shoot" and on April 10th 1950 the cry was heard again: "Celtic must find a leader." Mike dropped into the reserves and scored three in the first four minutes against Raith Rovers reserves at Parkhead on September 30th 1950. He made his debut at right-back versus Rangers in the Danny Kaye Charity Cup final (3-2 for Celtic) before 81,000 people at Hampden on May 6th 1950. He was right-back in the side that won the St Mungo Cup (1st August 1951) and the Coronation Cup on May 20th 1953 the year of his B. Comm. degree from Edinburgh University. 1953-54 was his best season as right-back of the side that won the Double under skipper Stein. He was capped for Scotland versus England at Hampden on a bleak wet Saturday (3rd April 1954) but found himself on the end of a 2-4 drubbing from Ronnie Allen and Johnny Nicholls. He regressed to his beginnings as inside-right at Hampden on April 21st 1956 in the incomprehensible Celtic team selection to play Hearts in the Scottish Cup final. He pulled the score back to 2-1 eight minutes after half-time but to no avail. His last game for Celtic was like his first: against Rangers in the Charity Cup (1st May 1957). This ex-Commando and captain in the Seaforth Highlanders emigrated to Indiana USA that same summer.

Appearances:
SL: 159 apps. 32 gls.
SLC: 45 apps. 7 gls.
SC: 29 apps. 5 gls.
Total: *233 apps. 44 gls.*

Mike Haughney

HAVERTY, Joseph

Role: Outside-left 1964
5' 4" 9st.6lbs.
b. Dublin, 17th February 1936

CAREER: Home Farm 1951/
St Patrick's Athletic 1953/
Arsenal 19 July 1954/
Blackburn Rovers 31 July
1961/Millwall Sept 1962/
CELTIC (month trial)
27 Sept 1964/Bristol Rovers
Dec 1964/Shelbourne 1965/
Chicago Spurs 1967/Kansas
City Spurs 1968.

*Debut v St Mirren (h) 4-1
(SL) 17.10.64*

Celtic had two left-wingers
of unfulfilled potential when they tried-out Joe
Haverty: Bobby Lennox and John Hughes.
Wee Joe was always a thrilling sight at the
Arsenal, full speed up the left before cutting in
to do havoc at the near post. Celtic fans were
hugely impressed by his one try-out but what
happened next is unclear: did Millwall order
him home from the Jungle to the Den? Were
Celtic repelled by a transfer fee of £3,000?
Whichever way, Parkhead cancelled his
registration on October 31st 1964.

>**Appearances:**
>*SL: 1 app. 0 gls.*
>**Total:** *1 app. 0 gls.*

♣ **Celtic note:** *While at Parkhead, Joe was capped
against Poland in Dublin on October 25th 1964
and appears in some international record books as
Haverty (Glasgow Celtic).*

HAY, Christopher Drummond

Role: Striker 1993 to date
5' 11" 11st.7lbs.
b. Glasgow, 28th August 1974

CAREER: Mearns Castle
School/Clarkston BC
/Giffnock North AFC/
CELTIC 27 May 1993.

*Debut v Partick Thistle (h)
1-1 (SL) 7.5.94*

Chris Hay

"Reserve scoring sensation" Chris
Hay, with seven goals in his last
four games (including three
versus Rangers on 30th April
1994) lined up with Simon
Donnelly on his debut to offer
Celtic some thrust in their vain bid
to clinch a UEFA Cup place for
1994-95. He started nervously, then
smacked a shot off the crossbar on
the stroke of half-time with the
score at 0-0 after beautiful work by
McLaughlin. Celtic went ahead
1-0 in 50 minutes but Thistle
equalised with four to go and, like
every other prize since the Year of
Revolutions 1989, Europe moved
out of Parkhead's reach. Veteran
John Burridge defied him at
Aberdeen on May 14th, the last
League game of the season. From being a
youngster on the dole training on a voluntary
basis at Parkhead in April 1993, he came on
for Willie Falconer with eight minutes to go
before 42,709 in the Mark Hughes testimonial
at Old Trafford (May 16th 1994).

>**Appearances:**
>*SL: 2 apps. 0 gls.*
>**Total:** *2 apps. 0 gls.*

HAY, David

Role: Midfield 1965-74
5' 11" 11st.7lbs.
b. Paisley, 29th January 1948

CAREER: St Mirin's BG/CELTIC (provisional)
Jan 1965/CELTIC (full) 20 Mar 1966/Chelsea
3 July 1974/CELTIC (guest)
17 May 1976/retired Sept 1979/
Chelsea coach Sept 1979/
resigned Oct 1979/Motherwell
asst. manager 26 Nov 1979/
acting-manager 26 Aug 1981/
manager 29 Sept 1981/resigned
26 May 1982/CELTIC manager
4 July 1983/dismissed 28 May
1987/Lillestroem manager 3 Nov
1988/Watford chief coach 7 June
1990/resigned 30 Nov 1990/
St Mirren manager 25 Mar 1991/
resigned 7 May 1992 (left 22 May
1992)/Tampa Bay Rowdies
youth director June 1992/
Swindon Town asst. manager

22 June 1993/resigned 19 May 1994/CELTIC chief scout 22 July 1994.

Debut v Aberdeen (h) 4-1 (SL) 6.3.68 (sub)

Sean Fallon was tipped-off about David Hay by the boy's Parish Priest and signed him "for the price of two footballs." The ex-St Mirin's Academy Victor Ludorum collected his first medal in the League Cup final against St Johnstone on October 25th 1969, in at left-back for Tommy Gemmell. His first goal for Celtic was a raging shot high over Gerry Neef's hands from 35 yards that put Rangers out of the Scottish Cup in a Parkhead mud-bath five minutes from time (21st February 1970). He made his Scotland debut against Ireland in Belfast on April 18th 1970. To the intense anger of Jock Stein, he was taken off by Bobby Brown against Denmark (11th November 1970) to placate the chants of "Jar - dine!" and the Rangers player sent on as substitute. A bad injury at Tynecastle in the Scottish Cup replay on March 27th 1973 saw him out of the game and considerably out of pocket until he became a first team regular again. When his plea for a better deal for injured players fell unheard, his first transfer request went in on September 1st 1973. He refused to train as of November 15th 1973 but was reconciled and saw the season out with unforgettable performances as a driving midfielder against England at Hampden (18th May 1974) and in

the World Cup at Munich. The transfer to Chelsea had a very disturbing effect on George Connelly and saw a dramatic downturn in Davie's own fortunes. He was on Cyprus July 1974 when Nicos Sampson declared Union with Greece. The Turks invaded to find Davie right in their path at Famagusta. At Chelsea he had five eye operations followed by crippling trouble with cartilage. Only Roy Aitken could compensate for the loss of Davie Hay as Celtic's midfield dynamo. When he came back to play for Celtic in the Jinky/Lemon testimonial of May 1976 the fans chanted "We want Hay!" throughout the game.

Appearances:
SL: 130 apps. 6 gls.
SLC: 45 apps. 5 gls.
SC: 30 apps. 1 gl.
Eur: 25 apps. 0 gls.
Total: *230 apps. 12 gls.*

David Hay in action against Dundee in the 1973 Scottish Cup semi-final.

HAY, James

J. HAY (Half Back)
SCOTLAND.

Role: Left-half,
left-back 1903-11
5' 8" 12st.0lbs.
b. Beith,
12th December 1880
d. 4th April 1940

CAREER: Woodside
Annbank Juniors/
CELTIC (trial)
3 May 1900/
Annbank FC
11 May 1900/
Ayr FC 12 Jan 1902/
Glossop Sept 1902/
CELTIC 19 Mar 1903/(Annbank loan (Ayrshire
Cup final) 21 Mar 1903)/Newcastle United
27 July 1911/(Ayr United loan 1 Dec 1915)/
RFA Mar 1918/(Hearts loan 15 Apr 1918)/
Clydebank 2 Jan 1919/Ayr United player-
coach 1919/Clydebank manager 1921/Ayr
United manager 11 June 1924/suspended sine
die 29 Jan 1926/reinstated 11 Nov 1927/
Newcastle United scout 1928.

Debut v Partick Thistle (h) 2-1 (SL) 15.8.03

Jimmy Brownlie paints a picture of Jimmy
'Dun' Hay: "Touch combined with strength...
neat stride, ground passes, lion-hearted
defence... vigorous tackler... shoulder-work
full of punch." At the age of 15, "a mere boy in
years but a man in stature" he signed for
Glossop but his father refused to let him go. A
tireless grafter, he cost Ayr United £2; Celtic
£50; and Newcastle £1,250. The Ayr officials
trudged miles through snow one quiet
Sabbath to obtain his signature. He played his
first game as a signed Celtic player against
Queen's Park in the Inter-City League at
Parkhead on March 28th 1903 and thereafter,
bar injury, was never out of the side. This man
of "tireless trot... gluttonous in his anxiety to
get the ball... subtle skill in every move," first
stepped-out in a half-back line reading Young,
Loney and Hay versus Airdrie at Broomfield
on January 9th 1904. He featured in each of
Celtic's six-in-a-row Championship seasons
1905-10, won the Scottish Cup in 1904, 1907,
1908 and 1911 and was team captain "as good
as Dan Doyle" from 1906-07 on. He captained
Scotland for the first time against Wales on
March 5th 1910 and led Scotland out against
England at Goodison Park on 1st April 1911.
He was a driving half-back by nature and

much of the impetus was lost to the Celtic
midfield when first McNair and then he were
drafted to perform totally defensive duties at
the heart of the defence in place of McLeod
and Weir. Jimmy took his benefit on 25th
April 1911 but within days had warned Celtic
on prospects: better terms or a move.
Magnificent player, great skipper, he got his
transfer nevertheless. He would probably have
liked a welcome back to Parkhead in 1915 but
lent his services to Ayr instead and did his bit
down the mines before conscription to the
guns with the Royal Field Artillery. While
manager at Ayr, he alleged that Ayr director
and SFA treasurer Tom Steen had offered
referee Tom Dougary a bribe at Cathkin on
March 28th 1925. When he refused to write
Steen a letter of apology, he was suspended for
life. SFA President Tom White and vice-
President Campbell then refused to work with
Steen after re-election (2nd June 1926) but
relented (to applause) three weeks later. Tom
Steen was voted off the treasurership May 4th
1927 and Dun Hay reinstated six months later.
He was an all-time great Celt. He is buried in
Ayr churchyard.

Appearances:
SL: 214 apps. 14 gls.
SC: 41 apps. 3 gls.
Total: *255 apps. 17 gls.*

HAYES, Martin

Role: Midfield 1990-93
6' 0" 11st.8lbs.
*b. Walthamstow,
21st March 1966*

CAREER: Arsenal am. 1981, app. June 1982, pro. 2 Nov 1983/ CELTIC 29 May 1990/ (Coventry City loan 23 Sept 1991)/free 7 Jan 1992/(Wimbledon loan 22 Feb 1992)/Swansea City 6 Jan 1993.

*Debut v Ayr United (h)
4-0 (SLC) 22.8.90*

Martin Hayes

"He's quick, is a strong runner, has an eye for goal" (Chris Morris 1990). Martin Hayes made an immediate impact on his first appearance at Parkhead. He scored two goals for Arsenal in the 1-5 destruction of Celtic on 1st August 1987 and by the start of October 1988 Celtic were alleged to be keeping tabs on him. Martin scored some fine goals for Arsenal more often than not as a substitute and sometimes to devastating effect as against France (preparing for Scotland) on February 14th 1989. Huddersfield almost landed him for £80,000 from Don Howe but Celtic paid George Graham £625,000. He played a fair game in Bryan Robson's testimonial (20th November 1990) then had to wait until 12th March 1991 for another start versus St Mirren in the League. He was open to transfer as of March 18th 1991 but was released from his contract by Liam Brady: "I wasn't a failure or a flop at Celtic. I didn't get the chance to be a flop... I find the free transfer a bit embarrassing" (24th February 1992). Darren Nesbit's administrations resulted in a broken leg and a further set-back on April 8th 1992: "I never saw him coming... It definitely wasn't a challenge for the ball." Martin went to Swansea with best wishes for the renewal of his career in the mind of a multitude Celtic fans almost as puzzled as himself as to his lack of opportunity at Parkhead.

Appearances:
SL: 7 apps. 0 gls.
SLC: 3 apps. 0 gls.
Total: *10 apps. 0 gls.*

HAZLETT, George

Role: Outside-left 1946-48
5' 8" 10st.0lbs.
b. Pollokshaws, 10th March 1923

CAREER: St Mary's BG/Blantyre Celtic/Glasgow Perthshire/Royal Navy/(Plymouth Argyle loan 1945-46) (CELTIC loan Nov 1945)/CELTIC 18 Feb 1946/free Apr 1948/Belfast Celtic 8 May 1948/ Bury 28 June 1949/Cardiff City 6 Aug 1952/Millwall July 1953/Guildford City July 1958/Bexleyheath & Welling Aug 1959/retired June 1960.

Debut v Motherwell (h) 3-0 (RL) 10.11.45

"Dapper little winger" George Hazlett, boyhood friend of Jimmy Mallan, was born on the day Celtic won through to their first post-Kaiser War Cup final 2-0 versus Motherwell at Ibrox. He made his debut at outside-right with another brand-new signing on the left: Pat O'Sullivan from Airdrie. George scored the leading goal for Celtic in 10 minutes in the 1-1 draw at Ibrox on Ne'erday 1947. He was a non-stop trier, and skilful, but his best football was played away from Celtic Park. He was in the Belfast Celtic team that played Linfield on the

George Hazlett

day of the infamous riot 27th December 1948 but although he toured the States with the Irish Celtic as they took their farewell of football, was not in the side that defeated Scotland (29th May 1949).

Appearances:
SL: 21 apps. 2 gls.
SLC: 2 apps. 0 gls.
Total: *23 apps. 2 gls.*
RL: 7 apps. 1 gl.
Total: *7 apps. 1 gl.*

HEALY, James

Role: Outside-right 1924-25
5' 8" 10st.9lbs.
b. Craigneuk, 14th September 1904
d. Craigneuk, 5th December 1969

CAREER: Shieldmuir Celtic/CELTIC (trial)
9 Feb 1924/CELTIC 21 Apr 1924/(Montrose
loan 9 Sept 1924)/(Stenhousemuir loan Sept
1924)/(Motherwell loan 28 Nov 1924)/
(Montrose loan 1925/free Apr 1925/Plymouth
Argyle 1925/Bristol City 1929.

Debut v Kilmarnock (h) 6-0 (SL) 8.11.24

Jimmy Healy "of whom much was expected
but who gets no show," was a sprinting
winger who tried-out for Celtic in the two-
referee experiment versus Third Lanark at
Cathkin on February 9th 1924. Shieldmuir
Celtic were one of the clubs to opt out of the
Scottish Junior FA and join the Intermediates
over the stealing of players by the seniors
without consultation or compensation. They
exempted Glasgow Celtic from this charge in
their dealings over Jimmy Healy. Willie Maley
paid a fee and sent a team to Craigneuk to
play a club benefit. "Well-built" Jimmy
"played a strong game" and was brought to
Parkhead as McAtee's successor just as
Motherwell thought they had landed him at
Fir Park. "He was in sparkling form" on his
debut "and sent over some beautiful crosses
after showing his speed on the run." His
second and last League game for Celtic was
on 15th November 1924 the same day
Sam Chedzgoy of Everton tested
whether a corner was a free kick or not
by hitting the ball once then hitting it
again. (The referee waved play on). The
second eldest in a family of twelve,
Jimmy returned to Scotland on
retirement and was employed
in the steelworks.

Appearances:
SL: 2 apps. 0 gls.
Total:
2 apps. 0 gls.

HEMPLE, Samuel

Role: Centre-forward 1952-54
5' 9" 10st.12lbs.
b. 3rd May 1929

CAREER: Parkhead White Rose 1949/
Auchinleck Talbot 25 Mar 1950/Parkhead
Juniors 1951/Rutherglen Glencairn July 1952/
CELTIC 11 Dec 1952/Albion Rovers 6 Aug
1954/retired 1955.

Debut v Stirling Albion (a) 1-2 (SL) 5.12.53

Sam Hemple

A nephew of
1920s Celt John
McKnight, Sam
Hemple joined
Celtic as the 23rd
forward on the
books and came
into the Double
side of 1953-54 in
the match at
Annfield where
Celtic experi-
mented for the
first time with a
white ball. Sam
was good in the
air and Celtic
scored 13 goals
in his first three
games and took six vital points. Clyde were
beaten 1-7 at Shawfield on Boxing Day 1953
(Sam scored the second goal) but John
McPhail was preferred at centre
for the Ne'erday match with
Rangers. Sam Hemple was a
builder's labourer and left his
mark on improvements to
turnstiles and other entrances
and exits at Celtic Park. He
quit the club over terms
and went to Cliftonhill to
replace Johnny McGrory.
Sam retired with a groin
injury that refused to
heal properly.

Appearances:
SL: 4 apps. 2 gls.
Total: *4 apps. 2 gls.*

Jimmy Healy

HENDERSON, Adam

Role: Outside-left 1897-98
b. Darlington, 16th June 1873

CAREER: Airdrie Fruitfield/
Airdrie/Preston North End
Mar 1893/CELTIC 1 May
1897/ Bristol St George's
21 May 1898/Preston North
End 1899/retd Nov 1901.

Debut v Hibernian (h) 4-1 (SL)
4.9.1897 (scored twice)

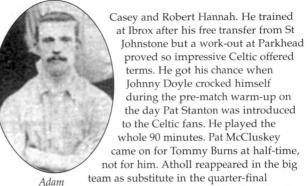

*Adam
Henderson*

Adam Henderson joined
Celtic from Preston with his great mate Willie
Orr as part of Celtic's new launch as a Limited
Company. He played his first game in the
Glasgow League versus Rangers on May 1st
1897 and got the equaliser in the 1-1 draw. He
was a brave winger, scored goals, but was
subsequently regarded as on a par with the
ineffectual Alex Crawford. He left Willie Orr
to prosper at Parkhead and followed Jack
Reynolds to Bristol. He retired to live in
Motherwell.

Appearances:
SL: 9 apps. 4 gls.
SC: 1 app. 2 gls.
Total: *10 apps. 6 gls.*

HENDERSON, Atholl

Role: Striker 1976-77
5' 10" 11st.4lbs.
b. 7th October 1957

CAREER: St Johnstone 'S'
form 1971/St Johnstone
21 Aug 1974/free 30 Apr
1976/CELTIC 29 July 1976/
free 30 Apr 1977/
Dunfermline Athletic 25 Aug
1977/Forfar Athletic 25 Nov
1977/Brechin City 1 Nov
1979 /released Dec 1982/

Atholl Henderson

St Johnstone coach Dec 1982-Oct 1987/Dundee
United coach Oct 1987-Dec 1987/Brechin City
coach & asst. manager Apr 1988-Apr 1992/
Dundee United community coach Apr 1992.

Debut v Dundee United (h) 1-1 (SLC) 1.9.76

Atholl Henderson was an Under-15 and
Under-18 schoolboy international playing in
the same teams as George McCluskey, Jim

Casey and Robert Hannah. He trained
at Ibrox after his free transfer from St
Johnstone but a work-out at Parkhead
proved so impressive Celtic offered
terms. He got his chance when
Johnny Doyle crocked himself
during the pre-match warm-up on
the day Pat Stanton was introduced
to the Celtic fans. He played the
whole 90 minutes. Pat McCluskey
came on for Tommy Burns at half-time,
not for him. Atholl reappeared in the big
team as substitute in the quarter-final
against Albion Rovers at Parkhead on October
6th. He played regularly for the second XI and
had scored 22 goals before a bad knock against
Rangers reserves in April 1977 ended his
season. Indeed, injury put an early end to
Atholl's career.

Appearances:
SLC: 2 apps. 0 gls.
Total: *2 apps. 0 gls.*

HENDERSON, John Neil

Role: Inside-forward 1895-97
b. Dumfries, c 1874
*d. Maxwelltown,
30th August 1930*

CAREER: 5KRV 1892/
Dumfries FC/CELTIC
Christmas 1895/Victoria
United 3 May 1897/Lincoln
City May 1898/Leicester Fosse
Dec 1900/Small Heath Mar
1901/Maxwelltown Volunteers
Sept 1902/Carlisle Aug 1905/
Maxwelltown Volunteers 1906
/KOSB(=Maxwelltown
Volunteers) 1908-Apr 1910/
Annan United Sept 1910 (one
game)/Nithsdale Wanderers
Nov 1910 (one game).

Debut v Clyde (h) 4-1 (SL)
12.12.1896

Wee John Henderson played and scored for
Celtic at Bury on Christmas Day 1895. He
made his League debut the day Billy Groves
began his two match come-back before a
"small attendance". His second points game
the following week was on an ice-rink against
Rangers at Ibrox. Rangers wore rubber soles
but Celtic their ordinary studs and Rangers

won 2-0, Celtic losing Groves for ever after ten minutes. John played inside-left to Willie Ferguson in the Arthurlie disaster of 9th January 1897 after Pat Gilhooly failed to show. He was a tobacconist in Dumfries at the time of his death. His elder brother James played for Rangers (and Notts County and Arsenal later) against Celtic at Ibrox at the Rangers/Clydesdale Harriers Sports on August 6th 1889. Celtic won 0-2 (Dowds 2) and the winners were rewarded with gold Alberts each.

Appearances:
SL: 3 apps. 0 gls.
SC: 1 app. 0 gls.
Total: *4 apps. 0 gls.*

HENDERSON, Samuel

Role: Wing-half 1962-68
5' 10" 10st.6lbs.
b. Garngad, 1945

CAREER: St Mungo's Academy 1959/Ashfield 13 Jan 1962/CELTIC 23 Feb 1962/(Morton loan 20 Jan 1964)/Stirling Albion 31 Jan 1968/Clydebank 9 May 1973/ Clydebank coach cs 1976/resigned 12 May 1988.

Sam Henderson

Debut v Dundee United (h) 1-0 (SL) 19.2.64

Louis Boyle, Ashfield team boss, reckoned Sammy Henderson "a better senior proposition than Crerand when he joined Celtic" (March 1963). Sammy played in the Celtic Trial of August 1st 1964: "The display of the young right-half handed out a warning to the first team men that, before long, he will be knocking on the door for promotion." He had excelled as an all-action schoolboy and junior and "showed promise" on his debut as deputy for John Clark, "but his inexperience left gaps in defence." Celtic still won both Sammy's Scottish League appearances. He moved to Stirling Albion on a guarantee of first-team football. Albion paid £5,000 for him and sold him on to Clydebank for £20,000. Sammy's career was ended by cartilage trouble.

Appearances:
SL: 2 apps. 0 gls.
Total: *2 apps. 0 gls.*

HEPBURN, Anthony

Role: Outside-right 1952-54
5' 8" 10st.0lbs.
b. 22nd May 1932

CAREER: St Paul's Whiteinch BG 1949/ Clydebank Juniors 1950/CELTIC (amateur) Jan 1952/(professional) 20 Mar 1953/ (Dumbarton loan 10 Aug 1953)/free 1 May 1954/Ayr United 11 Aug 1954/Distillery 27 June 1955/Morton 13 Aug 1957/ free 1958/Boston United 16 Aug 1958.

Debut v Queen's Park (a) 2-2 (GC) 3.9.52

Tony Hepburn, a fast tricky winger, signed for Celtic while reading for an MA degree at Glasgow University. He came into the League side on October 4th 1952 against Motherwell in place of Tully who was at Windsor Park giving Alf Ramsay a hard day. He zig-zagged his way past Redpath and Shaw to set Sean Fallon up for Celtic's second goal. The omens were favourable: "Celts find a new ace." He appeared again for Charlie, now suspended, at Airdrie on November 22nd 1952. Tony was preparing an LL.B degree and was commissioned in the RAF about the time he signed for Boston. His father was chief librarian at the Mitchell Library in Glasgow. Tony won an Irish Cup medal with Distillery as inside-right in 1956. He was playing with Celtic Old Crocks by June 7th 1963.

Appearances:
SL: 6 apps. 0 gls.
Total: *6 apps. 0 gls.*

HERON, Gilbert

Role: Centre-forward 1951-52
6' 0" 12st.7lbs.
b. Kingston, Jamaica, 9th April 1922

CAREER: USA 1939/Canadian Air Force (3 years)/Detroit Wolverines 1947/Chicago Sting/Detroit Corinthians/CELTIC 4 Aug 1951/free 17 May 1952/Third Lanark 1 July 1952/free 1953/Kidderminster Harriers cs 1953/Detroit Corinthians 1954/referee 1956-68.

Debut v Morton (h)
2-0 (SLC) 18.8.51
(scored once)

Celtic played
Chicago Polish
Eagles in Detroit
(8th June 1951) and
while in town were
recommended to
have a look at local
player, Gilbert
Heron, a profes-
sional photographer
when not playing
football. He
"exuded athleti-
cism" with boxing,
sprinting and soccer
on the side. Gil
came to Scotland,
played in the Public
Trial of August 4th
1951, scored twice,
and was signed
straight afterwards.
His impact at
Parkhead was
immediate: "He has

Gilbert Heron

ball control, magnificent headwork and can
trap like a veteran...took his goal with
camera-shutter speed." Gil beat the great
Jimmy Cowan in two minutes on his debut
but the goal was disallowed. His speed was
his undoing. As with Bobby Lennox later,
linesmen could not credit anyone could be so
fast off the mark and he kept being given offside. He dropped into the reserves (15 games,
15 goals) but the fans had taken to him: "Gil

Heron received
tremendous
vocal support.
He tried hard
but with little
luck" (1st
December
1951). The
first Annual
Rally and
Concert of
the Celtic
Supporters'
Associations
was held in
St Andrew's
Halls on

December 16th 1951. The guests of honour
were the team of 1938. Gil was on stage half-
an-hour just taking photographs. He had an
unfortunate start to 1952: ordered-off against
Stirling Albion reserves on January 2nd at
Celtic Park with a seven-day suspension
imposed on the 15th. Exactly one month later
he flew out from Prestwick to play for Jamaica
against Trinidad and Cuba. He was freed to
make room for James Swan and John
McDonald: "I may go home. I wouldn't get
the same thrill from another club." All the
same, he was as big an attraction at Cathkin as
at Parkhead. This stupendous all-rounder
played cricket for Poloc and Ferguslie, sang a
bit and fathered jazz musician Gil Scott-Heron.
He now lives in Detroit and has published two
books of poetry. The second collection (1993)
contains a piece called "The Great Ones" and
talks not only of Evans and Tully but of
Waddell, Young and Cox. Our interviewer
described Gil as "a great and supremely
interesting human being. If nothing else about
your book, this man will leave on me a lasting
memory."

Appearances:
SL: 1 app. 0 gls.
SLC: 4 apps. 2 gls.
Total: *5 apps. 2 gls.*

HEWITT, John

Role: Striker 1989-91
5' 8" 10st.8lbs.
b. Aberdeen, 9th February 1963

CAREER: Middlefield Wasps/Hilton
Academy 1979/Aberdeen 1979/CELTIC
14 Aug 1989/(Middlesbrough loan 4 Sept 1990
& 25 Sept 1991)/free 7 Jan 1992/St Mirren
20 Jan 1992/Deveronvale 14 Aug 1992/
St Mirren 4 Sept 1992.

Debut v Dumbarton (a) 3-0 (SLC) 16.8.89

"He's a big occasion player...quick, dangerous
and a handful for any defence" (Roy Aitken
19th September 1988). John Hewitt was Alex
Ferguson's first signing at Pittodrie and made
his first appearance (as a sub) versus Rangers
on January 12th 1980. He was a winger of pace
in the European Youth Championships in West
Germany May 1981 and in 1982 was being
praised for "explosive shooting, power, control
and incisive finishing." His finest hour was
surely at the Ullevi Stadium, Gothenburg

John Hewitt

HIGGINS, John

Role: Outside-right 1950-59
5' 9" 10st.0lbs.
b. Uddingston, 7th January 1933
d. 8th June 1994

CAREER: Our Lady's High 1949/St John's Uddingston BG/CELTIC 10 Jan 1950/ Queen of the South 1 Aug 1959/retired 13 Aug 1959/CELTIC coach 1961/chief scout 18 June 1967/resigned 3 July 1975.
Debut v Clyde (h) 0-0 (CC) 3.5.52

When Celtic played Bohemians for Willie Maley's benefit on August 10th 1953, the crowd went crazy over the outside-right: Jim Murphy of Blantyre Celtic. John Higgins was an unknown. If ever Celtic carried a 'sleeper' it was he. John got his first League game versus Queen of the South at Palmerston on 17th October 1953 but came intermittently and then late into the Double side. He could be said to have 'arrived' in the 1-7 defeat of Clyde at Shawfield on Boxing day 1953 when he scored twice. Yet he only began to play regularly as Fernie's partner and a goal-scoring winger in the Delaney mould (instead of Bobby Collins) as of 17th February 1954. He sealed the League title with a diving header past Tommy Younger at Easter Road four minutes from time on April 17th 1954 and had a fine game before 130,060 fans in the final versus Aberdeen at Hampden the following Saturday. In December 1954 this boy, unknown a year before, was nominated Celtic Supporters' Associations' Player of the Year. Almost immediately the trouble began that was to end his career: a broken toe during the 0-5 defeat of Hibs on December 11th 1954 followed by fluid on the knee when he attempted his comeback. John spent the Cup final of 23rd April 1955 in hospital. He missed most of 1954-55-56 and when he played in a friendly against Stirling Albion on April 7th 1956, the hope was to get him ready for the Cup final just two weeks away. His knee refused to stand up and Billy Craig went in against Hearts. Celtic played Airdrie at Broomfield on December 22nd 1956 in the League and led 3-4 at half-time (Higgins 4). His last hurrah was during the winter of 1957 with two fine games and a goal in each against Rangers

when he came on for Eric Black in the 86th minute and headed the goal from Mark McGhee's cross in the 111th that beat Real Madrid and took the Cup-Winners' Cup to Aberdeen (11th May 1983). Willie Miller seemed to think his departure for Celtic would benefit him: "There are some players can motivate themselves, there are others a change can do them good." John was hit by ligament trouble as of February 7th 1990 and seldom produced anything like his top form at Parkhead. He came on as substitute for Steve Fulton with 14 minutes to go in the League Cup final of October 28th 1990 versus Rangers. He was out of the team thereafter and under-went an operation on his knee on February 12th 1991. It is fair to say his best days were behind him in those fine teams of the Ferguson era at Aberdeen.

Appearances:
SL: 16 apps. 0 gls.
SLC: 5 apps. 0 gls.
Total: *21 apps. 0 gls.*

♣ **Celtic note:** *John Hewitt holds the record for the fastest goal in the Scottish Cup - 9.6 seconds for Aberdeen versus Motherwell at Fir Park on January 23rd 1982. He took 19 minutes to put Celtic out in the next round (13th February).*

John Higgins with the Scottish Cup in 1954.

in the Scottish Cup (4-4 at Parkhead on February 16th and 0-2 at Ibrox four days later). He saved Celtic for the moment with the equaliser against Kilmarnock in the semi-final on March 23rd and scored a hat-trick against Watford at Vicarage Road on April 4th. He managed only two matches out of eight on the US tour of 1957 before the knee went again, this time irrevocably, during the Public Trial of August 3rd 1957. John was reduced to walking exercise only. He seemed unconvinced the trouble was chronic and Queen of the South were prepared to give him a chance. After the Palmerston Public Trial of 3rd August 1959, the joint ballooned yet again and John Higgins, 'the new Delaney', announced his sad retirement.

> **Appearances:**
> *SL: 65 apps. 30 gls.*
> *SLC: 7 apps. 3 gls.*
> *SC: 12 apps. 7 gls.*
> **Total:** *84 apps. 40 gls.*

HILL, Dennis Aloysius

Role: Outside-left 1945-49
5' 7" 10st.0lbs.
b. Glasgow, 16th April 1926

CAREER: Ashfield/CELTIC 24 May 1945/ (Rhyl loan 1947)/free own request 11 Jan 1949.
Debut v Hamilton Academicals (h) 2-0 (RL) 15.9.45 (scored once)

Dennis Hill, a juvenile playing at Saracen Park, played initially for "a poverty-stricken Celtic side" in a Summer Cup first-leg against Albion Rovers and Jock Stein on 26th May 1945. He scored the opener in the (unofficial) Scottish League Division 'A' fixture at Parkhead on September 15th 1945 that gave Jimmy McGrory his first win as Celtic manager. Dennis was freed while in the Services.

> **Appearances:**
> *RL: 2 apps. 1 gl.*
> **Total:** *2 apps. 1 gl.*

HILL, John

Role: Outside-right
1913-14
5' 6" 10st.7lbs.
*b. Dumbarton,
17th January 1884*

CAREER: Clydebank Juniors/Dumbarton 15 Dec 1906/Dumbarton Harp 20 May 1912/CELTIC 7 May 1913/Vale of Leven 23 Oct 1913/ Renton 13 Oct 1915/Vale of Leven 6 Aug 1917 /retired 1918.

Debut v Rangers (h) 3-2 (CC) 10.5.13

Johnny Hill

"A nippy little player," Johnny Hill was "a neat and clever outside-left who, it is hoped, will fill a place that has been weak since the departure of 'Hammie'." Johnny, an electrical engineer with Wm Denny & Bros, and for seasons Dumbarton's top scorer (he played wing and centre), went straight into the team for the Charity Cup final against Rangers (two up in six minutes) and proved such a success he was awarded the match ball. He played with two other tyros on the big day: John McMaster and Barney Connolly, and a new goalie, Charlie Shaw. As the Parkhead fan said: "Celtic sign on boys at 2 o'clock and hand them out gold badges at five!" It must have made a change for Johnny; with Dumbarton he had been on the losing side in various Cup finals at least a dozen times. Alas for bright beginnings, the man definitively to replace Davie Hamilton was Johnny's inside partner on May 10th 1913, another son of the Rock, the great 'Smiler' Browning.

Appearances:
SL: 2 apps. 0 gls.
Total: *2 apps. 0 gls.*

HILLEY, Hugh

Role: Left-back 1921-30
5' 8" 11st.0lbs.
b. Garngad, 19th March 1899
d. Paisley,
14th September 1987

CAREER: St Anthony's/ CELTIC 16 May 1921/ (Armadale loan 27 Apr 1923) /(Dundee loan Spanish tour 12 May 1923)/free 1930/ retired 1930.

Debut v Third Lanark (a) 0-0 (SL) 4.3.22

Hugh Hilley

"Hilley is too reckless... he goes straight for his man... impetuous dashes that often fail... he must be coached... toned down... calmer judgement must be developed" (September 1923). "Hilley did things that stamped him as a really first-class back... only first-class men could do what he did" (13th October 1923). Hugh Hilley went on Celtic's 1922 tour of the new republic of Czechoslovakia and played against Johnny Madden's Slavia in Prague on May 25th. He became Joe Dodds' successor, first as Alec McNair's partner, then as Willie McStay's. In 1925 his nose was so frequently broken, his face was almost permanently in plasters. Against St Mirren in the Cup at Ibrox on March 9th with Celtic leading 1-0 and a minute to go, "I had lost so much blood I was seeing half-a-dozen balls. I missed my kick and Jean McFarlane brought down Gillies. Peter Craigmyle gave a free just outside the box but St Mirren would settle for nothing less than a penalty. They refused the free-kick and the hullabaloo ended with Craigmyle blowing for full-time." (Jean later admitted it was a penalty). On April 2nd 1927, England beat Scotland 1-2 at Hampden and skipper Willie

McStay had a bellow after the game: "If Hilley had partnered me... Scotland would not have lost!" Hugh was almost unable to finish against Hamilton Academicals on 20th August 1927 and left the field in state of exhaustion that led on to nervous breakdown. "Finally I decided my health came first. I gave up playing, set up in the ice-cream and catering business and I never looked back."

Appearances:
SL: 171 apps. 0 gls.
SC: 24 apps. 0 gls.
Total: *195 apps. 0 gls.*

HODGE, John McGeachie

Role: Outside-right
1899-1902
5' 6" 11st.4lbs.
b. Greenock, 5th May 1879

CAREER: Overbon Athletic/Newborn Thistle 1895/Port Glasgow Juniors/Port Glasgow Athletic 14 June 1898/CELTIC 7 Jan 1899/ (Morton loan 10 May 1902)/Portsmouth 22 May 1902/Morton 15 Apr 1903/ Thornliebank 11 Feb 1904 & 18 Aug 1904/ retired 1 May 1906.

Debut v 6th GRV (a) 8-1 (SC) 14.1.1899 (scored once)

Johnny Hodge

"Hardy little tyke," Johnny Hodge was a tearaway winger of great courage but a minimum of tactical awareness for which Sandy McMahon would frequently berate him. "He got there whatever way he could - and the way he thought shortest and best... a great lad... to see him try to shift Billy Foulke, the giant Sheffield United goalie, was a treat" (Jimmy Quinn). Johnny's Celtic debut saw a record crowd at Dalbeattie (700) and record receipts for the ground (£70). He won a Scottish Cup medal by scoring the clinching goal against Rangers on April 22nd 1899. He missed a lot of time out of 1899-1900 with an injury sustained against Morton on November

24th but came back brilliantly versus Hibs on March 3rd 1900 and had another magnificent game the following week when Rangers were put out of the Scottish Cup 4-0 (he opened the scoring himself in five minutes). "Spectators were spellbound by the brilliance of Celtic's forward play." He was selected against the English League on March 31st at Crystal Palace and was reckoned Jack Bell's most dangerous rival for a full cap versus England on April 7th at Parkhead. He won a second Scottish Cup medal against Queen's Park and a howling second half gale at Ibrox on April 14th 1900. Johnny's hobby was camping and he would discourse at length on the joys of the open air. He went to Morton in an exchange deal for goalkeeper Andrew McPherson.

Appearances:
SL: 34 apps. 17 gls.
SC: 8 apps. 5 gls.
Total: *42 apps. 22 gls.*

HOGG, Robert

Role: Right-back 1931-48
5' 8" 11st.7lbs.
b. Larkhall, 10th May 1914
d. Paisley, 15th April 1975

CAREER: Larkhall Academy/ Royal Albert/CELTIC 11 May 1931/free own request 19 Nov 1948/Alloa 23 Dec 1948/ manager 13 Apr 1949/ resigned 20 Oct 1949.

Debut v Queen's Park (a) 1-4 (SL) 17.9.32

Bobby Hogg, "mobile, fast, and sure in both tackling and kicking," experienced the heights (1938) and the depths (1948) as a Celtic player. His first game as Willie Cook's replacement was against Rangers at Ibrox on January 2nd 1933: "Bobby Hogg was the best back on the park." He won Scottish Cup medals in 1933 and 1937, Championship badges in 1936 and 1938 and was right-back for the Exhibition Trophy winners of

Bobby Hogg

June 10th 1938. He scored the goal of his life against Third Lanark at Cathkin in the Glasgow Cup on August 25th 1936, a 65-yarder into the Cathcart Road end goal with 3rds 'keeper Hall dazzled by the evening sun. Bobby was an utter gentleman of a player. Even when being skinned by the likes of Jimmy Caskie he would never resort to the foul or the plain crude maiming kick. Bobby probably stopped the Celtic team from leaving the field in the 70th minute of the Victory Cup semi-final replay at Hampden on June 5th 1946 in protest against Matt Dale's gratuitous award of a penalty to Rangers. Nevertheless, referee Dale indicted him in his report and Bobby's record card, hitherto unblemished, was endorsed by the gnomes of Carlton Place who "deplored his conduct." Bobby played right-back for Scotland in Prague on May 15th 1937 and was also right-back when Scotland won 2-3 against England in the Red Cross international at Newcastle on February 8th 1941. As Celtic skipper, he played his last game in the Charity Cup final against Rangers at Hampden on May 8th 1948. He asked for a free transfer and received it along with £500 from a grateful club. Ronnie Simpson's father, Jimmy, ex-Rangers, took him to Alloa. Bobby Hogg was totally committed to the club and is an all-time Celtic great.

Appearances:
SL: 278 apps. 0 gls.
SLC: 10 apps. 0 gls.
SC: 34 apps. 0 gls.
Total: *322 apps. 0 gls.*
RL: 179 apps. 0 gls.
RLC: 35 apps. 0 gls.
SWC: 2 apps. 0 gls.
Total: *216 apps. 0 gls.*

♣ **Celtic note:** *Bobby was so often travelling reserve for Scotland that by October 1st 1938 he had collected 11 jerseys and was able to equip an entire Scottish outfield during the hard days of clothing coupons during the Second World War.*

HOOD, Henry A.

Role: Striker 1969-76
5' 10" 11st.0lbs.
b. Glasgow, 3rd October 1944

CAREER: St Aloysius College/Holyrood Senior Secondary/Campsie Black Watch/ St Roch July 1961/Queen's Park 1961/ Brunswick BC 1961/Clyde June 1962/ Sunderland 9 Nov 1964/Clyde 7 Oct 1966/ CELTIC 16 Mar 1969/free 29 Apr 1976/ San Antonio Thunder as of 4 May 1976/ Motherwell 18 Aug 1976/free 2 May 1977/ Queen of the South 23 Sept 1977/retired 7 Sept 1978/Albion Rovers manager 4 Feb 1981/resigned 23 Apr 1981/Queen of the South manager 16 Feb 1982/resigned 19 Apr 1982.

Debut v St Mirren (a) 3-0 (SL) 29.3.69 (scored once)

"Harry has all it takes; control, physique, know-how but he must force himself into the action" (Jock Stein). Harry Hood trained at Parkhead as a schoolboy but when Celtic showed no interest joined Queen's Park and, to keep himself fit, played for

Brunswick in the summer. He signed for Clyde just the night before Sean Fallon came along to watch him. Celtic maintained an interest and the transfer looked on until the player refused terms on November 2nd 1964 and joined Sunderland. He and Jim Baxter were in the Roker Park team beaten 0-5 by Jock Stein's rejuvenated Celtic on August 7th 1965. He joined Celtic on the run-in to Stein's fourth Flag in a row and virtually won the League for Celtic with a last-gasp goal against St Johnstone in Perth (April 1st 1969). He won his first medal in the League Cup against St Johnstone (October 25th 1969). Harry was a graceful, skilful player, cool in front of goal and "possibly the outstanding sub of them all. When he goes on the field, the game takes on a new dimension." So much so, the Celtic fans would chant his name like a joyous mantra for Stein to send him on. The theme keeps repeating: "Hood transformed Celtic in the second half" (October 3rd 1970); "Davidson became a different player when he joined Hood in the middle" (November 28th 1970). He came on for Dalglish at Ibrox (August 18th 1973), beat three men at once in a dribble and set an 82nd minute goal up for Lennox. It was Harry who set-up four of Dixie Deans' six goals on November 17th 1973. On the debit side, Stein thought he failed to get fully involved in the 1-1 draw against Dunfermline in the Scottish Cup of February 13th 1971 but changed his mind about dropping him: "The players who have put us in trouble, they should get us out of it." On May 12th 1971 he became the first Celt to score with a penalty in a Scottish Cup final versus Rangers and is also the last to record a hat-trick against the Ibrox club (League Cup semi-final December 5th 1973 at Hampden). When he left Celtic, the team's flair went with him. A magnificent club servant.

Appearances:
SL: 189 apps. 74 gls.
SLC: 64 apps. 24 gls.
SC: 29 apps. 13 gls.
Eur: 30 apps. 12 gls.
Total: *312 apps. 123 gls.*

HUGHES, John

Role: Goalkeeper
1922-25
5' 8" 10st.7lbs.
b. Barrhead,
4th August 1901

CAREER:
Neilston Athletic/
Parkhead Juniors
1920/CELTIC
13 Sept 1922/
(Hibernian loan
9 Nov 1923)/
(Clydebank loan 4 Mar
1924)/(Ayr United loan
10 May 1924)/(Alloa loan
6 Mar 1925)/(Ayr United
loan 29 Apr 1925)/free cs 1925/Alloa 23 Sept
1925/free 18 June 1926/Vale of Leven 31 Jan
1927/St Anthony's cs 1927.

Debut v Motherwell (h) 1-0 (SL) 14.10.22

"Hughes played well versus Motherwell,
better versus Morton, but must be a clinking
clever chap to keep Shaw out." "Hughes is
goalie in a weak team... has not shown ability
to equal Shaw... against Ayr United he was
very poor... not protected as he should have
been... he has no claim to the position, not as
long as the veteran Shaw is on the books."
John Hughes succeeded Frank Collins as
Celtic's reserve 'keeper and played instead of
a perfectly fit Charlie Shaw against Rangers on
October 28th 1922 when only a Patsy
Gallagher goal in the last minute prevented a
0-3 whitewash. The executive were
unrepentant: "Hughes would require to go in
sometime" (Tom White). "I will play all the
young ones. If we do no more than keep our
place in the League and get a team for next
season, I'll be satisfied" (Willie Maley). Maley
had proposed wider goals to counteract
defensive football. When John Hughes lost
four to Ayr United on November 11th 1922, a
fan taunted the Celtic manager: "Hey, Maley!
Are your goals wide enough noo?" Charlie
Shaw was back between the sticks one week
later.

Appearances:
SL: 5 apps. 3 shut-outs.
Total: *5 apps. 3 shut-outs (60%).*

HUGHES, John

Role: Outside-left 1959-71
6' 2" 13st.7lbs.
b. Coatbridge, 3rd April 1943

CAREER: St Augustine's School/
Kirkshaw Amateurs/Shotts Bon Accord
6 Aug 1959/CELTIC 3 Oct 1959/Crystal
Palace 19 October 1971/Sunderland 23 Jan
1973/free May 1973/retired 8 October
1973/Baillieston Juniors coach Jan 1974/
Stranraer manager 28 Jan 1975, resigned
30 Apr 1976/Baillieston Juniors coach
again 15 May 1976/SJFA manager 14 Sept
1978, resigned 30 Jan 1982.

Debut v 3rd Lanark (h) 2-0 (SLC) 13.8.60
(scored once)

"Jeered one minute, cheered the next," big
John Hughes came into the side aged 17
and at once engendered a new optimism.
Rangers were beaten twice in five days by
a team of boys and Jimmy Millar told
Paddy Crerand he had never played

John Hughes once
scored five goals in a
game against Aberdeen
wearing Billy McNeill's
training shoes!

191

John Hughes gets in a shot despite an attempted tackle from Rangers' Doug Baillie.

against a better Celtic. 'Yogi' started as he was destined to go on until the arrival of Stein: displays of brilliance in the extreme mingled with moments of crassest ineptitude. He missed a sitter in 30 seconds on his debut then scored with an unstoppable header that Jocky Robertson never saw. Against Real Madrid on September 10th 1962 when every other Celt was playing out of his skin, big John just could not get started. For a man of such large physique, he was nimble as Johnstone with great close control, equally capable of a storming charge, then of allowing the likes of Ronnie Simpson at Hibs to pick the ball off his toe. John preferred the going heavy and detested hard pitches (he had a dreadful game on a rock surface for the Scottish Under-23s at Newcastle on February 5th 1964) until he caused a sensation but found the solution to his problem by turning out in 'sandshoes' versus Motherwell on a frozen pitch (Boxing Day 1964). They were Billy McNeill's (German) training shoes with a canvas upper and a rubber sole. He scored five wearing them versus Aberdeen (January 30th 1965). Under Stein, John's strength became allied to intelligence. He developed into an invaluable team man whose shooting was now invariably on target, who no longer fell over at the vital last second and of whom the fans sang: "Feed the Bear! Feed the Bear!" He had a great game for the Scottish League against the English at Hampden on St Patrick's Day 1965, scored two and gave Jack Charlton a torrid night. His first full Scotland cap was as outside-left against Spain in a bruising battle at Hampden on May

9th following. John's speciality number was a run that saw him beat man after man with the ball tied to his left boot, then a shift to his right and a booming shot high into the net as during Morton versus Celtic (January 25th 1964) and Crystal Palace against Sheffield United (December 4th 1971) (both featured on TV). How his psyche coped with the savage barracking to which he was subject from beginning to end of a match on an off-day before substitutes is beyond comprehension. His temper did have a snapping point as witness the notorious kicking of Cejas against Racing Club at Montevideo on November 4th 1967. He did not play in Lisbon on May 25th 1967 but got his chance against Feyenoord on May 6th 1970, another big occasion when Yogi took much of the game to get started. Benny Rooney clattered him in the 40th minute at Perth on February 6th 1971 and big John had to come off. While he was having stitches, St Johnstone went ahead 2-1. Stein sent him out for the second half. Yogi gave up after five minutes. Celtic lost 3-2. At the end of the season he went in to see Jock about more money. Stein was aghast: "A rise! What you did at Muirton coulda cost us the League!" John McPhail includes Yogi at outside-left in his all-time Celtic team.

Appearances:
SL: 255 apps. 116 gls.
SLC: 69 apps. 38 gls.
SC: 51 apps. 25 gls.
Eur: 41 apps. 10 gls.
Total: *416 apps. 189 gls.*

HUGHES, William

Role: Utility 1929-36
5' 10" 12st.0lbs.
b. Winchburgh

CAREER: Bellstane Birds/Bathgate 17 Mar 1927/CELTIC 12 Mar 1929/(Ayr United loan 31 Aug 1929)/(Hibernian loan 7 May 1932)/Clyde 22 Sept 1936/(Bo'ness loan 1938)/Arbroath 6 Dec 1938/(Hamilton Academicals loan 26 Oct 1940)/Hamilton Academicals 21 Jan 1941.

Debut v Motherwell (h) 2-0 (SL) 19.3.29

Willie Hughes

Celtic acquired one of their most versatile players when Bathgate went defunct in March 1929. Willie Hughes was signed as an outside-left but in spite of over 100 games played never properly established himself as a recognised first-teamer, not even after eight goals in Patsy Gallagher's benefit (January 4th 1932). (January 16th 1932: "Hughes' finishing was poor"). His outstanding other goalscoring feat was a magnificent solo, a run from deep in his own half finished off by a thunder shot ("he can shoot some") to equalise versus Rangers at the Rangers' end in the League at Parkhead on the stroke of half-time (September 8th 1934). In the Scottish Cup semi-final at Ibrox with Clyde on April 3rd 1937, he kept such a tight grip on Delaney that a fan invaded the pitch, seized the ball and could not be persuaded to part up until he had berated Willie thoroughly on the torrid time he was giving the great Jimmy. Willie's half-back game was forceful and eager but not strong on construction. Off the park, he ran a grocer's shop in Blantyre and married a sister of Bob Kelly.

Appearances:
SL: 94 apps. 11 gls.
SC: 10 apps. 1 gl.
Total: *104 apps. 12 gls.*

HUNTER, Alistair Robert

Role: Goalkeeper 1973-76
5' 11" 11st.4lbs.
b. Glasgow, 4th October 1949

CAREER: Hyndland Senior Secondary/BB/ Drumchapel Amateurs 1966/Rangers (trial) 1967/Leicester City (trial) 1967/Johnstone Burgh 20 May 1968/Kilmarnock 23 Apr 1969/ CELTIC 24 Jan 1973/Motherwell 15 Apr 1976/ free 25 Oct 1977/St Mirren (trial) 1 Nov 1977/ St Mirren 2 Dec 1977/free 27 Apr 1978/ Clydebank 4 & 10 Oct 1978/retired 1978.

Debut v Airdrie (a) 1-2 (SL) 27.1.73

"To the disgust of my friends at school I was always mad on Celtic." Celtic played Kilmarnock in the semi-final of the Scottish Cup on April 12th 1972 and although Deans hit form with two goals, Ally Hunter, a "fantastic young man in red," gave the Parkhead forwards such a game that "Johnstone shook his head in disbelief." Aged 17, Ally played for Rangers versus Queen's Park at the Albion ground: "No one talked to me on the way out. I got no expenses so I just forgot about it." Celtic bought him with a fifth of the £200,000 received for the Macari transfer of January 18th 1973. By mid-April: "Hunter is obviously the new Ronnie Simpson." Ally was turning in one near-miracle performance after another, one shut-out after another, culminating in a Scotland cap at Wembley on May 19th 1973 (where two stupendous saves on the half hour resulted in serious injury yet he played on) and a glory display versus Hibs in the Drybrough Cup of August 4th 1973. Then it happened: in the World Cup qualifier versus Czechoslovakia at Hampden on September 26th 1973, he lost a soft goal, a shot from well out that he had plenty of time to see. From that night on his self-confidence was dented. "He's a worrier," said Stein, "he blames himself for every goal." He continued as Celtic's regular 'keeper without missing a game until a back injury versus Hibs on January 23rd 1974 let Evan Williams in against Basle in Switzerland. Ally came back for Hearts on March 2nd. This time he played a full 90 minutes despite a damaged right leg which he could not use. Denis Connaghan played both matches against Motherwell in the Cup and retained his place against Basle at Parkhead with Ally on the bench. Ally came back for the League match against Dumbarton on March 30th and had a nightmare in the 3-3 draw. Denis Connaghan now went in against Atletico Madrid home and away and won a Scottish Cup medal on May 4th 1974 against Dundee United. Ally was Celtic's main 'keeper again as of October 1974 but his fate was sealed when Peter Latchford was brought on trial in February 1975. By September 13th 1975, he was up for transfer with no takers and when Latchford was dropped on January 21st 1976, Ally got one chance only and the big Brummie came straight back. Had he been blessed with the tough hide of an Alan Rough, this fine goalkeeper might indeed have made the new Simpson.

Appearances:
SL: 60 apps. 31 shut-outs.
SLC: 17 apps. 3 shut-outs.
SC: 10 apps. 6 shut-outs.
Eur: 4 apps. 3 shut-outs
Total: *91 apps. 43 shut-outs (47%).*

Ally Hunter

HUNTER, George Irwin

Role: Goalkeeper 1949-54
5' 9" 11st.4lbs.
b. Troon, 28th August 1930
d. Nottingham, 10th May 1990

CAREER: Crosshouses Waverley/Riccarton Glencairn/Neilston Juniors 1947/CELTIC 27 Dec 1949/free 30 Apr 1954/Derby County 10 June 1954/Exeter City Aug 1955/free 1960/Yiewsley 1960/Darlington June 1961/Weymouth 1962/Burton Albion 12 July 1963/Lincoln City Sept 1965/Matlock Town 1966.

Debut v East Fife (h) 4-2 (SC) 31.1.51

Chic Geatons persuaded Celtic to sign Sonny Hunter before Hearts did although the club already had its complement of goalkeepers. The Brig o' Lea boy is forever associated with a stand-out match in the third round of the Scottish Cup at Tynecastle (24th February 1951). Throughout the week Glasgow had been rife with rumour that Celtic were going to sign the excellent Roy Henderson of Queen of the South but on Saturday it was the boy Hunter who defied Conn, Bauld and Wardhaugh before a seething capacity crowd of 48,000 with "magnificent goalkeeping... clutching high balls... pulling them to him... saves from all angles that brought the house down." He earned his Scottish Cup medal versus Motherwell on April 21st 1951 before 133,343 fans at Hampden with a miracle save midway through the second half from a Wilson Humphries half-volley that was heading for the top corner of the net. He had an outstanding American tour and was in the team that won the St Mungo Cup on August 1st 1951. He hit his head on the post that night at Hampden trying to save Aberdeen's second goal, but there was much more than cuts and bruising wrong with him now: George had TB and was packed off to Switzerland for a cure. He came back to Troon on July 6th 1952 and was five pounds heavier and one inch taller when a big crowd turned out to see him with the reserves against Berwick Rangers (and Billy Houliston) on September 27th 1952. Alas, George was no longer "his usual sprightly self." His form had become "uncertain... he dropped balls time after time." On Ne'erday 1953, he erred horrendously against Rangers to let Billy Simpson score "the daftest goal I've ever let through." He asked to be dropped and got his wish ?ftc. the 2-4 defeat by Clyde on January 17th 1953. The way now opened for Johnny Bonnar to play in the Coronation Cup. When Bonnar broke his collarbone on August 20th 1953, Sonny came in but lost five goals to Aberdeen two days later, then four versus Rangers on September 3rd 1953. He was supplanted by Andy Bell. When Andy hurt his shoulder in turn, Sonny came back against Raith Rovers on October 10th. Each match he played the Celtic fans willed him back to form; "Every move brought a cheer." Johnny Bonnar had a try-out against Manchester City on October 28th at Maine Road and hit Coronation Cup form. In England, George proved a more than useful goalie. Bill Dodgin had played for Fulham against Celtic in the USA and took Sonny to Yiewsley on the memory of his fantastic shut-out performance at the Triboro' Stadium (27th May 1951).

Appearances:
SL: 31 apps. 6 shut-outs.
SC: 7 apps. 3 shut-outs.
Total: *38 apps. 9 shut-outs (24%).*

rge Hunter

HUNTER, John

John Hunter

Role: Goalkeeper 1941
5' 11" 11st.7lbs.
b. Coatbridge,
13th April 1916

CAREER: Coatbridge St Augustine's/ Lochryn Amateurs/ Shettleston Juniors/ Kilsyth Emmet Sept 1937/Kilmarnock Nov 1937/(Albion Rovers loan Aug 1940)/(CELTIC loan 17 May 1941)/ (Blantyre Victoria loan Aug 1942)/ Royal Navy/Kilmarnock again Apr 1945/ Stenhousemuir Sept 1948/ free 1949.

Debut v Queen's Park (a) 5-2 (CC) 21.5.41

John Hunter ("brings rare power and confidence into his work") was Celtic's fourth War-time goalie. He was part of the grand tradition of Kilmarnock goalkeepers and had one magnificent game out of many at Ibrox on November 6th 1937 when he played Rangers on his own. He helped put Celtic out in the third round of the Scottish Cup on March 5th 1938 and once with Celtic held his place until November 15th 1941 when his factory shift as a boilermaker (he had to work overnight before almost every game he played) prevented his getting away to face Falkirk at Brockville and let Jimmy Culley in. He had his last game for Celtic versus Hamilton Academicals on December 20th 1941 when the crowd at the start was 6,000 with long queues still outside buying tickets for the Ne'erday derby against Rangers. John was Kilmarnock's (Jimmy McGrory's) goalkeeper in the 1938 Scottish final against East Fife. He had one miracle save from Dougie Wallace of Clyde in the last minute of a League game (September 13th 1941) that epitomised his competence as a Celtic 'keeper.

Appearances:
RL: 17 apps. 1 shut-out.
Total: *17 apps. 1 shut-out (6%).*

HUTCHISON, Thomas

Role: Centre-forward
1896
5' 7" 10st.12lbs.
*b. Glasgow, April-
August 1871*

CAREER: Govan/
Stockton/Govan

Tom Hutchison

Whitefield 1889/Darlington 1890/Nelson
5 Aug 1893/West Bromwich Albion July 1894/
CELTIC 14 July 1896/Abercorn 6 Nov 1896/
Stockport County 1897.

Debut v Hearts (h) 3-0 (SL) 5.9.1896

Willie Maley says Tom Hutchison was brought
in from West Bromwich (where he made 14
League appearances out of a possible 30 in
1895-96) as a stop-gap. He played both his
Scottish League fixtures against Hearts. At the
home game, on his debut, the crowd was in
amazement at another novelty: the way
Celtic's new trainer, J.J. (Jack) Mullen sprinted
onto the pitch to the succour of the fallen. By
November 7th 1896, Tom was leading the
Abercorn attack against Celtic at Parkhead in a
5-0 defeat.

> **Appearances:**
> *SL: 2 apps. 0 gls.*
> **Total:** *2 apps. 0 gls.*

HYNDS, Thomas

Role: Centre-half 1898-1900
5' 10" 11st.6lbs.
b. Hurlford

CAREER: Hurlford Thistle/
CELTIC 5 Feb 1898/(Bolton
Wanderers loan 4 Mar 1899)
/(Clyde loan 7 Oct 1899)/
CELTIC again 9 Dec 1899/
resigned CELTIC Apr 1900
/(Bolton Wanderers loan
Sept 1900)/(Manchester City
loan 5 Oct 1901)/ Manchester City 27 Sept
1902/Arsenal 6 Dec 1906/Leeds City 15 May
1907/Hearts 19 May 1908/Ladysmith FC
(British Columbia) 1910/Scotland again Dec
1912/Musselburgh FC 9 Jan 1913/to USA
31 Jan 1914.

Debut v Rangers (n) 0-2 (CC) 7.5.1898

Tom Hynds

Tom Hynds was recommended to Celtic by
fellow Hurlford man Hugh Goldie and played
in the 3-1 defeat by Clyde at Barrowfield
(Glasgow League) on April 27th 1898 and had
his second defeat at the hands of "proud
Scotia's darling club" at 1st Cathkin Park on
May 7th. He went straight into the League
team for the first game of the season, Celtic
versus Third Lanark on August 20th 1898. One
week later he helped hansel the opening of
Shawfield Park as a football ground and the
new home of Clyde. He was subject to trainer
Dan Friel's deep fitness routines with training
twice a day and players being made to trot in
to Parkhead from drop-offs in Kirkintilloch,
Eaglesham and Hamilton. Tom moved over to
right-half when Harry Marshall arrived from
Hearts on January 28th 1899 but his chances
in the first team were few and club president
J.H. McLaughlin didn't fancy him much at all.
He was not "altogether satisfied at Parkhead."
He suffered from a perennial Celtic grievance:
"over-supply of players." Clyde had played
seven games for not a solitary point when
Celtic lent them Hynds, Somers and Doran.
Back with the green and white, he gave away
the third goal against Rangers in the
Exhibition Cup final of September 9th 1901 at
Gilmorehill when Jimmy Quinn was
screaming for the pass.
Tom Maley signed him for
Manchester City with
whom he won the Division
Two Championship in 1903
and an English Cup medal
in 1904 only to be
suspended from football
for being a "bonus
delinquent" in the
"scandal" over slush funds
that followed. He joined
Arsenal short-term. When
his playing days were over,
he returned to British
Colombia and coached out
there as well as in Italy.
Serie 'A' may well owe a
debt to a man who could
not find proper favour at
Celtic Park.

Appearances:
SL: 28 apps. 2 gls.
SC: 3 apps. 0 gls.
Total: *31 apps. 2 gls.*

JACK, John

Role: Centre-half 1950-59
5' 10" 12st.0lbs.
b. Bellshill, 9th March 1932
d. 22nd October 1988

CAREER: Mossend BG 1949/Stonehouse
Violet 29 June 1950/CELTIC 15 Oct
1950/Morton 19 May 1959.

Debut v Motherwell (h) 2-2 (SL) 22.12.51

"Not elegant but effective," John Jack (born
Jonas Kaduskeviechi) lived next door to the
Busbys at Bellshill and turned down an offer
to go to Old Trafford from the great Matt in
order to join Celtic. He signed as a left-back
and although reputed "one of the cleanest
kickers of the ball Lanarkshire football has
produced," he had a tendency to employ his
toe and Jimmy Gribben had him in on
Sundays until he had learned to use his instep
properly. John, "a magnificent physical speci-
men," was all man: he worked at the coal face
in Kirkintilloch, was up at 4.30 am daily and
trained at Parkhead in the evenings. He was
Joe Baillie's replacement on his debut in a half-
back line reading Evans, Stein and Jack but a
forgotten man by the time Big Jock broke his
ankle on August 31st 1955. Jock's immediate
successor at centre-half was Bobby Evans but
for the start of 1956-57
at Pittodrie (August
11th), John Jack was
pivot in a line reading
Evans, Jack and
Peacock. He had a
magnificent match
against Paddy
Buckley followed by
another against Max
Murray of Rangers
four days later. He
won a medal versus
Partick Thistle on
Hallowe'en 1956 as
pivot of the first
Celtic team ever to
lift the League Cup.
He held his place
into the end-of-
season US tour but
the 6-3 drubbing

John Jack

by Spurs on June
1st 1957 at the
Empire Stadium
Vancouver
signalled end of
tenure for the big
blond stopper. Bobby Evans moved back to
centre-half and John dropped into the
reserves.

Appearances:
SL: 48 apps. 0 gls.
SLC: 12 apps. 0 gls.
SC: 8 apps. 0 gls.
Total: *68 apps. 0 gls.*

JACK, Peter

Role: Centre-forward 1895

CAREER: Newton Thistle/(CELTIC trial 1895)
/Vale of Clyde 1895/Airdrie 23 Sept 1895.

Debut v Rangers (a) 1-1 (SL) 23.3.1895

Peter Jack was a Scottish junior international
of "pluck and judgement" who tried out for
Celtic in an Old Firm match on a day when
regular centre Johnny Madden was on
Scotland duty in Wrexham. Just once and that
against Rangers had to suffice for Peter who
had known "unqualified success" against
junior England just a week before. He seems
never to have played for Celtic again.

Appearances:
SL: 1 app. 0 gls.
Total: *1 app. 0 gls.*

JACKSON, John Bertram

Role: Utility 1917-18
5' 7" 10st.0lbs.
b. Dalry, 21st June 1893

CAREER: Ardeer Thistle/Clyde
25 Aug 1908/(CELTIC loan 4 Jan 1909
& 30 Oct 1912)/Leeds City 19 Dec 1913
/(Ayr United loan 23 Dec 1915)/(Clyde
loan 24 July 1916)/(Rangers loan
19 May 1917)/(CELTIC loan 8 Sept
1917)/Royal Scots Fusiliers May 1918/
(Clydebank loan 31 Jan 1919)/
Motherwell 29 Oct 1919/Dundee 24 Dec
1919/(Stevenston United loan 1920)/
free Apr 1922.

Debut v Rangers (h) 0-3 (GC) 22.9.17

"A heady, steady player, a useful man in attack at all times but at no time more useful than when a lead requires to be worked down." Rangers had "brainy player" and "tremendous worker" John Jackson on their books but unused, so he does not count as an actual combatant for both clubs. John "possessed a wonderful amount of devil for his size and weight" and played wherever Celtic needed him although his best position was right-half. He "would never acknowledge himself beaten" and during the Scottish Cup final first replay at Ibrox on April 16th 1910, had actually collapsed during extra time from his endeavours at inside-left on Clyde's behalf. Herbert Chapman took him to Leeds. For Celtic he had a stormer at right-half against Rangers on Ne'erday 1918 but on February 2nd the whole Hampden stand rose in outrage over his "none too gentle" treatment of flying winger Alan Morton of Queen's Park. He was right-half again in the Celtic side that won the War Shield final versus Greenock Morton at Hampden (May 4th 1918) and pocketed a Charity Cup medal versus Partick Thistle three weeks later at the same venue. John Jackson is the Celtic player who ran from Waverley Station to Easter Road on August 17th 1918 when his train was late and he could not get a taxi. Immediately before going off to the battlefields he engaged in the skirmish (ie the Glasgow Cup final) at Hampden on October 5th 1918 when Rangers wrestled to a 2-0 win and John was laid out by Tommy Cairns in the second half.

Appearances:
SL: 27 apps. 2 gls.
Total: *27 apps. 2 gls.*

JACKSON, Michael

Role: Inside-right 1957-63
5' 11" 11st.5lbs.
b. Glasgow, 25th August 1939

CAREER: Holy Cross Primary/Holyrood Senior Secondary/Holy Cross BG/Benburb Nov 1956/CELTIC 26 July 1957/St Johnstone 5 Apr 1963/Third Lanark 13 Feb 1964/ Drumcondra Apr 1966/Athlone Town 1966/ Partick Thistle (trial) 29 Oct 1966/Clyde (trial) 25 Jan 1967/Clyde Mar 1967/free Apr 1967/ Morton May 1967/Queen of the South 17 July 1967/Clydebank 14 May 1970/free 1971/ Hamilton Academicals (trial) 6 Aug 1971/

Mike Jackson

Benburb 1971/Albion Rovers reserve coach Aug 1973/dismissed 10 Mar 1974/Benburb 1974/Queen of the South coach Sept 1974/ manager 9 Aug 1975/Morton asst. manager 23 May 1978/dismissed 9 May 1983/Albion Rovers asst. manager 6 Apr 1984/Partick Thistle asst. manager 22 May 1984/resigned 14 July 1986/Queen of the South manager 4 Aug 1986/resigned 29 Apr 1987/CELTIC scout 1988.

Debut v Dundee (h) 0-0 (SL) 7.12.57

"A cultured forward in the Joe Cassidy mould," Mike Jackson was pursued by Manchester United while with Holy Cross Boys' Guild but opted for Celtic. Mike was a Kelly Kid, a silky inside-forward but just short on the sudden change of pace. He played 13 League games in 1959-60, fasted on medical advice (December 4th), was too weak for the home defeat by Dundee the following day and never got another chance. At Cathkin, he met up with Third Lanark's nemesis, Bill Hiddleston. He told Hiddleston he wanted to buy out his contract. The Thirds boss raised no objection: "I want £1,000 - cash." Mike got out for £150 (cash). He discovered his niche in coaching and management first of all at Queen of the South and then in tandem with Benny Rooney. During his second spell at Palmerston he had the Glasgow players training on the famous old turf at Cathkin (2nd Hampden Park). Negotiations between Billy McNeill and Jack McGinn at the end of May 1988 were held in Mike's house in Crosshill. Subsequently he "swept secretly" into places like West Berlin and Budapest to prepare dossiers and do player searches for Big Billy. He works currently with the YTS in Scotland.

Appearances:
SL: 57 apps. 23 gls.
SLC: 8 apps. 4 gls.
SC: 8 apps. 3 gls.
Eur: 1 app. 0 gls.
Total: *74 apps. 30 gls.*

JARVIS, Henry George

Role: Wing-half 1912-19
5' 8" 11st.0lbs.
b. *Glasgow, 3rd December 1889*

CAREER: Benburb/Cambuslang Rangers 1912/CELTIC 9 Nov 1912/(Motherwell loan Sept 1913)/(Vale of Leven loan 20 Dec 1913)/(Ayr United loan 28 Mar 1914 & 5 Sept 1914 & 2 Oct 1914)/(Clyde loan 30 Jan 1915)/(St Mirren loan 26 Feb 1915)/(Falkirk loan 29 Oct 1915)/Army 1916/(Clydebank loan 6 Aug 1917)/(Stevenston United loan Mar 1919)/Stoke (trial) 10 May 1919/Stoke 12 June 1919/Clydebank 7 June 1921/Dunfermline Athletic 20 Jan 1922/Ayr United reserves (amateur) 1924.

Debut v Motherwell (h) 1-2 (SL) 23.11.12

George Jarvis was an electrician in Fairfield's

Yard in Govan and played a trial for Celtic in the last Inter-City League match of all on November 5th 1912. Rangers won 4-0 at Ibrox and three days later the competition was scrapped for good. He was signed as understudy to Jim Young but the day of his League debut, Sunny wrenched a muscle and Celtic were outplayed for their first home defeat in 18 months. George was a whole-hearted trier within his limits but on April 5th 1913 these were stretched to breaking-point when he was brought-in as stop-gap for the unfit Quinn. He was geed-up by the other players to go at it like the great Jimmy, full-pelt and regardless of the kicks. George gave it his best but he couldn't get a goal. When Patsy Gallagher was within a month of death, gentleman George gave up his ticket to the Coronation Cup final of May 20th 1953 and went out to Scotstoun to listen to the game on the radio with the 'Mighty Atom'.

Appearances:
SL: 7 apps. 0 gls.
Total: *7 apps. 0 gls.*

JEFFREY, Robert

Role: Outside-left 1961-63
5' 8" 11st.0lbs.
b. *Ayr, 7th November 1942*

CAREER: Coltness United 1960/CELTIC 25 Oct 1961/Airdrie 4 Oct 1963/free May 1964/Rhyl/Altrincham/Pwllheli/Colwyn Bay/Cambridge City/Stranraer 24 Sept 1966/free May 1967.

Debut v Queen of the South (h) 0-1 (SL) 10.11.62

Bobby Jeffrey ("no failure, has a bit to learn") made his Scottish League debut against Willie Morrison, son of John of Celtic 1938. His Old Firm debut was in the Glasgow Cup replay at

Bobby Jeffrey

Parkhead the night Bobby Murdoch put Rangers out 3-2 (November 21st 1962). He played just his third League game ("somewhat slow on the draw") against Hibs on December 1st 1962 and was capped for the Scottish Under-23 side versus Wales at Pittodrie the following Wednesday. He "made good use of the ball" and scored Scotland's second goal in a 2-0 win. "Next kick" Celtic had dropped him for Frank Brogan as of Saturday 8th December. Frank had had a great Glasgow Cup tie against Partick Thistle on December 3rd and with a bone-hard pitch in prospect Celtic wanted him in against Hearts. Bobby played for his hometown club Airdrie beaten 9-0 by Celtic on October 26th 1963 the day Frank Haffey missed the penalty that would have made it ten.

Appearances:
SL: 5 apps. 1 gl.
SLC: 3 apps. 0 gls.
Total: *8 apps. 1 gl.*

JOHNSTON, Leslie Hamilton

Role: Centre-forward 1948-49
5' 8" 10st.8lbs.
b. Glasgow, 16th August 1920

CAREER: Hamilton Memorial Chuch/ Clydebank Juniors/Clyde 1 Dec 1941/ Hibernian 14 Feb 1947/Clyde 10 Oct 1947/ CELTIC 26 Oct 1948/Stoke City 28 Oct 1949/ Shrewsbury Town 22 July 1953/Hinckley Athletic Sept 1954.

Debut v Hibernian (a) 2-1 (SL) 30.10.48 (scored twice)

When Celtic signed ship's carpenter Leslie Johnston he became Scotland's first £30,000 footballer in accumulated transfer fees. The excitement was intense that Celtic had broken into the £30,000 offered for Middlesbrough's Wilf Mannion on October 13th 1948 and procured at last a proven goalscorer (for £12,000). Celtic had been after him since he won the Scottish Junior Cup with Clydebank in 1942. Jackie Gallacher was not dropped but continued at centre while Leslie played inside. Things looked so good for a while that even when Celtic were invited to bid for Mannion again, they refused: "We are not yet where we would like to be but we are on the right road" (Bob Kelly). Within weeks of finding the right road and with Leslie at inside-right, Celtic

were turfed out of the Scottish Cup at Tannadice by Division B side Dundee United (22nd January 1949). Leslie now moved his size 4½ boots to centre but the goals had dried-up (Leslie was essentially a stealer of pinches, not an elaborator)

Leslie Johnston

and within weeks of the start of 1949-50 he lost his place to Mike Haughney. Paddy Travers put his finger on the paradox of the much-travelled Johnston: "He was a one-club man - only at his best for Clyde."

Appearances:
SL: 24 apps. 8 gls.
SLC: 4 apps. 0 gls.
SC: 1 app. 0 gls.
Total: *29 apps. 8 gls.*

♣ **Celtic note:** : *Leslie Johnston came on at Hampden in 15 minutes as substitute for Tommy Bogan in the War-time international versus England on April 14th 1945. England scored in 28 minutes, Leslie got the equaliser 10 minutes later "and was engulfed by his ecstatic team-mates" (including ex-Celt Johnny Kelly). England ran riot in the second-half to win 1-6.*

JOHNSTON, Maurice

Role: Striker 1984-89
5' 9" 10st.7lbs.
b. Glasgow, 13th April 1963

CAREER: St Roch Primary School/St Roch Secondary School/Partick Thistle Under-16s/ Partick Thistle 18 Aug 1980/Milton Battlefield (farmed-out)/Watford 17 Nov 1983/CELTIC 11 Oct 1984/Nantes 1 July 1987/Rangers 10 July 1989/Everton 18 Nov 1991/free Sept 1993/Hearts 19 Oct 1993.

Debut v Hibernian (h) 3-0 (SL) 13.10.84

Mo Johnston's footballing assets were myriad. He was a player who had it all. Superb control, a stunning turn of pace, physical strength, power and bravery; he was also industrious, great in the air, but above all he was a supremely confident marksman who had the

Mo Johnston

wanted to stay with Celtic. Since then we have tried to contact him all over Europe but it seems the last to know his decision is his own club" (Billy McNeill 1st July 1987). "I'm never coming back to Scotland to play" (21st May 1988). "This baby will put the seal on his lifestyle. All his troubles are behind him now" (Bill McMurdo 19th August 1988). "Johnston has changed his mind about staying in France after a series of death threats..." (Press report 12th May 1989). "I've always wanted to be back with Celtic but I was never sure if I was wanted, until now, that is" (12th May 1989). "I'm sure things will be different this time" (Karen Bell 12th May 1989). "I am staying with Nantes" (30th May 1989). "Certainly I won't go to Rangers. They don't sign Catholics and anyway I don't want to go to Ibrox" (25th June 1989). "I think I can do a great job for Rangers" (21st July 1989).

Appearances:
SL: 99 apps. 52 gls.
SLC: 8 apps. 9 gls.
SC: 14 apps. 6 gls.
Eur: 6 apps. 4 gls.
Total: *127 apps. 71 gls.*

♣ **Celtic note:** *Everton were to play in Belfast in August 1992. Johnston represented to Howard Kendall he shouldn't go: "I'm liable to be shot by both sides." Kendall consulted Pat Nevin. Nevin: "I think he ought to go. He'd put 10,000 on the gate."*

golden gift of razor sharp reflexes in front of goal. His proven record of better than a goal every other game for Celtic is unquestionable. He was however, a precocious young man and an often inconsistent and outspoken temperament did him few favours down the years."I don't want to go to Parkhead. My career would be better off in England" (8th August 1983). "To move to such an ambitious club as Watford is unbelievable" (17th November 1983). "I would happily have been the first Catholic at Ibrox" (22nd December 1983). "There's only one team I'd come home for - that's Celtic" (22nd May 1984). "I pay no attention to the kind of pressure he puts himself under. Maybe he even enjoys it" (Jock Stein 18th February 1985). "I am the man to score goals for Manchester United... I'd be only too happy to shoot them out of trouble... If Celtic don't give me what I'm worth, I would like to go" (30th September 1986). "Johnston told me the last time we talked he

JOHNSTONE, George

Role: Goalkeeper 1940-41
6' 0" 12st.0lbs.
b. Caldercruix, 15th December 1914
d. Victoria Hospital, Kirkcaldy,
11th September 1974

CAREER: Bothwellhaugh Athletic 1934/ Benburb cs 1934/Aberdeen May 1936/(St Mirren loan 9 Mar 1940)/(CELTIC loan 20 Aug 1940)/Dunfermline Athletic player-trainer-coach 12 July 1949/resigned 8 Nov 1949/ Raith Rovers 5 May 1950/player-coach 1 May 1954/free 30 Apr 1955/Dumbarton Aug 1955/ Morton 6 Sept 1955/free Apr 1956/ Cowdenbeath trainer 1959/player 24 Oct 1959 ...[Thornton Hibernian/Newburgh/Nairn Thistle/Darlington by 1963 (all trainer-coach)].
Debut v Hamilton Academicals (h) 2-2 (RL)
10.8.40

George Johnstone, a baker by trade, was Benburb's goalie when they won the 1936 Scottish Junior Cup and played for Aberdeen against Celtic in the senior final at Hampden on April 24th 1937. Aberdeen beat Inverness Thistle 6-0 in the first round at Pittodrie

George Johnstone

in pitiless conditions on January 30th, a game so one-sided, George was given an overcoat to wear in the second half. Jimmy McStay asked for his services almost as soon as he became Celtic manager (14th February 1940) but Aberdeen only relented for 1940-41. George inspired Celtic against Rangers in the Glasgow Cup final at Ibrox on September 28th 1940 with save after save from the explosive shooting of Alex Venters. He came off the field with Jimmy Smith at half-time in either this game, or one of the two Southern League matches he played for Celtic versus Rangers (September 7th 1940: 0-0; Ne'erday 1941: Rangers 2 Celtic 3) and inquired politely of Joe Kennaway's estwhile scourge big Jimmy Smith: "Why don't you leave the goalkeeper alone? It doesn't do you any good." Smith had a notorious growl: "I don't like goalkeepers - especially Celtic ones!" George gave Celtic 100 per cent attendance for the season but charged the club with breach of contract over bonus money in September 1941. The SFA fined Celtic but threw George's case out (17th December 1941). The big goalie's reaction was so forthright he was fetched back into the chamber from the street to repeat his words. He was suspended sine die until he apologised on March 7th 1942. George was goalkeeper for the fine Aberdeen team that won the League Cup against Rangers on April 19th 1947 (he lost an horrendous first minute goal!) and was in the Dunfermline side at Hampden for the League Cup final of October 29th 1949 when the Athletic lost 3-0 to East Fife.

Appearances:
RL: 30 apps. 7 shut-outs.
RLC: 7 apps. 1 shut-out.
Total: *37 apps. 8 shut-outs (17%).*

JOHNSTONE, James

Role: Outside-right 1961-75
5' 4" 9st.8lbs.
b. Viewpark, 30th September 1944

CAREER: St John's Viewpark/Uddingston St Columba's/St Columba's BG/Blantyre Celtic 1960/CELTIC 8 Nov 1961/(Hamilton Academicals loan 24 Mar 1975)/free 9 June 1975/San Jose Earthquakes 17 June 1975/ Sheffield United 19 Nov 1975/free 14 June 1977/Dundee 6 July 1977/Shelbourne 4 Nov 1977/Elgin City 1978/dismissed 19 Aug 1979/Blantyre Celtic player-coach 24 July 1980/for transfer 26 Nov 1980/ ...CELTIC coach under Davie Hay.

Debut v Kilmarnock (a) 0-6 (SL) 27.3.63

'Jinky' Jimmy Johnstone, a ball-boy at Celtic Park since 1958, played for Scotland Juniors at Newtonards on St Patrick's Day 1962. His play was "nothing stereotyped... his tricks were the outcome of his skill." He roasted Jim Kennedy in the Public Trial of August 4th 1962 and apart from big Frank Haffey was Celtic's one success in the drawn Cup final versus Rangers on May 4th 1963 (but was dropped for the replay). Stein watched him playing for the reserves against Hibs on March 8th 1965. A casual conversation in the Gents at half-time and Jinky was inspired to score three in three minutes in the second half. He was not Stein's immediate choice at outside-right but his game took off as of the League Cup quarter-final against Raith Rovers (September 15th 1965) when Celtic won 1-8 at Stark's Park. He was a ball-playing genius but used by Stein as part of the plan. Stein blasted him (unnamed) in the *Celtic View* of November 9th 1966 after a 1-1 draw against St Mirren for refusing to stick to a pre-match strategy (ie wanting too much of the ball). He was substituted by George Connelly against Dundee United on October 5th and "made angry words and gestures to the dug-out." Stein pursued him up the tunnel for an apology. Like the great Patsy, Jinky took more than his share of kickings but unlike Patsy seldom bothered with the referee's blind side for his retaliation and was sent-off time after time in his career. At Ibrox on January 2nd 1967 he was fouled relentlessly

Jimmy Johnstone

and in such a state of bruising at the end there was no chance of his being fit for the match on the Saturday. Even in Di Stefano's benefit on June 7th 1967 he was hacked without scruple by Amancio but got his own back by beating five men in a dribble and setting up the goal for Lennox. It was the only way some opponents knew to pay tribute to his skill. Nor was he just a Flying Flea. As Helenio

Trainer Neil Mochan pours the bubbly for Jimmy Johnstone after Celtic's 1966 championship success... the first since 1954 and the first of the 'nine-in-a-row'.

Herrera looked on, he clinched the League for Celtic on an Ibrox mud-heap with two magnificent goals on May 6th 1967 as a prelude to Lisbon. After Lisbon and Montevideo (where he was sent off for trying to shake an Argentinian from his back) he was voted No. 3 in Europe in a France-Football poll of sports writers on December 25th 1967 and selected for the 1967 Earth team to play the Universe! He reached the total peak of performance 4-0 against St Etienne (October 2nd 1968) and Red Star Belgrade (November 13th). Jinky hated flying. Only a seat beside Lennox or Willie O'Neill kept him sane. Celtic went in at half-time drawing 1-1 with Red Star Belgrade at home. Stein promised him he wouldn't have to go on the plane to Yugoslavia for the second leg if Celtic won convincingly that night. The wee man went mad in the second half, scored two himself and saw Celtic home 5-1. He was one of the few successes against Feyenoord in the European Cup final of May 6th 1970 but again heavy tackling took its toll and Jimmy's ligaments suffered a lot of damage. His lifestyle mirrored his flamboyance on the park and Stein was left to pick up the tab: "No player has caused me more headaches since I went to Celtic and on no one has more time been spent to sort out his troubles." Jinky had another massive performance against Rangers in the Scottish Cup final replay ("The Jimmy Johnstone Spectacular") of May 12th 1971 but by the start of 1972-73 was rowing with Stein again and took off for Biarritz "on medical advice" to cure "traces of pleurisy." He was back to Parkhead by September 11th 1972 but

Jock was unrelenting: "It's up to Johnstone to show what he can do... so far this season he has done nothing for us - not unless he's playing well, that is. And he hasn't been playing well." Against Ujpest Dosza in the European Cup on March 22nd 1972, after a six week absence through injury, Jinky trotted on for Jim Brogan with about 20 minutes to go. Parkhead erupted and the Hungarians prepared. The night Atletico Madrid "assassinated football" at Celtic Park (April 10th 1974) Jock handed it to Johnstone: "He was provoked... he refused to retaliate... showed tremendous restraint... I'm proud of him." Jinky's final great game was for Scotland versus England at Hampden on May 18th 1974 three days after rescue from a rowing boat set adrift by Sandy Jardine of Rangers on the Firth of Forth. He was in the party to Munich for the World Cup but Willie Ormond did not play him (he had gestured at the press box at the end of the Hampden game and was involved with Billy Bremner in an incident in Oslo on June 2nd which almost got them both sent home). His free transfer was as much of a shock as those of his peers, McMenemy in 1920 or Patsy Gallagher in 1926. Jimmy Johnstone is an all-time Celtic great. Thank God for videotape.

Appearances:
SL: 308 apps. 82 gls.
SLC: 92 apps. 21 gls.
SC: 48 apps. 10 gls.
Eur: 67 apps. 16 gls
Total: *515 apps. 129 gls.*

JOHNSTONE, Peter

Role: Utility and
Centre-half 1908-17
5' 9" 11st.0lbs.
*b. Collessie, Fife,
6th July 1888
d. Killed in action,
12th-16th May 1917*

CAREER:
Buckhaven FC/
Kelty Rangers/
Glencraig Celtic/
CELTIC 9 Jan 1908.

*Debut v St Mirren (a)
1-0 (SL) 3.4.09*

Peter Johnstone, Celts'
Utility Man was a miner,
signed as replacement for
Peter Somers at inside-left. He
first turned out for Celtic when Peary
was within three days of the North Pole. As
of September 23rd 1911 at Kilmarnock he
dropped back into Jimmy Hay's old berth
and won his first Scottish Cup medal as a
left-half versus Clyde at Ibrox on April 6th
1912. Celtic met Clyde again in the final of
the Charity Cup on May 11th 1912 and won
by 7 corners to nil. Peter played centre-half:
"The softest job I've had all season."
February 8th 1913: "Celtic fans idolise Peter
Johnstone... a lion's courage... has played in
almost every position... never let the side
down." It was not until August 1913 that
the decision was taken to make him the
permanent centre-half and he joined the
roll-call of great Celtic pivots as Willie
Loney's successor in the Double side of
1914 (14 League goals only conceded). He
toured Central Europe bristling for War and
had to be restrained from starting early (he
had a sharp temper) on Burnley's "yappy"
Ulsterman Jimmy Lindley at the end of the
Ferencvaros Cup match in Budapest (May
20th 1914). With the Guns of August Peter
returned to the pits to assist the War Effort
but helped Celtic to the League
Championships of 1915 and 1916. To do his
bit more forcibly he attested on March 11th
1916 and was called up to the 14th Battalion

of the Argyll and Sutherland
Highlanders as Private
285250 (May 25th 1916).
He travelled overnight
by rail from training
camp in the south of
England to help
Celtic hoik Rangers
out of the Glasgow
Cup on September
23rd 1916 and won
his final medal (also
Glasgow Cup) on
October 7th 1916, 3-2
against Clyde in his
last-ever game for
Celtic. He transferred
to 6th Battalion of the
Seaforth Highlanders to
get quicker into the action
in France. On May 26th 1917
rumour swept Glasgow Peter
Johnstone had been killed in action
and the sad news was confirmed on June
6th: he had fallen in the Battle of Arras. He
lies in an unknown grave (Joe Cassidy went
looking for the spot) and is unmarked at
Parkhead also along with the other War
Dead: Donnie McLeod, Archie McMillan,
Bobby Craig, Joe Coen and Joe McCulloch.
He left a wife and two children Nellie and
Peter. John Conway, the Celtic poet of 35
Harvie St Bridgeton, wrote in 1913:

*A loyal servant you have been
Long may you wear the hoops of green
Your well-kent face of old be seen
On our own Paradise. No warmer Celtic heart
than thine
Long may your star ascendant shine
Full sure when Celtic made you sign
They booked a prize.*

Peter Johnstone was an all-time Celtic great.

Appearances:
*SL: 211 apps. 17 gls.
SC: 22 apps. 2 gls.*
Total: *233 apps. 19 gls.*

♣ **Celtic note:** *His name is on Bay 8 of the
Arras Memorial in the Faubourg d'Amiens
cemetery in the western part of Arras,
Boulevard du General de Gaulle, on the road to
Doullens.*

JONES, Walter Morris

Morris Jones

Role: Centre-forward
1940
5' 9" 11st.4lbs.
b. Bootle,
30th November 1919

CAREER: Bootle
Amateurs/South
Liverpool Dec 1937/
Port Vale 22 June 1939/
Army Sept 1939/
(CELTIC loan 29 Aug 1940)/
(Halifax Town loan 1943-44)/Swindon Town
14 Nov 1947/Crystal Palace May 1950/
Watford Mar 1951.

Debut v Albion Rovers (a) 3-1 (RL) 31.8.40
(scored once)

"Workmanlike leader," Morris Jones was a
soldier serving in Scotland and one of Celtic's
World War Two guests. The day of his debut at
centre, Joe Carruth was on the other side on
loan to Albion Rovers (and scored). Morris
was in the Celtic reserve side that played a
Polish Army XI at Celtic Park on October 5th
1940 and scored both goals in a 2-1 win. He
was demobbed in 1946 and rejoined Port Vale.

> **Appearances:**
> *RL: 3 apps. 1 gl.*
> **Total:** *3 apps. 1 gl.*

JORDAN, John

Role: Outside-right 1946-47
5' 9" 11st.0lbs.
b. Glasgow, 25th February 1924

CAREER: Possil Glenfield/Falkirk (trial)
1 Aug 1942/Queen's Park 8 Aug 1942/Scots
Guards 1944/(Fulham loan 1944-45)/CELTIC
2 Nov 1946/registration cancelled 10 May
1947/Edinburgh City 16 Aug 1947/Hearts
(trial) 1 Sept 1947/free 31 Oct 1947/Aberdeen
(trial) 15 Nov 1947/Alloa 23 Dec 1947/free
1948/Reading Oct 1948/Brentford 25 Oct
1949/free 1951/...Berwick Rangers as
unattached player 4 Aug 1955 (did not play).

Debut v Motherwell (a) 2-1 (SL) 23.11.46

Tommy Bogan broke his right leg against
Hamilton Acas in the third minute at
Parkhead on October 26th 1946 and although
Bobby Evans took over, Queen's Park flier
Jackie Jordan was signed as cover after a trial
for Celtic reserves versus Falkirk. 'Smiling
Jack' served Celtic as an amateur. Hearts tried
him at centre where he started brightly with
five against Leith Athletic on September 10th
1947. Jackie went professional at Reading.
After Brentford he trained with Pollok.

> **Appearances:**
> *SL: 3 apps. 1 gl.*
> **Total:** *3 apps. 1 gl.*

Jackie Jordan
(extreme left of the
front row) in an
early post-war
Celtic team group.

Back row (left to
right): Lynch,
McMillan, Hogg,
Miller, McDonald
and Milne.

Front row: Jordan,
Kiernan, Rae,
McAloon and
Hazlett.

KAPLER, Konrad

Role: Outside-left 1948-49
5' 7" 11st.0lbs.
b. Poland, 25th February 1925
d. Rochdale, 23rd October 1991

CAREER: Forres Mechanics July 1946/CELTIC
16 Aug 1947/free 1949/Rochdale May 1949/
Morecambe/Altrincham.
Debut v Third Lanark (h) 1-3 (GC) 10.9.47

Konrad Kapler

"Spotted playing for the Polish Army in Johnstone," Konrad Kapler was signed from Forres as cover at outside-left. A fair-haired wee winger, "strong and fast," who liked to shoot no matter how long the range, Konrad was unable to displace Johnny Paton. He had his chances in 1947-48 but was never out of the reserves the following season. He decided there was no future in Poland under Communism and gave up his nationality March 1948.

Appearances:
SL: 7 apps. 0 gls.
SLC: 1 app. 0 gls.
Total: *8 apps. 0 gls.*

KAVANAGH, Peter

Role: Outside-left 1929-32
5' 4" 9st.10lbs.
b. Dublin, 1910
*d. Glasgow,
15th February 1993*

CAREER: Munster Boys
(Drumcondra)/ Melrose
Celtic of Fairview/
Drumcondra/Bohemians
1927/CELTIC 29 Apr 1929/free May 1932/
Northampton Town 4 Aug 1932/Guildford
City 1933/Hibernian 5 Jan 1934/Stranraer

Nov 1935/
Waterford Feb
1936/ ...Babcock &
Wilcox by 1939.
*Debut v Hearts (h)
2-1 (SL) 10.8.29*

Peter Kavanagh was recruited for Bohemians by ex-Ranger Bobby Parker. This "splendid boy" was the youngest member of the Bohs' Clean Sweep team of 1927-28 and played against Celtic in a friendly at Dalymount (April 28th 1928). Alec Maley was sent to Ireland to watch a full-back in 1929 and reported home on the wonder kid seen at outside-left. James Kelly and Tom Colgan crossed to have a look and made the signing even though wee Peter didn't want to leave Dublin (yet Glasgow became his adopted city). His debut was doubly auspicious: the opening of the new north grandstand that lasted to 1971 and Jimmy McStay's first game as captain of Celtic. Peter scored his first goal for Celtic (0-3 down) against Aberdeen at Parkhead on August 24th 1929 with a bullet "that almost tore the roof off the net". He took over from Willie Hughes in the quest for a replacement for Adam McLean but "did not develop the thrust expected." At the end of his first season, Con Tierney was signed from Bo'ness on the same mission impossible. Despite the game of his life against St Mirren on February 21st 1931, Celtic would not accommodate him over re-signing terms and he missed the American

*Peter Kavanagh (centre) shows his two prized
Ireland caps to Chris Morris and Anton Rogan,
themselves Irish international Celts.*

tour. Wee Peter was capped twice for Ireland in 1931, each time versus Spain (in Barcelona 26th April and Dublin 11th December). He went to Northampton with Celtic's American-Scot Jimmy McGuire (who broke McGrory's jaw at the Brooklyn Dodgers' Ebbet's Field on 7th June 1931 and became a big wheel in FIFA after World War Two). Peter died in Leverndale Hospital.

Appearances:
SL: 32 apps. 5 gls.
SC: 3 apps. 0 gls.
Total: *35 apps. 5 gls.*

KAY, Robert

Role: Full-back 1977-78
5' 10" 11st.7lbs.
b. Edinburgh, 24th October 1949

CAREER: Gracemount Secondary/United Crossroads/Hearts 11 Jan 1968/free 1977/CELTIC 1 July 1977/free 22 Apr 1978/York City June 1978/Northallerton 1981/retired.

Debut v Ayr United (a) 1-2 (SL) 20.8.77

Roy Kay was one of Jock Stein's "sensation" signings. Roy had played 140 games for Hearts including one blinder against Celtic at

Roy Kay

Tynecastle (March 24th 1973) which probably stuck in Jock's memory. He was a casualty of Hearts' relegation from the Premier League in 1977 and represented a bargain signing "to strengthen the squad for Europe" as cover for McGrain and Lynch. He first appeared for Celtic in the National Stadium, Singapore on July 13th 1977 as a substitute with 15 minutes to go against the local Select. Roy made his League debut in place of Andy Lynch at Somerset Park in a match famous for the incident in which ref Cuthill blew up for hands against Johnny Doyle with two minutes to go. Doyle crossed, the ball struck Cuthill, Cuthill collapsed, came to, ordered Johnny off. Fan: "It couldnae hae been intentional. The way he wis playin', he'd ha' missed!" Roy was captain of York City and a virtual ever-present during his time there.

Appearances:
SL: 5 apps. 0 gls.
SLC: 4 apps. 0 gls.
Eur: 1 app. 0 gls.
Total: *10 apps. 0 gls.*

KELLY, Charles

Role: Goalkeeper 1891
b. 1867
d. Airdrie, 20th September 1898

CAREER: Broxburn Shamrock 15 Sept 1888/Glasgow Hibernian 1889/Hibernian 21 Dec 1889/(CELTIC loan Oct 1891)/Busby Cartvale 1893-94.

Debut v St Mirren (a) 2-1 (SL) 3.10.1891

Tom Duff took a dreadful soaking in goal against Dumbarton on September 26th 1891, the rain so bad at one point the teams had to shelter for ten minutes. "Rheumatics" set in as a result and Celtic had to borrow Charlie Kelly of Uphall and 16 John St, Coatbridge, versus Blackburn Rovers at Old Celtic Park for a friendly fixture on October 1st 1891. He kept goal in League and Glasgow Cup matches until the end of the month but Mick Dolan took over for November. Charlie's first match for Celtic was as Jimmy Bell's deputy against Bolton Wanderers at home on April 18th 1891. He died of the dropsy.

Appearances:
SL: 2 apps. 0 shut-outs.
Total: *2 apps. 0 shut-outs.*

KELLY, Charles

Role: Outside-left 1944-45
5' 6" 10st.7lbs.
b. Blantyre, 24th February 1925
d. 20th March 1986

CAREER: Cambuslang Rangers/CELTIC
12 Oct 1944/free 13 Dec 1945/Cambuslang
Rangers Jan 1946/Duntocher Hibernian
30 June 1947/Arthurlie Jan 1949/Bellshill
Athletic 4 July 1950/St Anthony's cs 1951/...
St Roch 1953/free 16 June 1954/Maryhill Harp
June 1954/coach by Feb 1955.

Debut v Third Lanark (a) 2-1 (RL) 18.11.44

"A grand little schemer and purveyor who
knows how to shoot," Charlie Kelly joined a
Celtic side in crisis with just 11 points from 13
games. He helped them garner six from his
four big team appearances but yielded his
place to Johnny Paton after December 9th 1944
just as the Germans opened the Battle of the
Bulge in the Ardennes and ex-Celt Willie Cook
was invalided home from the Far East to
hospital in Glasgow. Charlie was called-up to
the Navy after his release from Celtic. "A big
favourite with the crowd" as a junior inside-
left (with all Tully's tricks), he hit two wonder
goals for St Anthony's against Shettleston on
September 15th 1951 and there was
speculation that despite his age he might go
senior again.

Appearances:
RL: 4 apps. 0 gls.
Total: *4 apps. 0 gls.*

KELLY, Francis David

Role: Outside-right 1918
5' 8" 11st.0lbs.
b. Glasgow, 8th December 1892
d. Montagris, 5th May 1919

CAREER: Blantyre St Joseph's 1911/Blantyre
Victoria 1912/CELTIC (trial) Feb 1913/
CELTIC on tour 1914/Motherwell Aug 1915/
(Hamilton Academicals loan 16 Oct 1915)/
3 Cameronians (Scottish Rifles) 1917/
(CELTIC loan Feb 1918).

Debut v Queen's Park (a) 2-0 (SL) 2.2.18

Educated at Stonyhurst, Frank Kelly C.A. was
the eldest son of the great James Kelly and big

brother of the future Sir Bob. Celtic tried him
out as early as February 11th 1913 against the
Cameronians from Maryhill Barracks but
Frank was training as a stockbroker and his
Saturdays were fully taken-up. He managed to
go touring with Celtic on the eve of War 1914
and played in Leipzig on May 30th and Berlin
on June 1st. He had "the speed of a deer...
reminiscent of his father... a masterly crosser of
the ball who can shoot on the run". On loan to
Celtic in 1918 (McAtee had been conscripted
into the Army in January and Frank had lost
his place to Willie Lennie at Fir Park) he did
well for medals. He was in the side that beat
Morton in the final of the War Shield at
Hampden (May 4th 1918) and won the Charity
Cup against Partick Thistle also at Hampden
three weeks later. As Private 53182, Frank died
from his injuries after a train accident while
with the Army in post-War France. He is
buried in the north-west corner of Montagris
Communal Cemetery, Loiret, France. (Plot 29,
Row 8, Grave 23)

Appearances:
SL: 2 apps. 0 gls.
Total: *2 apps. 0 gls.*

KELLY, Francis

Role: Full-back 1943-47
b. Old Kilpatrick, 21st May 1923

CAREER: Renton BG/CELTIC 27 Feb 1943/
free Apr 1947/Ipswich Town (trial) 1947/Raith
Rovers (trial) Penman Cup 1947/Dumbarton
17 Sept 1947/free 2 Oct 1947.

Debut v Queen of the South (a) 0-0 (RL) 2.1.46

Frank Kelly, signed as a centre-half, made his
debut at left-back in place of the injured Roy
Milne. Jimmy Sirrel likewise made his first
appearance for Celtic and Queens had ex-Celt
John Connor at centre. Frank's second and
last big team game was at Brockville on
January 26th 1946. Now Falkirk had Chic
Napier at left-half and Doc Fitzsimons
outside-left. Frank lived at 12, West Bridgend,
Dumbarton.

Appearances:
RL: 2 apps. 0 gls.
Total: *2 apps. 0 gls.*

KELLY, James

Role: Centre-half 1888-97
5′ 8″ 11st.7lbs.
b. *Renton, 15th October 1865*
d. *Blantyre, 20th February 1932*

CAREER: Renton Wanderers/
Renton by 16 Nov 1884/
(Hibernian loan 16 Oct 1886)/
Hibernian Sept 1887/Renton
1887/CELTIC 28 May 1888/
director 13 Apr 1897/
reinstated amateur 3 Aug
1897/chairman Sept 1909 until
1914.

*Debut v Rangers Swifts (h) 5-2
(Inaugural Match) 28.5.1888
(scored once)*

Jimmy Kelly

Renton were Champions of the
World as of the 4-1 defeat of
WBA on 19th May 1888 and
their centre-half, lightning-fast
Jimmy Kelly (who did triple
somersaults to celebrate vital
goals) "could have named his
terms in any club in Britain.
His name was a household
word in the football world... when he decided
to join Celtic our lot were at rest for they knew
the calibre of the recruit both as a player and a
man meant the certainty of several others
throwing in their lot with Parkhead. His play
was always in deadly earnest and he couldn't
be bothered with the frittering and fancy work
of several of our greatest men. 'Get there first
and then diddle about afterwards' was always
his motto. His greatest game was in the
Glasgow Cup final of 1895-96 when Queen's
Park led us at half-time by 3 to 1. Kelly played
in that second half like a man possessed and
we won by 6 to 3... Celtic were lucky in
securing as their first skipper a man of model
character and ability as they did in Kelly... No
Kelly, no Keltic." (Willie Maley). Jimmy won
the Scottish Cup with Renton in 1885 and
1888. He was centre-half in the first Celtic side
to lift the Blue Riband of Scottish football on
April 9th 1892 and to win the League in 1893.
Scotland capped him eight times when caps
were far harder to come by than today. He was
as vital a Celtic chairman as he had been a
player. Celtic were trailing 0-1 to Clyde in the
League at half-time on September 2nd 1911
when Kelly burst out of the stand for the

pavilion dressing-
room, "face like thunder."
Result: two magnificent goals
from Jimmy Quinn almost at
once. As chairman one of his
duties was to hold the
Scottish Cup in his own
house for safe-keeping. His
resignation in 1914 is one of
the indicators of the end of
Celtic's first spring. We have
two portraits of Jimmy in
distress: when Celtic were
1-0 down against a packed
East Stirling defence in the
Scottish Cup on December
15th 1888 with three
minutes to go, muttering to
himself, "Isn't this terrible!
Isn't this terrible!"; then
very, very seasick with
Celtic from Fleetwood to
Belfast on the night of April
20th-21st 1889 in a raging
storm: "Give my purse and
my watch to my faither!"
Jimmy Kelly was an all-time
Celtic great.

Appearances:
*SL: 104 apps. 9 gls.
SC: 35 apps. 2 gls.*
Total: *139 apps. 11 gls.*

♣ **Celtic note:** *As a mere director in January
1928 Jimmy Kelly subscribed to his chairman's
theory that Celtic reserves were better off on a
Saturday watching the big team than having a
game themselves.*

KELLY, John

Role: Goalkeeper 1888-89

CAREER: Mearns Athletic/Busby
Cartvale/CELTIC 1888.

*Debut v Mitchell's St George's (h) 7-1 (Friendly)
31.12.1888*

Willie Dunning succeeded Mick Dolan and
was supplanted himself by John Kelly. John
kept goal for Celtic against English cracks, the
Corinthians in the mud at first Celtic Park on
January 3rd 1889 before a Scottish record
crowd of 21,000. He was the Celtic 'keeper in
the Snow Final at Hampden (Cathkin Park) on
February 2nd 1889 and lost the second goal

when unable to grip the ball for slush. He played a great game at the Oval in the return against the Corinthians on February 16th 1889 and the English papers were convinced they had seen a new Scottish star in action. However, Celtic took a 5-2 hammering from Renton in the Charity Cup back at 2nd Hampden on May 4th 1889 and John seems to have carried the can. He lost his place forthwith to Jim McLaughlin. John Kelly watched Celtic lose the Glasgow Cup final to Rangers on October 12th 1935 with Dan McArthur and Davy Adams. He was also on the guest list when Celtic celebrated their first 50 years at the Grosvenor Restaurant, Gordon St, on June 15th 1938.

Appearances:
SC: 2 apps. 0 shut-outs.
Total: *2 apps. 0 shut-outs.*

KELLY, John

Role: Goalkeeper 1929-30
5′ 9″ 12st.0lbs.
b. Wishaw, c 1902

CAREER: Wishaw YMCA/Vale of Fleet 1922/ Preston NE 20 Jan 1923/Motherwell 31 May 1923/Peebles Rovers 24 Sept 1925/Brighton & Hove Albion 6 Mar 1926/Gillingham 1926/ Crystal Palace 14 May 1927/Thames FC 21 July 1928/Nithsdale Wanderers cs 1929/ CELTIC 24 Aug 1929/(Nithsdale Wanderers loan 31 Aug 1929 & 8 Nov 1929 & 17 Apr 1930)/Carlisle United May 1930/Motherwell 1933.

Debut v Hibernian (h) 4-0 (SL) 2.11.29

John Kelly, a footballer-boxer who was class enough to spar with Tommy Milligan, "gave a good account of himself" in the Celtic preseason trial games of 1929 (Shawfield August 2nd; Parkhead August 7th) and got his chance of a spell in goal after Johnny Thomson's terrible injuries versus Airdrie on February 5th 1930. With Thomson out of action, Celtic signed Jock Britton, Dundee's 'keeper in the 1925 Cup final as John Kelly's understudy. Peter Wilson was sent off for protesting too vigorously to referee Mungo Hutton about a penalty to Hibs on March 8th 1930. He could have saved his breath: Kelly stopped Taylor's shot. Johnny Thomson returned to the team on March 29th 1930 and John Kelly went back to Crawick Holm. John played 77 games in three

seasons for Carlisle and befriended Bob Shankly when Shanks first appeared at Carlisle in 1932 from Glenbuck Cherrypickers.

Appearances:
SL: 9 apps. 6 shut-outs.
SC: 1 app. 0 shut-outs.
Total: *10 apps. 6 shut-outs (60%).*

KELLY, John Carmichael

Role: Outside-left 1938-41
5′ 7″ 10st.12lbs.
b. Paisley, 21st February 1921

CAREER: Mearns Amateurs/Arthurlie 1937/ CELTIC 2 Nov 1938/Morton Sept 1941/ Barnsley Dec 1945/Falkirk 24 July 1953/ Morton Oct 1955/Halifax Town 15 July 1956/ Portadown 1957/Barnsley scout 1958/ ...Shanks Welfare by 1963-64.

Debut v Cowdenbeath (a) 2-1 (SL) 26.8.39

Johnny Kelly

Johnny Kelly was the solution to Celtic's outside-left problem in the absence of Frank Murphy but was discarded much the same as Davie Duncan. He was immensely fast with control at top speed and a hard shot in either foot. November 1st 1942: Morton 2, Rangers 1: "Kelly... laddie Celtic had no use for, played merry hell with the Rangers defence... his winning goal tore the roof off the net... yet Celtic have been searching for years for an outside-left." Before the War was over, Johnny was left winger for Scotland versus England (he replaced Billy Liddell) when Hampden was Flodden not Bannockburn on April 14th 1945. Although he played on the left, he was born right-footed and at Barnsley took all the corners as inswingers from either side. "If we had eleven of him in the team, we'd be champions" (Angus Seed). Johnny lost more than a year out of his game between January 1951 and March 8th

1952 with knee operations. Matt Busby came to watch him on November 1st 1952 (and saw Tommy Taylor?). He played for Celtic Old Crocks against Rangers at Kirkintilloch on June 11th 1969 and was turning out for a Celtic-Rangers XI against Glasgow Police well beyond his sell-by date on May 23rd 1973.

Appearances:
SL: 1 app. 0 gls.
Total: 1 app. 0 gls.
RL: 29 apps. 3 gls.
Total: 29 apps. 3 gls.

KELLY, John

Role: Left-back 1939-40
b. c 1917

CAREER: Shawfield Juniors 1934/CELTIC 10 May 1939/free 12 Aug 1940/Shawfield Juniors 15 Aug 1940/St Mirren 24 Sept 1943/St Anthony's 1944/Shawfield Juniors 1945/retired 1947.

Debut v Clyde (h) 1-0 (SL) 2.9.39

John Kelly, "judgement and sure kicking," "an artist on the ball," "always smiling and obliging," won three junior caps for Scotland in 1938-39 (captain against the English) and made his Celtic debut on the last day before mass entertainment was suspended including League football as of September 4th 1939. This "grand little, clean-kicking left-back" hung up his boots to become coach and assistant trainer of Shawfield Juniors.

Appearances:
SL: 1 app. 0 gls.
Total: 1 app. 0 gls.
RL: 4 apps. 0 gls.
SWC: 1 app. 0 gls.
Total: 5 apps. 0 gls.

KELLY, John G.

Role: Wing-half 1960-62
5' 8" 10st.12lbs.
b. Glasgow,
14th December 1935

CAREER: Eastfield Rovers 1952/Whifflet St Mary's 1955/Shettleston Juniors

John G Kelly

1955/Kilmarnock (trial) spring 1956/Third Lanark 16 Oct 1956/Crewe Alexandra 8 Sept 1959/CELTIC 30 Mar 1960/(Morton loan 2 Dec 1961)/free 3 May 1962/Morton cs 1962/Barnsley 1963/Third Lanark 19 Jan 1967.

Debut v Sedan (a) 0-3 (Anglo-French Friendship Cup) 6.8.60

Schoolboy international Johnny Kelly aka "the Jet," was an all-action Third Lanark half-back in the Harry Mooney mould of total "zest and fitness... a human dynamo." Johnny was an engine fitter by trade and left Cathkin to get married and look for a job in the Manchester area as of May 8th 1959. Thirds accepted £1,000 from Crewe four months later. Bob Kelly felt his "souped-up" style might inspire the others but Celtic's youngsters needed a Fernie to slow them down and Johnny was never the same man with Celtic. Morton were glad to have him permanently once he was free. He rejoined Bobby Shearer's Thirds in the death throes of that grand old club still lamented by so many.

Appearances:
SL: 3 apps. 0 gls.
Total: 3 apps. 0 gls.

KENNAWAY, James

Role: Goalkeeper 1931-39
5' 10" 11st.7lbs.
b. Montreal, Canada, 25th January 1905
d. Johnston, (Providence RI), 7th March 1969

CAREER: Rosemount Juniors /Montreal Star/Gurney FC 1925/Canadian Pacific FC 1926/Providence (RI) FC Jan 1928/Fall River 1930/New Bedford autumn 1931/CELTIC 30 Oct 1931/to USA again 26 Oct 1939/SA Healey FC (White Plains) NY Sept 1940/Montreal Vickers player-manager by 1943/Fall River/Brown University soccer coach 1946.

Debut v Motherwell (a) 2-2 (SL) 31.10.31

Celtic lost 1-0 to Fall River on the US tour (May 31st 1931). Willie Maley cabled to Scotland: "Our people at home fancy John Thomson but they have his equal at Fall River where their goalkeeper saved them time after time with clever work." Joe had played for Canada versus USA at Ebbet's Field, Brooklyn on November 6th 1926, his one cap for Canada (they lost 6-2). After Johnny Thomson's death (September 5th 1931), Joe Kennaway got married, boarded ship with his new wife Loretta (23rd October 1931), was in Glasgow on October 29th and played his first game for Celtic two days later. "The new goalkeeper showed a safe pair of hands. He is quick too in getting to the ball in the air or on the ground. He is going to be a personality in Scottish football." Joe got injured on his debut and did not make his first appearance at Celtic Park until December 5th. The tributes poured in as for the young Thomson: "Superlative saving by Kennaway... never a hand wrong... an exhibition of goalkeeping as not seen in a long time... a round of applause all to himself as he left the field... clean clutching... a feature of his game." He rated the Scottish Cup final of April 15th 1933 as his greatest match: "Everything I did, I seemed to do at just the right time" (including one point-blank stop from George Stevenson). Before it was fashionable he used the throw almost as often as the kick to clear his lines. No Celtic goalie after Thomson or before Packy Bonner saved so many penalties. He dropped Davie Meiklejohn with a straight right (September 21st 1935) but saved the spot kick. He saved a twice-taken kick each time against Rangers in the Charity Cup final of May 14th 1938 at Hampden. During the Championship season of 1935-36 "Kennaway was like a rock" and conceded less than a goal a game throughout the campaign. With Joe in goal, Celtic won the Cup in 1933 and 1937; and the League in 1936 and 1938; his name is immortalised in the team that won the Exhibition Trophy on June 10th 1938. It was Joe kept Celtic in contention on May 25th when extra time had to be played with nine fit men against a fiercely physical

J. KENNAWAY

no-nonsense Sunderland side. He dropped out of the Celtic team with rheumatoid arthritis in September 1939 for which he was treated by Eddie McGarvie. Back in the States, he coached at Brown University, Rhode Island, and always made a point of going to see Celtic on tour "looking like a million dollars" (Charlie Tully). He visited Glasgow for the first time since 1939 in July 1965. He died suddenly from a heart attack. He is buried in Highland Memorial Park, Johnston, Providence, Rhode Island.

Appearances:
SL: 263 apps. 75 shut-outs.
SC: 32 apps. 8 shut-outs.
Total: *295 apps. 83 shut-outs (28%).*

♣ **Celtic note:** *Joe never played for the USA and despite the evidence of some record books missed his first Scottish cap versus Wales at Cardiff on October 4th 1933 with a broken finger. He kept goal once for Scotland (his father Charlie was from Dundee) against the mighty Austrians at Hampden on November 29th 1933.*

KENNEDY, James

Role: Left-back 1955-65
5' 10" 11st.3lbs.
b. Johnstone, 31st January 1934

CAREER: St Margaret's School Johnstone/ RAOC 1952/Johnstone Glencairn Juveniles 1955/Duntocher Hibernian 1955/CELTIC 3 Nov 1955/(Rangers loan 11 Mar 1959)/ Morton 13 Nov 1965/free 1968/CELTIC again 18 Aug 1968/free 1969.

Debut v Partick Thistle (a) 0-2 (SL) 23.4.56

Jim Kennedy left school and joined a Celtic Supporters' Club. He had no desire to play football and made no attempt to take the game seriously until National Service in Belgium. Even then he only joined Johnstone Glencairn a full six months after leaving the Army. He had two reserve games for Celtic then faced his ordeal against Johnny McKenzie, flying right-winger of Partick Thistle and Scotland. "Celtic fans were in raptures" following his performance against Clyde in the Charity Cup on May 5th 1956 and a great game against Rangers on September 10th 1960 led to talk of a Scottish cap. He missed the Cup final replay against Dunfermline with appendicitis having just given up his job in an Elderslie carpet factory on April 20th 1961 to go full-time. He was hugely popular with the Celtic support and could not believe his luck that he was playing for the club he would otherwise be following round Scotland. He was dropped in favour of Tommy Gemmell at the start of 1963-64: "I will always want to be with Celtic just as long as they need me." He received a new lease at left-half as of October 5th 1963 and it was as Celtic left-half he was capped by Scotland at left-back versus Wales on November 20th 1963. He played against England at Hampden in the 1-0 win of April 11th 1964. He held his place with Celtic until the arrival of Jock Stein who preferred John Clark. 'Pres' led Morton to promotion on April 9th 1967 at the same time as Bobby Evans was taking Raith Rovers up. He was appointed liaison officer between Celtic and the Supporters' Clubs on August 18th 1968 but re-signed as a reserve for a one-off against Morton the following evening.

Appearances:
SL: 170 apps. 0 gls.
SLC: 31 apps. 2 gls.
SC: 29 apps. 0 gls.
Eur: 11 apps. 0 gls.
Total: *241 apps. 2 gls.*

KENNEDY, John

Role: Goalkeeper 1965-67
6' 3" 12st.7lbs.
b. Newtonards,
4th September 1939

CAREER:
Distillery/CELTIC 10 Mar 1965/free 1967/Glentoran (Detroit Cougars) USA 23 May 1967/Lincoln City July 1967/retired 1 May 1974.

Debut v Raith Rovers (h)
4-0 (SLC) 22.9.65

Jack Kennedy

Jim Kennedy

Like Ronnie Simpson at Wembley in 1948, English teacher Jack Kennedy kept goal for the GB Olympic XI at Tokyo in 1964. Celtic paid £5,000 for him the day after Jock Stein took over as manager but Jack got small chance in competition with John Fallon and then his Olympic predecessor, Ronnie Simpson. John Colrain borrowed him to play in a US soccer tournament and shortly after he was off to Lincoln where he turned out 251 times for the Imps. He retired after 17 years in the game and was never once booked or cautioned.

Appearances:
SLC: 1 app. 1 shut-out.
Total: *1 app. 1 shut-out (100%).*

KIDDIE, Alexander Anderson

Role: Outside-right
1944-45
5' 9" 10st.7lbs.
b. Dundee,
27th April 1927

CAREER: Ashdale
Juveniles/Angus
Boys Amateurs/
Jeanfield Swifts
1943/Dundee
Stobswell 1944/
CELTIC 23 Dec 1944
/Aberdeen 9 Aug
1945/Falkirk 14 Dec
1950/Dundee (trial)
29 Nov 1952/free
14 Feb 1953/Arbroath
19 Feb 1953/Brechin 8 Aug 1953/Montrose
4 Aug 1956/free 30 Apr 1957.

Alex Kiddie

Debut v Airdrie (h) 4-2 (RL) 28.10.44

"Schoolboy sensation" Alex Kiddie ("Thrust
and speed with clever ball
control") was an amateur
during his time with Celtic
and did not turn professional
until June 21st 1948. He tried
out with Celtic reserves at Fir
Park on March 25th 1944 and
was signed after a friendly
against the full Dundee
United side at Tannadice in
December. He deprived
Johnny Pattillo of a first team
place at Aberdeen - where he
reminded older fans of Alec
Jackson - when Paddy
Travers brought the great
winger home to the Dons
from the USA. "He is the
Gordon Smith of Pittodrie...
great things are expected of
his combination with George
Hamilton." No matter how
exciting a prospect to the
connoisseur, young Alex was
much more intent on
acquiring a B.Sc. degree
(St Andrew's June 1948) and
securing his future outside
football as a schoolteacher
(St John's, Dundee). He had a
great game against Jock Shaw

for the Aberdeen team that won the League
Cup 3-2 versus Rangers at Hampden before
130,000 on May 11th 1946 (he made the second
goal). Alex did not give total satisfaction at
Pittodrie because of a "disinclination to mix
it". His two appearances for the Celtic big
team were both against Airdrie and he was in
a winning side each time. He played a major
role in the 6-2 destruction of Celtic at Pittodrie
on August 17th 1946.

Appearances:
RL: 2 apps. 0 gls.
Total: *2 apps. 0 gls.*

KIERNAN, Thomas

Role: Inside-right 1945-47
5' 8" 10st.10lbs.
b. Coatbridge, 20th October 1918
d. Coatbridge, 26th June 1991

CAREER: Viewpark Celtic 1935/Clydebank
Juniors Apr 1936/free Dec 1937/Albion
Rovers 3 Jan 1938/Royal Engineers 1940
(Chelsea & Southampton loan 1940)(Brentford,
Chelsea, Fulham &
Spurs loan 1941-42)
(Brentford loan
1942-43)(Brentford
& Fulham loan
1943-44)(Aldershot
& Fulham loan
1944-45)/CELTIC
11 July 1945/Stoke
City 25 Sept 1947/
Luton Town 12 Nov
1948/Gillingham
1950/St Mirren
14 Dec 1950/Barry
Town Aug 1951/
free 1952/Albion
Rovers 23 Sept 1952
/free 24 Apr 1954/
Alloa 10 Aug 1954/
free 1955/Barry
Town (tour of
Sweden) 1955/
Albion Rovers coach
16 Oct 1958.

Debut v Hearts (a)
2-2 (RL) 22.9.45

Tommy Kiernan

"He has all the talents of an internationalist... why they don't put him on top and - keep him there - is just one of the game's mysteries." Jimmy McGrory had "no definite rebuilding plan" in July 1945. "New blood will be brought in over a period." Two-footed Tommy Kiernan, "craft, forcefulness and unflagging energy," represents Celtic's first genuine post-War transfusion at the cost of £4,000. He had scored goals aplenty for Albion Rovers as a thrusting inside-forward and Celtic bought him both as scorer and provider for Jackie Gallacher. Tommy's displays such as his 4-1 destruction of Hibs on November 9th 1946 were rewarded with a League cap against England at Hampden (March 12th 1947), the highlight of his career, even though the English won 1-3. In the meantime, as of the friendly versus Aston Villa in Birmingham on March 1st 1947, Celtic had moved him to centre and the consensus of opinion saw a fine inside man being wasted as a spearhead. By August 30th 1947 Celtic were watching Dennis Westcott of Wolves and willing to listen to offers for Tommy. Bob McGrory got his signature on September 25th for a fee of £8,000. The transfer was as incomprehensible as Delaney's the year before and filled the support with comparable sadness. Tommy played for Alloa against Celtic in the Scottish Cup on February 5th 1955.

Appearances:
SL: 23 apps. 9 gls.
SLC: 8 apps. 6 gls.
SC: 1 app. 0 gls.
Total: *32 apps. 15 gls.*
RL: 26 apps. 0 gls.
RLC: 6 apps. 4 gls.
Total: *32 apps. 4 gls.*

KING, Alexander

Role: Utility 1895-1900
5' 9" 11st.2lbs.
b. Dykehead, 27th July 1871
d. Shotts, 12th December 1957

CAREER: Dykehead/Airdrie Mar 1893/Albion Rovers Apr 1893/Wishaw Thistle 24 Aug 1893/Darwen 4 Oct 1894/Dykehead 18 Apr 1895/Rangers (trial) 29 Apr 1895/Hearts 31 July 1895/CELTIC 6 May 1896/Dykehead 5 Sept 1900/St Bernard's 26 Oct 1900/Dykehead 31 Oct 1901/Airdrie 5 June 1903/Dykehead 4 July 1904/retired 1905.

Debut v Hibernian (a) 1-3 (SL) 15.8.1896

Alex King was 61 years a miner in the Shotts coalfield and worked under pit manager Mr Morton (Alan Morton's father). He was a destroyer of defences and made an indelible impression on Celtic when he scored a straight hat-trick against them on September 14th 1895 in a 0-5 win for Hearts. He came to Parkhead as an inside-left but proved a versatile performer. He took over in goal whenever Dan McArthur was off comatose and even started in goal versus Ancient City Athletic in St Andrews (October 18th 1897). He was left-half in the Celtic side which won the Scottish Cup 2-0 versus Rangers on April 22nd 1899 but signs of loss of confidence manifested in the autumn: "King waits for the ball and then gets rid of it as quickly as possible." To encourage him, Celtic reduced his wages then shortly after transferred him. Celtic played Rangers for his benefit at Dykehead on September 4th 1905. Alex of Hunter St., Shotts was a guest at the Hearts versus Celtic Scottish Cup final (April 21st 1956). He was capped six times for Scotland, four times with Celtic.

Appearances:
SL: 56 apps. 10 gls.
SC: 6 apps. 2 gls.
Total: *62 apps. 12 gls.*

KING, John

Role: Right-back, Half-back 1895-97
5' 9" 11st.11lbs.
b. Shotts, 19th January 1874

CAREER: Cleland Thistle 1892/Dykehead/Wishaw Thistle 1893/Airdrie Mar 1894/Dykehead 31 May 1894/Darwen 31 Aug 1894/Dykehead 18 Apr 1895/CELTIC 21 May 1895/East Stirling 3 May 1897/Dykehead 9 Feb 1898/reinstated amateur 12 Feb 1901/Albion Rovers 12 Feb 1901/Scots Guards 4 Dec 1903/discharged 11 Jan 1904.

Debut v Partick Thistle (h) 5-1 (GC) 2.11.1895

According to Ching Morrison, John King had a conceit of his abilities which resulted in a letter from an 'English scout' asking to meet him at the Alexandra Hotel in Bath Street. Almost the whole team accompanied John to advise him but no Englishman appeared. He was made scapegoat for the Day of Infamy of January 9th 1897 when Celtic were dumped out of the Scottish Cup by Arthurlie in the first round at Barrhead. He improvised a central defence with a half-stripped Barney Crossan which afforded Joe Cullen (the English 'scout') virtually no cover at all. John was summarily released to resume his career elsewhere.

Appearances: .
SL: 9 apps. 0 gls.
SC: 1 app. 0 gls.
Total: *10 apps. 0 gls.*

KIVLICHAN, William Fulton

Role: Outside-right 1907-11
5' 8" 12st.4lbs.
b. Galashiels, 11th March 1890
d. Glasgow, 5th April 1937

CAREER: St Joseph's Dumfries/Maxwelltown Juniors/Dumfries FC Mar 1905/Rangers 13 Nov 1905/CELTIC 16 May 1907/Bradford PA 29 Apr 1911/RAMC Nyasaland 29 Dec 1917/Police Casualty Surgeon Glasgow Central Division 1931.

Debut v Morton (a) 3-2 (SL)
24.8.07 (scored twice)

Willie Kivlichan

Willie Maley describes W. Fulton Kivlichan as a "good honest hard worker - never seemed to be just the class our people were looking for." Hugh Hilley places him at outside-right in the best Celtic side he ever saw. He sprang into prominence with the winning goal for Rangers at Ibrox Ne'erday 1907. Celtic took him on the Scandinavian tour that summer and he played his first game for the club as goalie in Copenhagen on June 5th 1907. Rangers met Celtic in the Scottish Cup on February 8th 1908; score: Rangers 1, Kivlichan ("worming about like an eel") 2. Willie graduated MA from Glasgow University in April 1908 and M.B. Ch.B. on July 21st 1917. He was set to join Partick Thistle from Celtic but was persuaded down to Yorkshire by Tom Maley. Captain Kivlichan served with the King's Own African Rifles and was reported seriously wounded on August 30th 1918. He was back in Scotland by September 1920 and down to play for Queen of the South reserves versus

St Mirren on October 2nd. Willie became Celtic club doctor and was in attendance at Ibrox the day of John Thomson's fatal accident (September 5th 1931). He died of a heart attack at his home in Crosshill, Glasgow, two days after watching Celtic beat Clyde 2-0 in the Cup semi-final at Hampden. He is buried at St Joseph's, Dumfries.

Appearances:
SL: 76 apps. 16 gls.
SC: 16 apps. 6 gls.
Total: *92 apps. 22 gls.*

♣ **Celtic note:** *Willie was a practising Catholic and a member of the Third Order of St Francis. Against Queen's Park at Hampden on October 1st 1910, the brown scapulars of the Order escaped from beneath his jersey and played in the breeze over his shoulders which "brought tears of joy to the eyes of the Parkhead faithful." (He also scored with a 40-yarder).*

KURILA, John

Role: Centre-half 1958-62
5' 11" 12st.8lbs.
b. Glasgow, 10th April 1941

CAREER: Holyrood Senior Secondary 1956/St Francis BG/CELTIC 5 Aug 1958/Blantyre Victoria (farmed-out) 1958/free 1 May 1962/Hamilton Steelers cs 1962/Northampton Town Aug 1962/Hamilton Steelers cs 1963/Bristol City Aug 1963/Northampton Town Nov 1963/Southend United July 1968/Colchester United May 1970/Lincoln City Dec 1971/Atherstone United 1973.

Debut v Motherwell (a) 0-2 (SL) 8.4.59

John Kurila was an ex-schoolboy goalie transformed at Parkhead into the last of Bobby Evans' and the first of Billy McNeill's understudies. It was a situation that afforded few enough chances to shine. John captained the Celtic reserves (half-backs; Crerand, Kurila and Clark) and won three 2nd XI

John Kurila

First Division in 1965-66. When he failed to settle at Bristol, Northampton paid a fee to get him back. John was in the Colchester side that sensationally knocked out mighty Leeds United 3-2 in the fifth round of the English Cup at Layer Road (13th February 1971). Big John was of Lithuanian extraction, his grandparents having settled in Scotland during 1914-18.

> **Appearances:**
> *SL: 5 apps. 0 gls.*
> *SLC: 4 apps. 0 gls.*
> **Total:** *9 apps. 0 gls.*

KYLE, James

Role: Left-half 1890-92
b. Glasgow, 22nd September 1870

CAREER: Benburb 1889/CELTIC 1890.
Debut v Cowlairs (a) 5-0 (SL) 29.4.1891

'Fish' Kyle was captain of Benburb and one of Celtic's many captures from "the Polmadie Greens" including Johnny Campbell, Barney Crossan, Joe Cullen and Johnny Cunningham. He was in the Celtic side that gave Cowlairs their first defeat on their new Springvale Park ground. He was also in the team that welcomed the reinstated Renton back in a friendly before 10,000 ecstatic fans at first Celtic Park on May 9th 1891. The Dumbartonshire men had fought the SFA through the courts and won. He has an Old Firm match on his record card, a 1-1 draw at Old Ibrox (May 7th 1892).

> **Appearances:**
> *SL: 2 apps. 0 gls.*
> **Total:** *2 apps. 0 gls.*

Championship medals along with a Reserve League Cup badge (versus Rangers May 10th 1960). He made his League debut at right-back in place of Duncan MacKay, preparing for Wembley duty in Bobby Evans' team. McNeill's knee joint bled against Third Lanark in the League Cup at Cathkin on August 27th 1960 and big John took over from him, same venue, same opponents, two nights later in the Glasgow Cup. He was in the inexperienced Celtic team beaten 1-5 by Rangers in the Scottish League on September 10th 1960. He took the suspended Crerand's place at right-half at an electric Firhill in the League Cup on the opening day of the season, August 12th 1960, when admission price rose to three shillings (15p) and Rangers fans stampeded to get into Cathkin. His free transfer in 1962 took the fans by surprise. He went on a tour of Canada with Bertie Peacock's XI under contract to Hamilton Steelers and returned a week early to sign for Northampton. Dave Bowen's 'Cobblers' used him as a wing-half and when his transfer value soared to £10,000 on October 1962, Steelers began to make noises. John was in the fine Northampton side that won the Third and Second Division Championships in successive seasons (1964 and 1965). He had one season in the English

LAFFERTY, James

Role: Centre-forward 1951-53

CAREER: Barrhead St Joseph's/Arthurlie 1950/CELTIC 1 Nov 1951/free 28 Apr 1953/ Lincoln City 6 July 1953/free own request Nov 1953/Larne 1953/Worcester City 21 Nov 1953 /Los Angeles Danes by 1955.

Debut v Partick Thistle (h) 2-1 (SL) 1.12.51

Jimmy McGrory signed "big, strong," Jim Lafferty as a centre-forward, "the best Arthurlie have had in years," then decided to develop him as an outside-left. Tully was on a month's suspension for kicking East Fife iron man George Aitken when Jim made his debut on the left wing. His second game coincided with Jock Stein's debut (December 8th 1951) by which time he was back in his familiar berth at centre in place of Gil Heron and scored twice against St Mirren. The first goal came "with a side-flick through a maze of black and white shirts." He missed an absolute sitter in eight minutes against East Fife in a 3-1 defeat at Methil on December 15th 1951 but was inspired to a "distinctive game" by Jimmy Walsh against Motherwell at Parkhead the following week. His last game for Celtic was in place of John McPhail in a 9-goal thriller versus Third Lanark at Parkhead on November 8th 1952 "when his wanderings had the Warriors in a spin." Lincoln City had been keen on him at Arthurlie yet played him at inside-left and outside-left almost exclusively in the reserves.

Appearances:
SL: 7 apps. 4 gls.
Total: *7 apps. 4 gls.*

LAMB, Peter

Role: Right-back 1945-47
b. New Monkland, 6th June 1925

CAREER: Arthurlie/St Anthony's/CELTIC 31 Dec 1945/free Apr 1947/Alloa 5 May 1947/ free 10 May 1949/Wigtown and Bladnoch 1949 until Dec 1955.

Debut v St Mirren (a) 1-0 (SL) 31.8.46

Peter Lamb, an inside man with Arthurlie, was converted to right-back by St Anthony's but always hoped for the chance to play forward again. His one appearance for the Celtic big

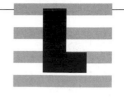

team was in "a match devoid of subtlety... the ball was biffed about." He got his solitary chance on one of Bobby Hogg's rare absences. With Pat O'Sullivan and George Gillan at Wigtown he helped give Third Lanark a hard passage in the Scottish Cup on February 7th 1953. Peter was five seasons a junior before joining Celtic.

Appearances:
SL: 1 app. 0 gls.
Total: *1 app. 0 gls.*

LATCHFORD, Peter

Role: Goalkeeper 1975-87
6' 0" 13st.0lbs.
b. King's Heath, Birmingham, 27th September 1952

CAREER: Broadmeadow Junior School/ Brandwood Secondary Modern/South Birmingham Boys/Monyhull Hospital FC/ Redditch Town (did not play)/Sutton Coldfield Town 1968/Finn Harps Birmingham GAA/West Bromwich Albion am. May 1969, pro. Oct 1969/(CELTIC loan 17 Feb 1975)/ CELTIC 14 July 1975/free June 1987/Clyde 18 July 1987/Arbroath coach (Danny McGrain).

Debut v Hibernian (a) 1-2 (SL) 22.2.75

Like Roy Aitken, Peter Latchford was a junior basketball star. Sean Fallon watched him in a reserve match at Huddersfield (February 15th 1975) and Celtic played him in a friendly at Ayr three days later. One week on from Huddersfield he was Celtic's goalie to the exclusion of Ally Hunter, Denis Connaghan and Graham Barclay. Despite soft goals lost, the support took to him at once as an "instinctive, athletic goalie." On March 8th 1975, "Latchford is beginning to look the part... the answer to Parkhead's prayers." A Brummie goalie behind a Glasgow defence had problems of communication: "Latchford seems to have overcome his 'language barrier' in goal and the whole defence benefited" (April 12th 1975). He got his first Scottish Cup medal against Airdrie on May 3rd 1975 and a special ovation all to himself at the end. Against Boavista in Portugal (October 22nd 1975) he saved an Alves penalty to get Celtic a

Peter Latchford

creditable 0-0 draw - the same night he felt a soldier's rifle muzzle on his back urging him to not to waste time at goal kicks! The start of 1976 was a disaster, 10 goals lost in four games, but Sean Fallon kept faith, dropped him for one game then brought him straight back. Against Dundee United at Tannadice in the League Cup (August 14th 1976) he had a save from a Paul Hegarty header in the 90th minute that sent the Celtic fans to the exits chanting his name. A save from Tom McAdam (Dundee United) on September 11th 1976 again at Tannadice was a replica of Banks' from Pele in the Mexico World Cup 1970. On one good leg against Rangers at Ibrox on March 19th 1977, he saved a Greig piledriver in the closing minutes which would have given Rangers a 3-2 win had it gone in. He won his second Scottish medal against Rangers after recovering from the Ibrox ankle injury (May 7th 1977). The Celtic Supporters' Associations nominated him their Player of the Year on February 26th 1978. His third

Scottish medal was also against Rangers (May 10th 1980). He broke his hand in training at the start of August 1980 and his effective career as a first-team Celt was over. He played his last game for the club in the Glasgow Cup final of May 7th 1987 versus Rangers when Lex Baillie defeated him with an own goal.

Appearances:
SL: 187 apps. 52 shut-outs.
SLC: 39 apps. 15 shut-outs.
SC: 27 apps. 9 shut-outs.
Eur: 19 apps. 6 shut-outs.
Total: *272 apps. 82 shut-outs (30%).*

LAVERY, Daniel O'Donnell

Role: Centre-forward 1948-49
6' 0" 12st.0lbs.
b. Sydney, Australia, 24th August 1925
d. Chorley, 19th March 1979

CAREER: Antrim GAA/CELTIC 30 Jan 1948/ (Glentoran loan 25 Oct 1948)/Ballymena United 1949/Dundalk 1949 until 1951/... Leyland Motors (Lancashire Combination League) by 1954.

Debut v Hibernian (a) 2-4 (SL) 3.4.48
(scored once)

Dan Lavery played a trial for Celtic reserves at Pittodrie on January 17th 1948 and was signed as a centre just before Jock Weir and just after Frank Walsh and Phil Gormley. He played against ex-Celt Alex Millar on August 14th 1948 and was described as "a doubtful quality... headed Millar's clearances for him." Dan got a another chance against Aberdeen at

Dan Lavery

Pittodrie the following Saturday but thereafter was a Celtic reserve. The high point of his stay with Celtic was surely the battle for two points at Dundee on April 17th 1948 as relegation threatened and Celtic without another game to play. He came straight from Gaelic football and however big his heart, the transition proved too hard. Glentoran received Dan and Jack Greenwood to keep in return for Bertie Peacock. Dan went to live at Buxton, Derbyshire, and worked for Ben Sayers, the manufacturer of golf equipment. He died at Chorley during a round on the links.

Appearances:
SL: 4 apps. 1 gl.
Total: 4 apps. 1 gl.

LAWRIE, William

Role: Goalkeeper 1919-21
5' 11" 11st.0lbs.
b. Dumfries, 4th August 1899

CAREER: Clydebank Juniors/CELTIC 20 Oct 1919/Aberdeen 25 May 1921/free 1923/ Peterhead 27 Sept 1924.

Debut v Queen's Park (h) 3-1 (SL) 25.10.19

Willie Lawrie

Willie Lawrie was "a lad of promise... full of enthusiasm, confident and hopeful... another excellent capture by Mr Maley." Charlie Shaw dropped out "with injuries and a cold" after his rearguard action in the 3-0 defeat by Rangers (October 18th 1919) in the League and Willie Lawrie came into the team for the next four games including a friendly won 3-4 at Cowdenbeath on October 29th. There were no clean sheets for Willie but he was never in a beaten team either. He played in the cauldron of Cappielow on November 1st 1919: Morton scored in five minutes, Adam McLean equalised in 40 and Jimmy McStay scored the winner with a penalty four minutes from time, the occasion of a field invasion to offer him congratulations. Willie was a blacksmith in Aberdeen by trade.

Appearances:
SL: 3 apps. 0 shut-outs.
Total: 3 apps. 0 shut-outs.

LEES, Walter Donald

Role: Centre-forward 1892-93; 1894
b. c 1870

CAREER: Cronberry Eglinton/CELTIC Sept 1892/Lincoln City 1893/CELTIC 29 May 1894 /Lincoln City 13 Oct 1894/Barnsley St Peter's 1895/Darwen 1896/Barnsley St Peter's 1897/ Watford Aug 1904/free Feb 1905/Barnsley Mar 1905.

Debut v Clyde (h) 3-1 (SL) 1.10.1892

Celtic were put on a proscribed list by the English FA when they induced Walter (Don) Lees back from Lincoln and put him out against Stranraer on June 8th 1894. No English club might meet them in a friendly until the matter was resolved. Celtic settled with Lincoln and came

Walter Lees

off the roster. Whatever his early promise, Don hit trouble at Watford after several drink-related breaches of training and despite a threat by Mrs Lees to descend from Barnsley and sort him out.

Appearances:
SL: 4 apps. 3 gls.
Total: 4 apps. 3 gls.

LEITCH, William Smith

Role: Outside-right 1923-26
5' 6" 11st.0lbs.
b. Saltcoats, 14th February 1901

CAREER: Irvine Meadow XI/Saltcoats Victoria/CELTIC 15 Sept 1923(St Bernard's loan 15 Nov 1923)(Armadale loan 22 Jan 1925) (Ayr United loan 17 Oct 1925)/Kilmarnock 3 June 1926/free 4 May 1927/Saltcoats Victoria Sept 1927/Irvine Meadow XI Aug 1933/ Saltcoats Victoria Aug 1934/Ardeer Recreation Sept 1936/Saltcoats Victoria 22 Oct 1938.

Debut v Queen's Park (a) 2-0 (CC) 6.5.24
(scored once)

Willie Leitch

"Clever but not ripe," Willie Leitch, a caulker in Ardrossan Shipyard, was farmed-out and recalled to Parkhead as necessary eg for the Charity Cup semi-final of May 6th 1924 and more famously for the Scottish Cup final against St Mirren on April 10th 1926 when he came in for Celtic's match-winner Adam McLean (injured) and Willie Malloy (likewise). He had a fair game in the Scottish final and was involved in the sensation in the 20th minute; McGrory rammed the inside of the post with a header from a Leitch cross and it took Bradford, the St Mirren goalie three attempts to get the ball clear with Celtic frantic to Peter Craigmyle it was in. Willie's trouble may have been a lack of pace: "Once he is speeded-up he ought to do well." After Ardrossan he worked with explosives at Ardeer. His career went on and on. "I'm kinda fond o' fitba'."

Appearances:
SL: 5 apps. 1 gl.
SC: 1 app. 0 gls.
Total: *6 apps. 1 gl.*

LENNOX, Robert M.B.E.

Role: Outside-left 1961-78; 1978-80
5' 8" 11st.7lbs.
b. Saltcoats, 30th August 1943

CAREER: St Michael's School Irvine/ Saltcoats Star of the Sea Amateurs 1959/ Ardeer Recreation 1959/CELTIC 5 Sept 1961/Houston Hurricane 29 Mar 1978/ CELTIC again 19 Sept 1978/retired 8 Nov 1980/CELTIC coach 8 Nov 1980, dismissed 10 June 1993.

Debut v Dundee (h) 2-1 (SL) 3.3.62

"He seemed to have a zest for the game... he was fast, alert and looked for the ball. In short, he seemed a footballer" (David Potter, having watched Dundee reserves vs Celtic reserves in February 1964). From being an orthodox left-winger, Stein moved Bobby Lennox to inside-left and gave him his role: "He got me lying well up-field... ready for the whip-through, on the move, in fact, before the pass was made." "My job was to look for space and run. Bertie Auld joined Bobby Murdoch in midfield and I was made" (eg with a true hat-trick against Rangers in the Glasgow Cup at Ibrox on August 23rd 1966 when Celtic won 0-4). Lennox was speed, striking power, fitness, a total team man and never a moment's trouble to his manager. A mere boy from the juniors against the almighty Real Madrid at Parkhead on the night of nights 10th September 1962, five years later he was the total menace scoring the goal for the European champions that beat the Spaniards at the Bernebeu packed to capacity for Di Stefano's benefit (June 7th 1967). He was the fastest man in Scottish football and the most dangerous, with his speed and opportunism sorely missed when Celtic went out of the European Cup 0-1 to AC Milan at Parkhead (March 12th 1969). His goals total for Celtic is second only to McGrory's and might even have been higher but for flag-happy linesmen down the years unable to believe anyone could be so fast on the break. The most notorious example of this was the disallowed last-minute counter at Anfield in the Cup-Winners' Cup semi-final on April 19th 1966 which would have seen Celtic through on the away goals rule and which even Liverpool players acknowledged was a

sound one. Very little rankles with Bobby Lennox bar that particular game. He was preferred to John Hughes for the European Cup in Lisbon on May 25th 1967 when he gave the Inter defence a torrid time. He was sent-off in the World Championship play-off in Montevideo (November 4th 1967) but was exonerated later by the SFA (March 4th 1968) as a case of mistaken identity. Bobby was one of the Celtic disappointments in the 1970 final against Feyenoord in the San Siro, Milan (May 6th). He just could not find his game on the night. His speed was always a special torment to Rangers as witness his bursting run up the left in the Scottish Cup final of April 26th 1969 culminating in Celtic's second goal. He set up the Celtic post-War record of 242 goals with a penalty on November 24th 1973 (but didn't know he'd done it). Unlike Jimmy McGrory, he got to Wembley and beat Gordon Banks all ends up to make it 0-2 in the 78th minute of Scotland's famous 2-3 victory over the 1966 World Champions on April 15th 1967. Unbelievably for a player who was on his way out as Stein arrived, Bobby holds eight Scottish Cup medals, eleven Championship badges and ten Scottish caps. Bobby Charlton paid him the supreme compliment after Ron Yeats' testimonial (May 13th 1974): "If I'd had Lennox in my team, I could have played for ever." 'Lemon' and 'Jinky' shared a testimonial at Celtic Park on May 17th 1976 and did a lap of honour together. Bobby Lennox is an all-time Parkhead great. Even the Queen recognised this with an M.B.E. on January 1st 1981 "for services to Celtic FC". Billy McNeill had paid him an even greater compliment on May 22nd 1979: "Bobby Lennox knows what wearing a Celtic jersey means."

Appearances:
SL: 335 apps. 167 gls.
SLC: 119 apps. 62 gls.
SC: 51 apps. 31 gls.
Eur: 66 apps. 13 gls.
Total: *571 apps. 273 gls.*

♣ **Celtic note:** *Willie Wallace gave him his nickname from a newspaper misprint: 'Celtic scorer: Lemon'.*

LIVINGSTONE, Dugald

Duggie Livingstone

Role: Full-back 1917-21
5′ 8″ 11st.0lbs.
b. *Alexandria,*
25th February 1898
d. *Harlow, Bucks,*
18th January 1981

CAREER: Parkhead
1915/ Ashfield 5 July 1916/CELTIC 3 Jan 1917
(Dumbarton Harp loan 11 Jan 1917)/CELTIC
again 13 Aug 1917(Dumbarton Harp loan
12 Dec 1917 & Oct 1918)(Clydebank loan
28 Dec 1918 & 11 Jan 1919)(Dumbarton Harp
loan 6 Jan 1921)/Everton 15 Apr 1921/
Plymouth Argyle Feb 1926/Aberdeen 11 Aug
1927/free Apr 1930/Tranmere Rovers 18 June
1930/Exeter City trainer 1935/Sheffield
United coach 1 July 1936/Sheffield Wednesday
manager 19 Jan 1947/resigned 14 Oct 1949/
Sparta Rotterdam Oct 1949/Eire coach Aug
1951/Belgium coach 1953 & World Cup 1954/
resigned 6 Dec 1954/Newcastle United
manager 8 Dec 1954/Fulham manager Jan
1956/Chesterfield manager May 1958 until
1962.

Debut v Ayr United (h) 4-0 (SL) 18.8.17

"Without being a big man, he is sturdily built
and relies on pure football... I liked his
judgement of position... his self-possession,
resolution and resource... strong capable
defender... all that he needs is a little more
speed." (Everton versus Manchester United
September 3rd 1921). Duggie Livingstone
made his Celtic debut just two days before the
horrific third Battle of Ypres opened in the
Flanders muck. He was "cool and resourceful
to a degree" against Hearts flier Willie Wilson
on October 30th 1920 and displayed "clean,
crisp kicking" versus Clydebank (8th January
1921). Everton had wanted his transfer for
years but Celtic were loath to let him go until
March 5th 1921 when a bad misunderstanding
with Charlie Shaw ("Livingstone is erratic
when pressed") put Celtic out of the Scottish
Cup against Hearts at Parkhead. He made his
main fame as coach and manager. The first
time he watched Newcastle they lost four
goals in seven minutes. As far as Jackie
Milburn was concerned the last thing the
Magpies needed was Duggie's innovative
methods and tactics (like chalking Bobby

Mitchell's boots to allegedly improve his
passing). Nevertheless he took them (with
Ronnie Simpson in goal) to the last Cup Final
win in their history on May 7th 1955. His team
selection for the big game was overruled by
Stan Seymour and the board. On May 11th
Duggie was told the club was reverting to old
established practice: the directors would pick
the side, Duggie would also no longer travel
to away matches; he would spend more time
on developing the third and fourth teams, and
was to move house from Sheffield to
Newcastle. Duggie moved on to Fulham with
"full control of team and tactics" and took
Johnny Haynes, Jimmy Langley, Macedo and
company to the Cup semi-final 1958. He was
watching Reading versus Carlisle just the
week before he died. Duggie followed in the
Peter Somers tradition of Celtic club pianist.

Appearances:
SL: 44 apps. 0 gls.
SC: 3 apps. 0 gls.
Total: *47 apps. 0 gls.*

LIVINGSTONE, George Turner

Role: Inside-forward 1901-02
5′ 9″ 11st.10lbs.
b. *Dumbarton, 5th May 1876*
d. *Helensburgh, 15th January 1950*

CAREER: Sinclair Swifts/Artizan Thistle/
Parkhead Juniors/Dumbarton 1895/Hearts
25 May 1896/Sunderland 30 June 1900/
CELTIC 1 May 1901/Liverpool 30 May 1902/
Manchester City May 1903/Rangers 5 Nov
1906/Manchester United 19 Jan 1909/RAMC
Oct 1915/Dumbarton manager Jan 1919/
Clydebank manager Aug 1919/Rangers
trainer July 1920/retired July 1927/Bradford
City trainer 9 July 1928/retired 1935.

Debut v Rangers (h) 1-0 (CC) 3.5.01

Geordie Livingstone was an immensely
physical player with a fearsome reputation as
a destroyer from the same mould as Alec
King. No game was ever lost while Geordie
was on the park. He represents as big a
signing coup for Celtic as Jack Bell and the
money must have been right, because George
was an astute businessman who earned ten
bob more a week than the great Billy Meredith
while at Manchester City. The Ne'erday game
of 1902 developed into a total rough house in
the second half under the histrionic control of

Geordie Livingstone

Hynds). He won an English Cup medal 1-0 versus Bolton Wanderers at the Crystal Palace on April 23rd 1904. He joined Rangers once the English FA decided on draconian measures against City for a bribes/wages scandal in the summer of 1906 and George found himself suspended from English football until New Year 1907. Like Willie Kivlichan he served with the RAMC in East Africa. He was Bill Struth's first trainer at Ibrox.

Appearances:
SL: 17 apps. 4 gls.
SC: 6 apps. 3 gls.
Total: *23 apps. 7 gls.*

LOCHHEAD, Ian

Role: Centre-forward 1958-61
5' 11" 10st.4lbs.
b. 26th September 1939

CAREER: St Gerard's Senior Secondary 1958/Drumchapel Amateurs 1958/Partick Avondale 1958/CELTIC 25 Sept 1958/free 2 May 1961/ Dumbarton 28 Dec 1961/free Mar 1962/retired.

Debut v Clyde (a) 4-3 (SC) 23.2.59

Drumchapel boy and apprentice C.A. Ian Lochhead, a great prospect, was signed by Celtic coach Jock Stein. He was troubled sore by cramp on his first appearance and was taken off during extra time. All the same he made his Old Firm debut for the injured John Colrain just five days later before an all-ticket crowd of 42,500 in a famous Scottish Cup victory, 2-1 at Parkhead when he gave Willie Telfer a torrid time. Max Murray scored for Rangers in the last minute, a goal greeted in utter silence. The Celtic forward line of McVittie, Jackson, Lochhead, Wilson and Divers was

Ian Lochhead

referee Nesbit. Even Rangers-daft Geordie Livingstone was booked for foul and abusive language to the Cowdenbeath whistler (who blew time three minutes early). George got his own back with four goals when Celtic beat Rangers 1-5 in the Inter-City League (March 1st 1902). Geordie played for Scotland in the Ibrox Disaster international of April 5th 1902 in place of the injured Johnny Campbell. (Dark rumour said Campbell had stood down so Celtic could tell Geordie: You got a cap with us, you owe us another season). Tom Maley got his transfer to Manchester City one day in Greenock. "And you signed with the pen held in both hands, didn't you, Geordie?" (Tom

Ian Lochhead scores for Celtic on a very muddy pitch at Stirling Albion.

on average one of the youngest ever fielded by the club with three 19-year-olds pitted against the might of Ibrox. This signalled the start of the Kelly Kids with Crerand, McNeill, Clark, Murdoch, Gallagher and Hughes all at Parkhead as part of Celtic's youth policy. In 1959 Celtic had a Cup team and a League team running separate, with Ian Lochhead at centre for the former. The result was a crashing defeat 4-0 versus St Mirren in the semi-final at Ibrox on April 4th 1959. That season Ian was also a member of the reserve side that won the 2nd XI Championship (April 27th 1959), Celtic's first since the 1930's, a feat for which each of the players was awarded the Golden Shamrock by the club. He played against Wolves on October 12th 1959, the night Stan Cullis's men hanselled Celtic's floodlights and gave such a clockwork exhibition of offside drill that the Parkhead crowd howled in disapproval. Along with the others, Ian got a silver cigarette case as a memento of the occasion. His last game was a home defeat 2-3 against Dundee on December 5th 1959 again in place of John Colrain.

Appearances:
SL: 7 apps. 3 gls.
SLC: 1 app. 0 gls.
SC: 4 apps. 1 gl.
Total: *12 apps. 4 gls.*

LONEY, William

Role: Centre-half 1900-13
5' 9" 11st.10lbs.
b. Denny, 31st May 1879
d. Glasgow, 6th March 1956

CAREER: Denny Athletic/CELTIC 5 June 1900 /(Belfast Celtic loan 2 May 1908)/Motherwell 24 Oct 1913/Partick Thistle 2 May 1914/ Clydebank 27 Aug 1915/retired 1917/Aston Villa scout 1935.

Debut v Hearts (a) 2-0 (SL) 17.9.00 (scored once)

Signed as a centre-half, Willie Loney played a fair amount of time at outside-right with "a galaxy of tricks and dodges." At centre-half, he was "Loney the Obliterator" the epitome of robust energy: *'We read of some great centre's raid/How could we e'er forget/The way he left his foes dismayed/And nearly burst the net!/We read his praises in the evening sheets/His worth I'm not gainsaying/But yet we seldom see such feats/When Willie Loney's playing!/A man may lead the halves a race/With many a mazy turn and twist/His name may find an honoured place/High up upon the scorers' list;/He may be greater than McColl/But this is all I'm saying/We scarcely see the chap at all/When Willie Loney's playing!'* "He was always edging forward for a shot and my, how he could shoot! The sting kept my hands tingling long after!" (Jimmy Brownlie). Loney had a magnificent game, second only to Quinn and equal with Somers in the Scottish final against Rangers on April 16th 1904 when Celtic came back from 2-0 down to win the Cup. He missed the finals of 1907 and 1909 through injury; a fractured wrist against Clyde in the Cup on February 25th 1911 cost him yet another medal. 'British cholera' struck him down in September 1911 but he was back in the team that won the Cup at Ibrox on April 6th 1912. When Celtic played all their football on the carpet, he one day hit a ball through the air to McMenemy. Napoleon: "Did you want me to bring a ladder?" Loney: "I was trying to drop it in your pocket!" He had a magnificent match against Rangers in the Charity Cup final at Parkhead on May 10th 1913, especially in the second half. It was his shot, crashing down from the bar, that Barney Connolly converted for Celtic's winning goal. Willie Loney and Jimmy McMenemy took the field at Celtic Park as escorts for Willie Maley at the

LONG, Hugh

Role: Outside-left 1942-44
5' 8" 10st.8lbs.
b. Glasgow, 2nd January 1923

CAREER: Mearns Amateurs
/Maryhill Harp 1 Sept 1941/
CELTIC summer 1942/free
18 Mar 1944/Clyde 22 Mar
1944/free 24 Apr 1954/
Worcester City 29 June 1954/
retired 1956.

*Debut v Dumbarton (h) 2-2
(RL) 8.8.42*

"He could never put the brakes on. Every game meant expenditure of 100 per cent effort... a human whirlwind... with the guts and go that so often accompany red hair." Paddy Travers called flame-headed Hugh Long "the toughest egg I ever met." For Clyde against Hearts on February 4th 1950 he refused to leave the pitch and played on with a broken jaw. Like Johnny Kelly and Davie Duncan, Hughie Long represents another War-time outside-left who made good elsewhere. Clyde took him as a winger but offered him his true niche at left-half. When Celtic won at Shawfield on December 23rd 1944 Hugh Long was a different player now possessed of "...dazzling skill and high fortitude... terrific energy, obvious football ability." On March 23rd 1946, Clyde thrashed Celtic 6-3 in the League Cup with magnificent displays by ex-Tims Long and John Riley. Hughie got his Scottish cap against Ireland in Belfast on November 27th 1946. He played for Clyde in the Scottish Cup final of April 23rd 1949 against Rangers before 120,162 at Hampden. He is probably the classiest left-half to have worn the famous white shirt (with red facings) in the history of the Bully Wee. "A fine constructive player."

Appearances:
RL: 24 apps. 3 gls.
Total: *24 apps. 3 gls.*

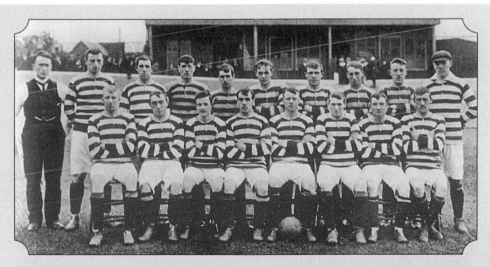

GOM's benefit match on August 10th 1953. He died at 62 White Street, Glasgow. He was a Celtic shareholder, centre-half of the six-in-row-team and an all-time great.

Appearances:
SL: 254 apps. 27 gls.
SC: 51 apps. 2 gls.
Total: *305 apps. 29 gls.*

Willie Loney (front row, with the ball at his feet) and his Celtic team-mates for 1905-06.
Back row (left to right): R.Davis (trainer), R.Campbell, D.McLeod, H.Watson, D.Hamilton, A.McNair, A.Wilson, E.Garry, J.McCourt, D.Adams. Front row: J.Young, J.Hay, A.Bennett, J.McMenemy, W.Loney, J.Quinn, P.Somers, W.McNair.

LONGMUIR, Archibald

Role: Centre-forward 1920-21
5' 9" 11st.0lbs.
b. Ardrossan, 17th April 1897

CAREER: Hall Russell's/Ardrossan Winton Rovers/CELTIC 11 May 1920/Blackburn Rovers 24 Nov 1921/Oldham Athletic 6 Aug 1923/Wrexham 16 June 1924/retired 1930.

Debut v Raith Rovers (h) 5-0 (SL) 27.11.20 (scored twice)

Archie Longmuir

27th November 1920: Sensation! Where was Tommy McInally? A midweek indiscretion at Seamill Hydro? No one knew and Celtic weren't saying. Longmuir took over at centre against Raith. Archie ("a grafter all the time... a real opportunist") had McInally's goal touch but not his speed. Celtic took him on the Lille, Paris tour of 1921 and although he didn't get a game he revisited the Battlefields where he had done his bit in the Kaiser War. He started 1921-22 as Celtic's centre after McInally had injured himself in the pre-season five-a-sides. He played his best football with Wrexham as a winger (223 games, 36 goals) and retired in his benefit year. He won a fortune, for the time, on the Pools: £16,982-11s-4d in December 1935 and set up in business.

Appearances:
SL: 10 apps. 6 gls.
Total: *10 apps. 6 gls.*

LYNCH, Allan

Role: Outside-left 1897-99
b. Portobello, 6th March 1879

CAREER: Scottish Rifles/CELTIC 16 Dec 1897 /Clyde 25 Sept 1899.

Debut v St Bernard's (h) 5-1 (SL) 18.12.1897

Allan Lynch seems to have been a soldier from Maryhill Barracks described as "inadequate" on his debut made in fog so dense that at times the crowd could barely see the pitch. He went with Celtic for a friendly to Dunfermline on January 3rd 1898 but it was an entire year and four days before he reappeared, this time for Cud Fisher and again at Parkhead but in pouring rain (January 7th 1899) before a "poor turn-out". He appears to have been alive and well in Portsmouth in 1946 and, as one who played for the Bully Wee, looking forward to the Pompey v Clyde (1939) Cup-winners' match.

Appearances:
SL: 2 apps. 0 gls.
Total: *2 apps. 0 gls.*

LYNCH, Andrew

Role: Left-back 1973-80
5' 10" 10st.12lbs
b. 3rd March 1951

CAREER: Lourdes School 1966/Glasgow Schools/Glasgow United/Renfrew Juniors 1968/Queen's Park 1968/Kirkintilloch Rob Roy 3 July 1969/Hearts 27 Aug 1969/CELTIC 7 Feb 1973/Philadelphia Fury 14 Apr 1980/ Montreal Manic 1981 & 1982/Team Canada asst. manager 1983 .../Albion Rovers asst. manager 23 June 1993/resigned 26 Jan 1994.

Debut v Partick Thistle (h) 1-0 (SL) 10.2.73 (sub)

Andy Lynch was a winger with Hearts first noticed by Jock Stein in 1971: "I liked the way he used his left foot." Andy was open-to-transfer on September 28th 1974: "He has never fitted into the scheme of things" (Stein). His turning-point was against Rangers reserves on January 3rd 1975 when he scored all the Celtic goals in a 4-3 win. He made it into the big team at Pittodrie on March 12th 1975 and showed speed and shooting power "at last" with both goals from outside-left in the 3-2 defeat. He was left-half against Dunfermline at East End Park on April 12th 1975, "attacking freely down the flank." Two weeks later at Perth he was left-back for the first time. One week on he collected a Scottish Cup medal against Airdrie (May 3rd 1975) as Celtic's new left-back. When Celtic were awarded the 18th minute penalty against Rangers in the Scottish final of May 7th 1977, Dalglish didn't want to take it and Andy had to wait until the Rangers players calmed down. "The moment Kennedy threw the ball to me, I knew I was going to score." He became Celtic captain as of October 8th 1977 after Danny McGrain's notorious ankle injury of the week before. His final glory night was the 4-2 League clincher against Rangers on May 21st 1979. He now runs the Inveresk Guest House at 8 Bank Street, Glasgow.

Appearances:
SL: 130 apps. 15 gls.
SLC: 31 apps. 6 gls.
SC: 13 apps. 4 gls.
Eur: 11 apps. 0 gls.
Total: *185 apps. 25 gls.*

Andy Lynch

LYNCH, Matthew

Role: Utility 1935-48
5' 8" 11st.0lbs.
b. 29th November 1916

CAREER: Linwood St Conval's/St Anthony's 1934/CELTIC 22 Aug 1934/free 5 May 1948/ Dumbarton 8 Aug 1948/free 6 May 1949.

Debut v Ayr United (a) 1-1 (SL) 20.11.37

"If I always got as clean a game as I get from Matt Lynch, then it would be a pleasure to play every Saturday" (Jimmy Duncanson of Rangers). Willie Buchan had just been transferred to Blackpool when Matt Lynch first turned out for Celtic as Chic Geatons' deputy. By the time of his fifth match on Christmas Day 1937, Jimmy McGrory had also gone. Matt played in the 3-0 win of Ne'erday 1938 before a crowd of 83,500 packed in so tight as to obscure the red shale of the Parkhead running track. The Championship was now well in prospect but Celtic had a very difficult match with Hearts a week later, many fans walking through the night to Edinburgh and queues forming outside Tynecastle at 6am. "Trust Celtic for the big occasion"; Lynch and his mates won 2-4. So great a draw were the Celts of '38 that for the Scottish Cup first round on January 22nd queues for the Cathkin turnstiles to see Lynch and Co. stretched away back down the Cathcart Road. Chic Geatons returned at Shawfield on January 29th 1938. Matt (he could hit the most beautiful crosses) moved to outside-right for Delaney's deputy Joe Carruth in a 1-6 win and scored his first goal as a Celt. With Geatons and Delaney fit, he became the capable reserve. He played right wing in the replay against Sunderland in the Empirex tournament on May 26th 1938 and in the semi-final versus Hearts on June 3rd. Although Matt's name was printed in the programme for the final, Delaney came back on June 10th versus Everton. It was Matt's finest season. With the onset of war, he became a mainstay in a side too often made to struggle as management experimented to blend boys with what genuine talent remained from 1938. On Ne'erday 1943, he joined Malky MacDonald in the dressing room at Ibrox, both ordered-off within minutes by Willie Davidson at 4-1, a fixture Rangers won eventually 8-1. Malky had been representing as Celtic's captain; Matt sent Charlie Johnstone sprawling

Matt Lynch BSc

on the Ibrox shale. Like Geatons, he was endowed with a long-range thunder shot (in either foot) and hit a screamer from 30 yards to put Celtic level 1-1 versus Rangers in the Summer Cup on June 19th 1943. Celtic teams were mostly lacking in "physique and experience" during the Hitler war but Matt could always be relied upon as the battler bringing "command and snap" on the wing, at centre or half-back. His game always heightened against Rangers and he had a magnificent match at outside-right at Ibrox in the Glasgow Cup on September 5th 1942 when a team of Celtic tyros including Airlie and a left-wing of McGowan and McAtee had Rangers on the rack and surrendered only in the second half of extra time. He played on a mudbath at Ibrox on Ne'erday 1945 in a half-back line of Lynch, Mallan and Paterson when Celtic "avenged" the 8-1 humiliation of two years previous with a spanking goal from George Paterson three minutes after half-time. Matt elected to stay out of the fracas over the 70th minute penalty kick during the Victory Cup semi-final replay at Hampden on June 5th 1946 and Rangers' Jimmy Duncanson later attested in writing to his impeccable behaviour. Referee MC Dale capped an erratic night's work by indicting him as having

incited the Celtic team to leave the field. On Ne'erday 1947 at Ibrox, Matt not only stood aloof from discord but as a good senior professional, acted as conciliator when tempers boiled over. Matt Lynch is the epitome of the out-and-out jersey player. He graduated B Sc from Glasgow on June 26th 1942.

Appearances:
SL: 48 apps. 2 gls.
SLC: 6 apps. 0 gls.
SC: 9 apps. 0 gls.
Total: *63 apps. 2 gls.*
RL: 119 apps. 25 gls.
RLC: 22 apps. 3 gls.
SWC: 2 apps. 0 gls.
Total: *143 apps. 28 gls.*

LYON, Thomas King

Role: Inside-forward 1939
b. Clydebank, 17th March 1915

CAREER: Clydebank High School/Clydebank Juniors Apr 1933/Motherwell 1 June 1933/ free 30 Apr 1934/Yoker Athletic 16 July 1934/ Albion Rovers 26 Sept 1934 (Airdrie loan 22 Feb 1936)/Blackpool 16 Mar 1937/ Chesterfield 16 Sept 1939/(Albion Rovers loan 1939)/(CELTIC loan Oct 1939)/paid-off Dec 1939/(Yoker Athletic loan 1940-41)/(Albion Rovers loan 1942-43)/14 Army (Burma)/ New Brighton 24 July 1948/free 7 May 1949/ Prescot Cables 1949/Oswestry Town 1949/ ...Clydebank Juniors coach June 1957.
Debut v Clyde (a) 0-2 (RL) 28.10.39

"Prodigious worker" Tom Lyon was Willie Lyon's wee brother, a qualified masseur and one of the earliest of Celtic's War-time guests. He played for the club at a time when "versatility in attack has been lost." His second game, a 0-3 defeat by Queen of the South was the team's fifth successive Saturday without a point. His last game was against Albion Rovers at Cliftonville in a 3-2 defeat on November 25th 1939 in downpour. He left Celtic sharing bottom place with Ayr United in the West/South League with two points from six games, the only club without a win. He scored five goals for Albion Rovers versus Falkirk on March 27th 1943.

Appearances:
RL: 3 apps. 0 gls.
Total: *3 apps. 0 gls.*

LYON, William King

Role: Centre-half 1935-44
6' 0" 12st.7lbs.
b. Birkenhead, 7th March 1912
d. Salford, 5th December 1962

CAREER: Kirkintilloch Rob Roy/
Cowdenbeath (amateur; one game Fife Cup
tie 1932-33)/Queen's Park 12 June 1933/
CELTIC 20 Apr 1935/Scots Grays 25 May
1940/(Chelsea loan 3 Sept 1940)/
(Aberdeen loan 15 Aug 1941)/retired
1944/Dundee asst. manager 18 Nov 1947/
resigned 11 Apr 1948.

Debut v Aberdeen (a) 1-3 (SL) 10.8.35

"Lyon is a coming centre-half... big, strong...
gets through a power of work... good head
and feet... cool, effective." (1932). Willie
Lyon, "hard as nails, mobile as a cowboy,
a hard man to circumvent," was a
dominating centre-half and an inspiring
skipper. "He wasn't so good in the air when
he came to Parkhead but he practised every
day and became one of the great centre-
halves in the game" (Jimmy McGrory). On
April 25th 1936, Willie Maley's 68th
birthday, he led "the cleverest young Celtic
team in years" to their 18th Championship
followed by a Charity Cup win 4-2 versus
Rangers at Hampden on May 9th. Like all
great captains, he led by example. When
Celtic were 2-3 down at half-time versus
Motherwell in the Scottish Cup on
St Patrick's Day 1937 and 2-4 immediately
after the re-start, Lyon led the fightback by
taking a 51st minute penalty himself. Celtic
won the replay at Fir Park and Willie took
them out before the biggest crowd ever to
assemble for a British club game, 146,433 at
Hampden on April 24th 1937 in the final
against Aberdeen. He was skipper of the
1938 Championship side and accepted the
Empire Exhibition Trophy on the field (a
novelty for the Scottish game at the time!)
at Ibrox from the Earl of Elgin on June 10th
1938. After a brief last flicker of the candle
6-2 versus Rangers (September 10th 1938
when Willie scored two, the second a
penalty) the light went out. He had a
penalty miss that was symbolic at 1-2

versus Hamilton Academicals on
September 17th 1938 and "seemed pretty
distressed about it." Celtic's dark night
began at that moment. Willie saw action in
North Africa and was decorated with the
Military Cross in October 1943 for his work
with an anti-tank unit of the 51HD in
Tunisia. He took part in the landings in
Sicily of 1943 but a bad leg wound in the
Normandy fighting in 1944 put an end to
his career. He entered the War a private and
came out a major. Flags flew at half-mast
and players wore black armbands at Celtic
versus Hearts on 8th December 1962 to
commemorate the early death of the man
Willie Maley called "Celtic's Bayard" (le
chevalier sans peur et sans reproche). Willie
Lyon was a magnificent skipper and an
all-time Celtic great.

Appearances:
SL: 146 apps. 16 gls.
SC: 17 apps. 1 gl.
Total: *163 apps. 17 gls.*
RL: 22 apps. 0 gls.
SWC: 2 apps. 0 gls.
Total: *24 apps. 0 gls.*

MACARI, Luigi

Role: Striker 1966-72
5' 6" 10st.10lbs.
b. Edinburgh, 4th June 1949

CAREER: St Michael's College Kilwinning/
Kilwinning Amateurs/CELTIC 21 July 1966/
Manchester United 18 Jan 1973/Swindon
Town manager 18 June 1984/dismissed 5 Apr
1985/reinstated 10 May 1985/West Ham
United manager 5 July 1989/resigned 17 Feb
1990/Birmingham City manager 7 Feb 1991/
Stoke City manager 18 June 1991/CELTIC
manager 26 Oct 1993/dismissed 14 June 1994/
Stoke City manager again 28 Sept 1994.

Debut v Ayr United (a) 2-0 (SLC) 27.9.67 (sub)
(scored once)

"Macari... as lethal as Greaves... a brilliant
opportunist" (October 9th 1971) was
recommended to Sean Fallon by a bookie.
He was a vastly popular and successful figure
during seven years at Parkhead but resented
for his "snapping" style by some fans who felt
the free-kicks he conceded broke up Celtic
attacks more often than the opponents'
defence. Lou ("fast, aggressive, dangerous
with an all-action style reminiscent of Steve
Chalmers") took knocks but he also gave them
as "the type of player who would kick his
grannie if he thought he could get a goal." Fit,
energetic, brave and, despite his diminutive
stature, outstanding in the air and clever on
the deck, Lou also possessed an indomitable
spirit that could inspire those around him on
the field. He won championship badges in
1970 and 1972, was a Scottish Cup winner in
1971 and 1972 and a League Cup finalist in
1971, 1972 and 1973. In the Scottish Cup final
replay versus Rangers on May 12th 1971, he
came in for Willie Wallace and scored the first
goal after Billy McNeill had dummied a low
corner (a Stein ploy). Despite having signed a
five-year contract just before the final, he
asked for a transfer on January 6th 1973:
"Scottish football is dying... I must better
myself." Jock Stein had just suffered a heart
attack but Sean Fallon and the directors had
no hesitation in agreeing little Lou could go.
It was "a loveless goodbye" for £200,000 - a
record fee for a Scottish player at the time -
and "the jackpot world of Manchester
United". It was the start of Celtic's decline
from the heights much as Jock might plead
this transfer was not the first of many. On the

way to Manchester with Crerand and Tommy
Docherty, Lou was nearly a goner when a
lorry took the side off the United manager's
three day old Mercedes. His charmed life
continued despite writing his own car off on
April 3rd 1973. As Scotland prepared for the
vital World Cup qualifier versus
Czechoslovakia on September 26th 1973, there
were reported suggestions that Lou diverted
his team-mates with his expertise as an
aficionado of the Stock Exchange. His relations
with ex-Celt Docherty were hardly
harmonious. On October 10th 1973, the United

Lou Macari the player...

boss put him on the transfer list and fined him two weeks wages for his reluctance to play in a benefit match. Lou later claimed 'victimisation' when substituted in 50 minutes versus Red Star Belgrade on August 8th 1976. He had asked for more money but Docherty couldn't see his way: "He's on £8,500! The Government won't allow it!" Lou won an English Cup medal versus Liverpool at Wembley on May 21st 1977 when his shot deflected off team mate Jimmy Greenhoff for the winner. He won 24 Scottish caps and scored five goals for his country, but had a poor 1978 World Cup in the Argentine and the SFA responded to an outburst in the press that he never wanted to play for Scotland again by imposing a life ban. He made conciliatory noises ("I'd play for Celtic for nothing these days") (January 20th 1983) prior to his testimonial, Manchester United versus Celtic of May 13th 1984 which attracted a crowd of 40,140 a record for a benefit match in England. At Swindon, his first managerial appointment, he and assistant manager Harry Gregg were sacked together in bizarre fashion for "irreconcilable differences" but the fans organised to procure Lou's reinstatement. Later at West Ham he resigned after an FA probe into allegations that he and Bevis Hillier had bet on Newcastle to beat their club Swindon in the English Cup 4th round tie of January 30th 1988. Lou was fined £1,000 on January 5th 1990. His appeal failed on April 3rd: "When you are innocent, even a penny is too much!" He won the Leyland Daf Trophy with Birmingham City at Wembley on May 26th 1991. Ramish Kumar, Blues' vice-chairman, accused him of reneging on a promise not to use the club as a stepping-stone when he walked out to join Stoke. Lou was back at Wembley to take the Autoglass Trophy to the Potteries on May 16th 1992. He was in court at Winchester on June 22nd 1992 charged with defrauding the taxman while at Swindon but was cleared on July 29th. The judge described him as "a naive shrinking violet, only looking after the players and knowing nothing of accounts." Three months later, back in court, he was cleared again, this time of running an illegal betting shop. He was mooted as Hay's assistant after the sacking of Frank Connor but turned the job down on July 18th 1986: "I'd have loved to have gone back but I would have rocked the boat. I didn't like what the people in charge had done to Sean Fallon when they got rid of him from the club" (January 20th 1988). When Stoke drew Manchester United in the early rounds of the League Cup in September 1993, Lou was delighted: "United's is the first score I look for on a Saturday night." The Celtic board finally landed him back as Brady's successor. According to *Celtic View*: "Lou Couldn't Say No To The Greatest Fans in the World" (although Celtic had reputedly offered him £150,000 a year). It was an uneasy alliance as internal strife dominated much of the 1993-94 season and the Board and Manager seemed unable to see eye to eye on various key issues. It culminated in summer 1994 when Fergus McCann sacked Macari after only eight months in the job for alleged infrequent attendance at Parkhead and inadequte supervision of his responsibilities.

Appearances:
SL: 58 apps. 27 gls.
SLC: 24 apps. 14 gls.
SC: 8 apps. 8 gls.
Eur: 12 apps. 8 gls.
Total: *102 apps. 57 gls.*

♣ **Celtic note:** *Lou Macari is the Celt who married in St Patrick's Cathedral, New York on 14th June 1970.*

... and Macari the manager.

MACKIE, Peter

Role: Midfield 1976-79
5' 7" 10st.7lbs.
b. 17th January 1958

CAREER: Celtic BC/
CELTIC ground staff
Apr 1974/Cumbernauld
United (farmed-out) 1974
/CELTIC full-time 3 Aug
1976/Dundee 21 Nov
1979/St Mirren 23 May
1984/free 1986
/Blackpool (trial) 26 July
1986/Partick Thistle
8 Aug 1986/free 13 May
1987.

Peter Mackie

*Debut v Stirling Albion (h)
1-1 (SLC) 26.10.77 (sub)*

"Blond-headed, razor-sharp" Peter Mackie
was in the Celtic Under-17 squad that won the
European Youth Cup at Celtic Park on April
15th 1974. He was hailed as "the new
Bremner," "the new Dalglish," the boy who
"must have studied Dalglish for hours, hitting
first time passes on the turn the way Dalglish
used to do" (May 8th 1979), Peter also
possessed a vicious shot but when he could
not oust Davie Provan from the first team,
Tommy Gemmell was able to secure him for
Dundee. At Dens he began really to show
what he could do and was proclaimed in
January 1980 "the bargain buy of the season"
at £30,000. Peter went to St Mirren in a straight
swap for defender John McCormack but his
best years were behind him at Dens Park.

> **Appearances:**
> *SL: 5 apps. 0 gls.*
> *SLC: 3 apps. 0 gls.*
> **Total:** *8 apps. 0 gls.*

MACKLE, Thomas

Role: Outside-left 1959-61
5' 4" 11st.4lbs.
b. 21st March 1938

CAREER: Renfrew St James' BG 1956/
Barrhead St John's/Johnstone Burgh/CELTIC
20 Nov 1959/free 2 May 1961/Dundee 18 May
1961/free 30 Apr 1964/Forfar Athletic cs 1964
/Raith Rovers Feb 1967/free 22 Mar 1968/
Forfar Athletic (trial) Apr 1968/Forfar Athletic
2 May 1968/free 30 Apr 1970.

*Debut v Raith Rovers (a) 1-2 (SLC)
8.8.59 (scored once)*

Bertie Auld was sent off for
retaliation in the last minute of
Holland 1, Scotland 2 in Amsterdam
on May 27th 1959 and when the new
season opened was in bad odour at
Parkhead. Into his boots stepped
Tommy Mackle, "a wee terrier of the
Collins school," who had "looked
very much the part" in the Public
Trial of August 4th 1959 and whom
Celtic wanted to play "at the first
opportunity." Tommy worried away
at the Raith defence "like a
Staffordshire bull terrier." His second
outing on Wednesday 12th August
was in another defeat, this time against Partick
Thistle, while the evening sky over Celtic Park
echoed to the slow handclap. Bertie Auld was
reconciled perforce and resumed normal
service on the left-wing to a huge roar of
acclaim. Tommy
reverted to the
reserves but
managed an Old
Firm debut in the
Glasgow Cup of
August 17th 1959
before scoring
two in a minute
against the wee
Rangers at
Parkhead
(September 4th
1959). Then the
Army took him
for National
Service. Apart
from Johnstone
Burgh, he
seems to have
enjoyed the
best time of his
career as a
midfield
general at Forfar
where his unfailing
vigour made him a very
popular team man.

*Tommy Mackle with the
West of Scotland Cup.*

> **Appearances:**
> *SL: 3 apps. 1 gl.*
> *SLC: 2 apps. 1 gl.*
> **Total:** *5 apps. 2 gls.*

MADDEN, John

Role: Centre-forward
1889-97
b. Dumbarton,
11th June 1865
d. Prague,
16/17th April 1948

CAREER:
Dumbarton Albion
1884/Dumbarton
Hibernian/
Dumbarton 27 Nov
1886/Gainsborough
Trinity/Grimsby Town
1887/CELTIC May 1888/
Dumbarton 1888/ CELTIC
Aug 1889/retired 1897/
Dundee 16 Sept 1897/
Tottenham Hotspur 27 Dec 1897/
retired 1898/FC Slavia Prague
coach 15 Feb 1905.

John
Madden

Debut v Rangers Swifts (h) 5-2 (Inaugural Match)
28.5.1888

Celtic's first centre-forward was a riveter at
Whiteinch; Jake Madden, "the Rooter." Celtic
were very anxious to have him and he was
down to play against Abercorn in the first
round of the World Exhibition Cup on August
1st 1888 but was dissuaded from leaving
Boghead by Dumbarton officials at the X-arena
in Gilmorehill. He turned out for Celtic at the
Rangers Sports a year and two days later and
bound himself to the club by playing in the
Scottish Cup against Queen's Park on
September 7th 1889. He was the Charlie Tully
of his day, famous for playing the dummy, the
back-heel, the spurt, the dead-stop and knew
too how to kill time at the corner flag like an
early-day Bertie Auld. In 1892, after the
Scottish League match at Tynecastle on
August 27th he went down to Sheffield, tried
out for the Wednesday at Sheaf House and
signed. By utter chance, he bumped into John
Glass and Willie Maley at Sheffield station
and, persuaded by the silver-tongued Glass,
joined the Celtic party on tour in England and
came home with them ten bob a week better
off than before (although officially still playing
the Scottish game for love alone). Partick
Thistle played Celtic at Inchview Park on
October 29th 1892 and were leading 1-0. First
Cynic: "Come on, Madden, show these
amateurs how it's done!" (Madden scores).

Second Cynic: "That was a £2 shot." Jake
gave Celtic unstinting service thereafter
as one of the hardest grafters ever to
wear the green and white vertical
stripes. He missed the Scottish
Cup win of April 9th 1892 but
was in the team that won the
Championships of 1893 and
1894. Celtic toured the new
republic of Czechoslovakia in
1922 and lost 3-2 to Johnny's
Slavia in a kicking match on
May 25th. He dared not return to
Scotland for fear of losing his
pension then had to spend the
years after March 15th 1939 in the
Reich Protectorate of Bohemia until
'liberated' by the Red Army in 1945.
His command of English diminished
with the years.

Appearances:
SL: 92 apps. 38 gls.
SC: 26 apps. 11 gls.
Total: *118 apps. 49 gls.*

♣ **Celtic note:** *Madden had a ferocious grass shot.*
According to Jerry Reynolds whenever he hit the
post it threatened to uproot the goals. Thus: 'The
Rooter'.

MADDEN, Richard Michael

Role: Goalkeeper 1962-64
5' 11" 11st.10lbs.
b. Blantyre, 27th July 1944

CAREER: Our Lady's High/Blantyre Celtic/
CELTIC 17 Aug 1962/free 9 June 1964/Albion
Rovers 5 Aug 1964/free 30 Apr 1967/
Clydebank 6 July 1967.

Debut v Kilmarnock (a) 0-6 (SL) 27.3.63

Dick Madden was Celtic's third choice goalie
during his short stint at Parkhead. He took
Frank Haffey's place the night of the Rugby
Park massacre when Celtic had McNamee,
McNeill, Murdoch, Hughes and Divers of the
regular first team all unfit against a crack
Kilmarnock eleven. He was with Celtic
reserves at Kilmarnock again the night the
news of President Kennedy's assassination
came through (November 22nd 1963). Dick
travelled as John Fallon's deputy to play
MTK in Budapest in the Cup Winners' Cup
semi-final on April 27th 1964. He wasn't a bad

'keeper at all and had some glory games for Albion Rovers and Clydebank. With Archie Longmuir and Bobby Evans: one of Celtic's football pools winners.

Appearances:
SL: 1 app. 0 shut-outs.
Total: *1 app. 0 shut-outs.*

MAIR, Matthew

Role: Centre-forward 1901-02
b. Dunlop, 3rd October 1880

CAREER: Newmilns/CELTIC 25 May 1901/Kilmarnock 12 July 1902.
Debut v Hearts (h) 1-2 (SL) 30.11.01

Matt Mair was a junior internationalist who first tried out for Celtic in a home friendly versus Notts County on April 27th 1901. He played in Davie Baird's benefit at Tynecastle (August 20th 1901) and scored twice against the full might of Hearts. He was Celtic's centre against Rangers in Danny McArthur's benefit six days later but got little chance other than in these early season benefits and friendlies. He was with Celtic in Dublin against Bohemians on Boxing Day 1901 when the referee was Mr Farrell IRA (Irish Referees' Association). His best month was March 1902 when he scored against Rangers at Ibrox in the Inter-City League on the 1st and was in the side that beat Newcastle 4-2 at Berwick Cricket Ground to help the wee Rangers celebrate their coming of age on the 13th.

Appearances:
SL: 1 app. 0 gls.
Total: *1 app. 0 gls.*

MALEY, Thomas Edward

Role: Outside-left 1888-92
5' 9" 11st.0lbs.
b. Portsmouth, 8th November 1864
d. 24th August 1935

CAREER: Cathcart FC/London Caledonian (under pseudonym) 1886/Partick Thistle 1886 /Third Lanark 1886/Hibernian 25 Dec 1886/Third Lanark 20 Aug 1887/Clydesdale Harriers Football Section 1887/CELTIC May 1888/(St Mirren loan 27 Dec 1891)/retired 1891/Preston North End am.

30 January 1892/CELTIC director 13 Apr 1897 /Manchester City manager Aug 1902/ suspended sine die 4 June 1906/suspension lifted July 1910/Bradford PA manager 25 Feb 1911/left Mar 1924.
Debut v Rangers Swifts (h) 5-2 (Inaugural Match) 28.5.1888 (scored three?)

"Speed, stamina, dash... all three were mine." 'Handsome Tom' Maley was recruited by John Glass and Brother Walfrid in December 1887 although absent from Argyll Place, Cathcart the night they called. Tom had leapt to prominence with Hibs when "I won a semi-final for them against Thirds" at 1st Cathkin on Christmas Day 1886 (it was actually a 6th round tie). Tom had trained as a teacher at Hammersmith College and was later to be headmaster of Slateford Industrial Schools in Glasgow and St Mary's Calton (1906). He first bound himself formally to Celtic by playing in the Scottish Cup tie of September 22nd 1888, the day the team inaugurated their passing game 8-0 versus Cowlairs. His greatest match

Tom Maley

was against Corinthians on the mud-heap of 1st Celtic Park on January 3rd 1889 when his speed through the glaur destroyed the London cracks. In 1889 also, he broke his honeymoon to plead for Groves at the SFA (22nd and 27th August); that Darlin' Willie was still an amateur despite having signed professional forms for Everton and accepted wages. As a manager, Tom took Manchester City out of Division Two in 1903 and led them to a Cup win on April 23rd 1904. The club was awarding bonuses under the counter and Tom paid with his career in 1906. Seldom a stranger to the lecture platform, he was likened to an "amateur recruiting sergeant" for his efforts in the First World War. He came back with Bradford PA (green and white hoops) and managed a Bradford Select at Celtic Park for Jimmy McMenemy's testimonial on January 6th 1920. He joined Celtic in the USA June 1931 on the long-projected trip. Brother Willie "took ill" on the way over and director Tom Colgan wired Tom to come out by next boat and manage the tour. Willie recovered fine and Tom enjoyed his first visit to the States. Tom probably accomplished far more for the early Celtic off the field than on it. He was an active committee-man and knew his football in a way that the founding fathers like John Glass and JH McLaughlin did not. In this sense alone, he is an all-time great.

Appearances:
SL: 2 apps. 0 gls.
SC: 7 apps. 6 gls.
Total: *9 apps. 6 gls.*

MALEY, William

Role: Half-back 1888-97
5' 10" 11st.10lbs.
b. Newry, 25th April 1868
d. Glasgow, 2nd April 1958

CAREER: Cathcart Hazlebank Juniors 1886/Third Lanark 20 Aug 1887/CELTIC May 1888/Ardwick loan Easter 1890/CELTIC player-secretary 15 May 1894/reinstated amateur 13 Aug 1895/ (Manchester City loan 24 Feb 1896)/(Everton loan 1 Jan 1897 & 3 Apr 1897)/CELTIC secretary-manager 3 Apr 1897/retired 1 Feb 1940.

Debut v Rangers Swifts (h) 5-2 (Inaugural Match) 28.5.1888

"Did you see Maley? He ran like a deer, dodged like a squirrel and shot like a catapult." As opposed to big brother Tom, Willie Maley was at home when Pat Welsh brought Brother Walfrid and John Glass out to Cathcart December 1887. He was a sprinter (SAAU 100 yards champion June 1896) and had played some football for Third Lanark mainly as a reserve but had met Rangers at the top level. This 19-year old made some strong impression on Glass and Walfrid and they recruited him forthwith. Jimmy Kelly too was struck by the vision of the big fair-haired boy among the Celtic players limbering up to play the Rangers on the evening of the opening match in May 1888. Willie was a stand-out in Celtic's first Scottish Cup triumph of April 9th 1892, his "blocking and feeding simply perfect... checking, returning, general engineering... immense." His mother used to walk a considerable distance to the shop on a Saturday to buy an evening paper to get the Celtic score. If they had lost, she was cast-down but would warn her son when he got home: "Never mind, Willie. It isn't a hanging matter." On the day of the Three Players' Strike (November 28th 1896) he turned out to play ("I was retired") but played again versus Dumfries Hibernian in a Friendly on April 14th 1899. His last game was on May 18th 1904 in Vienna after Sunny Jim Young was left stranded in Frankfurt railway station en route. Alec McNair says he played on the shady side of the pitch each half. We have at least one pep-talk extant from his career as Celtic manager: "If we win to-day, we have an outside chance of the Championship. The Rangers may have their bad time just as we have had ours - that will be our chance. And you can beat them if you start from the whistle to play the ball and keep playing it all the time. Now then, boys, go on determined to do your very best and remember the old Celtic spirit. Charlie Shaw will have a word to say to

Willie Maley

you on the way out" (Ibrox Ne'erday 1921; Rangers 0, Joe Cassidy 2). His resignation as Celtic manager was announced after Rangers 1, Celtic 1 at Ibrox on Ne'erday 1940.

Appearances:
SL: 75 apps. 2 gls.
SC: 21 apps. 0 gls.
Total: *96 apps. 2 gls.*

MALLAN, John (James)

Role: Full-back 1942-53
5' 8" 11st.4lbs.
b. Glasgow, 25th January 1927
d. Glasgow, 27th May 1969

CAREER: Holy Cross Primary/Holyrood Senior Secondary/St Mary's BG/Pollok/ CELTIC 1 Sept 1942/free 28 Apr 1953/ St Mirren (trial) 31 Aug 1953/St Mirren 9 Oct 1953/free Apr 1956/retired 1956.

Debut v Hearts (h) 3-0 (RL) 7.11.42

"Willie McStay has unearthed a rare centre-half in Jimmy Mallan" (20th January 1944). Born in Aikenhead Road below Hampden Park, amateur boxer Mallan began as a wing-half, moved to centre-half but is principally remembered as Bobby Hogg's successor at right-back in the team beginning Miller, Mallan and Milne. He was an utter Celt and played a game as centre-half to rival goalie Miller's in the Victory Cup semi-final at Hampden on June 1st 1946 in the 0-0 draw versus Rangers in dazzling sunlight at Hampden. Tully tells of the Glasgow Cup semi-final against Queen's Park (September 15th 1948). 38 minutes: Ronnie Simpson saves a Mallan penalty. Pat McAuley: "That's the last ******* penalty you take for Celtic!" 48 minutes: another penalty. Skipper McAuley sends it yards wide. Mallan: "That's the last ******* penalty *you* take for Celtic!" Jimmy was capped for the Scottish League against the English at Ibrox on March 23rd 1949 (his old school Holyrood stood agog) but despite a "fearless and confident display" missed selection for the 1-3 triumph of the full Scots (with Bobby Evans) at Wembley on 9th April. Jimmy's other finest hour to rival June 1st 1946 was again as centre-half on Celtic's 1951 tour of the USA, the battle against Eintracht Frankfurt in New York on May 30th for the Schaeffer Trophy when attack after attack by the Germans broke on

the rock that was Mallan. He was centre-half in the Celtic side that won the St Mungo Cup (Festival of Britain) versus Aberdeen at Hampden on August 1st 1951. It was this wonderful player's one and only major honour with Celtic. Jimmy's effective career at Parkhead was curtailed by a serious ankle break at Morton on September 1st 1951 and thereafter he was yesterday's man to the great sadness of the fans by whom he was vastly appreciated. He played for St Mirren in the League Cup final of October 22nd 1955 and scored an unavoidable own goal. When the Buddies released him he decided to concentrate on running his pub in Paisley.

Appearances:
SL: 90 apps. 0 gls.
SLC: 21 apps. 0 gls.
SC: 6 apps. 0 gls.
Total: *117 apps. 0 gls.*
RL: 59 apps. 0 gls.
RLC: 11 apps. 0 gls.
Total:
70 apps. 0 gls.

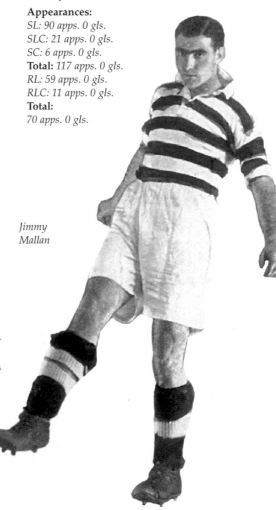

Jimmy Mallan

MALLOY, William

Role: Outside-right 1925-28
5' 8" 10st.8lbs.
b. Gateshead, April 2nd 1900

CAREER: Dumbarton Harp
1923/CELTIC 24 Oct 1925/
(Arthurlie loan 11 Nov 1926)/
(Ayr United loan 18 Nov
1927)/(Arthurlie loan 9 Dec
1927)/Dumbarton 7 Sept 1928/
Yeovil & Petters 1931/Bristol
City 1933/Falkirk 9 Aug 1934/
Dumbarton (trial) 6 Sept 1935/
free 4 Oct 1935.

*Willie
Malloy*

Debut v Dundee (a) 2-1 (SL) 17.3.26 (scored once)

"Prolific leader," Willie Malloy, Johnny
Madden's nephew, was wanted by Aberdeen
but had pledged himself to Celtic. He was
signed to understudy McGrory but took over
from McLean when wee Adam was injured in
the 6-1 win against St Mirren on March 9th
1926. Celtic tried to get Adam match-fit for the
Scottish final on April 10th 1926 but when he
failed the test, Willie Malloy was unfit in turn
and it was Leitch played outside-left in the 2-0
defeat by St Mirren. Willie Malloy played in
the Celtic side which clinched the
Championship on April 14th 1926 but "little
enthusiasm marked their success" (the fans
were still cast-down by the Cup defeat and
loss of the Double). It was a bitter-sweet day
for Willie because he was taken from Parkhead
to the Royal Infirmary with a chipped ankle
bone. He played in the Celtic trial of August
5th 1926 at centre
and had two more
games only for the
first team (4th and
11th September)
before being loaned-
out to Arthurlie.

Appearances:
SL: 7 apps. 1 gl.
SC: 1 app. 0 gls.
Total:
8 apps. 1 gl.

Gordon Marshall

MARSHALL, Gordon

Role: Goalkeeper 1971-72
6' 1" 12st.7lbs.
b. Farnham, 2nd July 1939

CAREER: Tynecastle
School/Balgreen Rovers/
Hearts 26 July 1956/Dalkeith
Thistle (farmed-out) 1956/
Newcastle United 24 June 1963/
Nottingham Forest Oct 1968/
Hibernian 18 Apr 1969/free 1971/
CELTIC 13 July 1971/Aberdeen 27 Jan 1972/
free 27 Apr 1972/Arbroath 30 June 1972/
retired 25 July 1975/Newtongrange Star
player-coach 1975/Arbroath again 1975/
retired 1977.

*Debut v St Johnstone (h) 4-2 (Drybrough Cup)
4.8.71*

Celtic's four goalies at the start of 1971-72
were Williams, Lally, Fallon (just getting over
an eight-month virus) and free transfer
acquisition Gordon Marshall. Gordon carried
the can for two of the St Johnstone goals on his
debut but got the nod for the first round
European Cup tie in Copenhagen versus
Boldklub 93 on September 15th 1971 after
Williams' injury against Rangers four days
before. It was a night in Europe when Celtic
were so awful that even Johnstone was booed
by the Danish crowd. Stein was obviously not
convinced Gordon was the new Ronnie
Simpson because the next month he bought
Denis Connaghan from St Mirren with
Connaghan deputising for Williams as of
October 27th. Big Gordon played his
last game for Celtic in a Challenge
Match at Annfield versus Stirling
Albion January 25th 1972. He didn't
catch fire at Aberdeen either but did
magnificent work in two stints at
Arbroath. Celtic players lined-up to
shake his hand after a superhuman
show for the Red Lichties on
December 16th 1972 at Gayfield.

Appearances:
Eur: 1 app. 0 shut-outs.
Total: *1 app. 0 shut-outs.*

♣ **Celtic note:** *Son of a Scottish soldier
based at Aldershot, Gordon lived the
first three weeks and two days of his life
in Surrey and thus qualified for an
England Under-23 cap.*

MARSHALL, Gordon George Banks

Role: Goalkeeper 1991 to date
6' 2" 12st.0lbs.
b. Edinburgh, 19th April 1964

CAREER: Tynecastle BC 1978/
Rangers S form 1979/Rangers
Jan 1980/(East Stirling loan
17 Aug 1982)/free 20 Nov 1982/
Broxburn Juniors Nov 1982/
East Fife 23 Dec 1982/Falkirk
20 Mar 1987/CELTIC 12 Aug
1991/(Stoke City loan 25 Nov
1993).

*Debut v Airdrie (a) 3-0 (SL)
23.11.91*

Gordon Marshall Jnr

Gordon Marshall junior, son of
Gordon of 1971, 6'1" tall at the
age of 15, broke his leg playing
for Rangers reserves at Alloa on July 29th
1981, the first casualty of the new season. He
went on monthly loan to East Stirling when
Charlie Kelly was injured and surrendered 32
goals in his first 13 games. At East Fife he
developed into a class goalkeeper, the best the
Bayview club had had for long years and
Celtic were interested in him before Falkirk
stepped in. Rangers wanted him as understudy to Goram in 1991 (the job Ally Maxwell
got) but Gordon opted for Celtic. Packy
Bonner's form shaded in the autumn of 1991
and when he dropped a ball at Dougie
Arnott's feet against Motherwell on November
20th 1991, Gordon Marshall's hour struck. He
had a shut-out on his debut and one followed
another. Liam Brady had made his best
signing since taking over as Celtic manager.
Andy Roxburgh gave Gordon his Scottish cap
against the USA at Mile High Stadium Denver,
where he had another shut-out in a difficult
game (May 17th 1992). Bonner's name was
linked with Chelsea but he was still Celtic's
second choice when Gordon had a stinker
against Hibs on September 12th 1992 and
blamed himself for all three goals including
the penalty. He was in goal at Cologne on
September 16th and played well in the 2-0
defeat but was now dropped as of Falkirk
September 19th 1992 (when Packy lost four of
the nine goals scored). His next game was a
shut-out versus Aberdeen on May 1st 1993
and he saw the season out with another two

against Thistle and Dundee.
What must this vastly
competent 'keeper have
wondered was wrong with
him when Carl Muggleton
was bought in for £150,000
as Bonner's replacement in
January 1994 by the
allegedly impoverished
Celtic? After all the
uncertainties and upheavals,
Gordon became Tommy
Burns' first choice goalie as
of 1994-95.

Appearances:
SL: 37 apps. 16 shut-outs.
SLC: 3 apps. 2 shut-outs.
SC: 4 apps. 2 shut-outs.
Eur: 2 apps. 1 shut-out.
Total:
46 apps. 21 shut-outs (46%).

MARSHALL, Henry James Hall

Role: Centre-half 1899-1903
5' 7" 12st.10lbs.
b. Portobello, 24th November 1872
d. Leith, 16th September 1936

CAREER: Portobello Thistle/St Bernard's/
Hearts 1892/Blackburn Rovers Oct 1892/
Hearts 16 May 1896/(CELTIC loan 28 Jan
1899)/(Blackburn loan Apr 1899)/(CELTIC
loan Apr 1899)/CELTIC 13 June 1899/(Alloa
loan 25 Sept 1900)/(Raith Rovers loan 25 Oct
1900)/CELTIC again 29 July 1901/Clyde
20 Aug 1903/reinstated amateur 15 Dec 1904/
Broxburn Athletic 16 May 1906.

Debut v St Bernard's (h) 3-0 (SC) 4.2.1899

"Beef" Marshall, the "Portobello Boatman,"
was so badly injured during his first stint with
Blackburn that he gave up football and went
back to hiring-out boats. Hearts were knocked
out of the Scottish Cup 4-1 at Ibrox on January
14th 1899 with Harry absent so Celtic seized
the chance to solve their centre-half problem
(Tom Hynds) by buying 'Beef' on loan. Harry
bottled up Rangers' RC Hamilton and helped
Celtic to victory in the Scottish Cup final at
2nd Hampden on April 22nd 1899. At the
speechmaking afterwards, Celtic chairman
JH McLaughlin was in a fulsome mood:
"Sectarianism is a dead letter in Scottish
football... We cull players from all quarters,

regardless of sect." Voice: "Or cost." (Beef's loan had cost £300, a lot of money in 1899). On April 14th 1900, Harry was captain of the Celtic side that won the Scottish Cup against Queen's Park in a hurricane at Ibrox. He won the toss and booked the gale for the first half. Celtic led 3-1 at half-time and held out (with much time-wasting) for a 4-3 victory. The Boatman was labouring on the new Musselburgh tramway in 1932.

Appearances:
SL: 29 apps. 5 gls.
SC: 17 apps. 0 gls.
Total: *46 apps. 5 gls.*

MARTIN, Allan

Allan Martin

Role: Centre-forward
1895-96
b. 1873
d. Springburn,
12th May 1906

CAREER: Northern 1889/Rangers 1892/ Hibernian 1 June 1893/CELTIC 4 June 1895/ Hibernian 22 June 1896 until 1899.

Debut v Dundee (a) 2-1 (SL) 10.8.1895
(scored once)

Allan Martin's first game in the green and white stripes was at the opening of Fir Park on August 3rd 1895 when he scored at least twice. Allan was a furnaceman in an iron works who refused to go full-time and put in some horrendous double shifts in order to be free for football. He played in the Glasgow Cup versus Linthouse at Govandale Park on September 21st 1895, scored in the first minute and the 90th and fainted from exhaustion as soon as the match was over. He hit goals freely for Celtic and was in the team that beat Rangers 6-2 at Parkhead on December 14th 1895 to clinch the third League flag. With Allan Martin at centre Celtic landed the Charity Cup 2-1 after extra time at Ibrox (May 16th 1896), the fifth time in five years they'd won it. His last game was for goalkeeper Charlie Kelly's benefit against Hibernian at Parkhead on May 21st 1896. Alec King was brought in from Hearts to replace him. Next time he saw Celtic was at Easter Road when he scored in a 3-1 win for Hibs (August 15th 1896).

Appearances:
SL: 17 apps. 18 gls.
SC: 1 app. 0 gls.
Total: *18 apps. 18 gls.*

MARTIN, Lee Andrew

Role: Full-back 1994 to date
6' 2" 12st.0lbs.
b. Hyde, Cheshire, 5th February 1968

CAREER: Tameside & Greater Manchester schoolboys/Manchester United assoc schoolboy Feb 1982, trainee June 1985, pro. May 1986/CELTIC 18 Jan 1994.

Debut v Aberdeen (h) 2-2 (SL) 19.1.94

"We have no right-back" (Lou Macari 8th January 1994). Lee Martin was the new manager's third signing after Wayne Biggins and Carl Muggleton and was apparently bought without the knowledge or approval of the Celtic board. He was out of contract at Old Trafford and the fee (United wanted £500,000) went to a tribunal. He came to Celtic much as Tom Barber in 1919: the scorer of a solitary goal that had won the English FA Cup (Manchester United v Crystal Palace in a

Lee Martin

replay at Wembley in May 1990). Lou Macari offered £150,000 for his transfer. Arbitration on March 14th 1994 adjudicated £350,000. Lee made his Old Firm debut in the Murray lock-out match at Ibrox on 30th April 1994. He was booked but had a great game in the makeshift Celtic defence. He looked a reliable, versatile defender who could slot in and do a good holding job for Celtic. He returned to Old Trafford in the makeshift Celtic side that won 1-3 in the Mark Hughes Testimonial on May 16th 1994. He broke his left leg in a freak accident (no one near him) versus Falkirk at Hampden on October 22nd 1994.

Appearances:
SL: 15 apps. 0 gls.
Total: *15 apps. 0 gls.*

MATHIE, Alexander

Role: Outside-right 1987-91
5' 10" 10st.7lbs.
b. Bathgate,
20th December 1968

CAREER: BB/Gairdoch BC/Celtic BC 1981/ CELTIC 15 May 1987/ Morton 10 Aug 1991/ (Port Vale loan Mar 1993)/ Newcastle United July 1993.

Debut v Motherwell (h) 1-2 (SL) 11.2.89 (sub)

Alex Mathie

Alex Mathie was a Celtic tip for the top after coming on as substitute for Tony Shepherd in Tommy Burns' testimonial against Liverpool (August 9th 1987) and was in the Celtic Youth side that went to Japan on January 11th 1989. He made his debut in the first of the "eleven Cup finals" Billy McNeill set Celtic to win in order to retain the Championship. He was fairly fast and looked useful but not hugely impressive on his rare appearances for the Celtic first team. He cost Morton £100,000 (a record for the Cappielow club which had once framed the £15,000 cheque received for Billy Steel in 1947) but didn't really want to leave: "I didn't like it. I think Liam Brady only saw me once before I was sold. When I wasn't on the Irish tour, I knew it was time to go." Alex repaid the Cappielow investment as a consistent goalscorer in the First Division. Morton

wanted £300,000 from Port Vale for his transfer in May 1993. Kevin Keegan got him for £285,000. He made his debut for the Magpies versus Sheffield Wednesday on September 13th 1993, coming on as a 72nd minute substitute. Four minutes later he set up a goal for Andy Cole and in the 83rd minute "scored with a stunning lob on the run over Chris Woods to give Newcastle the lead."

Appearances:
SL: 11 apps. 0 gls.
SLC: 1 app. 0 gls.
Total: *12 apps. 0 gls.*

♣ **Celtic note:** *"When he was burning out Dariusz Dziekanowski turned out for Celtic reserves against Partick Thistle in mid-winter. Alex Mathie slung cross after cross into the Thistle goalmouth all of which the Pole resolutely refused to chase. 'Jacki, Jacki, get into the box!' cried Alex. 'Shaud-aap' replied Dziekanowski." (Graham Spiers, November 21st 1993).*

MAXWELL, Hugh

Role: Inside-forward 1964-65
6' 0" 13st.0lbs.
b. Rigghead, 14th May 1938

CAREER: Shotts Bon Accord/Stirling Albion 3 Sept 1960/Bradford PA 29 Mar 1962/ Falkirk 27 Nov 1962/CELTIC 13 Nov 1964/ St Johnstone 11 June 1965/Dunfermline Athletic 23 Sept 1966/free 27 Apr 1967/ Hellenic (South Africa) May 1967.

Debut v Dundee (h) 0-2 (SL) 14.11.64

Hugh Maxwell's introduction to football at Celtic Park lacked nothing in terms of the dramatic: so torrential was the rain and threatening the lightning during the second half that the players had to shelter until the elements calmed down; one week later against his old club Falkirk, he scored in ten seconds, Celtic's fastest goal since the War, without a Bairn touching the ball. Hugh was tall and slim, fragile in appearance, and a prolific goalscorer at Falkirk (eg seven against Clyde on December 8th 1962). He was still Falkirk's top scorer two months after joining Celtic but at Parkhead the goals had now dried-up. Having shelled out £15,000 to buy him, the club exacted £10,000 for his transfer to St Johnstone (which helped to pay for Joe McBride). He was Dunfermline's second top scorer with 25 goals (just four behind Alex Ferguson) when the club released him.

Appearances:
SL: 8 apps. 2 gls.
Total: *8 apps. 2 gls.*

McADAM, Thomas Ian

Role: Centre-half
1977-86
6' 1" 12st.0lbs.
b. Glasgow,
9th April 1954

CAREER: Scotstoun School/Victoria Drive School (Scotstoun)/ Weir's Amateurs/ Clydebank Colts/ Weir's Recreation/ Dumbarton S form 1970/Dundee United 31 Oct 1975/CELTIC 6 Sept 1977/free 26 Feb 1986/Stockport County (trial) 26 July 1986/ Hamilton Academicals (trial) 18 Sept 1986/ Motherwell player-coach 13 Oct 1986/ Airdrie player-coach 15 Nov 1989/CELTIC coach 10 June 1993.

Debut v Rangers (a) 2-3 (SL) 10.9.77 (sub)

Tom McAdam

centre-half in the reserves as of April 7th. He started for the big team at number five against Partick Thistle on May 7th 1979 and played like "a hero in defence." He was centre-half for the fourth time two weeks later the night "ten men did extraordinary things" and Celtic pipped Rangers for the League title 4-2 at Parkhead. Centre-half or sweeper, he now "looked the part at the back... a tidy defender and a nifty goal-getter." He missed the 1980 Scottish final through automatic suspension but was in against Rangers on September 19th 1981 for the opening of "the brand-new Ibrox Bullring" when McNeill urged his team:

"Right, let's give them a day to remember." Tom went out and opened the scoring in 10 minutes. He was a fixture in the Championship sides of 1981 and 1982 but missed his second Scottish final on May 19th 1984 this time through injury. He got his medal at last in the 100th final (May 18th 1985) against Dundee United thanks to Aitken, Provan and McGarvey. Hibernian knocked Celtic out of the League Cup on penalties after a 4-4 draw and extra time on September 4th 1985 and Paul McGugan now came in for Tom. When McGugan broke his foot against Rangers Ne'erday 1986, Ronnie Coyle took over, then Pierce O'Leary. This fine defender played his last game for Celtic in the Scottish Cup against Queen's Park at Hampden on February 15th 1986.

Appearances:
SL: 261 apps. 37 gls.
SLC: 45 apps. 7 gls.
SC: 31 apps. 3 gls.
Eur: 25 apps. 1 gl.
Total: *362 apps. 48 gls.*

Rangers-daft Tom McAdam made his debut at Ibrox as substitute for John Dowie, also Rangers-daft. He was manager Jackie Stewart's first S signing at Dumbarton and taken on at Tannadice and then at Parkhead as a striker. He joined Celtic just as "alarming gaps" began to appear in defence and "McNeill needs a pace-man in his back four." Roddie MacDonald broke his ankle on March 28th 1979 and Big Billy began to play Tom at

McALINDON, John

Role: Centre-forward 1948-57
5' 11" 12st.0lbs.
b. Carlisle, 25th December 1930

CAREER: Carlisle Catholic Youth FC/Penrith Amateurs/CELTIC 19 May 1948/(Albion Rovers loan 12 Aug 1948)/(Worcester City loan 12 Mar 1953)/free 1957/Shrewsbury Town 1957.

Debut v Hearts (h) 2-2 (SL) 30.12.50
(scored twice)

Jack McAlindon was a fast, lively raider who understudied John McPhail and first played for Celtic 17 days after the big Celtic skipper was in the Scotland team beaten 0-1 by Austria, a result which provoked a severe crisis of confidence in the Scottish game as early as 1950. His

Jack McAlindon

"strength and purpose" worried Hearts pivot Bobby Dougan on his debut. Tully set up both goals, the second a hard-driven ball that gave great 'keeper Jimmy Brown no chance. Jack played against Partick Thistle in the Monday match April 16th immediately preceding the Scottish final of 1951 but it was McPhail who played, scored and lifted the Cup on the great day itself. He came in for Tully at outside-left at the start of Charlie's month's suspension on November 24th 1951 but had a poor game in a 4-0 defeat at Palmerston Park. National Service interrupted Jack's career including a spell in the Middle East as of February 1954. He was injured near the start of his time with Shrewsbury and returned to Glasgow to become maintenance electrician at Celtic Park with special responsibility for the Collins/Fernie floodlights.

> **Appearances:**
> *SL: 16 apps. 7 gls.*
> *SLC: 1 app. 0 gls.*
> *SC: 1 app. 0 gls.*
> **Total:** *18 apps. 7 gls.*

McALOON, Gerald Padua

Role: Inside-forward 1943-44; 1946-48
5' 9" 11st.0lbs.
b. Gorbals, 13th September 1916
d. 13th April 1987

CAREER: St Francis Juniors/Brentford 13 June 1934/Wolverhampton Wanderers 16 Mar 1939 /(Hamilton Academicals loan 19 Oct 1939)/ (Airdrie loan 7 May 1940)/(Albion Rovers loan 1941)/(Dumbarton loan 24 Sept 1942)/ (Dunfermline Athletic loan end of 1942-43)/ (CELTIC loan Sept 1943-44)/(Morton loan 9 Sept 1944-45)/Wolverhampton Wanderers again 14 Apr 1945/Brentford Jan 1946/ CELTIC 4 Oct 1946/Belfast Celtic 17 Aug 1948.

Debut v Hamilton Academicals (h) 1-0 (RL)
18.9.43 (scored once)

Celtic fans demonstrated outside the ground on September 4th 1943 demanding the club buy a centre. Gerry McAloon of the "bewildering footwork" was granted as the answer to their prayers: "He may prove the elusive link Celtic have long been looking for." Gerry, a silky and sometimes over-casual inside-man ("Play like blazes till you score, then take it easy. They can't drop you if you score!"), was the making of Jackie Gallacher. The highlight of 1943-44 was Celtic's winning all six matches in the qualifying stages of the League Cup in front of an aggregate of 100,000. With Gerry ever-present, "all balls led to Gallacher" who took his tally to 19 goals for the season when he scored five against Partick on April 8th 1944. Even if Gerry was inclined to coast (the reason Dumbarton released him in 1943) the move to Morton on loan was a puzzle. He rejoined Celtic in 1946 in a straight swap for George Paterson. The omens were not propitious. He was preparing for an office career in London and travelled up on Fridays "to get a good sleep" before the game. By the end of 1946-47 he had a job in Ireland and was flying across on Fridays if only to turn out for the reserves (with whom he was ordered-off at Morton

Gerry McAloon

on October 11th 1947). By 8th November McGrory wanted to exchange him for a Belfast Celtic forward called Tully but the Irish club wanted to see the outcome of the Morton business first. In the end Gerry went to our Ulster cousins but Tully came to Parkhead on the money received for Willie Corbett. Gerry was janitor of the Sacred Heart, Bridgeton for many years, one of the schools involved in the origin of the Celtic. The poor fellow died from hypothermia in 1987.

Appearances:
SL: 20 apps. 12 gls.
SLC: 5 apps. 1 gl.
SC: 1 app. 1 gl.
Total: *26 apps. 14 gls.*
RL: 21 apps. 10 gls.
RLC: 7 apps. 6 gls.
Total: *28 apps. 16 gls.*

McARDLE, John

Role: Outside-right 1926-27
5' 6" 10st.2lbs.
b. Gorbals, 1905

CAREER: St Francis Juniors 1922/St Anthony's 1923/CELTIC 12 June 1926/free 1927/St Roch's 1927/Blantyre Celtic 1932/retired 1934/St Francis Juniors Jan 1935/Rothesay Royal Victoria Aug 1936.

Debut v Dunfermline Athletic (h) 2-1 (SL) 2.4.27

"Who gets McArdle gets a good boy... he can score goals, make opportunities for others" (1924). "A warning to Pat Connolly: if McArdle gets a chance at outside-right, he will be difficult to displace" (1926). John McArdle "a quiet clean-playing little fellow, troubled by injuries," had his first game for Celtic when Willie Maley took a team down to Crawick Holm on August 18th 1925 to celebrate Nithsdale Wanderers' unfurling the Division Three flag. Adam McLean was outside-right for Scotland at Hampden before 111,214 when John had his 90 minutes of glory in a Celtic shirt before 4,000 at the Paradise. He was a crack junior, the toast of Garngad for St Roch. He broke his collarbone playing for the Franks in May 1936 but like Willie Leitch enjoyed his game too much and once under repair, was prepared to travel to the Isle of Bute for more.

Appearances:
SL: 1 app. 0 gls.
Total: *1 app. 0 gls.*

McARTHUR, Daniel

Role: Goalkeeper 1892-1903
5' 7" 10st.0lbs.
b. Old Monkland, 9th August 1867
d. 11th November 1943

CAREER: Parkhead Star/Parkhead Juniors/Cowlairs (trial) Nov 1891/CELTIC Apr 1892/free 1902/CELTIC again 20 Aug 1902/Clyde 25 July 1903/retired 29 Aug 1903/Queen's Park (once) 22 Aug 1904/to Canada Nov 1922/returned to Scotland Oct 1935.

Debut v Abercorn (h) 3-2 (SL) 10.9.1892

"If they're going to kill McArthur they'll have to shoot him" (Tom Hynds). Danny McArthur "the unbeatable little demon," kept goal at a time when 'keepers handled only as a last resort and God help the goalie caught with the ball by stampeding forwards. Dan got his first chance in the Celtic team because of the damage done to Joe Cullen at Sunderland on September 5th 1892. He was a fearless athlete, a marvellous goalie but the most frequently concussed of Celtic 'keepers prior to Willie Miller. Again and again he was kicked comatose and was mostly too black and blue

Dan McArthur

to achieve ever more than half a season's work for Celtic. Dan always managed "phenomenal goalkeeping," "unbeatable form," "really brilliant work," "consummate judgement and skill" against Rangers and took the kicks as they rained in from the likes of John McPherson and RC Hamilton. By the autumn of 1899, the battering had begun to take a toll. On May 9th 1900 he was too beat-up to play: "If I'd been at Magersfontein, they'd have sent me home." He lost the Scottish final against Hearts (April 6th 1901) by being at fault for each of Hearts' four goals. It was Celtic's first-ever season with nothing to show. Dan pulled his jersey off after a 3-0 defeat by Third Lanark in the Charity Cup final at Gilmorehill on May 24th 1901: "It's the unluckiest year I've ever had in football." He retired with broken ribs. Dan McArthur may quite possibly be Celtic's best-ever goalie.

Appearances:
SL: 104 apps. 33 shut-outs.
SC: 16 apps. 3 shut-outs.
Total: *120 apps. 36 shut-outs (30%).*

McATEE, Anthony

Role: Outside-left 1942-43
b. Croy, 25th February 1923

CAREER: Kilsyth St Pat's/Maryhill Harp 8 Aug 1942/Motherwell trial 15 Aug 1942/ CELTIC 15 Aug 1942/free 25 May 1943/ Ashfield 1943/Kilsyth Rangers 1947/free 1948 /Sligo Rovers (trial) summer 1948/Duntocher Hibernian 27 Nov 1948/Coltness United 1949/ free 13 June 1950.

Debut v Hamilton Academicals (h) 2-2 (RL)
22.8.42

Tony "hard as nails" McAtee was the nephew of the great Andy and worked down the same pit as his uncle. He scored three goals against Rob Roy on his debut for Maryhill Harp and was booked to try out for Motherwell at Shawfield. Motherwell decided they wanted him but Tony and Uncle Andy went off to Parkhead to sign for Jimmy McStay. He played in an Old Firm match, the Glasgow Cup first

McATEE, Andrew

Role: Outside-right 1910-24
5' 7" 12st.0lbs.
b. Cumbernauld, 2nd July 1888
d. Condorrat, 15th July 1956

CAREER: Croy Celtic/Mossend Hibernian July 1910/CELTIC 12 Sept 1910/RFA Sept 1917/(Ayr United loan 20 Apr 1918)/free 2 May 1924/New Bedford FC (USA) Oct 1925.

Debut v Partick Thistle (a) 1-1 (SL) 26.9.10

> *Here's to you Andy*
> *For sure you're a dandy*
> *We know you're a product of Croy's*
> *Long may you indulge in*
> *Your famous net-bulgin'*
> *And score many goals for the Bhoys!*

Andy McAtee came from a family of ten (five boys and five girls) and "with thighs like swelling oak," was the first outside-right adequately to replace the great Neilly McCallum. He was terrifyingly fast with a thunderbolt shot that would scud across the penalty box and bulge the net in the far corner.

> *The Kaiser, they say*
> *Only once saw him play*
> *And remarked, it is said*
> *"Dearie me!"*
> *My German artillery's*
> *Just fit for the pillory*
> *They can't shoot like young McAtee.*

He got one of these angled specials from 30 yards exactly one minute after Rangers had gone ahead in the League match of October 21st 1911 and yet another against Rangers from the edge of the penalty box on October 25th 1913. He set up each of Celtic's three goals against Hearts in the semi-final of the Scottish Cup (March 30th 1912) and in the final at Ibrox just a week later, made a prodigious run from deep in his own half followed by a great cross to John Brown that led to the second goal. He won his first representative honour in the Scottish League side that beat the English 4-1 at Hampden before 100,000 on St David's Day 1913 as "a strong, forcing forward." September 5th 1914: Celtic 2, Morton 2 (half-time). In the second half, Andy's target-practice outdid the Kaiser's artillery with four unstoppable shots for a 6-2 victory. In the Glasgow Cup semi-final against Rangers on September 23rd 1916, half-time was 0-0 with Celtic very disjointed. In the second half, McMenemy brought "Him-who-shoots-like-lightning" on to the game of his life for a 3-0 win. "McAtee the Main Man" was round at Ibrox on September 5th 1942, a 2-1 win for Rangers in extra time. His last first team game was at Cappielow a week later. At outside-left for Morton was the Celtic reject Johnny Kelly full of "flashing runs, accurate crossing and deadly finishing." Morton won 4-0. Ashfield converted him into a left-back but he joined Duntocher as a centre. His trial for Sligo Rovers almost cost him his career but the SJFA settled for a two months suspension as of 22nd December 1948. Andy was an "experienced goal-getter" but slipped out of the game with Coltness.

Appearances:
RL: 4 apps. 1 gl.
Total: *4 apps. 1 gl.*

McATEER, Thomas

Role: Centre-half 1910-12
5' 10" 12st.7lbs.
b. Glasgow, 18th November 1881

CAREER: Kilsyth Wanderers/Smithston

Hibernian 1897/Bolton Wanderers 1898/West Ham 1902/Brighton & Hove Albion 1903/ Dundee 24 May 1904/Carlisle United 1906/ (Clyde loan 28 Aug 1906)/Clyde 10 Feb 1908/ CELTIC 10 May 1910/retired June 1912/ Wishaw Thistle 1912/Albion Rovers Nov 1912 /Abercorn 30 July 1913/Broxburn United 13 Aug 1914/3 Cameron Highlanders Sept 1914.

Debut v Airdrie (h) 3-0 (SL) 17.8.10

"McAteer... this quiet reserved man... is a breaker-up... from hard work in the pit, he has become a hard grafter on the field... the oldest member of the Clyde team" (April 9th 1910). Tom McAteer came from the same miners' row in Croy as Jimmy Quinn and went to the same school in Kilsyth. A free-kick expert he played out of position at right-back on his debut on the first day of the 1910-11 season when Sunny Jim Young stood down on the occasion of his mother's death. He had captained Clyde in the three finals of the Scottish Cup against Dundee in 1910 and was signed

Andy McAtee

a potential match-winner every game he played. Celtic were struggling 0-0 against Clydebank in the semi-final of the War Fund Shield on April 27th 1918 with 15 minutes to go, then McAtee struck with two cannonball shots that left George McTurk helpless. Andy was outside-right of the four-in-a-row team 1914-17 and won Scottish Cup medals with Celtic in 1911, 1912, 1914 and 1923 (with his successor Paddy Connolly at outside-left). He served as a gunner in the Italian Alps with the famed 29th Division, heroes of Gallipoli 1915 and the Somme 1916. Andy McAtee is an all-time Celtic great.

> *His shooting's like lightning*
> *Custodians frightening*
> *And bringing the points to Parkhead.*

Appearances:
SL: 407 apps. 69 gls.
SC: 32 apps. 3 gls.
Total: *439 apps. 72 gls.*

♣ **Celtic note:** *Andy's 1922 Championship medal in solid gold came up for auction in Glasgow on February 2nd 1977. Celtic supporter Richard Gilmour of Ardenlea Street outbid the club to secure it for £60. He was prepared to go up to £200.*

as cover for Willie Loney. He came in as a last-minute replacement for the Denny man against Raith Rovers on Hogmanay 1910 and the following day got the equaliser against Rangers at Ibrox right on half-time in the 1-1 draw. Willie Loney fractured his wrist against Clyde on February 25th 1911 and big Tom played in two more Cup finals, this time against Hamilton Academicals. He got his winner's medal on April 15th 1911 at Ibrox when he hit a Loney-style screamer in the 90th minute for Celtic's clincher in the 2-0 victory. He was wounded fighting the Kaiser in 1915, was operated on in Aberdeen in October and was down the pit again at Kilsyth by 1920.

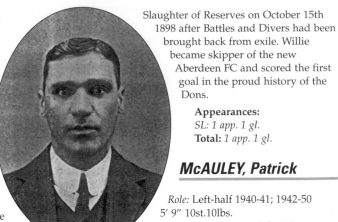

Tom McAteer

Appearances:
SL: 24 apps. 4 gls.
SC: 4 apps. 1 gl.
Total: *28 apps. 5 gls.*

McAULAY, William

Role: Inside-forward 1898
5' 9" 11st.0lbs.
b. Glasgow,
1st November 1879

CAREER: Cambuslang Hibernian/CELTIC 16 Apr 1898/free 15 Oct 1898/Sheffield Wednesday 21 Oct 1898/Dundee 10 Feb 1899/ Walsall Town Swifts 1899/Aston Villa Aug 1900/Portsmouth 3 May 1901/ Middlesbrough 1902/Aberdeen 4 July 1903/ Falkirk 16 May 1906/Hibernian 6 May 1907/ Alloa 6 May 1909 until 1913.

Debut v Third Lanark (h) 2-1 (SL) 20.8.1898 (scored once)

Willie McAulay

"Aberdeen have lost a great forward in McAulay" (August 1906). Willie McAulay was a very short time at Parkhead and got little chance to prove himself. He was part of the

Slaughter of Reserves on October 15th 1898 after Battles and Divers had been brought back from exile. Willie became skipper of the new Aberdeen FC and scored the first goal in the proud history of the Dons.

Appearances:
SL: 1 app. 1 gl.
Total: *1 app. 1 gl.*

McAULEY, Patrick

Role: Left-half 1940-41; 1942-50
5' 9" 10st.10lbs.
b. New Stevenston, 31st July 1921
d. Newarthill, 16th March 1970

CAREER: Douglas Hawthorn Juveniles/ Benburb (trial) 1940/CELTIC 29 July 1940/ free 21 Aug 1941/Arthurlie 23 Aug 1941/ free 18 Mar 1942/CELTIC 18 Mar 1942/Luton Town 16 Dec 1950/Kettering Town 1952/ Albion Rovers (trial) 23 Dec 1953/Albion Rovers 29 Jan 1954/free 24 Apr 1954.

Debut v Hibernian (h) 0-4 (RL) 26.10.40

"In all my experience, I have never come across a finer natural footballer" (Jimmy Hogan, Celtic coach 1950). Pat McAuley, "a football artist... a player of high culture... high intelligence... delightful footwork," began "a splendid partnership" as Delaney's inside man at the start of 1942-43. Within weeks he was being hailed as Celtic's general. He scored a magnificent solo goal against Falkirk at Parkhead on October 31st 1942 and walked through the Hearts defence at Tynecastle for another (February 13th 1943). Instead of making a team round McAuley, Celtic used McAuley to make up a team. He was outside-left in the 6-2 hammering by Hamilton (September 2nd 1944) when "the futility of playing him on the line" was apparent to all except the management. "Advice was shouted from all parts of the ground to shift him inside... a move made only when the game was lost." He had a "masterly match" against Torry Gillick in the Charity Cup final at Ibrox on May 14th 1947 (Rangers won 1-0). In 1948 Tully would not credit Celtic could be so low in the League with a craftsman like McAuley in the side.

Pat McAuley

"McAuley was the brains behind attack after attack" (December 11th 1948). His greatest game saw him destroy Rangers in the League Cup at Parkhead on August 13th 1949: "McAuley was the foundation stone of a splendid victory... a football artist... snake-hipped... with defence-splitting passes." Rangers players refused the tackle for fear of being left floundering. Pat wanted more money or a transfer and Joe Baillie took his place as of November 19th 1949. Pat played his last League game for Celtic (as a left-back) against East Fife at Parkhead on March 25th 1950. He was in the summer party for Rome and played left-half in Lazio's 50th birthday match (0-0) on May 30th. His was an instinctive genius which had the misfortune to play during Celtic's direst years when talent so rich was rewarded in paper pokes rattling with change. He was a crane operator at Ravenscraig at the time of his death.

Appearances:
SL: 78 apps. 4 gls.
SLC: 22 apps. 0 gls.
SC: 9 apps. 0 gls.
Total: *109 apps. 4 gls.*
RL: 90 apps. 20 gls.
RLC: 23 apps. 3 gls.
Total: *113 apps. 23 gls.*

McAVENNIE, Francis

Role: Striker 1987-89; 1992-94
5' 10" 11st.0lbs.
b. Glasgow, 22nd November 1959

CAREER: St Augustine's Milton BG/Kilsyth St Pat's/Kirkintilloch 200 Club/Johnstone Burgh Jan 1980/St Mirren 5 Nov 1980/ West Ham 13 June 1985/CELTIC 2 Oct 1987/ West Ham 22 Mar 1989/free May 1992/Aston Villa as free agent July 1992/Cliftonville as free agent 5 Nov 1992/South China as free agent Nov 1992/CELTIC (trial) as free agent 31 Dec 1992/CELTIC 26 Feb 1993/(Swindon Town loan 16 Feb-11 May 1994)/free 17 May 1994/Airdrie (month's trial) 10 Aug 1994/ Falkirk (month's trial) 13 Sep 1994/St Mirren (month's trial) 14 Oct 1994.

Debut v Hibernian (h) 1-1 (SL) 3.10.87

"He takes goals the way Denis Law did. You can't give any striker higher praise than that" (George Best December 7th 1985). "Great stamina and guts for a slightly-built kid... first to react to the goalie losing the ball even if playing in midfield" (David Pleat). "Celtic are the club I always wanted to play for more than any other" (October 2nd 1987). Frank McAvennie was no sooner at Parkhead than he was involved with Chris Woods, Graham Roberts and Terry Butcher at Ibrox on October 17th 1987 and charged with conduct likely to provoke a breach of the peace on November 1st. He was found not guilty (as every impartial observer knew) on April 15th 1988. The news "I want to leave Celtic" broke from London on April 30th 1988. Frank had not scored since March 2nd but got both goals in the last 15 minutes of the Scottish Cup final of May 14th 1988. By September 16th he was "raging" over stories that he wanted to be back to London. On the occasion of Frank's explosion ("I am fit!") at being played in the reserves (March 11th 1989), McNeill revealed that he had asked to go first of all in August 1988 and on three other occasions since. Celtic supporters felt badly let-down, although the consensus was that on the park McAvennie was the one player "doing the business regularly" (he fed off Joe Miller). He was booed against Hearts at Parkhead in the 5th round of the Scottish Cup a week later. His bravery was not in doubt. Butcher had rolled on his arm on January 3rd 1989 yet Frank had insisted he continue playing despite the break.

Frank went back to London to be closer to the woman in his life. It was Partick Thistle's turn to feel let-down when he came back to Scotland at the end of 1992. He paraded in Thistle's colours on Hogmanay, waved a Thistle scarf, and was John Lambie's player except for the form-signing. Then the 'phone rang and he went away to negotiate with Celtic. "We all make mistakes sometimes and I know now that I should have stayed at Celtic Park." He went back to Firhill on May 8th 1993. His name was not on the match pro-gramme and was omitted by the announcer over the tannoy. Frank scored the eighth goal of his Second Coming from a "ferocious" penalty to win the game.

Appearances:
SL: 85 apps. 36 gls.
SLC: 7 apps. 8 gls.
SC: 9 apps. 4 gls.
Eur: 4 apps. 1 gl.
Total: *105 apps. 49 gls.*

Frank McAvennie

McBRIDE, Joseph

Role: Striker 1965-68
5' 9" 11st.2lbs.
b. Govan, 10th June 1938

CAREER: St. Gerard's Senior Secondary 1954 /Kilmarnock Amateurs/Shettleston Town May 1956/Kirkintilloch Rob Roy June 1956/ Kilmarnock 13 Aug 1956/Wolverhampton Wanderers 26 Nov 1959/Luton Town 26 Feb 1960/Partick Thistle 24 Nov 1960/Motherwell 2 Nov 1962/CELTIC 5 June 1965/Hibernian 5 Nov 1968/Dunfermline Athletic 25 Dec 1970 /Clyde 7 Oct 1971/retired 29 Apr 1972.
Debut v Dundee (h) 0-2 (SLC) 21.8.65

"I have been asked to name the best Celtic centre-forward I've ever seen play and the man I choose may surprise you. He's Joe McBride. It was due to injuries that Joe only had a few seasons at Celtic Park. If he had been allowed a full career I am sure he would have become one of the all-time great goal scorers. He only played for half a season the year we won the European Cup, playing his last game before Christmas, yet he ended-up joint top scorer in Scotland. He was a tremendous header of the ball and could take a half chance on the ground. And his heart was in the right place" (Jimmy McGrory: *A Lifetime in Paradise* 1975). Joe was Jock Stein's first signing for Celtic and made his initial appearance in the colours on the George V Playing Fields in Douglas versus Motherwell on July 28th 1965 for Isle of Man Charities. Within twelve minutes he had clashed heads with John Martis and was taken-off, the blood streaming. He scored his first goals for Celtic against Shamrock Rovers at Dalymount on August 3rd and scored again against Sunderland in the 0-5 win at Roker Park four days later. He had hit it off with Motherwell but playing in a Celtic jersey now heightened his performance as never before. He was in the sides that beat Rangers in the League Cup finals of 1965 and 1966 and won Championship medals for 1966 and 1967 (despite his last game being on Christmas Eve 1966). He got the first of his two Scottish caps against Wales in Cardiff on October 22nd 1966 and the other against N.Ireland the following month at Hampden in a team that contained six Celts and was managed by ex-Celt Malcolm MacDonald. Joe's knee broke down against Aberdeen on Christmas Eve 1966. He was operated on at Killearn on March 10th 1967 and without playing another League game still ended-up top scorer in Division One with 33. He played his first full 90 minutes for points in a whole year on December 23rd 1967 against Morton at Cappielow and scored three. He seemed fit enough but after the League match at Shawfield on Ne'erday 1968 was no longer a significant factor in Stein's plans. He played as substitute against AC Milan in Jersey City on May 26th 1968 and also at altitude versus Necaxa in Mexico City on June 4th but Stein's strike force was now Wallace and Lennox with Joe one of several options as a reserve. He played his last game for Celtic (and scored) against Morton away in an all-ticket

Joe McBride

match on October 26th 1968. He joined Hibs as a replacement for Colin Stein and immediately found his old game not just as a striker but as a schemer making openings for others. Tom Hart, having sacked manager Willie McFarlane for putting Joe back in the team against Liverpool when he as Chairman had ordered him dropped, transferred the ex-Celt to Dunfermline on Christmas Day 1970. Hibs lost 0-1 to Dundee United on Boxing Day and from start to finish of the match, the supporters vented their feelings with a chant of: "Joe McBride! Joe McBride!" Celtic fans knew how they felt: "Joe! Joe! SuperJoe!" Stein defined him as the quintessential striker; the kind of player who, when he didn't know what else to do with the ball, stuck it in the net.

Appearances:
SL: 55 apps. 54 gls.
SLC: 21 apps. 24 gls.
SC: 8 apps. 3 gls.
Eur: 10 apps. 5 gls.
Total: *94 apps. 86 gls.*

McCABE, Patrick

Role: Outside-left 1915

CAREER: Laurieston Villa/East Stirling 12 Dec 1911/CELTIC 9 Mar 1915/(East Stirling loan 15 Mar 1915 & 5 Feb 1916)/(Vale of Leven loan 27 May 1916)/East Stirling 16 Sept 1916/ Scots Guards Dec 1916/East Stirling again 21 Oct 1919/Banknock Juniors Aug 1920.

Debut v Hamilton Academicals (a) 3-2 (SL) 16.10.15

Pat McCabe ("another star") first turned out for Celtic in a home friendly against Glentoran on March 13th 1915. "He started gingerly" on his League debut but "Gallagher gave him every opportunity to shine... with a few more outings he will be difficult to displace." In his second game against St Mirren at Parkhead he was marked by Hugh McGrory, big brother of a famous future Celt, but with Joe Cassidy "was the best man on view". "He had no real chance because of Browning's consistency... he is young enough and may yet get his chance with the team he loves" (Patsy Gallagher December 1916). Pat's grandson Jim, a goalie with Adelaide Lion and 25 caps for Australia, was training at Celtic Park in January 1960. Pat attended the big reunion of ex-Celts organised by the James Kelly (Blantyre) CSC in late 1951.

Appearances:
SL: 2 apps. 0 gls.
Total: *2 apps. 0 gls.*

McCAFFERTY, William

Role: Outside-right 1902-03
b. Rutherglen, 9th December 1882

CAREER: Rutherglen Glencairn/CELTIC 14 Mar 1902/(Bolton Wanderers loan 8 Nov 1902)/Stenhousemuir 7 Nov 1903/Bathgate 17 July 1905/Reading 9 Nov 1905/ Birmingham 1906/Bathgate 23 May 1907/ Portsmouth 7 Feb 1908/Brentford 5 Nov 1909/ Bathgate 6 Aug 1910.

Debut v Hibernian (h) 0-1 (SC) 26.4.02

Rutherglen's Willie McCafferty joined the Celtic first team too late for the League programme of 1901-02 but made his debut in a 0-5 win against Rangers in the Inter-City League on March 1st 1902 and played ICL, Charity Cup ties and various friendlies before and after his appearance in the Cup Final versus Hibernian (postponed two weeks because of the Ibrox Disaster on April 5th). He helped Berwick Rangers celebrate their 21st birthday with two in two minutes against Newcastle United on March 13th 1902 on Berwick Cricket Ground. His one League game was against Glasgow Rangers, a 1-1 draw at Parkhead (October 18th 1902).

Appearances:
SL: 1 app. 0 gls.
SC: 1 app. 0 gls.
Total: *2 apps. 0 gls.*

Steve McCahill

McCAHILL, Stephen Joseph

Role: Centre-half 1989-92
6' 2" 11st.8lbs.
b. Greenock,
3rd September 1966

CAREER: St Columba's High School Port Glasgow/ Gleniffer Thistle/Dumbarton 14 June 1984/St Etienne (trial) 27 Feb 1986/CELTIC 31 Jan 1989/free Aug 1992/ Morton 1 Oct 1992.

Debut v Dundee (a) 3-0 (SL)
25.2.89 (sub)

Notts County wanted Steve McCahill at the end of August 1984 but Dumbarton awarded him a two-year contract. This "tremendous prospect" was not for sale. He had a great game against Celtic in the Scottish Cup at Parkhead on January 28th 1989. "It mystifies me why Steve has never been bought. He should be playing in the Premier League..." (Jim George, Sons' coach). Three days later he moved for £100,000 and became the third Dumbarton player to be signed by Billy McNeill after MacLeod and Sinclair. Steve helped Celtic win the Dubai Super Cup against Liverpool in the desert on April 4th 1989 but broke his jaw in a collision with Bonner versus Motherwell at Fir Park eight days later. Despite a perfect recovery, his appearances for Celtic were sporadic thereafter and he seems hardly to have been considered before manager Brady splashed out on Gary Gillespie in August 1991. The ever-patient Steve spent most of his time at Parkhead as skipper of the reserves.

Appearances:
SL: 7 apps. 0 gls.
SLC: 1 app. 0 gls.
SC: 1 app. 0 gls.
Total: *9 apps. 0 gls.*

McCALLUM, Neil

Role: Outside-right 1888-90; 1891-92; 1905
b. Bonhill, 3rd July 1868
d. 5th November 1921

CAREER: Renton Athletic 1884/2nd Renton 1885/Renton 1886/(Rangers loan 18 Feb 1888)

/CELTIC May 1888/Blackburn Rovers 22 Feb 1890/CELTIC 17 Jan 1891/Nottingham Forest Aug 1892/Loughborough Town 1894/Newark Town 1894/Notts County 1895/Heanor Town 1896/...Gravesend player-groundsman Oct 1903/CELTIC (once)10 May 1905.

Debut v Rangers Swifts (h) 5-2 (Inaugural Match) 28.5.1888 (scored once)

Despite a flat-footed running style, Neilly McCallum was fast, clever, could shoot with hardly any backlift and no matter how oppressive the defence always got his crosses over. "The Shadow" did all the scoring in a 6-0 win for Renton over the Scottish Cup holders Hibs in 1887 and was invited to guest for Rangers against Aston Villa in Birmingham. He scored Celtic's very first goal in the 10th minute of their very first game. In the replay of the Snow Final on February 9th 1889, he scored the Celtic equaliser and the sight of his mates descending on him with congratulations was one that remained long in the memory of those who witnessed it. He signed for Blackburn "in a moment of weakness" but returned to Scotland under the amnesty of 1891 and was outside-right in the Celtic team that lifted its first Scottish Cup on April 9th 1892. When he induced Sandy McMahon to fly with him to Nottingham the following August, Celtic went after McMahon but decided enough was enough with Neilly. He came along to see "The Greatest Team on Earth" drubbed 5-0 by Stoke on November 7th 1892 but was allegedly shunned by his ex-team-mates. His loss to Forest was irreparable and bar Bobby Muir and Alec Bennett, the gap he left was never adequately filled until Andy McAtee in 1910. Neilly worked at Celtic Park as an odd-job man as of August 1905. His family seems to have had a Highland connection and Neilly himself wore an Inverness cape as part of his day wear.

Appearances:
SL: 20 apps. 9 gls.
SC: 13 apps. 8 gls.
Total: *33 apps. 17 gls.*

Neilly McCallum

Denis McCallum

McCALLUM, Denis

Role: Outside-right 1926-32
5' 11" 10st.10lbs.
b. Alexandria, 4th May 1908

CAREER: Vale of Leven mascot 1915/St Patrick's Dumbarton 1922/St Anthony's/Dumbarton/CELTIC 26 May 1926/(Clydebank loan 25 Feb 1928)/(Nithsdale Wanderers loan 5 May 1928)/(Dundee United loan 24 Oct 1930)/(St Bernard's loan 1931)/free May 1932/Glentoran 26 Sept 1932/Bangor Nov 1932/Coleraine 1933/Sligo Rovers 1935.

Debut v Falkirk (a) 1-4 (SL) 6.4.27

"McCallum will be a great understudy for Adam McLean... a star winger of the near future... he spanks along the wing like McAlpine, knows how to lob them over" (August 1926; Denis at outside-left). "He has reach, speed, determination... kicks a straight ball... afraid of no opponent... recovers quickly... crushes out a winger cutely... but he diddles with the ball in his own area..."

253

(September 1929; Denis at right-back). Denis, son of Charlie of Vale of Leven and grand-nephew of the great Neilly, "a sprinter with a wide reputation" was so tall and thin it looked as if Adam McLean had been transferred to make "Wafer" McCallum. He was subject to some of the most savage barracking ever heard at Parkhead. When Willie McStay left, Denis filled his boots also in the days of the "Celtic Waistcoat" team (it's got no back). He was tried out at full-back pre-season 1929 and proclaimed "the find of the Celtic trials." "He never put a foot wrong and his tackling and lengthy returns were a revelation to the Parkhead faithful." Denis was an erratic performer: against Kilmarnock on August 9th 1930 he hit an explosive goal at the start of each half and had a great game; against Falkirk one week later he was nobody.

Appearances:
SL: 39 apps. 3 gls.
SC: 1 app. 0 gls.
Total: *40 apps. 3 gls.*

McCALLUM, William Donald

Role: Right-back 1890-92
b. Kilbirnie,
24th October 1870

CAREER: Wishaw Thistle/Elm Park/ Dumbarton Athletic 1888/ Hibernian 1889/CELTIC 1890/ West Bromwich Albion 17 Jan 1892/Dumbarton 1892/Wishaw Thistle 1892/ Dundee Harp 1 Aug 1893/ Coatdyke Gaelic 4 Sept 1894.

Debut v Rangers (h) 1-0 (SC) 6.9.1890

Willie McCallum, stocky, red-haired "a steady back from Wishaw" was a printer with the *Glasgow News* and Celtic's reserve team skipper. He came in for Mick McKeown at Everton on April 5th 1890 the day that Mick, back in Glasgow, got the cap against England that went to his head in more ways than one. Celtic and Rangers met in the opening round of the Scottish Cup in "the first titanic struggle between the clubs" on September 6th 1890. Jimmy Kelly was suspended for setting up the Celtic versus Old Renton game of May 31st 1890 and Jimmy McLaren had burned his foot

so Willie Maley moved to centre-half with Willie McCallum on his left. Celtic went through thanks to a Groves wonder goal (Celtic linesman T E Maley waved his flag in delight).

Appearances:
SL: 1 app. 0 gls.
SC: 2 apps. 0 gls.
Total: *3 apps. 0 gls.*

McCANN, Daniel

Role: Inside-left 1910-11
5' 8" 10st.7lbs.
b. Hurlford, 18th March 1888

CAREER: Hurlford Thistle/Galston 15 Oct 1906/Nithsdale Wanderers 12 Sept 1907/Hurlford Athletic 25 Sept 1907/Dundee 13 Mar 1908/CELTIC 6 May 1910/ (Ayr United loan Mar 1911)/Dundee Hibernian May 1911/Nottingham Forest (trial) 2 Sept 1911 /Hurlford Athletic 26 Oct 1911/Galston 21 Mar 1914/(Dundee loan during WW1).

Debut v Airdrie (h) 3-0 (SL) 17.8.10

Dan McCann

Dan McCann, "a thin slip of a boy... resistant to all efforts to build up his physique," played for Dundee at Dens Park on September 4th 1909 as a stop-gap centre-forward. Rangers were 0-2 up at half-time but Dundee fought back and Dan first brought the crowd to its feet with the equaliser. Next he headed home the father and mother of all leading goals. He was concussed on landing and had to be carried off but he returned at outside-right and Dundee took the day 4-2. A week later, Dan received the match ball beautifully done out in dark blue and white and autographed by all his teammates. Willie Maley had been keen on the "dashing young forward" as a junior and at the end of the season Dan pleaded to be allowed to join Celtic. He played against Johnstone FC at Paisley in a friendly on May 10th 1910 and was pitched right into the big team for the start of 1910-11. The match was watched by a man from Mayo: Bro Dorotheus, ex-Headmaster of the Sacred Heart school Bridgeton 1888, one of the founders of Celtic. Dan was "a bit on the light side for the pushfulness which is injected into first-class senior play" and Jimmy McMenemy and Peter Johnstone were Celtic's inside men by August 27th 1910. With the arrival of John Hastie, Dan's chances of first team football were further diminished. He signed off with a nine minute goal against Hearts at Tynecastle in the League on April 1st 1911. He was playing great stuff at Hurlford again as of 1911, and Liverpool invited him for a trial in September 1913. Dan joined up at the start of hostilities in 1914 and was ranked corporal by November 1917.

Appearances:
SL: 7 apps. 1 gl.
Total: *7 apps. 1 gl.*

McCANN, Edward

Role: Outside-left 1893

CAREER: Broxburn Shamrock 1889/Bathgate Rovers 6 Sept 1890/Newcastle East End Nov 1890/Broxburn Shamrock 1891/CELTIC Mar 1893/Broxburn Shamrock 1893 until 1898.

Debut v Renton (a) 2-0 (SL) 25.3.1893

The Feast of the Annunciation 1893 saw Scotland play Ireland at Celtic Park with Willie Maley, Kelly, McMahon and Campbell on international duty. Eddie McCann of 8 Stuartfield, Broxburn, was brought in to do Johnny Campbell's job at Renton and helped Celtic to both points en route to their first Flag. He helped beat London Caledonians 3-0 on Holy Saturday April 1st 1893 but lost his place after the Easter Monday friendly at Ibrox where Rangers won 3-1.

Appearances:
SL: 1 app. 0 gls.
Total: *1 app. 0 gls.*

McCANN, John

Role: Half-back 1892; 1893
b. Uphall, 6th September 1867

CAREER: Broxburn Shamrock 1889/Bathgate Rovers 6 Sept 1890/Newcastle West End Nov 1890/Broxburn Shamrock 1891/(CELTIC loan

2 Jan 1892)/CELTIC Mar 1893/Hibernian 1893 /Preston North End Oct 1893/Broxburn Shamrock Dec 1893.

Debut v Renton (a) 2-0 (SL) 25.3.1893

Celtic lost to Dumbarton at Dalmarnock Street on Ne'erday 1892 "because they eight nothing." Peter Dowds had played left-half with his head in bandages. To avoid another humiliation the following day against Third Lanark at Govanhill, Celtic drafted in McCann and O'Byrne from Broxburn Shamrock, McCann to replace the wounded Dowds. Fourteen months later he came back again as a replacement for Jimmy Kelly on international duty and played the first of three League games in Celtic's first Championship season. His last was on May 2nd 1893 against St Mirren at Parkhead. The evening of that same day, on the motion of JH McLaughlin (Celtic), the SFA legalised professional football in Scotland.

Appearances:
SL: 3 apps. 0 gls.
Total: *3 apps. 0 gls.*

McCANN, William

Role: Centre-forward 1894-95

CAREER: Strathclyde/CELTIC 22 Dec 1894/ reinstated as amateur 18 Aug 1895/Clydebank United 7 Nov 1895/Abercorn 10 Sept 1896/ Partick Thistle 14 Nov 1896/Kilsyth Wanderers 17 Nov 1898.

Debut v St Mirren (h) 2-2 (SL) 22.12.1894

William McCann's debut was on a day so wild and stormy that Jerry Reynolds counted spectators individually as they arrived. Despite an appeal, the Scottish League decreed the result should stand. Willie played in the 3-0 Christmas Day reverse at Everton and also the 0-2 defeat at home by Burnley on Hogmanay. He turned out on a Tynecastle pitch thawed into a pond in the League on February 16th 1895 and had his first win with Celtic at Boghead for points on March 9th 1895 as inside-right.

Appearances:
SL: 3 apps. 0 gls.
Total: *3 apps. 0 gls.*

McCARRISON, Dugald

Role: Striker 1987-93
5' 8" 10st.7lbs.
b. Lanark, 22nd December 1969

CAREER: Celtic BC/CELTIC 17 Oct 1987/
(Ipswich Town loan 13 Dec 1990)/
(Darlington loan 31 Oct 1991)/Kilmarnock
26 Feb 1993.

Debut v Dundee United (h) 1-2 (SL) 24.10.87

Dugald McCarrison

Dugald McCarrison was in the Celtic side that won the BP Youth Cup in 1987. He made his first team debut one week after McAvennie and Woods had taken early baths at Ibrox. Mark McGhee was unfit so young Dugald went in as McAvennie's replacement versus Dundee United. A perennial reserve, he was on a month-to-month contract at Parkhead after July 1992. Tommy Burns paid £100,000 to take him to Kilmarnock on the day manager Brady definitively re-engaged the veteran McAvennie.

> **Appearances:**
> *SL: 4 apps. 1 gl.*
> **Total:** *4 apps. 1 gl.*

McCARRON, Francis

Role: Centre-half 1962-67
6' 1" 12st.2lbs.
b. Kinning Park, 1st October 1943

CAREER: Lourdes School Cardonald/CELTIC 28 May 1962/Parkhead Juniors (farmed-out) 1962/free 1967/Carlisle United Aug 1967/free Apr 1969.

Debut v Hibernian (h) 2-0 (SL) 6.4.63

Frank McCarron captained Scotland's Schoolboys Under-18s against England on April 18th 1962 and signed for Celtic the following month. He made his debut (marking Gerry Baker) on a day when Billy McNeill was

Frank McCarron

reserve with Scotland at Wembley. He took Jim Craig's place on the 'formation' tour of Bermuda and North America 1966 and after a bout of sunburn on Bermuda, made his tour debut in Kearny, New Jersey in the second half against the NJ All Stars, a match Celtic won 0-6. Frank came on for Big Billy in the second half against Hamilton Primo in Ontario exactly one year before Lisbon (May 25th 1966). He played for 14 minutes then sustained the ankle injury that ended his chances of playing again on the trip and also his prospects of a first-team breakthrough. He moved to Carlisle in the English Second Division but sustained a badly broken leg versus Millwall at the Den on Easter Monday 1968. The fracture was so serious as to require complicated surgery and put an end to Frank's playing career. His son, Frank junior, played for Montrose against Celtic in the Scottish Cup (January 25th 1992) at Parkhead.

> **Appearances:**
> *SL: 1 app. 0 gls.*
> **Total:** *1 app. 0 gls.*

McCARTHY, Michael

Role: Centre-half 1987-89
6' 2" 13st.3lbs.
b. Barnsley, 7th February 1959

CAREER: Our Lady's Junior School Worsbrough 1964/Barnsley Juniors 1970/ Worsbrough High School 1970/Worsbrough Miners' Welfare/Swaithe Miners' Welfare/ Worsbrough BC/Barnsley app. Dec 1973, pro.

July 1977/Manchester City 13 Dec 1983/CELTIC 20 May 1987/ Olympique Lyon 1 July 1989/ Millwall Mar 1990/caretaker-manager 18 Mar 1992/manager 18 Apr 1992.

Debut v Borussia Dortmund (a) 0-2 (UEFA Cup) 29.9.87

"Mick would pop your head off only in training" (Peter Grant). Long-throw specialist Mick McCarthy "big physique and a voice to match," was Davie Hay's last major signing. He played his first game for Celtic in a 3-0 defeat on the Scandinavian tour versus Stromstad on July 19th 1987 when he was taken off with badly torn abdominal muscles in the 75th minute. His appearances during the Double season were punctuated by injury and suspension and he played in only three Scottish Cup ties including the final against Dundee United on May 14th 1988. When 10 goals had been lost in five League games Ian Andrews and Mick McCarthy were dropped together as of September 24th 1988. Big Mick got his place back and had an immense game against Werder Bremen in the European Cup 0-0 draw in Germany on November 9th. Three days later Celtic beat Rangers 3-1 in the League but not before Mick had stuck his hand up to afford Rangers the lead with a gratuitous penalty. He repeated this same aberration against Motherwell on December 3rd. He won himself a second Scottish medal against Rangers on May 20th 1989 before his departure for France. Fans' opinion on him was very divided. Some were of the view that McCarthy (Celtic) and McCarthy (Ireland) were two different people. Mick was never less than a rock for the Republic. He was manager when Millwall played their last game at the Den on May 8th 1993.

Appearances:
SL: 48 apps. 0 gls.
SLC: 3 apps. 0 gls.
SC: 8 apps. 1 gl.
Eur: 5 apps. 0 gls.
Total: *64 apps. 1 gl.*

Mick McCarthy

McCLAIR, Brian

Role: Striker 1983-87
5' 10" 11st.7lbs.
b. Airdrie, 8th December 1963

CAREER: St Margaret's High School, Airdrie/ Coatbridge BG/Aston Villa app. June 1980/ free own request 1981/Motherwell 10 Aug 1981/CELTIC 20 June 1983/Manchester United 1 July 1987.

Debut v Brechin City (a) 1-0 (SLC) 24.8.83

Like Oliver Anderson in 1937, 'Choccy' had the choice of any club in Britain as a schoolboy including Celtic. He picked Aston Villa but felt Ron Saunders was only interested in first-teamers. With Motherwell as a 2nd Year student of Computer Maths at Glasgow University he scored the hat-trick in the 3-0 defeat of Rangers on January 3rd 1983 and the brace when 'well beat Celtic twelve days later. Billy McNeill signed him for £75,000 to replace

Charlie Nicholas but was gone from Parkhead himself before he had seen 'Choccy' play. Davie Hay's first match in charge against Basle on July 23rd 1983 was also McClair's first in a Celtic shirt. He scored one of the greatest goals ever seen at Celtic Park against Dundee United 15 minutes after half-time on August 18th 1984 with Celtic trailing 0-1 in the League. He collected the ball in his own box, raced the length of the field and with the United players expecting the pass, let fly an unstoppable shot past Billy Thomson. He asked for a transfer on November 23rd 1985: "I'm a proven goalscorer sitting on the bench... perhaps the Boss does not fancy me... he doesn't speak to me, I get the feeling I'm not wanted." He won his first honour with Celtic by coming on as substitute for Tommy Burns in the 65th minute of the 100th Scottish Cup final on May 18th 1985 with the score 1-0 to Dundee United. He won a League championship badge the following season and opened the scoring in six minutes against St Mirren at Paisley in the 'eery silence match' of May 3rd 1986 notching the fifth goal nine minutes after half-time with the score at Dens Park still Dundee 0, Hearts 0. McClair's goalscoring record was most impressive and by 1987 he was Scotland's Player of the Year and refused an offer of £80,000 a year from Celtic to re-sign. His transfer fee went to tribunal on July 30th 1987. Celtic wanted £1.5 million but had to be content with £850,000 which was robbery in the context of its time. 'Choccy' won an English Cup medal in 1990, a European Cup Winners' Cup medal in 1991 and in 1993 was in the first Manchester United side to land the League Championship in 26 years. In the Cup final versus Chelsea (May 14th 1994; the day United landed the 'Double') he came on for Kanchelskis in the downpour with five minutes to go and scored United's fourth goal in injury time.

Appearances:
SL: 145 apps. 98 gls.
SLC: 20 apps. 9 gls.
SC: 18 apps. 11 gls.
Eur: 16 apps. 2 gls.
Total: *199 apps. 120 gls.*

♣ **Celtic note:** *April 4th 1987; Celtic 0, Rangers 0 in the Premier League and McClair tangled with Souness. The Rangers' player-manager taunted him: "Show us your medals, sonny!" In the space of three minutes, Choccy twice hit penalties past Woods into the right-hand corner of the net. He had a quiet word with Souness after the second: "So where are your medals now then?"*

Brian McClair

George McCluskey

McCLUSKEY,
George McKinlay Cassidy

Role: Striker 1974-83
5′ 11″ 12st.1lbs.
b. Hamilton, 19th September 1957

CAREER: Holy Cross Hamilton/Celtic BC
1968/CELTIC ground staff 1973/Thorniewood
(farmed-out) 1973/CELTIC 22 July 1974/
Leeds United 26 July 1983/free 16 May 1986/
Hibernian 4 June 1986/Hamilton Academicals
8 Sept 1989/free 14 May 1992/Kilmarnock
25 July 1992/player-coach 26 Aug 1994/
Clyde 28 Oct 1994.

Debut v F.C. Valur (h) 7-0 (ECWC) 1.10.75 (sub)
(scored once)

George McCluskey played for Scottish
Schoolboys at Wembley on June 9th 1973 and
scored one of the goals in a great 2-4 victory.

He went full-time with Celtic in 1974 and was
seen as part of the team of '77. On his League
debut against Rangers (November 1st 1975),
he "looked the part... used the ball with
intelligence." As his career developed the
praise heaped on: "elegant... superb on the
ball... terrific shot... goals from impossible
angles... extremely talented." He did indeed
score some superb goals: a 30-yard free kick
against Dundee United at Parkhead in the
League on September 8th 1979; the opener
against Real Madrid in the European Cup
quarter-finals at Parkhead (March 5th 1980);
the stab-foot winner against Rangers in the
Scottish final (May 10th 1980); the 89th minute
strike against Cruyff's Ajax in the European
Cup at Amsterdam (September 29th 1982);
and against Thistle on November 28th 1981 he
sold Brian Whittaker the father and mother of
a dummy then let fly from 35 yards past Alan
Rough. He was in Jock Stein's provisional 40
of May 14th 1982 for the World Cup but like
that other exquisite ball player Tommy Burns,
did not make the final 22 for Spain. In terms of
instinctive genius he was one of the finest
forwards ever to wear the green and white.
But McNeill wanted aggression and felt
McGarvey and Nicholas had it more on offer:
"I would prefer that a striker is in among the
goals every week" (October 13th 1979); "I
want McCluskey to show me why he should
be in the Celtic team every week" (March 3rd
1983). Celtic's best side of recent years was the
team of the early '80s which won three titles in
five years and might well have done five in a
row. George McCluskey, great touch, ferocious
shot, was the Unsung Hero of that team and
Celtic lost a man with years of real football in
him when they refused to meet his worth in
terms of salary.

Appearances:
SL: 145 apps. 54 gls.
SLC: 28 apps. 7 gls.
SC: 18 apps. 12 gls.
Eur: 13 apps. 5 gls.
Total: *204 apps. 78 gls.*

McCLUSKEY, Henry John

Role: Wing-half 1942-47
b. Greenock, 30th August 1923

CAREER: St Anne's BG/St Mungo's
Academy/Queen's Park Victoria XI 1939/
Dumbarton reserves/CELTIC Oct 1942/Royal

Engineers summer 1943/(Fulham loan 1944-45)/free Apr 1947.

Debut v Partick Thistle (h) 3-3 (RL) 2.1.43

Matt Lynch got himself sent-off in the Ne'erday fiasco of 1943 for a stupid foul on Charlie Johnstone when Celtic were already down to ten men and losing 4-1. Harry McCluskey got Matt's place next day in a fighting draw at Parkhead after Celtic had been 1-3 down. He had a run of four games out of six in the qualifying stages of the League Cup and played against Rangers both at Ibrox (3-0) in the League Cup (March 6th 1943) and at Parkhead (0-4) in the Summer Cup (June 12th 1943). The Army then claimed him and put an effective end to his career as a Celt. On May 13th 1974, Henry McCluskey (52), a senior partner with William Fairhurst, the civil engineering firm, gave evidence in Glasgow for Rangers in a case brought against them as a result of the Stairway 13 disaster of January 2nd 1971. Rangers had employed him to examine all aspects of crowd control and safety at Ibrox. Harry had hired an aircraft to photograph Ibrox at various stages of a big game and had travelled to Barcelona, Munich and Milan to see how crowds were handled there. He found the stairways at Ibrox "adequate." He admitted his previous

knowledge of the ground had in the past been limited - mainly to the Celtic end!

Appearances:
RL: 2 apps. 0 gls.
RLC: 4 apps. 0 gls.
Total: *6 apps. 0 gls.*

McCLUSKEY, John Donnelly

Role: Striker 1973-79
5' 9" 11st.1lb.
b. Hamilton, 24th October 1960

CAREER: Holy Cross Hamilton/Celtic BC/ CELTIC 'S' form 1973/CELTIC 3 Aug 1976/ retired 1979.

Debut v Jeunesse Esch (a) 6-1 (EC) 28.9.77 (sub)

"He's a different class as a player... very direct... takes opponents on at pace... got a terrific shot" (Ronnie Glavin). Before Paul McStay, John McCluskey ('Friar') was Celtic's youngest-ever S form signing aged 13. He emulated big brother George's feat of scoring at Wembley for Scottish schoolboys 0-1 versus England (June 15th 1975): "He dribbled like a tanner ba' wizard round three completely baffled English defenders and slipped the ball coolly in the net." He was a "ball-playing

Muddy marvels: John McCluskey (extreme right, standing) and a group of jubilant young 'Bhoys'.

striker... surely guaranteed a future in the game." A massive blood clot in the leg first struck in February 1977 ("Jock Stein was never away from the hospital") but he recovered to play for Scotland Youth in the Polish tournament of 1978. Against Yugoslavia on May 12th: "He has been told to win this game for us" (Andy Roxburgh). Thrombosis now developed in his other leg and John spent Christmas 1978 in hospital after a warning that a blow on the limb could kill him: "I've been given tablets to thin the clot and no doubt I'll do all right but I know I'll never play football again." Poor John later suffered a heart attack in May 1992.

Appearances:
Eur: 1 app. 0 gls.
Total: *1 app. 0 gls.*

McCLUSKEY, Patrick

Role: Defence/Midfield 1969-77
5' 9" 12st.6lbs.
b. Kilsyth, 13th April 1952

CAREER:
Schools/ Millwall/Berwick Rangers / Albion Rovers/Chelsea (all trial) 1967/ Glasgow United 1967/Maryhill Juniors 1968/ CELTIC 20 May 1969/Maryhill Juniors (farmed-out)/(Sligo Rovers loan 11 Feb 1970)/ CELTIC (new contract) 25 May 1970/ Dumbarton 12 Aug 1977/ Darmstadt (trial) 1980/Airdrie 8 Oct 1980/Pittsburgh Spirit 1982/Queen of the South 9 Aug 1983/retired 1985.

Debut v Clyde (a) 1-2 (GC) 6.5.71

"Is there a better defender in the country?...

McCluskey is much more convincing than Connelly" (September 1974). Pat McCluskey, son of footballer and singer John McIvor (his professional name) won caps at centre for junior Scotland. His good mate Jimmy Quinn was injured on April 1st 1972. "I need a left-back," said Jock Stein, "anyone will do." Jim Brogan, only half-fit, played the first 45 minutes of the European Cup semi-final before 80,000 at the San Siro, Milan on April 5th and at half-time Celtic sent on 'anyone' ie the Tiger, Pat McCluskey. Result: Inter 0, Celtic 0. Stein appraised him in December 1973: "He's a good hard tackler... breaks things up... not a John Clark... more a young Bobby Murdoch in the back four." Pat was given Davie Hay's ball-winning role at the start of 1974-75: "He works on the principle, the bigger they are, the harder he hits them." Pat won League medals with Celtic in 1973 and 1974 and played on winning sides in the Cup finals of 1974 and 1975. He scored the third goal against Airdrie at Hampden with a penalty on May 3rd 1975. Pat's career took a down-turn after the Copenhagen night club rumpus with the Scotland international party on September 3rd 1975 when he was travelling as a member of the squad. He was suspended permanently from Scotland duty five days later and Celtic "censured him severely" on September 11th 1975. He lost his place to Pat Stanton and went on the transfer list as of October 2nd 1976. Davie Wilson took him to Dumbarton where he missed only three games in three seasons. Pat works nowadays on the North Sea oil rigs.

Appearances:
SL: 115 apps. 10 gls.
SLC: 40 apps. 1 gl.
SC: 14 apps. 1 gl.
Eur: 20 apps. 0 gls.
Total: *189 apps. 12 gls.*

McCOLGAN, Daniel

Role: Centre-half 1925-28
5' 9" 10st.10lbs.
b. Baillieston, 22nd February 1903

CAREER: Baillieston Juniors/CELTIC 9 June 1925/(Third Lanark loan 26 Nov 1926)/(Ayr United loan 26 Aug 1927)/(Third Lanark loan 27 Nov 1927)/(Raith Rovers loan 14 Mar 1928) /Third Lanark 27 Nov 1928/(Belfast Celtic loan 22 Oct 1929)/Third Lanark again 29 Apr 1930/Albion Rovers 17 Sept 1931.

Debut v Dundee
(h) 0-0 (SL)
31.10.25

Dan McColgan, "a tireless type, a thorough workman, a lad who believes in getting there first," played for Celtic in the five-a-sides at Hampden on June 6th 1925 and rumour buzzed that the club would use him as

Dan McColgan

a centre. He played centre-half (with Jimmy McStay right-half) on his debut and centre forward in place of McGrory on his second game (January 9th 1926). He was mainly appreciated at Cathkin Park where, as centre-half, "he strengthened and steadied the Warriors' middle line and bucked-up the whole side" (December 1926). At centre-forward he was "dashing, fearless... no finesse but shoots hard and often." Dan got a straight hat-trick for Thirds against Arbroath (February 5th 1927) and scored four for the Hi-Hi in the relegation battle versus Raith Rovers on January 5th 1929.

Appearances:
SL: 2 apps. 0 gls.
Total: *2 apps. 0 gls.*

McCOLL, James

Role: Centre-forward 1913-20
5' 7" 10st.10lbs.
b. Glasgow,
14th December 1892
d. Edinburgh, 7th March 1978

CAREER: Anderston Thornbank/St Anthony's 1911/CELTIC (trial) 20 Aug 1912/ CELTIC 27 Sept 1913/(Peebles Rovers loan 10 Oct 1913)/Stoke City 27 May 1920/Partick Thistle 1 Oct 1921/Hibernian 30 Sept 1922/ player-coach May 1926/Leith Athletic cs 1931 /Belfast Celtic coach 24 Sept 1932/Hibernian training staff 1934/asst. trainer 1937/trainer 3 Feb 1948/retired 1954.

Debut v Dundee (h) 1-0 (SL) 18.10.13

Celtic played Hibs at Ibrox in the frustrating 0-0 Scottish final of April 11th 1914. Jimmy McColl was drafted in at centre for the replay five days later and within ten minutes scored two goals "in slashing style." By August 21st 1915 the verdict was in: "It was just like old times to see a Celtic centre dash down the middle, no thought of numbers or distance. McColl is the new Quinn." "McColl the Sniper" was Celtic's centre in the Championship sides of 1915, 1916, 1917 and 1919 as well as during the great run of games without defeat between November 20th 1915 and April 21st 1917. Despite his slight build and lack of height, Jimmy McColl was brave as they come. Against Rangers in the League at Ibrox on October 20th 1917 he was in the box taking a buffeting Quinn-style yet still managed onto the end of Browning's cross to equalise for Celtic four minutes after Rangers had gone ahead. If Jimmy stayed clear of injury he could not help scoring goals and by May 5th 1917 had netted 89 in League and Cup since his debut. His second career lay with Hibs as "the best boy I ever signed" according to Alec Maley. He scored his first for the Edinburgh greens on October 21st 1922, rarely missed a game and the goals piled up over the years. Jimmy McGrory hit a hat-trick against Falkirk on January 7th 1928 to bring

Jimmy McColl

his League goals tally to 28. Right behind him was the Sniper, the veteran Hib, on 23. East played West for his benefit on September 13th 1927. A Hibs supporter was overheard on an Edinburgh tram in September 1928: "He's the best centre-forward in Scotland and he could be the grandfather o' some o' them! His fitba' boots are in his heid!" Jimmy was ever the available man at Easter Road and helped manager Walter Galbraith out after trainer Eddie Turnbull left on March 21st 1963. Hibs awarded him a gold watch in a public ceremony at Easter Road on August 2nd 1971.

Appearances:
SL: 165 apps. 117 gls.
SC: 4 apps. 6 gls.
Total: *169 apps. 123 gls.*

McCORMACK, Arthur Terence

Role: Right-back 1911-12
5' 11" 12st.0lbs.
b. Perth, 25th February 1887

CAREER: Perth St Leonard's 1908/
St Johnstone 1909/CELTIC 21 Aug 1911/
(St Johnstone loan 10 Jan 1912)/Merthyr Town
July 1912 until 1915.

Debut v Aberdeen (h) 1-0 (SL) 14.10.11

October 1911: "In McCormack Celtic have
made a great capture. Is he Scotland's coming
back?" Celtic played Rangers for Sunny Jim
Young's first benefit on
August 21st 1911 and
played junior
internationalist Arthur
McCormack at right-back
in the 0-0 draw. He was
signed immediately after
the game. Arthur had little
enough chance against
McNair and Dodds but had
also to compete for the
reserve spot with Tom
McGregor. Besides (which
is ominous) "he was a little
deficient in tackling and
did not kick a sufficient
length." Arthur seems to
have left Perth for Glasgow
during season 1909-10 and
was reading Law at the
University by October
1911. With Merthyr he had
"gained considerable speed
and improved immensely in his tackling"
(March 1915) and anticipated a return to
Scottish football.

Appearances:
SL: 1 app. 0 gls.
Total: *1 app. 0 gls.*

McCORMACK, Henry

Role: Inside-left 1917
5' 8" 11st.0lbs.
b. c 1897

CAREER: Denny Hibernian 1915/CELTIC
29 July 1917/Albion Rovers 18 Aug 1919/
Bathgate 7 Feb 1920.

Debut v Morton (a) 1-1 (SL) 1.12.17

"Brilliant junior" and "Class inside-left
forward" Harry McCormack played as Jimmy
McMenemy's deputy on the first two
Saturdays of December 1917 and scored
against Clydebank on December 8th. His
debut saw the diminutive Gallagher dismissed
for attentions to the robust and muscular Jacky
Wright (carried-off). (Patsy escaped with a
censure on the grounds of self-defence).

Appearances:
SL: 2 apps. 1 gl.
Total: *2 apps. 1 gl.*

McCREADIE, Bernard

Role: Goalkeeper 1955-57
6' 2" 12st.5lbs.
*b. Dumbarton,
23rd April 1937*

CAREER: Dumbarton
St Patrick's/Renfrew
Juniors/St Mirren (trial)
12 Feb 1955/Hibernian
(trial) 30 Apr 1955/
CELTIC 8 May 1955/
Rochdale 27 May 1957/
Oldham Athletic 17 Mar
1959/free 30 June 1959/
Clyde (trial) Aug 1959/
free 14 Sept 1959.

*Debut v Aberdeen (a) 1-0
(SL) 22.4.57*

Benny McCreadie

Benny McCreadie was one
of two junior goalies
taken-on by Celtic to cover
for the waning powers of Johnny Bonnar.
Benny got his one and only first team game
after the other tyro, Dick Beattie, had damaged
an ankle against St Mirren on April 17th 1957.
Bonnar played against Airdrie on Saturday
April 20th but "Big Ben" travelled to
Aberdeen on the Monday while "Coronation"
stayed behind in Glasgow to face Motherwell
in the 2nd XI Cup. Benny McCreadie was in
the USA by August 1966.

Appearances:
SL: 1 app. 1 shut-out.
Total: *1 app. 1 shut-out.*

McCULLOCH, Joseph

Role: Left-back 1940-41
5' 8" 11st.0lbs.
b. Ardrossan, 30th December 1918
d. Killed in action, 24th February 1945

CAREER: Ardrossan Winton Rovers/Third Lanark 19 March 1938/(CELTIC loan 23 Aug 1940)/6 Royal Scots Fusiliers 1941.

Debut v Hearts (h) 2-1 (RL) 24.8.40

A slater by trade and like Harry Dornan, a natural right-back, Joe McCulloch had his first game for Third Lanark on April 9th 1938. He was up against flying winger Kenny Dawson of Falkirk and showed himself "sharp in the tackle" with "ginger in the heels for recovery... a grand deputy for Jimmy Carabine." Joe won a Glasgow Cup medal with Celtic against Rangers at Ibrox on September 28th 1940. With Celtic he was reported "impetuous" in contrast with the initial studied cool of his successor, Roy Milne. He was capped for the Army in Scotland versus the Army in England (result 1-4) in place of Eddie Catlin of Sheffield Wednesday at Ibrox on November 30th 1940. He had his last game for Celtic at right-back for Bobby Hogg (playing for Scotland) in the 5-1 defeat of Partick Thistle in the League on February 8th 1941. He participated in the 1944 invasion of Europe and played for the 15th Division in matches to celebrate the liberation of Holland. As Warrant Officer Second Class (Company Sergeant Major), Joe lost his life travelling across difficult terrain near the Rhine in a turretless tank named the Kangaroo (so-called because it gave the impression of hopping). He is buried in Plot 9, Row E, Grave 5 in Jonkerbos War Cemetery, four kilometres south-west of Nijmegen. The son of Alexander and Jean McCulloch of Ardrossan, Joe belongs to the Roll of Honour of Celtic's Glorious Dead, especially as Third Lanark are now (sorrowfully) no more.

Appearances:
RL: 12 apps. 0 gls.
Total: *12 apps. 0 gls.*

McDERMOTT, Thomas

Role: Inside-forward 1901-03
5' 6" 11st.6lbs.
b. Bridgeton, 12th January 1878
d. Rutherglen, 1961

CAREER: Rutherglen Rosebank/Cambuslang Hibernian/Dundee 23 Sept 1899/CELTIC 26 Oct 1901/Everton 23 May 1903/Chelsea 16 Oct 1905/Dundee 17 Nov 1906/Bradford City (trial) 11 Apr 1908/Bradford City 6 July 1908/ Gainsborough Trinity 14 Nov 1908/ Kilmarnock 5 Jan 1909/Bradford City Mar 1909/Dundee Hibernian 10 June 1909/left Nov 1909/Anfield Royal Oct 1910/St Helen's Recreation Nov 1910/Wirral Railway 1911/ Vale of Leven 23 Feb 1912/Broxburn Shamrock 27 July 1912/Clyde 13 Apr 1913/ retired 1914/HLI (Black Watch) 1915.

Debut v Hearts (a) 2-2 (SL) 2.11.01

Tommy McDermott

"The finest footballer I ever saw. When I was a kid I used to watch him with intense delight when he played for Clyde. If ever there was a master of the ball it was Tommy. He could do what he liked with it" (Joe Cassidy 1924). "The greatest inside-forward of them all was that star of superlative brilliance, Tommy McDermott" (James Sharp: Memoirs). "He was the complete footballer. His ambling gait, the nonchalance with which he eluded tackles, his cleverness in spreadeagling a defence with a pass had the hallmark of genius. Bobby Walker, Jimmy McMenemy, Andy Cunningham, Alex James - Tommy could give them all points." (Dundee fan January 1951). Tommy McDermott and his Rutherglen pal Jimmy McMenemy both played in the Dundee pre-season trial of 1899. Both were offered terms but Napoleon returned to Glasgow. Tommy played a further trial against the famous English cracks, Wanderers, and was signed after the game. Celtic got him from Dundee for Davie Storrier and a fee. On his debut he "seemed under-trained, good for 20 minutes only." By the end of March 1902, McDermott was "now lasting the whole 90 minutes and getting more football in than anyone bar McMahon." It was Tommy made the back for Jimmy Quinn's climbing header in the last minute of extra time on June 17th 1902 at 2nd Hampden that beat Rangers 3-2 and brought the 1901 Glasgow Exhibition Cup to Celtic Park. He seems to have left Paradise amid a certain acrimony: "He had his own ideas of training and discipline... did not suit at Parkhead." By June 27th 1914 the verdict was in on this football nomad: "He simply could not stand prosperity. It was too much for him. Yet now that he is reduced to working for his living, I am proud to say that he gives every indication of becoming a good citizen." Tommy was alive and well in Rutherglen in 1959 and as a polished inside-forward in his time was inevitably critical of the modern game.

Appearances:
SL: 12 apps. 2 gls.
SC: 9 apps. 2 gls.
Total: *21 apps. 4 gls.*

MacDONALD, Malcolm (Calum)

Role: Utility 1932-45
5' 9" 11st.3lbs.
b. Glasgow, 26th October 1913

CAREER: St Roch's School/ Scottish Schools 1928/ Linwood St Conval's/ St Anthony's Aug 1931/ CELTIC 19 Mar 1932/ (Kilmarnock loan 15 May 1940 & 27 Oct 1945)/ Kilmarnock 31 Dec 1945/ Brentford 30 Oct 1946/ player-coach 1 June 1948/ Kilmarnock manager 9 Aug 1950/player again 1 Jan 1951/Brentford manager 1 July 1957/paid leave 2 Feb 1965/Kilmarnock manager 1 July 1965/Scotland interim manager Oct & Nov 1966/ dismissed at Kilmarnock 2 Apr 1968/Tottenham Hotspur scout 1970.

'Malky' MacDonald runs out onto Celtic Park to face Rangers in a Glasgow Cup semi-final match.

Debut v Partick Thistle (a) 2-0 (SL) 30.4.32 (scored twice)

Malky MacDonald was signed as a centre-half but in the League during 1932-33 "MacDonald was no third back. He came up with the ball and his passes were as good as you could wish. When it came to recovery, MacDonald was there." "MacDonald played centre-half like an inside-forward. He treated Neilly Dewar as if he did not exist." "MacDonald's footwork I have never seen excelled." "MacDonald is a born footballer with wonderful ball control but surely Celtic don't hope to start a revolution against the three-back game by playing him at centre-half? If they do, they may spoil a player who might be a star in any of the positions alongside or in front."

Q. Why was he so often out of the team in 1934?
A. "Because he is too clever."

Malky's role as pivot (Celtic did not play the third back game) was compromised by the arrival of Willie Lyon in 1935 as well as by chronic cartilage trouble starting in October. He recovered his fitness for 1936-37 and was the directorate's Golden Excuse for selling Willie Buchan in November 1937. He played a key role in the Glory Team of 1938 and got a hat-trick against Rangers on September 10th before appendicitis struck in November. Malky's game shaded with the outbreak of World War Two. He was working long night shifts and getting in only three hours training a week. All the same he was capped for Scotland at Newcastle on February 13th 1941 in the Red Cross international (right-half); at Wembley on October 4th 1941 (left-half) when he shook hands with Churchill; played in Delaney's come-back international at Hampden on April 22nd 1944 (right-back) and this time shook hands with Montgomery. His was one of the departures from Parkhead that broke the fans' hearts. Malky was as much part of the place as the crush barriers - if infinitely more subtle. On 19th January 1947, St Andrew's Halls were filled to capacity when he came back (with a broken jaw) for the presentation of his testimonial by the Celtic Supporters' Associations. "Perhaps this is the last link between Celtic and me but I ask you not to think of me as MacDonald of Kilmarnock or MacDonald of Brentford but as Malcolm MacDonald of Celtic." As Celtic's Dark Night deepened many diehards gave up in despair: "Ach, the only team I'm interested in now is Malky's!" Malky was a great club servant and an all-time great.

Appearances:
SL: 134 apps. 32 gls.
SC: 13 apps. 5 gls.
Total: 147 apps. 37 gls.
RL: 159 apps. 18 gls.
SWC: 2 apps. 0 gls.
RLC: 27 apps. 0 gls.
Total: 188 apps. 18 gls.

MacDONALD, Roderick

Role: Centre-half 1972-81
6' 1" 12st.9lbs.
b. Alness, 30th August 1954

Roddie MacDonald

CAREER: Invergordon Academy/ Easter Ross 1970/Brora Rangers 1971/CELTIC 5 Aug 1972/Hearts 7 July 1981/Morton 24 Sept 1987/ Partick Thistle 20 July 1989/free 6 May 1990/Queen of the South (trial) 1 Dec 1990/Irvine Meadow 10 June 1991.

Debut v Arbroath (a) 3-1 (SLC) 29.8.73

Big Roddie from Alness, Ross-shire was a Sammy Wilson discovery. Sammy recommended him to Celtic as a striker who had played trials for Leicester, Northampton and Morton aged 16. Celtic tried him out as a stopper against Queen's Park on August 2nd and Alloa on August 4th 1972 and after the 5-3 defeat by Hibs in the Drybrough Cup final on August 5th, Stein travelled north to sign the big Highlander. Billy McNeill played his last game for Celtic in the Scottish Cup final versus Airdrie on May 3rd 1975 with Roddie sitting on the bench. Jock Stein told him: "You'll be playing here next week" (versus Rangers in the Glasgow Cup final to celebrate Glasgow's 800th birthday). Roddie played his first Old Firm game, a 2-2 draw, under Jim Brogan's captaincy, before a crowd of 70,494. Like big Billy, he was an expert scorer of goals from set-pieces and earned a compliment from Rangers' Derek Johnstone: "He's as good as Douglas Bader in the air!" He was Sean Fallon's secret weapon at centre-forward against Sachsenring in the Cup-Winners' Cup in Zwickau (St Patrick's Day 1976) and scored a beauty with his head from a corner with five minutes to go, a goal annulled for a highly dubious infringement on Jurgen Croy. Roddie won everything in the air as a striker and certainly made room for Dalglish to play. He had the game of his life at centre-half in the Scottish Cup final of May 7th 1977 when Celtic beat Rangers 1-0. 1978 was far from a glory year for Celtic yet such were

Roddie's individual performances, his name was bruited for inclusion in the Scotland squad for the World Cup in Argentina, all the more so after Gordon McQueen's injury versus Wales on May 17th. On their day, Roddie and Johannes Edvaldsson were hailed as "the best centre-back pairing in Britain." Ally McCoist called the big Highlander "knife-sharp" as an opponent. A broken ankle against Morton on March 28th 1979 marked the beginning of the end of his fine stint as McNeill's successor and let Tom McAdam in. Celtic fans loved him and saw him leave for Tynecastle with regret. He played for Celtic again when they won the Old Crocks six-a-side UK Championship in 1992 along with Latchford, McGrain, Deans, Glavin, Sullivan, Casey and Joe Craig. Roddie scored the decisive penalty in the shoot-out after a 6-6 draw with Barnsley in the final.

Appearances:
SL: 166 apps. 22 gls.
SLC: 48 apps. 4 gls.
SC: 21 apps. 3 gls.
Eur: 17 apps. 5 gls.
Total: *252 apps. 34 gls.*

McDONALD, James

Role: Outside-right 1939; 1941-43
b. c 1922

CAREER: Blairhall Colliery/ CELTIC 28 January 1939/ paid-off Dec 1939/St Anthony's 1940/free 13 June 1941/CELTIC 13 June 1941/free 1943/Albion Rovers 3 June 1943/Armadale Thistle by 1946-47.

Debut v Hibernian (a) 1-0 (Summer Cup) 14.6.41

Blairhill Colliery was Celtic's Fifeshire nursery on the eve of World War Two and provided Celtic with Jimmy Birrell, Tom Harvey, James McMillan, Johnny Wilson and James McDonald. James was released for the Duration at the same time as Oliver Anderson and Tom Lyon but brought back just as Jimmy Delaney was resuming his career. He tried-out at inside-left in the pre-season trial of August 2nd 1941 and played against Rangers in the semi-final of the Glasgow Cup (September 29th 1941) when Celtic missed two penalties (MacDonald and Hogg) and scored one

(Dornan) in a 3-2 defeat at Hampden. Rangers had lost 8-1 to Hibs just two days before and Celtic fans in the 15,000 (quota) crowd kept the count up throughout the afternoon.

Appearances:
RL: 7 apps. 3 gls.
Total: *7 apps. 3 gls.*

McDONALD, John Neil

Role: Centre-forward 1951-53
5' 11" 12st.1lb.
b. Glasgow, 14th September 1931

CAREER: North Kelvinside School/Ashfield (trial) c 1948/Thermotank Amateurs Oct 1951/ Petershill Nov 1951/CELTIC 2 Dec 1951/ (Kilmarnock loan 6 Nov 1952)/(Leith Athletic loan 20 Dec 1952)/St Mirren 15 Dec 1953/ free 29 Apr 1954/ Petershill Aug 1954/ Berwick Rangers 1955 /Ardrossan Winton Rovers 1 Aug 1956.

Debut v St Mirren (a) 1-0 (SLC) 9.8.52 (scored once)

John McDonald

John McDonald left the RAF on October 8th 1951 and was suddenly a goal-scoring phenomenon with an average of two plus per game for Petershill as of November 17th (when he scored four on his debut). Grimsby offered £350 for his signature but Celtic took him and James Swan (Broxburn), another goalscoring junior at the same time. "Celtic's new Bhoy is worth watching" was the verdict on his debut. John managed only three appearances and one goal for Kilmarnock. That he failed to make the grade at either Parkhead or Rugby Park or Paisley was a source of wonder to many.

Appearances:
SLC: 2 apps. 2 gls.
Total: *2 apps. 2 gls.*

McDONALD, Patrick

Role: Left-back 1942-47
5' 9" 11st.0lbs.
b. Cambuslang,
19th April 1922

CAREER: St. Bride's
BG/Shawfield Juniors
26 Dec 1940/Airdrie
27 Nov 1941/free
31 Oct 1942/CELTIC
5 Dec 1942/Royal Navy
17 Feb 1945/(Raith Rovers
loan 14 Feb 1947)/
Dunfermline Athletic 1 Oct
1947/free 1 Dec 1949.

Pat McDonald

*Debut v Hamilton Academicals (a) 1-2
(RL) 5.12.42 (scored once)*

Airdrie took mining engineer Pat McDonald
as an inside-left and released him as "too
slow". He played his first game for Celtic at
outside-right on a day when both clubs were
in trouble putting teams out. The Hamilton
goalie was England great Frank Swift (died in
the Munich Disaster February 6th 1958)
serving with the Army in Scotland. Pat
McDonald beat him in the 89th minute at the
near post with a shot from the tightest of
angles. He took over at left-back from Harry
Dornan as of September 4th 1943 just before
the surrender of Italy. He was capped for
Scotland against the RAF (the virtual England
team) at Hampden on November 6th 1943:
"Time after time Matthews had the left-back
dizzy... but he never gave up." Pat was never
totally happy in a defensive role, always
wanting to play forward again and went on
the transfer list as of March 21st 1947. Raith
Rovers and Dunfermline both put their trust
in him as a defender and he was further
entrusted with the role of captain at East End
Road.

Appearances:
SL: 9 apps. 0 gls.
SLC: 5 apps. 0 gls.
Total: *14 apps. 0 gls.*
RL: 66 apps. 1 gl.
RLC: 9 apps. 0 gls.
Total: *75 apps. 1 gl.*

McDONALD, Thomas

Role: Inside-forward 1947-48

CAREER: Cleland St Mary's/
Royal Navy/St Roch's/Third
Lanark 24 Sept 1946/CELTIC
24 Oct 1947/Alloa 12 May 1948/
free 28 Apr 1949/Arbroath (trial)
25 Oct 1949/Crusaders (trial) Aug
1950/left Nov 1950.

*Debut v Queen of the South (h) 4-3
(SL) 25.10.47 (scored once)*

Third Lanark played Celtic in the
League Cup during their Hampden exile
on September 13th 1947 and reserve
McDonald scored twice in a 3-2 win ("Scoring
against Celtic was like having a tooth out").
(He had already scored three for the 3rds
reserves against Celtic on September 28th 1946
so the pain must have been intense). Tommy
was bought to solve a Celtic goalscoring crisis.
He had a magnificent game on November 15th
1947 when the
gates were closed
with 32,000
jammed inside
Firhill. Thistle led
2-0 inside 15
minutes then
Tommy scored to
make it 2-1 at
half-time. Thistle
went 3-1 ahead
ten minutes after
the interval,
Corbett scored
from a penalty
the next minute
and from that

Tommy McDonald

moment on, Celtic were a team inspired with
Tommy McDonald bringing Bogan onto the
game of his life. He got the final goal himself
in a 3-5 win and once again Glasgow echoed
to the news that Celtic were back! Celtic were
far from back and once into 1948 Tommy's
appearances in the big team were few as the
club struggled to stave off relegation.
Nevertheless he finished the season as club
top scorer on three goals less than ten.

Appearances:
SL: 13 apps. 7 gls.
SC: 1 app. 0 gls.
Total: *14 apps. 7 gls.*

McDONALD, William

Role: Full-back 1893-95

CAREER: Dumbarton Fern/CELTIC 8 Aug 1893/Everton 18 Mar 1895.

Debut v Leith Athletic (a) 0-5 (SL) 17.3.1894

Junior internationalist Willie McDonald played his first game for Celtic in a friendly against Battlefield on March 3rd 1894 when Dan Doyle was engaged in the International trials. The gate was a disaster: £2.16s. He went with Celtic on the Easter tour of Ireland where crowds were better. Willie came in for Tom Dunbar against Clyde in the Glasgow Cup (October 6th 1894) and played the next two Saturdays in the League at the time when Celtic were positively refusing a contribution to the Poor Children's Dinner Tables. His last game was in a friendly against Queen's Park on December 8th 1894. The Spiders won 4-0.

Appearances:
SL: 3 apps. 0 gls.
Total: *3 apps. 0 gls.*

McDOWALL, Daniel

Role: Inside-forward 1950-51
5' 10" 11st.0lbs.
b. Kirkintilloch, 22nd May 1929

CAREER: Kirkintilloch Rob Roy Juveniles/ Middlesbrough Feb 1947/Kilmarnock Nov 1949/CELTIC 21 Apr 1950/free 27 Apr 1951/ Workington Town Aug 1951/Lincoln City July 1953/Millwall June 1954 until 1956.

Debut v Dundee (a) 1-3 (SL) 20.1.51

Celtic made their final bid for Wilf Mannion at Ayresome Park on October 13th 1948. In April 1950 they signed the Middlesbrough Golden Boy's understudy, Danny McDowall and pitched him straight into the side that lost 3-2 to Irvine Meadow away in a benefit to raise money for the Catholic Young Men's Society annual outing for the OAPs. Danny played inside-right to Donald Weir. He made his big team debut out of position at outside-left to Bertie Peacock as a last minute replacement for the injured Tully. Dundee's South African right-back Gordon Frew, also a debutant, had been fully briefed on the opposition: "Tully likes a back to rush at him. Wait till he makes a move before you tackle." It was only in the

bath after the match he discovered he'd been holding off against Danny McDowall, not the great Charlie. Danny was released within six days of the Scottish Cup triumph of 1951. His career took up again in England ("He's the type who won't reach fruition until about 26") and Lincoln wanted the then quite considerable sum of £2,500 for his transfer in May 1954.

Appearances:
SL: 1 app. 0 gls.
Total: *1 app. 0 gls.*

McELENY, Charles

Role: Wing-half 1893-95; 1895-96
b. Glasgow, 6th February 1872
d. Greenock, 1st August 1908

CAREER: Greenock Volunteers/Abercorn/ CELTIC 2 Nov 1893/Burnley 9 Nov 1895/ CELTIC 2 May 1896/New Brighton 1897/ Aston Villa May 1899/Swindon Town May 1900/Brentford Aug 1901/Morton 20 Aug 1902.

Debut v Dundee (h) 3-1 (SL) 4.11.1893

Charlie McEleny collected his first medal against Queen's Park in the Charity Cup final on May 12th 1894 and from then on was an established first-teamer "with a never-tiring thirst for work." He won a second Charity Cup badge 4-0 versus Rangers at 1st Cathkin on May 25th 1895 with a typical sleeves-up-and-at-'em performance. For all his thunder on the field, Charlie was far from a fitness fanatic and the club's printed orders issued in August 1895 may well have had his lukewarm approach to training in view. Celtic's power-house left for Burnley and by March 1896 "Celtic (had) never parted with a better player." At Turf Moor he was arraigned for a formal apology to referee Straussen in front of witnesses including Jerry Reynolds after a rowdy altercation during the match.

> *Straussen: "Well, what have you to say for yourself?"*
> *Charlie: "You know it was no ****** penalty."*
> *(Exit).*

Burnley came to play at Parkhead on April 28th 1896 and Charlie ran the line for the black and gold. Back with Celtic, he collected his third Charity medal against Queen's Park after extra time on May 16th 1896. Again his stay at Parkhead was short, perhaps because he could no more stand the training disciplines of Jack Mullen than he had previously Tom Maguire's. Or maybe he was just a hard case.

Appearances:
SL: 30 apps. 1 gl.
SC: 4 apps. 0 gls.
Total: *34 apps. 1 gl.*

McELHANEY, Ralph

Role: Inside-right 1895
b. c 1877

CAREER: Dreghorn Juniors/Third Lanark 1894/CELTIC 27 Apr 1895/Clyde 2 Aug 1895/ Partick Thistle 24 Dec 1895/Tottenham Hotspur summer 1896/Swindon Town 1897/ Beith FC 13 Sept 1898/East Stirling 27 June 1899/Dunipace FC 28 Sept 1899/Brentford 31 Jan 1900/Grays United Jan 1903/Southall FC 1904.

Debut v Clyde (h) 2-0 (SL) 27.4.1895

Ralph McElhaney lined up for his Celtic debut with Charlie McEleny at right-half behind him and trialist Ching Morrison on his right. It was no humdrum end of season fixture. Clyde had twice beaten Hearts, the League champions, and were in special training to claim the championship of the East End. Next time Celtic and Clyde met at Parkhead on August 17th 1895, Ralph was at inside-left for the Bully Wee.

Appearances:
SL: 2 apps. 0 gls.
Total: *2 apps. 0 gls.*

McEVOY, Patrick George

Role: Half-back 1917-21
5' 7" 10st.10lbs.
b. Glasgow, 2nd May 1899

CAREER: St Anthony's/CELTIC (provisional) 1 Apr 1917/(full) 22 July 1918/(Dumbarton Harp loan 16 Aug 1919)/CELTIC again 29 Nov 1919 until spring 1921.

Debut v Hibernian (a) 3-0 (SL) 17.8.18

P.G. McEvoy (who won a prize for a hard trainer at Moore Park 1917-18) was recruited to see Celtic through the first half of 1918-19 when the club was strapped for choice of personnel. He made his Old Firm debut in the League at Parkhead on October 19th 1918

Pat McEvoy

when Celtic lost 0-3 but his glory day was just before the end of his stint as a first-teamer. Thistle had never beaten Celtic in the League but November 23rd 1918 was to be Der Tag. The fans were still queueing outside Firhill when Patsy got Celtic's goal three minutes before half-time. Inside Pat McEvoy and his mates held on throughout the second half for two precious points. Pat's contribution won him a Championship medal for 1919.

Appearances:
SL: 10 apps. 0 gls.
Total: *10 apps. 0 gls.*

McFARLANE, Hugh Morton

Role: Centre-half 1940
5' 11" 12st.0lbs.
b. Rutherglen, 1917

CAREER: Rutherglen Academy 1931/ Rutherglen Amateurs 1934/Rutherglen Glencairn 1934/Clyde May 1935/(Dumbarton loan 1936-37)/free 30 Apr 1938/Alloa 10 June 1938/(CELTIC loan 22 Mar 1940).

Debut v Dumbarton (h) 4-0 (RL) 23.3.40

Hugh McFarlane, "a tall bashful lad," was a newly-qualified doctor in Mearnskirk Hospital by the start of his loan period to Celtic in March 1940, brought in by his old boss at Recreation Park, Jimmy McStay. Ex-England international Clem Stephenson, manager of Huddersfield Town, had watched him at Recreation Park on August 12th 1939 and been hugely impressed. Hugh had played for Glasgow

Hugh McFarlane

Schools and Clyde as an inside-forward, been converted to half-back at Dumbarton and played his first game at centre-half for Alloa on December 3rd 1938. There were three centre-halves in the Celtic side on his debut: Teddy O'Neill, Malky MacDonald and himself. Willie Lyon had been dropped to let Hugh in but the rationale behind his recruitment as an addition to the glut of pivots was a mystery to the Parkhead faithful at a time when the attack cried out for strengthening.

Appearances:
RL: 5 apps. 0 gls.
Total: *5 apps. 0 gls.*

McFARLANE, John

Role: Left-half 1919-29
5' 7" 10st.10lbs.
b. Bathgate,
21st November 1899
d. 25th February 1956

'Jean' McFarlane

CAREER: Denbeath Star Juveniles/Wellesley Juniors/ Cowdenbeath (trial) Sept 1919/Raith Rovers (trial)/CELTIC Nov 1919/Middlesbrough 20 June 1929/Dunfermline Athletic 19 June 1934/retired 1935.

Debut v Motherwell (a) 0-0 (SL) 17.4.20

"Some player... his play lacked only devil." (Hughie Gallacher). John ('Jean') McFarlane, son of the manager of Bowhill Colliery, master of the "raking cross-field pass" was discovered by the immortal Pat Duffy as an inside-right with a "tea-team" and farmed out to Denbeath Star. Celtic signed him as an inside-right who "loved a fast sprint with the ball on his toe." In Patsy Gallagher's benefit versus Burnley on May 5th 1921 he came on for McMaster at left-half and supplanted the great Johnny's immediate deputy David Pratt nine days later in the Charity Cup final at Hampden when Celtic beat Rangers 2-0. Jean took part in the first post-War Scottish Cup triumph 1-0 versus Hibs on 31st March 1923 and from then on is identified with left-half in the Celtic memory. In 1923-24 no matter that Celtic were bad, McFarlane's game was pulling in the crowds. On Ne'erday 1924, he was "an artist all the time," "a glorious passer of the ball" and when Celtic beat Rangers in the Charity Cup

final on May 10th 1924, "McFarlane was in supreme form as a sixth forward." On September 26th 1924 Celtic beat Aberdeen 0-4 at Pittodrie. Chairman White in Glasgow: "I had to buy two papers to make sure my eyes were not deceiving me." Match report: "What a force McFarlane was!... he got the ball without difficulty... glided ahead, placed it where he chose." The Scottish final of April 11th 1925 is the match famous for Patsy Gallagher's equaliser but the winner is forgotten. It was a mighty goal scored by McGrory diving full-stretch to ram a perfect free-kick from McFarlane past future Celt Jock Britton. Jean McFarlane was a classic wing-half, a carpet artist and an all-time Celtic great.

Appearances:
SL: 268 apps. 11 gls.
SC: 36 apps. 2 gls.
Total: *304 apps. 13 gls.*

♣ **Celtic note:** *Jean McFarlane's (humorous) column was featured each weekend in the Weekly News. The player says it was a Celtic groundsman who first changed John to Jean.*

MacFARLANE, Robert

Role: Goalkeeper 1901-02
5' 11" 12st.2lbs.
b. Greenock, 14th May 1876
d. 27th July 1943

CAREER: Greenock Rosebery/Morton 17 Oct 1894/Third Lanark 9 May 1896/Everton 1897/ East Stirling 1898/Bristol St George's 1899/ New Brompton 1900/Grimsby Town Dec 1900 /CELTIC 6 May 1901/Middlesbrough Apr 1902/Aberdeen 2 July 1904/Motherwell 2 Feb 1909/retired 1909/to Australia 3 Sept 1909.

Debut v Third Lanark (n) 0-0 (CC) 9.5.01

"In his day a great goalkeeper" Rab MacFarlane was the original self-motivator: "When the ball is in midfield, he talks to himself, nods, gesticulates, exactly as though he were addressing a public meeting." Celtic brought him in as cover for McArthur but big Rab had none of wee Dan's suicidal tendencies: "It's better to lose a goal than a goalie." He played against Rangers in the Glasgow Cup final of October 26th 1901 "below form unless miracle saves required." In the Scottish Cup final at Parkhead (April 26th 1902), McGeachan of the Hibs nutmegged him with a back-heeler for the only goal of the game. He was sacked at Aberdeen on the (absurd) suspicion of having gifted Celtic a last-minute winner in the Scottish Cup semi-final at Pittodrie (March 21st 1908). Rab had his own confectionery business in Greenock in the '30s.

Rab MacFarlane

Appearances:
SL: 17 apps. 3 shut-outs.
SC: 6 apps. 1 shut-out.
Total: *23 apps. 4 shut-outs (17%).*

McGARVEY, Daniel

Role: Goalkeeper 1941
b. Clydebank, 16th September 1919

CAREER: Maryhill Harp 1940/(CELTIC loan 6 Dec 1941)/St Roch's 1945.
Debut v Dumbarton (h) 4-2 (RL) 6.12.41

Dan McGarvey was drafted in to play for Celtic when John Hunter was held up by War work and Jimmy Culley proved unavailable. He lost a goal in either half, the second to Gerry McAloon in 77 minutes by which time Dumbarton were fighting mad on the grounds that Delaney had handled for Celtic's third. Meanwhile, out there, the Japanese High Seas Fleet was steaming under radio silence towards Pearl Harbour...

Appearances:
RL: 1 app. 0 shut-outs.
Total: *1 app. 0 shut-outs.*

McGARVEY, Francis Peter

Role: Striker 1980-85
5' 10" 11st.0lbs.
b. Glasgow, 17th March 1956

CAREER: Colston Amateurs/Kilsyth Rangers Aug 1974/St Mirren 1974/Liverpool 4 May 1979/CELTIC 11 Mar 1980/St Mirren 12 June 1985/player asst. manager 20 Apr 1988/full assistant 9 May 1988/Queen of the South manager 6 July 1990/player-manager 8 Aug

1990/dismissed 6 Mar 1991/Clyde (trial) 21 Dec 1991/Clyde 20 Jan 1992/free 21 May 1993/Shotts Bon Accord cs 1993.
Debut v St Mirren (h) 2-2 (SL) 12.3.80

In 1974 Alex Ferguson took a chance on the waif-thin Frank McGarvey with a contract to the end of the season and saw his confidence rewarded as Frank's career took off after a summer of football on the sands in 1975-76. Jim Clunie summed the new star up: "He's brave and skilful in the box... the hallmark of all great goalscorers." Frank took a drop of £175 in basic wages to end the hiatus in his career at Liverpool and joined Celtic for a £325,000 fee. He was in the team that threw the 1980 League title away but which beat

Frank McGarvey

Rangers in the Scottish Cup final on May 10th. The Parkhead stand rose to its feet as the teams left the pitch at half-time on March 13th 1981 to applaud the glory of a McGarvey goal just scored. He had beaten defender after defender Patsy-style then crashed the ball past St Mirren's Billy Thomson. With Charlie Nicholas or George McCluskey for a partner, Frank spearheaded the Celtic attack in the Championship seasons of 1981 and 1982. Nicholas went off to sample the game in England in the summer of 1983 but Arsenal neglected to bid for McGarvey and Charlie, without Frank's "tireless running and tight control," would never be the same player anywhere again. Frank was now "the fastest striker in the Premier League, able to turn without losing momentum." Jock Stein watched him: "I wouldn't like to have played against him." Roy Aitken claimed the third goal against St Johnstone at Muirton Park on December 3rd 1983. Frank: "No, it was mine. I touched it in. That's my job." He was dropped for the home game against Aberdeen on March 31st 1984 and made his rejoinder: "I hope Jim Melrose gets a hat-trick." He accepted a year's contract in 1984 and became the first player to reach 100 Premier League goals (30 for St Mirren) on November 24th 1984. In the Scottish Cup final against Dundee United (May 18th 1985) after Celtic had trailed 1-0 until the 76th minute, it was his perfect header from Aitken's surge and cross that won the Cup with six minutes to go, a goal that paralleled almost to the second and the inch McGrory's of 60 years before. On the Monday following the miracle, manager Hay offered him a new contract which Frank described as "an insult." When Celtic won the League title at Love Street on May 3rd 1986, like everyone else, Frank knew they had left it late: "Celtic would have had the title wrapped up long ago had they held on to certain players." Frank McGarvey could fit into the attack of any Celtic side at any time in the club's history. He played seven times for Scotland.

Appearances:
SL: 168 apps. 78 gls.
SLC: 36 apps. 14 gls.
SC: 23 apps. 13 gls.
Eur: 18 apps. 8 gls.
Total: *245 apps. 113 gls.*

McGEE, Robert

Role: Centre-half 1922-24
5′ 10″ 11st.10lbs.
b. Mearns, 2nd September 1903

CAREER: Corkerhill Juniors/Eaglesham FC/ East Kilbride Thistle/CELTIC 22 Feb 1923 (St Mirren loan 26 Sept & 25 Oct 1923) (Stenhousemuir loan 8 Feb 1924)(Dumbarton loan 30 Apr 1924)/free 1924.

Debut v Rangers (a) 0-1 (GC) 15.9.23

Robert McGee

Joe Cassidy was selected as Celtic's centre for the match with Rangers but at kick-off time, Joe was a spectator; had the Dalbeth boy breached training regulations again? Or was his leg really that bad? The tyro McGee (not even a centre) lined up in his place. Once Rangers scored, 17 minutes into the second half, Adam McLean went into the middle and Robert more or less as a passenger to outside-left. Against Morton on February 2nd 1924 he was in his normal role of centre-half: "Memories of his first show... were obliterated from his first kick... and his long sweeping passes to either winger and an occasional deft slip up the middle evoked applause from the Parkhead followers." (Morton won 1-0). Robert was a highly-valued player at Ards and played centre-half for the Irish League against the League of Ireland during 1925-26.

Appearances:
SL: 1 app. 0 gls.
Total: *1 app. 0 gls.*

McGHEE, James

Role: Utility 1889; 1890-92
b. Lugar, Ayrshire
d. USA, circa 1945

CAREER: Cronberry FC 1878/Lugar Boswell Thistle 1880/Hibernian 1883/(St Bernard's loan 6 Apr 1889)(CELTIC loan 9 Aug 1889)/

Danny McGrain
is held aloft by
his team-mates
after leading
Celtic to the
championship
in 1982.

McGRAIN, Daniel Fergus M.B.E.

Role: Right-back 1967-87
5' 9" 12st.1lb.
b. Finnieston, 1st May 1950

CAREER: Camus Place Primary/Kingsridge Secondary/CELTIC 13 May 1967/QP Victoria XI (farmed-out) 1967/Maryhill Juniors (farmed-out) 1968/(Blackpool loan 1 Feb 1983) /free 12 May 1987/Rochdale Rovers (Brisbane) player-coach 8 July 1987/Hamilton Academicals 18 Aug 1987/coach 1988/ resigned 2 Nov 1988/Clydebank asst. coach/ Arbroath manager 10 Nov 1992/resigned 15 Jan 1994.

Debut v Dundee United (a) 2-2 (SLC) 26.8.70 (sub)

Sean Fallon was tipped-off about Danny McGrain by publican Tom Reilly but was warned the boy was a Rangers fan and playing for Scottish schools at Ibrox on May 13th 1967 (linkman in a 4-2-4). Sean visited the McGrain household, had tea with the parents, waited till Danny came home and left with the signature of an all-time Celtic great. At Parkhead, Danny made an immediate impression as a beautifully-balanced athlete of a full-back, a tigerish defender yet comfortable in attack (as great an exponent of the overlap as Jim Craig) with an almost telepathic under-standing to Dalglish. He was pitched into the Celtic side for the injured Davie Hay against Ujpest Dosza in the European Cup in Budapest (March 8th 1972) and "played like a king" against the likes of Horvath and Bene. He was in the Championship sides of 1973 and 1974 and won the Scottish Cup with Celtic in 1974 and 1975 as well as being the right-back in Dalglish's Double side of 1977. He was nominated Scotland's Player of the Year on April 26th 1977 and grew his Barabbas beard that summer in commemoration. He had an outstanding game for Scotland at Wembley on June 4th and on the SFA tour of South America gave Paolo Cesar of Brazil a very thin time at the Maracana on June 23rd. When Dalglish refused to tour Australasia in the summer of 1977, Danny took over as captain and was proclaimed "The Best Football Player Ever Seen in Australia." With Dalglish away to Liverpool, he became "the one world-class player left in Scotland." He published *'Celtic My Team'* on November 1st 1978 with reflections, shared already by most of the fans, on the awful season of 1977-78: (it was) "Bad enough to sit in the stand... after bad defeats, (but) certain players were swanning around, smiling to friends, signing autographs, not over-worried at placing the club at its lowest ebb in 13 years." Danny came back and skippered the Championship side of 1979. The only thing this master footballer did not possess was a decent shot. He tried one from long range in the Scottish Cup final of May 10th 1980 in the 17th minute of extra time. The effort was not a good one but George McCluskey stabbed at it, stranding Peter McCloy for the only goal, and shortly after Danny was lifting the Cup for Celtic. He was captain of the Champions of 1981, 1982, and 1986 besides raising the Cup for the second time on May 14th 1985. Celtic played his testimonial against Manchester United on August 4th 1980 before 45,000 at Parkhead and Glasgow honoured him with a civic medal for Services to Sport on September 14th 1987. Danny overcame a cracked skull (1972), diabetes (1974) and the mysterious but chronic ankle injury of 1977 that threatened his career. Scotland honoured him with 62 caps, a Celtic record until Paul McStay. The Queen awarded him the MBE on February 28th 1983. But above all, for a man who could have commanded his price like Hay, Macari and Dalglish, Danny was the Quality Street Kid who stayed.

Appearances:
SL: 439 apps. 4 gls.
SLC: 104 apps. 3 gls.
SC: 60 apps. 1 gl.
Eur: 54 apps. 0 gls.
Total: *657 apps. 8 gls.*

McGREGOR, Alexander

Role: Outside-right 1914
5′ 7″ 10st.10lbs.
b. Renfrew, 9th May 1896

CAREER: Renfrew Juniors 1912/Clydebank Juniors July 1913/CELTIC 27 Feb 1914/ (St Mirren loan 1914)/(Dumbarton loan Aug 1914)/(St Mirren loan 6 Mar 1915)/Clydebank 12 May 1916/Vale of Leven 1 Aug 1918/ Stevenston United Feb 1919.

Debut v Falkirk (a) 0-1 (SL) 28.2.14

Celtic tried out Alec McGregor ("fast, fairly clever and a good shot") against Wigtownshire then gave him his one and only League game at Brockville two days later in place of Andy McAtee. He played in the friendly against Middlesbrough on March 21st 1914 but did not go on the mid-European tour of that summer. He was in the Celtic squad for 1914-15 before moving down the Clyde to join the Sons.

Appearances:
SL: 1 app. 0 gls.
Total: *1 app. 0 gls.*

McGREGOR, Thomas

Role: Full-back 1910-19
5′ 8″ 11st.8lbs.
*b. Laurieston,
23rd November 1893*

Tom McGregor

CAREER: Laurieston Villa/ Kilsyth Emmet/CELTIC 14 Sept 1910/ (Motherwell loan Sept 1913)/(Dumbarton Harp loan Feb 1918)/ (Dumbarton loan Oct 1918)/(Clydebank loan 21 Dec 1918)/ (Dumbarton loan 21 Jan 1919)/ Motherwell 5 May 1919/(Alloa Athletic loan 6 Aug 1921)/ Alloa Athletic 29 Apr 1922/ retired 1924.

Debut v Hamilton Academicals (h) 3-0 (SL) 26.4.11

"There aren't many clubs who could have afforded to keep McGregor as a reserve for so long" (23rd February 1918). "McGregor possesses all the attributes of a first-class full-back." Celtic took "ruddy-countenanced Laurieston youth," Tom on the 1911 tour of Europe. Despite the total of first team games amassed, he was essentially a stand-by always ready to step in for McNair or Dodds as required. The high point of his career was

surely to be nominated reserve(!) right-back for Scotland against Wales at Parkhead on February 28th 1914. He got Alec McNair's place on the European tour of May 1914 and played in all five games including the bruiser against Burnley for the Budapest Cup on May 20th as well as in the replay at Turf Moor on September 1st 1914. He was in the Celtic side that beat Rangers 2-3 in the final of the Charity Cup at Ibrox on May 8th 1915 with the sinking of the Lusitania just hours before dominating the headlines. He cost Motherwell a substantial £400 when he moved from Parkhead. He went to Alloa on a year's transfer for £200 but Alloa paid another £200 to keep him in 1922.

Appearances:
SL: 77 apps. 0 gls.
SC: 3 apps. 0 gls.
Total: *80 apps. 0 gls.*

McGROGAN, Vincent

Role: Centre-half 1925-27
5′ 9″ 11st.7lbs.
b. Paisley, 12th November 1901

CAREER: Glenburn Rovers/Largs Thistle/CELTIC 12 Jan 1925/(Ayr United loan 28 Nov 1925)/(Armadale Thistle loan 18 Dec 1925).

Debut v Third Lanark (h) 7-0 (SL) 5.1.25

"McGrogan is a basher... not so much of it, Vincent, it doesn't pay." "McGrogan requires some subduing." Vincent McGrogan made his first appearance for Celtic on the day McInally ca'd the feet from under referee Russell and made his awful joke about preferring the Empire when ordered to the pavilion. Big Vinny took an early bath himself for "rough play" at Fir Park on January 17th 1925 ie trying to maim Hugh Ferguson. He and McInally appeared together for sentencing at 6, Carlton Place on January 21st 1925 while a huge crowd thronged outside. The Celtic mob were baying for the blood of referee Dougray who had ordered their Vincent off; the rest were Hi-Hi fans come to intimidate on behalf of McInally. Irony of fate: Vincent's knee took such a knock in the Scottish Cup against Solway Star on February 21st 1925 it ended his season and his career with Celtic.

Appearances:
SL: 5 apps. 0 gls.
SC: 1 app. 0 gls.
Total: *6 apps. 0 gls.*

McGRORY, James Edward

Role: Centre-forward 1922-37
5' 8" 11st.8lbs.
b. Garngad, 26th April 1904
d. Glasgow, 20th October 1982

CAREER: St Roch School/St Roch BG/St Roch Juniors/Bury (trial) 1921/CELTIC 10 June 1921/(Clydebank loan 7 Aug 1923)/Kilmarnock manager 18 Dec 1937/CELTIC manager 24 July 1945/Public Relations Officer 9 Mar 1965.

Debut v Third Lanark (a) 0-1 (SL) 20.1.23

"McGrory - you've got flat feet. People with flat feet cannot jump!" (Eddie McGarvie). "Shoulders like a young Clydesdale, neck like a prime Aberdeen Angus and a head the nightmare of every goalkeeper. He had the knack of connecting with his napper and directing the leather netwards with greater velocity and judgement than many a counterpart could accomplish with his feet" (Bill Paterson, ex-Arsenal May 23rd 1953). Jimmy McGrory saw himself as an inside-right and wondered how he could possibly displace a first-class reserve like Johnny McKay never mind Patsy Gallagher. Dun Hay made a centre of him at Clydebank as of September 29th 1923 but he was outside-left when he scored at Parkhead on March 4th 1924 "the goal that reminded Celtic I existed." Celtic took him on the tour of Lancashire over Easter 1924. He played but one game (versus Manchester United on April 16th) moving from left-wing to centre when Patsy was injured but doing enough to convince the Celtic officials that here was more than "just another india-rubber man." He opened the new season at Dundee on August 16th 1924: "Joe Cassidy's

The legendary Jimmy McGrory.

replacement was not wide-awake... he did not rise to the occasion." McGrory: "I didn't know where I was. I was being told Hold it! Give it! Out right! Out left! all at the same time." One week later: "Young McGrory was leading his forwards like a veteran... showed dash, distribution reminiscent of Jimmy Quinn." On April 11th 1925 Jimmy 'arrived' at Hampden in all sorts of ways when he flew through the air "from a seemingly impossible position" to meet a Jean McFarlane free-kick with minutes to go and butt it high into the net for a glory of a goal that won the Scottish Cup for Celtic.

The Jimmy McGrory goals which equalled and then beat Steve Bloomer's British record league tally of 352. No. 352 (left) came against Airdrie at Celtic Park in October 1935 and the 353rd (right) was a diving header against Aberdeen on New Year's Eve, 1935.

Jimmy McGrory with a very young looking Jock Stein (right).

No Celt since Sandy McMahon scored more goals with his head but Jimmy was no slouch when it came to footwork. At Ibrox on October 20th 1928, he hooked the ball over the head of one Ranger, then another, before crashing it past Jerry Dawson. In common with Jimmy Quinn, he took some stick. His nose was broken almost as often as Hugh Hilley's. Within a matter of weeks till his marriage, he had his jaw broken by future Celt and FIFA man Jimmy McGuire in the match against Brooklyn Wanderers on June 7th 1931. He scored the only goal of the 1933 Cup final on April 15th but had played on with two broken teeth and a cut lip after a collision with Jimmy Crapnell in the opening minutes. As the poet put it: *Oft indeed he feels most grateful/To escape from the attack/With his head upon his shoulders/And his jersey on his back.* Then there was the verbal abuse. Johnny Thomson complained when an opponent called him (a good church-going Protestant boy) a "Fenian bastard." "John, I get called that every game I play." "I know. It's all right for you. You are one!" Jimmy's second goal against England on April 1st 1933 inaugurated the Hampden Roar: "The tumult from 134,170 throats when McGrory took Scotland's goal eight minutes from time will never be forgotten." His own roar when Alan Craig put Bertie Thomson's cross through his own goal in the last seconds of the Scottish Cup final (April 11th 1931) was audible in the Hampden stand. His greatest headed strike was one that was disallowed (offside) versus St Mirren in the Scottish Cup 4th round on March 3rd 1934. With Celtic 1-0 down, Bobby Hogg hit a clearance out of his own half deep into the Buddies' penalty box. The Golden Crust "was off the mark like a flash" to meet the dropping ball on the 12 yard mark and thunder it past McCloy with

unbelievable force. Celtic trainer Jack Qusklay (who treated his broken teeth at Hampden in 1933) described it years later as the greatest headed "goal" he ever saw. Jimmy was a total jersey player and resisted all Willie Maley's subtle attempts to deliver him to Herbert Chapman in London going to and coming from Lourdes in the summer of 1928. He wanted Celtic and Celtic only. (Unknown to Jimmy, who was useless with money, his loyalty cost him a penalised wage packet for the rest of his time with Celtic). Jimmy equalled Steve Bloomer's British League goals aggregate on the half-hour against Airdrie at Parkhead on October 19th 1935 (352 goals) and passed it with six minutes to go. On a heavily-sanded pitch at Parkhead and the lochs frozen over in Argyll he passed Hughie Ferguson's aggregate of 364 League goals with a diving header from the edge of the six-yard box in the 36th minute on December 21st 1935. How he made contact with the ball no one knew. It was his favourite goal of the many he scored. His epitaph? "No ball too hopeless to chase... he never gave the defence a moment's peace." Jimmy McGrory was a Celtic all-time great. And then something.

Appearances:
SL: 378 apps. 398 gls.
SC: 67 apps. 74 gls.
Total: *445 apps. 472 gls.*

♣ **Celtic note:** *Jimmy was top League goalscorer in Europe 1926-27 (49) and 1935-36 (50).*

McGRORY, John

Role: Centre-half, centre-forward
1946-54
6' 1" 13st.1lb.
b. Linwood, 31st August 1928
d. Linwood, 12th November 1991

CAREER: Maryhill Harp/CELTIC
24 May 1946/Albion Rovers 18 Sept
1953/St Mirren 14 May 1954/Albion
Rovers (trial) 7 Aug 1956/retired
19 Dec 1956/Johnstone Burgh coach
1958.

Debut v Clyde (h) 3-6 (SLC) 9.10.48

"Celtic's one idea is to give the ball to
McGrory. He can shoot but he's got no
control" (February 14th 1953). Johnny
McGrory "arrived" first as a centre-
half in the Danny Kaye Charity Cup
final at Hampden versus Rangers
before a crowd of 81,000 on May 6th
1950 when Celtic won 3-2 and the
papers proclaimed the big Celtic
stopper "the new George Young." Other
voices advised caution. Johnny had been
pulled all over by place by a fast, mobile
centre called Lawrie Reilly at Easter Road on
February 4th 1950 and conceded three
penalties; another shifter called Neilly Mochan
virtually ended his career as a pivot with three
goals for Morton at Parkhead on September
9th 1950. Behind the scenes, Johnny was
known to his mates as "Derek Dooley"
because he enjoyed playing centre so much in
practice games. He was picked in the attack
against Montrose reserves on January 3rd 1953
and scored a hat-trick. In the Scottish Cup at
Eyemouth on January 24th he beat wonder
goalie Alex "Tension" Patterson four times to
send Celtic through 0-4 to Stirling (where he
scored again). The fight-back at Brockville in
the Scottish Cup on February 21st 1953 is
normally associated with Tully, Tully and
Tully. In fact, the score was 2-2 with five
minutes to go when centre forward McGrory
received the ball facing his own goal, turned
on a sixpence and shot deep into the Falkirk
net for the winner. He was so overwhelmed
with congratulations from his team-mates and
fans he had to have the attentions of trainer
Alex Dowdells before he could resume. Big
John had just abandoned his apprenticeship
when he broke his leg with St Mirren reserves
on February 26th 1955. He retired when he

*John McGrory (right) prepares for the 1951
St Mungo Cup wth Alec Boden.*

realised the limb was no longer up to the
demands of the first-class game. He did a
great job with the Four-Cup Johnstone Burgh
team of 1958-59. John got a great deal of
pleasure out of football. He was one of the
very few who look as if they are actually
enjoying themselves as they play.

Appearances:
SL: 38 apps. 3 gls.
SC: 9 apps. 0 gls.
SC: 11 apps. 8 gls.
Total: *58 apps. 11 gls.*

McGUGAN, Paul

Role: Centre-half 1980-87
6' 2" 12st.0lbs.
b. Glasgow, 17th July 1964

CAREER: Eastercraigs Amateurs/CELTIC
(provisional) Apr 1980/(full) 9 Oct 1980/
Barnsley 15 Oct 1987/(Chesterfield loan
24 January 1991)/Chesterfield 26 Feb 1991.

Debut v Hibernian (h) 3-2 (SL) 28.4.84

Paul McGugan first played for Celtic as a
substitute in the Glasgow Cup final versus
Rangers on May 13th 1982 and scored the

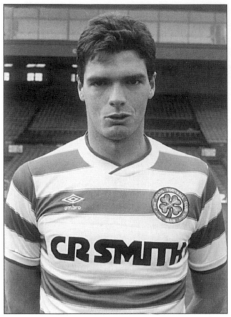

Paul McGugan

McGUIRE, Douglas John

Role: Striker 1984-88
5' 8" 11st.4lbs.
b. Bathgate, 6th September 1967

CAREER: Celtic BC/CELTIC 1984/
(Dumbarton loan 13 Feb 1988)/(Sunderland
loan 26 Mar 1988)/Coventry City 10 Aug 1988
/free Nov 1990/Cumnock Juniors Jan 1991/
Queen of the South 12 June 1991.

Debut v Falkirk (h) 4-2 (SL) 22.11.86 (sub)

Irvine boy and mazy dribbler Dougie McGuire
("the most wanted footballer in the country"
aged 13) went on the Celtic tour of Ireland in
1986 and came on as a sub for Owen
Archdeacon versus Longford on July 27th and
Cobh Ramblers on July 31st. He subbed again
for 'Dancer' against Aston Villa and Paul
Elliott on August 2nd 1986 and took over from
Tony Shepherd in the 70th minute on his
League debut. Eight minutes later he set up
Celtic's third goal for Mo Johnston. His
biggest night as a Celtic player was
undoubtedly going on for Andy Walker in the
away leg of the UEFA Cup (September 29th
1987) versus Borussia in Dortmund before
54,000 fans. He joined Coventry for £40,000
and was almost at once struck down by a form
of glandular
fever that
literally laid him
low in training.
He went into
hospital for tests
but was never
wholly a well
man with the
Sky Blues. On
his good days,
he was sheer
class. With
Scottish
schoolboys at
Wembley on
June 12th 1983
he inspired the
fight-back from
1-3 down to 3-3.

winner seven minutes from time. Such was his
form in the reserves, he was drafted into the
Celtic squad for the home leg of the European
tie versus Sporting Lisbon on November 2nd
1983. He had an outstanding match at Easter
Road (August 11th 1984) and showed "fine
touch for so big a player." He broke into the
first team against Hibs in Edinburgh as of
September 7th 1985 and capped some fine
performances with a headed goal from height
against Rangers in the ninth minute of the
Ne'erday game at Parkhead 1986. As he came
down, an awkward landing broke a bone in
his foot. He made a good recovery and shared
in an even better one when Celtic stole the
Championship from Hearts' grasp at the death
(May 3rd 1986) at Love Street. He missed the
Dubai Cup match against Liverpool on
December 9th 1986 through not being
inoculated in time. Barnsley paid £55,000 for
his transfer. He suffered a double fracture of
the left leg in a clash with Ipswich's Dalian
Atkinson (February 21st 1989).

Appearances:
SL: 49 apps. 1 gl.
SLC: 5 apps. 0 gls.
SC: 2 apps. 0 gls.
Eur: 3 apps. 0 gls.
Total: *59 apps. 1 gl.*

Appearances:
SL: 2 apps. 0 gls.
Eur: 1 app. 0 gls.
Total: *3 apps. 0 gls.*

*Dougie McGuire with
the Scottish Premier
League Championship
trophy.*

Jimmy McGuire

McGUIRE, James C.

Role: Right-back 1948-50
5' 11" 12st.7lbs.
b. Plains, 1927

CAREER: St Margaret's BG (Airdrie)/
Wolverhampton Wanderers Oct 1943/
Hibernian 28 Apr 1945/(Alloa loan 12 Aug
1946)/Aberdeen 5 Aug 1947/free 1948/
CELTIC 10 Aug 1948/free 1950/Shamrock
Rovers 1950/Waterford/Kidderminster
Harriers Aug 1952/Berwick Rangers July 1955
/free 5 May 1956/Stranraer 9 Aug 1956/free
1958.

Debut v Hibernian (a) 2-1 (SL) 30.10.48

Jimmy McGuire, an uncompromising full-back
nicknamed 'Killer' by the fans, made his debut
in place of Jimmy Mallan who had broken a
bone in his back in a rough-house against
Dundee the week before. Jimmy went on the
Highland Tour of 1949 when Tully and Weir
sang 'Home, Sweet Home' for the inmates of
Peterhead Prison (April 5th 1949); played in
the Battle of Millwall (April 25th 1949); and
missed a Charity Cup medal by losing to

Thistle in the sun at Hampden on May 9th
1949. The highlight of his stay at Celtic was
the opening day of the season 1949-50 when
Rangers were beaten 3-2 at Parkhead in the
League Cup on Bobby Collins' debut. He
brought Findlay crashing down for the
penalty that put Rangers in the lead on the
quarter-hour: "McGuire's awkward ways
must have been worrying to the Parkhead
crowd." Celtic played Hibernian in "a near
perfect display of the soccer arts" on
September 17th but "McGuire... frequently
threatened to disturb the harmony by the
sheer crudity of his tackling." Rangers were
Jimmy's nemesis: he lost his place for good
after a 4-0 massacre in the League at Ibrox on
September 24th 1949. With Shamrock Rovers
he was tipped for a League of Ireland cap
versus the Scottish League (17th January 1951)
and Aston Villa were reputedly taking an
interest.

Appearances:
SL: 14 apps. 0 gls.
SLC: 4 apps. 0 gls.
Total: *18 apps. 0 gls.*

McGUNNIGLE, Thomas

Role: Outside-right 1931-32
b. Glasgow, 31st March 1905

CAREER: Maryhill Hibernian/CELTIC 5 May
1931/Glentoran Oct 1932/Bangor Dec 1932/
Dumbarton 1933/Cork 1934/Brideville 1935/
Dumbarton 1936/Brechin City Oct 1937/
...St Roch by 1944.

Debut v Airdrie (a) 1-1 (SL) 9.4.32

With St Roch's in 1944, Tommy McGunnigle
(Peter's cousin) was "as nimble-footed and
alert as ever." He was Bertie Thomson's
understudy throughout his time at Parkhead
and got his chance at Broomfield in the rain
when Bertie was injured and Charlie Napier
playing for Scotland at Wembley. He went on
the tour of Ireland and had his last game for
Celtic in the shock defeat at Dundalk on April
19th 1932 (after which some Celtic players are
said further to have engaged opponents in the
dressing room areas).

Appearances:
SL: 1 app. 0 gls.
Total: *1 app. 0 gls.*

McILHATTON, John

Role: Inside-right 1940
5' 8" 11st.0lbs.
b. Ardeer, 3rd January 1921
d. Ardrossan, 13th February 1954

CAREER: Ardeer Recreation/CELTIC (trial)
23 Nov 1940/Albion Rovers 3 Jan 1942/
Everton 24 Apr 1946/Dundee 20 July 1949/
Raith Rovers 20 Nov 1950/Barry Town
summer 1951 to 1952.

Debut v Hamilton Academicals (a) 0-1 (RL)
23.11.40

Johnny
McIlhatton
played out-
side-right to
Tommy
Kiernan at
Albion Rovers
and together
they formed a
free-scoring
combination.
Webber Lees
persuaded
him to sign
for wee
Rovers after
Celtic told
him to wait a
bit. He was a
great dribbler,
a maker of
goals who
could also
score. Celtic

Johnny McIlhatton

wanted both him and Kiernan but by January
1946 McIlhatton, a welder in the Ardrossan
shipyards, was the hottest property in UK
football. He could have gone anywhere but
chose Everton who paid £5,000 for him, a
hefty sum in 1946. He played his last game for
wee Rovers (and scored) on the night he
signed for the Toffees. Theo Kelly, Everton
secretary, told Webber Lees a few weeks later:
"In Johnny McIlhatton we have as good a
player as Stanley Matthews." After Johnny's
early death Pat O'Sullivan organised
fund-raising for his widow and children.

Appearances:
RL: 1 app. 0 gls.
Total: *1 app. 0 gls.*

McILROY, James

Role: Centre-half 1950-56
6' 2" 12st.0lbs.
b. Glasgow, 19th July 1930

CAREER: Partick United/Duntocher
Hibernian 23 Jan 1950/CELTIC 19 July 1950/
Third Lanark 1 Mar 1956/free 1956/Barrow
26 June 1956.

Debut v Hibernian (a) 1-1 (SL) 6.12.52
(scored once)

Celtic played under lights in the UK for the
first time in the 20th century versus Doncaster
Rovers at the Belle Vue Ground on November
18th 1952. "Big, smiling Jimmy McIlroy" was
with the RAF locally and training with Peter
Doherty's Rovers so Celtic played him at
centre-half in the 3-2 defeat. His next game in
the colours was his League debut. He played
centre and was a sensation: "Big Jim Brought
Joy to Celtic!" He scored a "Wonder Goal":
picked up a George Hunter clearance, bored
right through the middle of the Hibs defence
and crashed a glory ball past Younger. He
played against Dundee at Parkhead the
following week and "led the line with the
coolness of a veteran." He scored in the last
minute from the tightest of angles in the box,
"a fleeting figure in the half-light." Jim's
promise faded over the New Year 1953. He
became Jock Stein's understudy in the Double
side of 1953-54 but experienced a disastrous
triple fracture of the leg and was in plaster
and on sticks until almost close season 1954.
Joe Harvey took him to Barrow.

Appearances:
SL: 11 apps. 3 gls.
SLC: 1 app. 0 gls.
Total: *12 apps. 3 gls.*

McILVENNY, Henry

Role: Centre-forward 1895-96; 1896-97; 1904-05

CAREER: Parkhead Juniors/CELTIC 24 Sept
1895/(Dumbarton loan Dec 1895)/Burnley
Sept 1896/CELTIC 6 Nov 1896/New Brighton
1897/Victoria United 6 Dec 1897/Belfast Celtic
Sept 1898/St Bernard's 27 Nov 1900/Hamilton
Academicals 8 Aug 1902/Partick Thistle
15 June 1904/CELTIC 29 Oct 1904/Hamilton
Academicals 1 June 1905/Ayr FC 13 Aug
1906/retired 1907.

Debut v Dumbarton (a) 3-2 (SL) 28.9.1895

Harry McIlvenny played his first game for Celtic at Preston on September 21st 1895 when the team appeared in an unfamiliar broad green stripe. He got his chance in his second phase as a Celtic player in the wake of the suspension of the three strikers, Battles, Meehan and Divers. During this second spell he played against Hibs at home on Ne'erday 1897 in a friendly with disaster just eight days off in the Scottish Cup: Arthurlie 4, Celtic 2. The Barrhead men scored in 12 minutes, Harry equalised in 20 but when it came to the post-mortem, he was summarily sacked. He returned to Celtic for a third spell seven years later. He played in the famous fixture at Ibrox on January 2nd 1905 when Mr Lewis of Blackburn abandoned the game because of the press of fans obliterating the touch-lines. His positively last game for Celtic was at Broxburn to raise funds for the local RC band on May 10th 1905

Appearances:
SL: 9 apps. 1 gl.
SC: 2 apps. 1 gl.
Total: *11 apps. 2 gls.*

McINALLY, Alan Bruce

Role: Striker 1984-87
6' 2" 11st.6lbs.
b. Ayr, 10th February 1963

CAREER: Ayr United BC/Ayr United 30 July 1980/CELTIC 12 May 1984/Aston Villa 20 July 1987/Bayern Munich 13 June 1990/retired summer 1992/Ayr United as free agent (one game) 30 July 1993/Kilmarnock 4 Feb 1994/free 14 May 1994.

Debut v Hibernian (a) 0-0 (SL) 11.8.84 (sub)

Alan McInally, son of the great Jackie of Kilmarnock in the 1960s, was a rare sight in his first season at Parkhead as the result of a mysterious back injury sustained during limbering-up at Love Street on September 22nd 1984. He was a hardly more common sight during 1985-86 and, but for a productive spell in his third and last season, his career as a Celt might well have vanished without trace. Graham Taylor took him to Aston Villa and would have sold him to St Mirren had not 'Rambo' again come to life and taken the English First Division by storm with 19 goals

Alan 'Rambo' McInally takes on his namesake Jim McInally, the Dundee United number four, once of Celtic (see over).

scored by the end of Boxing Day 1988: "At Celtic Park we were only back in the afternoons pre-season. At Villa I'm back regularly for specialised training for strikers" (October 11th 1988). At Bayern, Big Alan was a martyr to the knee trouble that forced his early retirement. He was working under physiotherapist Brian Scott at Parkhead in February 1993 in the hope of a come-back which started with Ayr against Kenny Dalglish's Blackburn Rovers. He trained with Everton at the start of 1993-94 without achieving a sufficient level of fitness to satisfy the club. Tommy Burns gave him his chance at Kilmarnock.

Appearances:
SL: 65 apps. 17 gls.
SLC: 11 apps. 4 gls.
SC: 5 apps. 1 gl.
Eur: 4 apps. 0 gls.
Total: *85 apps. 22 gls.*

McINALLY, Arthur

Role: Centre-half 1917
5' 9" 12st.3lbs.
b. Barrhead, 15th September 1900

CAREER: St Mungo's Academy/Barrhead Belmont/Kirkintilloch Rob Roy 1916/ St Mirren Juniors/Croy Celtic/CELTIC 9 July 1917/(Ayr United loan Oct 1917)/(Dumbarton Harp loan Feb 1918)/St Mirren 1 Aug 1918/ free 1919/Abercorn 5 Nov 1919/Dunfermline Athletic 22 Jan 1920/Armadale 8 July 1921/ Alloa 27 May 1922/(Clyde loan 6 Sept 1923)/ St Bernard's 28 Aug 1924/SL Div 2 referee 1 Aug 1929/St Anthony's secretary-manager 1935.

Debut v Motherwell (a) 4-3 (SL) 15.12.17

Arthur McInally

"A slow player but sure... a destroyer but also a builder," Arthur McInally was Tommy McInally's big brother (putative) and as occasion demanded, his agent. He played only 77 minutes of football for Celtic. Despite a delayed kick-off, Alec McNair failed to appear for the match against Motherwell and Celtic started with 10 men.

Within 13 minutes they were 0-2 down and Arthur was flung on to stem the flood. He made his debut for Dunfermline on January 31st 1920: "His ground passes were models of accuracy, his headwork was superb." He was involved in a very peculiar suspension in 1923 when Hamilton Academicals and Clyde got into a tangle over his transfer from Alloa. Arthur was banned from football for the best part of a season although he himself had broken no specific rules. He was described as "in a class by himself" in December 1921 and Celtic were rumoured to be manoeuvring to get him back. He was a schoolmaster when not playing football.

Appearances:
SL: 1 app. 0 gls.
Total: *1 app. 0 gls.*

McINALLY, James Edward

Role: Left-back 1980-84
5' 7" 10st.4lbs.
b. Glasgow, 19th February 1964

CAREER: Celtic BC/CELTIC 9 Oct 1980/ (Dundee loan 28 Mar 1984)/Nottingham Forest 18 May 1984/Coventry City 23 Jan 1986 /Dundee United 12 May 1986.

Debut v Dunfermline Athletic (a) 7-1 (SLC) 28.8.82

"A tireless, versatile player," Jim McInally was signed by Billy McNeill at the age of 16 and under McNeill was first reserve to Mark Reid. He played initially for Celtic against Queen's Park in the Glasgow Cup of October 13th 1981. Charlie Nicholas reckoned him "the best young player around" in April 1983, but Davie Hay came in as manager and Jim dropped to fourth choice left-back. Out on loan to Dens Park, he scored the goal that kept Dundee in the Premier Division in 1984. Hay offered him a new contract and a 50% salary rise but when the player thought his chances might be better elsewhere, let him go for "a nominal fee" to Forest as cover for Viv Anderson and Kenny Swain. Forest sold him on to Coventry for £80,000. At Dundee United he switched to midfield, where Jim McLean acknowledged him "the best in the position since George Fleming or Iain Phillip." Andy Roxburgh gave him his first Scotland cap on April 1st 1987. Jim marked Paul McStay out of the game at Parkhead on Boxing Day 1992 in the 0-1 defeat

Jim McInally

that extinguished Celtic's last hopes of the Flag for 1993. On the debit side, he was in the 'leaden-footed' Scotland team whacked 5-0 by Portugal on April 28th 1993. He scored his first goal of 1993-94 against Aberdeen on April 12th to put Dundee United into the Scottish Cup final versus Rangers on 21st May. After being a losing finalist in 1987, 1988 and 1991 Jim was part of Ivan Golac's Tannadice team that took the Cup from Rangers at Hampden and deprived them of a back-to-back treble.

Appearances:
SL: 1 app. 0 gls.
SLC: 1 app. 0 gls.
SC: 1 app. 0 gls.
Total: *3 apps. 0 gls.*

McINALLY, John

Role: Inside-forward 1934-37
5' 9" 11st.4lbs.
b. Blantyre, 17th May 1915

CAREER: Wishaw Juniors/CELTIC 17 Apr 1934/Arbroath 8 Sept 1937/(Motherwell loan 12 Jan 1940)/RAF 1941/ (Albion Rovers loan Sept 1943)/(Clachnacuddin loan 24 Nov 1945)/(Leicester City loan 1945-46)/ demobbed Mar 1946/free (from Motherwell) 24 Apr 1946/Arbroath again 12 Aug 1946/Queen of the South 7 Oct 1946/ Cowdenbeath 1947/Ballymena United 1947/ free own request 1948/Albion Rovers 30 Sept 1948/free 1 Nov 1948/to Los Angeles/ ...Wigtown & Bladnoch 29 Sept 1951.

John McInally

Debut v Kilmarnock (h) 4-1 (SL) 11.8.34
(scored once)

When John McInally signed for Celtic he was "as good a player as Wishaw has turned out in ten years." John was one of a bunch of new players in 1934: James Foley, Dan Clancy, a certain James Delaney and Carmyle boy Tom Ryan. "He likes the tackle before beating his man... he looks like helping to set Celtic on their previous lofty pedestal." John's promise did not evaporate. He just could not get his place against Buchan and Crum. With Arbroath and Motherwell he was outstanding. He turned Arbroath's 1937-38 season round and scored the clincher in a great 2-0 win over Celtic at Gayfield on October 9th 1937. He was at inside-left at Fir Park on October 19th 1940, the day Motherwell led 5-0 with three minutes to go and Malky MacDonald at last got one for Celtic. John was a bricklayer by trade and a Physical Training instructor in the Air Force.

Appearances:
SL: 9 apps. 4 gls.
Total: *9 apps. 4 gls.*

McINALLY, Thomas B.

Role: Centre-forward 1919-22;
inside-left 1925-28
5' 8" 11st.2lbs.
b. Partick, 18th April 1900 (?)
d. Paisley, 9th September 1955

CAREER: St Mungo's Academy/Croy Celtic 1915/St Anthony's 1917/Rangers (two trials) 1918-19/CELTIC 22 May 1919/Third Lanark 4 Sept 1922/CELTIC 12 May 1925/Sunderland 25 May 1928/Bournemouth 24 Nov 1929/free 2 June 1930/Morton (short contract) 31 Oct 1930/Derry City (short contract) Jan 1931/Armadale (Scottish Cup) 21 Jan 1933/Nithsdale Wanderers 1933 until 1937/CELTIC scout 16 Jan 1948.

Debut v Clydebank (h) 3-1 (SL) 16.8.19
(scored three)

"A lad of moods" with "a humour all his own that needs study to be appreciated," Tommy McInally had two stints at Celtic Park and one good season in each ie the first: 1919-20 and 1925-26. 'Snally' was hugely talented and Powderhall fast. As a centre he was "the apostle of direct action" with a vicious shot as soon as the gap appeared and as an inside-forward was Celtic's general when the League was won in 1926 and the Cup so narrowly missed. What he was unable to do was take his fitness seriously or a joke lightly. He degenerated into a lazy player, a prima donna, "a first-half man," if even that. By January 1922, he was

Tommy McInally

"completely dis-heartened" by bar-racking occasioned by his own lack of application. "His sensitive nature is very susceptible to this unfair treat-ment resulting in deterioration of form." His second spell at Parkhead wrought no change of heart. Celtic lost 1-2 to Motherwell in the League race on December 3rd 1927: "McInally was deficient in every phase... it is no use trying to walk through a match... his stand and wait policy cut no ice." Celtic suspended him on December 10th, no reason given and Tommy went off to watch Arthurlie. He and Maley were reconciled on Boxing Day. In early March 1928, on the eve of the vital Scottish Cup tie against Motherwell at Fir Park, he walked out of Seamill after his colleagues had played the old newspaper-reporter-on-the-phone trick against him. The executive vowed he would never play for the club again but as the prospect of the Double loomed, he came back on April 7th. Sunderland (who bought him to replace Charlie Buchan) even made him captain to encourage 90 minutes football out of him. Only Tommy Milligan, the Shieldmuir boy and avid Celtic supporter who was British middleweight champion from 12th July 1926 to 14th March 1928, could make him train and McInally was capped twice in 1926 as a result. Without Milligan's urging, his shadow grew ever bigger and his knees heavier. He came from St Anthony's as heir apparent to McMenemy but his wastrel talent was the occasion of two other great Celts leaving Parkhead prematurely: Jimmy McColl (1920) and Patsy Gallagher (1926). On either occasion McInally was expected confidently to assume their roles and do everything they had done. In fact he accomplished relatively little (the League in 1922 and 1926 and the Scottish Cup

in 1927). Not even his jokes sound funny today. In March 1925, he was again the object of Rangers' desire (Willie Wilton wanted him at St Anthony) and his transfer was on from day to day. Willie Maley indulged him end-lessly. It would be interesting to know how Bill Struth might have coped.

Appearances:
SL: 188 apps. 111 gls.
SC: 25 apps. 16 gls.
Total: *213 apps. 127 gls.*

♣ **Celtic note:** *The evidence of birth certificates in the National Registry in Edinburgh would tend to suggest that Tommy was not Arthur's wee brother in a strict biological sense. As with Tommy's self-destructive tendency, there is a mystery here.*

McINTOSH, James Boyd

Role: Full-back 1909-10
5' 9" 12st.7lbs.
b. Glasgow,
25th May 1886
d. 1959 (?)

CAREER: Wellwood Juveniles/Petershill Juniors/Scots Guards 17 Sept 1902 /Reading (trial) 1902 /discharged for £10 on 11 Oct 1902/ Glasgow Perthshire/ Third Lanark am. 2 Feb 1907/Aberdeen 10 May 1907/CELTIC 10 May 1909/ Hull City 2 May 1910/Scots Guards again 7 Dec 1914/(Hearts loan 19 Oct 1916)/(Hibernian loan 1918)/Dumbarton (trial) Feb 1919.

Jimmy McIntosh

Debut v Morton (a) 1-2 (SL) 11.9.09

'Napoleon' McMenemy rated Jimmy McIntosh at Aberdeen "one of the finest centre half backs in Scotland." Elsewhere he was reported as playing "with a vigour that knows no shrouding... is a glutton for work who simply revels in doing his own job well and assisting others." Jimmy, from 54, Calton Street, Glasgow, joined Celtic when they already had two centre backs in Loney and Dodds. "He was as a man lost at Parkhead... a really ser-viceable half-back but as a full-back a failure." He was essentially a reserve throughout his year with Celtic but played 106 games for Hull and skippered the Tigers. Jimmy was seconded to the USA by the Army in June 1917 to train Doughboys preparing for France.

Appearances:
SL: 8 apps. 0 gls.
SC: 3 apps. 0 gls.
Total: *11 apps. 0 gls.*

MacKAY, Duncan

Role: Right-half,
Right-back 1955-64
5' 9" 11st.7lbs.
b. Springburn,
14th July 1937

CAREER: St Mary's BG/
Maryhill Harp Apr 1953/
CELTIC 11 Apr 1955/
(Dumbarton loan Oct
1956)/Third Lanark

Dunky MacKay

6 Nov 1964/Croatia FC (Sydney) player-coach 1966/back to Scotland 13 Mar 1972/ St Anthony's player-coach 1972/Azzurri FC (Western Australia) coach 1974/Essendon Lions (Melbourne) player-coach 1977.

Debut v Clyde (a) 4-1 (SLC) 9.8.58

"An ideal and polished footballer," Dunky MacKay was one of the tyros taken on the US tour of 1957. He didn't get a game but made a strong impression on the Irish trip of 1958 and with John Donnelly in the Army, took over from the crippled Sean Fallon at right-back as of August 9th 1958. He was at once "a five-star proposition" and within weeks "the discovery of the season." By March 28th 1959 he rated as "the best defensive prospect in the country" and two weeks later in his first full season as a senior and only just out of part-time football, he stepped out at Wembley behind skipper Bobby Evans, the one player in the 22 not to wear shin-pads. Celtic fans had agonised for his inexperience but he gave England outside-left Doug Holden barely a look. He became Celtic's captain as of March 15th 1961 and led them in the two finals against Dunfermline. As of May 1961 Dunky decided openly he wanted to cash in on his speed and skill and join the haemorrhage of Scottish talent to England. No English club showed any real interest. Johnny Carey did watch him but saw a right-half playing full-back. As skipper, Dunky erred dramatically at Ibrox in the semi-final of the

Cup on March 31st 1962, winning the toss but gifting St Mirren a very strong wind. By half-time the Buddies were 3-0 up. This most stylish of full-backs and an attacker by nature who practised the overlap long before Jim Craig, never got his big money move to England. He lost the captaincy to Billy McNeill in August 1963 and his right-back spot to Ian Young as of October 5th. He joined Bobby Evans at moribund Third Lanark just months before Stein took over at Parkhead. He had years of good football left. Who knows what Big Jock might have made of him? It is significant that after the European Cup was won in 1967, the *Evening Times* polled its readers for the best Celtic side in living memory. Dunky MacKay walked in at right-back.

Appearances:
SL: 162 apps. 5 gls.
SLC: 37 apps. 0 gls.
SC: 33 apps. 2 gls.
Eur: 4 apps. 0 gls.
Total: *236 apps. 7 gls.*

McKAY, Donald

Role: Goalkeeper 1939-40
b. Milton, Glasgow, 14th September 1920

CAREER: St Roch/CELTIC 15 Aug 1939/Arbroath 8 May 1940.

Debut v Queen's Park (h) 2-2 (GC) 30.9.39

Celtic started 1939-40 with only one recognised goalkeeper, Joe Kennaway. Donald McKay, a railway carriage upholsterer, had played trials for Rangers and was "surely one of the most promising goalies in the Central League." Kennaway went down with rheumatoid arthritis just as War broke out and football was banned. When Celtic

Donald McKay

resumed with a friendly at home to Thistle on September 23rd 1939 it was the tyro McKay, newly-signed as Joe's cover, who was in goal. Young Donald made blunders - and what junior would not pitched into the first-class game on a mere three hours training a week? "McKay's mistakes are being magnified... those of some others minimised." Jimmy McStay took over as manager in February 1940 and looked at once for a new goalkeeper. Donald's last game for Celtic was in the first leg of the War Cup on February 24th 1940 when he carried the can for Raith Rovers' second goal.

Appearances:
RL: 16 apps. 1 shut-out.
SWC: 1 app. 0 shut-outs.
Total: *17 apps. 1 shut-out (6%).*

McKAY, James

Role: Centre forward 1944-45
b. Stirling, 11th June 1918

CAREER: Dunipace Juniors 1935/14th Army/ CELTIC 1 Sept 1944/free own request 24 Mar 1945/Alloa 23 July 1945/free 8 Feb 1946/ Portadown Oct 1947/Cowdenbeath (trial) 23 Aug 1948/free Oct 1948/Tranmere Rovers 5 Aug 1949.

Debut v Rangers (n) 2-3 (GC) 7.10.44
(scored once)

"Sharp-shooting" Jim McKay (a man who suffered sore with his knees as a junior and looked finished with football) came to Celtic "on direct leave" from Bill Slim's Army in Burma (he was with the Cameronians) to go into the "emergency attack" (Delaney and Jackie Gallacher were injured) at centre against Rangers in the Glasgow Cup final. It was one of the most unusual debuts for a Celt since the Charity Cup final of May 1913. Celtic were two up at one point, both goals from well-planned moves culminating in "devastating shots", the first from Matt Lynch, the second from Jim McKay. He played his last game against Hearts at Tynecastle on November 25th, his first appearance without scoring and by March 1945 was asking Celtic to grant him a free.

Appearances:
RL: 3 apps. 2 gls.
Total: *3 apps. 2 gls.*

McKAY, John Reid

Role: Inside-right 1919-21
5' 8" 10st.10lbs.
b. Glasgow, 1st November 1898
d. 6th February 1970

CAREER: 114 Coy BB/Townhead Benburb/ St Anthony's 1916/Royal Scots Fusiliers/ CELTIC 2 June 1919/Blackburn Rovers 11 Nov 1921/ Middlesbrough 10 Mar 1927/Hibernian 17 June 1936.

Debut v Queen's Park (a) 2-1 (SL) 13.3.20
(scored once)

Johnny McKay

Johnny McKay played "the highest type of Scots football and was at times unstoppable ... one of the cleverest players Blackburn Rovers have ever had... his understanding with Puddefoot delighted the Swedes and Danes on the club tour of 1926." Johnny came to Celtic as part of the St Anthony's intake of 1919 and made Jimmy McGrory wonder what was the point of joining Celtic to compete for a place with Patsy Gallagher and his deputy McKay, "a terrific player in his own right." Johnny won a Charity Cup medal on May 15th 1920 and may have been the factor that swayed the Board into telling Jimmy McMenemy he was free in June 1920. He had a great career in England and won a Scottish cap at Cardiff on February 16th 1924. Celtic backed McInally. Johnny McKay was a stayer and long-term would have been the better investment. During the Second World War he drove lorries in the Army.

Appearances:
SL: 10 apps. 6 gls.
Total: *10 apps. 6 gls.*

McKECHNIE, James

Role: Central Defence 1984-86
5' 10" 10st.7lbs.
b. Glasgow, 5th November 1964

CAREER: St Augustine's Milton/Celtic BC/
CELTIC S form Apr 5 1978/Nottingham Forest
13 Jan 1981/CELTIC 27 Jan 1984/(Norwich
City loan 7 Mar 1986)/free 1986/Derry City
1986.

Debut v Hibernian 0-0 (SL) 11.8.84 (sub)

Jim McKechnie

Jamie 'Jazzer' McKechnie had his Celtic S signing cancelled when his father obtained a job in England which then did not materialise. He played for Scotland Boys' Clubs in the eight-nation tournament at Nantes in spring 1979 and although Scotland came third, was nominated "Player of the Tournament". So anxious was Brian Clough to land him, he flew 14-year-old Jamie and his Dad to watch Forest in Cologne in the European Cup semi-final (April 25th 1979). With Celtic, Jazzer substituted for Frank McGarvey on his debut but started the whole 90 minutes on his second appearance for the green and whites, the 0-1 defeat by Jock Brown of Dundee (from a 25-yard free kick) on May 4th 1985.

> **Appearances:**
> *SL:* 2 apps. 0 gls.
> **Total:** *2 apps. 0 gls.*

McKEOWN, Michael

Role: Left-back 1888-91
5' 6" 11st.8lbs.
b. Dalmellington, March 1870 (?)
d. 25th October 1903

CAREER: Lugar Boswell/
Leith Harp/ Hibernian 1887/
CELTIC 1888/Blackburn
Rovers 25 Aug 1891/Cowlairs
May 1892/Fair City Athletic
Sept 1892/Motherwell Nov
1892/dismissed Jan 1893/

Morton 27 Sept 1893/3 Royal Scots Fusiliers
(Ayr) 5 Apr 1894/Ayr Parkhouse 18 May 1894
/Army discharge 17 Jan 1895/Hamilton Harp
29 Jan 1896/Lugar Boswell 26 Sept 1896/
Hibernian 22 May 1897/Carfin Shamrock
23 Oct 1897/Camelon FC 17 Mar 1898/
suspended Apr 1898/suspension lifted Oct
1899/Lugar Boswell 11 Oct 1899.

Debut v Shettleston (h) 5-1 (SC) 1.9.1888

"His green socks were a sort of club emblem... always in evidence where the action was thickest." Grey-eyed, brown haired Mick McKeown was left-back in the Hibs team that opened their first ground for Celtic versus Cowlairs on May 8th 1888. He first played for Celtic on August 1st 1888 in the World Exhibition Cup against Abercorn at Gilmorehill and "arrived" as a Celtic back against the Corinthians and the flying Fred Dewhurst on a pitch like glue at 1st Celtic Park on January 3rd 1889. His stay with Celtic was short but turbulent. Mick was ever threatening to go where his worth was more appreciated. The following appeared under 'Departures' in one of the Glasgow papers in October 1888: "Suddenly, at the Central Station, on the 11th inst., Michael McKeown for Burnley - Celtic, please accept this as the only intimation." *"Hard as the devil's was the kick/That sent the ball on high/Och, why did you go, Micky?/Why did you fly?"* Internal evidence might suggest he was the player who struck club secretary John O'Hara in a dispute over money (March 23rd 1889). He was capped as first choice versus Ireland on March 9th 1889 but won the major honour against England by default at 2nd Hampden on April 5th 1890 by which time, having resolved a feud with James Kelly, he had a new one going with Jerry Reynolds. He had been offered the captaincy of the new Glasgow Hibs in August 1889 and went absent in Ireland between August 24th and the vital Scottish Cup tie versus

Mick McKeown

Queen's Park on September 7th. On April 23rd 1890 he booked himself to play for the alternative Celtic at Oatlands and went public in the papers that Celtic had refused to release his kit. He resigned the club on May 3rd 1890 but difficulties were smoothed over and Mick was Celtic's left-back when the Scottish League began on August 16th 1890 and also left-back in the team first to lift a major trophy: the Glasgow Cup on Valentine's Day 1891. After Blackburn Rovers (he was warmly applauded onto the pitch at Parkhead for the friendly of October 1st 1891) it was downhill all the way. Mick had a drink problem. He was in and out of court and after 288 days in the Army was dismissed as "incorrigible and worthless". He began a nomadic existence as "The Ayrshire Wanderer", living on charity and his past repute. Dan Doyle had a chat with him in the street the night before his death. He was found asphyxiated in a lime kiln belonging to Robert Paul and Sons of Camlachie. A pauper's grave beckoned but Celtic did the decent thing and buried him.

Appearances:
SL: 14 apps. 0 gls.
SC: 16 apps. 0 gls.
Total: *30 apps. 0 gls.*

McKINLAY, Thomas Valley

Role: Left-back 1994 to date
5' 10" 11st.9lbs.
b. Glasgow, 3rd December 1964

CAREER: St Peter's (Partick) Primary/Celtic BC/Dundee Jan 1981/Hearts 7 Dec 1988/CELTIC 2 Nov 1994.

Debut v Dundee United (a) 2-2 (SL) 5.11.94

Tommy Burns sold McGinlay to Hibs on All Saints' and bought McKinlay from Hearts on All Souls' 1994. Like Pat, Tosh ('skilful and hard'), a Scotland Youth and Under-21 cap was Celtic daft and always had ambitions to play in the green and white before getting the chance on the brink of his more mature playing years. Burns bought him for £350,000 "to improve the balance of the team... Tom Boyd prefers his right foot... Tosh has natural ability and can put killer balls into the box and we need that. He's enthusiastic, looks for the ball, wants to create and can open the game with good quality diagonal passes... as he showed against us a few weeks ago!" (Hearts 1, Celtic 0; 15th October 1994).

'Tosh' McKinlay arrives at Celtic Park, November 1994.

McKNIGHT, Allen

Role: Goalkeeper 1986-88
6' 1" 12st.0lbs.
b. Antrim, 27th January 1964

CAREER:
Distillery/CELTIC 10 Aug
1986/ (Albion Rovers loan
10 Aug 1986)/West Ham
United 13 July 1988/free
19 July 1991/Falkirk (trial)
July 1991/Airdrie Aug
1991/Stockport County
Sept 1991/Rotherham
United Oct 1991/Walsall
Nov 1991/South China
(Hong Kong) Aug 1992/
Exeter City as unattached
player 24 Mar 1994.

Allen McKnight

Debut v Dumbarton (a) 5-1 (SLC) 26.8.87

Allen McKnight (who helped his father to
build the M25) and Anton Rogan were picked
to play against Yugoslavia in Sarajevo on
October 14th 1987, the first Celts in the
Northern Ireland squad since Peacock and
Tully, with Allen as replacement for the great
Pat Jennings. He got his first big opportunity
at Parkhead when Packy Bonner went down
with a virus in August 1987 but his chance of
chances came when Packy injured calf and
hamstring in training on May 9th 1988. Billy
McNeill kept it secret that Celtic's goalie for
the Scottish final against Dundee United five
days later would not be the Republic of
Ireland man but his Northern Ireland deputy.
In retrospect, Allen might wish he had spent a
longer apprenticeship at Celtic Park.
Indifferent goalkeeping conceded nine-man
Rangers the equaliser at Ibrox on October 17th
1987 and in the Scottish Cup final a clearance
punted short allowed Eammon Bannon to set
Kevin Gallacher up for the Dundee United
goal. Allen was spectacular but flaws in his
game quickly showed-up at West Ham. He
refused to commit a professional foul on Dale
Gordon on Boxing Day 1988 ("I was right not
to cheat") and he allowed Paul Merson to
squeeze a goal home at the near post in the
Cup on January 7th 1989 after the Hammers
had led 2-0. Billy Bingham seemed to
understate the case on February 6th 1989:
"If he has a fault, he does not know when to
commit himself." Allen's game was more
fundamentally at odds
with his superb basic
talent than that.

Appearances:
SL: 12 apps. 5 shut-outs.
SLC: 2 apps. 0 shut-outs.
SC: 1 app. 0 shut-outs.
Eur: 2 apps. 0 shut-outs.
Total:
17 apps. 5 shut-outs (29%).

McLAREN, James

Role: Left-half 1888-91;
1895-96
b. Lugar, 1860
d. Canada, 3rd January 1927

CAREER: Cronbery Eglinton/Lugar Boswell
Thistle/Hibernian 1883/(St Bernards loan
6 Sept 1886)/CELTIC June 1888/Morton June
1891/Clyde 1891-93/...CELTIC again 1895/
retired 1896.

Debut v Shettleston (h) 5-1 (SC) 1.9.1888

Jimmy McLaren "whose forte was splendid
pacing and headwork" was a left-half
(McGhee, McGinn and McLaren) in the great
team that lifted the Scottish Cup on February
12th 1887, the day of Hibs glory that inspired
the Celtic dream. He was in the Hibs team that
hanselled first Celtic Park versus Cowlairs on
May 8th 1888 and first played for Celtic in a
benefit match (3-3) for the new-founded club
against Mossend Swifts at Dalmarnock Street
on June 16th 1888; "the stand was packed...
deafening cheers every time Celtic equalised."
He was also in the side that contested the first
round of the World Exhibition Cup versus
Abercorn at Gilmorehill on August 1st 1888.
He fell out with the Celtic executive after an
indiscretion on the London trip of February
16th 1889 when his apology was tabled until
he would improve on it. Like Jimmy Delaney
at Hampden in the last minute against
England on April 13th 1946, James McLaren,
"The Oul' Giniral" won the undying love of
his generation when his famed left peg hit a
20-yard volley to score the 90th minute goal
against England at the famed Kennington
Oval on April 13th 1889 that gave Scotland a
2-3 win after being 2-0 down at half-time.
Even when England were two ahead "the
Saxon front line got sick of their repeated

Jimmy McLaren

failures to beat him... he has splendid judgement and seems to be wherever wanted." His health was specially singled out for proposal by the Scottish team at the Covent Garden Hotel after the official banquet at the Cafe Royal. Jimmy was unwell at the start of 1889-90 but returned to a massive reception versus Dumbarton on August 31st. He was Celtic's very first Scottish League goalkeeper on August 16th 1890. He did not have a good game in the 1-4 defeat by Renton (a result later expunged). Celtic played his benefit against Hibs 22 June 1895. He made his debut as a League referee on August 26th 1899 (Clyde versus Rangers). He emigrated to British Columbia in 1912 but served in France in 1917 and attended Sunny Jim Young's testimonial on January 3rd 1918 in the uniform of a Canadian Forester. He died on his ranch near Vancouver.

Appearances:
SL: 3 apps. 0 gls.
SC: 13 apps. 2 gls.
Total: *16 apps. 2 gls.*

McLAUGHLAN

Role: Left-back 1892

CAREER: Benburb/CELTIC Mar 1892/Albion Rovers Apr 1893.

Debut v Vale of Leven (a) 2-2 (SL) 2.4.1892

Dan Doyle was with Scotland losing 1-4 to England at Ibrox when Celtic seem to have tried out this "promising young back" from Benburb, the Polmadie Greens. There was no further interest.

Appearances:
SL: 1 app. 0 gls.
Total: *1 app. 0 gls.*

McLAUGHLAN, George

Role: Inside-forward 1923-24
5′ 8″ 10st.10lbs.
b. Bridgeton, 18th January 1904

CAREER: John St Secondary School Bridgeton/Greenhead Thistle Juveniles/ CELTIC 25 Apr 1923/(Clydebank loan Oct 1923)/(Stenhousemuir loan 7 Feb 1924)/ Clydebank 1 Mar 1924/free 1924/ Mid-Rhondda 1924/Clyde summer 1925/ Darlington 1925/Hull City June 1926/ Accrington Stanley summer 1927/Nelson 1928.

Debut v Partick Thistle (h) 1-2 (SL) 1.9.23

George McLaughlan received his kiss of doom the moment he was christened "the new McMahon." He made his one and only appearance in the first team the day Tom White and his cigar appeared in the dressing room to proclaim "No bonuses!" George won a Glasgow Cup medal with Clyde against Celtic on October 10th 1925. At Accrington Stanley he had "no superior in cleverness in the forward line."

George McLaughlan

Appearances:
SL: 1 app. 0 gls.
Total: *1 app. 0 gls.*

McLAUGHLIN, Brian

Role: Midfield 1968-77
5′ 8″ 10st.9lbs.
b. Falkirk, 7th October 1954

CAREER: CELTIC S form 27 Sept 1968/ Linlithgow Rose (farmed-out) 1968/CELTIC 4 Aug 1971/(Finn Harps loan 24 Jan 1976)/ Ayr United 4 Nov 1977/Motherwell 11 Sept 1979/(Hamilton Academicals loan 21 Jan 1983) /Hamilton Academicals 25 Mar 1983/Falkirk 16 December 1983/free own request 1985/ West Adelaide 20 Jan 1986/Ayr United 26 Sept

1986/player-coach 16 June 1987/St Mirren coach 1990.

Debut v Clydebank (h) 6-2 (SLC) 22.9.71

"McLaughlin has that cockiness which spells class and tons of natural ability" (August 19th 1972). "Don't let the tender years of McLaughlin fool you. This boy plays with a very old head indeed... he ghosts past players, uses the ball exceptionally well and has a keen eye for the goal-scoring chance" (versus Rangers August 18th 1973). Jock Stein regarded young Brian as a prospective all-time Celtic great and played him instead of Jimmy Johnstone in the quarter-finals of the League Cup 1971 aged just 16. After the Drybrough Cup final on August 4th 1973, Stein told Brian he was now definitively a first-teamer. An horrendous knee injury against Clyde and Willie McVie in the League on September 8th 1973 threatened his career and brought Stein to the verge of tears. Big Jock never lost hope: "It'll make a big difference once Brian's back... in the midfield with Kenny" (April 1974). But with Stein laid-up in Dumfries Infirmary, the boy Brian missed the start of training on July 14th 1975 and according to his girl friend, intended to give up foot-ball altogether. He had taken off for his parents' native Carrigart, Co.Donegal so the loan to Finn Harps was agreed. Brian had "no disagreement with Celtic, he just wants to keep out of the limelight for a while." He was back at Parkhead for 1976-77 but seemed to have burned his boats and was

Brian McLaughlin

off-loaded to Ayr United plus £15,000 for a full-back, Joe Filippi. In 1979, he was the Division One Player of the Year. "He hasn't missed a game since he came here and he's outstanding every week" (George Caldwell).

Appearances:
SL: 7 apps. 1 gl.
SLC: 11 apps. 0 gls.
SC: 1 app. 0 gls.
Eur: 1 app. 0 gls.
Total: *20 apps. 1 gl.*

McLAUGHLIN, Brian

Role: Forward 1992 to date
5' 4" 8st.9lbs.
b. Bellshill, 14th May 1974

CAREER: Celtic BC/Giffnock North AFC/Celtic groundstaff June 1990/CELTIC 7 July 1992.
Debut v Partick Thistle (h) 3-0 (SL) 6.11.93 (sub)

In an age of giants, Brian McLaughlin replaced Gerry Creaney with five minutes to go against Thistle on his debut as possibly the smallest player to turn out for Celtic since Bobby Collins, Jimmy Johnstone or Lou Macari and probably the smallest ever to perform in the Premier League. "It was a great day because so unexpected... since I was a boy it has been my dream to play for Celtic." Chief scout John Kelman had opposed 'Pele's' signing on the grounds of physique much as Jimmy Quinn had once feared for Patsy Gallacher. For long the darling of those who watch Celtic reserves, Brian is a pacy winger who holds a Glasgow Cup medal won against Partick Thistle on January 23rd 1991. He also won a Reserve League Cup medal with Celtic versus Dundee United at Tannadice April 18th 1994. Skill is the wee man's priority and along with Donnelly, Smith and Hay he is a signal of hope to the long-suffering Celtic faithful.

Appearances:
SL: 8 apps. 0 gls.
Total: *8 apps. 0 gls.*

Brian McLaughlin

McLAUGHLIN, James

Role: Right-back & Goalkeeper 1888-90
b. *Glasgow, 16th September 1864*
d. *Glasgow, 25th March 1946*

CAREER: Cowlairs Juniors 1880/Cowlairs 1883/Hibernian 1887/CELTIC June 1888/ Glasgow Hibernian 1889/CELTIC May 1889/ Battlefield 1890/Stockton 1891/Bootle 1892.

Debut v Albion Rovers (h) 4-1 (SC) 13.10.1888

Springburn man James McLaughlin started as a forward and before his career was over had played every position in the team including goalkeeper. He played at right-back in Celtic's second match versus Dundee Harp on June 9th 1888 and was used in the 3rd round of the Scottish Cup against Albion Rovers. He played in the riot friendly against Hibs in Edinburgh the following week before stepping down for Paddy Gallagher who handed on in turn to Pat Dowling. His next appearance was as Celtic's fourth goalkeeper (after Dolan, Dunning and John Kelly) in the North-Eastern final on May 11th 1889 against Cowlairs at Barrowfield when Celtic landed their first (albeit minor) trophy 6-1. He missed the Dyke Berry trundler from 30 yards that put Celtic out of the Scottish Cup 1st round replay 2-1 against Queen's Park at 2nd Hampden (Cathkin Park) with five minutes to go on September 14th 1889. James' last game in goal was against Third Lanark in the Charity Cup at home on April 19th 1890 when he conceded a 0-2 defeat within five minutes of the final whistle - (the papers vented on "Why Celtic Cannot Win a Cup"). Celtic were so anxious for a goalie when the new League started on August 16th 1890 that they drafted James McLaren, then broke the rules by playing Jamie Bell. On retirement, James became a much sought-after referee at the highest level in England and Scotland and prospered as a wine and spirit merchant in Airdrie.

Appearances:
SC: 3 apps. 1 shut-out.
Total: *3 apps. 1 shut-out.*

McLAUGHLIN, James

Role: Centre-forward 1947-48
5' 11" 11st.7lbs.
b. *Paisley, 11th February 1926*

CAREER: Royal Navy 1943/Barrhead St John's 1946/Renfrew Juniors 17 Dec 1946/ CELTIC 3 Apr 1947/(Glenavon loan 5 Mar 1948)/free Apr 1948/Walsall June 1948/ open to transfer 1950.

Debut v Morton (h) 3-2 (SL) 11.10.47
(scored once)

*Jim McLaughlin
(1947-48)*

Jim McLaughlin was a crack junior with a big physique wanted by Wolves and Hibs but who looked "awkward" on his Celtic debut. "Experience should rub-off the rough spots." He scored the winner with eleven minutes to go. This was the match during which Bobby Hogg screamed "Penalty!" on Morton's behalf after Roy Milne had handled McKillop's scoring shot. Nitshill boy Jim played centre-half at Walsall and applied for reinstatement to Renfrew in 1950 but was refused first time of asking at least on October 4th. Forfar Athletic were keen to get him. He played in goal for Celtic reserves on the end of a 6-0 hiding at Dundee when Ugolini was suspended (December 6th 1947).

Appearances:
SL: 2 apps. 1 gl.
Total: *2 apps. 1 gl.*

McLAUGHLIN, Joseph

Role: Utility 1938-40; 1941-45
5' 11" 13st.0lbs.
b. c 1920

CAREER: Douglas Water Thistle 1937/Bo'ness Cadora 1937/Blairhall Colliery 1938/CELTIC 27 Jan 1938/St Anthony's (farmed-out to cut costs) 22 Aug 1940/CELTIC 8 Feb 1941/ Hamilton Academicals 17 Nov 1945/Aberdeen 11 Oct 1946/Raith Rovers 12 Sept 1949/coach Nov 1951/free 1953/Albion Rovers 11 Aug 1953/Sligo Rovers 1954/retired 1955.

Debut v Partick Thistle (h) 5-1 (RL) 8.2.41

Play-anywhere Joe, "a big agile fellow, revealing a quick-thinking brain in low, measured passes," was one of the big Celtic intake from Blairhall Colliery at the end of the 30s. He himself was not a Fifer but lived at Longriggend. He was naturally right-footed but cast by Celtic as George Paterson's successor at left-half. He put through his own goal in 18 minutes against Rangers in the League Cup semi-final at Hampden on May 2nd 1942. Charlie Johnstone got a second in the 60th minute and Joe told Alex Dowdells

Joe McLaughlin

later it was the only time a Rangers goal had ever made him happy: it took the whole burden of defeat off his shoulders. As centre-half he won himself a Charity Cup medal against Third Lanark on March 22nd 1943 but his lack of pace was shown-up on October 30th 1943 at Easter Road when Tommy Bogan gave him a three yards start yet got to the ball first and scored Hibs' second goal. As centre-half he was appointed Celtic skipper for 1944-45, but was moved to inside-left against St Mirren on October 21st, allegedly to cure an attack of the jitters which was affecting his game as a defender. By nightfall on December 30th he had scored 15 goals in twelve matches including one outstanding performance against Clyde at Shawfield two days before Christmas. He did not score in the 0-1 win at Ibrox on Ne'erday 1945 but his shooting was the feature of the first half and his powerful tackling against Rangers on the rampage that of the second. He burst the rigging at Parkhead with a goal (April 21st 1945): "It was one of those shots I knew was a goal as soon as it left my foot" (Bobby Evans alerted him to the fact he'd ripped the net). Jimmy McStay took him to Hamilton where he now resented being used as at Celtic as "an all-over-the-field player." With Aberdeen he won a Scottish Cup medal at right-half (his favourite position) against Hibernian on April 19th 1947.

Appearances:
RL: 117 apps. 33 gls.
RLC: 33 apps. 2 gls.
Total: *150 apps. 35 gls.*

McLAUGHLIN, Paul Gerald

Role: Left-back 1989-91
5' 11" 13st.8lbs.
b. Johnstone, 14th December 1965

CAREER: Anniesland Waverley/St Mirren BC/Clydebank S form Aug 1982/Anniesland Waverley 1982/Clydebank 31 Dec 1982/ Queen's Park 14 Aug 1984/CELTIC 15 May 1989/Partick Thistle 15 Feb 1991/free 11 May 1993.

Debut v Motherwell (a) 0-2 (SL) 25.8.90 (sub)

Billy McNeill signed Paul McLaughlin from Queen's Park: "We have high hopes for him." The happiest moment of Paul's career was signing for Celtic. He had been pulled into the Clydebank side on trial at Stark's Park on

December 19th 1982 and had a blinder aged only 17 with no previous senior experience. He returned to Anniesland after four League games for 'bankies and played over 150 in the League for Queen's Park plus a Scottish Cup tie against Celtic (February 15th 1986). He describes Celtic versus Bohemians in Dublin on August 16th 1990 as the best match he ever played in. He moved to Firhill with goalkeeper Andy Murdoch for £150,000, enticed by the prospect of regular first-team football. John Lambie bought him and freed him: "He was given the chance to lose weight and didn't take it."

Paul McLaughlin

Appearances:
SL: 3 apps. 0 gls.
SLC: 2 apps. 0 gls.
Total: *5 apps. 0 gls.*

McLEAN, Adam

Role: Outside-left 1917-28
5′ 6″ 10st.10lbs.
b. Greenock, 27th April 1899
d. 29th June 1973

CAREER: Whiteinch Oaklea Juveniles/ Broomhill YMCA/Anderston Thornbank Juveniles/CELTIC 17 Jan 1917/Sunderland 27 Aug 1928/Aberdeen 16 Oct 1930/ Partick Thistle 25 July 1933/asst. trainer 26 Nov 1938/ Norway coaching summer 1939/Partick Thistle asst. manager 23 July 1962.

Debut v Dumbarton (h) 1-1 (SL) 20.1.17

A Partick Thistle fan and a Tom Colgan signing, Adam McLean was welcomed on his first approach to Parkhead by Jerry Reynolds at his most raucous: "Hey you! Whit's your name?" Adam, brought up in Belfast and now resident in Greenock, joined Celtic as a centre but on February 10th 1917 came into his own against Morton and iron man Billy Morrison at Cappielow when manager Maley asked

McLEAN, David Prophet

Role: Centre-forward 1907-09
5′ 9″ 12st.6lbs.
b. Forfar, 13th December 1890
d. Forfar, 21st December 1967

CAREER: Forfar Half-Holiday 1903/CELTIC (trial) 11 Mar & 8 May 1905/Forfar West End 1905/Forfar Celtic 1906/Forfar Athletic 9 Mar 1907/CELTIC 16 Apr 1907/(Forfar Athletic loan 18 Apr 1907)/(Ayr FC loan 17 Apr 1909)/ Preston North End 5 Nov 1909/Sheffield Wednesday Feb 1911/Forfar Athletic 19 May 1913/Sheffield Wednesday 31 Dec 1914/ (Dykehead loan 4 Sept 1915)/(Third Lanark loan 18 Dec 1915)/(Rangers loan 2 July 1918)/ Bradford PA 24 Oct 1919/Dundee Oct 1921/ Forfar Athletic May 1922/Dundee 4 Aug 1922/Forfar Athletic 20 Aug 1926/Dykehead 1932/Huddersfield Town scout 1940s.

Debut v Port Glasgow Athletic (h) 5-0 (SL) 2.11.07 (scored three)

Davie McLean, "a centre to grace any team in the first League," (November 1907) should be on the list of all-time Celtic greats yet few fans have ever heard of him. He was a prolific goalscorer and exceeded

Davie McLean

McGrory's aggregate but 80 goals scored for Forfar do not count as first-rank. "His greatest assets... were his fast reactions, his ability to get into top speed almost immediately and his willingness to shoot at any time, from almost any angle and almost any distance." He was

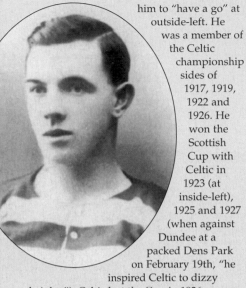

him to "have a go" at outside-left. He was a member of the Celtic championship sides of 1917, 1919, 1922 and 1926. He won the Scottish Cup with Celtic in 1923 (at inside-left), 1925 and 1927 (when against Dundee at a packed Dens Park on February 19th, "he inspired Celtic to dizzy heights"). Celtic lost the Cup in 1926 precisely because he was unfit to play. He was capped four times for Scotland. He rates as perhaps Celtic's greatest ever left-winger. McGrory reckoned him better than Alan Morton: "To me he had a lot more heart which counted a lot in days when the game was more robust than now." Jimmy McMenemy selects him at outside-left in his Celtic Team of the Century. In the 5-0 Scottish Cup semi-final of March 21st 1925 he was twin striker, just as restless as McGrory to get onto the end of Paddy Connolly's magnificent crosses. He pinched a Bert Manderson pass-back for the fifth goal. His departure from Parkhead with years of football in him was a tragedy that dogged Celtic for years. In 1928, as a senior player, he represented to the management at Seamill that their terms for a summer tour of the USA were not on. He next found his re-signing offer for 1928-29 startlingly reduced and his transfer to Sunderland ("I didn't want to go") began the endless saga of Celtic's search for an outside-left. Adam McLean was an all-time Celtic great. Celtic were irretrievably the poorer for his going.

Appearances:
SL: 367 apps. 119 gls.
SC: 41 apps. 19 gls.
Total: *408 apps. 138 gls.*

Quinn's natural successor but whereas Maley might tolerate the highs and lows of a McInally, he got rid of Davie ("Ah went to Maley and telt him") McLean. On September 12th 1908 Queen's Park and Celtic drew 4-4 in the Glasgow Cup. "Willie Maley came in and pitched into us in a black rage. There were seven internationalists and they sat there, dumb, and took it. I decided there and then no one was going to talk to me like that and get away with it." Davie's virtual farewell was the Charity Cup final versus Clyde on May 8th 1909 when he scored "two flashing goals" and was smothered in congratulations by his team-mates. Maley offered him to Liverpool who wanted a player exchange, then to Preston who paid £400. Celtic, it was said, did not want to stand in the way of the boy's career. As his fame burgeoned in England and Celtic hunted for a centre to replace Jimmy Quinn, Maley was asked why McLean had been allowed to go. The great manager revealed the secret: the boy had not possessed the Celtic spirit. Davie was capped first for Scotland versus England at Hampden on March 23rd 1912 with Templeton and Quinn as his wingers. He scored a hat-trick, burying every chance he got for Third Lanark against Celtic in a 1-3 League win on March 23rd 1918 which virtually ensured the Championship would go to Ibrox. In later years he recalled he had done the feat against Shaw, McNair and Dodds. In fact it was Shaw, McNair and Tom McGregor with Joe Dodds turning out for Fulham on the day.

Appearances:
SL: 28 apps. 19 gls.
Total: *28 apps. 19 gls.*

♣ **Celtic note:** *Celtic were European Champions when Davie chose his best-ever side on July 8th 1967: Adams; McLeod & Weir; Young, Loney & Hay; Bennett, McMenemy, Quinn, Somers & Hamilton. Reserves: McNair & Templeton.*

McLEAN, Finlay

Role: Outside-right 1904-05
5' 7" 11st.0lbs.
b. 1879

CAREER: Glasgow Perthshire/Hamilton Academicals 20 Dec 1902/CELTIC 2 July 1904/Hamilton Academicals 1 June 1905/Workington Town 1909/Hamilton Academicals 2 Apr 1910/Abercorn 11 Aug 1911/Renton 17 Nov 1911.

Debut v Partick Thistle (a) 2-0 (SL) 20.8.04 (scored once)

Finlay McLean was signed as Bobby Muir's replacement for 1904-05. After September 19th 1904 he lost his place to Alec Bennett but came back to the big team as of November 12th with Bennett moving to centre. He scored his fourth goal for Celtic against Dundee on a bone-hard surface at Dens Park (January 14th 1905) when the Celts' rubber-soled boots could get no hold and they had to retire one by one to change. By the time of the Barney Battles Family Benefit at Rugby Park on March 11th 1905, Celtic were experimenting with another McLean at outside-right, this one a mere boy, the formidable Davie. Hamilton Acas played Motherwell in Finlay's benefit on August 23rd 1909 by which time he had moved down to Workington.

Appearances:
SL: 15 apps. 4 gls.
Total: *15 apps. 4 gls.*

McLEAN, Lauchlan

Role: Centre-Forward 1909-10
5' 7" 11st.10lbs.

CAREER: Inverness Clachnacuddin Oct 1907/CELTIC 9 Aug 1909/Preston North End 2 May 1910/St Mirren 10 June 1911/Inverness Caledonian 13 Oct 1913.

Debut v Aberdeen (a) 1-0 (SL) 27.11.09

Lauchlan McLean ("like his namesake Davie he has the reputation of being a smart opportunist") played inside-left for a North of Scotland Select against Celtic in Inverness on May 3rd 1909 and turned out for Celtic first in Jimmy Quinn's benefit (August 18th 1909) when he scored the fifth and sixth goals in an 8-4 win against Rangers. Davie McLean went

south on November 13th 1909 and Lauchie stepped into his boots at centre at Pittodrie two weeks later. He totalled only three League games (the other two in March 1910) but Celtic won them all. He was the third McLean on the books when he joined Preston; Jimmy was English, Davie was a Scot and Lauchlan an Irishman.

Appearances:
SL: 3 apps. 0 gls.
Total: *3 apps. 0 gls.*

McLEOD, Donald

Role: Full-back 1902-08
5' 8" 12st.7lbs.
b. Laurieston,
28th May 1882
d. 6th October 1917

Stenhouse Thistle/Stenhousemuir 6 Aug 1901/CELTIC 10 May 1902/Middlesbrough 10 Oct 1908/(Inverness Caledonian loan 29 Nov 1913).

Donnie McLeod

Debut v Third Lanark (a) 2-1 (SL) 30.8.02

Edward VII was twenty days crowned when 'Slasher' McLeod "fearless... of tremendous speed," made his debut for Celtic and was an immediate hit: "McLeod is a speedy, two-footed player. Battles will have a hard job getting his place back." He was at right-back for the Quinn 3 Rangers 2 Scottish Cup final of April 16th 1904 and lined-up with Willie Orr in front of Davy Adams at the very beginning of the six-Championships-in-a-row on August 20th 1904. He joined Jimmy Weir for the first time in a home League match against St Mirren on April 27th 1907, the origin of one of the most effective defensive partnerships in the story of the Celtic. There was a problem with the scales during Celtic's Clean Sweep season of 1907-08: "McLeod grows rather adipose and would do well to mind his massage" (23rd November). It was Donnie brought Alec McNair to Celtic Park. He was the full-back who demanded of Davy Adams: "How the hell did you lose that ball?" Adams: "I havnae lost it. It's in the net!" Donnie was made scapegoat for the 4-4 draw against Queen's Park in the Glasgow Cup (September 12th 1908) and got his transfer to Middlesbrough within a month. As the papers said: "This will ensure an increase in their support" (ie of Celtic fans). When Jimmy Weir joined him again from Celtic, together they made "the most dogged, dour and fearless pair of backs in England" (September 1910). He ran the Lord Byron Hotel, Bridge St, Middlesbrough. Gunner 201979 McLeod served in 466 Battery of 65 Brigade, Royal Field Artillery and died from wounds sustained on the Flanders battlefield. He is buried in Dozingham Military Cemetery, Westvleteren, Belgium, Plot 5, Row G, Grave 7. Donnie left a wife and three children.

Appearances:
SL: 131 apps. 0 gls.
SC: 24 apps. 0 gls.
Total: *155 apps. 0 gls.*

MacLEOD, Murdo Davidson

Role: Midfield 1978-87
5' 9" 12st.4lbs.
b. Glasgow,
24th September 1958

CAREER: Douglas Academy/Partick Thistle BC/Partick Thistle S form 10 Mar 1971/Glasgow Amateurs/Dumbarton 21 July 1974/ CELTIC 2 Nov 1978/Borussia Dortmund 16 June 1987/ Hibernian player-coach 12 Oct 1990/free 11 May 1993/Dumbarton player coach 9 June 1993.

Debut v Motherwell (h) 1-2 (SL) 4.11.78

"I wish some of the players had the same spirit as the supporters" (Billy McNeill October 7th 1978). Within a month he had acquired just such a one. On his debut Murdo's "every touch brought ripples of applause." McNeill had bought a non-stop runner whose "tackles would demolish a single end." And could he hit a ball! Dead or moving it was struck with force to split granite. The like had not been seen since Charlie Gallagher. The only difference was Murdo used his left foot, Charlie his right. MacLeod never struck a free-kick but the defence trembled perceptibly. One

commentator complimented sports goods manufacturers on producing balls and nets able to withstand the impact. He was resolution personified: "MacLeod gave the impression that had there been a brick wall between him and the opposition, he still would have got the ball" (September 14th 1985). Murdo was the driving force behind everything Celtic accomplished in the 'eighties, the two Scottish Cups of 1980 and 1985, the League Cup of 1982, the three Championships of 1981, 1982 and 1986. When the Bear was ordered-off in the 39th minute of the Scottish Cup final versus Aberdeen (19th May 1984) Murdo went into defence and played like two Roy Aitkens. He came on for Strachan and his first cap in the 1-0 defeat of England at Hampden on May 25th 1985. He left the club with the whole-hearted good wishes of the support: "He's been a hell of a good servant to Celtic and he got an offer which at this stage of his career he couldn't turn down. He's kept us in touch all along with what's happening and I'm delighted for him" (Billy McNeill June 16th 1987). Caesar made two inspired signings during his first period as Boss at Parkhead. The first was Davie Provan; the second was the 'Wee Rhino'. Murdo was an all-time Celtic great. His departure was like Aitken's; it deprived the club of a lot more than just a player. A huge chunk of heart went with him.

Murdo MacLeod

Appearances:
SL: 281 apps. 55 gls.
SLC: 44 apps. 13 gls.
SC: 37 apps. 6 gls.
Eur: 32 apps. 7 gls.
Total: *394 apps. 81 gls.*

McMAHON, Alexander

Role: Inside-left 1890-1903
6' 0" 12st.4lbs.
b. Selkirk, circa 1871
d. Glasgow, 25th January 1916

CAREER: Harp Juveniles (Edinburgh)/
Hibernian Aug 1886/Queen's Park Juniors
(Edinburgh)/ Woodburn FC/Leith Harp
27 Aug 1887/ Darlington St Augustine's
(did not play) Sept 1888/ Hibernian Sept
1888/CELTIC 20 Dec 1890/Partick Thistle
7 Oct 1903/retired 1904.

Debut v Vale of Leven (a) 1-3 (SL) 24.1.1891

"McMahon can use his feet as other men do
their hands." Sandy McMahon played in a
ten-man team on his debut in Alexandria:
Mick McKeown missed his train and Duke
for a time was left-back. He had played first
for Celtic on Ne'erday 1891 at old Celtic
Park in a 1-1 draw against Dumbarton
"arms held high, spread out like ostrich
wings, head down, back slightly bent
forward, enormous feet." Viewed from the
terracing he was big, awkward, ungainly; at
pitch level he was pace, grace and elegance,
a dribbler of power who could take a
defence out with one swerve. Carfin's Hugh
Clifford, who commended him to Celtic,
had never seen anything so gawky until he
actually played left-half behind McMahon.
Nottingham Forest were very keen to have
him; he had a written agreement with the
River Trent club that prevented his playing
for Darlington; and Celtic never tried
harder to retrieve a player than when Sandy
fled to Forest with Neilly McCallum in July
1892. He was not an immediate success at
Celtic Park and hit a game for the first time
in the last fifteen minutes of a 3-1 defeat at
Cambuslang on March 7th 1891 as inside
man to Johnny Campbell. On form, the
Duke was almighty. Maley describes him as
"the best header of a ball I have ever seen...
he could almost hold a high cross with his
head... direct it with the greatest of ease... a
terror to defences at corner kicks." Celtic
beat Rangers 4-0 at 1st Cathkin on May 25th
1895. The Duke scored three goals, the last a
header "with a Ranger hanging on each

leg." His spectacular runs from deep "the
kind that tear at a defence" would have
rejoiced Jock Stein. If he had a fault it was a
tendency to "diddle and jink" - an over-
elaboration shared with Campbell and
Madden. They were so intent on doing
beautiful things with the ball that goals
were secondary. Sandy belongs to Celtic's
first team to win the Scottish Cup (April 9th
1892; he scored twice) and the first team to
win the Championship (May 9th 1893). He
is reputed to have been that rare football
phenomenon: a well-read man. When Celtic
beat Rangers 4-0 in the Scottish Cup 4th
round replay of March 10th 1900 the Duke
put it succinctly: "We have taken Kruger's
advice! We have staggered humanity!" He
is the first Celt to epitomise an era. After
him comes Jimmy Quinn.

Appearances:
SL: 174 apps. 126 gls.
SC: 43 apps. 45 gls.
Total: *217 apps. 171 gls.*

♣ **Celtic note:** *Duke was most probably named
(by Tom Maley) for the Duc de Mac-Mahon,
President of France 1873-79. When the great
man passed-over on October 17th 1893, a
Glasgow paper boy sold out his stock with cries
of: "McMahon deid! Whit'll the Cel'ic dae noo?*

McMAHON, Eamon

Role: Goalkeeper 1953-55
5' 11" 11st.0lbs.
b. Lurgan, 16th January 1933

CAREER: Clann na nGael (Lurgan GAA)/
CELTIC 30 Dec 1953/free 14 May 1955/
Glentoran 4 June 1955/retired 1960.

Debut v Queen of the South (h) 1-1 (SL) 16.10.54

Armagh played Kerry in the All-Ireland
Football final on September 27th 1953 and lost
0-13 to 1-6. Before a record crowd of 85,155
Eamon McMahon, between the sticks for the
Ulstermen, "gave a great exhibition of goalkeeping." Although Armagh lost, Eamon is in
the *Guinness Book of Records* as the one and
only 'keeper to play in every round of the All-
Ireland tournament without conceding a goal.
As the son of ex-Glenavon goalie, Peter
McMahon his pedigree was exceptional and
his display at Croke Park convinced Celtic's
Irish scout Peter O'Connor (Glenavon) that
this was a man for Parkhead. He was brought
over as cover for George Hunter after Johnny
Bonnar sustained a broken
collarbone (26th August
1953) and Bell damaged his
shoulder (5th October 1953).
He played his first game at
Parkhead versus Raith
Rovers reserves on October
17th 1953, but did not look
the same man as a soccer
goalie until Celtic took him to
Switzerland for the 1954
World Cup, a trip that seemed
to inspire him anew. He got
his first-team chance after
Bonnar wrenched his arm in
training but the goal he lost in
32 minutes was a 'keeper's
nightmare: "I advanced from
goal as Black shot from the
edge of the penalty box. I had
the ball covered low down to my right. As I
dived I got both hands to it but to my horror,
the ball squirmed from my grasp and
wriggled over the line. I can still recall the
banner headline in one of the Glasgow
evening papers reading 'Oh Eamon!' As a
young player I was devastated!" Eamon had
more success with Glentoran and played in
the final of the Irish Cup in 1956. He married
the great Alex Dowdells' daughter, Patricia.
He lived in Leicester and travelled to Belfast at
weekends to play for Glentoran. Nuneaton
Borough wanted him but Glens were reluctant
to let him go. He joined his father in business
in Lurgan in 1960 and today is a greyhound
trainer. His dog, Alan's Judy, won the Irish St
Leger in 1991.

Appearances:
SL: 1 app. 0 shut-outs.
Total: 1 app. 0 shut-outs.

McMAHON, Patrick

Role: Inside-forward 1967-69
5' 11" 10st.10lbs.
b. Kilsyth, 19th September 1945

CAREER: Ashfield/Yoker Athletic/Kilsyth
Rangers 1966/CELTIC 27 May 1967/free
2 May 1969/Aston Villa 11 June 1969/Portland
Timbers 1976, 1977/Colorado Caribous 1978/
Atlanta Chiefs coach-asst. manager 1979, 1980.

Debut v Partick Thistle (h) 5-0 (GC) 22.8.67
(scored once)

Pat McMahon

Jet-haired Pat McMahon
lived in Croy and played
junior without a single
overture from the
seniors. The Post Office
sent him to work in
London and Tommy
Docherty allowed him to
train at Stamford Bridge.
Kilsyth Rangers asked
him to do a Gerry
McAloon and commute
London-Glasgow-
London for the match
on Saturdays. Wee
Rangers won the Junior
Cup on May 24th 1967
the day before Lisbon
and one of big Jock's
first appointments on
return from Portugal
was to interview Pat and sign him. He took
Bertie Auld's place in the League Cup at
Aberdeen on September 2nd 1967 - and
scored; he lined-up in the League against
Clyde at Parkhead a week later - and scored;
he played in the quarter-final against Ayr on
September 13th - and scored. But Stein had no
intention of rushing him. "I think I got a bit

too cocky... so that when I was dropped, I went in a huff, I didn't show any interest in the reserves and that was the wrong attitude to take." Pat joined up with Tommy Docherty again at Aston Villa and scored 25 goals in 121 appearances, most of them as a midfielder. He played in the League Cup final at Wembley against Spurs on February 27th 1971 but got a loser's medal. He stayed in the USA running his own company supplying aluminium to industry.

Appearances:
SL: 3 apps. 2 gls.
SLC: 3 apps. 3 gls.
Total: *6 apps. 5 gls.*

McMANUS, Peter Thomas

Role: Wing-half 1895
5' 8" 11st.0lbs.
b. Winchburgh, April 1873 (?)
d. 1936 (?)

CAREER: Hibernian 1891/ Mossend Swifts 1893/ St Bernard's 9 June 1894/CELTIC 3 June 1895/ St Bernard's 23 Oct 1895/West Bromwich Albion June 1896/Warmley June 1898/Thames Ironworks 1899/retired 1900.

Debut v St Bernard's (a) 0-3 (SL) 16.9.1895

Peter McManus was in the St Bernard's side that won the Scottish Cup against Renton on April 20th 1895. His first game for Celtic was in Jimmy McLaren's benefit on June 22nd in that year versus Hibernian. He went on the autumn tour of England and got a game against Newcastle on September 4th 1895. He "lingered" south of the border with Doyle, Cullen and McMahon which meant Celtic were unable to field a reserve team to play Motherwell at Parkhead on September 7th. He must have had a good excuse for he came in for Peter O'Rourke just over a week later on his one and only League appearance. According to Willie Maley he was "not up to standard" but his southern adventure may have counted against him. At one time he was reckoned a better prospect than Barney Battles. In 1933 Peter was a garage hand in West Calder.

Appearances:
SL: 1 app. 0 gls.
Total: *1 app. 0 gls.*

Peter McManus

McMASTER, John

Role: Left-half 1913-23
5' 8" 11st.5lbs.
b. Port Glasgow, 4th January 1893
d. Greenock, 27th December 1954

CAREER: Menstrie Thistle Juveniles/Port Dundas Acrehill Juveniles/Carron Juveniles/ Clydebank Juniors/Vale of Leven 1910/ Dumbarton Harp 10 Oct 1911/ Clydebank Juniors 1912/CELTIC 3 May 1913/Royal Army Service Corps Aug 1916/(Fulham loan 25 Nov 1916)/Royal Engineers Apr 1918/(Birmingham loan Feb 1922)/ (Ayr United loan 24 Feb 1923)/free 1 May 1923/Queen of the South 7 July 1923/retired 1925.

Debut v Rangers (h) 3-2 (CC) 10.5.13

"He is one of those unobtrusive players who, while grafting well and often, do not get into the limelight." Electrician Johnny McMaster, "of the melancholy countenance," "a most reliable player," was centre-half in the Clydebank Juniors team of all talents in a club benefit versus Celtic on August 26th 1912. He signed for Celtic at the end of the following season and was in the first team versus Rangers in the Charity Cup final at Parkhead a week later on May 10th 1913 the day Celtic "signed on boys at two o'clock and handed them out gold medals at five." Celtic won 3-2 after being two goals down in six minutes and from that moment McMaster was the Parkhead left-half as successor to Johnny Mitchell and Jimmy Hay. He was in the side that brought the Cup home on April 16th 1914, then the League in 1915 and 1916 before the game of his life versus Partick Thistle in the Charity Cup final of May 13th 1916. Despite a certain deafness which saw him exempted originally, the Army took him for the Motor Transport

Johnny McMaster

Section of the Service Corps and he was training at Easter Road in the autumn of 1917. He obtained four days leave at the end of December but with his pass endorsed "not available for travel by train" (a sinister move in Celtic eyes). Undaunted, Johnny and four mates walked from Edinburgh to Glasgow on December 30th so he could offer his services to Celtic for Ne'erday 1918. He saw service in France and was wounded almost upon arrival in June 1918. He was a regular in the Championship side of 1922. He worked as an electrician with the *Daily Express* in Glasgow after football. Johnny McMaster was a rock solid Celt, dependable, straight and wholesome, an all-time great. Only Hugh Brown and Jean McFarlane were good enough to replace him.

Appearances:
SL: 204 apps. 6 gls.
SC: 14 apps. 0 gls.
Total: *218 apps. 6 gls.*

McMENEMY, James

Role: Inside-left 1902-20
5′ 7″ 11st 7lbs.
b. Rutherglen, 23rd August 1880
d. Robroyston, 23rd June 1965

CAREER: Rutherglen Young Celtic Juveniles 1898/Cambuslang Bluebell Juveniles 1899/Dundee (trial) Aug 1899/ Cambuslang Hibernian 1900/Rutherglen Glencairn 1901/Everton (trial) Apr 1902/ CELTIC 6 June 1902/(East Stirling loan 1902)/(Stenhousemuir loan 12 Mar 1903)/ (Linfield loan 22 Apr 1919)/free 20 June 1920/Partick Thistle 22 June 1920/ (Stenhousemuir loan 1922)/Partick Thistle player-coach 1922/retired May 1923/ Partick Thistle coach 15 July 1932/paid-off 28 Apr 1934/CELTIC coach 15 Oct 1934/ coach-trainer 27 May 1935/paid-off by 18 May 1940.

Debut v Port Glasgow (h) 3-0 (SL)
22.11.02 (scored once)

Adam Scott Duncan played for the Scottish League against the English in a War Fund match. He was out of position on the left-wing but his inside man was Jimmy McMenemy. "I don't think I ever played a better game. Anyone could play with McMenemy. He's one of the few to whom the term genius has been applied without hysterics." 'Napoleon' McMenemy lost two years out of his football career with working in a glass factory that "played havoc with my feet." He took a job elsewhere making chairs and Celtic first tried him out against Motherwell in a friendly on August 16th 1900 as inside man to Johnny Hodge. With Glencairn he played alongside Alec Bennett and Tom Sinclair. He was "Smith" against Blackburn Rovers at Parkhead on April 16th 1902 ("a promising display") but played trials for

Jimmy McMenemy (left) and Celtic team-mate Alec Bennett on the occasion of their first Scotland international together.

Jimmy McMenemy

both with Celtic ("Keep the heid!") and Scotland (he once admonished Mr Sutcliffe, the England umpire, a high FA official, that his place was on the line and not on the pitch tending to an injured England player). Jimmy retired for a time in June 1918 (he was due for call-up in October) but the stand rose to its feet when he came back versus Dumbarton on December 14th to lead Celtic to yet another League title. Tommy McInally swore by Jimmy McMenemy. Had Celtic retained his services in 1920 instead of rewarding this great servant with peremptory dismissal, they might have got a lot more out of McInally than they did. McInally would not credit Celtic could just let him go to save on the wage bill. Nap came back and must take a lot of credit for the Celtic successes of 1936-38. He took Jack Qusklay's job as trainer in 1935 and was himself supplanted (without announcement) by Alex Dowdells in 1940. He was feted by the Celtic Supporters' Associations on December 2nd 1962; in his speech he was sure Celtic would be back to winning again soon. He saw the 1965 Scottish Cup come home but what a pity this all-time Celtic great and utter gentleman could not have had a fuller experience of the Stein era. Napoleon was a Celtic giant.

Everton also and turned-out against Celtic at Parkhead on April 28th 1902. He signed for Willie Maley "up a close in Union Street." He was inside-right to Bobby Muir in the 3-2 defeat of Rangers in the Scottish Cup final of April 16th 1904. Nap served Celtic as general of the attack for almost two decades and was inside-forward of the six-in-a-row side (1905-10), of the four-in-a-row (1914-17) and the Championship side of 1919. Patsy Gallagher's "control and passing" in his opening game on December 2nd 1911 "were comparable to McMenemy's." Jimmy had fantastic speed over 20 to 30 yards, was a beautiful header of the ball and had a net-bulging shot almost as powerful as Quinn's or McAtee's. Against Rangers on Ne'erday 1914, the 4-0 match, he beat five men in a dribble just two minutes before half-time and crashed the ball into the rigging high behind Johnny Hempsey. He was perennially the voice of sanity on the park

Appearances:
SL: 456 apps. 144 gls.
SC: 59 apps. 24 gls.
Total: *515 apps. 168 gls.*

♣ **Celtic note:** *Jimmy brought home his Scottish Cup medal won with Partick Thistle versus Rangers on April 16th 1921 and asked his wife: "What'll I do with it?" She: "Oh, just chuck it in the drawer with all the others." (He had won six with Celtic besides his eleven Championship medals and all his badges for the Glasgow and Charity Cups).*

McMENEMY, John

Role: Inside-right 1925-28
5' 8" 10st.4lbs.
b. Glasgow, 9th February 1908
d. 5th February 1983

CAREER: St Andrew's Schools/
St Mungo's Academy 1923/St
Anthony's/St Roch's/CELTIC
1 December 1925/(Motherwell
loan 11 Feb 1927)/Motherwell
25 Oct 1928/Partick Thistle
3 Sept 1936/St Mirren 12 Jan
1938/retired 1939.

John McMenemy

Debut v Falkirk (a) 1-4 (SL) 6.4.27

John McMenemy, second of Nap's large family
of footballer sons, "a carpet slippers player,
dainty in every move... the same brainy player
as his famous sire," was St Mungo's Victor
Ludorum at Celtic Park on June 13th 1925 and
booked for St Roch's. He signed for St
Anthony's so as to stay with his school pals
Felix Gillon and Hugh Coyle. "Never showy
but valuable," he went to St Roch's when he
failed to fit in at Moore Park. With Celtic he
was "methodical, some say slow, not as astute
as Alec Thomson but with a powerful shot...
often sluggish." Jimmy McGrory had two ribs
broken on young John's debut just a week
before the Scottish Cup final against East Fife.
Celtic decided to play Tommy McInally at
centre in place of McGrory and half an hour
before kick-off manager Maley told John he
was in the team (that won Celtic's 12th
Scottish Cup). Manager John Hunter at
Motherwell had wanted him as a junior and
when young John failed to fit at Parkhead it
was at Fir Park that he made his career. He
played against Celtic in the two finals of 1931
and also in the final of April 15th 1933. He
helped a fine Motherwell side to the League
championship of 1932 by providing the
ammunition for the prolific Willie McFadyen.
John's big brother Harry (Newcastle United)
was selected to play for Scotland versus Wales
at Cardiff on October 4th 1933. When he
dropped out through injury John took his
place and got his one and only Scottish cap in
a 3-2 defeat.

Appearances:
SL: 15 apps. 2 gls.
SC: 1 app. 0 gls.
Total: *16 apps. 2 gls.*

McMILLAN, Duncan

Role: Centre-half 1945-49
5' 11" 12st.0lbs.
b. Glasgow, 18th January 1922
d. Grimsby, 20th May 1992

CAREER: Maryhill Harp/
CELTIC 6 Sept 1945/Grimsby
Town 8 Mar 1949/free own
request Nov 1954/Dundee
United (trial) 22 Nov 1954/free
21 Dec 1954.

*Debut v Hamilton Academicals (h)
2-0 (RL) 15.9.45*

Dunky McMillan was Jimmy McGrory's first
signing for Celtic and made his debut on the
day the Golden Crust won his first match as
manager. Dunky had a great game despite a
2-1 defeat by Morton on December 7th 1946
and it seemed as if the Bhoys had found their
ideal centre-half. In 1948 he was intended by

Dunky McMillan

new coach Jimmy
Hogan for Celtic's
first genuine
stopper but went
down with
ptomaine
poisoning on the
eve of the new
season (August
13th). Alec Boden
seized his chance
and Dunky's
undoubted
promise was
again frustrated.
His last game for
Celtic was in an
away friendly
against the club

he was shortly to join (February 19th 1949).
The move to Grimsby was a complete success
("Are there any more like you in Scotland?")
and he made a career of 188 first team games
and two goals with the Mariners.

Appearances:
SL: 18 apps. 0 gls.
SLC: 5 apps. 0 gls.
SC: 2 apps. 0 gls.
Total: *25 apps. 0 gls.*
RL: 19 apps. 0 gls.
RLC: 1 app. 0 gls.
Total: *20 apps. 0 gls.*

McNALLY, Mark

Role: Defender 1987 to date
5' 9" 10st.7lbs.
b. Motherwell, 10th March 1971

CAREER: Celtic BC/CELTIC 15 May 1987.
Debut v Motherwell (h) 3-1 (SL) 6.11.90

The official Celtic line on Mark McNally was to hail him as a young gun who "has matured into a reliable and consistent defender." Mark himself was grateful for what he called manager Brady's "commitment to giving young players a genuine chance to prove themselves in the first team." Whereas other players were dropped for one error, Mark seemed to have apparent carte blanche to make mistakes at leisure. A nightmare against Aberdeen on December 2nd 1992 did not affect his tenure and when he headed a ball straight down for Iain Ferguson to score in 40 seconds for Hearts at Tynecastle on December 19th he was rewarded with praise: he had put the blunder behind him and got on with the game! Even the Dash to Europe was arrested at Fir Park on April 3rd 1993 when Mark nodded a pass-back into Stevie Kirk's path for Motherwell's first in a 2-0 defeat for UEFA

aspirants Celtic. Another year, another Dash but the pass-back headed short to Bonner and the vital point dropped was again down to Mark in a 1-1 draw versus St Johnstone on April 27th 1994. On the credit side, such was the improvement in his general game during 1993-94, he can probably lay better claim to the role of central defender than anyone else at Parkhead. In a purely destructive, get-the-ball-away role he is unsurpassed. Like Peter Grant he is also Celtic in the bone and there have been few enough of his sort on the books at Parkhead lately. Thus he is to be cherished but as a central defender not a full-back. His distributive game also needs to be worked-on.

Appearances:
SL: 103 apps. 3 gls.
SLC: 8 apps. 1 gl.
SC: 7 apps. 0 gls.
Eur: 7 apps. 0 gls.
Total: *125 apps. 4 gls.*

McNALLY, Owen

Role: Centre-forward 1927-30
5' 8" 11st.0lbs.
b. Denny, 20th June 1906

CAREER: Denny Hibernian/CELTIC 26 Feb 1927/(Arthurlie loan 16 Aug 1927)/(Hamilton Academicals loan 23 July 1928)/CELTIC again 29 Apr 1929/(Hamilton Academicals loan 23 Feb 1929)/Bray Unknowns 17 Sept 1930/ Cardiff City 1931/Bray Unknowns 1932/FC Lausanne 1934/Sligo Rovers 1935/Distillery 1935/Leicester City Apr 1936/Racing Club de Paris 1937/Shamrock Rovers 1938.

Debut v Dundee United (a) 3-3 (SL) 9.4.27

Owen McNally made his debut for Celtic just a week before the Scottish Cup final versus East Fife in place of Jimmy McGrory (broken ribs). He must have had a chance of selection but Tommy McInally and John McMenemy were preferred on the day. Celtic leased him to Arthurlie in Division Two and immediately his goal touch as a junior returned: he scored eight against Armadale on October 1st 1927. He made his Old Firm debut in a 1-0 defeat at Ibrox on October 26th 1929.

Appearances:
SL: 11 apps. 4 gls.
Total: *11 apps. 4 gls.*

Mark McNally

McNAMARA, John

Role: Centre-half 1970-76
5' 9" 12st.0lbs.
b. Glasgow,
19th September 1952

CAREER: Lochend
Secondary/Eastercraigs
Amateurs/Cumbernauld
United Aug 1970/ CELTIC
(provisional) 28 Oct 1970/
(full) 30 Mar 1972/
Hibernian 1 Sept 1976/
Morton player-coach
12 June 1985/retired as
player 17 Dec 1987/
resigned as coach 11 May 1988/Hamilton
Academicals coach 1988/resigned 15 May
1989/Morton scout 1989/coach 5 Mar 1990/
Berwick Rangers asst. manager 25 May 1990/
resigned 5 May 1992.

Jackie McNamara

Debut v TPS Turku (h) 3-0 (EC) 3.10.73 (sub)

The myth says that Cumbernauld took
McNamara on as a 5ft 2ins stop-gap but in fact
Jackie was a highly-regarded juvenile and
snapped-up by Frank Meechan for Celtic after
just two games for United. In Jock Stein's
opinion, "Jackie could be as good if not better
than Dalglish... he has all the skills... he's just a
slow developer." His League debut was made
on the day Dixie Deans scored six against
Partick Thistle and Jackie (who came on for
Bobby Lennox) got to autograph the match
ball. His manifesto appeared in *The Leveller* of
December 12th 1975: "I am a Communist...
football is a sick business... the management
pulls all the strings and everyone looks out for
himself... Celtic and Rangers... take a shy and
you see the hate on the faces... it's a shame...
Celtic Park... not many politically conscious at
all... in for the wages and that's all." 'Boris'
moved to Hibs in a swap for Pat Stanton and
made his career at Easter Road where he was
enormously popular ('Mr Hibs') in Stanton's
sweeper role. He also had his Trade Union
moments. He threw his jersey at referee Joe
Timmons at Love Street on November 6th 1982
after being ordered off ("It wasn't even a
foul!") and was suspended for four games.
The SFA imposed a further punishment of £50
(January 10th 1983) for bringing the game into
disrepute. Jackie refused to pay ("I'm being
punished twice for the same offence!") and

invoked the General and
Municipal Workers' and
Boilermakers' Union to which the
Scottish Professional Footballers'
body was affiliated, demanding
right of appeal or a court action.
Pat Stanton resolved the fine
would be paid; Hibs had been
without their big key man for far
too long. Jackie's knees refused to
co-operate after four cartilage
operations and forced his
retirement at 32.

Appearances:
SL: 21 apps. 1 gl.
SLC: 15 apps. 2 gls.
SC: 2 apps. 1 gl.
Eur: 5 apps. 0 gls.
Total: *43 apps. 4 gls.*

McNAMEE, John

Role: Centre-half 1959-64
6' 0" 12st.7lbs.
b. Coatbridge, 11th June 1941

CAREER: Bellshill Athletic/CELTIC 13 Aug
1959/Hibernian 17 Apr 1964/Newcastle
United 30 Dec 1966/Blackburn Rovers Nov
1971/(Hartlepool United loan Dec 1972)/free
1973/Morton 20 Dec 1973/Lancaster City
1973/Workington Town manager 19 June
1975/dismissed Dec 1975/Cockermouth local
soccer coach 1975.

Debut v Hibernian (h) 2-0 (SL) 18.2.61

Parkhead coach Jock Stein signed John
McNamee after the 17-year-old had refused
Manchester United because he wanted Celtic.
Nottingham Forest had even offered Bellshill
Athletic £800. He made his debut when Billy

McNeill had 'flu
and was preferred
to Paddy Crerand
after the Ne'erday
fiasco of 1963. He
played a double
centre-half role
with Billy McNeill
and saw action in
both Scottish Cup
finals of 1963, May
4th and 15th. John

John McNamee

had family in the south of Ireland and was due to skipper Celtic against Cork Hibs on May 29th 1963 but was sent home for infringing curfew the night before. Joe Harvey took him to Newcastle: "The first time I saw him I ducked." At Blackburn "he brought self-respect and steel to the team." John was the Celtic player booked with the reserves at Tannadice on February 15th 1964 for arguing with his own goalie, Frank Haffey.

Appearances:
SL: 27 apps. 2 gls.
SLC: 2 apps. 0 gls.
SC: 7 apps. 1 gl.
Eur: 2 apps. 0 gls.
Total: *38 apps. 3 gls.*

McNEIL, Hugh

Role: Centre-half 1900-01

CAREER: Dalziel Rovers/Motherwell 22 Aug 1899/CELTIC 1 June 1900/Hamilton Academical 27 Dec 1901/Morton 2 Aug 1902/Motherwell 6 June 1904/free 1914/Motherwell 31 Oct 1914/Wishaw Thistle 31 Dec 1917/retired 1919.

Debut v Kilmarnock (h) 1-0 (SL) 27.10.1900

Celtic played Everton in a friendly at Parkhead on October 20th 1900 and gave junior internationalist Hughie McNeil a try-out in place of Tom Hynds. Celtic won 1-0 and when Hughie left the field after the Kilmarnock game a week later, Celtic had still to lose a goal with him in the team. His Nemesis arrived with the visit of Hearts on November 17th when top-of-the-League Celtic lost 1-3. He went on the December tour of England and played against Blackburn on Christmas Day, Grimsby on Boxing Day then did Celtic's Highland trip in May 1901. As an Accies' player he guested for Celtic versus Everton at Parkhead on April 28th 1901 and when Morton played Celtic in the final of Rangers' Ibrox Disaster Tourney (September 24th 1902) Hugh was at centre-half for the Greenock blues. He made his career with Motherwell and became so identified with Fir Park it was hard to remember he had a Celtic connection. He survived a serious motorcycle crash in September 1913.

Appearances:
SL: 2 apps. 0 gls.
Total: *2 apps. 0 gls.*

McNEILL, William M.B.E.

Role: Centre-half 1957-75
6' 1" 12st.0lbs.
b. Bellshill, 2nd March 1940

CAREER: Mossend Primary/Hereford Schools/Our Lady's High/CELTIC 20 Aug 1957/Blantyre Vics (farmed-out)/retired 3 May 1975/Clyde manager 1 Apr 1977/Aberdeen manager 9 June 1977/CELTIC manager 29 May 1978/Manchester City manager 30 June 1983/Aston Villa manager 22 Sept 1986/dismissed 8 May 1987/CELTIC manager 28 May 1987/dismissed 22 May 1991.

Debut v Clyde (h) 2-0 (SLC) 23.8.58

Big Billy's first strike at Hampden with his head was an own goal for Holyrood against Our Lady's High (May 9th 1957). He signed as Willie McNeill for coach Jock Stein and became Billy only as a Celt. He came on at half-time for John Jack in the Public Trial of August 6th 1957 and Bobby Collins sat in the bath afterwards amazed that this big gangly boy could fit in so quickly and so well. Bobby Evans damaged his back against Clyde in the League on August 20th 1958 and Billy's hour as Celtic's centre-half struck that night. He replaced Dunky MacKay as Celtic captain at the start of 1963-64 and lifted the Glasgow Cup, the club's first trophy since 1957 on March 25th 1964. His name was linked strongly with Spurs during the summer of '64 but, however much tempted, Billy decided to give it one more year with Celtic. The corner was turned with the arrival of Stein in 1965. Billy drilled home the first of his famous headed goals in the 81st minute of the Scottish Cup final on April 24th 1965 to bring Celtic a major trophy at last, 3-2 against Dunfermline. The next - which made the normally imperturbable Simpson do handstands - was in the last minute against Vojvodina at Parkhead on March 8th 1967 to send Celtic into the semi-final of the European Cup. Against Rangers in the 4-0 final on April 26th 1969, Billy struck earlier and not so cleanly but still welcome as ever. This 1969 final apart, he had probably his outstanding game as a Celtic centre-half in the semi-final second leg, the rearguard

Billy McNeill

Left: Billy McNeill lifts the European Cup in 1967 and (above) heads a 3rd minute goal in the 1969 Scottish Cup Final victory over Rangers - the first in 65 years. Below: Billy the boss.

action against Dukla in Prague (April 25th 1967). The Czechs sent their giant left-back Novak forward to contest corners and free-kicks, but Billy won every one in an atmosphere that was fraught with tension for the entire 90 minutes. In a sense, Jock Stein made McNeill but what would Jock have done without big Billy at the heart of his defence? Jock called him "One of the greatest Celts of all time, an inspiring captain and a model for every young footballer." Billy played 831 competitive games for the club all-told, took part in 12 Scottish Cup finals and got a winner's medal seven times; won nine Scottish League Championships; played in nine League Cup finals and was a winner in six; played 29 times for Scotland (it should have been more) and is the Celtic skipper who raised the European Cup over his head at Lisbon on May 25th 1967. Even in defeat he showed magnificence. He was the one Scottish success in the 9-3 thrashing at Wembley on April 15th 1961 (his international debut); but for him (and Haffey), Rangers would have taken the Scottish Cup by a far wider margin than 3-0 on May 15th 1963. Under Stein, Cesar (for Cesar Romero, svelte and smooth in his Duke Santos role) became Caesar (for conquering general, hero of the legions, master of the Earth). Big Jock and Big Billy formed one of the most potent manager/captain combinations in the history of the game. "He's my voice on the park" said Stein. McNeill, the best centre-half Celtic have ever had, led the

greatest Celtic team in history (most of them relics of that awful year of 1963) to glory in victory and defeat. There were no more Celtic fans streaming out early after Stein's return on March 9th 1965 and Big Billy's first Scottish Cup medal of April 24th 1965. Billy McNeill is an all-time Celtic great. And even that's an understatement.

Appearances:
SL: 486 apps. 22 gls.
SLC: 138 apps. 2 gls.
SC: 94 apps. 7 gls.
Eur: 72 apps. 3 gls.
Total: *790 apps. 34 gls.*

McOUSTRA, William

Role: Inside-forward 1899-1902

CAREER: Heather Rangers/Ashfield/CELTIC 21 Sept 1899/(Stenhousemuir loan 18 Nov 1899)/Manchester City 1 Feb 1902/Blackpool 9 Oct 1907/Stenhousemuir 29 July 1909/ Abercorn Nov 1909/Alloa 10 May 1910/ retired 1911/G Coy 2 Battalion Scots Guards May 1915.

Debut v Queen's Park (a) 2-0 (SL) 8.9.1900

Willie McOustra

Speed merchant Willie McOustra was tried out against the Kaffirs from Orange Free State at Celtic Park on September 21st 1899 and got his first match as a signed Celt in Bummer Campbell's benefit at Rugby Park on January 2nd 1900 in a 6-0 defeat. He first played in the Inter-City League versus Hibernian at Parkhead on March 3rd 1900 and scored twice in a 4-1 win. Willie was "a class man... a hard worker... a dashy, speedy player." Celtic exploited his pace on both wings but Willie was often so fast he had an embarrassing tendency to over-run the ball. Celtic retired to the Lorne Hotel, Rothesay, to prepare for "The Cup-tie of the Century" versus Rangers on January 12th 1901. Celtic took it 1-0 with a McOustra goal in 22 minutes. After a form slump he and Jimmy Drummond were off-loaded to Manchester City "for enormous prices... do Celtic really want to win the Cup?" Tom Maley's great Manchester City side of 1904 was destroyed by the English FA inquiry into illegal payments and a new team with a new style was built around McOustra who took on his shoulders the work once shared by giants like Meredith, Livingstone and Turnbull. Willie served on the Western Front during World War I. He was a committeeman at Stenhousemuir and when not working in the foundry at Keppochhill was Jerry Reynolds' assistant doing odd jobs around Parkhead.

Appearances:
SL: 23 apps. 6 gls.
SC: 7 apps. 3 gls.
Total: *30 apps. 9 gls.*

McPHAIL, John

Role: Utility 1941-56
6' 0" 13st.7lbs.
b. Lambhill, 27th December 1923

CAREER: St Mungo's Academy/Strathclyde Aug 1941/CELTIC (provisional) 14 Aug 1941/(full) 27 Oct 1941/(Ballymoney United loan summer 1947)/retired 5 May 1956.

Debut v Partick Thistle (h) 1-1 (RL) 25.10.41

'Hooky' McPhail broke into the Celtic League team as a play-anywhere type and had the best game of his young career against Thistle at Firhill on January 22nd 1944 at inside-right: "McPhail's assiduous purveying was a feature... it's a long time since I've seen such consistently brilliant dribbling, feinting and lobbing from an inside-forward and full of Tommy McInally cheek too." His physical strength and power in the tackle was a major factor in the 0-1 defeat of Rangers at Ibrox on Ne'erday 1945 but by the start of 1946-47 he was seriously ill in Ruchill Hospital and lost the entire season from the Victory Cup tie versus Raith Rovers on May 18th 1946 until his come-back on April 12th 1947 at Easter Road. He was made captain at the start of 1948-49 and the unalloyed affection the fans felt for him was demonstrated by the mighty roar that greeted his name as back in the team after absence on Christmas Day 1948. He got his first cap for Scotland as "a roving, dashing centre-forward" against Wales on November 9th 1949 and scored the opening goal at a fog-bound Hampden. *In the war against Rangers/In the fight for the Cup/Big John McPhail put the Celtic one up.* The Cup in question was the Charity trophy (in the Danny Kaye final on May 6th 1950)

Captain John McPhail scored the only goal of the game in Celtic's 1951 Scottish Cup final victory over Motherwell.

when he got a hat-trick with three strikes between the 40th and 48th minutes. Big John captained Celtic in Rome against Lazio in the Italian club's Golden Jubilee match of May 30th 1950. He and Remondini were ordered-off after half an hour for fighting. According to John, it was the Italian who was ordered-off. The referee asked him to go too "in order to to placate the crowd." It was big Hooky's goal at Ibrox on November 29th 1950 that saw the Scottish League beat the English 1-0. At Tynecastle in a pulsating Cup-tie on February 24th 1951, McPhail and Tully passed and re-passed their way through the packed Hearts defence for his 33rd minute goal that won the match 1-2 for Celtic. He made his Celtic fame for ever when he led the attack at sun-drenched Hampden on April 21st 1951. He was ever "the danger man... the mastermind of the Celtic attack... and played the skipper's part" when he broke down the middle in 13 minutes after incessant Motherwell pressure and lobbed the diving Johnny Johnstone for the only score of the game ("a gem of a goal") and Celtic's first Scottish Cup since 1937. Celtic sailed to America and while Jimmy McGrory carried "McPhail's Cup" everywhere in a paper bag until he was sick of it, it was big John who paraded it before every match so the Yanks could see what he'd won for Celtic. His last hurrah was at left-half in the Celtic side that beat Hibs in the Coronation Cup final of May 20th 1953. He was a shock choice for Scotland at centre-forward in Belfast on October 3rd

1953 and when he failed to appear for Celtic versus Aberdeen the week previous rumours were rife as to his fitness. Scotland took it 1-3 but could as easily have lost and "McPhail just won't do." Weight problems dominated 1954 and he was sent to a health farm in Tring to diet off the excess. With the poundage problem he was more and more reluctant to play in the middle but did lead the attack in the Scottish Cup final against Clyde on April 23rd 1955. He was dropped for the replay. John McPhail was Celtic through and through and beloved of the fans of his time. In the further words of the old parody quoted earlier: *Hail John McPhail! The Pride of Parkhead!* He worked as a journalist for the *Daily Record* and later for the club newspaper on retirement.

Appearances:
Sl: 142 apps. 54 gls.
SLC: 38 apps. 16 gls.
SC: 24 apps. 17 gls.
Total: *204 apps. 87 gls.*
RL: 106 apps. 11 gls.
RLC: 25 apps. 2 gls.
Total: *131 apps. 13 gls.*

♣ **Celtic note 1:** *His all-time Celtic team: Miller; Hogg & Gemmell; Geatons, McNeill & Murdoch; Johnstone & Malky MacDonald; Billy McPhail; Tully and John Hughes.*
♣ **Celtic note 2:** *John was 'Hooky' to the fans because of "the extraordinary way he jab-cuts the ball with his right foot."*

McPHAIL, William

Role: Centre-forward 1956-58
5' 11" 11st.0lbs.
b. Glasgow, 2nd February 1928

CAREER: Queen's Park 23 Sept 1944/Clyde
10 May 1947/Army (Black Watch) 4 Jan 1948/
demobbed Nov 1949/CELTIC 5 May 1956/
retired 28 Aug 1958.

Debut v Aberdeen (a) 2-1 (SLC) 11.8.56

"Billy McPhail uses his head... not with the
power of a McGrory but he knows all the
angles" (written after William had scored five
for Clyde against Cowdenbeath on October
6th 1951, four of them headed). Ladies'
hairdresser, restaurateur, "player of audacious
deliberation," Billy McPhail joined the Celtic
just as big brother John retired. Billy was
stylish, elegant and he scored goals. His first
for Celtic was typical; a header from a Peacock
free-kick that bulleted into the East Fife net at
Parkhead in the League Cup on August 18th
1956. With his two goals against Clyde on
October 6th, Celtic won their way into
uncharted territory: a League Cup final, the
competition in which they had failed with
total consistency since its inception in 1941.
They had to play Partick Thistle twice in the
final but won their most elusive trophy by 3-0

on October 31st 1956, with the first two
counters from McPhail. He went on the US
tour of 1957 and lined-up with Sammy Wilson
as his inside-left partner for the first time
against Hibernian on August 31st in the
League Cup at Parkhead. Each scored and
Billy had found his perfect foil: he knocked
them down, Slammin' Sammy hammered
them in. The first full League points in 22
years were won 2-3 at Ibrox on September 21st
1957 (McPhail 54, Wilson 64), a mere appetiser
for the League Cup final at Hampden in the
sun (October 19th 1957). Billy scored three (53,
67, 80) in the greatest game of his career. His
knee broke down in the Celtic trial of August
2nd 1958 and he never played again. He was
two short seasons at Celtic Park. He was
expected to make a difference and he did.

Appearances:
SL: 33 apps. 13 gls.
SLC: 20 apps. 21 gls.
SC: 4 apps. 4 gls.
Total: *57 apps. 38 gls.*

McPHERSON, Andrew Forbes

Role: Goalkeeper 1902-04
b. Greenock, 22nd September 1879

CAREER: Morton Juniors/Morton 10 June
1898/CELTIC 19 May 1902/Hibernian 22 Apr
1904/reinstated
amateur 1905/
Stenhousemuir Sept
1905/Port Glasgow
Athletic Jan 1906.

*Debut v Hearts (h) 3-1
(CC) 19.5.02*

Andy McPherson
succeeded Bob
McFarlane between
the sticks for Celtic
and was Davy
Adams' immediate
precursor. He came
from Morton in
exchange for John
Hodge. He first
played for Celtic in
the 2-0 defeat of
Rangers in the Inter-
City League on May
9th 1902 but lost six
goals against Hibs in

*Celtic goalscorers in the 7-1 League Cup Final thrashing of Rangers in 1957.
Left to right: Willie Fernie, Billy McPhail, Neilly Mochan and Sammy Wilson.*

the Charity Cup final at 2nd Hampden on May 31st 1902. He collected his first medal with Celtic at the same venue on June 17th when Rangers were beaten 3-2 after extra time in the final of the Ibrox Disaster British Championship. He played his first League match on August 16th 1902 and was "nervous and excited at crucial moments" versus Hibernian in Edinburgh. So much so, Celtic re-signed Dan McArthur. He was in the Celtic side which beat his old comrades Morton for gold watches in the final of the Rangers Benefit tournament (September 24th 1902). His finest hour guarding the Celtic net was in the Scottish Cup first round (third replay) against St Mirren on February 14th 1903, a display that so inspired the Celts that at last they saw off a very tough Buddies side, 4-0. Andy was the first Celtic goalie to wear the hoops as opposed to the stripes on August 15th 1903.

Appearances:
SL: 27 apps. 6 shut-outs.
SC: 5 apps. 3 shut-outs.
Total: *32 apps. 9 shut-outs (28%).*

McPHERSON, James

Role: Left-half 1890
b. Kilmarnock, c 1866
d. Springburn, March 1926 (?)

CAREER: Kilmarnock 1884/Cowlairs summer 1885/(Rangers loan)/(CELTIC loan Oct 1890)/ Kilmarnock Apr 1894.

Debut v Carfin Shamrock (a) 3-1 (SC) 4.10.1890

Brother of the more famous John "Kytie" McPherson (who also assisted Celtic), Jamie played left-half for the Cowlairs team that hanselled the first Celtic Park with a match against Hibs on May 8th 1888 (Kytie played outside-left). He helped the green and whites out versus Sunderland on Thursday October 2nd 1890 in place of Jimmy McLaren and turned out at Byresknowe Park to see the Shamrock off in the Scottish Cup second round replay. He had played for Cowlairs against Celtic in their first ever final, the (phantom) World Exhibition Cup on September 6th 1888. He belongs to the list of players who saw action with both Celtic and Rangers.

Appearances:
SC: 1 app. 0 gls.
Total: *1 app. 0 gls.*

McQUILKEN, James

Role: Left-back 1989 to date
5' 9" 10st.8lbs.
b. Glasgow, 31st October 1974

CAREER: St John Bosco Academy/Celtic BC/ CELTIC 'S' form Apr 1989/CELTIC 28 June 1991.

Debut v Falkirk (h) 1-0 (SL) 20.4.93

Govanhill boy Jamie McQuilken, a Parkhead YTS probationer and not yet a signed professional, was first mentioned in the Celtic big team context versus Partick Thistle on February 20th 1993. He came on for Dariusz Wdowczyk against Shelbourne in the 50th minute at Tolka Park (March 3rd 1993) and had some experience of sitting a game out on the bench unused before he started a full 90 minutes work on a Tuesday night against the Bairns. Joe Miller came on for Charlie Nicholas in 66 minutes and Jamie now found he had a new freedom to go forward and worry Ian Westwater with some samples of his speciality: the deep cross from the left. Jamie was in the Celtic side that won the Reserve League Cup at Tannadice (April 18th 1994).

Appearances:
SL: 1 app. 0 gls.
Total: *1 app. 0 gls.*

Jamie
McQuilken

McSTAY, James

Role: Centre-half 1920-34
5' 8" 11st.0lbs.
b. Netherburn, 1st April 1895
d. 3rd January 1974

CAREER: Larkhall Thistle summer 1917/ Royal Scots Fusiliers 1918/CELTIC 13 Nov 1920/free 1934/Hamilton Academicals 28 Sept 1934/(CELTIC loan May 1936)/Dublin Brideville player-coach-manager 9 Aug 1937/ Alloa manager 21 Apr 1938/CELTIC manager 15 Feb 1940/dismissed 24 July 1945/Hamilton Academicals manager 14 Feb 1946/resigned 13 July 1951/CELTIC chief scout 21 Dec 1951/ resigned 1961.

Debut v Clyde (a) 1-0 (SL) 4.11.22

"You never see the younger McStay get caught in possession... he gets rid quickly and to best advantage" (December 1925). "He is not one for the new Third Back style. He likes to get forward as much as possible" (January 1926). "Quiet, unostentatious, often better than he looks," Jimmy McStay joined Celtic as a left-half but proved such a poor distributor of the ball he had to work hard to avoid the free transfer which Tom White was anxious to award him. He was not tried at centre-half until the two-referee experiment at Cathkin on February 9th 1924. He now found his niche as one able to "pump the ball forward and keep pumping it forward." "He's not flashy but 90 minutes on the field with McStay as opponent makes you realise you've a lot to learn... the quietest player I've ever opposed... no shouting, no intimidating." Jimmy had few faults bar a lack of style.

Jimmy McStay (centre, front) heads a group of 1931 Celts.

Herbert Chapman called him "a good, steady, plodding centre-half." He took over as skipper from big brother Willie in 1929 and had his best game for Celtic in the Glasgow Cup final of October 11th 1930, 2-1 versus Rangers: "He raised the enthusiasm of the crowd to high pitch by his brilliant display." In the Scottish Cup final of April 11th 1931 with Celtic 2-1 down and Bertie Thomson footering about so as to be able to claim the match ball, it was quiet man McStay who bellowed at him: "Get it across, man!" He captained the Scottish League against the English at Celtic Park on November 7th 1931 when the Scots won 4-3. On that day his proudest epitaph was written: "Jimmy McStay refused to allow Dixie Dean to get going." Jimmy played centre-half for a fine Hamilton Acas team beaten 1-2 by Rangers in the Scottish Cup final of April 20th 1935.

Appearances:
SL: 409 apps. 6 gls.
SC: 63 apps. 2 gls.
Total: *472 apps. 8 gls.*

♣ **Celtic note:** *Celtic tradition would not allow the complete adoption of the Third Back game as practised by every other club in the country as of 1925-26. Jimmy McStay was expected to get forward as Loney used to do and angle for the shot. Once McStay warned "I'm going up," the onus was on the goalkeeper to be ready to risk his neck if the centre got away.*

Paul McStay

McSTAY, Paul Michael Lyons

Role: Midfield 1981 to date
5' 10" 11st.0lbs.
b. 22nd October 1964

CAREER: Meadowhill United BC/Holy Cross
Hamilton/Hamilton Thistle/CELTIC S form
1975/Celtic BC/CELTIC full pro. 20 Feb 1981.
Debut v Queen of the South (h) 4-0 (SC) 23.1.82

"McStay, of course, is exceptional... for all their
huge investment in players... Rangers quite
simply do not possess a talent to compare
with his... home-grown McStay is in a class of
his own" (Alan Davidson March 21st 1988).
Paul McStay scored two goals at Wembley for
Scotland schoolboys in the wonderful 4-5 win
of June 7th 1980 over England. In the
European Youth Championships in West
Germany on May 25th 1981, Scotland beat
Austria 1-0: "His performance sent shivers of
delight down the spines of every football
lover. He was the springboard for everything
good. What enormous talent this young Celtic
star has!" Paul was extra at senior level too.
He broke into the Championship side of 1982
and won a League Cup medal against Rangers
at Hampden in heavy rain on December 4th of
that year, the last time Celtic won the trophy.
He brought the ten-man Celtic hope in the
Scottish Cup final of May 19th 1984 with an
equaliser five minutes from time against
Aberdeen. He was "the pedigree player of
Scottish football" and some days, as against
Hibs on January 16th 1985, his form was so
unbelievable that "wave after wave of
applause" broke out. He won his first Scottish
Cup medal (although taken off injured)
against Dundee United on May 18th 1985 and
scored the fourth goal when the Celtic stole
the League at Love Street on May 3rd 1986. In
the club's Centenary Season 1987-88 he was
enormous in midfield and Celtic's key man in
the side that brought home the Double.
Against Rangers in the Scottish Cup final of
May 20th 1989 Paul again was Celtic's five-star
player. He became the third in his family to
skipper Celtic as of January 13th 1990 when he
took over from Roy Aitken. He also succeeded
big Roy as Scotland skipper (until 13th
October 1993 versus Italy in Rome when he
was dropped by Craig Brown) and on October
14th 1992 versus Portugal at Ibrox he surpassed Danny McGrain's Parkhead record of
62 Scottish caps. The most ominous gesture at

Paul McStay

the end of Liam Brady's empty first term at
Parkhead was Paul McStay stripping off his
jersey and throwing it to the Jungle on May
2nd 1992. The dreaded goodbye looked as if it
were being said. Paul stayed on at Paradise
but his game went into eclipse during 1992-93.
It revived during Frank Connor's brief
interregrum after Brady and before Macari: "I
told him to stay off the play, to get his passes
in rather than take players on. I told him to be
selfish." Paul had two magnificent matches,
1-0 versus Sporting Lisbon on October 20th
1993 and the 1-2 defeat of Rangers at Ibrox in
the League ten days later. His 1993-94 season
ended prematurely on April 16th and he
entered hospital for a hernia operation. He
should be the figure dominating Celtic's
performances but since 1992 has been largely
anonymous, almost as if something else was
thrown away with his jersey on May 2nd. Nor
is he any longer an automatic choice for
Scotland. One school of thought believes he
might be a better player without the burden of
the Celtic captaincy.

Appearances:
SL: 440 apps. 53 gls.
SLC: 47 apps. 7 gls.
SC: 54 apps. 6 gls.
Eur: 38 apps. 0 gls.
Total: *579 apps. 66 gls.*

McSTAY, William

Role: Full-back 1912-29
5' 9" 12st.0lbs.
b. Netherburn, 21st April 1894
d. 3rd September 1960

CAREER: Larkhall Thistle 1909/Ashgill Rovers 1910/Larkhall Thistle 1911/Tottenham Hotspur (trial) 1 Jan 1912/CELTIC 13 Jan 1912 /(Vale of Leven loan 25 Jan 1912)/(Ayr United loan 29 Nov 1912)/CELTIC again 19 July 1916 /North Irish Horse 1917/(Belfast Celtic loan 8 Aug 1917)/CELTIC again 23 Jan 1919/New York Giants (once) May 1923 /Hearts 30 Aug 1929/ retired Oct 1930/ reinstated am. 1931/ Kirkmuirhill Juniors 1931/Glentoran manager 25 Nov 1932 /resigned Oct 1933/ Coleraine manager 1933/resigned 1935.

Debut v St Mirren (a) 5-1 (SL) 19.8.16

"When Willie McStay was my left-back, I never had to worry about crosses from the right" (Jimmy Brownlie). Willie McStay served his apprenticeship at Ayr then played for Celtic throughout the Championship season of 1916-17 before helping Belfast Celtic to their first ever Irish Cup on April 4th 1918. He missed the Championship campaign of 1919 on active service but won a League badge again in 1922 and went on the tour of Czechoslovakia where he and John Gilchrist were sent off for what manager Maley called "ordinary fouls" against Johnny Madden's Slavia on May 25th. Despite the lifting of the Scottish Cup on March 31st 1923 (he played left-back, his favourite position), Celtic reduced wages all round and Willie went AWOL on May 5th when

Willie McStay

Celtic lost 0-1 to Rangers in the semi-final of the Charity Cup. There was soccer in the USA at £12-£14 a week and he and Willie Crilly crossed to reconnoitre prospects. Celtic suspended him ("He left us in the lurch!") but Willie was soon back and reconciled by August 21st. He was made Celtic skipper after Billy Cringan as of September 24th 1923. He ordered the hold-'em-then-hit-'em strategy for the 5-0 defeat of Rangers in the Cup semi-final of March 21st 1925. Although he led Celtic to victory in the "Gallagher Final" of April 11th 1925, he always regarded his greatest match as being the Glasgow Cup final of October 9th 1926; Celtic held out against Rangers and a hurricane the whole of the first half then snatched the trophy with a McGrory goal in the second. Willie was first capped for Scotland on Valentine's Day 1925 at Tynecastle when the mud so obliterated the jerseys Scotland had to change into a set of Hearts' blue at half-time and Wales into red supplied by Hibs. He took over as captain of Scotland one year later, on February 27th versus Ireland at Ibrox. Willie skippered the Celtic team that won the League but lost the Cup final in 1926 and won his third and last Scottish Cup medal against East Fife on April 16th 1927. He went open-to-transfer on May 8th 1929 and Celtic were without a genuine replacement until Willie Cook. Willie was a well-read man with considered views on world issues. He had a car to get the kids to school but otherwise preferred to walk. His passion was breeding pedigree dogs.

Appearances:
SL: 399 apps. 36 gls.
SC: 47 apps. 3 gls.
Total: *446 apps. 39 gls.*

McSTAY, William James

Role: Full-back 1977-87
5' 11" 11st.7lbs.
b. 26th November 1961

CAREER: Holy Cross
Hamilton/Hamilton Thistle/
CELTIC S form 23 Dec 1977/
Celtic BC/CELTIC 3 Aug
1979/Huddersfield Town
12 Mar 1987/Notts County
26 Feb 1988/ (Hartlepool
United loan Nov 1989)/
(Partick Thistle loan 1989-
90)/Kilmarnock 16 July 1990
/Sligo Rovers player-
manager Oct 1992/CELTIC
coach 26 July 1994.

*Debut v Motherwell (h) 3-0
(SL) 2.4.83 (sub)*

"Fleet-footed, a good user of
the ball," Willie McStay, big
brother of Paul, grand-
nephew of Willie and Jimmy,
first played for Celtic in the
Glasgow Cup versus Clyde
on April 29th 1981 and was
hailed before he had kicked a
ball as an outstanding
prospect. He began the first

Willie McStay

of his four seasons as a Celtic
first-team player against
Brechin City in the League Cup on August
27th 1983 playing sweeper behind Roy Aitken.
He never properly made a big team spot his
own but filled-in for Aitken and McGrain.
Tom McAdam was unfit for the Scottish Cup
final of May 19th 1984 and Willie played centre-half in the 2-1 defeat. Of his two goals for
Celtic, the more famous was against Rangers
in the 3-0 League victory at Parkhead (April
2nd 1984). 1-0 down, Rangers were going all
out for an equaliser in the second half until
"Willie McStay ran onto a short free kick... hit
a long-range shot... McCloy dived too late...
could only touch the ball onto the post and
into the net." Willie was seldom as
comfortable on the ball as Paul but on his day
might exhibit such exquisite control as to
suggest he was play-maker as well as rugged
defender. He won a Scottish Cup medal
against Dundee United on May 18th 1985 in

grand-uncle Willie's
position at right-back and a
League Championship
badge in 1986. After a sticky
start at a Sligo club on the
brink of collapse, Willie led
Rovers to the League of
Ireland Shield, the First
Division Championship and
on May 15th 1994 to the FAI
Cup 0-1 versus Derry City at
Lansdowne Road. He was
being hailed as Ireland's
new Jack Charlton before
returning to Celtic as a
coach in the summer of
1994.

Appearances:
SL: 67 apps. 2 gls.
SLC: 12 apps. 0 gls.
SC: 7 apps. 0 gls.
Eur: 4 apps. 0 gls.
Total: *90 apps. 2 gls.*

McVITTIE, Matthew

Role: Inside-right 1953-59
5' 7" 10st.0lbs.
*b. Calderbank,
30th September 1937*

CAREER: Chapelhall St
Aloysius/Calderbank BG/
Wishaw Juniors 17 July
1953/CELTIC (provisional)
29 July 1953/(Albion Rovers loan Sept 1953)
/(full) 9 Dec 1953/Army Feb 1956 to Feb 1958
/St Johnstone 25 Nov 1959/free own request
1962/Cambridge Town 17 Aug 1962/
Baillieston Juniors coach.

Debut v Clyde (h) 4-0 (GC) 23.8.55

Matt McVittie aged 13 was commended to
chief scout Jimmy McStay: "You must see him.
He looks like a man playing among boys."
Matt had a "splendid debut" aged 17 with
"ball control and an excellent idea of the
game." He was in Stein's side which won the
2nd XI Cup on an 8-2 aggregate versus
Rangers (March 21st 1958). Triumph then
disaster: he broke his arm on the Irish tour
against Derry City at the Brandywell on May
18th 1958. At Ibrox on Ne'erday 1959 so
atrocious were the conditions he was found to
be suffering from exposure at the final whistle

Matt McVittie

and had to be got into a hot bath fast. His finest hour was surely the defeat of Rangers in the Scottish Cup on February 28th 1959 when he not only played well, he put Celtic 2-0 up 12 minutes after the interval. He won a Charity Cup medal against Clyde on May 9th 1959 but lost his wing spot to Steve Chalmers in mid-September 1959. His second last game was in the "Lambs-to-the-Slaughter" Celtic side that played Wolves under the Parkhead lights (October 12th 1959). Bobby Brown offered him a house, top wages and a job on the ground staff to come to St Johnstone. Jim Sharkey recommended Alan Moore to take him to Cambridge.

Appearances:
SL: 33 apps. 9 gls.
SLC: 6 apps. 0 gls.
SC: 5 apps. 3 gls.
Total: *44 apps. 12 gls.*

McWILLIAM, Ian

Role: Centre-forward/Centre-half 1977-78
6' 5" 12st.4lbs.
b. *Malta, 19th March 1953*

CAREER: Glasgow Police Cadets 1973/ Duntocher Hibernian 1974/Queen's Park 1975 /CELTIC 2 Aug 1977/free 22 Apr 1978/Seiko (Hong Kong) 3 Aug 1978/Blackpool (trial) 24 Jan 1981/Rutherglen Glencairn.

Debut v Jeunesse Esch (h) 5-0 (EC) 14.9.77

Davie McParland tried to take police cadet Ian to Partick Thistle in 1973 but eventually landed him as a centre-half for Queen's Park where he had "an outstanding season 1976-77" and was "a real personality." It was Davie took him (now a taxi driver but still an amateur) to Parkhead as centre-half cover. On his Premier League debut (September 17th 1977) at Pittodrie, Celtic went ahead thanks to a Willie Garner own goal (49) but big Ian reciprocated for the Dons (58). His last full game for Celtic was a rain-lashed League Cup

quarter-final at Love Street on November 9th 1977. He came on as substitute for Joe Craig in the second leg at Parkhead a week later and the rest is silence. Surely the tallest player ever to have turned out for Celtic in all their time? John Curran and Eddie Dowdells (1949) were a mere 6ft 4ins and Eddie didn't make the first team.

Appearances:
SL: 1 app. 0 gls.
SLC: 2 apps. 0 gls.
Eur: 1 app. 0 gls.
Total: *4 apps. 0 gls.*

McWILLIAM, Robert McMillan

Role: Outside-left 1928-29; 1932
b. *Camelon, 24th May 1909*

CAREER: Auchinsharry Juveniles 1928/ Denny Hibernian July 1928/CELTIC 15 Aug 1928/Watford 1929/Leith Athletic 8 Aug 1931 /free Feb 1932/CELTIC 18 Feb 1932/Yeovil and Petters United Dec 1932/Newry Town 1933/Larne Aug 1933/Coleraine Oct 1933.

Debut v Kilmarnock (h) 3-0 (SL) 8.9.28

Manchester City wanted Bob McWilliam and manager John Hodge was willing to pay £130 for the brand new Denny Hib. Bob wanted to go to Parkhead and Willie Maley took him for £100 less. His debut was "a mistake. A month or two ago he was only a juvenile... he is immature, inexperienced, green. He requires nursing, not shoving into the team as if he were a ready-made winger... Celtic directors will spoil him if they treat him as a matured and experienced product." Against Third Lanark on November 24th 1928 he showed "very clever" and played in the final of the Dental Hospital Cup versus Partick Thistle at Hampden four days later, a tie which went to extra time and represents a one-off trophy that Celtic did not win. Bob came back to Parkhead when Leith Athletic folded and went straight into the team in place of Peter Kavanagh versus Clyde at Shawfield February 20th. This was his last game for Celtic. A week later he was playing for the reserves at Dens Park where he "gave a magnificent display of dribbling and his crossing was dangerously accurate."

Appearances:
SL: 7 apps. 0 gls.
Total: *7 apps. 0 gls.*

MEECHAN, Francis

Role: Full-back 1952-59
6' 0" 13st.2lbs.
b. Condorrat, 27th October 1929
d. Croy, 20th August 1976

CAREER: Holy Cross (Croy) BG 1948/
Glenboig St Joseph's/Holy Cross (Croy) BG
again/Armadale Thistle 1950/free 1951/
Petershill (trial) 1951/Notts County (trial)
1951/Petershill 1951/Hibernian (provisional)
25 Aug 1951/free 1952/CELTIC 1 July 1952/
(Stirling Albion loan 11 Nov 1958)/free 1959/
CELTIC scout until July 1975.

Debut v Hibernian (a) 0-3 (SLC) 30.8.52

Red-headed Frank Meechan from Croy is
identified in the Celtic memory as Mike
Haughney's left-back partner. Big Frank
claimed to enjoy the camaraderie of the pit
and was a part-time footballer until 1955-56.
Essentially right-sided with no left foot to
speak of, he became Celtic's left-back for the
first time against Rangers in the League on
September 20th 1952 instead of Sean Fallon
but lost his place in the Coronation Cup c
ompetition to Alex Rollo after a bad game versus Aberdeen on April 15th 1953. He returned
to do great deeds in the Double side of 1954
and won a Scottish Cup medal on April 24th
1954. In the Cup final of April 23rd 1955, he

Frank Meechan challenging Aberdeen's George
Martin in the 1954 Scottish Cup final.

and Johnny Bonnar combined to lose Archie
Robertson's 88th minute corner-kick in-
swinger at the near post that gave Clyde the
equaliser and a replay. Frank was never again
automatic first-team choice but he had a good
tour of the USA in 1957 and started the new
season at right-back as partner to Sean Fallon.
All went well until the League Cup qualifier at
Easter Road on August 17th when Frank
gifted Willie Ormond the lead in five minutes
and put through his own goal in eleven. John
Donnelly now took over as Celtic's right-back.

Appearances:
SL: 86 apps. 0 gls.
SLC: 11 apps. 0 gls.
SC: 19 apps. 0 gls.
Total: *116 apps. 0 gls.*

MEEHAN, Peter

Peter Meehan

Role: Right-back
1895-97
5' 9" 13st.13lbs.
b. Broxburn,
28th February 1872
d. Nova Scotia, July 1915

CAREER: Broxburn
Shamrock/Hibernian
Feb 1892/Sunderland
12 Aug 1893/CELTIC 20 May
1895/Everton 6 Jan 1897/Southampton Aug
1898/Manchester City 15 Sept 1900/Barrow
1901/Broxburn 14 Mar 1902/Clyde 22 Aug
1903/Broxburn Shamrock 14 May 1904.

Debut v Queen's Park (a) 1-0 (CC) 14.5.1895

Linlithgowshire miner Peter Meehan saw his
best days with Sunderland and was probably
never a completely well man for the rest of his
career. He took over from Jerry Reynolds for
1895-96 and secured a Charity Cup medal
almost immediately in the 4-0 win over
Rangers at 1st Cathkin on May 25th 1895. He
was in the team that beat Rangers 6-2 on
December 14th 1895 to secure Celtic's third
League Flag and also when the fifth Charity
Cup in five years was won (May 16th 1896).
Peter played his last game for Celtic in the
Glasgow Cup final defeat by Rangers on
November 21st 1896 and with Battles and
Divers, refused to strip versus Hibs at
Parkhead the following week unless the press
box was purged. With Everton his career
reached almost Sunderland pitch again and he

went to Southampton for a record fee of £200. With the Saints he won a loser's medal in the English Cup final of April 21st 1900.

Appearances:
SL: 25 apps. 1 gl.
Total: *25 apps. 1 gl.*

MELROSE, James

Role: Striker 1983-84
5' 9" 10st.1lb.
b. Glasgow, 7th October 1958

CAREER: Whitehill School /Partick Thistle 'S' form 1973/Eastercraigs Amateurs/Sighthill Amateurs 1975/Partick Thistle 8 July 1975/ Leicester City 10 June 1980 /Coventry City 13 Sept 1982/CELTIC 11 Aug 1983/(Wolverhampton Wanderers loan Sept 1984)/Manchester City 7 Nov 1984/Charlton Athletic 24 Mar 1986/ Leeds United 25 Sept 1987/(Shrewsbury Town loan 6 Feb 1988)/Shrewsbury Town 25 Mar 1988/Macclesfield Town Oct 1990/St Mirren reserves (trial) 1991/Curzon Ashton 22 Oct 1991/Halesowen Harriers 1992/Bollington Athletic (Cheshire) manager.

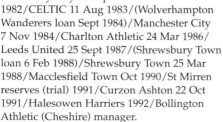
Jim Melrose

Debut v Rangers (n) 0-1 (GC) 13.8.83 (sub)

"Fast off the mark, never giving the defence peace," Jim Melrose came on for Danny Crainie in the 100th Glasgow Cup final at Hampden on his debut while Rangers fans mocked the Celtic end: "Where's your Charlie gone? Far, far away." Jim with his "harassing pace" took his chance at Firhill when Joe Craig moved to Celtic. "He's so fast, sometimes he doesn't take time to size the situation up properly" (Bertie Auld). Jock Wallace brought him to Leicester for £250,000 where the flame-haired forward was enormously popular and the support was cast into dudgeon when Gordon Milne swapped him for Tommy English. He played for Celtic reserves in a 3-4 win at Ibrox on January 4th 1984 and scored a straight hat-trick past Peter McCloy, wee Rangers' first defeat in 18 starts. Jim was a substitute in the two Cup final defeats of 1984, the League Cup versus Rangers (March 25th) and the Scottish Cup versus Aberdeen (May 19th). He started 1984-85 still unable to establish himself in the first team. With Wolves

on trial he scored four goals in four games but Tommy Docherty could not afford the transfer fee. He came back to Celtic on November 5th 1984 and Billy McNeill, looking to boost City's successful promotion drive, took him to Maine Road as "the steal of the season" at £40,000 two days later.

Appearances:
SL: 30 apps. 7 gls.
SLC: 8 apps. 3 gls.
SC: 4 apps. 1 gl.
Eur: 6 apps. 0 gls.
Total: *48 apps. 11 gls.*

♣ **Celtic note:** *At White Hart Lane on February 21st 1981, Jim "went into the challenge" on Spurs' Paul Miller "and then darkness." He was rushed to hospital in deep concussion with what many players on the field described as the most frightening injury they had witnessed. With Shrewsbury on February 20th 1988 he was attacked by Swindon's Chris Kamara after the match and required surgery on a fractured cheekbone. Kamara was fined £1,000 in court for assault.*

MILLAR, Alexander

Role: Centre-half 1935-38; 1940
5' 10" 11st.3lbs.
b. Mossend, 21st October 1911
d. 28th January 1978

CAREER: Mossend Celtic/Parkhead Juniors 1933/free 1934/Shawfield Juniors 1934/ CELTIC 22 May 1935/Preston North End 13 Oct 1938/(CELTIC loan 5 Oct 1940)/ (Albion Rovers loan 30 Nov 1940)/free from Albion Rovers Feb 1941 and temporary retire-ment/(Newarthill Hearts loan Aug 1942)/ (Motherwell loan Feb 1943)/(Blairhall Colliery loan 1943)/(Motherwell loan Aug 1944)/ Motherwell Feb 1945/Dundee United summer 1946/Morton 24 Oct 1947/free 1949/Inverness Caledonian (trial) 3 Sept 1949/Stranraer 24 Oct 1949/... Middlesbrough scout 1955.

Debut v Kilmarnock (a) 1-1 (SL) 5.10.35

Alex Millar was of Lithuanian parentage, one of three children, two boys and a girl. A schoolboy outside-right, he was a practised stowaway "in the old brake club days" and used to follow-follow Celtic "as far away as

Perth or Dundee." His tragedy was to join up at Parkhead (through Steve Callaghan) at the same time as Willie Lyon although it was as outside-right in place of Jimmy Delaney on international duty that he made his debut. With big fair-haired Alex at centre-half, Celtic reserves won the Alliance League and the 2nd XI Cup in 1935-36. He played in both legs of the Champions' Match against Sunderland on September 16th and 30th 1936 and made his Old Firm debut in a 1-1 draw at Parkhead in-between on September 19th. Alex was "a great boy without a doubt... a host in himself... what a boy to be in reserve team football!" He had his best period in the Celtic first team with five League games out of six (and none lost) between September 18th 1937 and October 23rd when he played his last game in the 6-0 defeat of St Johnstone. Alex asked away at the same time as Johnny Divers (November 15th 1937) so as to play first team football and Tommy Muirhead took him to Deepdale where he found he had left Willie Lyons' shadow for Tom Smith's. This vastly-talented player-er was Morton's centre-half in the great side of 1947-48 and "played Jock Weir out of the park" at Ibrox in the Scottish Cup semi-final (March 27th 1948). Both he and Johnny Divers blamed each other for the Cappielow club's success: "Having a centre-half behind you who seldom puts a foot wrong gives forwards confidence" (Divers after the 4-0 defeat of Celtic on January 17th 1948). He figured prominently also in the two finals of 1948 against Rangers. He was secretary of the Scottish Players' Union until November 1950 and condemned the nascent power of FIFA as a Bosses' Plot to deprive the players further of a decent livelihood. He married a Motherwell girl while at Preston and was the father of ten children, nine of them surviving.

Alex Millar

Appearances:
SL: 9 apps. 0 gls.
Total: *9 apps. 0 gls.*
RL: 1 app. 0 gls.
Total: *1 app. 0 gls.*

♣ **Celtic note 1:** *Alex's big brother, Charlie, played with Jimmy McGrory in the St Roch's Scottish Junior Cup-winning side of 1922 and was with Exeter City for 13 years after.*
♣ **Celtic note 2:** *Johnnie Wilson tells how Celtic players were forbidden to use cars. Maley's spies told him Alex was breaking the rule and parking in Alexandra Parade to walk to the park. Maley upbraided his centre-half, but Alex protested that George Paterson drove to the ground and left his vehicle right outside yet nobody said a thing. Maley: "Paterson is different. He's a first-team man, and besides, he does work for the YMCA!"*

MILLER, Andrew

Role: Outside-left
1920-24
b. Bo'ness,
27th February 1899

CAREER: Croy Celtic /CELTIC 25 Aug 1920/ (Dumbarton Harp loan 29 July 1922)/(Dumbarton loan 5 July 1923)/ Nottingham Forest 1924/ Bo'ness 10 July 1925/Camelon Juniors 1927/ Montrose 3 Oct 1930.

Andrew Miller

Debut v Hamilton Academicals (h) 2-1 (SL) 11.9.20

"A product of Newtown Park Bo'ness," Andrew Miller was "stoutly built, stands well on his legs and has pluck and strength." The one goal he scored was "coolly taken and overall, his display pleased the Parkhead critics" (Celtic 3 Hibs 0; 21st April 1921). Andrew acted understudy to Adam McLean and played for Celtic first when wee Adam was injured and Celtic were unbeaten in five League games since the start of the season but already two points behind Rangers. He next played in Charlie Shaw's benefit on October 5th 1920 against a strong Central League XI that included Joe Dodds and Arthur McInally. Andrew was competing with David Pratt and Jean McFarlane for a first team place. Pratt and McFarlane went on the Battlefields tour of May 1921 but not Andy. He played his last game for Celtic in the semi-final of the Lord Provost's Unemployment Tourney versus Third Lanark on November 29th 1921 with Tully Craig as his inside-left.

Appearances:
SL: 5 apps. 1 gl.
Total: *5 apps. 1 gl.*

MILLER, Joseph

Role: Outside-right 1987-93
5' 8" 10st.4lbs.
b. Glasgow, 8th December 1967

CAREER: Glasgow Schools/Aberdeen S form 1980/Celtic BC 1982/Aberdeen Dec 1984/ CELTIC 13 Nov 1987/Aberdeen 28 July 1993.

*Debut v Dundee (h) 5-0 (SL) 14.11.87
(scored once)*

At Pittodrie Joe Miller wore the No. 7 shirt and operated through the middle. Except for three fine games in May 1989, Joe was expected to wear the No. 7 shorts and attack down the right with Celtic. Against Aberdeen on September 20th 1989 at Hampden, he came on at half-time for Stevie Fulton in the League Cup semi-final. Another 22 minutes and Billy McNeill had replaced him with Andy Walker. The humiliation hit Joe hard and he asked to go: "I was never a winger at Aberdeen!" He and McNeill were reconciled but Joe was still employed wide and fared no better under manager Liam Brady. There was no attempt to exploit him through the middle not even during periods of goal drought when Celtic's predicament would have seemed to cry out for experiment. Joe earned immortality in the 42nd minute of the Scottish Cup final versus

Rangers on May 20th 1989 by stealing Gary Stevens' pass-back and drilling home the winner past Chris Woods' left hand. Just weeks before Celtic had been 1-2 down against Rangers in the League (April 1st 1989) and were awarded a penalty. Joe insisted he would take it. Chris Woods parried his shot and Joe put the rebound over the bar. His greatest game at Parkhead was another Scottish Cup-tie: Celtic 2, Rangers 0 (5th round; St Patrick's Day 1991). He and Stevie Fulton were sold to part-finance the purchase of Pat McGinlay from Hibs (30th July 1993).

Appearances:
*SL: 152 apps. 26 gls.
SLC: 13 apps. 2 gls.
SC: 21 apps. 2 gls.
Eur: 9 apps. 1 gl.*
Total:
195 apps. 31 gls.

Joe Miller

MILLER, William

Role: Goalkeeper 1942-50
5′ 9″ 11st.0lbs.
b. Glasgow, 20th October 1924

CAREER: Woodside Secondary/St Rollox United BB/St Rollox YMCA/Maryhill Harp 3 Jan 1942/CELTIC 20 May 1942/Clyde 1 Aug 1950/(Stirling Albion loan 19 Apr 1952)/free 28 Nov 1953/Hibernian 29 Jan 1954/retired 1956.

Debut v Hamilton Academicals (h) 2-2 (RL) 22.8.42

1942: "Miller, helpless against the two shots that beat him, pleased the Parkhead fans highly..." (August 22nd). "Miller... daring and magnificent" (Rangers 2, Celtic 1; September 5th). **1943:** "Willie Miller was in distress from the 15th minute but insisted on playing on. Despite his lameness, he saved Celtic from a rout" (Celtic 0, Rangers 4; June 12th). "Miller's brilliance in the opening stages inspired his defence..." (Rangers 0, Celtic 1; September 11th). "Miller's brilliance defied Hearts time after time in the first half" (Hearts 0, Celtic 0; September 25th). **1944:** "Excellent goalkeeping by Miller" (Hearts 2, Celtic 0; November 25th). **1945:** "Miller had a magnificent second half" (Rangers 0, Celtic 1 Ne'erday). "Miller was a great Celtic goalie. Some of his saves - especially one from Mathie - were wondrous to behold" (Celtic 1, Motherwell 1; February 10th). "Miller - two superb saves from Bill Shankly" (Celtic 2, Falkirk 1; February 17th). "Miller got balls he had no right to..." (Falkirk 1, Celtic 0; March 24th). "only miraculous saving by Miller kept the score down" (Hibernian 2, Celtic 0; June 24th). "Miller has few superiors at the moment... impeccable timing of nasty balls" (Celtic 3, Motherwell 0; November 10th). **1946:** "A keeper in a million... a golden Miller... inspired... more thrilling saves seen in 90 minutes than since the New Year... salmon-like leaps... Thornton screechers knuckled over the bar... electric Miller... the darling of stand and terracing and not among Celtic supporters only" (Celtic 0, Rangers 0; June 1st). "Miller, half-blinded and limping, refused to leave the field and played in a dazed condition most of the match. Thistle players rushed to shake his hand at the end" (Partick Thistle 4, Celtic 1; November 16th). **1947:** In the Inter-League match on

March 12th, Willie was concussed and had his nose broken in two places trying to prevent FP Kippax's second goal. He went off but within two minutes was back to a roar that rent the afternoon sky over Hampden. At Parkhead the following day his body was a mass of welts. Willie kept goal in the traditional Celtic style - behind a defence with no stopper. When the ball was lobbed down middle his duty was to dash off his line and make a neck or nothing save at the centre's feet. He must have had near enough 100 stitches in his scalp. When he moved to Clyde he was inundated with mail from Celtic supporters bewailing his departure as an all-time Celtic great.

Appearances:
SL: 94 apps. 21 shut-outs.
SLC: 23 apps. 4 shut-outs.
SC: 6 apps. 3 shut-outs.
Total: 123 apps. 28 shut-outs (23%).
RL: 117 apps. 26 shut-outs.
RLC: 25 apps. 10 shut-outs.
Total: 142 apps. 36 shut-outs. (25%).

♣ **Celtic note:** *The fans protested outside Parkhead on September 4th 1946 after the 1-4 defeat by Third Lanark. "Only Miller stood between Thirds and a glut of goals." Willie appeared (on his way home) to an enormous cheer. Minutes later all the bad feeling vanished and the demonstration dispersed.*

Willie Miller

Ronnie Mitchell

out of his Parkhead career to HM Forces. On his debut he played right wing to Willie Gallagher ("a lively onslaught") on a day when Jimmy Mallan joined Bogan as another Celtic casualty with broken ribs on the half hour and Roy Milne was crippled moments after. Mallan took Ronnie's outside-right spot in the second half and Ronnie missed a chance to equalise Bobby Flavell's goal for Hearts before himself going off for repairs in a game of no quarter.

Appearances:
SL: 1 app. 0 gls.
Total: *1 app. 0 gls.*

MITCHELL, John

Role: Left-half 1906-13
5' 8" 11st.6lbs.
b. c 1885

CAREER: Baillieston Thistle/CELTIC 26 Nov 1906/(Forfar Athletic loan 3 Mar 1911)/ Cowdenbeath 2 Sept 1913/retired summer 1916.

Debut v Partick Thistle (h) 4-1 (SL) 1.12.06

John Mitchell

"Everything Mitchell did was marked by coolness and confidence in his own powers." Johnny Mitchell whom Patsy Gallagher called "a champion grafter at left-half," amassed almost 100 games for Celtic but was only a regular during 1912-13. He got his first opportunity when Celtic played Arsenal at Plumstead on Christmas Day 1906. Willie Orr was injured in 20 minutes and Johnny replaced him in the second half. He went on the Copenhagen tour of 1907, played goalie in the first match on June 3rd then came on for Jimmy McMenemy at half-time two days later. He got a Glasgow Cup medal 2-1 versus Rangers on October 26th 1907 and started a run in the League team as of Ne'erday 1908 until March 7th while Dun Hay was out with appendicitis. Thus he helped bring two prizes home out of four in the season Celtic won everything they played for. Johnny's last major occasion at Parkhead was the defeat by Hearts in the Scottish Cup on March 8th 1913 before 66,000 fans with the gates shut long before kick-off. By the start of 1913-14 Celtic had discovered John McMaster and Johnny Mitchell went to serve at Cowdenbeath.

Appearances:
SL: 89 apps. 0 gls.
SC: 6 apps. 0 gls.
Total: *95 apps. 0 gls.*

MITCHELL, William

Role: Inside-left 1918-19
5' 8" 11st.10lbs.

CAREER: St Anthony's/CELTIC 22 July 1918/ (Hamilton Academicals loan Oct 1918)/ (Clydebank loan 28 Dec 1918)/(Dumbarton loan 10 Jan 1919)/Partick Thistle 14 Aug 1919 /Alloa 23 Apr 1920.

Debut v Dumbarton (a) 5-0 (SL) 26.10.18

The Spanish 'flu epidemic played rags with team selections in the autumn of 1918 and the kick-off at Boghead on October 26th was delayed half-an-hour so both clubs could put eleven men together. Celtic pulled in "particularly fine inside-forward" Billy Mitchell from Hamilton Academicals and played him five times up to December 21st for four wins and a draw in a Championship season. Patsy Gallagher said he had a tendency to hold on to the ball just a bit too long. "He needs to sharpen-up to replace

McMenemy." Elsewhere he is described as "on the slow side... needs to find a yard of pace." Willie was "the most methodical member of the Partick Thistle attack... very elusive" in the 0-0 draw against Celtic at Parkhead on November 22nd 1919.

Appearances:
SL: 5 apps. 0 gls.
Total: *5 apps. 0 gls.*

MOCHAN, Neil

Role: Outside-left 1953-60
5' 7" 12st.0lbs.
b. Larbert, 6th April 1927
d. Falkirk, 28th August 1994

CAREER: St Francis' School Falkirk/Dunipace Juniors (juvenile)/Morton (provisional) 1943/ (full) 22 June 1944/Middlesbrough 8 May 1951 /CELTIC 8 May 1953/Dundee United 17 Nov 1960/free 29 Apr 1963/Raith Rovers 4 July 1963/CELTIC coach 8 Feb 1964/ kit manager June 1991.

Debut v Queen's Park (a) 3-1 (CC) 9.5.53 (scored twice)

Neilly Mochan scored the second goal against Manchester United in the semi-final of the Coronation Cup on May 16th 1953 and with 10 minutes of the first half to go in the final against Hibs hit a ball with his "wrong" foot (his right) but with all the force of McAtee from 35 yards out into the evening sun and high past Tommy Younger in the Mount Florida-end net. Alan Breck nominated it the Goal of 1953: "a wonderful shot... hurling past Younger... a goal of memory-stamping ingredients... surprising in its speed... thrilling as the net bulged... it took Celtic into distinction." Neilly had won two medals with Celtic (Charity Cup and Coronation Cup) before he had even kicked a ball at Celtic Park. He was the catalyst that inspired the dull, poor Celtic side of 1952-53 and was the inspiration again of the team that did the Double in 1954. Celtic went to Edinburgh needing two points for the Flag on April 17th 1954 in what promised to be a tense, desperate finish against a very good Hibs side with Easter Road packed full and

overflowing. Within a minute Neilly had scored. Within three minutes of the second half he had scored again. The Championship was coming home courtesy of Mochan for the first time since 1938! He won his first cap against Norway on May 19th 1954 and went with Scotland to the World Cup in Switzerland. He was in the side beaten 0-7 in suffocating heat by Uruguay in Basle on June 19th 1954. Neilly appeared in the dressing-room at the end and sat down rubber-legged: "We could have beaten them!" Because of a private grievance of Chairman Kelly's, this fine player sat out both finals against Clyde on April 23rd and 27th 1955 even though Celtic were desperate for a forward with pace and a shot. He won his first League Cup medal against Partick Thistle on October 31st 1956 and his second in the 7-1 rout of Rangers when he skinned Bobby Shearer down the left at Hampden on October 19th a year later. He

Neil Mochan

MORRISON, Alexander

Role: Right-half 1907
b. Campsie, 5th September 1887

CAREER: Kilsyth Emmet/Kirkintilloch Rob Roy/Ayr FC 5 Sept 1906/(CELTIC loan Apr 1907)/CELTIC 8 May 1907/Clyde 11 Oct 1907/Ayr FC 21 July 1908/Ayr Parkhouse 27 Apr 1910 until 1911.

Debut v Hibernian (a) 1-0 (SL) 8.5.07

Celtic had already won the League for the third time in a row on April 24th 1907 before Sandy Morrison was given a try-out against Hibs who had ex-Celt Willie McAulay in their line-up. He played in a few benefit matches at the start of 1907-08 including one against Clyde on September 10th which may have moved the Bully Wee to ask for him. When Celtic went to Shawfield on League business on November 9th 1907 Sandy was at centre-half for Clyde. Celtic won it 0-2.

Appearances:
SL: 1 app. 0 gls.
Total: *1 app. 0 gls.*

MORRISON, John

Role: Left-back 1929-40
5' 8" 11st.2lbs.
b. Kilsyth, 9th November 1909
d. Croy, 25th May 1992

CAREER: Croy Celtic/CELTIC 5 Oct 1929/ (Morton loan summer 1940)/free 11 Sept 1941.
Debut v Aberdeen (h) 1-0 (SL) 6.12.30

Jock Morrison was a right-back commended to Celtic by Jimmy Quinn. He went on the USA tour of 1931 but did not get a game, Bob Whitelaw going in at full-back when Willie Cook was not playing. Jock played left-back for the first time in place of Peter McGonagle at Cowdenbeath on November 28th 1931 and then began the long and patient wait for another chance. He broke into the first team at Kilmarnock on October 5th 1935 and before the season was out had won a Championship medal as one of Willie Lyon's men. Jock had a temper but never one to equal Peter's. All the same, he brought the same verve and high octane energy to his performance and Celtic made the smooth transition from one great left-back to another. The reward of patient fidelity was soon being reaped: the Charity Cup 4-2 versus Rangers (May 9th 1936); the

John Morrison (extreme right) with the 1937 Scottish Cup-winning team.
Back row (left to right) - Hogg, Paterson, Buchan, Lyon, Mr W.Maley (manager), Crum, Delaney, Morrison. Front row: McGrory, Geatons, Kennaway and Murphy.

Scottish Cup 2-1 over Aberdeen (April 24th 1937); the Scottish League (April 23rd 1938); the Charity Cup 2-0 versus Rangers (May 14th 1938); the Empirex Trophy (June 10th 1938); the Glasgow Cup 3-0 versus Clyde (October 15th 1938). He missed the Glasgow Cup final of May 15th 1937 (the 3-4 win against Queen's Park) because of injury at 3-0 in the 8-0 defeat by Motherwell on April 30th. He played his last game for Celtic in the Regional League on April 28th 1940. As of 1940-41, work in the pits left him too exhausted for football. He worked coal until his retirement. Jock Morrison was a man of '38 and a Celt who played every match like a Cup-tie simply because he was playing for Celtic.

Appearances:
SL: 161 apps. 1 gl.
SC: 17 apps. 0 gls.
Total: *178 apps. 1 gl.*
RL: 21 apps. 0 gls.
SWC: 1 app. 0 gls.
Total: *22 apps. 0 gls.*

MORRISON, Thomas

Role: Outside-right 1895-97
b. Belfast, 1874

CAREER: Stormont FC/ Glentoran Aug 1891/Burnley Feb 1894/CELTIC 27 Apr 1895/Burnley 20 Feb 1897/ Manchester United Dec 1902/ Colne FC Sept 1904/Burnley trainer-coach 1906/Glentoran coach 1907/ ...Glentoran trainer 1915.

Debut v Clyde (h) 2-0 (SL) 27.4.1895

Tom 'Ching' Morrison

The "cat-witted Ching's" impact on Scottish football was as instantaneous as Tully's much later. As with Tully, Celtic were beseeched to rein-in "Sandy Row's" antics and curb his tongue. Ching's first League fixture for Celtic was strictly speaking a try-out against Clyde and he was signed only after the game. He had played against Celtic for an East End select in Belfast on April 16th and been invited over to Glasgow then. He was injured against Newcastle on September 4th 1895 and out of the game until Celtic beat Rangers 6-2 on December 14th 1895 to clinch the League title. The second half saw rain, darkness and four Celtic goals in five minutes concluding with one by Tommy 'Ching' Morrison. He was a proud member of the side that beat Aston Villa 3-1 at Parkhead for the Championship of the World on April 20th 1896. His season got off to another scintillating start in 1896-97 in the 2-7 win against Clyde despite the non-stop rain of August 17th but, when Celtic met Rangers at Ibrox on a pitch that was frozen and unplayable on December 19th, Ching was again turning out for only his first game in three months. He scored Celtic's only goal in the 6-1 thumping by Everton on Christmas Day 1896 as the Parkhead club's form and team morale sagged lower and lower until finally, with the players' connivance, Arthurlie threw them out of the Scottish Cup 4-2 at Barrhead on January 9th 1897. In a month Ching was on his way back to Turf Moor where they still held his English registration. Celtic received £300. Glentoran played Linfield for his benefit on May 5th 1933.

Appearances:
SL: 15 apps. 2 gls.
SC: 1 app. 0 gls.
Total: *16 apps. 2 gls.*

♣ **Celtic note:** *"Ching" is probably a corruption of Ah-Sin from some racist doggerel by Bret Harte about a Chinese card-sharp cheating some Simon Pure white chaps. Tommy's game was supposed to resemble Ah-Sin's jugglery with the cards: That for ways that are dark/And for tricks that are vain/The heathen Chinee is peculiar. The "Sandy Row" nickname is more obviously derived.*

MORRISON, William

Role: Inside-left 1951-53
5' 9" 11st.0lbs.
b. 10th October 1939

CAREER: Craigen Juveniles/Loanhead Mayflower/CELTIC 24 Nov 1951/(Leith Athletic loan 20 Dec 1952)/free 1953/ Loanhead Mayflower 5 Aug 1953.

Debut v Raith Rovers (a) 0-1 (SL) 12.1.52

Willie Morrison was wanted by Rangers, Hibernian and Celtic. He played a trial for Celtic on November 24th 1951 versus Berwick

Rangers at Parkhead and gave such satisfaction he was signed after the game. (This was the day the wee Rangers appeared with no kit and played in Celtic's white shirts with a shamrock on the breast). Jimmy Walsh had 'flu for the match at Kirkcaldy in January and although John Higgins travelled, Celtic sent Willie out to play at inside-left. "The occasion was too much for Morrison... it was a tactical error by skipper Evans to move him to outside-right when Collins had the beating of McNaught." Willie waited fifteen minutes for his first touch, a flick which almost brought a goal. George Johnstone was in miracle form and saved point-blank from Willie in the second-half before the switch to outside-right. He moved to Leith with Jim Swan and gave Loanhead Mayflower long years of fine service on reinstatement.

Appearances:
SL: 1 app. 0 gls.
Total: *1 app. 0 gls.*

MOWBRAY, Antony Mark

Role: Centre-half 1991 to date
6' 2" 13st.2lbs.
b. Saltburn, 22nd November 1963

CAREER: Schools/Middlesbrough Nov 1981/ CELTIC 6 Nov 1991.
Debut v Aberdeen (h) 2-1 (SL) 9.11.91

Everyone can remember what he/she was doing at the news of President Kennedy's death; Tony Mowbray was being born. His was the fresh face promised by manager Brady after the 5-1 xamaxing at Neuchatel (October 22nd 1991), a countenance that put some in mind of Sunny Jim Young. Tony had made his debut for Middlesbrough under Bobby Murdoch and after 331 competitive matches came to Celtic on a £1 million transfer but with a warning: "I am no Gary Pallister... Celtic paid a lot of money for me and I do not want the public to be misled in any way." Ian Baird thought otherwise: "I reckoned him better than Pallister" (who cost Manchester United £2.3m). That he brought a new resolution to the Celtic back four was patent. In the downpour at Hampden before the Scottish Cup semi-final against Rangers on March 31st 1992 "Mowbray prowled among the players giving last minute instructions." There is a feeling this is a job he might do

Tony Mowbray

even better as captain. According to Peter Grant: "He is not slow to put players right if they are in wrong positions or not doing their job properly." Tony: "I am just trying to do what I am good at... I have almost had stand-up fights... but I feel the more players are like this in the team, the more successful the team will be." For a battling centre-half, he is almost as conscientious a placer of the ball as Gary Gillespie. He was a virtual ever-present at Ayresome Park but has lost a lot of time through injury since the move to Parkhead. He refused a transfer back to Middlesbrough on 16th November 1993. His best period as a Celt began under Lou Macari's management. He scored against Dundee United at Tannadice on 2nd April 1994 and was given a standing ovation as he left the field in honour of his impending marriage the following day to Bernadette Devlin. Tony's young bride was a very sick girl and he was granted leave of absence until April 30th when the team bus picked him up on its way to Ibrox. "His redoubtable stance at the heart of the defence was a monument to his character... his inspiration coursed through the team." (Patrick Glenn 2nd May 1994).

Appearances:
SL: 62 apps. 4 gls.
SLC: 3 apps. 0 gls.
SC: 3 apps. 0 gls.
Eur: 2 apps. 0 gls.
Total: *70 apps. 4 gls.*

MOYES, David William

Role: Centre-half 1978-83
6' 2" 12st.0lbs.
b. Glasgow, 25th April 1963

CAREER: Bearsden Academy/ Celtic BC 1974/Drumchapel Amateurs/CELTIC 17 Oct 1978 /Cambridge United 30 Oct 1983/ Bristol City 1985/Shrewsbury Town 30 Oct 1987/ Dunfermline Athletic 20 Aug 1990/Hamilton Academicals player-coach 18 Aug 1993/ Preston NE 18 Sept 1993.

Debut v Hibernian (h) 4-1 (SLC) 15.8.81 (sub)

Davie Moyes

Andy Roxburgh had a terrific opinion of Davie Moyes as Scotland Youth Coach: "A future Celtic captain, I'd say." Gianni Trapattoni watched Davie on his debut for fear he might be in the team against Juventus on September 15th 1981 at Parkhead. Davie didn't play but he was right-back for Danny McGrain (broken leg) at the Stadio Communale on September 30th in the 2-0 defeat. He had been carrying an injury and Billy McNeill had his doubts: "Will you kick a door to prove your foot is okay?" Davie: "Certainly. Which door would you like?" He held his place till Danny came back on December 5th but played often enough to win a Championship medal on May 15th 1982. He was in the team for the 2-2 European Cup tie versus Ajax (September 15th

1982) and came on as substitute for Paul McStay with 12 minutes to go in the 1-2 win at Amsterdam two weeks later. He occupied the bench for the 2-1 win versus Rangers (December 4th 1982), did not get into the game but took a lap of honour with the League Cup at the end. Then, the new broom of 1983: "Davie Hay... made it clear... I wasn't wanted at Parkhead... I left Celtic when I didn't want to. Nobody wants to leave Celtic and it's something I sometimes regret having done." Davie was John Docherty's skipper at Cambridge and Asa Hartford's at Gay Meadow. He joined Dunfermline as Shrewsbury's second top scorer. He played at Wembley in John Beck's Preston side defeated 2-4 by the English League's latest newcomers, Wycombe Wanderers, in the (new) Third Division play-offs (28th May 1994).

Appearances:
SL: 23 apps. 0 gls.
SLC: 9 apps. 0 gls.
Eur: 2 apps. 0 gls.
Total: *34 apps. 0 gls.*

MUGGLETON, Carl David

Role: Goalkeeper 1994
6' 2" 11st.10lbs.
b. Leicester, 13th September 1968

CAREER: Leicester City app. 1985/pro. Sept 1986/(Chesterfield loan Sept 1987)/(Blackpool loan Feb 1988)/(Hartlepool United loan Oct 1988)/(Stockport County loan Mar 1990)/ (Liverpool loan Sept 1990)/(Stoke City loan Aug 1993)/(Sheffield United loan Nov 1993)/ CELTIC 12 Jan 1994/Stoke City 20 July 1994.

Debut v Dundee United (h) 0-0 (SL) 22.1.94

Lou Macari bought Carl Muggleton for £150,000 as the fifth goalkeeper on Celtic's books after Packy Bonner, Gordon Marshall (on loan to Stoke), Stewart Kerr (on loan to

Swindon) and Shay Given. It was an odd signing also in that just three days later manager Macari was deploring the fact he had to play the same squad of players game after game: "We are so short of cash, I have no other option." Carl was on the bench versus Motherwell

Carl Muggleton

at Fir Park on the night of his signing and made his debut the following day against St Patrick's Athletic in Dublin. He had a shaky League debut but produced one almighty clawing save from Craig Brewster in the closing seconds that saved Celtic the point. A local lad, capped at England Under-21 level and highly regarded by fans at Filbert Street who felt Celtic had got a bargain, he saved a penalty in Leicester's (old) Division Two play-off final defeat at Wembley against Blackburn in May 1992. At Liverpool he had understudied the great Bruce Grobbelaar and was on loan at Stoke who were keen on a permanent transfer when Macari moved to Celtic. A magnificent display at Easter Road on March 19th 1994 gave Carl his sixth Premier League shut-out in a row. An unsteady but not a culpable performance in the 2-0 defeat by Kilmarnock on April 16th 1994 saw him drop out of the team to let Packy Bonner back. Although he was a fine instinctive shot-stopper, it was felt Carl needed to work on his judgement and positional sense. In summer 1994, with Bonner back at Celtic after his 'free transfer' saga, Carl moved on for £200,000 to Stoke, a club who had always been keen on securing his services.

Appearances:
SL: 12 apps. 6 shut-outs.
SC: 1 app. 0 shut-outs.
Total: *13 apps. 6 shut-outs (47%).*

MUIR, Robert

Role: Outside-right 1903-04
5' 8" 11st.0lbs.
b. Kilmarnock, 23rd September 1876
d. Toronto, 1953

CAREER: Kilmarnock Deanpark/Clyde 19 June 1896/Kilmarnock 7 July 1897/Bristol Rovers 1901/CELTIC 1 May 1903/Notts County 20 Apr 1904/Norwich City 1905/ retired 1908/Eaton FC Canada player-secretary-manager.

Debut v Partick Thistle (h) 2-1 (SL) 15.8.03

Mick Dunbar recruited Neilston boy Bobby Muir from Bristol Rovers in 1903 as a man "plain done before he left Scotland," according to the press. He was outside-right in the first Celtic team to wear the hoops (in torrential rain) on August 15th 1903. Against Queen's Park in the Glasgow Cup (September 12th 1903) he proved "the best man in his position since Neil McCallum... a bewilderer with clean and clever footwork." His greatest game for Celtic was the Scottish final of April 20th 1904 when Celtic took the Cup 3-2 with Jimmy Quinn's third goal and seven minutes to go. Bobby retired with back problems in 1908 and Norwich played his benefit on December 3rd 1908. He emigrated to Canada and was associated with Eaton FC for 30 years as well as being secretary and treasurer of the Ontario FA. He met the Celtic on tour in Canada (June 15th 1951) and wrote a piece for the Celtic Football Guide of 1951-52.

Appearances:
SL: 20 apps. 4 gls.
SC: 5 apps. 3 gls.
Total: *25 apps. 7 gls.*

Bobby Muir

MULROONEY, John

Role: Goalkeeper 1911-13
5' 9" 12st.0lbs.
b. Hamilton,
1st August 1886
d. 26th July 1914

CAREER: Cadzow Hibernian/Quarter Huttonbank/ Burnbank Athletic/ Earnock Rovers/ CELTIC 4 Nov 1911/ (St Johnstone loan 19 Aug 1913).

Debut v Queen's Park (a)
4-1 (SL) 9.12.11

John Mulrooney

Big panther goalie John 'Caruso' Mulrooney succeeded Davy Adams between the sticks for Celtic on a snow-topped Hampden in December 1911. He performed heroics in the second half of the Scottish Cup final versus Clyde and a hurricane wind at Ibrox on April 6th 1912. On May 11th he won a Charity Cup medal when Celtic beat Clyde again, this time 7-0 on corners. It was John who saved Celtic for a 1-1 draw in the Cup-winners' match at rain-soaked Parkhead (September 3rd 1912) against a hard and ruthless Barnsley side to whom the voice of sanity, Jimmy McMenemy appealed in vain for quarter. John looked the part in the yellow jersey and socially was an early-day Frank Haffey, "the life and soul of many a Celtic trip," especially on the 1912 tour of Norway and Denmark. He was the first Celtic goalie to experience the restriction of using hands inside the penalty area only (1912-13). He came in for criticism latterly for "lack of anticipation" but it was allegedly a rheumatic condition that made Celtic pay a transfer fee for Charlie Shaw in May 1913. Big John kept for St Johnstone when they won the Consolation Cup against St Bernard's at Dens Park on April 25th 1914, his final season. Celtic players in pre-season training were devastated to hear the news of his early death. *He loved the team that graced Parkhead/And sang the glories of the Old Brigade.*

Appearances:
SL: 42 apps. 19 shut-outs.
SC: 9 apps. 7 shut-outs.
Total: *51 apps. 26 shut-outs (51%).*

♣ **Celtic note:** *Big John may well be the Mulrooney who played in the Port Glasgow trial when they were looking for a successor to Charlie Shaw on August 10th 1907.*

MULVEY, Michael

Role: Inside-left 1892-93
b. Shettleston, 3rd July 1869

CAREER: Drumpelier Aug 1886/ Hibernian 1888/Newcastle East End Nov 1888/Airdrie/Newcastle East End Sept 1890/Airdrie 1892/ Carfin Shamrock mid-Oct 1892/ CELTIC end-Oct 1892/Dundee Harp 25 July 1893.

Debut v Hearts (h) 5-0 (SL) 5.11.1892 (scored once)

Duke McMahon had his leg put in splints by Dr Scanlan in a 0-3 defeat by Sunderland on October 6th 1892 and was replaced by the semi-retired Mick Dunbar for League matches and Tom Towic for Cup-ties. Mick Mulvey came in for Dunbar on his debut but the Duke was back by November 19th so Mick did not get another chance to show until March 18th 1893. Celtic Park had a new telegraphic link with England open that day but reporters from the *Glasgow News* and the *Scottish Referee* were refused access which is of interest in relation to the three players' strike of November 28th 1896. Mick Mulvey played his last game for Celtic on April 22nd 1893 (some reports give reserve J.Gibb) in a 0-6 defeat of Thirds at 1st Cathkin which gave him a 100 per cent record and a goal a game in his short time as a Celt.

Appearances:
SL: 4 apps. 4 gls.
Total: *4 apps. 4 gls.*

MUNRO, Daniel

Role: Outside-right 1907-10
5' 8" 10st.7lbs.
b. Peterhead, 2nd March 1887

CAREER: Forres Mechanics/CELTIC 5 May 1908/Bradford City 5 Nov 1910/Burslem Port Vale 1914/Clydebank Dec 1918.

Debut v Clyde (h) 2-0 (CC) 9.5.08

Now Murdoch "a majestic stroller of a player... able to put the best-planned defence in a fankle with one pass, one flick" strutted his stuff and it was Rangers' turn to quiver as witness the Glasgow Cup (August 23rd 1966) at Ibrox when Bobby did as ordered by Stein and claimed the midfield; Jimmy Johnstone had a balmy night and Celtic won 0-4. Johnstone summed-up his personal contribution: "Murdoch was on form. He turns me on." Bobby won eight League Championships with Celtic; five Scottish Cup medals; six League Cup medals; a European Cup medal and Scottish Player of the Year 1969. He fell out of favour when Big Jock decided he wanted a running half-back (ie Steve Murray). Stein had saved Bobby's career but again what would Stein have done without Murdoch? Bobby Murdoch is an all-time Celtic great. Middlesbrough supporters sit at the Scarborough Cricket Festival and reminisce on the greatest half-back the Reds ever had. 'Tis a pity he got bored.

Appearances:
SL: 291 apps. 62 gls.
SLC: 83 apps. 19 gls.
SC: 53 apps. 13 gls.
Eur: 57 apps. 11 gls.
Total: 484 apps. 105 gls.

Bobby Murdoch (left) shows off the European Cup on Celtic's triumphant return home.

Frank Murphy

MURPHY, Francis

Role: Outside-left 1932-45
5' 8" 11st.0lbs.
b. Gartcosh, 6th December 1915
d. Airdrie, 12th February 1984

CAREER: Glenboig BG/Coatbridge BG/Croy Celtic/CELTIC (provisional) 7 Apr 1932/ St Roch (farmed-out) 1932-33/CELTIC (full) 11 May 1933/(Albion Rovers loan 15 Aug 1942)/RAF Feb 1943/(Tranmere Rovers loan 6 Nov 1943)/(Aldershot loan 1943-44)/ free 1945/Limerick Jan 1946.

Debut v Airdrie (a) 4-2 (SL) 7.4.34 (scored twice)

Celtic won at Ibrox for the first time since 1920-21 on September 21st 1935 and "Celtic supporters invaded the field to congratulate their team." Celtic had found their attack: Delaney and Buchan; McGrory; Crum and new left-winger Murphy who had scored the equaliser. "Light, nippy and clever," wee Frank was at last the answer to Adam McLean and began to whip in the crosses on which McGrory thrived. One header from a Murphy ball was of such perfection at Pittodrie on September 25th 1937 that even the Aberdeen players congratulated McGrory; Frank set the Golden Crust up for another tearing bullet against Sunderland (October 6th 1937) and the

Roker Park crowd rose to its feet in acclaim. He was also able to "slice" a corner kick so as to "break" the flight of the ball which caused havoc in the opponents' goalmouth. And he could dribble! At Easter Road on November 9th 1935, he beat Brady, Peter Wilson, Wilkinson and Souter in a mazy run then thundered the ball past Jimmy Culley for a goal Jimmy McMenemy nominated as his all-time best. Frank was capped for Scotland against Holland in Amsterdam and scored the second goal in a 1-3 win on May 22nd 1938, a burst through the Dutch defence at speed and then a tearing shot that gave the 'keeper no chance. For Alan Breck of the *Glasgow Evening Times* it was one of the finest goals he had ever witnessed in a long career of reporting foot-ball. Frank took the penalties for Celtic and free-kicks just outside the box. He was a man of '38 who won two Championship medals (1936 and 1938) a Scottish Cup medal (1937), and the Empirex Trophy at Ibrox (June 10th 1938). All the same he reckoned the team of 1967 was better and his yardstick was the regularity with which they beat Rangers. Frank would have fitted very well into the team of '67. With his speed and control he could have done Bobby Lennox's job. Like Bobby, he knew what a Celtic jersey meant.

Appearances:
SL: 144 apps. 46 gls.
SC: 17 apps. 4 gls.
Total: *161 apps. 50 gls.*
RL: 66 apps. 21 gls.
SWC: 2 apps. 0 gls.
RLC: 14 apps. 6 gls.
Total: *82 apps. 27 gls.*

MURPHY, James B.

Role: Full-back 1920-23
5' 8" 11st.10lbs.
b. Possil, 20th September 1897

CAREER: Glasgow Perthshire 1914/(Abercorn loan 22 Jan 1916)/ Parkhead Juniors 5 July 1916/Royal Scots Fusiliers (Salonika) WW1/CELTIC 3 July 1920/(Clydebank loan 16 Jan 1923)/ Clydebank 7 Aug 1923/Glasgow Perthshire 1927.

Debut v Partick Thistle (h) 1-0 (SL) 11.12.20

Jim B. Murphy, "Perthshire's stylish half-back," in the autumn of 1915 was "one of

Jim B. Murphy

Celtic's coming men" in 1920-21. A "keen tackler of the never-tiring order... He can trap, kick a ball in any position and is a feeder of the first degree... he seldom wastes a ball... pushes it along the carpet... a dandy passer." Jim won a Scottish Junior Cup medal at Hampden as right-half on May 29th 1920 when Parkhead beat Cambuslang Rangers 1-0. On his Celtic debut as one of the replacements for the injured Gilchrist, he "displayed all the coolness of an experienced player." In the team of 1920-21 he was a virtual regular playing anywhere in defence and went on the French Battlefields tour after winning a Charity Cup medal in the side that beat Rangers at Hampden (14th May 1921). He became less prominent during the Championship season of 1922 but was in the side which won the Alliance League before Celtic scrapped their reserves. He played in the 2-0 defeat at Ibrox on Ne'erday 1923 and may have overdone the Alec McNairs: "Is Murphy of the Celtic not just a trifle too cool at times?" Celtic were criticised for loaning him out since it meant whittling the playing staff down to a minimum and leaving not a single experienced player for cover in emergencies.

Appearances:
SL: 35 apps. 0 gls.
SC: 3 apps. 0 gls.
Total: *38 apps. 0 gls.*

MURPHY, James F.

Role: Inside-left 1921-24
5' 8" 11st.4lbs.
b. Hamilton, 25th January 1902

CAREER: East Kilbride Thistle/ CELTIC 15 Apr 1921/(Ayr United loan 24 Feb 1923)/(Clydebank loan 7 Aug 1923)/(Ayr United loan 15 Dec 1923)/Ayr United 27 May 1924/Mid-Rhondda summer 1925 /Charlton Athletic 14 June 1926/ Merthyr Town 1927/Morton 8 Aug 1927/ free 9 Nov 1929.

Debut v Dundee (a) 1-0 (SL) 23.9.22 (scored once)

Jim F. Murphy, "a neat tackler, a splendid purveyor," accompanied the Celtic tour party to Prague where he got a game against Sparta in a 2-0 defeat on May 28th 1922 and against Preussen in Berlin in the (projected 1916)

Olympic Stadium two days after. On his League debut, Adam McLean and Willie McStay were both hirpling on damaged knees when Jim F. won the points with a goal three minutes from time. He had proved himself "the goods" and afforded "a pleasing display on his initial senior show." He played his last game for Celtic on January 27th 1923 in the Scottish Cup against Hurlford before starting on loan since there was no reserve football for him at Parkhead. On January 5th 1924, Ayr United smashed Rangers' 100% record in the League 2-1 at Somerset Park. Left-half Jim Murphy had a stormer.

Jim F. Murphy

Appearances:
SL: 6 apps. 2 gls.
SC: 1 app. 0 gls.
Total: *7 apps. 2 gls.*

MURRAY, Michael

Role: Outside-right 1890; 1892
b. Stirling, 3rd November 1872
d. 31st January 1925

CAREER: Campsie FC/CELTIC reserves Jan 1890/Glasgow Hibernian 6 Sept 1890/CELTIC May 1892/Abercorn 19 Aug 1893/Johnstone FC 14 Mar 1894/reinstated amateur 21 Aug 1894/Campsie FC Aug 1894/Hibernian 1 Dec 1894/St Mirren 18 Sept 1895/Johnstone FC 22 Jan 1896 until summer 1898.

Debut v Renton (h) 4-3 (SL) 20.8.1892

Mick was one of a family of footballing brothers from Campsie in the 1890s and represents Celtic's initial attempt to replace the fugitive Neilly McCallum. He went on the tour of England as of September 1st 1892 and played four games in five days (Sunday was a rest) against Sheffield United, Middlesbrough, Newcastle East End and Sunderland. He has the distinction of having been in the Celtic team that opened St James' Park, Newcastle on Saturday, September 3rd 1892. He came back from tour and played his last League game against Abercorn at Dalmarnock Street on September 10th. Some reports give him at

outside-right versus Pollokshaws Athletic at Maxwell Park in the Glasgow Cup the following Saturday yet others give Tom Fitzsimmons. But with September 1892, Mick Murray effectively vanishes from the Celtic story until he plays for Abercorn against Celtic on February 11th 1893 when the Paisley team wins 4-3. The Abbies' fans are exulting in front of the pavilion until Johnny Madden speaks: "The way you're going on, you'd think you'd won the Cup!" The mood turns ugly, Johnny Campbell knocks a spectator's teeth out and Jerry Reynolds is arrested for this same assault. What Mick did in the fracas is not known. He became a successful publican in Lennoxtown and Kilsyth.

Appearances:
SL: 2 apps. 0 gls.
Total: *2 apps. 0 gls.*

MURRAY, Patrick

Role: Outside-right 1902-03
b. Currie, 13th March 1874
d. Edinburgh, 25th December 1925

CAREER: Quarter Huttonbank FC/Royal Albert 26 June 1895/Hibernian 11 Oct 1895/Darwen 1896/East Stirling 8 Sept 1897/Preston North End May 1898/East Stirlingshire 13 June 1899/Wishaw Thistle 18 Jan 1900/Royal Albert 1900/Nottingham Forest 1 Dec 1900/CELTIC 8 Nov 1902/Portsmouth 1903/East Stirling 23 Nov 1904/Royal Albert 8 Mar 1905.

Debut v Partick Thistle (h) 4-1 (SL) 15.11.02
(scored once)

Celtic began 1902-03 without a recognised right-winger. Alec Crawford was not up to standard and Quinn, Somers, Walls and McCafferty were all tried before Paddy (Larkie) Murray, a Scottish internationalist as a Hib, was brought in. In the Scottish Cup, Paddy broke the deadlock against St Mirren in the third replay of round one with a goal in 30 minutes, the first of four, on February 14th

1903. When Celtic lost 0-3 to Rangers in the third round two weeks later, Paddy moved to inside-right with James Walls on the wing. Mick Dunbar went down to Bristol at the end of May to sign Bobby Muir and Paddy played his last game against the Hibs (with whom he made his fame) in a Charity match in Edinburgh on May 11th 1902.

Appearances:
SL: 11 apps. 2 gls.
SC: 5 apps. 1 gl.
Total: *16 apps. 3 gls.*

MURRAY, Stephen

Role: Right-half 1973-76
5' 9" 11st.3lbs.
b. Dumbarton, 9th October 1944

CAREER: St Patrick's Dumbarton/Dundee 6 Aug 1963/Aberdeen 16 Mar 1970/CELTIC 1 May 1973/retired 6 Sept 1975/CELTIC again 27 Dec 1975/retired 22 Jan 1976/ Dundee United scout 1979/player 17 Nov 1979/Clydebank (trial) 1979/retired Apr 1980/ Forfar Athletic manager 19 Aug 1980/resigned 22 Aug 1980/Montrose manager 17 Apr 1982/ Dundee United coach 1986/asst. manager 20 June 1989/dismissed 20 Nov 1989.

Debut v Dunfermline Athletic (h) 6-1 (Drybrough Cup) 28.7.73

"Murray does not hog the limelight but gets through a tremendous amount of work and is seldom out of the action." Jock Stein wanted a wing-half more mobile than Bobby Murdoch and bought Steve Murray ("He never stops running for an instant"; Evan

Steve Murray

Williams September 7th 1974). With the aggregate score at 5-5 over two legs, Steve headed Celtic into the semi-final of the European Cup against Basle at Parkhead in the eighth minute of extra time on March 20th 1974. He helped Celtic to their ninth Championship in a row on April 27th and then won a Scottish medal against Dundee United a week later when the team circumvented SFA regulations with a "spontaneous" lap of honour before receiving the Cup. The beginning of the end of his career happened during the 6-3 League Cup final versus Hibs on October 26th 1974 (he damaged his right ankle) and the following week in the League against Aberdeen at Parkhead (he damaged his right big toe). He soldiered on to his second Scottish Cup medal versus Airdrie on May 3rd 1975 but training had now become an agony and he retired for the first time. He made a brief come-back on a Fir Park mudheap as of December 27th (when Sean Fallon gave him the option of playing or not), before cracking a bone in the same right foot during training on January 22nd 1976.

Appearances:
SL: 62 apps. 11 gls.
SLC: 20 apps. 5 gls.
SC: 8 apps. 4 gls.
Eur: 10 apps. 1 gl.
Total: *100 apps. 21 gls.*

♣ **Celtic note 1:** *Steve won £55,000 for wrongful dismissal against Dundee United on February 6th 1991.*
♣ **Celtic note 2:** *While at Aberdeen, he was a student at Stirling University and known as "Back Seat" for his habit of swotting in the rear of the team coach on the way to games.*

NAPIER, Charles Edward

Role: Forward 1928-35
5' 9" 11st.4lbs.
b. Bainsford, 8th October 1910
d. Falkirk, 5th September 1973

CAREER: Grangemouth Sacred Heart Celtic/
Cowie Juveniles/Alva Albion Rangers 1928/
CELTIC 10 Oct 1928/Maryhill Hibernian
(farmed-out) 1928/Derby County 12 June
1935/Sheffield Wed 12 Mar 1938/Falkirk loan
26 Oct 1939/suspended sine die 13 Feb 1941/
suspension lifted 5 July 1943/Falkirk 29 Sept
1945/Stenhousemuir Sept 1946/free Apr 1948
/Luton Town scout 28 Aug 1948/
...Bonnybridge Juniors coach Jan 1955.

Debut v Queen's Park (h) 2-1 (SL) 19.10.29

Happy Feet made his debut for Celtic just five
days before Wall Street crashed: "I liked the
way Napier varied his moves. He is no
touchline slave. He knows when to cut-in...
when to hold... when to cross
first-time into a scattered
defence." Charlie was never
fussy about conditions or
where he played. In fog and on
a pitch like flint he was at
inside-left versus Cowdenbeath
on November 16th 1929: "The
juggling and artistry of Napier
captivated the shivering
onlookers... his ball control,
manipulation and passing were
perfect... he must only shoot
oftener." Charlie obliged with a
seven minute goal at Parkhead
on Ne'erday and another when
Celtic beat Rangers 2-1 in the
Glasgow Cup final (October
11th 1930). In the Scottish Cup
final of April 11th 1931, 2-0 up
with eight minutes to go,
Motherwell expected a blast of
a free- kick. Instead Charlie
found McGrory with a lob and
the greatest fight-back in the
Celtic story had begun. The fine
Celtic side of 1931 slumped
after John Thomson's death on
September 5th but Airdrie were
beaten 6-1 on December 12th:
"Everything Napier did was
stamped with class... skill allied
to strength... a most dangerous

attacker... a Parkhead idol now." In the
Scottish Cup against Falkirk (January 16th
1932), "Napier did all the things for Celtic
Patsy Gallagher used to do..." "dazzling
footwork, feinting and passing put him in a
different grade." At Muirton a fortnight later
in pouring rain, he played centre and showed
all the skill "to exploit the greasy ground and
strength to thump the ball that looked like a
ton weight" (he scored three). In the Scottish
Cup final versus Motherwell again (April 15th
1933), "Napier often gained 30 to 40 yards by
clever footwork and elusive running." He
appeared at right-half at Dens Park on October
1st 1934, after the removal of cartilage, and
played "football that was breathtaking,
scientific and pure" with both knees bandaged
like an Egyptian mummy. Charlie had a
magnificent match and two goals against
Wales at Aberdeen on November 21st 1934 as
inside-left to Dally Duncan. From then on he
was in and out of the Celtic team and was
played more often at right-half than anywhere
else. Scotland maintained faith
in him and picked him at
outside-right versus England at
Hampden on April 6th 1935.
He didn't have a great game
but took the two corners from
which Duncan got the Scottish
goals. Charlie refused to re-sign
in May 1935 unless he were
guaranteed his benefit. George
Jobey saw his chance and
Happy Feet took off for the
Baseball Ground: "I'm sorry to
leave Celtic Park. I've made
friends I'll never forget... I
know my faults and it won't be
for want of trying if I don't get
over them." Chic Napier was
an all-time Celtic great, with
control in both feet, the owner
of a booming shot and, like
Jimmy McMenemy, frightening
speed over 20/30 yards. He
was also the first Celt to play at
Wembley (April 9th 1932).

Appearances:
SL: 176 apps. 80 gls.
SC: 24 apps. 12 gls.
Total: *200 apps. 92 gls.*

Chic Napier

NAUGHTON, William A.

Role: Inside-right 1890
b. Garnkirk, 16th July 1868

CAREER: Carfin Shamrock 1887/(Hibernian loan 7 Jan 1888)/(Uddingston loan 23 Feb 1889)/CELTIC Mar 1889/(Carfin Shamrock loan 20 Apr 1889)/Glasgow Hibernian 1889/Wishaw Thistle Oct 1890/Stoke 1890/Southampton 15 May 1895/Carfin Rovers 8 Mar 1898/retired 1899.

(Debut v Renton (h) 1-4 (SL) 16.8.1890)

Billy Naughton

Carfin boy Billy Naughton, nickname "Chippy" or "The Antelope," played for Hibs when the Edinburgh Irishmen hanselled first Celtic Park against Cowlairs on May 8th 1888. He turned out for Airdrie St Margaret's on Christmas Day 1888 and "had a demon game" in the 2-1 defeat of Celtic. With Hibs on his debut, he "made the best right-wing seen at Easter Road for some considerable time" (January 7th 1888). Billy first appeared for Celtic in a 4-4 draw against Abercorn in a Merit Friendly on March 2nd 1889. He played for the club in its very first League match against Renton on Aug 16th 1890, a 1-4 defeat. Renton were expelled for being tainted with professionalism and the result expunged. They fought their case through the courts and were vindicated which justifies Billy's inclusion in this record as a Celtic League appearance. He was "a good outside-right, very clever on the ball and a rare good shot." At Stoke in 1891 he was suspended for receiving money and registered as an amateur. When "The Greatest Team on Earth" (Celtic) came down to play for the Hanley Church Restoration Fund on November 7th 1892, Billy played outside-right against them in the 5-0 drubbing. "We're looking for Billy Naughton's house," was Dan Malloy's excuse for the Celtic party's presence in Carfin the night of Jerry Reynolds' kidnapping (September 6th/7th 1889).

Appearances:
(SL: 1 app. 0 gls.)

NEILSON, John

Role: Left-half 1897
5' 8" 11st.6lbs.
b. Renfrew, 26th December 1874

CAREER: Renfrew Victoria/Abercorn Jan 1897 /CELTIC 31 Jan 1897/Abercorn 1 May 1897/ Third Lanark 31 Aug 1899/Bristol Rovers May 1900/Third Lanark 2 May 1902/Wishaw Thistle 6 Oct 1907/Albion Rovers 25 Aug 1908.

Debut v St Mirren (a) 0-2 (SL) 13.3.1897

John Neilson was first selected to play for Celtic at Dundee in the League on February 20th 1897 but was found at the last moment to be ineligible for reasons unclear. John had made his debut against Sunderland in a friendly on Wearside two weeks before. His League debut coincided with the day John Glass had the 2nd XI Cup (won 13-1 versus St Mirren February 21st 1891) burgled from his home.

Appearances:
SL: 1 app. 0 gls.
Total: *1 app. 0 gls.*

NELSON, David

Role: Outside-left 1942
5' 8" 11st.3lbs.
b. Douglas Water, 3rd February 1918
d. Greenwich Conn., USA, September 1988

CAREER: Douglas Water Thistle/St Bernard's 1935/Arsenal 27 May 1936/(Motherwell loan 23 Mar 1940)/(CELTIC loan 3 Jan 1942)/ (Tottenham Hotspur loan 1943-44)/Fulham 11 Dec 1946/Brentford Aug 1947/Queens' Park Rangers Feb 1950/Crystal Palace Mar 1952/Ashford Town player-manager 24 Mar 1953.

Debut v Clyde (a) 1-2 (RL) 3.1.42

A corporal in the Wiltshire Regiment, David Nelson was a "a cute passer" with "a little, whippy style." He joined Arsenal as an inside-right from St Bernard's and was converted to outside-left on April 10th 1937. He was part of the package that took Ronnie Rooke to Highbury from Fulham. He emigrated to St Louis, Missouri in December 1955 to take up work in a car plant. He played

David Nelson

in a Celtic forward line reading: James McDonald and Fagan; Paterson; Divers and Nelson. David was skipper of Queen's Park Rangers in 1950.

Appearances:
RL: 1 app. 0 gls.
Total:
1 app. 0 gls.

NELSON, James Park

Role: Outside-left 1941-43
b. Lanark, 1st December 1921

CAREER: Douglas Water Primrose/CELTIC 14 Aug 1941/free 25 Feb 1943/Vale of Clyde 1943/Wishaw Juniors/Coltness United 1946/ Douglas Water Thistle 1947/Douglasdale/ Shotts Bon Accord 7 Sept 1950.

Debut v Queen's Park (h) 2-0 (RL) 30.8.41

Hibernian beat Rangers 8-1 at home on September 27th 1941. Celtic went through to Easter Road on October 11th for a very creditable 1-3 victory which allegedly avenged Rangers' defeat. Jimmy Nelson opened the scoring in 28 minutes after Harry Dornan had missed a penalty in ten. Jimmy played in Celtic's first home defeat of 1941-42 against Rangers on Ne'erday and then made way for big brother David of Arsenal versus Clyde at Shawfield. He was back at outside-left for the start of 1942-43 but after August 15th lost his place to Tony McAtee, Long, McLaughlin, McGowan, Duncan, Riley, Paton, whoever happened to be handy.

Appearances:
RL: 14 apps. 3 gls.
Total: 14 apps. 3 gls.

NICHOL, William Douglas

Role: Centre-forward 1911-12
5' 7" 11st.9lbs.
b. Easington, Co. Durham, January 1887

CAREER: Royal Warwickshire Regt 16 Mar 1903/Northumberland Fusiliers/Nottingham Forest/Notts County (professional)/Seaforth Highlanders 12 May 1909/Fort George (Aberdeen) 15 May 1909/Aberdeen 1 Apr 1910/Army discharge own request 31 Mar 1911/CELTIC 26 July 1911/(Stenhousemuir loan Feb 1912)/(Ayr United loan 22 Apr 1912) /Bristol City 11 May 1912/Queen's Park Wednesday Juniors (Aberdeen) Aug 1913/ Seaforths again 6 May 1915.

Debut v Rangers (n) 1-2 (CC) 10.5.11
(scored once)

Celtic signed ex-soldier Willie ('Thunderbolt') Nichol as cover for Jimmy Quinn. An amateur with Aberdeen (as required by his Army service), he slipped out of the Granite City at 5.20 a.m. on May 1st 1911 to spend with Celtic the three months stipulated before he could turn professional. Without a word to the angry Wasps, Celtic played him in the Charity Cup final and put him straight into the team for the tour of the Continent where he scored five goals against Etoile Rouge in the final game at Montmartre, Paris (May 28th 1911). "He bears a marked likeness to Quinn in features and style but there the resemblance ends." "He can shoot but lacks the touch to make him exceptional." Willie got a game only if the Croy Express was unfit and played his last match for Celtic on April 20th 1912 when the Titanic had been four days on the bed of the Atlantic. He blamed his English origins for a certain unpopularity with the fans at Parkhead but seems not to have lost his love for Celtic. At Bristol he was reserve to Ebb Owers. With the Seaforths in Mesopotamia he was wounded at Sanni-i-Yat on February 22nd 1917, gazetted DCM on June 18th 1917 for "conspicuous gallantry and ability" and commissioned Lieutenant the following October.

Appearances:
SL: 16 apps. 9 gls.
Total: 16 apps. 9gls.

NICHOLAS, Charles

Charlie Nicholas

Role: Striker 1979-83; 1990 to date
5' 10" 11st.4lbs.
b. Cowcaddens, 30th December 1961

CAREER: St Columba of Iona
Maryhill/Celtic BC/CELTIC
18 June 1979/Arsenal 22 June
1983/Aberdeen 7 Jan 1988/
CELTIC 6 July 1990/free 17 May
1994/CELTIC again 20 July 1994.

*Debut v Kilmarnock (a) 3-0 (SL)
16.8.80 (sub)*

Charlie Nicholas stood out on his
Glasgow Cup debut against
Queen's Park on August 14th
1979: "He looked sharp... he's got
penalty-box ability which is going
to bring him a lot of goals in the
future." "The teenage wonder
boy... can't help scoring goals...
his flicks, vision, distribution are
worth the admission money
alone." In the League Cup semi-
final at Tannadice (November
12th 1980) with Dundee United
winning 1-0 Celtic fans sang
"Char-lee! Char-lee!" for McNeill
to let him loose. He came on (with
Frank McGarvey) in 68 minutes
and got the equaliser with eight to
go. Rangers led 0-1 at half-time in
the Premier League on February
21st 1981. Big Billy told him at
half-time that if he (Nicholas),
was a top-class striker, then he
(McNeill), was thinking of
making a come-back: "Lie up
on them! Make them turn!"
Charlie went out, did as asked,
scored two, and Celtic took it 3-1.
The papers began to urge his
transfer. Charlie made his answer:
"I just want to stay with Celtic... I don't want
to go anywhere else. I've always supported
Celtic and they are the only club I've wanted
to play for" (March 31st 1981). He helped
Celtic to the Championship of 1981 then lost
his place to George McCluskey as a result of a
mystery "illness" prior to St Mirren 1, Celtic 5
(McCluskey 3) in the Premier League on
August 22nd 1981. He broke his leg with the
reserves in a clash with Joe McLaughlin at
Cappielow on January 18th 1982 and was out
of the game until the Labbatt's Tournament in
Toronto in July. He worked his way back into
the first team and by December 27th 1982
'Charles de Goal' had struck for the 30th time
in the season. The winner against Rangers at
Ibrox on Ne'erday was number 31. Big Billy
knew siren voices were calling a player with
such fabulous skills and genuine charisma:
"He must mature among friends, the terracing

and the team" (February 14th 1983). "It's not the money," said Charlie, "I just want to sample the game in England." He made his Scotland debut alongside Dalglish versus Switzerland at Hampden on March 30th 1983 and scored a spectacular second goal to equalise in the 2-2 draw. He was voted Scotland's Player of the Year on April 26th 1983 but had a terrible game versus England at Wembley on June 1st and was taken off. Terry Neill and Don Howe set up a £650,000 deal and gave him £100,000 to sign-on at Highbury plus a £2,000 a week salary. Despite all the 'Champagne Charlie' hype and the unwavering adulation of the North Bank he accomplished very little at Arsenal bar a League Cup medal on April 5th 1987 against Liverpool at Wembley (albeit he scored both goals for the Gunners). Integrating his often dazzling but ultimately inconsistent virtuoso skills into the Arsenal style was always a problem. After a £400,000 move to Aberdeen he was in the side that beat Celtic 9-8 on penalties in the Scottish Cup final of May 12th 1990. His Second Coming to Parkhead did not effect the change in Celtic's fortunes predicted. He had one glory moment: a stunner of an opening goal against Rangers in the League at Ibrox on March 21st 1992. Into 1994 he was being hailed as Celtic's Cantona or Beardsley, the "thinking man's centre-forward": he "has the gift for passing the ball and embroidering play with moments of unexpected pleasure, a shimmy here, a flick there... he has the capacity to play the game the supporters enjoy." (Mike Aitken 14th February 1994). Charlie is still skilful enough to make a fool of defenders but has lost that vital burst of speed that stopped him being marked out of a game. To the sorrow of many Macari freed him in May 1994 but Tommy Burns believed Charlie still had much to offer and re-signed him on taking over at Celtic Park.

Appearances:
SL: 176 apps. 85 gls.
SLC: 29 apps. 25 gls.
SC: 11 apps. 7 gls.
Eur: 20 apps. 7 gls.
Total: 236 apps. 124 gls.

NICOL, David

Role: Goalkeeper 1927-29
5' 10" 11st.8lbs.
b. 20th September 1907

CAREER: Cadder United/Maryhill Hibernian 1926/CELTIC 28 June 1927/(Ayr United loan 26 Aug 1928)/(Third Lanark loan 1 Dec 1928)/(Montrose loan 7 Jan 1929)/Hamilton Academicals 26 Sept 1929/Maryhill Juniors 1931.

Debut v Hamilton Academicals (a) 1-1 (SL) 29.9.28

David Nicol

A "splendidly endowed 'keeper of great promise," David Nicol had a good job outside football and no particular desire to go senior until Celtic sought him out as cover for John Thomson. As a Celtic provisional he had a poor game for Junior Scotland against Wales on May 19th 1928, then a great one, Maryhill Hibernian 6, Burnbank Athletic 2 in the Junior Cup final the following Saturday, each time at Firhill. Thomson came out of the Glasgow Cup against Third Lanark at Cathkin on September 24th 1928 with "split fingers" (the referee got stoned). David was called in to play just at the time Alexander Fleming was discovering penicillin (no more the septicaemia bogey for footballers!). His last game for Celtic was at Hampden versus Queen's Park in the Charity Cup (May 4th 1929) when he conceded five goals but Celtic won 5-6 after extra time. "An injury with Hamilton versus Rangers ended his senior career." In the 1940s, David ran the MacDonald Arms Hotel in Balbeggie and was coach to the local team (Perth Amateur League).

Appearances:
SL: 1 app. 0 shut-outs.
Total: 1 app. 0 shut-outs.

O'BRIEN, John (?)

Role: Goalkeeper 1895
b. Blantyre, 3rd August 1877(?)

CAREER: Mossend Brigade Juniors/CELTIC (trial) 30 Mar 1895/Benburb Sept 1895.

Debut v Leith Athletic (a) 6-5 (SL) 30.3.1895

Dan McArthur was playing for Scotland against Ireland at Parkhead on March 30th 1895 so Celtic invoked the services of a top tyro at Beechwood Park. John (?) had played for Scotland Juniors versus England in Glasgow just two weeks before: "His display... brilliant and seldom surpassed at either junior or senior level." In Edinburgh with the Celts John (?) "did not play up to his reputation as Scotland's best junior goalkeeper and was responsible for at least three of the five goals conceded. He was very nervous."

Goalkeeper John O'Brien

Appearances:
SL: 1 app. 0 shut-outs.
Total: *1 app. 0 shut-outs.*

O'BYRNE, Fergus

Role: Centre-half 1892; left-half 1893-94
b. West Calder, 19th August 1871

CAREER: Broxburn Shamrock/Newcastle West End Nov 1890/Broxburn Shamrock 1891 /(CELTIC loan 2 Jan 1892)/Broxburn Shamrock June 1892/CELTIC May 1893/ Broxburn Shamrock 14 Feb 1894/retired 1896.

Debut v Third Lanark (h) 5-0 (SL) 12.8.1893

Jimmy Kelly, Celtic centre-half and skipper, was injured against St Mirren on Boxing Day 1891. For the Ne'erday holiday game at Dalmarnock Street, Celtic drafted in guest star John Cherrie of Clyde. Dumbarton won 0-8. The following day, against Thirds at Calder Street, Fergus O'Byrne played. Celtic won 1-3. When he next appeared for Celtic he was a registered professional in a friendly against Hibs on August 5th 1893. He managed an Old Firm game with the semi-final of the Glasgow Cup (November 18th 1893) at Ibrox and also played in the first-ever Celtic-Rangers Ne'erday fixture in 1894. His last match was the 0-4 friendly against Everton the following day. Charlie McEleny took over his position.

Appearances:
SL: 7 apps. 0 gls.
Total: *7 apps. 0 gls.*

O'CONNOR, John

Role: Outside-left 1888;
Centre forward 1892
b. Greenock, 7th January 1867

CAREER: Vale of Leven Hibernian/CELTIC Aug 1888/Glasgow Hibernian 7 Sept 1889/ Renton 3 Oct 1889/Warwick County 1889/ Hibernian 1889/Aston Villa Jan 1890/Burslem Port Vale 1891/CELTIC Mar 1892/Nottingham Forest 1892.

Debut v Shettleston (h) (SC) 1.9.1888

Gallowgate man John O'Connor ("He's a good 'un") of 148, Comelypark Street played in many of Celtic's early games. His first appearance was at Mavisbank in the 0-6 defeat of Airdrie in a friendly on August 11th 1888. His formal debut was made on the club's first-ever Scottish Cup tie against Shettleston at Dalmarnock Street. He also played in Celtic's first-ever final, for the World Exhibition Cup against Cowlairs at the X-arena at Gilmorehill on September 6th 1888 (lost 2-0). Tom Maley had John O'Connor as his inside-left for the 5th round Scottish Cup tie (Celtic 0, Clyde 1) of January 24th 1889 (the result successfully protested-against on the grounds of time-wasting). John returned to the team on March 19th 1892 when Michael Davitt MP laid a sod of Donegal turf on New Celtic Park then returned to Dalmarnock Street to kick-off (for Clyde) with John O'Connor facing him.

Appearances:
SL: 1 app. 0 gls.
SC: 2 apps. (1 unofficial) 0 gls.
Total: *3 apps. (1 unofficial) 0 gls.*

O'DONNELL, Francis

Role: Centre-forward 1930-35
6'0" 11st.10lbs.
b. Buckhaven, 31st August 1911
d. Macclesfield, 4th September 1952

CAREER: Wellesley Juniors Aug 1930/
CELTIC 8 Sept 1930/Preston North End
19 May 1935/Blackpool 30 Nov 1937/Aston
Villa 10 Nov 1938/(Blackpool loan 1939-40)
/(Hearts loan 30 Mar 1940)/(Wolverhampton
Wanderers & Brighton loan 1941-42)/(Fulham
& Brentford & York City loan 1942-43)/
(Tottenham Hotspur & York City loan 1943-44)
/(Blackpool & Brighton & Tottenham Hotspur
loan 1944-45)/(Brighton loan 1945)/
Nottingham Forest Jan 1946/free 22 Mar
1947/Buxton FC player-manager 22 Dec 1948.

Debut v Hamilton Academicals (a) 0-1 (SL)
23.1.32

Pat Duffy had no sooner sent Joe Cowan to
Celtic than he found his successor, a big, long-
striding boy, with a thump of a shot: Frank
O'Donnell. Frank was "a brainy footballer...
forceful, bustling... makes his presence felt... a
cool calculating shot... he chases... regains the
ball... shows good fighting spirit." Then the
riders that explain the barracking which drove
him out of Parkhead: "He needs to speed up
his game... he's too gentlemanly." "Sixty per

Frank O'Donnell

cent of his dribbling runs take him across the
field... he likes to dribble the ball into a scoring
position instead of storming through... not a
heaven-born centre... too often he gets
possession facing his own goal... slow on the
turn... opportunities are lost because of his
immobility." At Preston Tommy Muirhead
allowed him to concentrate on playing centre
as opposed to all over the forward line when
with Celtic. He also learned to play the whole
ninety minutes instead of running out of puff
as so often at Parkhead. He did not become a
better player in England but for every four
pinches he missed he scored one (thus football
expert and Spurs' fan non-pareil Patrick
Sugrue who watched him as a boy guesting at
White Hart Lane during the War). Scotland
capped him six times (unthinkable as a Celt)
including the England game at Hampden on
April 17th 1937 and at Wembley on April 9th
the following year. He is somewhere rated as
one of the four best buys Blackpool ever made
(for £8,000 and two players). Frank wasn't a
bad manager either and took Buxton to the 3rd
round of the English Cup at Doncaster
(January 12th 1952).

Appearances:
SL: 78 apps. 51 gls.
SC: 5 apps. 7 gls.
Total: *83 apps. 58 gls.*

O'DONNELL, Hugh

Role: Outside-left 1932-35
5' 7" 10st.7lbs.
b. 11th December 1915
d. Preston, 9th May 1965

CAREER: Wellesley Juniors Aug 1930/
CELTIC 19 Mar 1932/Preston North End
19 May 1935/Blackpool 16 Mar 1939/RAF
1940/(Hearts loan 30 Mar 1940)/(Manchester
United & Preston North End loan 1940-41)/
(Burnley loan 1942-43)/(Lincoln City loan
1943-44)/(Birmingham loan 1944-45)/free 22
Feb 1947/Rochdale 4 Mar 1947/Halifax Town
Mar 1948.

Debut v Clyde (h) 3-1 (GC) 20.9.32

"Neat, artistic, polished," Hugh O'Donnell
never attracted the boos the way big brother
Frank did. After five long years he was the
first genuine left-winger to compensate for
the loss of Adam McLean. "A wonderful
opportunist," he had "half a dozen ways of

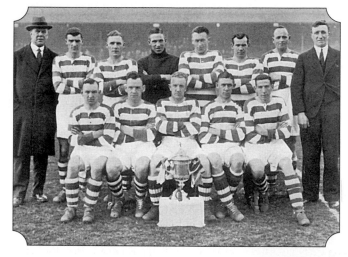

Hugh O'Donnell (extreme right of front row) with a 1933 Celtic line-up.

Back row (left to right): W.Maley (manager), A.Thomson, Hogg, Kennaway, Napier, McGrory, McGonagle, Quaskey (trainer).

Front row: R.Thomson, Geatons, J.McStay, Wilson, O'Donnell.

beating a man" and was "a sound but not a brilliant ball-player." He showed himself "infinitely more subtle than Frank in approach" with "useful speed and an ability to cross at the right time." Where Frank got caps, Hugh won Cups eg the Scottish trophy with Celtic on April 15th 1933: "Sorry, Frank, you didn't get a medal." "Don't worry, if it's in the house, it's all right." He won the English Cup with Proud Preston on April 30th 1938 and in War-time the English League Cup also with Preston (at Ewood Park) on May 31st 1941 after a drawn game at Wembley on May 10th. He hadn't wanted to leave Parkhead but Frank was being driven out and it was a case of "Love me, love my brother." Preston were glad to have them both.

Appearances:
SL: 75 apps. 20 gls.
SC: 15 apps. 7 gls.
Total: *90 apps. 27 gls.*

O'DONNELL, Philip

Role: Midfield 1994 to date
5' 10" 11st.0lbs.
b. Bellshill, 25th March 1972

CAREER: Motherwell BC/Motherwell 30 June 1990/CELTIC 9 Sep 1994.

Debut v Partick Thistle (a) 2-1 (SL) 10.9.94 (scored twice)

Phil O'Donnell, one cap for Scotland, was Tommy Burns' long-coveted first signing and at £1.75 million, Celtic's most expensive ever.

Phil O'Donnell

He came into the team immediately as replacement for the suspended Paul McStay and made an instant and startling impact with both Celtic goals on his debut. "Phil is the outstanding young talent in the country... I'm not bothered by the fee because it's not my money. It was the fans who spent more than £3 million on season tickets who provided it. They wanted a top quality player... and they are entitled to have their money spent on what they want." (Tommy Burns 9th September 1994).

O'HARA, Daniel

Role: Inside-forward 1959-62
5' 9½" 11st.0lbs.
b. Airdrie, 28th August 1937

CAREER: Fauldhouse United/CELTIC 24 Apr 1959/(Cork Hibernian loan 22 Oct 1960)/ (Mansfield Town loan June 1961)/Albion Rovers Aug 1962/free 1963/Coltness United (trial) summer 1963/Armadale Thistle 31 July 1963.

Debut v Kilmarnock (h) 2-0 (SL) 19.8.59

Dan O'Hara

Dan O'Hara came in for the injured Mike Jackson on his League debut in a "slick Conway, O'Hara combine... O'Hara, fast, strong and dangerous... blasted the ball as though he hated the sight of it." He had another great game against Raith Rovers (August 22nd 1959) in brilliant sunshine on a perfect pitch when Jim Conway played decoy to let Dan and Charlie Gallagher through the middle in a Celtic attack packed with "real punch. Parkhead's period of mourning is over." Despite his running and thunderous shooting, Dan reverted to the reserves as of August 29th when Jackson and Divers resumed the role of first-team inside men. He played in the floodlight friendly versus Everton (January 27th 1960) and was inside-right in the 7-1 debacle at Roker Park three days later. His last game was at Pittodrie on February 6th 1960 when Celtic lost 3-2 and Neilly Mochan got the goals from penalties. Celtic won the Reserve League on April 30th 1960 which gave Dan a medal to take with him when he left Parkhead.

Appearances:
SL: 7 apps. 1 gl.
SLC: 2 apps. 0 gls.
Total: *9 apps. 1 gl.*

O'KANE, Joseph

Role: Centre-forward 1914-26
5' 9" 12st.0lbs.
b. Glasgow, 12th January 1896

CAREER: St Andrew's Schools/Maryhill Juniors July 1913/CELTIC 6 June 1914/ (Clydebank loan 29 Aug 1914)/CELTIC again 24 Dec 1914/(Clydebank loan 26 Dec 1914)/ Royal Irish Regiment May 1915/Royal Engineers 1916/(Clydebank loan 25 Feb 1916) /CELTIC again 8 Apr 1916/(Clydebank loan 3 Aug 1917)/(Clyde loan 15 Dec 1917)/ (Airdrie loan 12 Oct 1918)/(Stevenston United loan 2 Sept 1920)/(Stockport County loan 4 Nov 1920)/(Stevenston United loan 14 Feb 1921)/(Stockport County loan 17 Oct 1921)/ (Stalybridge Celtic loan 1922)/(Dundee Hibernian loan 27 July 1923)/(Dundee United loan 25 Apr 1924)/(Arthurlie loan 19 Feb 1925) /Helensburgh 19 Apr 1926.

Debut v Falkirk (a) 2-0 (SL) 8.4.16 (scored once)

"But for certain peculiarities, I fancy O'Kane might have been another Jimmy Quinn"

(Jimmy Brownlie, 1940, not being more specific). "O'Kane is the best Hibs forward. He has some real football in him" (September 29th 1923)."Big Maryhill boy" Joe O'Kane first turned out for Celtic on Christmas Day 1914 at Old Trafford. Celtic lost 2-1 but Joe's first goal for the club saw them turn round 0-1 up at half-time. He came into the Celtic side proper for the injured Jimmy McColl at exciting times. Celtic were chasing Falkirk's 1908 record of 103 goals in 34 League games. When Joe scored just before half-time on his debut he took Celtic to 98 in 33. The 34th

Joe O'Kane

game was against Raith Rovers at Parkhead the following Saturday (April 15th 1916). Joe got the Celts off to a flying start with two goals in 25 minutes, Patsy Gallagher next scored three in a row before Joe Dodds smashed the record with a screamer from 40 yards. On Easter Monday 1916, Joe O'Kane scored a straight hat-trick against Third Lanark at Parkhead, followed by a brace against Partick Thistle on April 29th. He won a Charity Cup medal at Hampden versus Thistle on May 13th 1916 and in the Glasgow Cup semi-final on September 23rd versus Rangers, he bored through the middle like Jimmy Quinn to get Celtic's second goal in 81 minutes. He had now reached his high point. McColl came back from his knee injury, Joe shifted to inside-right but was destined never to score so regularly again. He played his last game for Celtic at Pittodrie on March 24th 1917 when Patsy's work in the Clydebank shipyards precluded travel. He helped Celtic to two Championships (in 1916 and 1917).

Appearances:
SL: 20 apps. 13 gls.
Total: *20 apps. 13 gls.*

O'LEARY, Pierce

Role: Central defender 1984-88
5' 11" 11st.2lbs.
b. Dublin, 5th November 1959

CAREER: Shamrock Rovers 1977-80/ Philadelphia Fury 1978/Vancouver Whitecaps 1981-82-83-84/CELTIC 29 Nov 1984/free 7 May 1988/retired 1988.

Debut v Hamilton Academicals (a) 2-1 (SC) 30.1.85

Pierce O'Leary came to Celtic "heavily recommended" but nursing a groin injury and lacking match-fitness enough for manager David Hay. He had to wait until the second half of the practice game versus Hibs in Edinburgh on 26th January in the snowbound winter of 1985 to make a firm impression. Celtic's defence was so porous as to have conceded four goals by half-time. Pierce's "unhurried use of the ball" throughout the second half brought a "calming influence" and "one defence-splitting pass to Mark Reid to create the goal for Paul McStay was in Pat Crerand class." Pierce won a Scottish Cup

Pierce O'Leary (left)

medal on May 18th 1985 by coming on for the injured Paul McStay in 74 minutes. He was already an Irish international and had won an FA of Ireland Cup medal with Shamrock Rovers in 1978. At Hampden on May 18th, he went into defence thus releasing Roy Aitken to storm Dundee United from midfield. Out with pelvic trouble again (the legacy of the Whitecaps) for the first part of 1985-86 he came back on January 11th 1986 after Paul McGugan had broken his foot against Rangers on Ne'erday. He qualified for a badge when the Championship was won at the last gasp at Paisley on May 3rd 1986 after both Davie Hay and Alex Ferguson had conceded it to Hearts (April 12th). At Highbury on August 5th 1986 he skippered Celtic versus Arsenal in big brother David's testimonial. 10,000 Celtic supporters came down and David went home £150,000 richer than Pierce. Celtic won 0-2. He nowadays (1994) runs a thriving cleaning company (founded with Packy Bonner) based in Rutherglen with a full-time staff of five plus 100 part-time cleaners.

Appearances:
SL: 39 apps. 1 gl.
SLC: 2 apps. 0 gls.
SC: 6 apps. 0 gls.
Eur: 2 apps. 0 gls.
Total: *49 apps. 1 gl.*

OLIVER, James

Role: Goalkeeper 1909
b. Dumfries, 1st August 1889

CAREER: Creetown Volunteers 1905/(Morton loan Mar 1907)/(CELTIC loan Jan 1909)/ Girvan Athletic 4 Aug 1909/reinstated amateur 8 Aug 1909/Creetown Volunteers Sept 1909/Port Glasgow Athletic 12 Aug 1910 /Morton 29 Apr 1911/Maybole 5 Aug 1911.

Debut v Hearts (h) 1-1 (SL) 9.1.09

Davy Adams was injured versus Rangers Ne'erday 1909 and Sunny Jim Young kept goal in the League against Kilmarnock at Rugby Park the following day (Celtic lost 3-1). Celtic tried Kane of Carson Thistle on January 4th at East Stirling then borrowed Morton reserve Jim Oliver for the game against Hearts managed by old Celt Jimmy McGhee. Davy Adams came back the following week but Jim played in the wee Celtic team that put Rangers out of the 2nd XI Cup 1-0 the same day at

Parkhead. His last game was against Partick Thistle before a "small attendance" which produced a £17 gate (guarantee: £50!) at Parkhead on a Monday afternoon (March 29th 1909).

Appearances:
SL: 2 apps. 1 shut-out.
Total: *2 apps. 1 shut-out.*

O'NEIL, Brian

Role: Midfield 1989 to date
6' 1" 12st.7lbs.
b. Paisley, 6th September 1972

CAREER: Old Kilpatrick/Celtic BC/CELTIC 2 Nov 1989/(Porirua Viard United (NZ) loan summer 1991)/CELTIC again 10 July 1991.

Debut v Falkirk (h) 4-1 (SL) 17.8.91 (sub)

Brian O'Neil

"He reminds me so much of Murdoch" (Alex Smith March 14th 1992). In the summer of 1992, with Paul McStay's departure virtually certain, all was not total despair. If Maestro did leave, there was always Brian O'Neil. Not since Paul himself in 1982 had a debutant made a bigger impact. He had tired before the end of 1991-92 but if McStay moved on, surely Brian was his natural successor? Pele had watched him in the World Youth Cup on June 16th 1989 and called him "a skilful boy who can dictate play... he has vision and superb passing skills." Brian played defence or midfield and scored the goal against Portugal (June 20th 1989) that put Young Scotland into the final. On the big day itself, June 24th, he had a penalty saved by the Saudi 'keeper in normal time then missed another in the shoot-out. He first appeared for Celtic against Spurs at Parkhead on August 4th 1991, made his European debut at Ekeren on October 1st and scored his first goal for the club in the 5-1 xamaxing at Neuchatel exactly three weeks later. Despite talent in abundance he showed a tendency to play off the pace of the game and was largely a fringe player (injuries contributing) throughout 1992-93. Liam Brady was asked why his young star was not making progress: "How should I know? I'm not a psychologist!" Brian scored the last minute winner at Ibrox in the League in injury time on October 30th 1993 after coming on moments before as substitute. New manager Macari drafted him into the starting line-up as a striker against Partick Thistle on November 6th 1993. Brian is no striker yet is unable to command a place in midfield. He won a Reserve League Cup medal with Celtic at Tannadice on April 18th 1994. Tommy Burns sees his future as a Celtic centre-half: "The forwards will love it because they've got someone who'll pass the ball as opposed to launching it over their heads." He scored the goal, with a gliding header in 99 minutes, that beat Aberdeen at Ibrox on 26th October 1994 and took Celtic into the League Cup final.

Appearances:
SL: 72 apps. 6 gls.
SLC: 6 apps. 0 gls.
SC: 4 apps. 0 gls.
Eur: 5 apps. 1 gl.
Total: *87 apps. 7 gls.*

O'NEILL, Felix

Role: Right-half 1910-11
b. Motherwell, 21st December 1889

CAREER: Shotts United/CELTIC 21 Dec 1910 /(Alloa loan 26 Jan 1911)/CELTIC again 3 Nov 1911/Bathgate 7 Sept 1912/Dykehead 25 Sept 1912.

Debut v St Mirren (a) 1-1 (SL) 18.3.11

After "some great games for Shotts United," Felix O'Neil played his solitary League match for Celtic in place of Sunny Jim Young in a half-back line reading O'Neil, McAteer and Mitchell. At Alloa he played against Celtic in a friendly at Recreation Park on March 4th 1911 alongside ex-Celt Willie McOustra at centre-half with Pat Geehrin and John Young also in the line-up (Alloa won 2-1).

Appearances:
SL: 1 app. 0 gls.
Total: *1 app. 0 gls.*

O'NEILL, Hugh

Role: Centre-half 1938-40
5' 10" 11st.7lbs.
b. Motherwell, 15th February 1913
d. 24th September 1964

CAREER: Holytown United Juveniles/ CELTIC (trial) 11 Sept 1936/St Anthony's Oct 1936/St Andrew's United 1937/CELTIC 9 Oct 1937/Wishaw Juniors (farmed-out) Apr 1938/ free 21 Aug 1940/Arthurlie (as senior) 24 Aug 1940/free 23 July 1941/Dunfermline Athletic 9 Aug 1941/Comrie Colliery/reinstated junior Aug 1946/Lochgelly Albert Sept 1946.

Debut v Queen's Park (h) 0-1 (SL) 3.1.39

'Teddy' O'Neill made his debut in the throes of a Celtic slump blamed by the programme on muddy pitches and poor refereeing. He was Celtic's pivot in the last Scottish League team (September 2nd 1939) before Chamberlain declared War on Germany the following morning. Teddy got his first

Teddy O'Neill

protracted run in the big team as of March 9th 1940 but mainly as left-back for John Morrison. He played his last game in a 1-3 win at Palmerston (April 17th 1940) the day Celtic ended Queen of the South's Regional League title hopes. He joined Arthurlie but when the SJFA refused unreinstated seniors in the junior game, War or no War, the Barrhead club retained him yet stopped his wages. Teddy was suing them for back pay in June 1942. He was Kelty Rangers' representative on the SJFA council by March 29th 1951.

Appearances:
SL: 5 apps. 0 gls.
Total: *5 apps. 0 gls.*
RL: *11 apps. 1 gl.*
Total: *11 apps. 1 gl.*

O.NEILL, John Joseph

Role: Striker
5' 10" 10st.4lbs.
b. Glasgow, 3rd January 1974

CAREER: Queen's Park 25 July 1991/CELTIC 13 May 1993.

Debut v Partick Thistle (h) 0-0 (SL) 9.11.94 (sub)

A Macari signing, John O'Neill first played for Celtic in the Mark Hughes Testimonial at Old Trafford on May 16 1993. He lasted fifteen minutes before coming off with a pulled hamstring. A work colleague from the same bank as ex-Queen's Parker and fellow Celt Malky Mackay, he came on for another old Spider, Simon Donnelly, on his debut in a vain effort to add bite to a toothless Celtic attack.

O'NEILL, William

Role: Full-back 1959-69
5' 10" 11st.7lbs.
b. Glasgow, 30th December 1940

CAREER: Sacred Heart School/Our Lady of Fatima BG/St Anthony's 1959/CELTIC 12 Oct 1959/Carlisle United 13 May 1969/retired 1971/St Roch's coach 1972/...Rutherglen Glencairn coach 30 Mar 1982.

John O'Neill

Debut v Dunfermline Athletic (n) 0-2 (SC) 26.4.61

"Willie O'Neill was the best back I've come up against including Bob McNab and Cyril Knowles, the back I've had least success against when I've had to face him" (Willie Henderson, September 1968, attempting perhaps a put-down of Tommy Gemmell). Willie was a left-half with St Anthony's, "a cool and cultivated player... puts the accent on precision passing... in the mould of an old Ant like John Gilchrist." He got his share of shocks at the start of 1961: he stood on a live cable in February and was paralysed all down one side; on the eve of the Scottish Cup final replay he was pitched into the team for his first senior game (Jimmy McGrory warned Celtic fans not to worry: "He's got the temperament for the Big Time"). Willie rejoined the reserves but didn't just play football; he kept Johnstone happy. Jinky came out for the second half of the Public Trial on August 9th 1965 barely able to stand as a result of some joke O'Neill had just told him. It was Willie's low-key, mordant humour kept the wee man distracted on plane trips later on the European and American odysseys with Stein. Willie broke into the first team in place of Ian Young in the second half of the match against the Bermuda Select (May 12th) on the "formation tour" of 1966. Gemmell and O'Neill were Big Jock's first-choice backs at the start of the annus mirabilis 1966-67. In the League Cup final against Rangers on October 29th 1966 he came from nowhere to kick a certain Rangers goal off the line in the second half. Celtic won 1-0. Willie held his place until the 3-2 defeat by Dundee United on Hogmanay 1966 when Stein decided a change was called-for. Craig and Gemmell lined-up against Dundee one week

Willie O'Neill

later and Willie became a squad man. He captained Carlisle from left-half in the 1-0 victory over Celtic on August 2nd 1969. He played fifteen League games for the Cumbrian club but a chronic ankle injury sustained in the gym forced his retirement.

Appearances:
SL: 55 apps. 0 gls.
SLC: 20 apps. 0 gls.
SC: 3 apps. 0 gls.
Eur: 8 apps. 0 gls.
Total: *86 apps. 0 gls.*

O'ROURKE, Peter

Role: Half-back 1894-97
5' 7" 11st.7lbs.
b. Newmilns,
22nd September 1874
d. Bradford,
10th January 1956

Peter O'Rourke

CAREER: Mossend Celtic/Hibernian (trial) 2 Feb 1895/CELTIC (trial) 9 Feb 1895/CELTIC 21 Feb 1895/Burnley May 1897/Lincoln City July 1899/Third Lanark 12 Nov 1900/

Chesterfield Nov 1901/Bradford City June 1903/reserve team coach 1904/acting-secretary-manager Oct 1905/secretary-manager 14 Nov 1905/retired as player Dec 1905/resigned as manager 16 June 1921/Pontypridd manager summer 1921/Dundee Hibernian manager Dec 1922/resigned 22 Mar 1923/USA 1923/Bradford PA manager Apr 1924/retired Feb 1925/Bradford City manager May 1928/resigned 23 June 1930/Walsall manager 31 Oct 1930/Llanelly manager 1932/retired 1933.

Debut v Third Lanark (h) 4-4 (SL) 23.2.1895

A Scottish Junior International versus England in January 1895, Peter O'Rourke was Jimmy Kelly's cover at centre-half but as often as not played alongside his skipper. He won a Charity Cup medal 4-0 at 1st Cathkin on May 25th 1895 and caused havoc to Rangers with his massive throw-ins. He made his fame as a manager at Bradford City. He joined them as they entered the English League (Division 2), took them into Division One 1908 and brought home the FA Cup (ie the present trophy as won for the first time) on April 26th 1911. He was much affected by the death of a son in Newfoundland in October 1919. His other two sons, Mike (Military Medal June 1918) and Peter junior, played for Dundee Hibs when he was at Tannadice.

Appearances:
SL: 9 apps. 0 gls.
Total: *9 apps. 0 gls.*

ORR, James

Role: Full-back 1895-98
5' 7" 11st.1lb.
b. Dalry, 24th July 1871
d. Knockintiber, 2nd October 1942

CAREER: Kilmarnock Winton/Kilmarnock Roslyn/Kilmarnock Shawbank/Kilmarnock Athletic 1899/Kilmarnock FC summer 1890/Darwen June 1892/CELTIC 15 Aug 1895/Kilmarnock Athletic 31 Aug 1898/Galston 18 May 1899/retired.

Debut v Cambuslang (h) 6-1 (GC) 19.10.1895

"A clean player but respected as a hard opponent," James "Duster" Orr was a full Scottish international capped against Wales on March

26th 1892 and signed by Celtic as cover for Peter Meehan and Dan Doyle. He first turned out against King's Park in Stirling in scorching heat on August 17th 1895 and played versus Preston at Deepdale on September 21st 1895. He was in the team for Bury and Everton on the tour of Lancashire over Christmas 1895 then played against Everton again when they came to Parkhead on January 2nd 1896. Duster got his chance in the League side after Peter Meehan went on strike (November 28th 1896) but missed the Arthurlie Scottish Cup debacle on January 9th 1897 with a (genuinely) damaged knee. He lost his place to Jim Welford signed in the summer of 1897. His last game was a Glasgow League match against Clyde at Barrowfield on April 27th 1898. He is buried in Kilmaurs churchyard.

Appearances:
SL: 7 apps. 0 gls.
Total: *7 apps. 0 gls.*

ORR ,William

Willie Orr

Role: Left-half, left-back 1897-1907
5' 9½" 12st.2lbs.
b. Shotts, 20th June 1873
d. 26th February 1946

CAREER: Airdrie Fruitfield/Airdrie/Preston North End Oct 1894/CELTIC 1 May 1897/ retired 1908/Airdrie director 1909/secretary-manager Oct 1921/Leicester City manager July 1926/resigned 14 Jan 1932/Falkirk manager 17 June 1932/suspended sine die 4 Apr 1935/suspension lifted Feb 1937.

Debut v Hibernian (h) 4-1 (SL) 4.9.1897

"Veteran", concluding his *History of the Celtic* in December 1931, puts Willie Orr at left-half in his all-time team. With his good mate Adam Henderson, Willie was one of the "dons" recruited from England in the summer of 1897 by the new Football & Athletic Company Limited in the hope that a good team would pay its way and a substantial dividend. Celtic won the League for the fourth time in Willie's first season (February 12th 1898). He missed the April 1899 Scottish Cup win with injury but won his first trophy medal with Celtic in the Charity Cup 0-2 against Rangers on May 27th 1899. He weathered the Scottish Cup Hurricane Final 4-3 against Queen's Park on April 14th 1900 and was left-half on June 17th 1902 when Rangers were relieved of the 1901

Exhibition Cup at 2nd Hampden. Parkhead on October 18th 1902 saw a 1-1 League draw that was "all Rangers in the first half, all Willie Orr in the second." Celtic played Third Lanark in the Glasgow Cup final the following Saturday: "Orr missed his train and Celtic the Cup." Willie was left-back and captain when Quinn beat Rangers 3-2 in the first Scottish Cup final to be played at Hampden (April 16th 1904). He led Celtic to the Championships of 1905 and 1906, the first two of the six-in-a-row before handing over as captain to Jimmy Hay. He played his last game in a friendly at Forfar on October 14th 1907 in thanks for the transfer of Davie McLean. As a manager, Willie led the greatest team in the history of Airdrieonians (with Bob McPhail and Hughie Gallacher) to a Scottish Cup triumph in 1924 but got into trouble at Brockville for a bribe allegedly offered to Bobby Russell not to turn out for Ayr versus Falkirk in March 1935. (He was succeeded by ex-Celt Tully Craig as manager).

Appearances:
SL: 165 apps. 17 gls.
SC: 47 apps. 6 gls.
Total: *212 apps. 23 gls.*

O'SULLIVAN, Patrick

Role: Outside-left 1945-48

CAREER: Saltcoats Victoria/St Anthony's June 1941/Airdrie 23 Oct 1943/CELTIC 5 Nov 1945/free 1947/Alloa 23 June 1947/free 29 Apr 1948/Stirling Albion (trial) 28 Aug 1948/Stirling Albion 30 Aug 1948/Newton-Stewart by Oct 1948/Coleraine Jan 1949/Wigtown & Bladnoch summer 1950 until 1955/Saltcoats Victoria match secretary by 1956.

Debut v Motherwell (h) 3-0 (RL) 10.11.45

A free-scoring winger with Airdrie (he got two against Celtic at Parkhead on October 28th 1944), Pat O'Sullivan, famous for his "ferocious Sandy Archibald-type crosses," was an unlucky man with cartilage problems at Celtic Park and when fit, just could not find the net for the green and white. He played his last game for Celtic on February 22nd during the hard, bitter winter of 1947 just as Blackpool freed his predecessor Hugh O'Donnell. He was left-half and skipper at Wigtown and spoke of his time at Trammonford Park as the happiest he had spent in football. Pat's son John played centre-half for Ardeer Recreation and was attracting Celtic's interest in March 1967.

Appearances:
SL: 4 apps. 0 gls.
Total: *4 apps. 0 gls.*
RL: 13 apps. 0 gls.
Total: *13 apps. 0 gls.*

OWERS, Ebenezer

Role: Centre-forward 1914
5' 10" 11st.6lbs.
b. West Ham, 21st October 1888
d. June 1951 (?)

CAREER: Leytonstone & District Schools/Bashford FC/ Leytonstone/Leyton 1906/ Blackpool 1907/WBA Nov 1907/ Chesterfield 1908/Darlington 1909 /Bristol City June 1910/Clyde 5 Mar 1913/(CELTIC loan 6 Dec 1913)/Clyde again 12 May 1914/ Footballers' Battalion Kaiser War/ retired 1919.

Debut v Third Lanark (h) 3-0 (SL)
6.12.13 (scored once)

Willie Maley was scouring the earth for a centre-forward to replace Jimmy Quinn. Ebenezer (Ginger) Owers had lost his place to Pat Allan at Shawfield and was delighted to get the chance: "I felt like doing the tango!" Celtic players (ten clean sheets in a row) were obsessed with the prospect of defeat at Kirkcaldy in December as they caught the train at Queen Street: it was the 13th of the month; 13 weeks since a reverse; the 13th year of the century... All they surrendered was the clean sheet. Ebb got the winner in 77 minutes. Against Ayr at Somerset Park one week later he scored the last four goals in the 0-6 victory. He didn't score on Ne'erday 1914 but Rangers claimed he had obstructed Hempsey to let Sunny Jim in for Celtic's first in the 4-0 win. Where it all went wrong was in the Scottish final at Ibrox on April 11th 1914. Will Allan was in miraculous form in the Hibs goal but the consensus says Ebb should have scored at least three and his fate was sealed when Willie Smith hit the post in the last minute and almost stole the Cup for Hibs. Ebb was dropped for the replay. He may not have won a medal at Ibrox but he helped bring home the 1914 Championship in Celtic's last Double season for forty years.

Appearances:
SL: 13 apps. 10 gls.
SC: 3 apps. 1 gl.
Total: *16 apps. 11 gls.*

Ebenezer Owers (right) is intercepted by Hibs' Bobby Templeton in the 1914 Scottish Cup Final.

PATERSON, George Denholm

Role: Left-half 1932-46; 1952-53
5' 7" 11st.5lbs.
b. Denny, 26th September 1914
d. New Zealand, Christmas 1985

CAREER: Denny High School/Denny YMCA /Carrowbank Juveniles/Dunipace Thistle Juveniles/CELTIC 23 Mar 1932/RAF Cleveleys Lancs 1941/(Leicester City loan 1940-41-42)/(Blackpool & Tranmere Rovers loan 1943-44)/(Blackpool & Wolverhampton Wanderers loan 1944-45)/(Blackpool & Arsenal loan 1945-46)/Brentford 4 Oct 1946/ Yeovil Town player-manager 1 Oct 1949/ Stirling Albion manager 26 Oct 1951/player 19 Apr 1952/resigned 3 June 1952/ CELTIC assistant-trainer-scout 23 Sept 1952/ CELTIC reserves (one match) 29 Apr 1953/ free as player 1953/coach 1953-56.

Debut v Rangers (a) 1-2 (GC) 11.10.33

"He reminds me of Jimmy Hay... every action is calculated... all his passes on the ground... a democrat in distribution... a master in bringing the ball down dead." The great Billy Steel was a younger contemporary of George Paterson at school in Denny and had such respect for him as footballer and athlete, he used to step off the pavement to let George go by with access unimpeded. George signed for Celtic as a centre straight from the juveniles and "something of a Hughie Gallacher; he cuts in for goals big fellows wouldn't think of." As of October 6th 1934 he became Celtic's regular left-half. The great midfield line of Geatons, Lyon and Paterson was born at Aberdeen in a 3-1 League defeat on August 10th 1935 at the start of Celtic's first Championship season in ten years. George was a main man in the triumphs of 1936, 1937 and 1938 and hugely popular with the Celtic fans. He joined the RAF to serve as a pilot but spent his War working in rehabilitation. At Leicester City,

Always smiling - George Paterson hurdles Jimmy Delaney during a training session. Chic Geatons and Jimmy McGrory offer the support.

manager Tom Bromilow called him "One of the best wing-halves I have ever seen." He was capped three times for Scotland during 1945-46 but saw Jackie Husband preferred for the England match at Hampden on April 13th. George was in the Celtic team on Wednesday night June 5th 1946 at Hampden in the semi-final replay of the Victory Cup. At half-time he reported the smell of drink on the breath of referee MC Dale. When the erratic Matthew awarded Rangers a gratuitous penalty in 70 minutes, Paterson, normally the most equable of men, seized the ball and invited Dale to perform with it "an act anatomically impossible." He was ordered-off for the first time in his career, followed by Jimmy Mallan and received a draconian three-month suspension as of August 10th 1946 which was still in operation at the time of his transfer to Brentford. When the Bees came to Parkhead on September 26th 1949, George scored their second goal with a 30-yarder "then hung his head... looked hangdog and ashamed." At Yeovil he had a reputation as one of the most enterprising managers since David Pratt. The end at Annfield was signalled by the incident with Jimmy Steadward after the Scottish Cup tie at home with Falkirk on February 13th 1952 when George berated the big goalie for the

loss of the goals and the press reported the dressing-room rumpus. Celtic gave him a medal marked "Coach" to commemorate his part in bringing home the Double in 1954. George was whipper-in when Celtic ran to the top of Ben Lomond on July 20th 1954 (1. Collins; 2. Fallon; 3. Hugh Fletcher; 4. Evans). He was a totally committed Celt, one of the greatest ever, with the widest smile ever seen at Parkhead prior to Tully's.

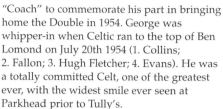

Appearances:
SL: 175 apps. 15 gls.
SC: 20 apps. 1 gl.
Total: *195 apps. 16 gls.*
RL: 80 apps. 1 gl.
SWC: 2 apps. 0 gls.
RLC: 6 apps 1 gl.
Total: *88 apps. 2 gls.*

PATON, John Aloysius

Role: Outside-left 1942-49
5' 7" 11st.2lbs.
b. Glasgow, 2nd April 1923

CAREER: St Mary's Calton/Dennistoun Waverley 1939/CELTIC 28 May 1942/RAF July 1943/(Manchester City loan 1943-44)/ (East Fife loan 2 Oct 1943)/(New York Americans loan (Starlight Park, Bronx) 1944)/ (Arsenal, Crystal Palace & Leeds United loan 1944-45)/(Millwall loan 1945-46)/(Chelsea loan 6 Dec 1946)/CELTIC again 30 May 1947 /Brentford 9 Sept 1949/Watford July 1952/ player-coach 1955/player-manager mid-1955-56/Arsenal coach 1961-65.

Debut v St Mirren (a) 2-0 (RL) 16.1.43

Johnny was the son of a Celt, Johnny Paton senior (1898-1974), an inside-left from the famous Pale Ale (with Willie Crilly) and Shawfield 1919, who never managed a League or Cup game for the club but was as lively and good for copy in his day as Tommy McInally (at 5' 5" wee Johnny played for New York Giants during summer 1923). Johnny Paton junior, a schoolboy (1937) and junior (1939) internationalist, was "cool and heady... the right stuff to mould into a clever player." He first appeared for Celtic against Partick Thistle in a 2-1 Summer Cup win at Parkhead on May

Johnny Paton

30th 1942 as outside-right having previously done some useful work behind the Parkhead goals and elsewhere in his civilian job as a junior press photographer for the *Scottish Daily Express* and the *Sunday Express*. The RAF took him to Canada in February 1944 where he qualified as a navigator/bomb aimer that same year. He played outside-left for the RAF (as often as not virtually the great England team of the War years) against Sweden and Denmark in 1945 with Stanley Matthews on the other wing. He returned to Celtic to score a wonder goal against Rangers in the League at Parkhead in the 58th minute on August 30th 1947. He beat Sammy Cox on the left, began a meander across field past Ranger after Ranger before wheeling suddenly and crashing the ball high past Bobby Brown from outside the penalty box. Against Hibs at Easter Road on December 13th 1947 (working a ploy suggested by Chic Geatons) he picked up a Frank Walsh pass into space to score the Celtic equaliser with a shot of such terrific force it hit the stanchion and came out, a goal so instantaneous that the vast majority of the 38,000 capacity crowd did not realise it had been scored. Johnny was Frank Murphy's lineal successor on the left wing. By 1948-49, such was the roar that used to greet Tully's name at inside-left, no one was ever certain whether Johnny Paton was in the side or not until the teams appeared on the field. Tully gave him all the ball he could take but according to the press, if Johnny had a fault, it was his tendency "to cut inside... getting dispossessed while Charlie waits for the return." Apart from football and accreditation as a press photographer, he was a well-regarded amateur boxer (ATC welterweight champion 1942). He came back to Parkhead with George Paterson and Malky MacDonald for a 2-2 draw in the friendly versus Brentford of September 26th 1949. Johnny won his full English FA coaching badge in 1951 and did some fine work as coach and player-manager at Watford. While Metropolitan League side manager (with scouting duties) at Highbury he was responsible for the development of many of the Arsenal Double side of 1971: Bob Wilson, Jon Sammels, Peter Simpson, George Armstrong, John Radford and Peter Storey.

Appearances:
SL: 52 apps. 11 gls.
SLC: 15 apps. 3 gls.
SC: 5 apps. 2 gls.
Total: *72 apps. 16 gls.*

RL: 26 apps. 11 gls.
RLC: 10 apps. 2 gls.
Total: *36 apps. 13 gls.*

♣ **Celtic note:** *Johnny's grandfather, Billy McVey, held Celtic Season Ticket No.2 and as a child Johnny sat on Billy's knee watching Celtic from stand seat No.2 behind the Directors' Box. Billy ran a confectioner's opposite St Mary's, Abercromby St, and on Celtic nights, used to supply the committee and company with cakes.*

PATON, Robert

Role: Inside-right 1957-61
5' 8" 10st.10lbs.
b. Glasgow, 20th June 1942

CAREER: St Mungo's Academy 1956/CELTIC 14 Nov 1957/Maryhill Harp (farmed-out) 1957/free 2 May 1961/Derry City 1961/free 1962/Shamrock Rovers 1962/Drogheda 1964 until 1966.

Debut v Clyde (h) 1-1 (SC) 18.2.59

A Celtic ballboy of 1955, Roy Paton was one of the many St Mungo's Former Pupils at Parkhead by 1959 including Stephen Lynch, John Curran and John Colrain. Roy was dogged first by cartilage and then by ligament trouble which saw his ankle more often in plaster than out. As one of Celtic's youth signings, great things were expected of him. On his debut, John Colrain set him up six yards out in the 42nd minute with the score at 0-0 but Roy lofted his shot high over the bar. He was so plainly out of his depth that he swapped positions with outside-right Matt McVittie in the 70th minute. Roy returned to the reserves to acquire more experience.

Appearances:
SC: 1 app. 0 gls.
Total: *1 app. 0 gls.*

PAYTON, Andrew Paul

Role: Striker 1992-93
5' 10" 11st.7lbs.
b. Burnley, 23rd October 1967

CAREER: Burnley apprentice 1980/Hull City YTS 1983/Hull City July 1985/Middlesbrough 15 Nov 1991/CELTIC 14 Aug 1992/Barnsley 24 Nov 1993.

Debut v Dundee United (h) 2-0 (SL) 15.8.92

Andy Payton

Liam Brady watched Andy Payton with Hull versus Darlington on October 26th 1991 just before the player moved to Middlesbrough. Andy had an unhappy time with injuries right from the start at Ayresome Park and the Celtic manager got him in a straight swap for Chris Morris. Andy resembled McBride, Wallace and Deans in physique but instead of scoring regularly in his first period, tended to get singles in clutches with long fallow periods in between. As of February 1993 with McAvennie to feed-off, the goals began to come and against Rangers on March 20th 1993 he hit his eighth in seven games to send Celtic into a 2-0 lead in the second half, the counter that brought effectively to an end the Light Blues' run of 44 games without defeat. Andy's last game for Celtic was when he came on for Gerry Creaney in the 64th minute at Ibrox in the League on October 30th 1993. Three minutes later Rangers scored but thanks to Collins and O'Neil it was to be Celtic's day (1-2). He was the first of new manager Macari's transfers out and went to Yorkshire in part-exchange for Wayne Biggins.

Appearances:
SL: 36 apps. 15 gls.
SLC: 5 apps. 5 gls.
SC: 2 apps. 0 gls.
Eur: 3 apps. 0 gls.
Total: *46 apps. 20 gls.*

PEACOCK, Robert

Role: Left-half 1949-61
5' 8½" 11st.0lbs.
b. Coleraine, 29th September 1928

CAREER: Killowen School/Coleraine YMCA/Coleraine 1947/Glentoran 1948/CELTIC 28 May 1949/Coleraine player-manager 18 May 1961/(Morton loan 30 Apr 1962)/(Hamilton Steelers (Ontario) player-coach loan summer 1962)/N.Ireland team manager as of 7 Nov 1962/resigned 1 Sept 1967/retired as player 1969.

Debut v Aberdeen (h) 1-3 (SLC) 31.8.49

"Peacock worked like a legion of Trojans... his vitality is astonishing." Bertie scored Glentoran's only goal versus Barney Cannon's Derry City in the Irish Cup final of April 16th 1949 but was not spotted by Celtic scout and Glenavon full-back Peter O'Connor until the RUC Fives of that summer. At Parkhead he came under the benign influence of coach Jimmy Hogan as reserve to Willie Taylor at inside-left. He played against St Mirren at Love Street on March 18th 1950: "Peacock's through balls were every bit as good as Pat McAuley's." He won his first honour with Celtic in the 3-2 defeat of Rangers in the Danny Kaye Charity Cup final of May 6th 1950 and scored his first goals in a friendly at Dens Park four days later, two in three minutes near the end, then travelled to Rome for the "partita bruta e fallosa" against Lazio on May 30th. He became Celtic's established inside-left as of 1950-51 with a goal against East Fife on the opening day, August 12th. He was Tully's left-wing partner in the youngest-ever Celtic team to win the Scottish Cup when Motherwell were beaten at Hampden on April 21st 1951. His industry on

Bertie Peacock

Bertie Peacock

the park rivalled Bobby Evans' to the extent
that the two self-styled craftsmen McPhail and
Tully began to refer to him as their "labourer."
Bertie went on the USA tour of 1951 and
discovered what it was to be loved when the
team arrived back at the Central Station in
Glasgow on June 30th. He won a St Mungo
Cup medal against Aberdeen on August 1st,
four days after Mrs Peacock had presented
him with their first child, a son. Northern
Ireland picked him and Tully as left-wing at

Windsor Park on October 6th 1951 but the Wee
North surrendered 0-3 to Scotland with Bobby
Evans at right-half. Bertie took Charlie's place
at outside-left for much of 1952-53 and
dropped back to left-half for the first time
when Joe Baillie tore ligaments at Broomfield
on November 22nd 1952. Bertie could blast
long-range bombs in the tradition of Geatons
and Lynch and when Tully set him up against
Manchester United in the semi-final of the
Coronation Cup (May 16th 1953) he gave Jack

Crompton no chance with a booming drive in 24 minutes. The great half-back line of Evans, Stein and Peacock lined up for the first time in a League match at Parkhead on December 13th 1952 but only became permanent as of Ibrox on September 19th in the Double Season of 1953-54. Jock Stein was now playing "with two human dynamos" on either side of him. Bertie was left-half in the first-ever Celtic team to win the League Cup on October 31st 1956. He was appointed captain aboard the SS Mauretania in mid-Atlantic en route to the USA in 1957 and on return, it was his happy duty to lift the League Cup to show to the delirious support after the 7-1 defeat of Rangers at Hampden on October 19th. He was part of the wonderful Irish performance in the World Cup of 1958 when his energy so impressed the Swedish journalists they nicknamed him "The Little Black Ant" because his jet mop seemed to be everywhere on the park against Czechoslovakia, Argentina, West Germany and the Czechs again (when, badly hurt, he still managed to "score" a disallowed goal in extra time in the play-off at Malmo on June 17th). Bertie came back from injury to lead a Celtic team not so much in decline as trying to find a game plan until the events of spring 1961. He damaged his knee in 4th round of the Cup against Hibs at Parkhead on March 11th (total silence then pandemonium when Chalmers equalised five minutes from time). Young John Clark took over at left-half. Bertie was fit for the Cup final replay on April 26th but was told he could play for Northern Ireland in Rome if he wanted. Celtic lost the Cup while the discarded skipper played the three games of his life against Italy, Greece and West Germany and all away from home. The ever-smiling Bertie was an all-time Celtic great and not a bad manager either: he took his beloved Coleraine to their first-ever Irish League Championship in 1974.

Appearances:
SL: 318 apps. 33 gls.
SLC: 79 apps. 10 gls.
SC: 56 apps. 7 gls.
Total: *453 apps. 50 gls.*

POWER, Patrick

Role: Left-half 1894-95
b. Glasgow, 11th July 1876

CAREER: Blantyre Victoria Apr 1892/CELTIC 10 Oct 1894/Airdrie 17 May 1895/Blantyre FC Aug 1895 until 1898.

Debut v Dumbarton (h) 6-0 (SL) 20.10.1894

Jimmy Kelly was injured against Clyde on October 13th 1894 and Willie Maley moved to centre-half for the next two games with reserve Pat Power on his left and Charlie McEleny on his right. Pat's one League match was against the great Dumbarton now in sad decline. The following week he played against Cowlairs at Springvale Park in the Glasgow Cup semi-final. The crowd was "immense" (about 7,000) and "the gates... besieged before kick-off." His last game seems to have been a friendly against Queen's Park (April 6th 1895) in a half-back line reading O'Rourke, McEleny and Power. Celtic lost 0-4. He played centre-half for Blantyre versus Celtic in a club benefit on August 26th 1895.

Appearances:
SL: 1 app. 0 gls.
Total: *1 app. 0 gls.*

PRATT, David

Role: Outside-left
1919-21
5' 11" 11st.10lbs.
b. Lochore,
5th March 1896

CAREER: Lochore Welfare 1913/ Lochgelly United 1913/ Cameron Highlanders 1914/Hearts o' Beath 1918/CELTIC 2 June 1919/(Bo'ness loan 2 Jan 1920)/Bradford City 14 Nov 1921/Liverpool Jan 1923/Bury Nov 1927/Yeovil & Petters United player-manager 1929/Clapton Orient manager 17 Mar 1933/Notts County manager Apr 1935/Hearts manager June 25 1935/ resigned 4 Feb 1937/Bangor City manager July 1937/resigned Oct 1937/RAF WW2/Port Vale manager 29 Dec 1944/resigned 11 July 1945.

David Pratt

Debut v Falkirk (h) 1-1 (SL) 8.11.19

David Pratt was one of a large family of brothers and by September 1918 had been

Aberdeen, the new Champions of 1955, (who received a very warm welcome from the 45,000 crowd) in the 2-1 win of April 16th. With his mane of hair and face of a Renaissance nobleman, Ian is a distinctive figure in team groups of the time. He was a much-valued player at Alloa who were keen to sign him when he went free from Celtic.

Appearances:
SL: 4 apps. 1 gl.
Total: *4 apps. 1 gl.*

REID, Mark

Role: Left-back 1977-85
5' 9" 11st.5lbs.
b. Kilwinning, 15th September 1961

CAREER: St Andrew's Academy Saltcoats/ Celtic BC 1975/CELTIC S form 1975/CELTIC 1 Sept 1977/Charlton Athletic 29 Apr 1985/ free 1991/St Mirren 26 July 1991/retired 25 Oct 1992.

Debut v Dundee United (a) 1-1 (SLC) 12.11.80

"He's unflappable... a nice, classy player... got awareness and composure... he can tackle a bit... a good left foot... I've never doubted his ability" (Billy McNeill 3rd March 1981). Mark Reid made his first appearance for Celtic as a midfield substitute with the reserves against Rangers in the Glasgow Cup of May 16th 1978 but it was as left-back he broke into the first team. By April 22nd 1981 he had won himself a League Championship medal in a team which his predecessor, ex-Lisbon Lion Tommy Gemmell proclaimed "the best in years." Mark began taking the penalties as of April 14th 1982 at Broomfield on the run-in to another Flag and sank a beauty in Rotterdam on August 8th 1982 to level the scores 3-3 against the hosts in the final of the Feyenoord Trophy. With another penalty versus Rangers in the League Cup final on March 25th 1984 he brought Celtic level 2-2 in the last minute. As with many good players on the Parkhead roll, Davie Hay seems not to have the same high opinion of Mark Reid as Billy McNeill and the majority of the fans. This perfectly sound and consistent defender found himself contesting left-back with both Graeme Sinclair and Brian Whittaker but held his place after a magnificent match versus Nottingham Forest in the UEFA Cup at the City Ground on November 23rd 1983. It was a Mark Reid

penalty rifled past Jim Leighton of Aberdeen on St Patrick's Day 1984 that put Celtic into the League Cup final. Still Hay was not satisfied. "I wasn't keeping my place in the first eleven. I'd play about five or six in a row, then be out for the same. As this went on, I felt the writing was on the wall. Charlton made an offer. I took up the challenge." Mark Reid left for London to the incomprehensible regret of his multitude of admirers. Hay had to resort to using playmaker Tommy Burns at left-back.

Appearances:
SL: 124 apps. 5 gls.
SLC: 23 apps. 6 gls.
SC: 17 apps. 1 gl.
Eur: 14 apps. 0 gls.
Total: *178 apps. 12 gls.*

♣ **Celtic note:** *Rangers played Hearts in the Scottish Cup at Hampden on May 1st 1976. The fans were entertained before the match with a penalty kick competition for schoolboys against a famous ex-Celtic goalie. The winner beat him five penalties out of five. The 'keeper was John Fallon; the tyro Mark Reid.*

Mark Reid

RENNET, William James

Role: Outside-left 1949-51
5' 8" 10st.7lbs.
b. Perth, 25th October 1924

CAREER: Perth Celtic/Beechwood Juniors (Dundee)/Lochee Harp/Stirling Albion (trial) 1945-46/Perth Celtic/Stenhousemuir (trial) 24 Apr 1948/Aberdeen (trial) 26 Mar 1949/CELTIC 27 Aug 1949/free 27 Apr 1951/Blackburn Rovers (trial) 3 May 1951/Arbroath 16 June 1951/free 1957.

Debut v Rangers (a) 0-4 (SL) 24.9.49

The great Steve Callaghan was re-appointed scout to help Celtic out of their post-War doldrums. His first discovery was "wee winger," Bill Rennet, a goods checker at Dundee West railway station. Bill's father had played 20 years with Perth Celtic

Bill Rennet

with innumerable offers to go senior but none from Glasgow Celtic, the only club he wanted. Bill junior made his debut at Ibrox on a day of boycott by the Parkhead fans. The Celtic end was barely one-tenth full as he trotted on the field and the support had room enough to sit on the terracing in the second half and watch the disaster. He played against Brentford two days later and scored a brilliant equaliser in the last minute: "Rennet is a natural outside-left... a distinguished career lies ahead." He was a player of "steadiness and cool control... with much more than a small degree of skill." Coach Jimmy Hogan called him "a natural footballer... one of the best prospects I've come across in a long time." Against Clyde on Guy Fawkes' Day 1949 he scored a hat-trick in a match when "McAuley, Tully and Rennet made a brilliant triangle." "He is freely quoted as the best left-winger to wear the green and white since Frank Murphy." His low point came in the Scottish Cup against Aberdeen on February 25th 1950. John McPhail scored for Celtic in seven minutes to uproarious acclaim

but the goal was disallowed against Rennet for offside. Aberdeen scored 28 minutes later and took the tie 0-1. Scott Duncan wanted to take him to Ipswich in 1951 but Bill preferred to hold on to his job as a clerk with the railways in Glasgow and while doing his training at Cathkin, gave Arbroath instead fine service as a Red Lichtie. His career petered out the more his job precluded his playing on Saturdays. Bill was an ice hockey fan and a keen follower of Perth Panthers.

Appearances:
SL: 14 apps. 4 gls.
SC: 1 app. 0 gls.
Total: *15 apps. 4 gls.*

REYNOLDS, Jeremiah

Role: Right-back 1889-95
5' 8" 12st.0lbs.
b. Maryhill,
15th April 1867
d. 26th December 1944

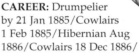

Jerry Reynolds

CAREER: Drumpelier by 21 Jan 1885/Cowlairs 1 Feb 1885/Hibernian Aug 1886/Cowlairs 18 Dec 1886/Carfin Shamrock 1888/(CELTIC loan Feb 1889)/(Glasgow Hibernian loan 1889)/CELTIC 7 Sept 1889/Burnley May 23 1895/left 1899/retired 1900/Mossend Swifts 1 Sept 1900/retired 1901/Shettleston Celtic trainer 1920s.

Debut v Queen's Park (h) 0-0 (SC) 7.9.1889

Jerry Reynolds, a right-back of "heavy, solid physique," replaced Pat Dowling in the Celtic side. Jerry "was dauntless in defence... flung himself like a fury at the fray... he knew all there was to know about tactics... with a little repose... would have taken his place among the greatest backs of his time." He became an early object of adulation as a Celt and was mobbed at Paisley's Gilmour Street station on September 12th 1891 by young women screaming "Jerr—ee! Jerr-ee!" He seems to have been regularly the last to know. He was giving his all in the first Scottish final against Queen's Park on March 12th 1892 when Jimmy Kelly told him to ease up: "We're playing a friendly." Walking down London Road with McCallum and McMahon after training in July 1892, he left them for a moment to pop into a tobacconist's. When he emerged, his two pals had disappeared for Nottingham, hot-foot for English gold. Dan Doyle showed him the bales of straw to keep the frost off the pitch for the Cup match versus 3rd Lanark (January 14th 1893): "Have you heard it now? They want us to sleep in the pavilion." Jerry sought out John Glass to protest. In the riot at Abercorn on February 11th 1893, Johnny Campbell knocked three teeth out of a Paisley fan's mouth. The police brought the casualty into the dressing room where he identified the totally innocent Jerry. "It was him!" On the playing field Jerry "never thought twice about heading a ball flying at knee-height with an opponent's feet less than a yard away." His headers were as powerful as shots. Neilly McCallum stuck his face into Jerry's one day: "And if you had a boot on your heid, you would be the best back the world has ever seen or ever will see!" (and hared out of the pavilion before Reynolds could hold him). The break with Celtic was signalled by a violent row with some Parkhead committeemen in the theatre at Hanley on November 7th 1892 over Dan Doyle's conduct that afternoon versus Stoke. It was then he says he resolved to go when he got the chance. He took over as gateman of the covered enclosure at Parkhead in 1911 and was notorious for his raucous opinions on games and players. He was buried at Dalbeth on December 28th 1944. His grandson (also called Jerry Reynolds and a right-back) was with Glasgow Perthshire in 1957.

Appearances:
SL: 74 apps. 0 gls.
SC: 25 apps. 0 gls.
Total: *99 apps. 0 gls.*

Jack Reynolds

REYNOLDS, John

Role: Left-half 1897-98
5' 4" 9st.7lbs.
b. Blackburn,
21st February 1869
d. Sheffield, 12th March 1917

CAREER: Portglenone & Ballymena Schools/Park Road FC (Blackburn)/ Witton FC/Blackburn Rovers 2nd XI 1884/Park Road FC 1886/East Lancs Regt 1 Dec 1886/Distillery 1888/left Army 27 Dec 1889 /Ulster FC June 1890/West Bromwich Albion Mar 1891 /(Droitwich Town loan 1892)/Aston Villa Apr 1892 /CELTIC 3 May 1897/free 14 Jan 1898/Southampton St Mary's 28 Jan 1898/ Bristol St George's July 1898 /New Zealand as coach 1902/Stockport County 1903/Willesden Town 1903/Cardiff City coach 1907-08.

Debut v Rangers (n) 1-4 (CC) 11.5.1897
(scored once)

A stumpy wee man but a lion of a player, Jack Reynolds was thin on top from a young age and the most unlikely looking footballer. Yet "Baldy" won English Cup medals in 1892, 1895 and 1897 and had played five times for Ireland before it was discovered he was Lancashire-born and England began to throw caps at him. He had played for Ireland at Parkhead on March 28th 1891 and Celtic made moves to sign him. His lack of thatch misled some of the Parkhead committee into stereotyping: with so little hair he had to be an old man whose best days lay behind him. When Celtic did eventually land their catch, Jack's baldness might really have represented exhausted force and he was destroyed by McKenzie of Clyde in the Glasgow Cup (September 18th 1897). He made only two appearances for Southampton and when his glorious football career was over, earned a living in the Yorkshire coalfield.

Appearances:
SL: 4 apps. 1gl.
Total: *4 apps. 1 gl.*

RIBCHESTER, William

Role: Outside-right 1916-19
5' 6" 10st.0lbs.
b. Govan, 28th July 1898

CAREER: St Mungo's Academy/Townhead Benburb Juveniles 1915/Parkhead Juniors summer 1916/CELTIC 11 Dec 1916/Army 1917/OTC Machine Gun Corps 1918/CELTIC again 5 Apr 1919/Albion Rovers 16 Aug 1919 /St Johnstone 3 Aug 1922/Dunfermline Athletic 5 Oct 1924/Armadale 1 Sept 1925/ St Mirren 12 Feb 1927.

Debut v Queen's Park (a) 3-1 (SL) 11.11.16

Bill Ribchester

"Light, fast and fearless..." "Slim of build but clever and speedy. A real topper at corner kicks and able to get the goal an odd time. A toff on and off the field"; Bill Ribchester, son of a headmaster, signed for Celtic and was the youngest first League player in Scotland in November 1916. He had two games in succession as deputy for Andy McAtee in the Championship season of 1916-17. His debut was a "picnic" but for the second he had no McMenemy to feed-off and was up against a powerful tackler in Jimmy McMullan of Partick Thistle. His game improved tremendously in the forces "and he scarcely plays for the regiment without scoring... he is hoping to don the green stripes once more." He was a Lieutenant by 1918 and watched Celtic with a wound stripe up on September 7th after being strafed in a tank engagement. With Albion Rovers he equalised from a penalty against Rangers in the first of the three semi-finals at Celtic Park (March 27th 1920) and was outside-right in the Rovers team beaten in the Cup final by Kilmarnock at Hampden (April 17th 1920). While with St Johnstone Ribby trained at Ibrox until 1923-24.

Appearances:
SL: 2 apps. 0 gls.
Total: *2 apps. 0 gls.*

RILEY, John Lochery

Role: Outside-right 1941-43
5' 9" 11st.0lbs.
b. Gorbals, 20th July 1920

CAREER: Glasgow Perthshire 1940/CELTIC 23 Apr 1941/free 1943/Petershill July 31 1943/ Glasgow Perthshire summer 1944/Clyde 30 June 1945/Arbroath 18 July 1949.

Debut v Partick Thistle (h) 1-2 (CC) 24.5.41

It took hot favourites Glasgow Perthshire three games to bring home the Scottish Junior Cup against Blantyre Victoria (and ex-Celt Johnnie Wilson) in 1941. Outside-right John Riley, the boy with the 'cleek legs' just could not get going until the third match at Tynecastle on April 26th 1941 (when Blantyre played ten men for 80 minutes). John joined Celtic just as Jimmy Delaney was making his comeback and was employed mainly on the left wing. He made his debut while the Royal Navy was hunting the Bismarck in the North Atlantic. Trouble with his cartilage began at Falkirk on November 15th 1941. He was Seton Airlie's immediate replacement on March 14th 1942 when the big Carmyle boy left for the Artillery. When Celtic lost 2-1 to Motherwell in the Summer Cup on June 20th 1942 he was one of four Celtic forwards (including Johnny Crum) described as "third-class". Paddy Travers took him to Shawfield. Clyde beat Celtic 6-2 in the League Cup Section D of the qualifying rounds on March 23rd 1946. It was inside-right John Riley (with Hughie Long) who destroyed the Celts.

John Riley

Appearances:
RL: 17 apps.
5 gls.
RLC: 5 apps.
5 gls.
Total: *22 apps.*
10 gls.

RILEY, Joseph J.

Role: Inside-forward 1928-30
5' 8" 10st.8lbs.
b. Bonnybridge

CAREER: St Mungo's Academy/Cardown
St Joseph's/Cambuslang Bluebell/Rutherglen
Glencairn/Maryhill Hibernian 1927/
Hibernian (trial) 1927/CELTIC 2 June 1928/
(Ayr United loan 2 Mar 1929)/(Nithsdale
Wanderers loan 2 Oct 1929 & 17 Apr 1930)/
free 1930/St Mirren 8 July 1930/free 29 July
1931/Alloa 28 Aug 1931 until Jan 1932.

Debut v Dundee (a) 1-0 (SL) 11.8.28

J.J. Riley was
rejected by
Glencairn as "not
much use" but won
a SJFA Cup winner's
medal with the all-
conquering Maryhill
Hibs of 1928 and
stepped into the
Celtic big team on
his debut as the man
who was going to
take Tommy
McInally's place.
His play at Dens

J.J. Riley

Park on his debut was described as "sharp
and correct." Joe was reading for a B.Sc.
degree at Glasgow University and by 1931 had
a job as a teacher at the Higher Grade School,
Coatbridge. His son Anthony of Our Lady's
High Motherwell and a prospective student of
Medicine at Glasgow signed as a right-half for
Bob Shankly at Falkirk September 25th 1950.

Appearances:
SL: 10 apps. 2 gls.
Total: *10 apps 2 gls.*

RITCHIE, Andrew

Role: Midfield 1971-76
6' 1" 14st.0lbs.
b. 23rd February 1956

CAREER: Bellshill Academy/Bellshill YMCA/
Celtic BC/CELTIC S form 1971/Kirkintilloch
Rob Roy (farmed-out) 1971/CELTIC 10 Feb
1973/Morton 27 Oct 1976/Motherwell 26 July
1983/Clydebank (trial) Jan 1984/East Stirling
(trial) Feb 1984/Hannover 96 (trial) 1984/

Albion Rovers Mar 1984/player-coach 30 June
1984/resigned 27 Aug 1984/retired Jan 1985/
Barbican YMCA London 1985/St Mirren coach
12 Oct 1992/CELTIC BC coach 7 Sept 1994.

Debut v Dunfermline Athletic (h) 6-0 (SL)
29.12.73 (sub)

"If laziness was a trade, big Andy would be in
business for himself... he makes valium look
like a pick-me-up." At 16, Andy Ritchie "the
idle idol" had "the poise of a veteran," like a
new George Connelly. On his debut he was
"one to watch... a wallop in his right foot..."
"I played against Leeds (February 11th 1976),
scored Celtic's goal, had Norman Hunter
going round in circles, got a standing ovation
at half-time. So Stein told me to have a bath:
'You're too lazy.'" Andy went to Morton in
exchange for Roy Baines plus £15,000 and
began at once to score prolifically not least as a
dead ball specialist. He hit thunderous free-
kicks that swung right and left and could
almost bend a ball round a corner. So why had
Celtic let him go? "I know I didn't give my all
in my last two years at Parkhead but then I
wanted away." Big, heavy and slow but with
superb touch he was the buy of the season in
1976-77, "a Jekyll and Hyde player... with a bit
more effort he could develop into a real
personality." "I like to have a breather and
have a chat with the fans... I'm lazy. I like to
entertain people. That's how I see my role."
His role ("Play the game, lads, some of us are
trying to get some sleep out here") won him
the Player of the Year award on April 24th
1979. "The bookies are offering 6/4 I'll make
the speech sitting down."

Appearances:
SL: 9 apps. 1 gl.
SLC: 1 app. 1 gl.
Total: *10 apps. 2 gls.*

Andy Ritchie

ROBERTSON, David Vallance

Role: Goalkeeper 1930-31
5' 9" 10st.8lbs.
b. Kirkcaldy, 16th August 1906

CAREER: Tranent Juniors/St Mirren 12 Feb 1927/York City 1928/Rosslyn Juniors 1929/ CELTIC 22 Oct 1930/(Clydebank loan 9 Mar 1931)/Cowdenbeath June 1931/Rosslyn Juniors 1931.

Debut v Motherwell (a) 3-3 (SL) 25.10.30

John Thomson was playing for Scotland against Wales at Ibrox on the day when engineer David Robertson first pulled on the scarlet sweater. His second League game was at Love Street on February 21st 1931 when the Laddie frae Cardenden was at Windsor Park keeping Ireland out in a 0-0 draw.

Appearances:
SL: 2 apps. 0 shut-outs.
Total: *2 apps. 0 shut-outs.*

ROBERTSON, Graham Baird

Role: Half-back 1929-31
5' 9" 11st.3lbs.
b. Buckhaven, 22nd September 1907

CAREER: Aberhill Public School (Methil)/ Kirkland Wanderers/Milton Violet/Denbeath Star/Thornton Rangers/Wellesley Juniors/ Partick Thistle (trial) Aug 1928/St Mirren (trial)/East Fife (trial)/CELTIC 6 Apr 1929/ free Apr 1931/Cowdenbeath 3 June 1931/ St Mirren 5 Mar 1932/Cowdenbeath 10 Mar 1932/Alloa (trial) 6 Aug 1934/left 14 Sept 1934.

*Debut v Clyde (a) 1-1
(GC) 7.9.29*

For the second Public trial of August 7th 1929 Celtic returned to Parkhead from exile at Shawfield since the pavilion fire of March 28th 1929. All eyes were on James Gallagher, Peter Kavanagh and

*Graham
Robertson*

Pat Duffy's latest discovery, Graham Robertson, "reputed to be the finest wing-half in the Kingdom of Fife." Two-footed Graham, an ex-centre-forward, was destined as fellow-Fifer Jean McFarlane's first successor at left-half. "Big, powerful and plucky," he gave Celtic good service but was counselled to stand down for sake of his health as of September 9th 1930. He did as advised but made a comeback with Cowdenbeath (manager: Adam Scott Duncan) and had at least one magnificent game on a frozen pitch against Rangers at Ibrox on January 28th 1933.

Appearances:
SL: 34 apps. 1 gl.
SC: 3 apps. 0 gls.
Total: *37 apps. 1 gl.*

ROBERTSON, William Smith

Role: Outside-left 1909-10
b. Stirling, 7th June 1887

CAREER: Denny Hibernian/CELTIC 30 Oct 1909/Preston North End Sept 1910/St Mirren 26 June 1911.

Debut v Kilmarnock (h) 2-1 (SL) 4.12.09

Celtic lost right-winger Willie Kivlichan, injured versus Airdrie on November 20th 1909, and after trying John Young, brought in Langcroft boy, Willie Robertson ("clever and promising") for his senior debut in fog on a frostbound pitch before a wetched 6,000 crowd. Two prodigious goals were witnessed: a long range effort from Loney and the mother of all headers from Quinn. The following week, Willie partnered Jimmy McMenemy in such downpour that the Parkhead executive relented and opened the stands to the drowning. His last game was at Rugby Park on Christmas Day at outside-left to Peter Johnstone when Quinn scored a rampage of a goal on the stroke of half-time, right down the middle with the whole Killie defence in pursuit. Willie played for the reserves against the first team before 10,000 fans in the North End pre-season trial of August 27th 1910 and with Lachlan McLean "gave a wing display, the superior of which has not been seen in Preston for many years."

Appearances:
SL: 3 apps. 0 gls.
SC: 1 app. 0 gls.
Total: *4 apps. 0 gls.*

RODGERS, Patrick Edward

Role: Outside-left 1944-46
5′ 7″ 10st.0lbs.
b. Grangemouth, 9th September 1924

CAREER: Bowhill St Ninian's/CELTIC 4 Sept 1944/(Raith Rovers loan 23 Feb 1946)/free 1946/Workington Town 1946/Rosyth Recreation July 1947/Lochgelly Albert/ (Lochee Harp loan June 1950)/Crossgates Primrose/Thornton Hibernian 1951/retired Dec 1954.

Debut v Dumbarton (a) 3-0 (RL) 16.9.44

Celtic were a team without an outside-left when they lost 6-2 to Hamilton on September 2nd 1944. They were destroyed by Accies' left-winger Billy McCall, a 3rd Lanark supporter but with green and white proclivities. To buy McCall seemed the obvious answer. Instead Celtic went for a juvenile from John Thomson country "pawky Pat Rodgers... He's wee but he has a big say when the Parkhead attack is on." Inverkeithing boy Paddy was a trier but never able to hold down a regular first-team place. Pat O'Sullivan was taken from Airdrie to replace him in November 1945. Dunfermline Athletic were interested in making a senior of him again in the summer of 1950. Pat hung up his boots from arthritis.

Pat Rodgers

Appearances:
RL: 18 apps. 1 gl.
RLC: 1 app. 0 gls.
Total: *19 apps. 1 gl.*

ROGAN, Anton

Role: Left-back 1986-91
5′ 11″ 11st.6lbs.
b. Belfast, 25th March 1966

CAREER: St Paul's Belfast GAA/Distillery/ CELTIC 9 May 1986/Sunderland 1 Oct 1991/ Oxford United 6 Aug 1993.

Debut v Hamilton Academicals (h) 8-3 (SL) 3.1.87

"Rogan has pace, heading ability, is a ferocious tackler and supremely fit." Celtic went to Ibrox on Sunday March 20th 1988 on Championship business. Joe Miller was off form and substituted in 64 minutes by Anton Rogan. Anton immediately began to run at Rangers and from two of his headers, first McStay scored with a ferocious left-foot volley, then Andy Walker chested the winner past Woods with 11 minutes to go. It was Centenary Year and the Celtic fans left Ibrox singing "Happy Birthday to Us!" Anton started the full 90 minutes of the Cup final versus Dundee United on May 14th 1988 and it was his snake-hipped run into the box that set McAvennie up for the late equaliser. He got his second Scottish Cup medal in the defeat of Rangers on May 20th the following year and was beloved of the Parkhead faithful. There were two ghastly blunders against Rangers in the space of six weeks, April 1st and May 12th 1990 when he gave away a pair of penalties through totally gratuitous handball. He missed a vital spot-kick in the Scottish Cup final shoot-out against Aberdeen on May 12th 1990 so when he approached the manager for a pay-rise, McNeill was adamant: "The deal he's offered is the one he gets." Anton was

Anton Rogan

axed from the pre-season tour, refused to accept a monthly contract, and had his wages stopped on August 10th 1990. He made his peace with Celtic and then his comeback against Rangers (September 15th 1990). His transfer to Sunderland came as a shock to the fans. Tommy Boyd had to be procured for an adequate replacement. Anton had a great first season at Roker and was Malcolm Crosby's left-back in the Sunderland side beaten 2-0 by Souness' Liverpool in the Cup final of May 9th 1992. He was handed a winner's medal by mistake. A broken leg in 1992-93 and Terry Butcher's re-shuffle ruined his hopes at Roker and a move to Oxford followed.

Appearances:
SL: 129 apps. 4 gls.
SLC: 13 apps. 0 gls.
SC: 19 apps. 1 gl.
Eur: 8 apps. 0 gls.
Total: *169 apps. 5 gls.*

ROLLO, Alexander

Role: Left-back 1948-54
5' 10" 12st.0lbs.
b. Dumbarton, 18th September 1926

CAREER: St Theresa's Possilpark BG/ Ashfield Juveniles/Springburn United/ Ashfield Juniors 13 May 1948/CELTIC 10 Oct 1948/King's Own Scottish Borderers/free 30 Apr 1954/Kilmarnock 25 May 1954/ Dumbarton 28 May 1956/Workington Town 11 June 1957/Sligo Rovers player-coach Sept 1960/retired 1962.

Debut v Motherwell (a) 1-2 (SL) 6.1.51

On January 20th 1951 Alex Rollo was the Celtic left-back first to have to cope with Jimmy Delaney on his return to Paradise almost five full years after his departure in February 1946. Alex played subsequently in the first Celtic side to win a post-war Scottish Cup 1-0 against Motherwell (April 21st 1951). He went on the tour of the United States and was with the team mobbed at Central Station on their return (June 30th 1951). He won a St Mungo's Cup medal against Aberdeen (marking Tommy Bogan) on August 1st 1951. His solitary Scottish Cup goal for Celtic was a fine piece of heroics against 3rd Lanark in the first round replay (February 4th 1952; a Monday afternoon kick-off, attendance 27,344

Alex Rollo

at a time of full employment). Alex was carried-off at half-time. He hobbled out for the second half but was taken off again. Back he came for another try as passenger on the wing but this time scored the equaliser with his damaged left peg. Once more he was carted off but *again* limped back on for extra time. The leg put him out for the rest of the season. He returned to beat George Niven with a mis-hit cross from outside-right at Parkhead on September 20th 1952, the day of Jackie Millsop's funeral, and was Joe Baillie's immediate stop-gap at left-half on December 6th 1952. He re-established himself as a first-team back in time for the Coronation Cup. When Celtic beat Hibs at Hampden before 117,000 on May 20th 1953, Alex regarded it as a bigger occasion than winning the Scottish Cup in 1951. A free spirit, he gave up full-time football to clean windows in 1955. Later he was a crane operator in Workington.

Appearances:
SL: 37 apps. 1 gl.
SLC: 13 apps. 0 gls.
SC: 9 apps. 1 gl.
Total: *59 apps. 2 gls.*

ROOSE, Leigh Richmond

Role: Goalkeeper 1910
6′ 1″ 13st.6lbs.
b. Holt, nr Wrexham,
27th November 1877
d. Killed in action, 7th October 1916

CAREER: UCW Aberystwyth/
Aberystwyth Juniors 1897/
Aberystwyth Town 1898/Ruabon
Druids 1900/London Welsh
Juniors 1899/Stoke Oct 1901/
Everton Oct 1904/Stoke Aug
1905/Sunderland Jan 1908/
(CELTIC loan Mar 1910)/
Huddersfield Town Apr 1911/
Aston Villa Aug 1911/Arsenal
11 Dec 1911/Aberystwyth Town
1912/Llandudno Town 1914/
9 Royal Fusiliers 1914.

Debut v Clyde (a) 1-3 (SC) 12.3.10

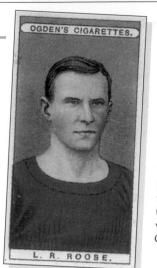

OGDEN'S CIGARETTES.

L. R. ROOSE.

and shook his hand in
congratulation. Football
note: Goalies were stopped
from handling outside the
18-yard box because of Dick
Roose's "antics in carrying
forward the ball." Lance-
corporal Roose won the
Military Medal during
World War I. He was killed
in the bloodbath of the
Somme but has no known
grave. He is commemorated
with the Royal Fusiliers on
the Thiepval Memorial and
we may claim him for one of
Celtic's Glorious Dead.

Appearances:
SC: 1 app. 0 shut-outs.
Total: *1 app. 0 shut-outs.*

"Provided the game's conditions are
favourable, Roose will generally be found
sitting propped up by the goalpost with an
assumption of careless indifference to his
surroundings" (and there are photographs that
prove it!). An idiosyncratic amateur who
reputedly could only play "in one particular
long-bottomed jersey made in one particular
way by one particular person," Dick Roose
was a doctor of Bacteriology and reputedly a
very rich man who once hired a train to get
him on time to an Aston Villa fixture. By
December 1908, "his daring gymnastics in
goal" had made him "the hero of every boy in
the land." He was also a practical joker who
might turn up for a match with his hands
wrapped in bandages, saying not to worry, he
could play. He was in goal for Wales against
Scotland at Rugby Park on March 5th 1910. At
Parkhead, Davy Adams was down with
pneumonia and Jimmy Quinn's brother Phil
kept goal in a friendly versus 3rd Lanark. For
the Scottish Cup semi-final the following week
at Shawfield, Celtic engaged Dick Roose's
services by way of compensation for the way
Llewellyn Davies had put Jimmy McMenemy
out of the tie with the cynical kicking
administered at Kilmarnock. There was little
the famous goalie could do to forestall the
Clyde but he did exhibit one lovely touch:
after Clyde's third goal in the 55th minute, the
big Welshman ran after the scorer Chalmers

ROSS, Andrew

Role: Inside-right 1898-1900
b. Hurlford, 17th February 1878

CAREER: Hurlford Thistle/Kilmarnock (trial)
May 1898/CELTIC 17 Sept 1898/Galston
19 Apr 1900/Barrow 1901.

Debut v St Bernard's (a) 3-2 (SL) 29.10.1898

Hurlford natives Hugh Goldie and Tom
Hynds recommended their townie Andrew
Ross to Celtic. He played in the Rood Fair Day
friendly against Dumfries Hibs on September
30th 1898 and scored for Celtic at Dundee in
Alec Keillor's benefit match (October 10th). As
such a recent signing, he escaped the Massacre
of the Reserves five days later and made his
League debut in place of Johnny Divers at
Logie Green before a small attendance. His
final appearance for the green and white
vertical stripes was on April 14th 1899 in the
0-10 defeat of Dumfries Hibs at Cresswell Park
when he scored the fourth goal, the first of the
second half.

Appearances:
SL: 1 app. 0 gls.
Total: *1 app. 0 gls.*

ROUGH, Alan Roderick

Role: Goalkeeper 1988
6' 1" 13st.6lbs.
b. Gorbals, 25th November 1951

CAREER: Lincoln Amateurs/Partick Thistle
S form 1966/Sighthill Amateurs (farmed-out)/
Partick Thistle Amateurs (farmed-out)/Partick
Thistle 20 Oct 1969/Hibernian 26 Oct 1982/
free 19 Apr 1988/Orlando Lions player-coach
1988/CELTIC 9 Aug 1988/Hamilton
Academicals 23 Dec 1988/free 12 May 1989/
Ayr United 26 Sept 1989/free 15 May 1990/
Glenafton Athletic player-coach 18 July 1990/
manager 27 Sept 1990.

Debut v Ayr United (h) 4-1 (SLC) 17.8.88

Packy Bonner was recuperating from a back
operation; Andy Murdoch damaged his ankle
in Switzerland on July 12th 1988; Hamish
McAlpine came in as a stop-gap at Winterthur
on July 16th 1988; Celtic signed Ian Andrews
to replace Bonner and got ex-Scotland
internationalist Alan (adulated here, execrated
there) Rough as cover. Scruff got his chance
when big Ian went down with a sudden virus
after the Hearts game on August 13th 1988. He
seemed delighted to be playing for Celtic: "I'm
just sorry I didn't get the chance years ago."

Alan Rough

Packy Bonner was back in action by October
22nd 1988 and big Alan moved to Hamilton:
"I'm just glad to be able to say I played for
Celtic" (December 30th 1988). The pleasure
was all Celtic's. Under manager Rough's
tutelage, Glenafton Athletic won the Scottish
Junior Cup on May 23rd 1993.

Appearances:
SL: 5 apps. 1 shut-out.
SLC: 1 app. 0 shut-outs.
Eur: 1 app. 1 shut-out.
Total: *7 apps. 2 shut-outs (33%).*

♣ **Celtic note:** *Alan came on as an outfield sub for
Glenafton on January 4th 1992. Athletic were
awarded a penalty. He took it and missed. Minutes
later he headed home from a corner!*

ROWAN, James

Role: Inside-right 1952-56
5' 10" 12st.0lbs.
b. Glasgow, 29th June 1934

CAREER: L.Pieters 1950/Shettleston Juniors
1951/CELTIC 9 Oct 1952/(Stirling Albion loan
20 Dec 1955)/free 30 Apr 1956/Clyde 13 May
1956/(Stirling Albion loan 1957-58)/free 1959
/Dunfermline Athletic 9 May 1959/Stirling
Albion 11 Dec 1959/Airdrie 24 May 1962/
Falkirk 16 June 1965/player-coach 1968/
caretaker manager 29 Sept 1968/coach only
24 Oct 1968/dismissed as coach 16 Oct 1968/
free 4 May 1969/Chairman Scottish PFA
5 May 1969/Clyde player-coach 8 Aug 1969/
Partick Thistle player 14 Sept 1969/East
Stirling manager 26 Mar 1970/dismissed
30 Aug 1971/CELTIC scout 1971/Clyde
acting-manager 29 Aug 1973.

*Debut v Dundee (h) 4-1 (SL) 18.12.54
(scored once)*

"An opener-out of play with long carpet
passes," Jimmy Rowan was a fitter with
Harland and Wolff and went to Switzerland
with Celtic where the 1954 World Cup made
as profound an impression on him as an
enthusiast for the game, as on Jock Stein as a
strategist. He was a highly-valued utility
player with leadership potential wherever he
went. Because he was playing "too much
football" in defence at Airdrie he was moved
to centre and began to score freely. He hit an
equaliser at Parkhead on March 2nd 1963
which was greeted with a mighty roar of

Jim Rowan (centre) and a group of Celts admire the Player of the Year trophy won by John Higgins in 1953-54. Left to right: W.Gillies, J.Higgins, E.Smith, J.Rowan, M.Conroy, J.McPhail and groundsman C.Docherty.

sardonic acclaim so awful were Celtic on the day. At Falkirk he fell foul of manager Willie Cunningham's bristly new broom approach for observations on the changes at Brockville to the local press. By 1968 as he signed-on for his 17th season, Jim was the father of four daughters. He was a far-seeing and conscientious manager at East Stirling until the directors lost patience with his youth policy and brought in Alex Ferguson.

Appearances:
SL: 2 apps. 1 gl.
Total: *2 apps. 1 gl.*

RUSSELL, David

Role: Centre-half 1896-98; 1899-1903
5' 8" 12st.7lbs.
b. Airdrie, 6th April 1868

CAREER: Shotts Minors/Stewarton FC/ Broxburn FC/Preston NE 1888/Hearts 1890/ Broxburn FC by Mar 1890/Nottingham Forest 1891/Preston NE 1892/Hearts 1895/CELTIC May 1896/Preston NE 2 May 1898/CELTIC 10 May 1899/Broxburn 18 Aug 1903.

Debut v Hibernian (a) 1-3 (SL) 15.8.1896

Sandy-haired miner Davie Russell ("one of the finest centre-halves that ever played") was Jimmy Kelly's first successor at Celtic. He had won an English Cup medal with Preston's 'Invincibles' on March 30th 1889 as a "fumbling centre-forward" with a reputation for a "bruiser" and scored the only goal when Hearts beat Dumbarton in the Scottish final of February 7th 1891. One of his best games for Celtic was a mere friendly at the Manor Park Plumstead against Woolwich Arsenal (February 15th 1897). Arsenal (with ex-Celt Jimmy Boyle) led 4-1 before Davie went to work scoring a hat-trick in a great 4-5 fight-back. He was renowned for

Davie Russell

his long-distance shooting and got a stunning goal from 40 yards in Johnny Madden's benefit on September 7th 1897, 1-3 versus Rangers. His brother died on Hogmanay 1898 but Davie insisted on turning out for the vital Ne'erday match at Parkhead (abandoned at 70 minutes for encroachment). The race for the League went on. At Dundee a fortnight later, Dan Doyle put a penalty yards wide at 1-1. The referee ordered a retake. Davie Russell stepped up, spat on his hands and scored. The Scottish League was won on February 12th 1898 and Davie earned another Scottish Cup medal when Celtic beat Queen's Park 4-3 on April 14th 1900. He was skipper of the Celtic side that lost the final 4-3 against Hearts (April 6th 1901). After football he worked full-time down the Greenrigg pit in Fauldhouse and was severely crushed in a roof fall on October 16th 1906.

Appearances:
SL: 71 apps. 11 gls.
SC: 13 apps. 0 gls.
Total: *84 apps. 11 gls.*

RYAN, Vincent

Role: Utility 1953-58
6' 0" 12st.0lbs.
b. c 1936

CAREER: Home Farm/CELTIC 31 Aug 1953/ St Mirren 7 Feb 1958/Drumcondra 1959.

Debut v Hamilton Academicals (h) 1-0 (SL) 26.4.54

"Vince Ryan is the most promising player I have ever seen" (Duggie Livingstone, Eire Youth coach 1953). Matt Busby and Johnny Carey implored young Vincent to Old Trafford but the boy was allegedly set like concrete on Celtic. He played his first game at right-back and had been employed in every position except goal before he left Parkhead. Versus Hearts as late as December 28th 1957 (at centre-forward) it emerged he was even a deep-throw specialist as well as owner of a thunderous long-range shot. In a Floodlight Friendly at Elland Road on December 3rd 1956 he played the game of his life and scored an incredible goal right on half-time in a 3-4 win against Leeds. Vincent's trouble was he blew hot and cold. Against Dunfermline 12 days after Leeds, he had a superlative first half yet spent the second 45 minutes in total eclipse. He went on the US tour of 1957 and had a fine game against Spurs in Montreal on June 9th 1957 yet once back home, was out of the first team frame until December 28th when he began his last clutch of matches. At Parkhead on Ne'erday 1958, Sammy Wilson set up chance after chance but Vincent, of all people, could not finish. Against Aberdeen (January 18th 1958), his final appearance for Celtic, he put a penalty well wide in 36 minutes that might have won the game 2-0. As it was Ewen equalised with six minutes to go and Aberdeen went home with a hard-earned point.

Appearances:
SL: 22 apps. 3 gls.
Total: *22 apps. 3 gls.*

Vince Ryan (2nd left) at Southampton Docks before departing for Celtic's 1957 tour of America.

Robbie Sanderson

SANDERSON, Robert (Turnbull?)

Role: Inside-right 1908
5′ 8″ 11st.10lbs.
b. *Peebles, 15th March 1887 (?)*

CAREER: Vale of Leithen/Peebles Rovers Nov 1902/CELTIC 1 May 1908/(Kilmarnock loan 28 Aug 1908)/Spennymoor United 1909/Barnsley 1909/Hearts 2 May 1910.

Debut v St Mirren (a) 2-2 (SL) 30.4.08

Celtic met a Border XI at Mossilee, Galashiels on April 18th 1906 and Robbie Sanderson of Peebles Rovers played centre for the Select. He opposed Celtic again in the Scottish Cup on Burns' Day 1908, this time at inside-right in the Rovers side beaten 4-0 at Parkhead. His debut for Celtic was in the nature of a trial in place of Jimmy McMenemy in the 34th and final League match of Celtic's Clean Sweep season 1907-08. He showed "nice touches and much promise." He got a goal against Rangers for Peter Somers' benefit on a wet, bad night (August 26th 1908). He was also in the team that put Rangers out of the 2nd XI Cup 1-0 at Parkhead on January 23rd 1909.

Appearances:
SL: 2 apps. 0 gls.
Total: *2 apps. 0 gls.*

SCARFF, Peter

Role: Inside-left 1928-33
5′8½″ 11st.0lbs.
b. *Linwood, 29th March 1908*
d. *9th December 1933*

CAREER: Linwood St Conval's/CELTIC 27 Aug 1928/Maryhill Hibs (farmed-out) 30 Aug 1928.

Debut v Arthurlie (h) 5-1 (SC) 19.1.29

"Scarff is a worthy successor to Jimmy McMenemy... he has McMenemy's dragging touch and the same ease with the long opening pass to the other wing." Peter Scarff joined Celtic, "a second-class team," in 1928-29 from a "second-class juvenile club," Linwood St Conval's. He was a "utility man... no artiste... strong in limb and body... tireless... tremendous capacity for work." He got his first medal on October 11th 1930 when Celtic beat Rangers 2-1 in the Glasgow Cup final. He played in both Scottish finals against Motherwell in 1931 and figured with Bertie Thomson in the notorious pursuit of referee Peter Craigmyle round the Celtic end goal claiming a penalty for hands against John Johnman in the first half of the first game (April 11th), an incident Craigmyle denied had ever happened, despite photographic evidence. He went on the 1931 tour of the USA and when Celtic turned up a jersey short against Montreal Carsteels on June 13th, played in an ordinary (pale green) dress shirt and scored five. He watched with concern as John Thomson was carried-off to die at Ibrox on September 5th 1931. Eighteen days later, in Willie Fleming's benefit at Ayr, he was unable to resume for the second half and Denis Currie went on in his place. His last game for Celtic was at left-half versus Leith at Parkhead (December 19th 1931) and on Jan 12th 1932 he was admitted to the Bridge of Weir sanatorium seriously ill with pulmonary tuberculosis. Despite periods of remission giving rise to

Peter Scarff

false hope, it was announced on July 29th 1933 that Peter Scarff would never play football again. He was buried at Kilbarchan (December 12th 1933) and Willie Maley laid a Celtic jersey on the coffin before interment. Peter was beloved of the fans of his time and the news of his death was greeted with anguish.

Appearances:
SL: 97 apps. 51 gls.
SC: 15 apps. 4 gls.
Total: *112 apps. 55 gls.*

♣ **Celtic note:** *On a visit to the Education Offices in Bath Street to trace some old teachers in summer 1989, Celtic writer Tom Campbell was shown a box containing Scarff family souvenirs of the great Peter including medals and newspaper cuttings that made his historian's heart race.*

SCOTT, Robert

Role: Inside-left 1893
b. 2nd October 1870

CAREER: Airdrie May 1888/(CELTIC loan Apr 1893)/retired 1899.

Debut v Rangers (h) 3-0 (SL) 29.4.1893

On Willie Maley's 25th birthday (April 25th 1893) Celtic entertained Everton at Parkhead for a £40 guarantee before 4,000 fans, and played guest stars, viz Johnstone of Airdrie and Adams, Baird and inside-left George Scott of Hearts. Four days later, before 14,000, they borrowed another Scott, also an inside-left, Robert from Airdrie and Aitchison Street, a future internationalist (March 31st 1894). Under the rules of the time he was able to take Mick Mulvey's place and help see Rangers off on the run-in to the Bhoys' first League Championship

Appearances:
SL: 1 app. 0 gls.
Total: *1 app. 0 gls.*

SEMPLE, William

Role: Outside-left 1907-09
5' 5" 10st.10lbs.
b. West Maryston, 18th April 1886
d. Southport, 4th June 1965

CAREER: Baillieston Thistle/CELTIC 14 Oct 1907/Millwall Aug 1909/Carlisle United 1910

/Haslingden July 1911/Southport Central 1912/1st Battalion 7th King's Regt WW1/Southport 1919/player-coach 1923/retired 1926/asst trainer 1926/trainer 1939/head groundsman 1947/retired Christmas 1963.

Debut v Rangers (n) 0-0 (GC) 19.10.07

Davie Hamilton was suspended for two months on October 17th 1907 and Celtic transferred out-of-favour left-wing virtuoso Bobby Templeton to Kilmarnock the following day. This meant the club was without a recognised outside-left for the Glasgow Cup final replay. As a result, wee miner Billy Semple played his last junior game on Monday October 14th 1907 and trotted out into the cauldron of Hampden the following Saturday as a signed Celtic player before an Old Firm crowd of 55,000. For the second replay on October 26th, Billy was dropped; Celtic used Jimmy Quinn at outside-left and played Davie McLean at centre. Billy went into the League side on November 2nd 1907 in a 5-0 win over Port Glasgow and held his place until Davie Hamilton returned four days before Christmas. He was "a prime favourite" at Millwall and Carlisle (from where there was talk of Celtic bringing him back) but above all at Southport where he served the club a total of 51 years in all and as groundsman, produced a Haig Avenue pitch with the reputation of the best playing surface in England outside Wembley.

Billy Semple

Appearances:
SL: 8 apps. 2 gls.
Total: *8 apps. 2 gls.*

SHARKEY, James

Role: Centre-forward 1954-57
5' 11" 11st.7lbs.
b. 12th February 1934

CAREER: Sacred Heart Primary School/Pirn St Secondary/RAF Stranshaw 1952/Haverill Rovers/League Hearts 1954/CELTIC (provisional) Apr 1954/Rutherglen Glencairn (farmed-out) 1954/CELTIC (full) 1 Dec 1954/Airdrie 8 Nov 1957/Raith Rovers 30 May 1961/free Apr 1962/Portadown (trial) 18 May 1962/Cambridge Town 1962/Wisbech Town 1964/Corby Town/Bury/Newmarket Town/Girton United player-manager 1969/retired 1972.

Debut v Raith Rovers (h) 2-0 (SL) 1.10.55 (scored once)

Apart from the RAF, greenkeeper Jim Sharkey's football experience had been confined to half-a-crown-a-head games. He was taken-up by Jimmy McStay as a brainy

inside-forward and converted into Celtic's 27th centre since 1946. He lacked speed over the first few yards but was "slick in avoiding the tackle... does a nifty line in double shuffles." "My idol used to be Gerry McAloon, the greatest of them all at the double shuffle. I watched him and tried it myself." Jimmy set a goal up for Matt McVittie with a glorious dummy on his debut. He had his greatest game for Celtic in the Glasgow Cup final replay at Hampden Boxing Day 1955 when he dribbled George Young into bewilderment and scored two beautiful goals in the 5-3 defeat of Rangers, caressing the ball with his foot each time before crashing it high into the net behind George Niven. Jimmy was so seriously injured by a ball driven into the face at Morton on February 4th 1956 that for months at home he was dogged by black-outs. Nevertheless, he continued to play and scored for Celtic in the second minute of the semi-final versus Clyde on March 24th. An alleged misdemeanour at Seamill was reported to Chairman Bob Kelly and he was dropped as inside-right in favour of full-back Mike Haughney for the Scottish Cup final on April 21st 1956. Jimmy later made his feelings plain to the Chairman at the defeat celebration, apologised to the Directors on April 24th, but knew thereafter his days had numbers on. His last League game was at outside-right in the 2-3 victory of September 21st 1957 when Celtic collected their first full points at Ibrox in 22 years. He was a huge success at Airdrie, "The Tully of Broomfield," both from his performances on the field (he gave Bobby Evans and Eric Caldow some hard games) and the good atmosphere he engendered in the dressing room. When Airdrie reached second top of the Scottish League (October 11th 1958) it was largely down to a man called Sharkey. He left the Waysiders under a cloud after rumours of not trying against Celtic in the Cup semi-final on April 1st 1961. He broke his ankle versus St Mirren at Love Street on January 20th 1962 with no one near him and missed the rest of the season 1961-62. Jimmy is nowadays porter at Pembroke College, Cambridge and looks as fit as in his prime.

Appearances:
SL: 23 apps. 7 gls.
SLC: 2 apps. 0 gls.
SC: 2 apps. 1 gl.
Total: *27 apps. 8 gls.*

Jim Sharkey

SHAW, Charles

Role: Goalkeeper 1913-25
5' 6" 12st.0lbs.
b. Twechar, 21st September 1885
d. New York City, 27th March 1938

CAREER: Baillieston Thistle/Kirkintilloch Harp/Port Glasgow Athletic 18 Apr 1906/ Queen's Park Rangers May 1907/CELTIC 2 May 1913/(Clyde loan 13 Feb 1925)/ New Bedford FC (USA) 6 June 1925.

Debut v Third Lanark (a) 2-1 (CC) 6.5.13

"The wondrous little goal-keeper," Charlie Shaw had a splendid debut: "Celtic have a gem of a custodian in the man from QPR" (where he played 223 games and missed only three). In his first League match against Ayr at Parkhead on August 16th 1913 there were "deafening roars of delight at Shaw's saves" and two weeks later in a quiet match, "the crowd was anxious to see more of Shaw." He was slim-built like Joe Cullen but took the ball in a vice of a grip reminiscent of another great Celtic 'keeper: *"How oft your cat-like spring recalls/McArthur's way with treach'rous balls."* Shaw, McNair and Dodds formed "one of the prickliest defensive zarebas" in British football. With Charlie between the sticks, Celtic just stopped conceding goals. When Kilmarnock won on April 21st 1917, his average yield after 37 League matches was a goal every other game. He took over as skipper from Sunny Jim Young in September 1916 and "his voice could be heard shouting advice all over the field" (Charlie was a barker at the Parkhead Cross Fair). After the Kaiser War as Rangers moved into the ascendant, he spent many an anxious second half playing them on his own in a one-man bid to compensate for Celtic's lack of reserves, brawn and stamina. Celtic fans were singing his name within minutes of the kick-off at Dundee on September 23rd 1922, a novelty which struck one local reporter as an "extraordinarily stupid idea." When Celtic played West Ham for charity at Upton Park on April 10th 1924, the London crowd, remembering Charlie's displays for QPR burst into fervent applause as he took up his position. He was still a top-flight goalkeeper when replaced by Peter Shevlin and played his last game for his beloved team on January 17th 1925. Charlie had a lot to say on footballers' affairs, especially low wages, and the Parkhead executive had been trying to move him on for years. He was renowned for his "Get it back to Charlie" understanding with Alec McNair but had already astutely organised the pass-back with Joe Breslin (later Motherwell) when they were togther at Kirkintilloch. Charlie Shaw was one of the finest goalkeepers who ever played for Celtic. He won Scottish Cup medals in 1914 and 1923 and was in the Championship sides of 1914 to 1917, 1919 and 1922. He died of pneumonia in New York. Celtic fathers used to lull their babes to sleep with a murmur that began: Shaw, McNair and Dodds; Young, Loney and McMaster... Charlie shielded the Celtic net long and gloriously.

Charlie Shaw

Appearances:
SL: 420 apps. 227 shut-outs.
SC: 16 apps. 13 shut-outs.
Total: *436 apps. 240 shut-outs (55%).*

SHAW, Hugh Crawford

Role: Outside-right 1906
b. Uddingston, 31st July 1879

CAREER: Scottish Amateurs/Queen's Park
Mar 1903/Hamilton Academicals 23 Mar 1904
/Albion Rovers Sept 1905/Rangers Oct 1905/
CELTIC Feb 1906/Kilmarnock Mar 1906/
Albion Rovers 7 Sept 1906.

Debut v St Mirren (a) 1-3 (SL) 17.2.06

An Uddingston cricketer, Hugh Shaw helped
Rangers beat Celtic 3-2 in the League on the
100th anniversary of Trafalgar (October 21st
1905) and scored the second goal. Celtic used
him to less effect at Love Street in place of
Alec Bennett ("lashed with boot and tongue"
by Bo'ness in the Cup on February 10th). He is
described as having Bennett's "pallid
intellectuality" and a "mincing, lawn-tennis
sort of style."

> **Appearances:**
> *SL: 1 app. 0 gls.*
> **Total:** *1 app. 0 gls.*

SHEA, Daniel

Role: Inside-right 1919
5' 6" 11st.6lbs.
b. Wapping, 6th November 1887
d. 25th December 1960

CAREER: Builders' Arms FC Stratford/Manor
Park Albion/West Ham Nov 1907/Blackburn
Rovers 4 Dec 1912/(West Ham loan 28 Aug
1915)/(Birmingham loan Jan 1918)/(Fulham
loan Apr 1918)/(CELTIC loan Jan 1919)/
(Nottingham Forest loan 1919)/West Ham
May 1920/Fulham Dec 1920/Coventry City
summer 1923/Clapton Orient Feb 1925/
Sheppey United October 1926/Winterthur
(Zurich) coach 21 Aug 1928.

Debut v Clyde (h) 2-0 (SL) 2.1.19

"At Fulham in 1920-21, I had as my inside-
right, one of the greatest ball artists who has
ever played for England - Danny Shea. His
manipulation was bewildering" (Peter
Gavigan July 10th 1954). England international
Dan Shea "the prince of partners, the
intellectual footballer" was born on a day of a
certain significance: the formal inauguration of
the Celtic football club in an upstairs room at
St Mary's, Abercromby Street. Dan was a

Dan Shea

superstar of his
time. When he
signed a three
and a half year
contract for
Blackburn it was
estimated he
would cost
Rovers in the
vicinity of £20 a
match, a colossal
sum for 1912.
His was also the
first (sensational)
£2,000 transfer.
At Blackburn he
made a famed
combination
with outside-
right Jocky
Simpson and at
West Ham during the Kaiser War with Sam
Chedzgoy. The fair-haired wee man's
appearance for Celtic caused consternation
once his identity was rumoured through the
crowd. Even Patsy Gallagher moved to outside-left to accommodate him. At West Ham
he superceded ex-Celt Willie Grassam in
1908-09 and won the Victory Shield with
Nottingham Forest versus Everton in 1919.

> **Appearances:**
> *SL: 1 app. 0 gls.*
> **Total:** *1 app. 0 gls.*

SHEPHERD, Anthony

Role: Midfield 1983-89
5' 9" 10st.7lbs.
b. 16th November 1966

CAREER: St Aidan's High School (Wishaw)/
Celtic BC/CELTIC 11 Aug 1983/Gartcosh BC
(farmed-out) 1983/Carlisle United summer
1989/(Bristol City loan Dec 1988)/Motherwell
9 July 1991/free 11 May 1993/Portadown
summer 1993.

Debut v Queen's Park (h) 2-1 (SC) 15.2.86

Scotland Schoolboys U-15s beat England 0-1 at
Wembley on June 5th 1982 and the Man of the
Match with "poise and bite" was the powerful
Scots midfielder Tony Shepherd. English team
manager Jim Morrow saw him as "a player of
rare talent in every part of the game." Celtic
looked to have found the new Bobby Evans in

this big fair-haired lad with his drive, energy and non-stop commitment. On his debut, Celtic trailed Queen's Park 0-1 as of the 50th minute until Tony set goals up for McClair (54) and Aitken (61). He had the extraordinary experience, unknown for a Celt since the time of Johnny Madden, of being ordered off and then recalled, this in the League Cup final with two minutes to go on October 26th 1986. Mo Johnston had just been sent off by David Syme. Tony appealed: "Have a heart, ref!" at which moment Syme was struck by a coin and thought the Celt had hit him. Tony was recalled on the intervention of the linesman. The fact that this hard-working runner did not make the grade at Parkhead after a promising start was a source of real disappointment to many.

Appearances:
SL: 28 apps. 2 gls.
SLC: 5 apps. 0 gls.
SC: 2 apps. 0 gls.
Eur: 3 apps. 0 gls.
Total: *38 apps. 2 gls.*

Tony Shepherd

SHEVLANE, Anthony Christopher

Role: Right-back 1967-68
5'8½" 11st.0lbs.
b. Edinburgh, 6th May 1942

CAREER: Edina Hearts/Hearts 5 July 1959/ Loanhead Mayflower (farmed-out) 1960/free 1967/CELTIC 21 June 1967/free 1 May 1968/ Hibernian 16 May 1968/free 21 Oct 1971/ Morton 28 Oct 1971/free 28 Apr 1973 and retired.

Debut v Partick Thistle (h) 5-0 (GC) 22.8.67

Chris Shevlane "an inspiring, attacking captain" of Scotland's U-23s in 1964 was seen as Jim Kennedy's successor in the full international side and a certainty for the 1966 World Cup campaign. It was not to be. Hearts released him after a warning an arthritic ankle might land him in a wheelchair. Chris sought a second opinion which favoured the resumption of his career. Jock Stein interviewed him on June 17th 1967 with an eye to strengthening the squad and Chris was signed to help compensate for the departure of John Cushley. Although he looked every bit the part in a Celtic jersey (he played his first game at right-back with Willie O'Neill on the left against Cowdenbeath at Station Park on August 7th) he was never realistically expected to displace Craig or Gemmell of the Lisbon Lions. He made his League debut for Celtic at home against Clyde on September 9th 1967 in place of Jim Craig injured versus Penarol four days before. He was 'Cairney's' deputy again at Parkhead in the League on December 2nd versus Dundee United the day Willie Wallace was ordered-off with five minutes to go for an 'assault' on Davie Wilson. He played in the League Cup quarter-final at Somerset Park the night Billy McNeill was spoken-to by the referee then booked for making a salaam. Released by Celtic, Chris went straight off on Hibs' tour of West Africa. He runs "Shevlane's Bar" in Springburn but at one time took a keen interest in the antiquarian and second-hand book trade.

Appearances:
SL: 2 apps. 0 gls.
SLC: 1 app. 0 gls.
Total: *3 apps. 0 gls.*

Chris Shevlane

SHEVLIN, Peter

Role: Goalkeeper 1924-27
5' 9" 11st.4lbs.
b. Wishaw, 18th November 1905
d. Manchester, 10th October 1948

CAREER: Pollok Juniors 1923/St Roch 1924/
CELTIC 11 Oct 1924/South Shields July 1927/
Nelson summer 1929/free 21 Mar 1931/
Shelbourne 26 June 1931/player-manager
9 Dec 1931/Hamilton Academicals 3 Apr 1933
/(CELTIC loan 22 May 1934)/Albion Rovers
7 May 1935.

Debut v St Johnstone (a) 0-0 (SL) 18.10.24

"A goalie of class" as a junior (and reputedly
on Newcastle's books as an amateur), Peter
Shevlin was signed by Chairman White in
person and cost Celtic £120 as Charlie Shaw's
replacement. Charlie had kept goal for the first
10 League matches of 1924-25: seven wins,
three draws and only seven goals conceded.
Peter Shevlin took over for no pressing reason,

Peter Shevlin

Ronnie Simpson

SIMPSON, Ronald

Role: Goalkeeper 1964-70
5' 10½" 11st.13lbs.
b. Glasgow, 11th October 1930

CAREER: King's Park Secondary/Queen's
Park 2 June 1945/(Rangers loan 16 Apr 1947)/
Royal Armoured Corps (Catterick) Feb 1949/
Third Lanark 28 June 1950/demobbed July
1950/Newcastle United 12 Feb 1951/
Hibernian 4 Oct 1960/CELTIC 3 Sept 1964/
retired 7 May 1970/Hamilton Academicals
manager 11 Oct 1971/resigned 28 Sept 1972/
Pools Panel as of 25 Nov 1972.

Debut v Barcelona (a) 1-3 (Fairs Cities' Cup)
18.11.64

Celtic asked Queen's Park for the loan of
boy-goalie Ronnie Simpson, son of Jimmy of
Rangers, when Willie Miller was on
international duty at Wrexham (October 19th
1946). Ronnie had made his debut for the
Spiders at the age of 14 years 304 days. When
he won his first Scottish cap he was 36 years
196 days old and no stranger to Wembley: he
had been there in the 1948 Olympics and won
Cup medals with Newcastle in 1952 and 1955.
He had also played for the Magpies against

and by January 10th 1925, out of his 14 games, 3 had been won, 3 drawn, 8 lost and 22 goals conceded. Shevlin's "clutching of high balls was uneasy" and by January 1925 he was "still too nervous to do himself justice." "His guardianship is not distinguished by complete confidence... he seems unable to take defeat philosophically." Peter had his days however, and won a Scottish Cup medal in his first senior season when Celtic beat Dundee 2-1 on April 11th 1925. He pulled-off his greatest save in the Scottish Cup semi-final versus Aberdeen at Tynecastle on March 20th 1926. Jock Hutton had just made it 1-1 from a penalty in the 56th minute. Straight from the kick-off, the Dons came back and centre-forward Tom Pirie hit a ball full force from point-blank that the Celtic goalie performed a miracle to stop. ("Shake Hands With Shevlin!") He had to carry the can for defeat in the Cup final of April 10th 1926 when he let Davie McCrae have a free header from a corner in two minutes and allowed a shot

from Jimmie Howieson to pass over his hands in 26. He was dropped after Celtic's 3-6 win in the Scottish Cup at Brechin on February 5th 1927 and replaced by John Thomson, although his main understudy had been the big American-Swede Julius Hjulian. His game took off again at South Shields and Celtic thought of him as replacement for Thomson. He played once more for the club at Roubaix in place of Joe Kennaway (May 27th 1934). He was picked to play in goal for Hamilton Acas versus Rangers in the Scottish Cup final of April 20th 1935 but had to stand down with damaged fingers in favour of Jimmy Morgan (who had a great game). Peter was machine-gunned and battered with shrapnel during the Midlands blitz of spring 1941 and spent until December in hospital.

Appearances:
SL: 86 apps. 28 shut-outs.
SC: 17 apps. 8 shut-outs.
Total: *103 apps. 36 shut-outs (35%).*

SHIELDS, James... see over

Celtic at Parkhead in the Cup-winners' match September 12th 1951. Sean Fallon secured him from Jock Stein at Hibs for half the asking price of £4,000. He became Celtic's regular goalie as of September 25th 1965 when Celtic beat Aberdeen 7-1 in the League. His youth was suddenly renewed: first League Championship medal, May 7th 1966; first cap, April 15th 1967; first Scottish Cup medal, April 29th 1967; Scotland's Player of the Year, May 5th 1967; European Cup winner's medal May 25th 1967 (with the tears running down

his face at the end). Ronnie's shoulder went out for the first time at Shawfield on February 12th 1969. He was sidelined until October 4th but the arm dislocated again nine days later and he said goodbye to the first-class game after almost 25 years. He took the field with the other Lisbon Lions to salute the fans before the Clyde game of May 1st 1971. The players didn't call him 'Faither' just because of his age. He stamped his authority on the team of Celtic's golden era. How would Stein have done without him? He ranks with Celtic's best between the sticks: McArthur, Adams, Shaw, Thomson, Kennaway and Miller. Ronnie Simpson seldom made a mistake. He is an all-time Celtic great.

Appearances:
SL: 118 apps. 54 shut-outs.
SLC: 29 apps. 14 shut-outs.
SC: 17 apps. 10 shut-outs.
Eur: 24 apps. 13 shut-outs.
Total: *188 apps. 91 shut-outs (48%).*

Ronnie Simpson keeps Inter Milan at bay in the 1967 European Cup final.

SHIELDS, James

Role: Inside-forward 1939-47

CAREER: St Mungo's Academy/Arthurlie 1938/CELTIC 15 June 1939/(Dumbarton loan Jan 1940 & 6 Aug 1940)/RAF July 1941/ (Bolton Wanderers & Rochdale loan 1941-42)/ (Blackpool loan 1942-43)/free 1947/Raith Rovers (trial) 17 May 1947/Dumbarton 19 June 1947/free 1948/retired 1948.

Debut v Third Lanark (h) 3-2 (CC) 18.5.40

A student at Jordanhill College, Jimmy Shields was "paid-off" for the duration by Celtic with Tom Lyon and Oliver Anderson in December 1939 but was recalled to Parkhead for the Charity Cup in May 1940. He made his Old Firm debut in the semi-final at Ibrox at inside-left to Johnny Kelly in the 5-1 defeat. He next played for Celtic as a newly-demobbed serviceman on August 10th 1946, the first of three games all at out-side-left. His last appearance for Celtic was on August 17th when Aberdeen (with Alex Kiddie) won 6-2 at Pittodrie. Bobby Evans was brought in to take Jimmy's place. Jimmy retired to concentrate on his career as a PE teacher and Youth Club instructor.

Appearances:
SL: 3 apps. 0 gls.
Total: *3 apps. 0 gls.*

SINCLAIR, James Graeme

Role: Left-back 1982-85
5' 9" 11st.12lbs.
b. 1st July 1957

CAREER: Camphill School/St Mirren S form 1969/Eastercraigs Amateurs/Dumbarton Oct 1975/ CELTIC 12 Aug 1982/ (Manchester City loan 16 Nov 1984)/(Dumbarton loan 22 Feb 1985)/free 19 May 1985/ St Mirren 13 June 1985/retired 1985/ St Mirren coach 1988.

Debut v Dunfermline Athletic (a) 7-1 (SLC) 28.8.82 (sub)

Graeme Sinclair

Elvis Presley impersonator and pacy defender, Graeme Sinclair was in 1978 reckoned the "best marker" in the First Division. Billy McNeill paid £65,000 to get him as the man who "could eventually replace Danny McGrain." His glory night arrived early when he played versus Ajax in Amsterdam in the European Cup (September 29th 1982) and put the shackles on the great Johann Cruyff. Against Dundee United on February 5th 1983, "Sinclair tied Sturrock up every way." Graeme hit pre-season fitness trouble against Lausanne on July 27th 1983 when he was taken off with torn knee ligaments and flown home for treatment. He fell out of favour after the 1-1 draw at Dumbarton (September 8th 1984), a team display described by Davie Hay as "an absolute disgrace". Graeme tried out for his old boss McNeill at Maine Road, before injuries forced premature retirement at St Mirren.

Appearances:
SL: 52 apps. 1 gl.
SLC: 12 apps. 0 gls.
SC: 5 apps. 0 gls.
Eur: 7 apps. 0 gls.
Total: *76 apps. 1 gl.*

SINCLAIR, Thomas S.

Role: Goalkeeper 1906
5' 11" 12st.0lbs.
b. Glasgow

CAREER: Rutherglen Glencairn 1900/ Morton 6 June 1903 /Rangers 25 Oct 1904 /(CELTIC loan 17 Aug 1906)/ Newcastle United 28 Mar 1907/retired 1912/Dumbarton Harp 31 Dec 1912/ Dunfermline Athletic 3 Apr 1913/Army 1914-16/Stevenston United 25 July 1916/ Kilmarnock 24 Feb 1917/Stevenston United 30 Mar 1917/ retired summer 1919.

Debut v Motherwell (a)
6-0 (SL) 18.8.06

Davie Adams
lacerated his palm on
a rogue nail at Ibrox
during Finlay
Speedie's benefit
(August 16th 1906)
and with the start of
the League just two
days away Rangers
offered reserve goalie
Sinclair until the

Tom Sinclair

wound healed. Tom left Celtic without
conceding a goal for points up to and
including September 29th 1906 (six matches
from his debut, a record equalled but not
beaten by Carl Muggleton on March 19th
1994). He did lose four in the Carlton FC
benefit match versus Queen's Park on August
21st but none in a first-class fixture until
Tommy Fairfoul put two past him in the
Glasgow Cup final at Ibrox on October 6th
1906. The first was straight from the kick-off
and according to Alec McNair, the big Ranger
was not at all pleased. Celtic won 3-2 and Tom
took a medal won with Celtic back with him
to Govan. He played for Kilmarnock against
Celtic as late as February 24th 1917.

Appearances:
SL: 6 apps. 6 shut-outs.
Total: *6 apps. 6 shut-outs (100%).*

SINCLAIR, Thomas Mackie

Role: Left-back 1927-28
5' 11" 12st.0lbs.
b. Alva, c 1907

CAREER: Alva Albion Rangers 26 May 1927/
CELTIC 1 Nov 1927/South Shields 1928/Alloa
(trial) 10 Sept 1934.

Debut v Aberdeen (h) 1-1 (SL) 25.2.28

Partick Thistle wanted "nicely-built defender"
Tom Sinclair and were disappointed when
Celtic stumped up £30 for his transfer. Peter
McGonagle split his head open against St
Mirren on February 21st 1928 which presented
young Tom with his first opportunity in the
Cetic big team. He did not get a second chance
until April 23rd in a 0-3 defeat by Raith
Rovers. He played 174 games for South
Shields and was there in 1929 when the club

changed its name to Gateshead. He tried-out
for Alloa but the Wasps did not take up the
option.

Appearances:
SL: 2 apps. 0 gls.
Total: *2 apps. 0 gls.*

SIRREL, James

Role: Inside-forward 1945-49
5' 7" 10st.0lbs.
b. Glasgow, 2nd February 1922

CAREER: Riverside Secondary School/
Bridgeton Waverley/Renfrew Juniors/CELTIC
31 Dec 1945/Royal Navy 1946/free Apr 1949/
Bradford PA 12 May 1949/Brighton Aug 1951
/Aldershot Aug 1954/trainer-coach 1955/
player (once) Apr 1956/Brentford coach 1960
/acting-manager Mar 1967/manager summer
1967/Notts County manager 10 Nov
1969/Sheffield United manager 16 Oct 1975/
dismissed 27 Sept 1976/Notts County
manager 5 Oct 1976/general manager
1982/director 29 June 1984/team manager
19 Apr 1985 until end season/retired 2 June
1987/Derby County scout.

Debut v Queen of the South (a) 0-0 (SL) 2.1.46

"I thoroughly enjoyed my career at Celtic
Park, particularly the atmosphere and the
reception from the supporters when you ran

Jimmy Sirrel

out of the tunnel at the start of a game" (Jimmy Sirrel December 1993)." Sirrel is the best thing that's happened to Parkhead for a long time. There's not much to him but he's a worker and full of craft" (February 9th 1946). Jimmy took Tommy Kiernan's place at inside-right on his debut and became thus the penultimate Celt to partner the great Jimmy Delaney. He was a first-team regular at inside-left as of February 9th with wing partners Pat O'Sullivan, Johnny Paton and Jackie Gallacher. In June 1946, he played in both Victory Cup semi-finals versus Rangers but was crippled throughout much of the replay on June 5th with a pulled muscle. He was still on the pitch but almost a total passenger after the loss of Paterson, Mallan and Gallacher. Jimmy was at right-half at Douglas Park on August 28th 1946 when Manager McGrory noticed he seemed to be shirking in the tackles. An X-ray revealed that the wee man was playing with a flake fracture of the ankle bone, an injury which put him out of the game until the last match of the season versus Motherwell at home on May 3rd 1947. Things got rough after Joe Rae sent Celtic 3-1 up with a penalty and moments later, two of the finest exponents of the inside-forward's art in Scotland, Jimmy Sirrel and Jimmy Watson, were sent-off together. On top of the damaged ankle, Jimmy was bothered throughout much of his time at Parkhead by an injury to the sciatic nerve sustained at Fir Park on a bone hard pitch on February 9th 1946. He was ever a popular figure with the fans and his free transfer in 1949 was a cause of deep regret to many. He made his main fame in the game as manager at Meadow Lane. He joined the Magpies in Division 4, left them in Division 2, came back and took them into Division 1 on May 2nd 1981. He was also the manager who brought Jimmy Johnstone to Sheffield United. Jimmy Sirrel celebrated his testimonial at Notts County on November 3rd 1981.

Appearances:
SL: 13 apps. 2 gls.
SLC: 5 apps. 0 gls.
Total: *18 apps. 2 gls.*
RL: 4 apps. 1 gl.
RLC: 6 apps. 1 gl.
Total: *10 apps. 2 gls.*

SLATER, Malcolm

Role: Outside-right 1958-59
5' 9½" 11st.2lbs.
b. Buckie, 22nd October 1939

CAREER: Buckie Academy/Buckie Thistle 17 Nov 1956/Army 1957/CELTIC 15 Nov 1958/(Buckie Thistle loan Sept 1959)/free own request 5 May 1960/Buckie Thistle 5 May 1960/Inverness Caledonian 1961/Montrose 7 Dec 1962/Southend United 25 Oct 1963/ Leyton Orient Jan 1967/(Colchester United loan Oct 1969)/free 1970.

Debut v Queen of the South (a) 2-2 (SL) 24.1.58

Malcolm Slater and Alex Scott of Rangers were in the Pay Corps together in Edinburgh and Malcolm training at Ibrox when Celtic signed him as an amateur. He remained a Simon Pure throughout his time at Parkhead and was even capped for Scotland at Coleraine on February 21st 1959. Against Falkirk at Brockville (February 7th 1959) "Slater lacked experience." On the verge of going professional, he experienced an horrendous personal bereavement: the loss of his two brothers Sandy and Andrew in a drowning tragedy on June 14th 1959. He was released to Buckie at his own request in 1960. Montrose paid £1,500 for him and Southend £6,000. Malcolm played just four games for Colchester and then returned to Scotland. Outside football he was a tax officer in Aberdeen.

Appearances:
SL: 5 apps. 1 gl.
Total: *5 apps. 1 gl.*

Malcolm Slater

SLATER, Stuart Ian

Role: Outside-right 1992-93
5' 9" 11st.6lbs.
b. Sudbury, 27th March 1969

CAREER: Schools/West Ham 1987/CELTIC
14 Aug 1992/Ipswich Town 30 Sept 1993.
Debut v Dundee (h) 1-0 (SLC) 19.8.92 (sub)

"Slater is fast and able to take the ball with
him when in full flight - a rare talent these
days - but too much of his work is done far
away from the opposition's goal. He does not
penetrate enough." Signed by Liam Brady for
a hefty £1.5 million Stuart had netted only 11
times in 141 games for West Ham with a
virtual goalscoring sabbatical during 1991-92.
Early in his time at Parkhead he was met by
one of Celtic's legion of affable supporters.
They chatted and then the punter made his
move: "Do you mind if I give you a bit of
advice? Don't hide during a game. The fans
will forgive you anything as long as you keep
trying." Stuart ("who runs with the ball
extraordinarily close to his feet") scored his

first goal as late as December 2nd 1992 and
gave the Jungle a cheery wave. The official
line was to credit him as more a creator rather
than a scorer of goals. Unfortunately most of
the time Stuart simply looked an expensive
luxury. He joined Ipswich (where he trained at
14) for £750,000 and linked up again with
former Hammers stalwart John Lyall in the
hope of rebuilding his career, but was reported
against Leeds on January 15th 1994 as looking
"a shadow of the player who used to thrill
Upton Park."

Appearances:
SL: 43 apps. 3 gls.
SLC: 5 apps. 0 gls.
SC: 3 apps. 0 gls.
Eur: 4 apps. 0 gls.
Total: *55 apps. 3 gls.*

SLAVEN, Patrick

Role: Outside-right 1897
b. Rutherglen, 22nd April 1878

CAREER: Fauldhouse Hibs/CELTIC 6 Feb
1897/Motherwell 5 June 1897/Dykehead
1 Sept 1898/Carfin Emmet 21 Jan 1900/
Dykehead 20 Apr 1900/Albion Rovers
4 Aug 1900/East Benhar Rangers 17 Oct
1900/reinstated amateur 13 Aug 1901.
Debut v St Mirren (a) 0-2 (SL) 13.3.1897

Celtic were in the throes of transforming
the charity into a Limited Company and
designing a cycle track for the World
Championships at the time Pat Slaven
tried-out as Ching Morrison's
replacement. The new business was also
planning a big splash with the import of
"dons" from England for the new season
1897-98 so Pat's role seems to have been
that of stop-gap before he moved to
Motherwell. He played his first game in
the green and white vertical stripes
against 3rd Lanark at Parkhead in the
Glasgow League on February 27th 1897
and scored the opener in a 3-1 win. He
played nine Scottish League games for
the Fir Parkers.

Appearances:
SL: 1 app. 0 gls.
Total: *1 app. 0 gls.*

Stuart Slater

SMITH, Barry Martin

Role: Defender 1991 to date
5' 10" 12st.0lbs.
b. Paisley, 19th February 1974

CAREER: Giffnock North AFC/CELTIC
21 June 1991.
Debut v Falkirk (a) 3-4 (SL) 19.10.91 (sub)

Mike Galloway was injured on the half-hour at 1-1 at Brockville in October 1991 and came off for Cascarino who went to centre-half. Falkirk were winning everything in the air and at 4-2, in the 68th minute, Big Tony departed in turn to let 17-year old Barry try. Celtic conceded no more goals. According to manager Brady, the boy had been brought along mainly to help on the hamper. Barry is a versatile performer but has looked decidely useful at right-back, a Celtic problem position. He came on for Mark McNally in 24 minutes against Airdrie on April 6th 1993 after an absence of over a year from the first team and as a marker, found himself given an unfamiliar ball-carrying role in a 4-0 win. He started his initial full 90 minutes of the season for the big team versus Falkirk on April 20th 1993 as deputy for McNally. He was skipper of the Celtic team that lifted the Reserve League Cup 1-3 at Tannadice (April 18th 1994) and

Barry Smith

made his first successive big team starts against Dundee on April 23rd and St Johnstone four days later. His Old Firm debut followed in the Ibrox lock-out match on the last day of the month. He was booked but played impressively throughout. According to some observers Celtic may at last have discovered a genuine successor to Danny McGrain. He played in the patchwork Celtic side that beat Manchester United 1-3 in the Mark Hughes benefit on May 16th 1994.

Appearances:
SL: 16 apps. 0 gls.
Total: *16 apps. 0 gls.*

SMITH, Hugh

Role: Inside-forward
1930-34
5' 7" 10st.8lbs.
*b. Port Glasgow,
c 1913*

CAREER: High Holm School/Clyde United/Port Glasgow Juniors/ CELTIC 17 May 1930 free 6 June 1934/Ayr United 15 June 1934 /Tunbridge Wells Rangers (trial) 27 Dec 1934/ Morton Aug 1935 /free 30 Apr 1938/Alloa 9 June 1938 until 1940.

Hugh Smith

*Debut v Hibernian (h) 6-0 (SL) 23.8.30
(scored once)*

"Hughie Smith has the Gallagher wiggle and the McInally nonchalance... he is going to be one of the best captures Celtic ever made... like Bob McPhail he looks slow but is one of the fastest dribblers we have... his sharpness is amazing for one so young... he lacks height but he plays the traditional Scottish game... trails the ball, looks deliberately at colleagues as if to indicate the pass then flicks the ball the other way... a fascinating player... Celtic's new Patsy Gallagher." Steve Callaghan signed Willie Cook's pal Hughie "a player with all the dodges... one of the trickiest and most subtle inside men in recent years," whom even Maley acknowledged as "one of the finest passers of the ball of his generation" (Tynecastle October 1st 1932). Celtic took him on the USA tour of 1931 when he played one match (the club's first under lights in the 20th century) at Baltimore on June 30th. When Willie Hughes scored eight goals in Patsy Gallagher's testimonial on January 4th 1932, it was Hughie Smith serviced him with ball after ball through the middle to chase. Nevertheless, his first-class game revealed flaws that disqualified him from being another Gallagher: "His frame is not strong enough... he is too easily bumped off the ball... he is deft but his finishing lets him down." At Ayr he was advised to give up on medical grounds but made his comeback at Cappielow where he and Dan McGarry made a formidable left-wing. This "dapper little fellow with the courteous way" was working in the shipyards in 1940.

Appearances:
SL: 25 apps. 2 gls.
SC: 2 apps. 0 gls.
Total: *27 apps. 2 gls.*

SMITH, John Eric

Role: Utility 1953-60
5' 6" 11st.7lbs.
b. Glasgow, 29th July 1934
d. Dubai, 12th June 1991

CAREER: St Andrew's Juveniles 1951/Pollok 1951/Benburb 1952/ CELTIC 2 Apr 1953/ Army 1954/Leeds United 11 May 1960/free own request 28 Apr 1964/ Morton 13 July 1964 /coach 1966/Pezoporikos Larnaca (Cyprus) 29 Nov 1970/Morton manager 20 May 1972/ Hamilton Academicals manager 28 Dec 1972/ Sharjah (UAE) manager 29 Apr 1978/Al Nasr asst manager by June 1982/ dismissed 10 May 1983/Al Shaab (UAE) manager by 1984/ Peziporikos manager by 1987.

Eric Smith

Debut v Queen of the South (h) 1-1 (SL) 16.10.54

Eric Smith (at 17, "the best juvenile inside-forward since Bobby Collins") had hardly made his League debut ("playing in the Joe Cassidy mould") before he was turning out for Western Command alongside Dave Mackay, Ralph Brand and Bobby Charlton. He went on

the Irish tour of May 1955 but the rest was silence until he was cast dramatically at inside-left against Rangers in the League Cup at Ibrox (Aug 27th 1955) and scored two inside five minutes in the first half towards a 1-4 win. The second goal was a screamer, a wonder ball, bulging the rigging high past George Niven. He led a famous fight-back from 0-3 down against Rangers in the Glasgow Cup at Parkhead (August 21st 1956) with a goal immediately after half-time. Celtic exploited his versatility at half-back, on both wings and at inside forward. His no-nonsense, all-action style with great physical courage made him very popular with the support. He broke into the first team proper during 1957-58 only and played right-half for Scotland on tour versus Jutland, Holland and Portugal in 1959. But back at Parkhead, Scotland full-back Dunky MacKay was right-half and Scotland right-half Eric Smith was inside-right. By 1960 he was what he wanted to be: right-half again (but only as the club's third choice). He was outside-right when he saved Celtic from an ignominious draw with the winner two minutes from time versus Elgin City (away) in the Scottish Cup on March 5th 1960. Don Revie took him to help build a team at Leeds. Eric had astounding success as a coach. His tactics at Morton were "the most professional of any among the provincial teams in Scotland." He is credited with discovering Joe Jordan, Joe Harper and John Brown (Rangers). He worked with Don Revie again at Al Nasr. He died from a heart attack on holiday while manager at Pezoporikos.

Appearances:
SL: 95 apps. 12 gls.
SLC: 16 apps. 3 gls.
SC: 19 apps. 5 gls.
Total: *130 apps. 20 gls.*

SMITH, Mark Alexander

Role: Outside-right 1986-87
5' 9" 10st.0lbs.
b. Bellshill, 16th December 1964

CAREER: St Mirren 'S' form/
Queen's Park 14 Dec 1983/
CELTIC 6 June 1986/
Dunfermline Athletic 9 Oct 1987
/(Hamilton Academicals loan
8 Sept 1989)/(Stoke City loan
Mar 1990)/Nottingham Forest
22 Mar 1990/(Reading loan Dec
1990)/(Mansfield Town loan Mar
1991)/Shrewsbury Town 20 Sept
1991.

*Debut v Airdrie (h) 2-0 (SLC)
20.8.86*

Mark Smith

St Mirren discarded "very nice
lad," Mark Smith as "too wee, too
thin." He hit his game with Eddie Hunter's
Queen's Park and this whippet of a winger
with a direct approach and few frills made
things hot for Celtic in the Scottish Cup at
Parkhead on February 15th 1986. He turned
Leicester City down to join Davie Hay's Celtic.
He began brightly enough but injury at
Falkirk (September 28th 1986) put him out of
the game for ten weeks. A pasta diet got his
fighting weight up to 10 stone by February
1987 but the new management team of
McNeill and Craig (May 1987) were
unimpressed: "You're not good enough." Jim
Leishman took him to Dunfermline where a
different style lent a new enjoyment to his
football: "There's a great spirit here. At
Parkhead it was different. You had only to
look at the faces of some of the players to see
the pressure they were under." Leishman
spoke of "his speed... a nightmare for any
defence." Souness' Rangers soon caught the
blast. Mark ran them out of the Scottish Cup
on February 20th 1988 and collapsed in the
dressing-room after. He scored the opener
himself in six minutes from a "bad cross" then
set-up the second goal. The only way to stop
him was to whack him and John Brown was
ordered-off for exactly that. Brian Clough paid
£100,000 to take him to Forest but he never
made a first team outing.

Appearances:
SL: 6 apps. 0 gls.
SLC: 2 apps. 0 gls.
Total: *8 apps. 0 gls.*

SMITH, Robert Hoynes

Role: Goalkeeper 1940
5' 10" 11st.7lbs.
b. Beith, 19th May 1918

CAREER: Beith Caledonia/Ayr
United 1935/Dundee United
summer 1938/paid-off Feb 1940
/(CELTIC loan 1 Mar 1940)/
free summer 1940/Arthurlie
17 Aug 1940.

*Debut v Raith Rovers (a) 0-3
(SWC) 2.3.40*

Jimmy McStay's priority on
becoming manager on February
14th 1940 was to find a goalie to
replace the inexperienced Don
McKay. He tried to get George
Johnstone but finally engaged
Bob 'Farmer' Smith, Ayr United's 'keeper
when they won the 2nd Division
Championship in 1937. Bob's debut was not
auspicious. Celtic were knocked out of the
Scottish War Cup
5-4 on aggregate at
Kirkcaldy and he
was troubled
throughout by
Johnny Maule's
crosses. Against
Hamilton Accies on
April 3rd 1940,
Bertie Harrison
(ex-Rangers, who
assisted Celtic in
Ireland in May
1936) hit a shot
straight at him only
for the ball to burst
in flight and

Bob Smith

swerve into the net for the first goal of a 5-0
defeat. His last match was in the Charity Cup
semi-final at Ibrox on May 22nd 1940 when
Rangers won a bad-tempered game 5-1. While
with Celtic, Bob worked for the Government
as a meat distributor in Greenock. He was
alive and well and writing to the papers in
March 1968.

Appearances:
RL: 14 apps. 1 shut-out.
SWC: 1 app. 0 shut-outs.
Total: *15 apps. 1 shut-out (7%).*

SNEDDON, Alan

Role: Right-back 1977-81
5' 11" 11st.2lbs.
*b. Baillieston,
12th March 1958*

CAREER: Larkhall
Academy/Fairholm
United Amateurs/
Larkhall Thistle 1975/
CELTIC 22 Aug 1977/
Hibernian 9 Jan 1981/
free 11 May 1992/
Motherwell 23 July 1992/
free 11 May 1993/East
Fife 27 July 1993/asst
manager 25 Aug 1994.

*Debut v Dundee (h) 7-1
(SC) 6.2.78*

Alan Sneddon

for Celtic versus Hearts
at Parkhead on
December 13th 1980.
Hibs got years of great
service out of Alan for
the £60,000 he cost
them. They played his
testimonial versus
Aston Villa in October
1991. He was still
hitting through balls
(against Celtic) at Fir
Park on October 17th
1992.

Appearances:
*SL: 66 apps. 1 gl.
SLC: 15 apps. 0 gls.
SC: 9 apps. 0 gls.
Eur: 8 apps. 0 gls.*
Total: *98 apps. 1 gl.*

Larkhall Thistle wanted
apprentice fitter Alan Sneddon to stay with
them until they won the Junior Cup or were
eliminated. Alan knocked them out himself
with an own goal against Beith and was in the
Celtic first team after three reserve
appearances and a practice match against Ayr
on January 29th 1978. He took over from Joe
Filippi (replacing the injured McGrain) and
was hailed by Billy McNeill as "the best young
full-back in Scotland." For a full-back Alan
was a beautiful exponent of the through ball
and set George McCluskey up for two of the
Celtic goals on his debut. He was Celtic's Man
of the Match in the League Cup final versus
Rangers on March 18th 1978. His League
appearances were four only during the
Championship season of 1978-79 but he
started 1979-80 at right-back with Danny
McGrain on his left and made both goals
against Real Madrid in the third round (first
leg) of the European Cup at Parkhead on
March 5th 1980, a shot that Ramon could not
hold (George McCluskey) and a cross for
Johnny Doyle. He collected a Scottish Cup
medal against Rangers on May 10th 1980
while the fans battled down below on the
park. Alan played often enough (15 games) to
qualify for a League medal in the
Championship season of 1980-81 but lost his
place after the defeats 3-0 by Rangers and 0-2
by Aberdeen of November 1st and 8th 1980.
McNeill now opted for a full-back pairing of
McGrain and Reid. He played his last match

♣ **Celtic note:** *Alan played 14 games for Hibs in
1980-81 and won a First Division medal; two
Championship medals in the same season!*

SOLIS, Jerome

Role: Outside-left 1931-32
5' 7" 10st.10lbs.
b. Glasgow, 6th October 1909 (?)

CAREER: St Aloysius College/Woodside
Rovers/Dennistoun Amateurs/Maryhill Hibs
1928/CELTIC 11 July 1931/Coleraine Feb
1932/Linfield June 1932.

*Debut v Cowdenbeath (h) 7-0 (SL) 26.8.31
(scored once)*

"Although a wee yin," Jerry Solis, reputedly
Celtic's solitary Jewish star, was "as clever as
they are made... he is not afraid of hard work
and is a football box
of tricks with the ball
in possession." Jerry
came to Celtic at the
end of the
Intermediate
dispute in 1931
having spent the
entire season 1930-31
out of the game.
He was an
inside man
employed by
Celtic on the

Jerry Solis

left touchline. He played three League games in a row beginning with his debut but Charlie Napier went in against Rangers on September 5th 1931 the day John Thomson was injured unto death. (Jerry had played inside-right to Yoker's Sam English for the Glasgow and District Association versus Ayrshire at Dalry on January 2nd 1929). At Parkhead on September 12th he was back in the team with a black band on his arm and lined-up before kick-off for Two Minutes Silence and the Last Post. He played his final game for Celtic at home to Aberdeen on January 11th 1932 the day before Peter Scarff entered the sanatorium. Jerry won an Irish Cup medal with Coleraine on May 7th 1932.

Appearances:
SL: 9 apps. 3 gls.
Total: *9 apps. 3 gls.*

STANTON, Patrick Gordon

Role: Central Defence 1976-78
5' 9" 11st.0lbs.
b. Edinburgh, 13th September 1944

CAREER: Holy Cross Academy/United Crossroads/Salvesen BC/Dunfermline Athletic (trial) 1961/Edina Hearts/Bonnyrigg Rose Athletic 1961/Hibs (provisional) 1961/ (full) summer 1963/CELTIC 1 Sept 1976/ retired 5 Aug 1978/Aberdeen asst manager 16 Aug 1978/resigned 2 Jan 1980/Aberdeen scout 30 May 1980/Cowdenbeath manager 13 Aug 1980/Dunfermline Athletic manager 16 Dec 1980/Hibernian manager 2 Sept 1982 /resigned 30 Apr 1983/reinstated 2 May 1983 /resigned 16 Sept 1984/Musselburgh Athletic manager 21 Nov 1989.

SOMERS, Peter

Role: Inside-left 1897-1909
5' 9½" 10st.10lbs.
b. Avondale,
3rd June 1878
d. 27th November 1914

CAREER: Mossend Celtic/Cadzow Oak/ Hamilton Academicals 1897/CELTIC 29 Nov 1897 /(Clyde loan 7 Oct 1899)/ (Blackburn Rovers loan 9 Feb 1900 & 16 July 1900)/CELTIC again 26 Aug 1902/ resigned Dec 1909/Hamilton Academicals 15 Jan 1910/retired Apr 1911/Hamilton Academicals director May 1912.

Debut v Third Lanark (h) 4-0 (SL) 4.12.1897 (scored once)

"The beauty of the the movements of the McMenemy, Quinn and Somers trio is unsurpassed in football" (April 13th 1907). *"Somers and McMenemy/Masters two of trickery /Back up Jimmy Quinn."* "I never played against a harder left-wing than Somers and Harold Paul for the Scottish League against the English League in 1909 at Parkhead" (Bob Crompton). Willie Maley called Peter Somers "Celtic's powder monkey," after the boys who serviced the guns aboard battle ships in the days of Rodney and Nelson.

Blackburn Rovers paid £200 to borrow him as "a quiet worker who allowed others to profit by his skilful, unselfish, if unobtrusive play." He came home and played against the Glasgow Junior League at Parkhead on May 2nd 1900: "Somers' all-round play is so much above the others he could step into the first team now. But who is to make way for him?" From the unobtrusive hard worker at Blackburn he became the general of the Celtic attack and in the Quinn Cup final of April 16th 1904, his voice could be heard in the stand: "Hold it!" "First time!" as he read the opposition. He was the brains of the six-in-a-row team 1905-10 and won the Scottish Cup with Celtic in 1904, 1907 and 1908 as well as playing in both finals when the Blue Riband was withheld in 1909. In the 1907 final against Bobby Walker's Hearts, he scored twice, both walk-in goals from Alec Bennett crosses and was awarded the match ball after. He was renowned for "a tongue as sharp as a lance." Tom Fitchie went in high on Tom Sinclair on September 22nd 1906 and Peter reprimanded him: "Play the game, Fitchie!" Fitchie pursued the Celt: "How should I play the game?" "I dunno. Just watch me." Jimmy Galt of Rangers was a great man on the links. Peter confronted him

Debut v Rangers (h) 2-2 (SL) 4.9.76

"Stanton is a world-class player whose absence from the Scotland team seems absurd on any grounds" (August 1972). Celtic played Dundee United in the League Cup on September 1st 1976 and introduced Jock Stein's latest shock signing at half-time: the great Pat Stanton of Hibs. Film star Sean Connery turned-up to watch his debut. With Stanton at his back, Ronnie Glavin, given complete freedom to run, developed into a powerhouse in midfield and Roddie MacDonald grew in confidence game by game. Stein had signed not one new player but three. By February Celtic were "playing with skill, excitement, confidence... ready for Continental football again." Pat won the first leg of the 1977 Double with Celtic at Easter Road on April 16th and was in the side that

in the heat of a game: "You teach me to play golf an' I'll teach you to play fitba.'" After much provocation, he kicked out at Larry Abrams of the Hearts. "What was that for?" "It was for you. Don't tell anybody!" Also, according to referee Jock Bell, he "used the little whisper. If an opponent was getting the ball, he would call almost under his breath, 'Nice ball' or 'Give it here' or 'I'll take it'. I would penalise him and he'd start asking, 'Why all these free-kicks against me today, ref?' I'd point to my ears: 'Look, Peter, these aren't feathers growin' out the side of my head.'" He was an accomplished pianist and rendered for a packed house at the St Mungo's Halls on March 6th 1907 on the night of the presentation to Jimmy Quinn. The death of this all-time great followed the worst fate that could befall a footballer: the amputation of part of a leg. Celtic fans everywhere were plunged into gloom.

Appearances:
SL: 186 apps. 52 gls.
SC: 33 apps. 10 gls.
Total: *219 apps. 62 gls.*

♣ **Celtic note:** *Peter's wee brother played for Celtic versus Bohemians in Dublin on St Patrick's Day 1904 and a son at centre-half for Ulster United against Celtic in Toronto on June 27th 1931.*

won the Cup 1-0 versus Rangers at Hampden on May 7th. Dalglish left for Liverpool on August 10th and Celtic fans now looked to Pat and Alfie Conn to inspire the team in Europe. On August 13th 1977, against Dundee United at Tannadice, Conn was stretchered off minutes before half-time. At 4.25pm Pat Stanton was carried-off with the injury that ended his career and Celtic's season crumbled there and then. Pat may not have been skipper of the side but he led Celtic to the Double of 1977 nonetheless. It would not have happened without him.

Appearances:
SL: 37 apps. 0 gls.
SC: 7 apps. 0 gls.
Total: *44 apps. 0 gls.*

Pat Stanton

STARK, William

Role: Midfield 1987-90
6′ 1″ 11st.3lbs.
b. Glasgow, 1st December 1956

CAREER: Rangers Youth/
Anniesland Waverley/St Mirren
29 July 1975/Aberdeen 5 June
1983/CELTIC 2 July 1987/
Kilmarnock 6 July 1990/
Hamilton Academicals 4 Oct
1991/asst manager 8 Oct 1991/
out of contract 13 May 1992/
Kilmarnock asst manager
20 May 1992/player 3 Aug
1992/CELTIC asst manager
13 July 1994.

*Debut v Morton (a) 4-0 (SL) 8.8.87
(scored once)*

"One of the most casual players
in football," St Mirren's Billy
Stark was transformed by
manager Alex Ferguson into an
all-action midfielder who also
scored goals. At Pittodrie, he
had a hard act to follow as
Gordon Strachan's successor but
by 1986 had won five medals in
three years and made and
scored goals aplenty. Billy
McNeill brought him to
Parkhead in the scramble to get
a team together for the
Centenary season. Stark's
signing must rate on a par with

Billy Stark

Stein's capture of Stanton ten years before. On
August 29th 1987, within five minutes of kick-
off at Parkhead, he scored the only goal of the
game against Rangers to signal that Celtic
were on their way to a Very Happy 100th
Birthday. (He was the victim of the late tackle
that saw Graeme Souness sent off after 54 minutes). He scored another vital goal on the way
to the Centenary double in the Scottish Cup
4th round replay at Easter Road (February
24th 1988) when he was right on the spot in
the 79th minute to shoot home the rebound
after Peter Grant had hit the bar. By April 23rd
1988, Billy had won a Celtic Championship
medal to go with his two from Aberdeen and
went on as substitute in the Cup final against
Dundee United on May 14th. He was also on
the bench for the final against Rangers on May
20th 1989 but did not actually play. Achilles

trouble put him out of the side for almost all
of 1989-90 but by April 28th when he made his
comeback at Motherwell, he was still sixth top
all-time Premier League goalscorer on 101. He
played in the penalty kick shoot-out Cup final
versus Aberdeen on May 12th 1990. His
talents were probably too hastily disposed-of
by Celtic both as player and coach. He helped
Tommy Burns to take Kilmarnock into the
Scottish Premier on May 15th 1993 and
followed Tommy back to Parkhead in the
summer of 1994.

Appearances:
SL: 64 apps. 17 gls.
SLC: 5 apps. 4 gls.
SC: 10 apps. 3 gls.
Eur: 5 apps. 1 gl.
Total: *84 apps. 25 gls.*

STEIN, John C.B.E.

Role: Centre-half 1951-57
5' 11" 11st.7lbs.
b. Earnock, 6th October 1922
d. Cardiff, 10th September 1985

CAREER: Greenfield School Burnbank/
Burnbank Athletic (did not play) 1938/
Blantyre Victoria 1938/Albion Rovers 14 Nov
1942/(Dundee United loan 10 Apr 1943)/
Llanelly 10 May 1950/CELTIC 4 Dec 1951/
retired 29 Jan 1957/CELTIC coach summer
1957/Dunfermline Athletic manager 13 Mar
1960/Hibernian manager 1 Apr 1964/CELTIC
manager 9 Mar 1965/Scotland interim
manager 13 May 1965 to 7 Dec 1965/resigned
CELTIC 28 May 1978/Leeds United manager
21 Aug 1978/Scotland manager 4 Oct 1978.

Debut v St Mirren (h) 2-1 (SL) 8.12.51

Jock Stein first pulled on a Celtic jersey when
a Parkhead Five were a player short at
Coatbridge in the summer of 1945. He won a
wallet along with Pat McAuley, Pat McDonald
and Jimmy Mallan. Jock went full-time only at
Llanelly in response to newspaper
advertisements placed by Jack Goldsborough
for "players of proven ability. Transfer fees no

detriment... only top players need apply." It
was on assistant trainer Jimmy Gribben's
recommendation that Celtic brought him to
Parkhead. The plan was for Jock to bring
along the reserves but Jimmy Mallan had
aggravated his USA groin strain; Alec Boden
had a sore back; Johnny McGrory was
recovering from cartilage so the Burnbank
man walked into the team and was never
dropped once. "Stein made a quiet debut,
attempting nothing spectacular." By
November 1st 1952, "Evans, Stein and Baillie
were the perfect half-back line." By December
18th: "The Celtic faithful feel they owe Jock
Stein an apology... the man who would never
do when he first arrived is one of the chief
factors they are up among the leaders... a quiet
type of player who seldom gets credit for the
work he does." Two days later, Sean Fallon
cracked his armbone after a clash with Jimmy
Delaney. Jock now took over as Celtic captain
on December 27th 1952 in a half-back line
reading Evans, Stein and Peacock. He had
only ever won a single medal: the Lanarkshire
Cup with Albion Rovers. Now he led the
no-chance Celtic into the Coronation Cup of
1953 and was immense in all three games
against Arsenal, Manchester United and Hibs.
He led Celtic to their first Double in 40 years

Jock Stein (3rd left, front row) lines with Celtic's 1954 Double side.
Back row (left to right): Jimmy Walsh, Bobby Evans, John Bonnar, Mike Haughney, Frank Meechan.
Front row: Bobby Collins, Sean Fallon, Jock Stein, Bertie Peacock, Willie Fernie, Neil Mochan.

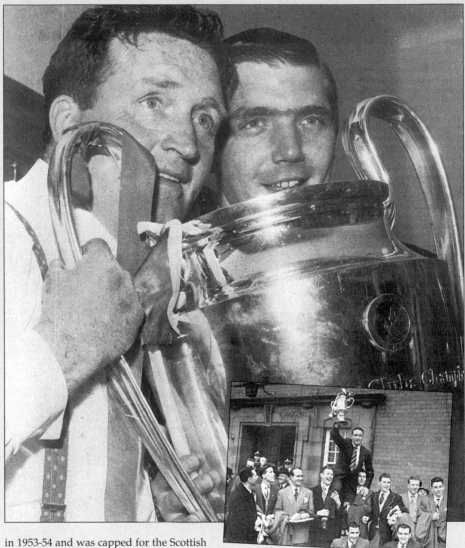

Jock Stein led Celtic to success as both a player and manager.

in 1953-54 and was capped for the Scottish League against the English at Stamford Bridge on April 28th 1954. He had a good game but the Scots lost 4-0. The ankle injury that was to finish him happened against Rangers at Parkhead on August 31st 1955.

Jock resisted the temptation to be instructed by Jimmy McGrory as a manager or by Willie Johnstone as a trainer. He took charge of the Celtic reserves and schoolboys and persuaded the club to purchase Barrowfield, Bridgeton Waverley's old ground (not Clyde's) as a training field. He won his first trophy as a manager, the 2nd XI Cup, 8-2 on aggregate versus Rangers on March 21st 1958. Jock had done great things for Celtic as a player. His

true legendary greatness now lay in store but Celtic were very lucky to get him back. Bob Kelly later confected the myth: "He had to learn his trade" (January 31st 1965). Hibs delayed the announcement of his return to Celtic to allow Churchill a quiet burial.

Appearances:
SL: 106 apps. 2 gls.
SLC: 21 apps. 0 gls.
SC: 21 apps. 0 gls.
Total: *148 apps. 2 gls.*

STEWART, Thomas Earley

Role: Right-half 1918
b. Renfrew, 29th December 1889

CAREER: Cambuslang Rangers/Rutherglen Glencairn/Fulham 1913/Dumbarton Harp 9 Nov 1915/(CELTIC loan Jan 1918)/ Dumbarton Harp Feb 1918/St Mirren 2 Aug 1918/Dumbarton Harp 4 Dec 1918.

Debut v St Mirren (a) 0-0 (SL) 5.1.18

Alec McNair was injured in Sunny Jim Young's testimonial on January 3rd 1918 and for the League match at Love Street Sunny's successor Jimmy Wilson was placed at right-back and ex-Craven Cottager Tom given a day to remember at right-half in a line reading Stewart, Cringan and Jackson.

Appearances:
SL: 1 app. 0 gls.
Total: *1 app. 0 gls.*

STORRIER, David

Role: Left-back 1898-1901
5' 11" 13st.0lbs.
*b. Arbroath,
25th October 187?
d. Arbroath,
27th January 1910*

CAREER: Arbroath Dauntless/Arbroath 1892/ Everton 1893/CELTIC 4 May 1898/ Dundee 26 Oct 1901/Millwall 2 Sept 1902/retired 1904.

Debut v Third Lanark (h) 2-1 (SL) 20.8.1898

Davie Storrier

Journalist RM Connell ('Bedouin') met Davie Storrier by chance playing billiards in the Bee Hotel, Liverpool on May 3rd 1898. Storrier told him Everton wanted rid of their Scottish imports: "Any chance of Celtic needing a back?" Connell telegraphed JH McLaughlin who "never crossed the street for a player." The Celtic chairman wired back that Willie Maley and Mick Dunbar would be on the Night Mail; meet them at the Matlock Clinic, Hyde Road, Manchester. Davie Storrier signed for Celtic the next day. He was not an instant sensation but in the Glasgow Cup semi-final versus Rangers at Ibrox (October 15th 1898) with two minutes to go and Celtic 1-0 down, "he took aim deliberate and deadly from 45

yards" and the ball flew past Matt Dickie for the equaliser. 1899 was Davie's year. He was not only capped versus Wales, Ireland and England (at Villa Park, April 8th, on a field of snow and slush), he skippered Scotland against the Irish at Parkhead on March 25th. He was also captain of the Celtic team that won the Scottish Cup 2-0 versus Rangers on April 22nd 1899 but later on was suspended by the club on a suspicion of malingering (April 8th 1901). In fact he was probably not a wholly well man. He went to Dundee as a makeweight for Tommy McDermott and got his chance at Millwall through another random encounter this time with Bob Hunter, the Lions' manager on holiday in Scotland. After football he resumed business interests in Arbroath. "Ever the soul of good nature" he also played cricket for Arbroath United.

Appearances:
SL: 34 apps. 0 gls.
SC: 6 apps. 0 gls.
Total: *40 apps. 0 gls.*

STRANG, William

Role: Full-back 1903-04
5' 8" 12st.0lbs.
b. Dunfermline, 16th September 1878

CAREER: Dunfermline Athletic Juniors Aug 1897/Orion FC (Aberdeen) 6 Sept 1899/ Dunfermline Athletic 19 Feb 1901/ CELTIC 23 Apr 1903/(Renton loan 6 Nov 1903)/Calgary Caledonian 1905.

Debut v Partick Thistle (h) 2-1 (SL) 15.8.03

"Wull" Strang played his first game for Celtic in green and white vertical stripes versus Dundee at Parkhead in the Inter-City League on May 2nd 1903. He made his League debut as Barney Battles' full-back partner, on a day of torrential rain, in the very first Celtic team to wear the hoops, and impressed with his lusty clearances. He achieved another first when Celtic opened East End Park for the Zebras (Dunfermline Athletic) four days later. Wull is not to be confused with Thomas William Strang of Penicuik who was on Celtic's books in 1902 and made his fame with Aberdeen 1904-07 (and founded Strang's Pools); nor with his own brother Sandy who played a trial for Celtic versus King's Park at Forthbank on April 29th 1903 and returned to

Dunfermline on May 5th. Wull played for Celtic reserves during a season when the executive tried very hard indeed to keep them active with a game every Wednesday, mostly against University opposition. He went on the Irish trip of March 1904 and played in both matches against Bohemians and Belfast Celtic. Having played in the very first League game of 1903-04, he played also in the very last, a 6-1 win against Kilmarnock on April 23rd. Whatever they got up to, Wull and Sandy were both suspended by the SFA in 1904 and emigrated to a new life in Canada.

Appearances:
SL: 2 apps. 0 gls.
Total: *2 apps. 0 gls.*

SULLIVAN, Dominic

Role: Midfield 1979-83
5' 11" 11st.4lbs.
b. Glasgow, 1st April 1951

CAREER: Provanmill Gasworks/St Roch July 1969/Clyde 19 Oct 1969/ Aberdeen 10 Apr 1976/ CELTIC 26 Oct 1979/free 28 June 1983/Dundee United (trial) 2 Sept 1983/ Manchester City (trial) 12 Sept 1983/Morton 8 Nov 1983/free July 1985/ Alloa (trial) 17 Aug 1985/ Alloa 20 Sept 1985/player-manager 1986/dismissed 4 Nov 1987/Kirkintilloch Rob Roy coach 13 Aug 1988/Falkirk coach 5 Sept 1988/acting-manager 1989/dismissed 24 May 1990/East Stirling manager 16 Nov 1990/resigned 7 Dec 1992/Arbroath asst manager 1993/resigned 15 Jan 1994/CELTIC youth coach Aug 1994.

Debut v Rangers (h) 1-0 (SL) 27.10.79

Clyde signed Dom Sullivan as an outside-right and Ally McLeod took him to Aberdeen. Celtic bought his transfer as a "silky-smooth right-side midfield player" with "tons of skill if a little short on dig." He scored the goal of his life against Hearts on January 31st 1981, a magnificent build-up by Celtic followed by Dom's crashing finish in the 68th minute. He was part of "easily the best Celtic team in years" that won the Premier League in 1981

Dom Sullivan

with record goals and points totals and which beat the host team and Dukla Prague for the Feyenoord Trophy in Rotterdam on July 31st and August 2nd 1981. He missed December 1981 and January 1982 with injury but once fit again, ran the right midfield in the side that brought another Championship home on May 15th 1982. That was also the year of Paul McStay's arrival and Dom dropped out to make room for Maestro. With Celtic director Tom Grant, he ran the Railway Hotel, Denny which was reputed at one time to have a poltergeist on the premises.

Appearances:
SL: 84 apps. 12 gls.
SLC: 13 apps. 2 gls.
SC: 9 apps. 0 gls.
Eur: 7 apps. 1 gl.
Total: *113 apps. 15 gls.*

SYME, David

Role: Goalkeeper 1918-19
5' 7" 11st.0lbs.
b. Govan, 11th December 1891
d. Irvine, 20th April 1962

CAREER: Irvine Meadow XI 1913/ St Anthony's 5 July 1916/CELTIC 15 Aug 1918/free 1919/Stevenston United (trial) May 1919/Irvine Meadow XI 1919.

Debut v Kilmarnock (a) 1-1 (SL) 12.10.18

Invalided out of the trenches in 1917, David Syme was part of Steve Callaghan's Team of All Talents at St Anthony's that furnished Celtic with so many fine players in the immediate aftermath of the Kaiser War. He was signed as cover for Charlie Shaw and got his chance when the Dalmuir man went down with Spanish 'flu just a month before the Armistice after 228 consecutive games for Celtic - his first absence since joining in May 1913. David's second and final game for Celtic was a 0-3 defeat in the League by Rangers at Parkhead a week later when he had to pick the ball out of the net in the first minute. A shipyard worker in Irvine, he died there at 62, Rankine Drive. He was the father and grandfather of referees Willie and David, both beloved in their day of Jock Stein.

Appearances:
SL: 2 apps. 0 shut-outs.
Total: *2 apps. 0 shut-outs.*

TAYLOR, David

Role: Left-back 1919
5' 10½" 13st.4lbs.
b. *Govan, 29th September 1883*
d. *Bridge of Allan, 6th August 1949*

CAREER: Bannockburn Juniors/Ashfield 1906
/Rangers 19 Sept 1906/(Motherwell loan
24 May 1909)/Bradford City 29 Sept 1910/
Burnley Dec 1911/(Ayr United loan Jan 1916)/
(Rangers loan 27 Apr 1916)/(Chelsea loan
2 Sept 1916)/(Falkirk loan Jan 1918)/(CELTIC
loan 31 Dec 1918)/Burnley again Jan 1920/
St Johnstone manager 6 May 1924/resigned
4 Apr 1930/Blackburn Rovers coach 20 Nov
1934/Dunfermline Athletic manager 5 June
1936/Carlisle United manager 1938/
Wolverhampton Wanderers scout by 1948.

Debut v Rangers (a) 1-1 (SL) 1.1.19

Davie Taylor was in the same league as Joe
Dodds as a sprinter yet was rejected early by
Falkirk as "too slow". A centre-half to begin
with, he guested for Stenhousemuir against
Celtic in a Tryst Fair friendly on September
11th 1906. He played against Jimmy Quinn for
Rangers at Parkhead on October 27th
following and gave him the heave with his
shoulder. "That's all right, young fella," Quinn
told him, "as long as that's all I get, I'll no'

David Taylor

grumble." Davie
won two English
Cup medals, one
with Peter
O'Rourke's
Bradford City on

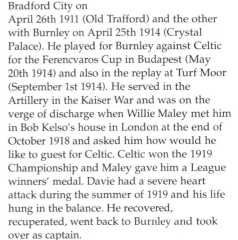

April 26th 1911 (Old Trafford) and the other
with Burnley on April 25th 1914 (Crystal
Palace). He played for Burnley against Celtic
for the Ferencvaros Cup in Budapest (May
20th 1914) and also in the replay at Turf Moor
(September 1st 1914). He served in the
Artillery in the Kaiser War and was on the
verge of discharge when Willie Maley met him
in Bob Kelso's house in London at the end of
October 1918 and asked him how would he
like to guest for Celtic. Celtic won the 1919
Championship and Maley gave him a League
winners' medal. Davie had a severe heart
attack during the summer of 1919 and his life
hung in the balance. He recovered,
recuperated, went back to Burnley and took
over as captain.

Appearances:
SL: 5 apps. 0 gls.
Total: *5 apps. 0 gls.*

TAYLOR, William

Role: Inside-left 1948-51
5' 10" 11st.7lbs.

CAREER: Glencairn Juveniles 1947/CELTIC
5 Feb 1948/free 27 Apr 1951/Carlisle United
(trial) 12 Apr 1951/Alloa 31 May 1951/Ayr
United Feb 1953.

Debut v Third Lanark (a) 2-0 (CC) 2.5.49

"A real ball worker," "a hard grafter whose
head never goes down," Willie Taylor was a
Tommy McInally "discovery" (but in fact a
much sought-after commodity) who scored
four goals in 10 minutes in the Glasgow Police
Sports 5-a-sides at Hampden on June 11th
1949. This gingertop played inside left to Tully
on breaking into the League team (September
3rd 1949) but lost his place to Charlie after the
3-0 defeat at Dundee (October 22nd 1949). He
came back against Rangers on January 2nd
1950 for another short run including the
aborted Cup-tie (snow) and field invasion at
Cathkin (February 11th 1950). Celtic wanted
him full-time at the start of 1950-51 but not for
money enough to compensate for the loss of
his job as a motor mechanic with Glasgow

Corporation. He re-signed on September 9th but got no more big team opportunities. His last game was against Derry City at Parkhead April 24th 1950. He tried-out for Bill Shankly at Carlisle.

Appearances:
SL: 14 apps. 4 gls.
SLC: 1 app. 0 gls.
SC: 2 apps. 0 gls.
Total: *17 apps. 4 gls.*

TEMPLETON, Robert Bryson

Role: Outside-left 1906-07
5' 9" 11st.3lbs.
b. Coylton, 22nd June 1879
d. Kilmarnock,
2nd November 1919

CAREER:
Irvine Heatherbell/
Westmount
Juveniles/
Kilmarnock Roslyn
1896/Neilston
Victoria/Kilmarnock
Rugby XI July 1897/
Aston Villa May 1898/
Newcastle United Feb
1903/Woolwich Arsenal
8 Dec 1904/CELTIC 17 May
1906/Kilmarnock 18 Oct 1907/
Fulham 22 Aug 1913/Kilmarnock
Apr 1915/retired 1915.

Debut v Kilmarnock (h) 5-0 (SL)
25.8.06 (scored once)

Bobby
Templeton

Celtic signed the 'Wizard of Dribble' in 1906 and immediately added him to the tour party for Germany, Bohemia and Hungary. He may well have played his first game in a Celtic jersey versus FC Altona in Hamburg on May 20th. His greatest game for Celtic was in the semi-final of the Scottish Cup on April 13th 1907 when he devastated Hibs, the club that had once tried to diddle Aston Villa out of his signature. He was outside-left in the team that won the Scottish Cup at Ibrox 3-0 versus Hearts a week later and which clinched the third League title in a row at Firhill on April 24th 1907. Celtic lost the Charity Cup final to Rangers (and a Bob Campbell goal) at 2nd Cathkin on May 18th 1907 and Bobby was blamed for "a very selfish display." Matters

came to head in Copenhagen on tour on June 3rd and 5th 1907 when he dribbled himself dizzy in "a silly, selfish display" (according to Willie Maley but not Jim Young; according to Sunny, the crowd knew "Temple - TON!" from touring with Newcastle and wanted a repeat performance); he was made to keep goal for the final two matches. His days as a Celt were now numbered and he was sold on to Kilmarnock even though it meant the club had no recognised left-winger for the Glasgow Cup final replay against Rangers on October 18th 1907. His career revived at Rugby Park most notably when he was picked for the Scottish team that beat England on April 2nd 1910 and played a draw on March 23rd 1912, each time at Hampden. After football, Bobby ran a pub in George Street, Kilmarnock with Sunny Jim. Bobby is also the footballer who got into the cage at Bostock and Wombwell's menagerie in New City Road on August 22nd 1908 (after a game at Parkhead) and twisted the lion's tail for a bet. The proprietors awarded him a gold medal for bravery. He died of heart seizure one Sunday morning just "pulling on his boots." The Ibrox Disaster on April 5th 1902 is said to have been caused by the swaying of the crowd occasioned by one of the "Blue Streak's" mazy runs.

Appearances:
SL: 29 apps. 5 gls.
SC: 7 apps. 0 gls.
Total: *36 apps. 5 gls.*

♣ **Celtic note:** *Bobby married on April 18th, 1916 but his brother Andrew, hard-up, gave away a box of his medals in Australia in 1928 in gratitude for a gift of money. The recipient gave them all back to the Templeton family in 1956 on a visit to Scotland.*

THOM, James

Role: Right-half 1895

CAREER: Parkhead Juniors/CELTIC (trial)
Jan 1895/Parkhead Juniors.

Debut v Hearts (a) 0-4 (SL) 16.2.1895

James Thom tried out for Celtic reserves on January 19th 1895 and was scheduled to make his big team debut at home versus Leith Athletic the following week. The game was frozen-off. He played at Tynecastle in a thaw, with pools of water all over the pitch. His display was "disappointing" but the spirit of disharmony prevailed in the Celtic camp: Charlie McEleny and Willie Maley were missing without explanation; Madden had had an "accident"; Doyle ran the line with a "cold." A bad time for a boy to be in the first team.

Appearances:
SL: 1 app. 0 gls.
Total: 1 app. 0 gls.

THOMAS, Daniel

Role: Left-half 1895
b. Glasgow, 30th March 1872

CAREER: Mossend Celtic/CELTIC (trial)
23 Feb 1895/Hibs May 1895/Motherwell
7 Aug 1895/Carfin Rovers 26 Aug 1897/
Albion Rovers 4 July 1898/Carfin Rovers
26 Oct 1898.

Debut v Third Lanark (h) 4-4 (SL) 23.2.1895

The week after James Thom, Newmains boy Danny Thomas got his chance for Celtic who had not won a match since January 2nd 1895 and were strengthened by the guest appearance of Scotland right-back Watty Arnott. Celtic fought back from 0-3 and 1-4 down to square the game.

Appearances:
SL: 1 app. 0 gls.
Total: 1 app. 0 gls.

THOMSON, Alexander

Role: Inside-forward 1922-34
5' 9" 11st.0lbs.
b. Buckhaven, 14th June 1901
d. 1975

CAREER: Glencraig Celtic/Wellesley Juniors/ CELTIC 9 Oct 1922/(Ayr United loan 31 Aug 1923)/Dunfermline Athletic 16 June 1934/free Apr 1937/retired 1937.

Debut v Clyde (a) 1-0 (SL) 4.11.22

"Celtic can be doing with more of Thomson's calibre if that youth's first appearance in a green and white jersey is anything to go by." "The Fife youth showed many clever touches." "I was impressed with Thomson. His execution was faulty at times but his ideas were finely conceived." Precision passer Alec Thomson was Jimmy McMenemy's natural successor in the Celtic team and got his chance in November 1922 because he happened to be available (ie not loaned-out) on a day when Celtic were so reduced for reserves, several first-teamers played with injuries. He was "a craftsman to the fingertips, not a move of the game that is not known and exploited by the Celtic inside-right... a smart lad on his feet... nerve, sinew and heart... he possesses all the essentials... a first-class inside-forward." Sweet-moving Alec was an outside-right for Wellesley Juniors, "the best trapper of a ball I've ever seen on the touchline," according to John Richardson. East Fife took him for a try-out but "I wasn't required" (he was asked to play linesman). Alec established himself as a first team man in the 3-0 defeat of Morton on September 24th 1923 but his solitary flaw, the lack of dig in front of goal, manifested early. Against Rangers on October 27th 1923 with the score 0-0 and a minute to go, Alec missed a sitter. He made up for it with the first goal on Ne'erday 1924 and scored the fourth in the 5-0 defeat of Rangers in the Scottish Cup semi-final (March 21st 1925) at Hampden. The sinewy Alec beat man after man including Alex James for a Patsy-style goal versus Raith Rovers a week later and won his first Scottish Cup medal versus Dundee in Gallagher's final on April 11th 1925.

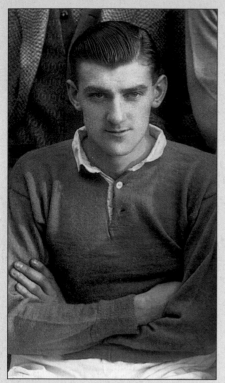

Alex Thomson

Against Cowdenbeath on Boxing Day 1925, "Thomson was the outstanding Celtic forward, tireless, tricky, all mazy runs and swinging passes." He won a Championship medal in 1926 and was in the Celtic sides that won the Cup in 1927, 1931 and 1933. Versus the English League at Villa Park (November 3rd 1928), "the brainiest work in the game came from the Celtic inside-right." Alec was the first of the three Thomsons to play at the same time in the Celtic team. He was also the last of the three to leave. He was an all-time Celtic great. His epitaph? "Not a strong player but he used to lay on beautiful passes for me" (Jimmy McGrory).

Appearances:
SL: 392 apps. 85 gls.
SC: 59 apps. 13 gls.
Total: *451 apps. 98 gls.*

THOMSON, John

Role: Goalkeeper 1926-31
5' 8½" 10st.8lbs.
b. Buckhaven, 28th January 1909
d. Glasgow, 5th September 1931

CAREER: Bowhill West End 1924/Bowhill Rovers 1924/Wellesley Juniors 1925/CELTIC 1 Nov 1926/(Ayr United reserves loan Dec 1926).

Debut v Dundee (a) 2-1 (SL) 12.2.27

"Wellesley have unearthed a champion goalkeeper in Thomson from Bowhill. He is a youngster yet but should develop" (*Fife Free Press* October 1925). "Thomson is coolness personified. His anticipation is positively uncanny. High shots, low shots, point-blank or long range, Thomson deals with them all in masterly fashion and his cutting-out of crosses from either wing is well-nigh perfect... not big as goalkeepers go, but in his lithe, boyish frame is the agility of a tiger and his brain is like ice." "Time and time again Thomson saved brilliantly. His clutching of the ball was perfect and his anticipation wonderful... still in his teens... clever as a veteran..." (February 23rd 1927). "Falkirk were denied an almost certain goal by the alertness of Thomson... a Ritchie through-pass almost reached Martin but for the goalie's anticipation although the save cost him an injury" (August 27th 1927). "I hesitate to describe the display of the Celtic goalkeeper as flawless... he miskicked and mispunched... but he made some saves which none but a goalkeeper in the top flight could have accomplished" (November 12th 1927). "I should like to see Thomson take his own goal kicks. Apart from this, he is good enough to keep goal for Scotland at any moment" (March 17th 1928). "John Thomson, the Hero of Birmingham!... the crowd took young John to their hearts and cheered him to the echo... midway through the second half... he went after a terrific shot from Hine like a cat... another John Thomson day" (November 7th 1928). "Thomson was injured going down at Fleming's feet for the second goal" (Ibrox, Ne'erday 1929). "Twice Thomson averted the fall of his goal by a daring dive at the feet of the forward boring in. The third time he got a knock on the head that caused concussion" (December 14th 1929). "Young Thomson seems to be making a habit of getting hurt and

John Thomson - a brave save at the feet of Sam English in September 1931 cost him his life.

carrying on... he had to be forced off the field for attention after concussion" (December 21st 1929). "Thomson sustained a double fracture of the collarbone; a broken jaw; a broken rib; two teeth lost..." (February 5th 1930). "Towards the end when knocked by Smith, Thomson staggered out 10 or 15 yards but would he, did he, relax his grip? No, sir!" (October 11th 1930)." Only one real success - John Thomson magnificent... a marvel... the crowd cheered him to an echo as he retired at the interval... several saves bordered on the miraculous..." (English League 7, Scottish League 3; White Hart Lane, November 5th 1930). John Thomson of 23, Balgreggie Park, Cardenden, kept goal in an era when 'keepers did not stand up to oncoming forwards. They were expected to go down head first and fast at a marauder's feet. In John's case his task was made doubly difficult in that Celtic refused to use a third back as dictated by the 1925 change in the offside law. In front of him often yawned a hole in which lurked the opposition centre-forward while the Celtic centre-half was upfield being "constructive". John hesitated at least twice before coming out to meet Sam English on September 5th 1931 and although he timed his dive correctly enough the save was to cost him his life. He died that night in the Victoria Infirmary, Langside, at 9.25.

Appearances:
SL: 163 apps. 57 shut-outs.
SC: 25 apps. 7 shut-outs.
Total: *188 apps. 64 shut-outs (34%).*

♣ **Celtic note 1:** *John signed for Celtic's Steve Callaghan on the lid of a roadside fuse box at the top of Gallowtown (Galton) after a persuasive talking-to in a single-deck tram car during the Miners' Strike of November 1926.*
♣ **Celtic note 2:** *John maintained to Bill Paterson it was Peter McGonagle broke his jaw with a clearance kick in the melee of 5th February 1930 not Bobby Skinner of Airdrie as popularly alleged.*
♣ **Celtic note 3:** *John belonged to a Protestant sect called the Church of Christ whose members took services themselves without a delegated minister. His funeral was conducted by a miner and family friend, John Howie.*

THOMSON, Robert Austin

Role: Outside-right 1929-33
5' 6" 10st.6lbs.
b. Johnstone, 12th July 1907
d. 17th September 1937

CAREER: Broomfield Juveniles/Possil Hawthorn/Glasgow Perthshire 1927/ CELTIC 17 Oct 1929/Blackpool 21 Aug 1933/ Motherwell 30 Nov 1934/Brideville (Dublin) 4 Mar 1936.
Debut v Cowdenbeath (h) 2-1 (SL) 16.11.29

"He can box, he can sing, he can play the soccer game and play it beautifully." "Every time Thomson got the ball the crowd was on its toes and they were seldom disappointed" (October 25th 1930). "Fine, aggressive player Thomson" put across the inswinger at the Mount Florida end of Hampden in the dying moments of the Scottish Cup final versus Motherwell on April 11th 1931 that Alan Craig headed into his own goal for the 2-2 draw after Celtic had been 2-0 down. Bertie told how he dallied on the wing in order to claim the match ball since he wasn't going to get a medal but hearing no whistle from Mr Craigmyle, said "Goodbye, ball!" and gave it a careless welt with his left into the Motherwell box with instant tragedy to the claret and amber and delirium to the Celts. He scored two goals in the replay four days later and in the final of 1933, exactly two years on, wormed his way into the Motherwell goalmouth to set up McGrory for the only chance of the game. By this time however, he was already persona non grata with the Parkhead executive. After the 4-1 drubbing by Queen's Park on September 17th 1932, manager Maley bawled him out for "unsatisfactory play and physical condition" and ordered double training for Monday September 19th which Bertie refused to do. He was suspended sine die the following day, apologised on October 1st but had his letter left on the table until November 12th when the suspension was lifted. Bertie trained at Parkhead for six weeks before the transfer to Motherwell. As he took the field against Celtic in Glasgow on December 8th 1934, the fans presented him with a decorative horseshoe in green and white. He was poorly supported, "with no running power to speak of" and proved "but a pathetic relic of his glory days

Bertie Thomson (second right, front row) with a 1931 Celtic line-up.
Back row (left to right): W.Maley (manager), Geatons, Cook, J.Thomson, McGonagle, Wilson, W.Quinn
(trainer). Front row: Napier, Scarff, McGrory, J.McStay, R.Thomson, A.Thomson.

at Parkhead." A "live-for-the-day" type, Bertie epitomised gallus. He had no idea of the value of a pound and spent his wages as he earned them without a thought for the morrow. He died of heart trouble in his mother's arms on his daughter Roberta's third birthday. His death went largely unremarked. Jimmy McGrory went to his funeral: "I didn't even know that he was ill." The wee man's gravestone says it all: "Bertie of Celtic."

Appearances:
SL: 113 apps. 22 gls.
SC: 18 apps. 8 gls.
Total: *131 apps. 30 gls.*

THOMSON, William

Role: Centre-half 1895

CAREER: Wishaw Hibs/CELTIC (trial) 16 Mar 1895/Wishaw Hibs.

Debut v Leith Athletic (h) 4-0 (SL) 16.3.1895

On Billy Thomson's debut, Marshall, outside-right of Leith Athletic, was tackled by Dan Doyle early in the first half and broke his leg. The snap was so distinctly heard it made patrons in the north stand (the Jungle) flinch. The poor fellow had to wait until half-time for an ambulance but a substitute, Hamilton, took

his place, courtesy of Celtic. Billy seems to have played for Celtic once more in a friendly at Renton on May 23rd 1895 when the downpour was so bad the clubs settled for 35 minute halves.

Appearances:
SL: 1 app. 0 gls.
Total: *1 app. 0 gls.*

TIERNEY, Cornelius

Role: Outside-left 1930-32
5' 4" 11st.4lbs.
b. Kilbirnie, 22nd April 1909

CAREER: Rosewell
Rosedale/Bo'ness/(CELTIC loan 21 Apr 1930)/CELTIC 30 July 1930/(St Johnstone loan 23 Jan 1931)/(Forfar Athletic loan 8 Aug 1931)/(Belfast Celtic loan 4 Sept 1931)/Guildford City 1 Aug 1932/Exeter City 31 July 1934.

Debut v Queen's Park (a) 4-1 (CC) 3.5.30

"Con Tierney is the most promising player Celtic have tried at outside-left since Adam McLean departed." If Con had a flaw, it was "a penchant for too-frequent cutting-in." He played in the Charity Cup final versus Rangers on May 10th 1930, a 2-2 draw and 4-4 on corners after extra time. Jimmy McStay lost the toss of the coin which gave Rangers the clean sweep of the season. Con was in the USA 1931 publicity photograph taken by Frank Agnew at Parkhead on September 6th 1930 but not destined to tour the States with Celtic.

Appearances:
SL: 7 apps. 0 gls.
Total: *7 apps. 0 gls.*

TOBIN, John

Role: Goalkeeper 1888
6' 0" 12st.0lbs.
b. Bathgate, 13th June 1868

CAREER: Morton 1883/Hibernian Aug 1885/ Celtic Sept 1888/Glasgow Hibs 7 Sept 1889.
Debut v Clyde (h) 0-1 (SC) 24.11.1888

John Tobin ("a giant in stature") won a winner's medal with Hibs in the Scottish Cup final on February 12th 1887 and was in goal for the Edinburgh Irish when they hanselled first Celtic Park against Cowlairs on May 8th 1888. He played his first game for Celtic in a Merit Friendly at Dalmarnock Street on September 18th 1888 against Dumbarton Athletic. He was living at 60, Franklin Street, Bridgeton and played instead of Willie Dunning in the 5th round of the Scottish Cup 1888. It was a 0-1 defeat but Celtic managed a successful protest on grounds the game had ended in darkness because three Clyde players had caused a late start by having to remove illegal cross bars from their boots. John scouted talent like James Coleman for Glasgow Hibs and later (a dangerous occupation at the time) for English clubs. When Willie Groves died in penury, there was shock then resolve that this must never happen again. A letter to the *Glasgow Observer* in 1908 suggested a fund for John Tobin (ex-17, Norman Street) also struggling to survive in straitened circumstances. His son David played for Shettleston and Strathclyde and signed for Albion Rovers in August 1912.

Appearances:
SC: 1 app. (unofficial) 0 shut-outs.
Total: *1 app. (unofficial) 0 shut-outs.*

Willie Toner

TONER, William

Role: Centre-half 1948-51
6' 0½" 12st.1lb.
b. Shettleston, 18th December 1929

CAREER: St Paul's Shettleston BG/Queen's Park Strollers 1947/CELTIC Feb 1948/RAF 1948/free 27 Apr 1951/Sheffield United May 1951/Guildford Town Oct 1954/Kilmarnock 1 Nov 1954/Hibernian 1 Apr 1963/Ayr United player-coach Nov 1963/Dumbarton manager 3 Oct 1964/resigned 23 Sept 1967/Shettleston Juniors manager.
Debut v Stirling Albion (h) 2-1 (SL) 18.2.50

Darleith Street boy Willie Toner signed for Celtic just before National Service and what chance he had at Parkhead was further spoiled by cartilage trouble. He played in two Celtic half-back lines: Toner, McGrory and Baillie on his debut and Evans, Toner and Baillie on March 4th 1950. He was invited to join Sheffield United and did some great work at centre-half at Bramall Lane, winning a Division Two Championship medal in 1953. He left the Blades in a dispute over terms and took a job driving a van in Glasgow as well as being prepared to travel south to Surrey each weekend to play. Malky MacDonald took him to Rugby Park where he made his main mark with two caps for Scotland and played for Kilmarnock against Rangers in the Scottish Cup final of April 25th 1960. He was the winning nomination for *Sunday Mail* Player of the Year on February 19th 1961 and in 1962 became chairman of the Scottish Footballers' Association. Walter Galbraith bought him for Hibs to stave off the threat of relegation. Willie played for Celtic Old Crocks versus Rangers at Kirkintilloch on June 11th 1969. His son Kevin was the Shettleston Juniors midfield dynamo in 1979, aged 19, and ran the line for the Celtic versus Dundee League Cup tie on August 19th 1992.

Appearances:
SL: 2 apps. 0 gls.
Total: *2 apps. 0 gls.*

TOWIE, Thomas

Role: Outside-right 1892-93
5' 9½" 11st.0lbs.

CAREER: Dumbarton Union/Preston NE 1891-92/Renton 1891-92-93/(CELTIC loan Oct 1892)/Derby County 1893-94/...Renton 29 Aug 1895 until 1897.
Debut v Partick Thistle (a) 2-1 (GC) 29.10.1892

Renton were seldom out of dispute with the SFA and season 1892-93 was no exception. Celtic were able to borrow Tom Towie but for Cup fixtures only. He "won" the Scottish Cup for Celtic in the "Pretend" final versus Queen's Park at Ibrox on February 25th 1893 with a goal in 70 minutes but when the match was played for real on March 11th 1893, the Spiders took it 2-1.

Appearances:
SC: 5 apps. 2 gls.
Total: *5 apps. 2 gls.*

TRAVERS, Patrick

Role: Inside-forward 1911-12
5' 8" 11st.6lbs.
b. Beith, 28th May 1883
d. Dublin, 5th February 1962

CAREER: Renfrew Victoria/Thornliebank 1901/Barnsley 18 Jan 1904/Thornliebank 15 Aug 1904/New Brompton 14 Nov 1904/Renton 22 Jan 1907/Clyde 19 Nov 1908/Aberdeen 11 May 1910/CELTIC 29 Aug 1911/Aberdeen 3 June 1912/Dumbarton 24 June 1914/Clydebank 3 Aug 1918/Vale of Leven 1919/Dumbarton Harp Mar 1920/Bergen, Trondheim, Stavanger (Norway) coach May to Dec 1920/Dumbarton 16 Dec 1920/manager Apr 1921/Aberdeen trainer 1922/manager 2 Aug 1924/Clyde manager 22 Nov 1937/retired 19 July 1956.
Debut v Clyde (h) 3-2 (SL) 2.9.11

Paddy Travers was so anxious to join Celtic he had himself reinstated junior and amateur and did not cost Parkhead a penny in transfer fees. It was Paddy who was dropped on December 2nd 1911 to make way for Patsy Gallagher. He did not get another game until Christmas Day when his goal beat Belfast Celtic in Ireland as 10,000 looked on in a downpour. He came

Paddy Travers

TRAYNOR, John Francis C.

Role: Full-back 1983-89
5′ 10″ 10st.6lbs.
b. Glasgow, 10th December 1966

CAREER: Celtic BC/CELTIC Jan 1983/free
16 May 1989/Clydebank 11 Aug 1989/Ayr
United 7 Nov 1991.
Debut v Motherwell (h) 3-1 (SL) 28.9.88

"I don't care whether I play right-back,
sweeper or midfield" (John Traynor after a
hat-trick for Ayr as a midfielder versus
Clydebank on February 1st 1992). John played
for Scottish Schools U-15s alongside Tony
Shepherd in the 0-1 win at Wembley (June 5th
1982). He made his debut in the Glasgow Cup
at Firhill on March 10th 1987 and first stepped

back at inside-left on Ne'erday 1912 at
Parkhead, kept John Brown fed with the ball
while Brown in turn fed Quinn a hat-trick for
the 3-0 win. Paddy's Celtic career virtually
ended when he was injured at Firhill on
March 16th 1912. Aberdeen were glad to have
his services again. Paddy managed the great
Aberdeen side which failed so gallantly
against Celtic in the 1937 (April 24th) final as
well as the Clyde teams which lifted the
Scottish Cup on April 22nd 1939 (versus
Motherwell) and April 27th 1955 (versus
Celtic). Wild rumours used to fly through
Glasgow that Paddy Travers had taken over
the Celtic managership as Maley's successor.
Before marriage, he would take his holidays
on the Isle of Man in the company of Mr and
Mrs Bill Struth sharing many a happy jest at
the silliness of the religious divide in Scottish
football.

Appearances:
SL: 18 apps. 3 gls.
SC: 4 apps. 3 gls.
Total: *22 apps. 6 gls.*

John Traynor

out with the Celtic big team against Ajax in the Viareggio Tournament (July 31st 1988). His Premier League debut was in the Billy Stark role of midfielder with a nose for goals. Manager McNeill set Celtic a six out of six target for their remaining League matches as of April 8th 1989. Celtic promptly lost 2-0 at Douglas Park where Hamilton Accies hadn't scored once since December 10th. Hope of the Flag still glimmered. When Chris Morris went down with appendicitis before the Motherwell game four days later, McNeill called John Traynor in. Within moments of the start the Celtic manager was racing along the touchline to complain bitterly about a late Colin McNeil challenge on his new young right-back. The 2-2 draw was young John's last game for Celtic. His free transfer was a major surprise. He missed 18 months out of his career at Kilbowie Park through injury.

Appearances:
SL: 4 apps. 0 gls.
Total: *4 apps. 0 gls.*

TRODDEN, Patrick

Role: Right-half 1895

CAREER: Shawbank Sept 1892/Kilsyth Hibs/ Kilmarnock (trial) 1893-94/Queen's Park (trial) 6 Apr 1895/ CELTIC (trial) 4 May 1895/Kilmarnock Athletic Aug 1895.

Debut v Dundee (h) 2-1 (SL) 4.5.1895

Paddy Trodden was an orphan from Quarrier's Home who played in place of Peter O'Rourke on his debut. He played in a half-back line with Jimmy Kelly and Charlie McEleny and helped Celtic fight back from a goal down in two minutes to take both points in the final League match of the season.

Appearances:
SL: 1 app. 0 gls.
Total: *1 app. 0 gls.*

TULLY, Charles Patrick

Role: Inside-left 1948-59
5' 8" 10st.7lbs.
b. Belfast, 11th July 1924
d. Belfast, 27th July 1971

CAREER: Whiterock Juniors/Belfast Celtic 1938/(Cliftonville loan 1940)/(Ballyclare Comrades loan 1941)/Belfast Celtic II 1942/Belfast Celtic 1943/CELTIC 28 June 1948/(Stirling Albion loan 25 Dec 1958)/ (Rangers loan 11 Mar 1959)/free by 2 Sep 1959/Cork Hibs player-coach-manager 13 Oct 1959/Bangor manager 7 Jan 1964/ resigned 29 Apr 1965/Portadown manager 16 Dec 1965/Bangor manager 1967-68.

Debut v Morton (h) 0-0 (SL) 14.8.48

"Tully was giving Billy Wright a hard time to remember... Tully went through the English defence like a hot knife from the right-half position... Tully swerved and weaved through a half-lost English defence... sent in a shot Swift could not hold..." (Ireland versus England, Windsor Park, October 9th 1948). Charlie was the second of twelve children and "an inside-forward to the manner born... the greatest soccer import Scotland has had in years... a classic footballer." Tully arrived at Parkhead and Celtic began to play to crowds every match of a size unknown for humdrum fixtures in their previous history: 412,000 for the first ten games of 1948-49. The legend of Tully and the Three Gers was born at Parkhead on

Ireland cap Charlie Tully

Best Wishes
Charlie Tully

September 25th 1948: "Tully dribbled about almost at will..." "The miraculous Irishman bewildered, badgered... mesmerised Rangers. Every time he got the ball... three Ibrox men were with him and none dared to tackle... he kidded McColl, Cox, anyone who came within his orbit... he brought repose to Celtic, panic to Rangers... and goals as well." Charlie won his first Celtic medal when the Scottish Cup came home at last on April 21st 1951 for the first time since 1938 through a goal scored by his great friend John McPhail. When Celtic came off the Liverpool train from the USA tour at Glasgow Central on June 30th 1951 they, and above all Tully, were engulfed by the ecstatic Celtic support. Charlie gloried in his element as the entertainer beloved of his fans. Against Aberdeen in the St Mungo Cup final (August 1st 1951) "Tully took corners right and left and throw-ins of equal menace" (including a shy off Davie Shaw's back in 40 minutes that led to the corner from which Sean Fallon put Celtic back in the game). He conversed with his marker, the future Sir Alf, before kick-off at Windsor Park on October 4th 1952: "Do you enjoy playing for your country, Mr Ramsey?" "I do, Mr Tully." "Make the most of it today then - it might be the last chance you get!" Charlie must have known he was on his game. "Tully took a corner with his right foot. The in-swinger sailed waist-high and at speed, swerving into goal at the last moment. Merrick sensed the danger... but the swerving ball bounced out of his arms and over the line." (This sort of thing was old hat to Celtic fans who had seen him do it twice within minutes at Falkirk on February 21st previous). Charlie did not play in the Coronation Cup final but he got Celtic there with a magnificent show versus Manchester United at Hampden on May 16th. He was outstanding in the Double Year of 1954 but so pestered for tickets prior to the Scottish Cup final, that he spent the night before (April 23rd) at Jock Stein's to get some decent rest. Charlie's last great day was the October Revolution League Cup final against Rangers at Hampden in the Sun in 1957 when he and Evans each had a glory match despite a fist fight at Parkhead on Thursday October 17th over a remark in Charlie's column in the *Evening Citizen*. Just two months before (August 19th 1957) he had even coaxed applause out of the Rangers end for a great 40 yard run in the Glasgow Cup at Ibrox. His last big show was in the Ford Fives Festival "Night of a Thousand Stars" at Meadowbank on February 10th 1971 when he displayed all the old tricks. He died in his sleep. One of his last acts had been to commend Bangor goalie Billy Irwin to Celtic. For his funeral to

Milltown Cemetery (July 29th 1971), the Falls Road was as thronged as Glasgow Central 20 years before. Johnny Bonnar surveyed the sight and turned to Stein: "Charlie would have loved this, Jock." Charlie Tully was an all-time Celtic great. He is one of the players who epitomise an era in the history of the club.

Appearances:
SL: 216 apps. 32 gls.
SLC: 68 apps. 8 gls.
SC: 35 apps. 7 gls.
Total: *319 apps. 47 gls.*

♣ **Celtic note:** *At a Glasgow auction on September 8th 1971, Celtic paid £19 for lot 229: Charlie's loser's medal from the 1955 Cup final.*

Charlie Tully

TURNBULL, David

Role: Left-half 1927-28
5' 9½" 11st.0lbs.
b. Hurlford, 4th April 1904

CAREER: Kilbirnie Ladeside/CELTIC 26 Feb 1927/(Ayr United loan 26 Aug 1927)/Ayr United 3 Sept 1928/free own request 22 Dec 1931/Glentoran 1932.

Debut v St Johnstone (a) 0-1 (SL) 23.4.27

Q. Will Celtic join the new Provincial League? Or is it better for colts to watch their seniors than to play serious football?

A. No. Celtic allow reserves like David Turnbull to play for clubs like Ayr United. A reserve side is superfluous to Celtic's progress.

David Turnbull was the hottest junior property on the go when Celtic acquired his signature. He played an excellent Public Trial (August 9th 1927) and was pawned out to Ayr United. Willie McStay took him to Glentoran.

> **Appearances:**
> *SL: 2 apps. 0 gls.*
> **Total:** *2 apps. 0 gls.*

TURNBULL, Thomas

Role: Full-back 1899-1900

CAREER: Falkirk Dec 1893/East Stirling 3 May 1899/CELTIC 19 May 1899/Sheffield United 13 Sept 1900/Stenhousemuir 6 Mar 1903/Partick Thistle 17 Oct 1903.

Debut v Clyde (h) 3-2 (SL) 19.8.1899

Celtic's full-backs for 1899-1900 were Welford, Storrier, Davidson and Tom Turnbull, "a young man of great promise." The club started the season with neither manager nor trainer; both Maley and Dan Friel were incapacitated by injury and ex-Seaforth Highlander Tom Maguire (who had marched with Roberts from Kabul to Kandahar) was forced into a comeback. Tom Turnbull was in the team on October 28th 1899 when the wonder of the age was opened, the two-tier Grant Stand with plushbottom tip-up seats and weatherproof steam-up windows. He went to Sheffield United in a double transfer with Pat Gilhooly. Tom was regarded as too good a back to lose but was unable to command a regular first team spot. He joined Thistle at the same time as Duke McMahon but neither lasted long.

> **Appearances:**
> *SL: 11 apps. 0 gls.*
> **Total:** *11 apps. 0 gls.*

TURNER, Patrick

Role: Inside-right 1963-64
5' 8" 11st.0lbs.

CAREER: Shamrock Rovers 1957/Shelbourne 1960/Morton 20 Nov 1961/CELTIC 31 May 1963/Glentoran 16 June 1964/Dundalk 1965/Bohemians 1971 until 1973.

Debut v Rangers (h) 0-3 (SLC) 10.8.63

Morton brought motor mechanic Paddy Turner and goalkeeper Finnbarr Flood from Ireland in 1961. Each proved a big success at Cappielow and Paddy was in the Eire team that beat Scotland in Dublin on June 9th 1963. Bob Kelly seemed to see the fair-haired Turner as the new Tully and Paddy looked to have football stamped all over him. Celtic fans clapped approval of his cultured performance in the Public Trial of August 5th 1963 when the Hoops beat the Whites 8-0. He played inside to Steve Chalmers and in the second trial on August 8th was partner to Jimmy Johnstone. 1963-64 started where the old season had left-off with a 0-3 cuffing by Rangers for Paddy's debut and then another two weeks later at Ibrox. Celtic fans were now streaming out long before the end of Old Firm (mis)matches. After the 2-2 draw against Dunfermline on October 5th, Paddy was dropped for the young Murdoch and only played again when Bobby was unfit. Paddy's last game was on a snow-covered pitch at Broomfield on February 22nd 1964. He had football in him but nothing the no-plan Celtic of the time could harness to advantage.

> **Appearances:**
> *SL: 7 apps. 1 gl.*
> *SLC: 6 apps. 0 gls.*
> *SC: 1 app. 0 gls.*
> **Total:** *14 apps. 1 gl.*

Paddy Turner

UGOLINI, Rolando

Role: Goalkeeper 1944-48
5′ 9″ 12st.0lbs.
b. Lucca, 4th June 1924

CAREER: Armadale Thistle/Hearts (trial)
20 Feb 1943/CELTIC 23 Mar 1944/
Middlesbrough 22 May 1948/Wrexham 5 June
1957/Dundee United 17 June 1960/free May
1962/Berwick Rangers (trial) 1962.

Debut v Partick Thistle (a) 1-1 (CC) 5.5.45
(Celtic 9-2 on corners)

Born in Italy in the town where Caesar,
Pompey and Crassus divided the Roman
Republic among them into spheres of
influence, Rolando
Ugolini was
brought to Scotland
as a toddler of
three. He was a
reluctant
goalkeeper but a quite magnificent one and
Rangers seem even to have wanted his
services for January 15th 1944 but Rolando
was unfit on the day. He was unable to break
into the Celtic big team on account of Miller's
brilliance and got only an occasional chance as
on October 19th 1946 when Willie was on
international duty. He made his fame at
Ayresome Park. Hair sleeked back, sleeves
pushed up, he played tremendous football for
Middlesbrough in the Wilf Mannion era,

battling with one
fearless performance
after another to keep the
Reds out of Division
Two. He looked the part
and was "spectacularly
agile" with "safe hands".
He became a great
thrower of the ball on
George Hardwick's
advice: big punts down
the middle were food
and drink to the
opposition. He returned
to Parkhead on League
duty on December 10th
1960. Rolando was in
Ronnie Simpson's class
as a low-handicap golfer.
He played for Celtic Old
Crocks as late as 1973
still looking as good as
in his prime. Frank
Walsh describes 'lando
as the life and soul of
every Celtic team bus
and the team's personal
turf agent.

Appearances:
SL: 4 apps. 0 shut-outs.
SLC: 1 app. 0 shut-outs.
Total:
5 apps. 0 shut-outs.

Rolando Ugolini

VATA, Rudi

Role: Utility 1992 to date
6' 1" 12st.5lbs.
b. Shkodar, 4th September 1969

CAREER: Vllaznia Shkodar/Dinamo Tirana/
(FC Tours loan 1991)/CELTIC 14 Aug 1992.

Debut v Dundee (a) 1-0 (SL) 3.10.92

Rudi Vata became possibly the first Albanian to play in British football when he turned out for Celtic reserves versus Rangers at Parkhead on August 22nd 1992. He had defected after the France versus Albania international in Paris 1991 and was spotted by manager Brady playing as a central defender with fine command in the air against the Republic of Ireland in May 1992. Celtic tried him out on tour versus Cork City July 21st and UCD July 23rd 1992. His transfer was bought from Dinamo for £200,000 at the same time as Stuart Slater and Andy Payton signed on for Celtic. "I was signed as a centre-half but Mr Brady told me I would need to speak English better before I could play there." Parkhead used him wide on the right and his first game in central defence was not until April 20th 1993 against Falkirk at home. He is a popular figure with the support: "There was one delicious moment at Firhill when the Albanian suddenly realised that the chanting which had been going on for some time was actually his name... the delight on Vata's face was quite wondrous. He applauded the troops who chanted some more. A star is born." (Partick Thistle 2, Celtic 3 SL 5th December 1992). As a Celtic player Rudi has been capped eight times for Albania up to May 1994.

Appearances:
SL: 32 apps. 3 gls.
SLC: 2 apps. 0 gls.
SC: 1 app. 0 gls.
Total: *35 apps. 3 gls.*

Albanian Rudi Vata (centre) joined Celtic from Dinamo Tirana in a triple transfer swoop which also saw the arrival of Andy Payton and Stuart Slater.

WADDELL, William

Role: Centre-half 1940-41
5' 9" 11st.2lbs.
b. Glasgow, 7th December 1918

CAREER: Strathclyde/Renfrew Juniors/Aberdeen 30 May 1938/(CELTIC loan 8 Aug 1940)/(York City & Huddersfield loan 1941-42) /Kettering Town summer 1950.

Debut v Hamilton Academicals (h) 2-0 (RL) 10.8.40

Celtic had a new look team out for the start of 1940-41: Ferguson and Gillan from Alloa; Conway from Glencraig; a new trainer Alex Dowdells; George Johnstone and apprentice plumber Willie Waddell both from Aberdeen. Willie Lyon was away to the Army and Willie his replacement at centre-half. He got a medal almost straightaway in the Glasgow Cup final: Rangers 0, Celtic 1 (September 28th 1940) and was again a winner at Ibrox in the 2-3 game of Ne'erday 1941. He was in the Celtic side that won its League Cup qualifying section on April 5th 1941 after Divers, MacDonald and Hogg had negotiated a £25 per man special pay-day with Tom White (to whom bonus spelt anathema) if they managed to bring it off. Willie was a solid and consistent centre-half who looked magnificent in a Celtic kit and rendered the club fine service over a season and a half (100% attendance in 1940-41) until he handed over to Willie Corbett on 13th December 1941. Waddell and Lyon were together battling Rommel in the Western Desert in July 1942. Willie emerged unscathed from the fighting in Italy in January 1944 and was with the BAOR in 1945. He won a Scottish Cup medal with Aberdeen 2-1 versus Hibs at Hampden on April 19th 1947. He walked out on the Dons for non-League football where better terms were on offer. Kettering played his benefit against Leicester City in 1956 with player-manager Tommy Lawton intending to play and promises too of appearances by Bobby Mitchell and Jackie Milburn.

Appearances:
RL: 48 apps. 0 gls.
RLC: 5 apps. 0 gls.
Total: *53 apps. 0 gls.*

WALKER, Andrew

Role: Striker 1987-92; 1994 to date
5' 9" 10st.8lbs.
b. Glasgow, 6th April 1965

CAREER: Partick Thistle Youth/Toronto Blizzard/Baillieston Juniors 1983/Motherwell 31 July 1984/CELTIC 1 July 1987/(Newcastle United loan 20 Sep 1991)/(Bolton Wanderers loan 9 Jan 1992)/Bolton Wanderers 11 Feb 1992/CELTIC again 13 June 1994.

Debut v Morton (a) 4-0 (SL) 8.8.87 (scored twice)

"Goals come easily to Andy Walker... we ask him to play to his strengths, holding the ball up, bringing others into the game and getting on the end of things" (Bruce Rioch before Andy headed Liverpool before the English Cup January 13th 1993). Andy from Burnside had played with Partick Thistle straight from school but after injury was allowed to drift, even as far as Canada where getting a work permit proved the snag to a career with Toronto Blizzard. Dundee United were keenly interested but Billy McNeill bought him to replace Brian McClair and Andy, delighted to be a Celt at last, had a magnificent season as the quintessential striker. He possessed a thunderous shot, was a superb header of the ball and even chested home a brilliant goal against Rangers in the League crunch match at Ibrox on March 20th 1988. He won the Scottish Cup semi-final with a strike in the last minute versus Hearts at Hampden on April 9th that sent Celtic fans into delirium. He was a sine qua non of the Celtic side that landed the Double in the club's Centenary Year. When Dundee looked like coming back into the game at 1-0 on April 23rd 1988, it was Andy's two goals in the 75th and 76th minutes that clinched the Championship for Celtic. He missed the 1989 Cup final because of an horrendous injury at Aberdeen on April 29th when Brian Irvine smacked a ball into his face that almost detached a retina. Andy spent too much time on the bench during 1989-90 and his goal touch seemed to have deserted him. He was a virtual discard as of 1990-91 and Celtic decided he could go on May 14th 1991. At Burnden Park, he was regarded as the hottest property since the great Nat Lofthouse. Frank Stapleton described him as "the best striker outside the Premier League." Lou Macari (at Stoke): "It's only a matter of time

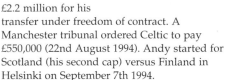

before someone offers seven figures for him." Andy: "I'm playing the best football of my career. I feel I'm going to score every time I play" (33 goals from 44 games in 1992-93). Andy temporarily ended this finest period in his career with a worrying cruciate ligament injury at home to Martin Hayes' Swansea City on April 12th 1993. He made his comeback as Bolton's "trump card" to a massive roar of acclaim in the last 15 minutes of an epic Cup-tie versus Arsenal at Burnden Park with the Trotters 1-2 down (5th February 1994). At Highbury in the replay, he appeared again as substitute and scored in Bolton's shock 1-3 win on February 9th. Bolton wanted £2.2 million for his transfer under freedom of contract. A Manchester tribunal ordered Celtic to pay £550,000 (22nd August 1994). Andy started for Scotland (his second cap) versus Finland in Helsinki on September 7th 1994.

Appearances:
SL: 107 apps. 40 gls.
SLC: 14 apps. 8 gls.
SC: 11 apps. 6 gls.
Eur: 7 apps. 2 gls.
Total: *139 apps. 56 gls.*

WALLACE, John

Role: Goalkeeper
1932-34
5' 10" 11st.4lbs.
b. Falkirk, 20th June 1910
d. Fallin,
17th November 1992

CAREER: Blantyre Victoria/Stonehouse Violet/CELTIC 5 Nov 1932/(East Stirling loan 1933)/free 30 Apr 1934/Coleraine 16 May 1934/Derry City 1935/Hartlepool United Aug 1938/Belfast Celtic 6 Sep 1941.

John Wallace

Debut v Third Lanark (a) 4-0 (SL) 26.11.32

Joe Kennaway had 'flu when ex-Stonehouse Violet left back and "very good capture" Jock Wallace got his first chance for Celtic and made an "impressive debut" with "good clutch, good anticipation." A flaw in his game showed up on 17th December 1932 when "although no Carnera," he began to clutch the ball and then invite the shoulder charge. Chairman White in the stand was apoplectic: "Get it away, boy! Get it away!" Stonehouse miner Jock played in a sensational match versus Hearts at Parkhead on February 11th 1933. Half-time was 0-0 but within six minutes of the restart Hearts were 0-2 up. The Celtic fight-back began and McGrory scored the winner with five minutes to go "amid tremendous excitement." He played in the 3rd

Andy Walker

round of the Scottish Cup in brilliant weather against Partick Thistle before 55,595 at Parkhead a week later. Again Celtic had to fight back for a 2-1 win. In the 4th round against Albion Rovers at Cliftonhill on March 4th, the teams were presented to Sir Harry Lauder. When Celtic signed John 'Pot' Doherty from Derry he was reserve 'keeper to the excellent Jock who had left Coleraine over terms.

Appearances:
SL: 15 apps. 3 shut-outs.
SC: 3 apps. 0 shut-outs.
Total: *18 apps. 3 shut-outs (17%).*

WALLS, James

Role: Outside-right 1901-03
b. Beith, 27th June 1883

CAREER: Dalmuir Thistle 1894/Duntocher Harp 1895/Beith FC/Hamilton Academicals/ (CELTIC loan Jan 1902)/CELTIC 31 May 1902 /(Beith FC loan 1902)/Ayr FC 19 Aug 1903/ Johnstone FC Aug 1904/Beith FC 13 Aug 1904 /Morton 21 Jan 1905.

Debut v Thornliebank (h) 3-0 (SC) 11.1.02

Jimmy Walls from Main Street, Lochwinnoch was tried at outside-right in season 1901-02 when everybody and anybody except John Glass JP was being given a turn as Celtic tried

WALLACE, William Semple Brown

Role: Striker 1966-71
5' 8" 11st.6lbs.
b. Kirkintilloch, 23rd June 1940

CAREER: Kilsyth Rangers/Stenhousemuir 28 Jan 1958/Raith Rovers 22 Oct 1959/ Hearts 25 Apr 1961/CELTIC 6 Dec 1966/ Crystal Palace 19 Oct 1971/Dumbarton 12 Oct 1972/Apia (Sydney) 28 Mar 1975/

Partick Thistle (trial) 8 Mar 1977/Ross County player-coach 15 Mar 1977/player-manager 27 May 1977/Dundee coach 17 June 1977/Apia and Leichhardt (Sydney) coach 8 Dec 1979 until July 1982.

Debut v Motherwell (h) 4-? (SL) 10.12.66

William Semple Brown (WSB='Wispy') Wallace followed Rangers home and away as a boy yet came out onto the pitch at Lisbon on May 25th 1967 singing the Celtic Song as lustily as Bertie Auld or Ronnie Simpson.

Willie Wallace scored twice as Celtic built a 3-1 first leg lead against Dukla Prague at Celtic Park in the 1967 European Cup semi-final.

to find an outside-right to replace Neilly McCallum now ten years away. Jimmy had his best run in the first team as of March 1903 when he played three Scottish League and four Inter-City League matches with a goal versus Queen's Park (ICL) on 28th March 1903. Then Bobby Muir was bought from Bristol City and there was no more place for wee Jimmy. He played his last game in an away friendly against Ayr FC on May 13th 1903 in a forward line of Walls and Campbell; Bennett; Somers and Hamilton.

Appearances:
SL: 4 apps. 0 gls.
SC: 1 app. 0 gls.
Total: 5 apps. 0 gls.

WALSH, Francis

Role: Centre-forward 1947-49
5' 8" 11st.0lbs.
b. Overtown Wishaw, 15th September 1923

CAREER: St Ignatius School Wishaw/ Mossend BG 1940-42/Wishaw Juniors Aug 1942/Wishaw BG 1942-43/Ardeer Recreation Sep 1943/Kilmarnock Aug 1944/Ardeer Recreation (farmed-out) 1944/CELTIC 12 Nov 1947/free Apr 1949/Torquay United (trial) Aug 1949/Southport 3 Oct 1949/ (Stranraer loan 21 Jan 1950)/Hamilton Academicals 7 Aug 1950/Limerick Feb 1952/ Ards 13 Dec 1952/East Stirlingshire 1953/ retired 1956.

Willie ("a masterstroke in the buying market") was signed to take over from alleged veteran Steve Chalmers but came in effectively as McBride's replacement once SuperJoe's knee went at the end of 1966. As a striker, Willie was almost as potent as Joe but more mobile and skilful (like working the ball past Drew Rogerson of Stirling Albion with an ingenious piece of heelwork at Annfield on February 25th 1967) and with a relish for the physical, an area in which, like Auld, he was rarely bested. As a trainer and a dressing room good influence, he was Stein's ideal. His two most famous goals for Celtic were against Dukla at Parkhead in the European Cup semi-final of 12th April 1967 that sent Celtic to Prague 3-1 up and won him his cap (in place of the injured Jinky) in a famous win at Wembley against the World Cup holders ten days later. Another week on and he scored both goals in the 2-0 defeat of Aberdeen in the Scottish Cup final. Then there was Lisbon. But on August 30th 1967 Celtic, the holders, had to beat Rangers in the qualifying stages of the League Cup at Parkhead or go out of the competition. There was a 75,000 all-ticket crowd in spite of the fact that "The Fugitive" (on which the nation was riveted) was putting out its final episode on TV and the bookies were laying odds who dunnit. Celtic trailed 0-1 from the 8th minute and Rangers got a penalty in the 76th. Kai Johansen struck the bar and hit the rebound himself. Wispy - who else? - went straight down the park and scored the

equaliser. Parkhead erupted. Five minutes later Murdoch made it 2-1 and the Parkhead stand resounded to the stamp of feet. Stein described the night as "Celtic's greatest win since I became manager" (and Wallace made it). Willie left Parkhead in a peculiar fashion, Stein allegedly not wanting him to go and Willie under the impression that he did. Willie Wallace is an all-time Celtic great.

Appearances:
SL: 142 apps. 89 gls.
SLC: 36 apps. 21 gls.
SC: 27 apps. 12 gls.
Eur: 29 apps. 13 gls.
Total: 234 apps. 135 gls.

*Debut v Partick Thistle (a) 5-3 (SL) 15.11.47
(scored once)*

"Speedy and opportune," Frank Walsh scored
more than 70 goals all told in his time with
Kilmarnock and was Scotland's leading
goalscorer on 23 in 1945-46. He got a goal
against Celtic in the League at Parkhead on
February 16th 1946 in the 33rd minute and
broke his shoulder just before half-time. An
ex-Bevin Boy from down the Dalmellington
Pit, Frank first appeared for Celtic in a "false
dawn" match before a 32,000 crowd packed
into Firhill and the gates closed long before
kick-off. Thistle beat Rolando Ugolini twice in
the first 13 minutes and led 3-1 after 55. The
Celtic fight-back began through goals from
Corbett and Bogan before Frank put the Bhoys
ahead 3-4 in the 68th minute. Colonel John
Shaughnessy declared Celtic would be great
again soon and according to the *Daily Herald*,
Celtic had recovered the will to win and
"Walsh has to a large extent solved the leadership problem." Frank was a fast mover who
liked the going hard and sunny but was
dropped after a 0-4 defeat on a muckheap at
Ibrox on January 2nd 1948. Celtic bought Jock
Weir and Frank played his last big game in a
5-1 thumping by 3rd Lanark on March 29th
1948 two days after the sickening extra-time
defeat by Morton in the Cup semi-final at
Ibrox. He expected to be in the team for the
vital relegation match at Dundee on April 17th
1948 but instead turned out with the reserves
and suffered a double fracture of his right leg
at Celtic Park. Frank celebrated his comeback
with five goals against Albion Rovers colts on
January 22nd 1949 but made only one more
appearance again with the reserves versus
Queen of the South the following week. He

was always a handy man to have around and
scored a hat-trick on his debut for Limerick
(his grandparents lived in Newcastle West).
Frank finished with football at 33: "That left an
enormous hole in my life, when you don't
have that piece of green pitch, the ball, wet or
dry, and the goals." He worked in the
Lanarkshire Steelworks for 22 years until
redundancy and began retraining as a capstan
setter in Bellshill at the end of November 1977.

Appearances:
SL: 10 apps. 3 gls.
Total: *10 apps. 3 gls.*

♣ **Celtic note:** *Despite the intimation of his death
(1981) in Bill Donnachie's otherwise excellent
'Who's Who of Kilmarnock FC', Geoff Wilde the
Southport FC historian assured us Frank was alive
and well in Cambusnethan (1993) and put us in
touch with this utter gentleman to prove it. One of
his sons, Frank junior, is Sir William Dunn
Professor of Experimental Pathology at Guy's
Hospital, London.*

WALSH, James

Role: Inside-forward 1949-56
5' 9" 11st.0lbs.
b. Glasgow, 3rd December 1930

CAREER: Valleyfield Colliery/Bo'ness United
1949/CELTIC 21 Oct 1949/Leicester City
13 Nov 1956/Rugby Town 1964.
Debut v Hibernian (a) 1-3 (SL) 30.4.51

Jimmy Walsh was "a fast-raiding forward, not
afraid to eat up ground and go through on his
own... he can excavate a defence and release
wonder shots... he does not pass the buck!"

Jimmy Walsh tests Falkirk 'keeper Slater at Brockville.

(September 1950). Fair-haired Jimmy was a Fifer from famous Rintoul Avenue in the well-known football village of Blairhall. He made his debut in a forward line reading Weir and Collins; Walsh; Peacock and Millsop. In 1951-52 he began to wear a bow-tie. Alex Dowdells counselled against. "But Tully wears one!" "Aye, but that's Tully, son." Jimmy did not go to the States on tour but went straight into the team for the first round of the St Mungo Cup on Bastille Day 1951 as inside-right to Bobby Collins and got a hat-trick against Raith Rovers in the semi-final two weeks later. "Walsh has a high sense of position and has given the Celtic attack a stimulus and new finishing power." He scored the winning goal in the great fightback from 2-0 down against Aberdeen in the final of August 1st 1951 and got his first Celtic honour: a silver tankard. He played in all three games of the Coronation Cup tournament and scored the clincher against Hibs at Hampden in the final with two minutes to go (20th May 1953). He helped bring the League Championship home in 1954 but was pressed into service in an unfit condition against Thistle at Firhill (20th March 1954) and missed the Cup semi-finals versus Motherwell and the final against Aberdeen. He played inside-left against Clyde in the Cup final of 23rd April 1955 but when Collins was unaccountably dropped for the replay on the 27th Jimmy moved over to plug the gap at outside-right. For the 1956 final versus Hearts on April 21st it was his turn to be out of favour and take a seat in the stand. He followed Alex Dowdells to Leicester and tossed for ends with Danny Blanchflower, skipper of Spurs' great Double side at Wembley in the English final of of May 6th 1961. Something happened to his timing in 1963 and again Alex Dowdells intervened with good advice: try contact lenses.

Appearances:
SL: 108 apps. 46 gls.
SLC: 21 apps. 8 gls.
SC: 15 apps. 5 gls.
Total: *144 apps. 59 gls.*

♣ **Celtic note:** *Leicester City beat Manchester City 8-4 in a battle for First Division survival on February 22nd 1958. Jimmy Walsh scored four.*

Jimmy Walsh

WATSON, Charles

Role: Outside-right
1919-21
5' 7" 11st.0lbs.
b. Coatbridge,
21st May 1895

CAREER: Ashfield / Airdrie 5 June 1913 / Albion Rovers 14 Sep 1914 / Clyde 12 June 1916 / Albion Rovers 16 Sep 1916 / Clyde 23 Mar 1917 / Stevenston United 20 Oct 1917 / Johnstone FC 7 Mar 1918 / Dumbarton Harp 10 Aug 1918 / CELTIC 28 May 1919 / free June 1921 / Bathgate 8 Feb 1922 / Dykehead 13 Sep 1922 / Albion Rovers 28 Jan 1924.
Debut v Clydebank (h) 3-1 (SL) 16.8.19

A seasoned campaigner, Charlie Watson belonged to a famous Coatbridge footballing family and was brought to Celtic as cover for Andy McAtee and wing partner to Patsy Gallagher. In the summer of 1919, "perhaps Celtic's most important signing was that of Watson, the outside-left of Dumbarton Harp who last season was easily the best man in the West of Scotland in that position." Charlie won a Charity Cup medal against Queen's Park on May 15th 1920 after being sent off in the semi-final against Rangers on May 8th in a case of mistaken identity. It was Johnny McKay struck Jimmy Gordon. Charlie was an innocent bystander. He was in the Celtic League team that enhanced his home town by hanselling the new pavilion and stand at Albion Rovers (August 21st 1920). He got a bonus medal in gold (courtesy of the Celtic board) as a member of the team that beat Clyde 3-0 for the Retired Priests Fund (Argyll and the Isles) at Parkhead on April 5th 1921. He was not included in the Battlefields Tour party of May 1921 and played his last game for the Celts against the Internationals at Ibrox in the Robert Hay Testimonial of May 2nd 1921.

Appearances:
SL: 18 apps. 4 gls.
Total: *18 apps. 4 gls.*

Hugh Watson (4th left, back row) lines up for Celtic in 1905-06.
Back row (left to right): R.Davis (trainer), R.Campbell, D.McLeod, H.Watson, D.Hamilton, A.McNair,
A.Wilson, E.Garry, J.McCourt, D.Adams.
Front row: J.Young, J.Hay, A.Bennett, J.McMenemy, W.Loney, J.Quinn, P.Somers, W.McNair.

WATSON, Hugh

Role: Right-back 1901-06
5' 9" 12st.0lbs.
b. Maybole, 20th August 1882

CAREER: Trabboch Thistle/CELTIC 29 May
1901/Kilmarnock 20 Oct 1905/free May 1906/
Belfast Celtic Oct 1906.

Debut v Clyde (h) 3-0 (GC) 14.9.01

Hugh joined Celtic as a wing-half but became
Celtic's undisputed right-back as of his debut,
displacing Bobby Davidson and linking-up
with Barney Battles. He was joined at left-back
by Donnie McLeod in the 2-7 first round
defeat of Rangers to raise money for the Ibrox
Disaster Fund on August 20th 1902 and
together they won gold watches in the final
versus Morton (24th September 1902). Hugh
was no subtle back like his successor Alec
McNair: "Watson stakes everything on one
desperate move and if it fails he blames
everyone else, especially Battles." Rangers and
Celtic drew 2-2 in the Inter-City League at
Ibrox on April 13th 1903: "The leather medal
must go to Hugh Watson... a superb display of
headless muddling... spoiled Adams and
McLeod... practically gifted the two goals to
Rangers." Yet his endeavour was famous and

Patsy Gallagher remembered how as a boy he
heard Hugh spoken-of with awe. He was on
the verge of Scotland honours when tragedy
struck on Celtic's first-ever visit to Broomfield
on January 9th 1904: a double fracture of the
leg in the 52nd minute. He returned to the
Celtic side on March 31st 1906 in the Glasgow
League (0-3 against Rangers at Parkhead) and
was given an extended run including tour
matches at Bolton and Bradford City in April
and the Highlands in May. He was no longer
the Hugh of old and was released after Bobby
Craig at last signed-on. Hugh broke his shin
on March 7th 1908 against Linfield in the
semi-final of the County Antrim Cup.

Appearances:
SL: 49 apps. 0 gls.
SC: 9 apps. 1 gl.
Total: *58 apps. 1 gl.*

WATSON, Philip Ross

Role: Centre-half 1902-03
b. Dykehead, 29th April 1881

CAREER: Shotts Hawthorn/Dykehead
16 Aug 1900/CELTIC 18 Dec 1902/(Dykehead
loan 10 Feb 1903)/Ayr FC 9 Oct 1903/
(Dykehead loan 4 July 1904 & 17 Mar 1905)/
Dykehead 3 Aug 1906/Bathgate 25 Apr 1907/

Hamilton Academicals 22 July 1907/
Motherwell 13 May 1912/Dykehead 20 Aug
1914/retired 1918.

Debut v Morton (h) 1-1 (SL) 20.12.02

Phil Watson tried out for Celtic against the
Junior Internationalists to raise money for
Parkhead FC's ground improvement scheme
on 6th May 1902, then played in a friendly
against Clyde in John Hodge's last game four
days later. He made his League debut at
left-half on the day Hibs won the Flag (20th
December 1902) and played just two more
matches for points this time at centre-half (7th
and 14th March 1903). Phil made his fame at
Douglas Park and played for Hamilton against
Celtic in the two Scottish finals (8th and 15th
April 1911) and displaced ex-Celt Hughie
O'Neil at Fir Park for a time in 1912.

Appearances:
SL: 3 apps. 0 gls.
Total: *3 apps. 0 gls.*

WATTERS, John

Role: Inside-forward 1935-47
5' 8" 11st.4lbs.
b. Waterside, 5th September 1919

CAREER: St Aloysius' College/CELTIC
(provisional) 1935/St Roch's (farmed-out) Oct
1936/CELTIC 9 Jan 1937/Royal Navy 1940/
(Newcastle United loan 1941-42)/free Apr
1946/re-signed 1946/free Apr 1947/Airdrie
30 Sep 1947/...Pollok FC trainer and
physiotherapist Apr 1949/Sunderland
physiotherapist 1956/retired 1982.

*Debut v Arbroath (a) 2-0 (SL)
26.11.38*

Malky MacDonald went down
with appendicitis on 23rd
November 1938 and schoolboy
wonder centre-forward Jackie
Watters took over at inside-right.
In his second game under the
control of referee M.C. Dale
(having one of his erratic days but
in Celtic's favour), the green and
whites beat Hibs 5-4 and Jackie

scored two. He scored another brace in the 2-2
draw against Hearts on a frozen pitch at
Parkhead on Hogmanay and was held up as
proof that "Celtic can produce a young player
fit for League duty at any time." He played at
Ibrox in the Ne'erday thriller of 1939 before a
world record League match crowd of 118,730
and is credited in some reports with a part in
Joe Carruth's wondrous fightback goal 15
minutes from time. Celtic now went into a
slump and Jackie scored his final goal in the
3-8 defeat of Burntisland Shipyard in the Cup
on January 21st 1939 the day the Kirkton Park
amateurs matched Parkhead goal for goal
until 3-4. He had studied physiotherapy and
served six and a half years as a medic in the
Royal Navy but with no football. Jackie took
part in the D-Day invasion of June 6th 1944
aboard HMS Warspite which was engaged in
both bombardment of the Normandy coast
and the landing of troops. After a year with
Celtic reserves, he resumed his career as a
hospital physiotherapist. At Sunderland he
claimed credit for the discovery of 'keeper
Jimmy Montgomery and was in attendance on
the Wearsiders unforgettable day at Wembley
on May 5th 1973. Jackie's four children, two
girls and two boys, are all honours graduates
of the University of Newcastle: one in Classics,
two in Law and one in Medicine.

Appearances:
SL: 9 apps. 4 gls.
SC: 1 app. 1 gl.
Total: *10 apps. 5 gls.*
RL: 9 apps. 0 gls.
Total: *9 apps. 0 gls.*

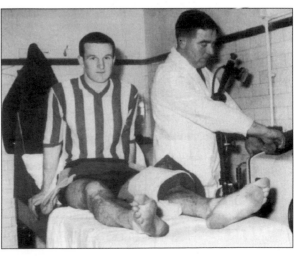

*Jackie Watters (right) takes care of
Sunderland's George Mulhall
during his time as physiotherapist at
Roker Park.*

WDOWCZYK, Dariusz

Role: Left-back 1989-94
5' 11" 11st.11lbs.
b. Warsaw, 25th May 1962

CAREER: Gwardia Warsaw (schoolboy) 1973/
(professional) 1983/CELTIC 17 Nov 1989/free
17 May 1994/Falkirk (trial) 3 Aug 1994/
Reading 9 Aug 1994.

Debut v St Mirren (h) 1-1 (SL) 22.11.89

Chief Scout John Kelman watched Shuggie in
Warsaw on September 5th 1989 and then Billy
McNeill took in the Poland versus England
game on October 11th. A week later it was
announced Celtic had dropped out of the race
and left the field clear for Manchester United.
Nine days on the Polish internationalist and
captain was Parkhead's for £400,000. As a
player Dariusz was nothing if not cultured but
on the debit side he tended towards the
robotic and "plays as if he's got his best suit
on." He was the best striker of a dead ball at
Parkhead since Tommy Gemmell. Against
Rangers in the St Patrick's Day Massacre of
1991 he hit a 35-yarder off Terry Hurlock that
flew on unstoppably past Chris Woods for
Celtic's second goal. In the Paul Davis
Testimonial at Highbury on July 30th 1991
with Celtic trailing 2-1 he hit a free-kick from
about the same distance high into the net
behind the helpless David Seaman who had
barely moved, a goal in a million. He also
passed a ball beautifully and took a mean
corner. One of new manager Macari's more
successful experiments was to use Dariusz in
central defence. In the Ne'erday disaster of
1994 he injured his thigh and did not play
again until April 23rd. He had a big part in a
much better Celtic performance at Ibrox before
the all-Rangers crowd in the Murray lock-out
match of April 30th. For 1994-95 Dariusz was
offered such a reduced weekly wage (with an
appearance money clause in the club's favour)
as to be the recipient of what was virtually a
free transfer. He moved on to link up with
ex-Celt Mark McGhee, manager at resurgent
Reading. As a Celtic player he had been
capped 12 times for Poland up to May 1994.

    Appearances:
    SL: 116 apps. 4 gls.
    SLC: 11 apps. 0 gls.
    SC: 13 apps. 1 gl.
    Eur: 8 apps. 0 gls.
    Total: *148 apps. 5 gls.*

WEIR, Donald

Role: Inside-forward 1948-52
5' 11" 11st.7lbs.
b. Cadder East, 1930
d. 18th September 1959

CAREER: Kilwinning Rangers/CELTIC 2 Nov
1948/free May 1952/Portadown 5 July 1952/
...Ards (trial) Dec 1953/...Coatbridge Burgh
Police FC 1954/resigned 1955/Canterbury
City July 1955/Forfar Athletic 7 Aug 1956.

Debut v Third Lanark (h) 1-2 (SL) 16.4.49

Donald Weir played inside-right on his debut
with Tommy Docherty at inside-left. Together
"they lacked the necessary guile to draw the
defence." Celtic beat Rangers 3-2 in the League
on September 23rd 1950. The game was
deadlocked 0-0 until seven minutes after half-
time when "after a mazy piece of interpassing
among Tully, McPhail, Peacock and Weir,"
Donald scored with a diving header from
Bertie's lob. This capped a splendid display of
"perfect passes right, left and centre. Where on
earth have Celtic been hiding him?" After the
defeat at Aberdeen on October 14th 1950,
Donald was dropped for Willie Fernie and did
not get another chance until Celtic 1, Hearts 3
(September 29th 1951). Jimmy Walsh and Sean
Fallon both pulled a muscle and he ended up
playing right-back (he had played full-back for
the reserves) in what was his last game for the
big team. Portadown believed in him enough
to offer him £9 a week and a house. Donald
was killed in the Aughengeish pit disaster. He
lived at 14, Hillhead Avenue, Chryston.

    Appearances:
    SL: 6 apps. 1 gl.
    SC: 1 app. 1 gl.
    Total: *7 apps. 2 gls.*

WEIR, James

Role: Left-back 1907-10
5' 9" 12st.6lbs.
b. Muirkirk, 23rd August 1887

CAREER: Benfoot Hill Thistle/Dunaskin Lads
FC/Ayr FC 30 Apr 1904/CELTIC (trial) 27 Apr
& 8 May 1907/CELTIC 13 May 1907/
Middlesbrough 24 Aug 1910/retired 1920.

Debut v St Mirren (h) 1-1 (SL) 27.4.07

Dun Hay tipped Celtic off about Burns' Songs
specialist and fierce battler Jimmy Weir who

Dariusz Wdowczyk

was no sooner signed than he was off on the June 1907 trip to Copenhagen playing left-back with Bobby Craig on his right. As of August 15th 1907 Celtic's full-back partnership was McLeod and Weir, reckoned by Davie McLean the best in the history of the club. Jimmy went into the challenge with a warning cry: "Get rid of the ball!" that was as full-blooded as the tackle itself. Alec McNair joined Jimmy at full-back against Rangers in the Scottish Cup at Ibrox on February 8th 1908. Jimmy took a severe kicking against Dundee on March 28th 1908 so much so that

manager Maley protested on the pitch to the referee at half-time. He recovered for the Scottish Cup final of 18th April 1908, the 5-1 game, when St Mirren's forwards could make nothing of the Weir man at all. Celtic won the Double and all else in 1908 and Jimmy Weir played a full part. Jimmy lost Donnie McLeod as his neighbour after the 4-4

Jimmy Weir

draw with Queen's Park in the Glasgow Cup on September 12th 1908 and Alec McNair now joined him permanently. They loitered on the pitch hoping for extra time at the end of the Cup final replay on 17th April 1909 and as they were ordered to the pavilion, the Hampden Riot began. Celtic then had to play eight games in 11 days for the Championship and Jimmy played in them all. He was out of favour at the start of 1910-11 and went to Ayresome Park to rejoin his mate, Slasher McLeod. The departure of these two great backs was much lamented by the fans of the time and meant the loss of the midfield drive of McNair and Hay called to replace them.

Appearances:
SL: 82 apps. 1 gl.
SC: 14 apps. 0 gls.
Total: 96 apps. 1 gl.

♣ **Celtic note:** *Jimmy and his son were running the Crown Hotel in Redcar in 1956.*

WEIR, John

Role: Outside-right 1948-52
5' 8" 11st.7lbs.
b. Fauldhouse, 20th October 1923

CAREER: Leith Renton/Hibernian 1941/ Royal Navy (Fleet Air Arm)/(Cardiff City loan 1941-42)/(Brighton loan 1944-45)/Blackburn Rovers 30 Jan 1947/CELTIC 17 Feb 1948/ Falkirk 16 Oct 1952/Llanelly 28 July 1953/ Dumbarton 16 Dec 1953.

Debut v Motherwell (h) 1-0 (SC) 21.2.48

For Jock Weir's "zest, ever-eager pursuit, ability to snap-up the impossible chance," Celtic paid £7,000 - more than double the fee

Jock Weir

paid for his predecessor at Hibs, Tommy Bogan. Jock was ever a tireless performer. According to Eddie Hapgood at Blackburn he was too fast for the rest of the team. Jock was virtually taking throw-ins and receiving them himself! He started at centre for Celtic with Bogan at outside-right, missed a three yards sitter at 0-0 in the 13th minute of extra time in the Cup semi-final versus Morton (27th March 1948) at Ibrox, then scored the hat-trick at Dens Park that allegedly saved Celtic from relegation (17th April 1948). "Whole-hearted" Jock was outside-right in the first Celtic team to lift a post-War Scottish Cup (21st April 1951) and went to the USA on tour. He played against Eintracht for the Schaeffer Trophy on May 30th 1951 when there was fighting in the crowd, fighting on the field, and Jock told his marker Kudrass: "I was paid two bob a day during the War to kill big ******* like you!" Jock and Charlie Tully were great mates. Charlie could never get over how the Weir man signed for Celtic then spent 15 months living in the Kenilworth Hotel at the club's expense. For Charlie, this proved Jock was that special something that Glasgow calls 'gallus'.

Appearances:
SL: 81 apps. 22 gls.
SLC: 10 apps. 2 gls.
SC: 15 apps. 9 gls.
Total: *106 apps. 33 gls.*

WEIR, John

Role: Midfield 1978-82
6' 1" 10st.11lbs.
b. Coatbridge,
18th February 1960

CAREER: Coatbridge High School/Celtic BC/Gartcosh United/CELTIC ground staff May 1974/Petershill (farmed-out) July 1977/CELTIC 1978/free 8 May 1982/Winterslag (trial) 19 Sep 1982/ Airdrie 1 Oct 1982/Alloa 8 July 1983/ Cumbernauld United 1984.

Debut v Dundee United (a) 1-1 (SLC) 12.11.80

John Weir was captain of the Celtic BC U-14s who lifted the European Youth Cup at Parkhead on April 15th 1974. He was "tall, skinny, slow to settle but quite a player." Jim Lumsden called him "a hard worker and a good listener." He had 15 games for Celtic in

John Weir

1980-81 (starting with the League Cup semi-final first leg at Tannadice and including Sammy Nelson's testimonial at Highbury on November 25th). John was the midfield grafter with a crunching tackle and looked the part but had to give way to Mike Conroy as suffering from "mental and physical tiredness" (ie finding every game a very hard one and one ordeal seeming to follow the other without respite). He reverted to the reserves but won a Glasgow Cup medal just after he was set free (13th May 1982). John studied Civil Engineering at Strathclyde University.

Appearances:
SL: 11 apps. 0 gls.
SLC: 2 apps. 0 gls.
SC: 1 app. 0 gls.
Total: *14 apps. 0 gls.*

WELFORD, James William

Role: Right-back 1897-1900
5' 10½" 13st.7lbs.
b. Barnard Castle, 27th March 1869
d. Renfrew, 17th January 1945

CAREER: Barnard Castle FC/ Bishop Auckland 1890/Mitchell's St George's 1892/Aston Villa Aug 1893/CELTIC 3 May 1897/(Belfast Celtic loan Aug 1899)/Distillery 24 Feb 1900/Hamiton Academicals 5 Oct 1901 until 1903.../retired 1906.

Debut v Rangers (n) 1-4 (CC) 11.5.1897

Tom Maley was sent to Birmingham in May 1897 to bring Campbell home and came back with the great Johnny plus Jack Reynolds and the cricketer-footballer Jim Welford. Welford was not on his shopping list. "He shaped awkwardly to begin with... broke down against Rangers on his debut... but a better bargain the club never made." He had his first experience of a certain extra edge in the Scottish game at Tynecastle on September 11th 1897: "This crowd didn't come for football but to get men killed." He was in the team that took Scottish Cup revenge on Arthurlie (8th January 1898 at infamous Dunterlie Park) and played the role of overlapping full-back. In the next round (21st January), the defeat by 3rd Lanark, he and Doyle argued bitter on the field like Reynolds and McKeown in bygone days of yore. In the Glasgow League against Queen's Park on April 23rd 1898, so incensed was Jim by the award of a penalty to the Spiders ("It wasn't even a free kick!") that he pulled 'keeper Forbes out of goal to let RS McColl

Jim Welford

hit a trundler. The press had a sneer: "Children at play." He became the first Englishman to hold Scottish and English Cup medals when Celtic beat Rangers 2-0 in the final of April 22nd 1899. He had a woeful match when Kilmarnock beat Celtic 6-0 at Rugby Park for Bummer Campbell's benefit (2nd January 1900). Celtic downgraded his wages and although he began to train daily, he asked for a transfer on 13th January. He watched Celtic beat Rangers 5-0 in the semi-final of the Scottish Cup on 21st March 1925.

Appearances:
SL: 38 apps. 0 gls.
SC: 6 apps. 0 gls.
Total: *44 apps. 0 gls.*

♣ **Celtic note:** *A middle order batsman, Jim played minor counties cricket for Durham as of 1891 but had a senior season with Warwickshire in 1895.*

WELSH, Francis

Role: Centre-half 1971-75
6' 0" 11st.9lbs.
b. 14th May 1954

CAREER: Avoca Amateurs/CELTIC (provisional) 29 Dec 1971/ Shettleston Juniors (farmed-out)/(full professional) 30 Mar 1972/free 13 Sep 1975/Coventry City (trial) Sep 1975/Hamilton Academicals (trial) 4 Oct 1975/Kilmarnock 5 Feb 1976/ Partick Thistle 8 Aug 1980/free 14 May 1983/Morton 15 Aug 1983/Hamilton Academicals Sep 1984/Morton Dec 1984/free 10 May 1985/Hamilton Academicals (trial) 3 Sep 1985/Morton 20 Dec 1985.

Frank Welsh

Debut v Aberdeen (a) 0-0 (SL) 29.4.74

Celtic had just won their ninth Championship in a row when Frank Welsh got his chance in place of Billy McNeill. He played his last game for Celtic on March 22nd 1975. Throughout his final season at Parkhead he was crippled by the groin strain that had dogged him for three years. He was a good man in the air and Celtic certainly conceded very few goals with Frank in the team. For a time, it was a fine line's difference between him and Roddie MacDonald for McNeill's successor. Bertie Auld took him to Thistle for £10,000.

Appearances:
SL: 5 apps. 0 gls.
Total: *5 apps. 0 gls.*

WHITEHEAD, George

Role: Centre-forward 1913
5' 9" 12st.0lbs.
b. Galashiels, 24th February 1890

CAREER: Dalkeith Thistle/Newtongrange Star/Hearts 30 Aug 1911/(CELTIC loan 16 Oct 1913)/Motherwell 19 Dec 1913/Newtongrange Star 1915/Royal Naval Division 1915/ (Cowdenbeath loan Jan 1921)/Newtongrange Star 1921/Falkirk 3 Mar 1924/St Bernard's 9 Aug 1924.

Debut v Dundee (h) 1-0 (SL) 18.10.13

"Whitehead is a fine dribbler... smart in taking opportunities... one who will make his mark in Scottish football" (January 1912). Third Lanark put a Quinnless Celtic out 1-0 in the semi-final of the Glasgow Cup on October 7th 1913 and the press bewailed "Celtic's stingless forwards... a scoring centre must be found." Dod Whitehead was borrowed from Hearts for the Dundee fixture. Verdict: "Whitehead lacks speed but has good control." Dod played against Rangers the week following his debut and scored the second goal in a 0-2 League win before 65,000 at Ibrox. His next goal was at Boghead on 15th November when the mill outside the ground was so heavy three Dumbarton players could not get in. Sons kicked-off with eight men and the crowd sat on the touchline in merciless rain throughout. Dod played his last game against Airdrie on November 23rd 1913. He may not have been a great goalscoring centre but "he brought balance to the line" and Celtic won every one of his seven League appearances. His luck held during the Kaiser War when he was torpedoed twice and survived each time.

Appearances:
SL: *7 apps. 2 gls.*
Total: *7 apps. 2 gls.*

WHITELAW, Robert

Role: Left-half 1930-32; 1934
5' 8" 10st.8lbs.
b. 2nd November 1907

CAREER: Larkhall Thistle/ Doncaster Rovers July 1926 /CELTIC 16 Aug 1930/(Albion Rovers loan 1931)/free 1932/Bournemouth June 1932/free 1933/Glentoran July 1933/Queen of the South 1933/CELTIC again 1934/Cowdenbeath 4 June 1934/Albion Rovers 12 Aug 1935/ Glentoran 1936/ Southampton May 1936/ Kidderminster Harriers 1937.

Debut v Hamilton Academicals (a) 0-0 SL 13.9.30

Bobby Whitelaw

"A whole-hearted 90 minutes player," Bob Whitelaw won a Glasgow Cup medal 2-1 versus Rangers on October 11th 1930 when the 70,000 crowd stood bareheaded for a minute's silence before kick-off to commemorate the victims of the R101 airship disaster being buried that day at Cardington. He was the one import in the team on a day when Tom White congratulated himself on the Celtic policy of raising their own. He took Graham Robertson's place in the side to begin with but was himself mainly second choice to Chic Geatons. He went on the USA tour of 1931 and played in six out of the nine games, two at right-back. At Bournemouth he was considered "on the light side" and played reserve to Billy Moralee who was just two pounds heavier. He scored with three penalties for Kidderminster Harriers in a game versus Worcester City in 1939 and was for many years landlord of the 'Corn Exchange', New Road, Kidderminster. He appeared at Parkhead in Army uniform during World War Two and told Jimmy McStay he was in Intelligence as an Interpreter: explained the Scots to the English and vice-versa.

Appearances:
SL: *17 apps. 0 gls.*
SC: *1 app. 0 gls.*
Total: *18 apps. 0 gls.*

WHITNEY, Thomas John Black

Role: Outside-left 1931
b. At sea, 6th March 1910

CAREER: St Mary's BG/Dalry Thistle/ Bridgeton Waverley/CELTIC 11 July 1931/(Stenhousemuir loan 11 Feb 1932) /free May 1932/Larne Nov 1933.

Debut v Leith Athletic (a) 3-0 (SL) 8.8.31

The Intermediate dispute in Scottish Junior football was resolved while Celtic were in America 1931. The first question Willie Maley put to Steve Callaghan on coming off the SS Transylvania was: "Who have we got?" Answer: "Tom Whitney." (Rangers got Sam English). Tom played for the green and whites in the Public Trial of August 4th 1931: "A cool customer... he can beat a man with almost as much craft as Bertie Thomson... gets his crosses in so as to find his target every time." Tom played the first four League fixtures of 1931-32 but by the time Celtic played a benefit for Bridgeton Waverley in gratitude (31st August 1931) his effective career as a Celt was over.

Tom Whitney

Appearances:
SL: *4 apps. 1 gl.*
Total: *4 apps. 1 gl.*

WHITTAKER, Brian

Role: Left-back 1983-84
6' 0" 11st.9lbs.
b. Glasgow, 23rd September 1956

CAREER: Cumbernauld High/BB/Sighthill Amateurs/Crystal Palace (trial) 1971/Partick Thistle 26 July 1974/Borussia Dortmund trial /Hertha Berlin (trial) (both Oct 1980)/CELTIC 19 Aug 1983/Hearts 22 May 1984/Falkirk 11 Aug 1990/Hearts coach 25 June 1993.

Debut v Brechin City (h) 0-0 (SLC) 27.8.83

Bertie Auld's first signing for Partick Thistle was Brian Whittaker, "one of the few naturally

Brian Whittaker

left-sided defenders in Scotland" on whom Bertie put such a high value as a potential international that Rangers shied-off from paying Thistle's asking price (27th June 1978). Brian tried out in Germany as the first Scottish star to take advantage of the new Freedom of Contract legislation which came into operation as of May 18th 1980. Parkhead was not one of Brian's luckier grounds. He knocked Nicholas down on March 18th 1981, stamped on him and was ordered-off in the 35th minute none of which endeared him the more to Thistle manager Peter Cormack. Cormack went public on what he felt was Brian's poor approach to the challenge when Thistle were knocked-out of the Scottish Cup by Dumbarton at Firhill on January 24th 1982. Mark Reid was supposed to lack class enough so Brian went to Celtic as one of David Hay's first signings (for £50,000 and John Buckley) and for a time looked like the new Gemmell. He was too late for Europe and by 23rd November 1983 Reid had played more games in the UEFA Cup than in the Premier League where he had been supplanted by the big ex-Jag. He scored his first goal on October 1st 1983 and bowed to the Jungle. Brian dropped out of the team through injury but was prepared to fight to get his place back when Alex MacDonald came in for him. Hay let him go for £25,000 ("It just didn't work out") at the same time as Jim McInally went to Nottingham Forest (£30,000). He came back to Parkhead with Hearts as a second-half substitute on 15th September 1984 under orders to let John Colquhoun know quickly who was boss. Brian (who seldom took prisoners anyway) got a yellow card for his first tackle and was ordered off for his second within five minutes of the re-start. He had still to kick the ball.

Appearances:
SL: 10 apps. 2 gls.
SLC: 6 apps. 1 gl.
Total: *16 apps. 3 gls.*

WHYTE, Derek

Role: Central Defence 1985-92
6′ 0″ 12st.7lbs.
b. Glasgow, 31st August 1968

CAREER: Cumbernauld Colts/Hamilton Thistle/CELTIC 14 May 1985/Celtic BC (farmed-out)/Middlesbrough 12 Aug 1992.
Debut v Hearts (h) 1-1 (SL) 22.2.86

"He's a tremendous player. What a prospect he is for the future!" (Billy McNeill 26th September 1987). Derek Whyte was born on a propitious Saturday, the day Bobby Lennox went nap against Partick Thistle at Firhill (1-6) and the wee Celtic beat the wee Jags 12-0 at Parkhead. "I'd had trials with Motherwell and been approached by Rangers before I chose to sign for Celtic when I was 13. I chose Celtic simply because their coaching is better than any other club I have seen" (February 1984). His impact as a defender was immediate and so much did he remind people of the young McNeill (but with muscles) that he seemed destined for a future Celtic captain. Hearts were odds-on certainties for the League title in February 1986 when big Derek played against them on his first team debut. He played in the 'eery silence game' of May 3rd 1986 as everyone listened on his/her transistor at Love Street to the events befalling the Maroons at Dens Park and Celtic prepared to seize the 1986 Flag at the last gasp. He got another Championship badge in 1988 plus Scottish Cup medals in 1988 and 1989. In the 1989 Scottish Cup final he cleared a Mark Walters shot off the line just after Joe Miller had scored for Celtic. He made his Scotland debut by coming on as substitute versus Chile on May 30th 1989. Abruptly the progress stopped. He recognised as much himself when he scored the opener in the second half versus Rangers on September 15th 1990: "It was the first goal I've headed in two years. It's about time I did something in the air." The strike transformed an outclassed, overrun Celtic into a new team. He had a dreadful first half of the season 1991-92 when the ability to clear his lines with of all things his good foot, his trusty left, deserted him and his stock slumped dramatically. He hit form again in the new year and had a great game against Rangers on 21st March 1992. He left Celtic over terms and his rejuvenation continued at Middlesbrough.

Derek Whyte

Andy Roxburgh recalled him to the Scotland squad (four caps with Celtic) but as the Reds began to struggle for survival in 1993 so did Derek. His time at Parkhead was a fairly successful period. It's just a great pity he was not another McNeill.

Appearances:
SL: 215 apps. 7 gls.
SLC: 20 apps. 0 gls.
SC: 26 apps. 0 gls.
Eur: 15 apps. 1 gl.
Total: *276 apps. 8 gls.*

WHYTE, Francis

Role: Centre-forward, Right-half 1951-56
5' 10" 11st.10lbs.
b. Govanhill,
18th April 1935

CAREER:
St Gerard's Senior Secondary/
St Paul's Whiteinch BG /CELTIC 8 Aug 1951/Maryhill Harp (farmed-out) 1951/free 30 Apr 1956/ Swindon Town June 1956.

Frank Whyte

Debut v Partick Thistle (a) 1-0 (SLC) 27.8.52

Signed as a schoolboy centre, Frank Whyte got his main first-team opportunity after Jock Stein's ankle injury versus Rangers (31st August 1955). Bobby Evans converted to pivot and somebody was needed for right-half. Eric Smith, Ian Reid, Willie Fernie were tried, then Frank, then Mike Conroy and Alec Boden. Frank played six times in a half-back line reading Whyte, Evans and Peacock, and once (his very first game at right-half) Whyte, Jack and Mochan. His final match was at Palmerston Park on Hogmanay 1955.

Appearances:
SL: 7 apps. 0 gls.
SLC: 2 apps. 0 gls.
Total: *9 apps. 0 gls.*

WILLIAMS, Samuel Evan

Role: Goalkeeper 1969-74
5' 10" 11st.7lbs.
b. Dumbarton, 15th July 1943

CAREER: St Michael's BG/Duntocher Juveniles/Vale of Leven June 1962/Third Lanark 16 Oct 1964/Wolves 8 Mar 1966/Aston Villa (trial) Aug 1969/CELTIC 14 Oct 1969/ free 6 May 1974/Clyde 18 July 1974/free 29 Apr 1975/Arbroath reserves (trial) Aug 1975/ Falkirk 22 Apr 1976/Vale of Leven manager 4 July 1976/Albion Rovers asst manager 10 Feb 1981.

Debut v St Mirren (h) 2-0 (SL) 1.12.69

Aston Villa offered Evan Williams a contract as cover for John Dunn and the deal was on until Frank Munro warned him in the heat of combat: "Look behind your goal when you

Evan Williams

can. I'm sure that's Sean Fallon standing there," at a Wolves versus Liverpool reserve fixture October 1969. Evan exchanged playing in the Central League for the European Cup. In the semi-final against Leeds at Elland Road on April 1st 1970, he collapsed in the goalmouth, leg spouting blood, appealing for Neilly Mochan, only to hear Stein: "Get up! Get up! Get on with the game!" But for him, Celtic's defeat by Feyenoord in the final of May 6th in Milan might well have been heavier. He carried the can for the 4-1 defeat by Thistle in the League Cup final of 23rd October 1971 and Denis Connaghan was bought to replace him. Evan came back and against Ujpest Dosza in Hungary (8th March 1972; the night Richard Burton and Elizabeth Taylor threw a £5,000 party for the Celtic support) he had an outstanding game and was again magnificent at the San Siro versus AC Milan on April 5th. He took the blame for the 5-3 defeat by Hibs in the Drybrough Cup final on August 5th 1972 and another fine display against Ujpest in the European Cup on 8th November 1972 was not enough to satisfy Stein. Ally Hunter was bought from Kilmarnock in January 1973. Evan took his curtain call in Europe against Basle on 27th February 1974 when he set the Swiss on the way by letting Hitzfeld's shot slip from his grasp in 27 minutes. But over all, as Ronnie Simpson's successor (a hard act to follow), he served the Celtic extraordinarily well. He won Championship medals in 1970, 1971, 1972 and 1973 and Scottish Cup medals in 1971 (against Rangers) and 1972.

Appearances:
SL: 82 apps. 36 shut-outs.
SLC: 25 apps. 8 shut-outs.
SC: 19 apps. 6 shut-outs.
Eur: 22 apps. 9 shut-outs.
Total: *148 apps. 59 shut-outs (40%).*

WILSON, Alexander

Role: Half-back 1905-07
b. Muirkirk, 9th April 1883

CAREER: Newmains Thistle/Cambuslang Rangers 1901/Morton (trial) 7 Jan 1905/ CELTIC 9 Jan 1905/(Ayr FC loan 28 Apr 1905 & 12 Apr 1906)/Kilmarnock 25 July 1907/ Hamilton Academicals 23 Oct 1908.

Debut v Partick Thistle (a) 3-0 (SL) 4.11.05

Alex Wilson

Future Scottish international centre Andy Wilson played trials for Celtic in the autumn of 1904 ("You find the space, I'll give you the ball": Jimmy McMenemy) and sat at home one night in January 1905 waiting for the signing-on papers. Instead, the Celtic rep went to another house and signed the wrong A. Wilson, Alex not Andy. Alex aka 'Tug' started well as deputy for the crippled Sunny Jim: "He never knows when he's beaten... a most promising debut... twice he came within an ace of scoring." In the summer of 1906, he "was probably least known of all the Celtic players" but had his best run as a Celt between 13th October and 24th November 1906 when he played centre-half in place of Willie Loney. His final two games for Celtic were in "the best match of the season" on March 2nd and "the fastest match of the season" (16th March 1907).

Appearances:
SL: 14 apps. 0 gls.
Total: *14 apps. 0 gls.*

WILSON, James

Role: Half-back 1913-19
5' 9" 11st.5lbs.
b. Glasgow, 1894

CAREER: Townhead Emerald/Cambuslang Rangers/CELTIC 18 Oct 1913/(Vale of Atholl loan 6 Dec 1913)/(East Stirling loan 12 Aug 1914 until Apr 1916)/CELTIC again 15 Apr 1916/(Dumbarton loan 17 Nov 1917)/(Vale of Leven loan 25 Jan 1919)/Albion Rovers Mar 1919/East Stirling July 1920/free Dec 1921/ Kent Mills Soccer Club (Philadelphia) player-coach by 1926.

Debut v Ayr United (a) 1-0 (SL) 2.9.16

"Rare player" and Glasgow East End boy Jimmy Wilson was signed as a centre-half but "took up the mantle of Sunny Jim in the Celtic team and... is pleasing immensely." "Gritty and keen," Jimmy played as a regular first-teamer from September 2nd 1916 until

September 29th 1917 and won a Championship medal in 1917. During the 1917-18 season he was no longer a regular but filled-in as required both at right-back and a stop-gap outside-right. He moved to Coatbridge and played for the wee Rovers against Celtic at centre in the Victory Cup on March 15th 1919 and was right-half versus Kilmarnock in the Scottish Cup final of 17th April 1920.

Appearances:
SL: 47 apps. 0 gls.
Total: *47 apps. 0 gls.*

Paul Wilson

WILSON, Paul

Role: Left Midfield 1967-78
5' 9" 10st.7lbs.
b. Milngavie, 23rd November 1950

CAREER: St Ninian's High School/CELTIC 19 Dec 1967/Maryhill Jnrs (farmed-out)/ Motherwell 20 Sep 1978/Partick Thistle 12 July 1979/free 30 Apr 1980/Blantyre Celtic 24 Aug 1980/retired 14 Jan 1982/Drumchapel Amateurs coach 1984.

Debut v Dundee (h) 5-1 (SLC) 23.9.70 (sub) (scored once)

"He appears to have it all - balance, poise, two good feet, speed, the ability to beat a man, but too often he gets caught in possession by either overrunning the ball or by trying too much..." Paul Wilson both resembled Willie Fernie in his straight-backed running style and the elegance he lent to the Celtic kit every time he appeared on the park. He was a spectacular raider with speed, control and a net-burster of a shot as witness against Basle in the European Cup (27th February 1974). Yet he was unable consistently to command a place in the Celtic first team. "He has blown hot and cold... he has to believe in himself... he could be the hard-running man to support Deans and Dalglish" (Jock Stein March 1974). He had his best season in 1974-75 when he started straight-off as a first-teamer without a run in the reserves and scored with a brilliant header against Rangers in the Drybrough Cup on August 3rd 1974. Even when Rangers won 3-0 on 4th January 1975 he was easily the best man on the field. (He would invariably raise his game against Rangers). Scotland capped him against Spain in Valencia (5th February) and he scored Celtic's first two goals in the defeat of Airdrie in the Scottish Cup final of May 3rd. One week later he gave a magnificent exhibition of running, shooting and control against Rangers again in the Glasgow Cup final to celebrate the city's 800th birthday. He got both Celtic's goals within 20 minutes in a 2-2 draw. But in 1976, Paul was "the oldest youngster in the game... still learning," and Ronnie Glavin was given the free-running role. When Alfie Conn arrived in March 1977 it was Paul Wilson made way for him. He was still part of Jock Stein's plans for the assault on Europe 1977-78 as an attacker with Lennox and Conn and hit two goals by way of rehearsal against the Arsenal at the Sydney Cricket Ground 24th July 1977 in the 'World of Soccer' Cup. But Celtic had a disastrous season and he virtually dropped out of the side after the 1-2 defeat by St Mirren (25th February 1978). The passing of Paul's massive talent from Parkhead was a source of deep regret to the many who had followed him from his time of high promise in the reserve team and confidently expected he would one day be an all-time Celtic great in succession to Johnstone or Lennox. John Hughes capped him for Junior Scotland against Eire at Irvine Meadow on October 4th 1980.

Appearances:
SL: 131 apps. 29 gls.
SLC: 48 apps. 13 gls.
SC: 15 apps. 4 gls.
Eur: 20 apps. 6 gls.
Total: *214 apps. 52 gls.*

WILSON, Peter

Role: Right-half 1923-34
5' 10" 11st.2lbs.
b. Beith, 26th March 1905
d. Beith, 13th February 1983

CAREER: Beith Amateurs/Beith Juniors (once) 6 Feb 1923/CELTIC 5 May 1923/ (Ayr United loan 1 Sep 1923 & 16 Nov 1923) /Hibernian 24 Aug 1934/free 30 Apr 1938/ Dunfermline Athletic player-manager 6 May 1938/manager 1939/Royal Navy 1941/Pollok Juniors coach June 1947/Derby County scout 29 Mar 1948/Kilmarnock coach 1953.

Debut v Motherwell (a)
1-0 (SL) 16.2.24

"Peter Wilson didn't pass the ball, he stroked it." "Peter Wilson with the ball in front of him, nothing could be finer" (6th October 1928). "Football draughtsman," Peter Wilson first played for Celtic in the two-referee experiment at Cathkin Park on 9th February 1924. He told the story how he reported to Maley's Bank Restaurant in Queen Street the following Saturday, boarded a bus with the other players, got to Fir Park (didn't know where he was) and was

told he was marking the fastest left-winger in Scotland, Bob Ferrier. Peter's was a "cool style," "easy-oasy." "I like the way Wilson surveys the position before he makes a pass. He is cool, quick-thinking and a shrewd constructor. The crisp, inch-accurate passes to a well-placed colleague stamp him as a half-back who knows just what is required and when... no flurry or hurry... just cool and calculating... he will be a top-notcher yet" (1924)."Carpet artist" Peter was not always an iceman. Celtic players mobbed referee Mick Quinn twice for a penalty versus Hearts at Parkhead on October 11th 1924 and were refused. Later, when a spot-kick was at last awarded, goalie White saved from Patsy Gallagher then Adam McLean put the retake over the bar. Referee Quinn ordered a second retake. Unbidden, the boy Wilson took it and scored off the underside of the bar. There were 13 minutes left and he spent them in a cold sweat. Peter was a formation influence on the young Malky: "Right MacDonald, you've lost the ball. Away and get it back." Peter Wilson was an all-time Celtic great.

Appearances:
SL: 344 apps. 14 gls.
SC: 51 apps. 1 gl.
Total: *395 apps. 15 gls.*

WILSON, Samuel

Role: Inside-left 1957-59
5' 8" 10st.10lbs.
b. Glasgow, 16th December 1931

CAREER: Uddingston BC/Renfrew Juniors/
St Mirren 1 Sep 1951/free 1 May 1957/CELTIC
3 May 1957/free 1959/Millwall July 1959/free
24 June 1960/Northampton Town July 1960/
free summer 1961/Ross County 30 June 1961/
Brora Rangers manager.

Debut v East Fife (a) 4-1 (SLC) 14.8.57

Bob Kelly snapped Sammy Wilson up when
he came free from St Mirren and was
delighted to land him. John McPhail watched
the Public Trial of August 3rd 1957 and found
him "miscast at inside-forward." In the second
Trial three days on, "Wilson failed to click."
He played right-half on his debut and then it
happened. He lined-up as inside-left to the

Sammy Wilson

younger McPhail in the 6-1 defeat of East Fife
on August 28th 1957 when he and big Billy
scored two goals each. Slammin' Sammy had
arrived! He was using the open space and
feeding off McPhail, the best provider of
chances in the game. By September 11th and
the 6-1 defeat of Third Lanark, he was "an ace
schemer... snappy ground passer... positionally
intelligent... a revelation." He and McPhail
each scored a goal versus Rangers in the 2-3
win of September 21st 1957 that saw Celtic
take their first full League points from Ibrox in
22 years. At Hampden in the Sun on October
19th, a month later, Sammy scored the first
goal of the 7-1 rout in 22 minutes (yet was
back at work in the garage the following day
to do time lost to football he had promised to
make up). On Ne'erday 1958 he was "in
devastating form... ripped open Rangers'
defence... made a beautiful combination with
Colrain." 1957-58 was Sammy's golden year
with Celtic. When Billy McPhail retired in
August 1958, his game never
reached the same heights again.
But he goes down in perpetuity
as one of the heroes of the 1957
October Revolution.

Appearances:
SL: 48 apps. 26 gls.
SLC: 14 apps. 13 gls.
SC: 8 apps. 7 gls.
Total: *70 apps. 46 gls.*

WRAITH, Robert

Role: Goalkeeper 1968-69
5' 10" 11st.4lbs.
b. Largs, 26th April 1948

CAREER: Gourock Athletic
Youth 1964/Largs Amateurs
1965/Largs Thistle 1965/Port
Glasgow Rangers 1966/Dalry
Thistle 30 Jan 1967/CELTIC
26 Apr 1968/free 2 May 1969/
Southport 22 July 1969/Formby
FC 1971-73 [& 1976-78]/Police
football.

*Debut v Hamilton Academicals (a)
4-2 (SLC) 25.9.68*

An Ibrox diehard, Bobby Wraith
had follow-followed Rangers
down to Leeds in the Fairs Cities'
Cup just three weeks before he

Goalkeeper Bobby Wraith (extreme left, middle row) in a Celtic line-up which includes some all-time greats.
Back row (left to right): Brogan, McGrain, McBride, Cattanach, Connelly, Fallon, Simpson, Gallacher, Quinn, Clark, Dalglish, O'Neill. Middle row: Wraith, Hughes, Hay, Craig, Clark, Gemmell, McKellar, Murdoch, Murray, Chalmers, Livingstone. Front: McMahon, Johnstone, Macari, Wallace, Davidson, McNeill, Wilson, Lennox, Clarke, Auld, Gorman.

signed for Celtic. He played for the local Thistle against a Celtic select at Dalry on Thursday April 25th 1968 and Jock Stein invited him to try out against Home Farm at Parkhead the following night. Celtic won 7-2 and Bobby signed on as a Bhoy after the game. He travelled to San Siro for the European Cup quarter-final versus AC Milan on 19th February 1969. Ronnie Simpson had just suffered his first dislocated shoulder so John Fallon played in the 0-0 draw while Bobby, barely out of the juniors, watched from the bench. Bobby played representative football for the British Police versus Holland and Norway. He lives nowadays at Ormskirk.

Appearances:
SLC: 1 app. 0 shut-outs.
Total: *1 app. 0 shut-outs.*

WYLIE, John McLaren

Role: Right-half 1943
b. Glasgow, 20th January 1923

CAREER: Celtic 29 Jan 1943/free 1943/ Petershill Juniors 31 July 1943.
Debut v Hearts (a) 3-5 (RL) 13.2.43

An amateur, John Wylie came in for Hugh Long on his one and only appearance for Celtic in a half-back line reading Wylie, McLaughlan and Mallan. He saw Joe Rae have a great game (two goals) and Pat McAuley walk through the Hearts' defence for Celtic's third.

Appearances:
RL: 1 app. 0 gls.
Total: *1 app. 0 gls.*

YOUNG, Andrew

Role: Inside-right 1944-45
5′ 8″ 10st.10lbs.
b. Oakley Fife, 21st June 1925

CAREER: Steelend Victoria Juveniles/
Dunfermline Athletic (trial) 1943/CELTIC
5 Feb 1943/(Raith Rovers loan 15 Feb 1945)/
free 1945/Raith Rovers 17 Sep 1945/retired
1960/CELTIC scout/Leeds United scout/
Dunfermline coach 11 Jan 1968/Lochore
Welfare manager.

Debut v Hibernian (h) 2-2 (RL) 12.2.44

"Andy Young is the most neglected player in
Scottish football... serves up tremendous
stuff... not a better right-half in Scotland...
when asked to move forward, has unfailingly
put new life into the Raith front line... Yet

*Andy Young (right) training with
Willie McNaught (left) and Andy
Leigh during his long career at
Raith Rovers.*

never a glance from the selectors despite one storming game after another" (1953). Andy played a trial for Celtic reserves at Boghead and was signed after the game by Jimmy McStay at Willie Maley's Bank restaurant in Queen Street, still the epicentre of Celtic operations a full four years after the dropping of the pilot. He was on £2 for a first team game, £1 the reserves (both taxable). He played inside to the great Delaney on his debut and was taken-off with the blood streaming from a gash over the eye. Andy left Celtic because the exigencies of War-time meant he was employed full-time down the pit at Oakley on night shift. Sheer exhaustion and the difficulties of travel made Stark's Park a much more attractive proposition in terms of a career in football. Andy made his fame at Raith Rovers in the Kirkcaldy team's greatest ever half-back line of Young, Colville and Leigh in the 'forties and the 'burglar-proof' line of Young, McNaught and Leigh in the 'fifties. He played in the League Cup final versus Rangers on March 12th 1949 and had a magnificent game. Derby County offered £10,000 for him in January 1951 but Andy, ever a home-loving man, was reluctant to move. He was inside-right versus Celtic in the semi-final of the Scottish Cup at Hampden on March 31st 1951 as likewise in the semi-final of the St Mungo Cup also at Hampden on July 28th that same year. As Rovers battled for a second-half equaliser, Young's "weaving tactics bamboozled everyone." He moved to centre for Raith during 1950-51 and ended-up club top scorer. He hardly missed a game and after going part-time in 1952-53, played his 350th League and Cup match on September 15th 1956. He would play anywhere and once went went into goal when the Rovers' 'keeper was injured at Dumfries. His last chance of a medal vanished when Falkirk put Raith out of the Scottish Cup semi-final in a replay on March 27th 1957. Andy scouted in the east of Scotland after retirement and became George Farm's youth coach at Dunfermline. He had frequent offers to turn manager and once turned Raith Rovers down at the last minute. At the famous Lochore Welfare he brought on the careers of Tommy Callaghan, Bud Johnston, Doug Rougvie and Ian Porterfield.

Appearances:
RL: 3 apps. 0 gls.
Total: *3 apps. 0 gls.*

YOUNG, Ian

Role: Right-back
1961-68
5' 10" 11st.7lbs.
b. 21st May 1943

CAREER: Neilston Waverley/CELTIC 28 June 1961/Neilston Juniors (farmed-out)/free 1 May 1968/St Mirren 1 July 1968/free 27 Apr 1970/Saltcoats Victoria coach 1970s.

Debut v Third Lanark (n) 1-1 (GC) 5.5.62

Ian Young

Celtic took centre-half Ian Young (training at Ibrox) and centre-forward John McGaw from Neilston Waverley at the same time. Young John got a free transfer in 1962 but apprentice industrial chemist Young played his first game for Celtic in the Glasgow Cup final of 1962 at Hampden after Dunky MacKay had chipped his elbow bone in the rough house against Uruguay at the same venue two days before. He won his first medal in the replay on Friday May 11th. He became Parkhead's right-back in succession to Dunky on October 5th 1963 and had his finest ninety minutes in a green and white shirt when Celtic beat Slovan 0-1 in Bratislava to reach the semi-final of the Cup-Winners' Cup on March 4th 1964. He won a Scottish Cup medal on April 24th 1965 and it was the power of an Ian Young tackle right at the start of the League Cup final of October 23rd 1965 that destroyed the threat to Celtic of Willie Johnston's speed down the left. Rangers maintained 'Bud' had been sorted-out; Celtic that it was no cruder a challenge than was typical of Old Firm encounters. Ian also won a Championship badge for 1965-66 at the beginning of the nine-in-a-row. Stein experimented with Gemmell and O'Neill on the North American tour of 1966 and at the start of the Annus Mirabilis 1966-67 had decided on Tam and Willie as his full-backs. Ian got two games all season and having ousted Dunky MacKay, the chemist lost his place in turn ultimately to the dentist, Jim Craig. Yet Young and Gemmell is as memorable a combination as Craig and Gemmell: they were the full-backs at the start of it all (the Glasgow Cup final win of March 25th 1964 that marked the presence of the talent that the Big Man would exploit?).

Appearances:
SL: 101 apps. 2 gls.
SLC: 31 apps. 1 gl.
SC: 13 apps. 0 gls.
Eur: 19 apps. 0 gls.
Total: *164 apps. 3 gls.*

Sunny Jim Young

YOUNG, James

Role: Right-half 1903-17
6' 0" 12st.7lbs.
b. Kilmarnock, 10th January 1882
d. Kilmarnock, 4th September 1922

CAREER: Lilliemount Juveniles/Dean Park/Kilmarnock Rugby XI/Kilmarnock (trial) 10 Aug 1901/Stewarton FC/Shawbank FC/Barrow Feb 1902/left June 1902/Bristol Rovers June 1902/free 1903/CELTIC 1 May 1903/retired 12 May 1917.
Debut v Hibernian (n) 0-0 (CC) 16.5.03

"With me, one club was as good as another as long as the money was right." Jim Young signed for Mick Dunbar in the Black Swan, near Eastville, Bristol Rovers' ground, despite the fact he was appointed for interviews with West Bromwich Albion and Bristol City the next day. As an engineering apprentice in Kilmarnock, he used to watch as Celtic's Tom Hynds made his way to catch the train to Glasgow to play. The moment he pulled on a Celtic jersey (green and white vertical stripes) for the first time, there began a love affair with the club that lasted until his tragic death nineteen years on. He sold himself heart and soul to a team for which he had previously felt nothing. He started with Celtic as a centre-half but moved to right-half against Dundee in the first replay of the Scottish Cup third round tie against Dundee at Dens Park on February 27th 1904. With Sunny as the common denominator, the constant factor, the catalyst in midfield, Celtic won 10 Championships (the six-in-a-row 1905-10 and the four-in-a-row 1914-17); five Scottish Cups (suspended during the Kaiser War - it might have been more!); seven Glasgow Cups and nine Charity. He was probably as great an influence on the triumph of the Celts between 1903 and 1917 as Stein between 1965 and 1977 yet to date

Sunny Jim (holding Scottish Cup) with Celtic's double-winning side of 1913-14.
Back row (left to right): W.Maley (manager), McMaster, Dodds, Shaw, McNair, Johnstone, McColl,
Quinn (trainer). Front row: McAtee, Gallagher, Young, McMenemy, Browning.

his contribution has been overlooked and the tribute muted. He looked "a very common player" on his debut but within days was hailed as "a glutton for work... a splendid tackler... a hardy strong fellow who never admits defeat." On the park, he was the picture of earnestness, and claims he was first called 'Sunny Jim' (from the advertisement for Force breakfast cereal) in irony, versus St Mirren at Paisley on August 22nd 1903. Sunny is the Celtic player who got lost off the train in Frankfurt Station on the way to Vienna (May 17th 1904) (he had five minutes to stretch his legs but understood 25) and claimed he could not have caught up with the tour party at all "if it hadnae been fur ma command o' languages" (he spoke broad Ayrshire). He took over from Jimmy Hay as skipper in 1911 and urged Celtic on by bark (his "Come away, boys! Get into that ball!" could be heard from the Ibrox press box on April 11th 1914 in the Scottish final) and by bite (he hit the Hibs' post with a 40-yarder in the 80th minute). When Celtic were under the hammer "Young's face set like a summons" and he would relax only when he knew his beloved Bhoys had the points safe (eg like stealing Joe Dodds' penalty kick on January 2nd 1913). He came back from the tour of Scandinavia (14th June 1912) and stood on the platform of York station as the team changed trains: "Well, boys, I'm prouder than ever to be a Celtic player." Until the injury that finished him, he was leader of the side that went 66 games without defeat from

20th November 1915 through the whole of 1916 until 21st April 1917. No Rangers skipper ever shook hands with Sunny in the middle of the park without knowing his team were in for a game against Young's Celtic. He damaged his knee irretrievably against Hearts on September 30th 1916 and was in hospital till the end of February 1917. With his departure from Parkhead, Celtic went into a decline that would be reversed only with the advent of Stein. He died aged 40 from injuries sustained when the motorbike on which he was a pillion passenger was in collision with a tramcar on the Wellington Bridge between Kilmarnock and Hurlford. Jock Stein was born just six weeks after his death. Who then on grass was the greatest of the Celts? The question seems otiose and the answer obvious. First is Patsy Gallagher, second Jimmy Quinn, third McGrory. In fact, the truth is Parkhead's forgotten man: Sunny Jim Young. Sunny was the greatest Celt ever. See Matthew 7.16. John Riggins ("Riggie") Celtic's Gallowgate balladeer described him thus:

"One fine big Celtic boy, would play without
the money,
Parkhead's endless inspiration, salute Jim,
the genial Sunny!"

Appearances:
SL: 392 apps. 13 gls.
SC: 51 apps. 0 gls.
Total: *443 apps. 13 gls.*

YOUNG, James

Role: Outside-right 1918

CAREER: Lochgelly United May 1917/(Raith Rovers loan Aug 1917)/(Kilmarnock loan 5 Jan 1918)/(CELTIC loan 9 Feb 1918)/Rangers 20 Feb 1918/Army May 1918/Dumbarton Jan 1919.

Debut v Hearts (h) 3-0 (SL) 9.2.18

Celtic played "Black" in place of Gunner McAtee against Hearts and although "he did a lot of clever things... he was hampered by the ground conditions... and did nothing brilliant." Lochgelly wanted £250 but Celtic wanted another look. Rangers stepped in and signed the boy. At Ibrox he did not live up to his reputation as a junior and lacked "the necessary football skill to accompany his fine physique." Rangers were 3-0 down to Morton in the War Fund Shield semi-finals on April 27th 1918 when James got a late goal. Instead of grabbing the ball and dashing back up the park to go for another, young Jim set off on a trek for handshakes. Geordie Livingstone took him to Dumbarton. Like Geordie, he belongs to the list of players who have seen action for both Celtic and Rangers.

Appearances:
SL: 1 app. 0 gls.
Total: *1 app. 0 gls.*

YOUNG, John

Role: Inside-right 1908-11
5' 6" 10st.2lbs.
b. 1888

CAREER: Strathclyde Juniors/CELTIC 27 Oct 1908/(Morton loan 19 Nov 1908)/(Ayr FC loan 22 Jan 1910)/(Alloa loan 19 Sep 1910)/(Dundee Hibs loan 21 Aug 1911)/Dundee Hibs 17 Nov 1911.

Debut v Aberdeen (a) 0-0 (SL) 27.11.09

John Young joined Celtic and was farmed out at once to Morton "for experience." He came in for Willie Kivlichan on his League debut at Pittodrie and played in the very last match of the six-in-a-row Championships, a 0-0 draw at Dundee on April 30th 1910 (after a magnificent match there in the Herbert Dainty benefit of April 11th against stuffy half-back Bert Lee). In 1952, on April 28th, Celtic played a benefit for the descendants of James (Finnie) Young, "son of the old Celt John Young (1908)." The benefit had been scheduled originally for January 3rd 1952 to raise funds to fly Finnie to Germany (just seven years after Armageddon) for essential medical treatment. The game was postponed because of bad weather and Finnie, son of John, had died in the meantime.

Appearances:
SL: 3 apps. 0 gls.
Total: *3 apps. 0 gls.*

John Young (fifth left, back row) and the 1910-11 Celtic team.
Back row (left to right): D.Adams, A.McNair, P.Geehrin, D.Munro, John Young, J.Mitchell, P.Johnstone, T.McAteer. Front row: W.Kivlichan, J.McMenemy, J.Dodds, J.Hay, W.Loney, J.Quinn, D.McCann, D.Hamilton.

THE FAITHFUL IN ARMS

Tho' our soldiers have gone at the call of the drum
To many a field afar,
Their fancy flies to the Paradise
No matter where they are.
The Green and White like a beacon light
Upon their paths has shone,
And the question slips from Celtic lips,
How Did The Boys Get On?

Tho' seas divide, they think with pride
Of the team they left behind.
They are faithful still through good and ill,
They bear the Celts in mind.
So memory clings in their wanderings
To lighten a trooper's load,
The tramp of feet down Janefield Street,
Or a vision of the London Road.

Far across the surf, they can see the turf
That came from the shamrock shore,
The team tripping out, the welcome shout,
They heard in days of yore.
They read with zest of Britain's best
And the mighty deeds they've done.
When the mail comes through, one thought in view:
"Have The Good Old Celtic Won?"

(Celtic Football Guide 1942-43)

172 CHARLIE HUGHES, Dumbarton
173 F.J. LEE, Ford, Plymouth, Devon
174 ROBERT TAGGART, Cranhill, Glasgow
175 BERNADETTE RASMUSSEN, Greenock
176 MARTIN O'KANE, Ballybay, Co.
     Monaghan
177 DANIEL A. JONES, Bearsden, Glasgow
178 DAVID JOHN LEWIS, Portland, Dorset
179 VINCENT PINTERICH, Hamilton,
     Lanarkshire
180 ALDO BOVE, Parkhouse, Glasgow
181 A.N. OTHER, West Cheshunt, Herts
182 THOMAS McCULLOCH, Airdrie
183 WILLIAM, CLARE, CHARLES &
     WILLIAM (Jnr) AGNEW, HighWycombe
184 JOHN ANTHONY GORRY, Grangemouth,
     Stirlingshire
185 EOIN GERARD CRAMPSEY,
     Grangemouth, Stirlingshire
186 Fr. BRIAN GOWANS, Falkirk
187 MICHAEL JARDINE, Paisley
188 PAUL JOHN GALLACHER, Horfield,
     Bristol
189 ALAN LEISTER, London
190 R.S. OLIVER, East Kilbride
191 JOSEPH MURTY, Milford, Connecticut,
     U.S.A.
192 MARTIN KINNAIRD, Glasgow
193 GLEN CLARK, Calgary, Alberta, Canada
194 ANTONY JENKINS, Longstanton,
     Cambridge
195 EDDIE BRESLIN, Broughty Ferry, Dundee
196 ANTHONY McCANN, Levenvale,
     Alexandria
197 PATRICK SHERIDAN, Lisburn, Co. Antrim
198 DAVID CHRISTIE, Finzean, Banchory
199 SEAN O'HANLON, Elephant Butte,
     New Mexico, USA
200 SETON M. AIRLIE, Barbourne, Worcester
201 JOHN & ELLA WILSON, Blairhall, Fife
202 Miss ELLEN O'MALLEY, Motherwell
203 ANDREW MURPHY, Montrose, Angus
204 J.A. GILMARTIN, Kempen, Germany
205 DAVID SHIELDS, Glasgow
206 BRIAN GALLAGHER, Glasgow
207 JOHN ARRAS McMASTER, Baillieston
208 MARTIN SIMONS, Bekkevoort, Belgium
209 MARISA MEECHAN, Irvine, Ayrshire
210 ANDREW WALKER, Dundee
211 JOHN WYNNE, Penilee, Glasgow
212 JAMES RAFFERTY, Olney, Bucks
213 RONNIE GORDON, Bishopmill, Elgin
214 THOMAS COOPER, Redcar, Cleveland
215 DAVID ROBERTS, Rutherglen
216 JOHN BURNETT, Burnt Island, Fife

217 "GEORDIE" BRIAN H., Collyhurst,
     Manchester
218 STEVE WOLSTENCROFT, Kinning Park,
     Glasgow
219 T. MURPHY, Coatbridge, Lanarkshire
220 HUGH O'NEIL, Glasgow
221 BRIAN JOHN JONES, King's Park,
     Glasgow
222 ALAN O'DONNELL, King's Park, Glasgow
223 GERALD DOWNEY, Cambuslang
224 Mr HEMER, Jarrow, Tyne & Wear
225 Mr HEMER, Jarrow, Tyne & Wear
226 JOHN McCLELLAN, Berkhamsted, Herts
227 ANTHONY C. MARTIN, Coatbridge,
     Lanarks
228 JIM DONALDSON, Falkirk
229 COLIN JOSE, Hamilton, Ontario, Canada
230 G.T. ALLMAN, Essington, Wolverham,pton
231 ROGER HARRIS, Hove, East Sussex
232 TONY WOODWARD, Harthill, Sheffield
233 PAUL O'CONNOR, Worcester
234 LIZ O'CONNOR, St. Johns, Worcester
235 FRANK GLENCROSS, Dalbeattiie,
     Kircudbrightshire
236 HUGH M. BROWN, Barassie, Troon,
     Ayrshire
237 E. STOKKEL, Almere, Holland
238 JAMES GALLAGHER, Scarborough,
     Ontario, Canada
239 RAYMOND SHAW, Sutton in Ashfield, Notts
240 GARY SHELLARD, East Farndon,
     Leicestershire
241 BILL COOK, Randlay, Telford, Shropshire
242 GRAEME KELLY, Dringhouses, York
243 DICK BARTON, Lexden, Colchester, Essex
244 J. RETTER, Tuxford, Newark, Notts
245 CANDIDA BASKCOMB, Melbourne,
     Australia
246 BOBBY BASKCOMB, Worth Matravers,
     Dorset
247 CAMILLA BASKCOMB & DAVE GILLAN,
     Battersea, London
248 RUPERT BASKCOMB, Wimbledon, London
249 LEIGH R. PEARCE, Quorn, Leics
250 JULIAN BASKCOMB, Leicester